Beyond Metropolis

Beyond Metropolis

The Planning and Governance of Asia's Mega-Urban Regions

Aprodicio A. Laquian

Woodrow Wilson Center Press
Washington, D.C.

The Johns Hopkins University Press
Baltimore

EDITORIAL OFFICES

Woodrow Wilson Center Press
Woodrow Wilson International Center for Scholars
One Woodrow Wilson Plaza
1300 Pennsylvania Avenue, N.W.
Washington, D.C. 20004-3027
Telephone: 202-691-4029
www.wilsoncenter.org

ORDER FROM

The Johns Hopkins University Press
Hampden Station
P.O. Box 50370
Baltimore, Maryland 21211
Telephone: 1-800-537-5487
www.press.jhu.edu/books/

2 4 6 8 9 7 5 3 1

Library of Congress Cataloging-in-Publication Data

Laquian, Aprodicio A.
    Beyond metropolis : the planning and governance of Asia's mega-urban regions /
Aprodicio A. Laquian.
        p. cm.
    Includes bibliographical references and index.
    ISBN 0-8018-8176-5 (cloth : alk. paper)
    1. Urbanization—Asia. 2. City planning—Asia. 3. Regional planning—Asia.
4. Municipal services—Asia. 5. Municipal government—Asia. I. Title.
    HT147.A2L38 2005
    307.1′416′095—dc22

                                                                    2004030993

ABOUT THE CENTER

The Center is the living memorial of the United States of America to the nation's twenty-eighth president, Woodrow Wilson. Congress established the Woodrow Wilson Center in 1968 as an international institute for advanced study, "symbolizing and strengthening the fruitful relationship between the world of learning and the world of public affairs." The Center opened in 1970 under its own board of trustees.

To my grandson, Jackson Daniel,
for his virtual journeys to infinity and beyond . . .

Contents

Tables and Figures

Foreword

The new millennium has been tagged as both the urban and the Asia-Pacific century. Indeed, between 2000 and 2030, the world's urban population is expected to increase by 2.1 billion, and most of that increase will be in Asia, where 60 percent of the world's population already lives. At the beginning of the nineteenth century, only the city of Beijing had a population of more than 1 million. By 2015, fourteen of the world's twenty-two mega-cities with populations of 10 million or more will be in Asia. Tokyo continues to be the world's largest mega-city, followed closely by Dhaka, Mumbai (formerly Bombay), Delhi, Jakarta, Kolkata (formerly Calcutta), Karachi, Shanghai, Metro Manila, Beijing, Istanbul, Osaka, Seoul, and Tianjin. At the same time, other Asian cities, such as Bangkok, Chongqing, Hyderabad, and Lahore, are growing and vying for inclusion in the list of mega-cities.

Since its inception, the Comparative Urban Studies Project (CUSP) of the Woodrow Wilson International Center for Scholars has focused on the developmental roles as well as the problems and challenges faced by the world's rapidly growing cities. Historically, urbanization has been a vital instrument for achieving economic and social development. At the same time, cities are acknowledged to suffer from the effects of rapid population growth, lack of material and financial resources, environmental degradation, poverty, social inequality, ethnic fragmentation, political instability, and terrorism. These positive and negative aspects of urbanization have engaged the scholarly efforts of fellows, researchers, and staff members associated with CUSP. Through comparative field studies, seminars, workshops, and publications, CUSP has sought to understand the complex interplay between these positive and negative aspects in an effort to identify policies and programs that might help to fulfill the developmental potentials of urban settlements.

The policy orientation of CUSP is embodied in the mission of the Woodrow Wilson International Center for Scholars, which was created by the United States Congress in 1968 as the official memorial to Woodrow Wilson, the twenty-eighth president of the United States. The Center is a nonpartisan institute for advanced study in key policy areas. In its regular activities, the Center brings together groups of thinkers and doers, scholars and policymakers, and academic and business leaders, as well as civil society leaders and other stakeholders in a series of dialogues that may lead to better understanding and evaluation of policies and programs. Through its fellowship program, the Center provides the opportunity for individuals to join their colleagues as members of a community of scholars focused on key policy issues crucial to economic, social, and political development.

In this book, Aprodicio Laquian, one of the Woodrow Wilson Center's fellows in 2002–3, explores the processes of planning and governance in the largest cities in Asia. On the basis of research he has conducted during the past twelve years, he notes that it may now be rather inaccurate to refer to these large urban settlements as mega-cities, because their developmental "fields" of influence have expanded dramatically and they have been transformed into sprawling mega-urban regions. Thus, instead of a Shanghai of 12.8 million people, Laquian focuses on a mega-urban region of 76 million inhabiting the whole Yangtze River Delta, with Shanghai designated as the "head of the dragon" and other cities like Hangzhou, Nanjing, Suzhou, and Wuxi providing the economic and social energy for the region's rapid growth. Similarly, Jakarta Raya is much larger than the metropolitan area of 11 million named as Indonesia's capital. The built-up urban areas in the Jakarta region have spread to the neighboring regencies of Bogor, Tangerang, and Bekasi, creating the so-called Jabotabek planning region. Turning to Laquian's native city of Metro Manila, he does not see a metropolitan area composed of thirteen cities and four towns holding a population of 12.6 million but a vast region covering parts of the provinces of Cavite, Laguna, Batangas, Rizal, and Quezon, or the so-called Calabarzon region. In this wide-ranging study, Laquian attempts to analyze and explain the planning and governance processes in these city-regions that now dominate urban development in Asia.

Laquian's efforts in this book are noteworthy because instead of describing prevailing conditions in individual cities, he uses a comparative perspective that cuts across individual city studies and focuses on policy issues concerned with planning and governance. He analyzes individual urban services such as transportation, water and sewerage provision, waste collection and disposal, and housing and basic urban services, sorting out programs that have worked or have not worked and specifying lessons learned in each city-region. He cites successful and unsuccessful efforts to use physical master plans and comprehensive strategic plans in areawide regional development. He also probes into programs that develop inner-city areas as well as efforts to achieve rational development on urban peripheries. He asks if expanding mega-urban regions are sustainable from an environmental, economic, social, and political perspective. He utilizes actual case studies or urban projects as the basis for generalizations and insights into how huge city-regions are planned and governed.

In his efforts to compare and find commonalities and differences among unique conditions in a wide variety of urban settlements, Laquian makes distinctions among Asian mega-urban regions, such as (1) East Asian city-regions in wealthy and technologically advanced countries such as Osaka, Seoul, and Tokyo; (2) centrally planned Chinese cities like Beijing and Shanghai; (3) Southeast Asian city-regions characterized by primacy, such as Bangkok, Jakarta, and Metro Manila; and (4) South Asian city-regions, such as Delhi, Dhaka, Karachi, Kolkata, and Mumbai. In addition, Laquian pays special attention to rapidly changing cities in China like Guangzhou, Hong Kong, and Tianjin, as well as Vietnamese cities like Hanoi and Ho Chi Minh City. By focusing on the political, economic, and social character of these city-regions, Laquian attempts to explain how actors and stakeholders in each urban region are attempting to face up to the myriad challenges that confront them.

An underlying theme in this book is the relationship between globalization and the emergence of mega-urban regions. Laquian defines globalization operationally as a process that includes four key elements: (1) the rapid dissemination and receiving of information worldwide, (2) unfettered trade and commerce across national boundaries, (3) easier movement of people internationally, and (4) the immediate effects and impact of significant global events on people's lives. Basing his understanding of globalization on the role of very large cities, Laquian also adds other elements, such as (5) the nearly instantaneous transfer of financial resources between cities, (6) the increased influence and power of transnational corporations and international financial institutions, (7) the use of international legal regimes and standards, and (8) the rapid spread of sociocultural influences from dominant urban nodes.

After his analysis of the linkages between globalization and urbanization, however, Laquian contends that in Asia, the so-called global cities phenomenon does not seem as important and crucial in the development process as has been suggested by researchers like Saskia Sassen, Manuel Castells, and John Friedmann. Mainly, Laquian argues that in most Asian countries, very large cities have closer linkages to the nation-state than to other urban centers in other parts of the world. This is particularly true in cities that function as national capitals, where local affairs tend to be dominated by the national government officials and political leaders who live there. With the possible exception of Singapore, which seceded from the Federation of Malaya and became a city-state, most Asian city-regions have strong economic and political linkages with their hinterlands. Even a global city like Tokyo, with its vital financial ties to cities like London and New York, functions predominantly within the context of the Japanese economic and political context.

Building on his early studies of Metro Manila, Laquian stresses in this book the role of the city in nation building. As city-regions spark the economic development of nation-states, Laquian contends that they also exert a positive effect on the spread over the whole country of positive tendencies related to social and political behavior. Thus, it seems only natural for local political leaders in capital cities to be considered as potential candidates for national office. Modernizing messages related to key aspects of political development—such as the formation of political parties based on issues rather than personalities, voting for the most qualified candidates, and resorting to referendums or recalls to change erring local officials—tend to spread from urban areas to the more traditional countryside.

The concepts of planning and governance used by Laquian in this book parallel the comprehensive and strategic approaches used by CUSP in its comparative studies of cities all over the world. The set of Asian mega-urban regions studied by Laquian suggests a commonality in themes and concerns that may also apply to big cities in Africa, Latin America, and other developing global regions. We at CUSP welcome this book as a significant contribution to the growing literature on the developmental potentials and sustainability of the world's cities. We look forward to more studies of a comparative nature to further our understanding and commitment to the developmental roles of cities and mega-urban regions.

Joseph S. Tulchin
Co-Chair
Comparative Urban Studies Project
Woodrow Wilson International
Center for Scholars

Preface

In the early 1960s, when I first became interested in the planning and governance of big cities, there were only four Asian cities with populations of more than 5 million (Tokyo, Shanghai, Beijing, and Osaka). At the time, New York was the largest city in the world, followed closely by London, Paris, and Los Angeles. Not a single city in Latin America or Africa ranked among the world's top ten cities. Buenos Aires, Mexico City, and Cairo were rapidly expanding, but they were not yet designated mega-cities. My home city of Manila, with fewer than 3 million inhabitants, did not make the list of the thirty biggest cities in the world.

By 2005, almost half of the world's population of 6.2 billion will be urban. The number of mega-cities with populations of 10 million or more has expanded to eighteen, with twelve of these in Asia (Tokyo, Mumbai, Kolkata, Dhaka, Delhi, Shanghai, Jakarta, Osaka, Beijing, Karachi, Metro Manila, and Seoul). The United Nations projects that by 2015, there will be twenty-two mega-cities worldwide, and fourteen of these will be in Asia (Istanbul and Tianjin will gain mega-city status). Though there will be four mega-cities in Latin America (São Paulo, Mexico City, Buenos Aires, and Rio de Janeiro) and two in Africa (Lagos and Cairo), not a single city in Europe will qualify as a mega-city. Only two cities in North America, New York and Los Angeles, will rank as mega-cities, with the former sliding down from first to eighth place.

In the span of four decades, the mega-city phenomenon has shifted from North America and Europe to Asia, Latin America, and Africa. In almost all the mega-cities mentioned above, urban development has sprawled into the surrounding countryside, enveloping villages, towns, and small and medium-sized cities. Many mega-cities have been transformed into "extended metropolitan regions." In some cases, the field of expansion of mega-cities has joined up with those of other large cities, creating sprawling "mega-urban regions."

On the question of the developmental role of big cities, I confess that I have always held an optimistic view of urbanization. This optimism is probably rooted in the fact that I grew up in the slums and squatter settlements of Metro Manila and later managed to pursue an international career in urban planning and management. During the turbulent years in the Philippines after World War II, our family moved to Manila to escape from the ravages of the Communist Huk insurgency in Central Luzon. In the capital city, we lived as squatters in a succession of makeshift shanties, somehow managing to stay at least one step ahead of the demolition crews of the city's Public Works Department. By the time I finished high school in 1954, our family had been evicted half a dozen times. Happily, in the Philippines of my time, it was possible to get an education by managing to get good grades. The American Fulbright scholarship program also made it possible for me to go abroad and get a doctoral degree in urban affairs at the Massachusetts Institute of Technology. Because of these early life experiences, it seemed only natural for me to become a researcher, author, practitioner, and professor of urban and regional planning.

I first became involved in urban affairs in 1965, as the head of an urban community development program attempting to solve the housing problems of squatters and slum dwellers in Tondo, Manila's largest informal settlement. In this program, we conducted pilot projects in urban community development focused on self-help, progressive housing consolidation, mutual aid, and community upgrading. As indicated in my book *Slums Are for People* (1969), it became clear after launching the project that Manila's housing and basic urban services problems could not be solved by piecemeal efforts. Onsite development, though effective, usually required moving people out of the target communities. Low-cost housing projects also faced the problem of "gentrification," as project beneficiaries sold their plots and housing allocations to wealthier families and moved to other squatter areas. Often, these families moved to sites on the urban periphery, in a process that some sociologists have called "premature suburbanization." It became quite obvious to me at the time that individual community projects would not solve the problems—an areawide or metropolitan approach was needed to deal with the complex issues involved in providing poor people with affordable housing and basic urban services.

In my view, urbanization and the growth of very large cities are inevitable and irreversible. Despite the observation by some demographers that big city growth has declined significantly or that it has been reversed, I am not convinced that this is the case. To me, the so-called polarization reversal in big city growth may just be the result of a statistical artifact. The central cities in big metropolitan areas may not be growing (some may even be losing population), but growth rates in peripheral areas continue to be high. Metropolitan area statistics may be showing declining population growth rates, but this is because city-regions are "underbounded" by formal definitions of city or standard metropolitan statistical area boundaries. Adjusting the political and administrative boundaries of city-regions in the light of the actual "fields" of economic and social influence of urban settlements clustered into an urban network will most likely reveal the actual geographic scope and continued growth of urban agglomerations.

The truth is that the city-regions of Asia are continuing to grow. Though urban residents have lower levels of fertility than their rural counterparts, sharp declines in death rates are adding to the population of cities There is also ample evidence indicating that efforts to keep people down on the farm have not worked. Such programs as busing migrants back to their villages in the Philippines or issuing identification cards only to bona fide city residents in Indonesia have failed. The use of the household registration system, or *hukou,* in China and Vietnam, worked only for a number of years. As soon as these "socialist" countries shifted to a more market-oriented system, the migration toward cities continued. In the light of the fact that mega-urban regions will continue to grow, I believe that it is time to reconsider policies designed to control or reverse big city development.

It is my contention in this book that planning efforts for developing and managing very large human settlements need to start with the urban built environment and how it affects the urban core and its hinterland. This means that planning has to be geographically inclusive, as well as functionally comprehensive, covering the whole urban field of influence and dealing holistically with the full range of economic and social factors that determine citizens' quality of life. Governance structures should be set up to encompass whole mega-urban regions, and such structures should avoid the political fragmentation that is a serious hindrance to areawide cooperative and coordinated action. The twenty-first century is an urban one, and the planning and governance of mega-cities and mega-urban regions is the major challenge facing people interested in urban development. I hope that this book on the planning and governance of Asia's mega-urban regions will help to shed some light on these urban-regional issues.

The basic ideas in this book originated from a perception among faculty members at the School of Community and Regional Planning (SCARP) at the University of British Columbia (UBC) that a new view of urbanization in the twenty-first century was needed. In 1991, when I was appointed professor of planning and director of the Centre for Human Settlements (CHS), the research arm of SCARP, there was dissatisfaction among my academic colleagues with the extremely negative view of urbanization that dominated the planning literature. We felt that a shift to a new human settlements paradigm was needed to effectively deal with problems of urbanization in the coming new millennium. We saw the fields of planning and governance as two possible mechanisms for bringing about positive developmental changes.

CHS was founded in 1976 after the First United Nations Conference on Human Settlements (Habitat I) in Vancouver. Before Habitat I, quite a number of researchers perceived development in the developing world as basically rural-agricultural. They saw urbanization as dehumanizing, politically corrupting, morally degrading, and disruptive of the natural environment. In this, they were merely perpetuating the notion—shared by many thinkers, philosophers, and romantics from Confucius to Marx and from Rousseau to Engels—that rural places were good and natural and cities were evil and artificial. The prevailing view at the time was that the problems of developing countries could be solved if donor agencies focused on how to develop miracle rice, hybrid corn, fast-growing fish, and nitrogen-fixing legumes through scientific and technological breakthroughs that would enhance rural development—not dealing with the problems of cities.

The creative approaches and popular initiatives shown in Habitat I, however, indicated that urban residents, especially urban poor people, were capable of solving their own problems. Participants in the Nongovernmental Organization Forum, composed mainly of popular-sector organizers, community-level activists, and other civil society representatives, came up with creative ideas for dealing with issues like squatting and slum dwelling, low-cost transport, garbage recycling, and other urban ills. This more positive view of urbanization encouraged CHS faculty members to seek policy and program solutions to problems of rapid urbanization through planning and governance approaches. In this, many of the UBC faculty members were influenced by the results of studies by Charles Abrams, Jorge Hardoy, Alfred van Huyck, Otto Koenigsberger, William Mangin, Lisa Peattie, Janice Perlman, Colin Rosser, John Turner, and others who argued that urban poor people living in slum and squatter areas, instead of being the cause of urban problems, were actually the solution to those problems.

In 1990, the Canadian International Development Agency named the UBC Centre for Human Settlements an International Centre of Excellence in development planning. It awarded CHS a grant of $5.8 million to carry out a study of the effects and impact of rapid urbanization in three Asian countries (China, Indonesia, and Thailand), with a special focus on the mega-cities of Beijing, Shanghai, Guangzhou, Bangkok-Thonburi, and Jakarta-Bandung. The objective of the study was to analyze the various factors influencing rapid urbanization and to suggest planning and governance mechanisms that could help make cities more sustainable human settlements. To carry out the study, the Asian Urban Research Network (AURN) was established in 1991. When UBC offered me the directorship of CHS (which also included acting as project coordinator and principal investigator of the AURN), I decided to resign from the United Nations and moved from New York to Vancouver.

My early interest in big city planning and governance had begun while studying at MIT in the early 1960s, where I wrote my doctoral dissertation on the role of Metro Manila in the economic, social, and political development of the Philippines. In my first book, *The City in Nation-Building: Politics and Administration in Metropolitan Manila* (1966), I had argued that big urban centers like Metro Manila played a modernizing role in the process of national development and that this role went beyond their significance as engines of economic growth. The surveys I conducted on the careers of Metro Manila political actors showed that they invariably played prominent roles in national politics. My studies also made me aware of the management inefficiencies in the delivery of urban services in a system of governance suffering from the acute political fragmentation of local governments.

When I was invited by D. E. Regan and William R. Robson to contribute a chapter on Manila to their classic volume *Great Cities of the World* (1971), I was already committed to the idea of unified governance for sprawling mega-urban regions. These ideas were finally put in legal form when I was asked to draft legislation for the creation of the Metro Manila Commission (MMC) in 1975. Unfortunately, the vision of a unified regional governance structure for the whole Metro Manila area was shattered by the appointment of First Lady Imelda Marcos as governor of the MMC and the eventual ousting of her husband, Ferdinand, from the presidency.

In my other policy studies, I focused on the adjustment of migrants in slum and squatter communities to urban life. In these studies, I was vastly impressed by the capacity of squatters and slum dwellers to gain access to shelter and basic services through their own efforts while, at the same time, effectively dealing with punitive and repressive government policies. I also started believing that solving big city problems required the rationality of planning and governance, but that the success of these efforts eventually depended on the support of people and their organized actions at the community level. In 1966, I had a chance to test some of my theories in an action-research project on urban community development conducted in Tondo, Manila's largest slum.

In my second book, *Slums Are for People* (1969), I documented the amazing capacity of low-income people to organize and cooperatively carry out projects that enabled them to build their own shelter and gained them access to water, sanitation, and other basic services. In subsequent policy studies—covering the evaluation of World Bank–financed sites-and-services and slum-upgrading projects in Manila; Dakar, Senegal; San Salvador, El Salvador; and Lusaka, Zambia—I confirmed the merits of housing and basic service provision programs that relied on the human, financial, and organizational capabilities of poor people themselves. The results of these studies were published in *Basic Housing: Policies for Urban Sites, Services and Shelter in Developing Countries* (1983).

In taking on the leadership in the AURN project, I carried as twin components of my intellectual baggage the ideas that (1) urban residents, especially urban poor people, are capable of effectively dealing with their own problems through cooperative and coordinating efforts; and (2) unified metropolitan or regional governance is needed for the efficient management of areawide urban services and infrastructure. These two ideas represented different poles in a theory of governance and constituted the basic dilemma of officials attempting to govern large mega-urban regions. The first highlighted the need for full citizen participation in all aspects of governance and the need for transparent processes and representative structures that ensured the responsiveness of officials to people's demands. Often, that approach involved concepts like local government autonomy, decentralization, community-based planning, and "grassroots democracy." The other called for objective and neutral processes of governmental action that would effectively and efficiently deliver urban services without regard for particularistic interests and lobbying by various interests. That usually took the form of special-function authorities, centralized bureaucracies, top-down planning, and unified second-tier metropolitan governance structures. These polar and seemingly contradictory frameworks constituted the main policy approaches in the AURN project.

As project coordinator and principal researcher for the AURN, I set out to organize a network of research teams in selected Asian cities. Members of the network were researchers, teachers, planning practitioners, policymakers, and community leaders in partner Asian cities. Research teams were organized in the following institutions: the Institute of Architectural and Urban Studies at Tsinghua University, Beijing; the Department of Architecture and Urban Planning, Tongji University, Shanghai; the Centre for Urban and Regional Studies, Zhongshan University, Guangzhou; the Department of Regional and City Planning, Faculty of Civil Engineering and Planning, Institute of Technology, Bandung; and the Institute of Urban and Regional Planning, Faculty of Architecture, Chulalongkorn University, Bangkok. In 1994, Chulalongkorn University was replaced in the project by the Department of Sociology, National Center for Social Sciences and Humanities, Ho Chi Minh City.

The main themes covered in the present volume grew out of the research findings of the AURN project, which was primarily concerned with the rapid growth of large cities that had expanded beyond their formal boundaries and thus become mega-urban regions. As such, the project focused on these mega-urban regions: (1) the Beijing national capital region, which extends along the Beijing-Tianjin-Tangshan (Jing-Jin-Tang) "development corridor" in China's northeast; (2) the Jakarta-Bogor-Tangerang-Bekasi (Jabotabek) development region on Indonesia's island of Java; (3) the "growth triangle" region made up of Guangzhou, Hong Kong, and Macao in China's Pearl River Delta; (4) the Ho Chi Minh City region in south Vietnam, which extends to the coastal areas of Vung Tau; (5) the Bangkok region; and (6) the "head of the dragon" development region of Shanghai in China's Yangtze River Delta.

The AURN project was concluded in 1998, and I wrote and submitted a formal report to the Canadian International Development Agency, the donor agency that supported it. City reports were also written and published by research partners on metropolitan development in Bangkok, Beijing, Guangzhou, Ho Chi Minh City, Jakarta, and Shanghai. Several book-length manuscripts were written and published in English and Chinese. At least three Ph.D. dissertations and a dozen master's theses were based on data gathered in the project. A book titled *Rehabilitating the Old City of Beijing: A Project in the Ju'er Hutong Neighbourhood* (1999), was written by Wu Liangyong and published by the University of British Columbia Press.

The AURN project, therefore, was the first stage in the writing of this book. The second stage started in 2002, when I was awarded a fellowship by the Woodrow Wilson International Center for Scholars in Washington to support the writing of a book on the planning and governance of Asia's mega-urban regions. At the Woodrow Wilson Center, I decided to expand the more narrowly focused themes and city coverage of the AURN project. I also took advantage of the access to information made possible by my stay in Washington to update the data in my study.

By 2002, the number of big cities with populations of at least 10 million in Asia had increased to twelve. With the resources made available to me through the Woodrow Wilson Center's grant, I decided to study developments in other big cities in Asia and compare these with the findings of the more intensive studies we had conducted in the six urban regions covered in the AURN project. I also gathered more recent information on the six AURN city-regions to verify developmental trends. Limitations of time and resources did not permit the same level of efforts in my study of other Asian cities, but analysis of secondary data and reviews of country-project documents available in Washington (data sources from the World Bank, the International Monetary Fund, Environmental Protection Agency, U.S. Agency for International Development, and the Department of Housing and Urban Development; and materials from the Library of Congress, George Washington University, University of Maryland, and Georgetown University) yielded additional information and insights for this book.

This book, therefore, incorporates primary data from the AURN project as well as more recent secondary data on other Asian mega-cities, such as Delhi, Dhaka, Karachi, Kolkata, Mumbai, Osaka, Seoul, and Tokyo. Using the main conceptual framework developed for the AURN project, I have attempted to compare certain conclusions and generalizations derived from that study and to check their applicability to development in the other city-regions. In these efforts, I have tried to focus more intensely on policy concerns and to expand on key lessons learned from the AURN project and their relevance to the planning and governance of the other mega-urban regions of Asia.

Acknowledgments

This book has taken more than a decade to write, and it is only to be expected that in the process, I have incurred many debts of gratitude to countless individuals. In carrying out the Asian Urban Research Network (AURN) project that initially covered six cities in four countries, I have called on the support and cooperation of many people without whose help, this book would never have been written. First of all, I am deeply indebted to the Canadian International Development Agency for funding the AURN project, particularly to the officers who managed the project in Ottawa, Patricia Campbell and Keith Olson. At the University of British Columbia's School of Community and Regional Planning, many thanks are owed to Brahm Wiesman, who wrote the original AURN project proposal; and Alan Artibise, Anthony Dorcey, and William Rees, who were directors of the school during the life of the project. At the Centre for Human Settlements, Peter Boothroyd, Penny Gurstein, Basil van Horen, Thomas Hutton, Michael Leaf, and You-tien Hsing all contributed to the substantive and methodological evolution of the project. The hard work and patience of Elizabeth Zook, research manager, Christine Evans, publications editor, and Karen Zeller, project secretary, strongly contributed to the smooth operations in this project. The contributions of my students in PLAN 570 and PLAN 573, especially their reactions to some of my well-worn "Prod's stories" and outlandish generalizations about planning and governance in Asian mega-urban regions will, unfortunately, be more difficult to trace in this book because my theories kept changing as the years progressed.

In Asia, the dedication and efficiency of our AURN partners are gratefully acknowledged. Mao Qizhi, Wu Liangyong, Zhang Jie, and other faculty members and students at Tsinghua University played key roles in the studies in Beijing. In Shanghai, Zhai Min, Zheng Shiling, and others made sure that the tasks were completed well and on time. The team in Guangzhou, headed by Xu Xueqiang, assisted ably by Yan Xiaopei and others, was a model of efficiency and timely delivery. In the initial years of the project, the contributions of the Bangkok team at Chulalongkorn University, especially that of Suwathana Thadanitti, are gratefully acknowledged. The Bandung team—headed by Tommy Firman and Mochtarram Karyoedi, who were assisted by Teti Argo, Johnny Patta, Krishna Nur Pribadi, and others—contributed immensely to completing the work in that city. In Ho Chi Minh City, the leadership of Nguyen Quang Vinh of the Centre for Sociology and Development and the assistance of Le Thanh Sang, Ngo Thi Kim Dung, and Nguyen Vi Nhuan are gratefully acknowledged.

In the final year of writing this book, I was supported by a grant from the Woodrow Wilson International Center for Scholars in Washington, which made it possible for me to update my data and to conduct additional research on other Asian mega-cities. For this opportunity, I am grateful to Lee Hamilton, the president of the Woodrow Wilson Center, and to the members of the Scholars Selection Committee for selecting me as a resident scholar for the year 2002–2003. I am also grateful to Richard Stren, of the University of Toronto, who first suggested that I apply for the Woodrow Wilson Center grant, and to Ellen Brennan-Galvin and Howard Wolpe, Center fellows, who encouraged me to develop my research proposal. During my year in Washington, I was greatly helped by Blair Ruble and Joseph Tulchin, the co-directors of the Woodrow Wilson Center's urban development group, who led me to new sources of information and invited me to join the advisory committee of the Comparative Urban Studies Project. Joseph Brinley, director of the Woodrow Wilson Center Press, expressed early interest in the publication of this book. I am deeply indebted to the four anonymous reviewers of the initial book manuscript, who suggested extremely useful suggestions to improve the book. Rosemary Lyon, coordinator of the scholars selection program, and Arlyn Charles, who efficiently looked after all administrative and financial details related to my fellowship, were of tremendous help. Lindsay Collins, who always had a positive response to every issue, is owed a great deal of gratitude. I am also indebted to Lisa Hanley and Diana Varat, who managed the urban projects group with efficiency and good humor.

I greatly benefited from the many discussions held with the other fellows at the Woodrow Wilson Center, who freely shared their ideas and comments through intense Work-in-Progress sessions, brown bag seminars, leisurely lunchtime discussions, and fun-filled Friday social hour occasions. The

Center's librarians, particularly Dagne Gizaw, Michelle Kutler, and Janet Spikes, promptly responded to all my requests for books and materials and were especially sympathetic and understanding when I returned borrowed items late. The coordinator of the Center's information system, Rositta Hickman, helped me in my desperate efforts to surf the Internet and responded quickly to frantic calls for help when I was confronted with inevitable computer glitches. On a more personal plane, I am indebted to my research assistant, Joshua Lee, who relentlessly pursued data from the Library of Congress, the World Bank, the U.S. Agency for International Development, and other agency files.

Washington was a great place to write a book such as this one. It made it possible for me to carry out extensive discussions with colleagues at the World Bank, such as Billy Cobbett and Mark Hildebrand of Cities Alliance; Tim Campbell and Barjor Mehta of the World Bank Institute; and my compatriots at the World Bank like Kim Cuenco, Emmanuel Jimenez, and Julie Viloria. Discussions and meetings with Bruce Ferguson of the Inter-American Development Bank; Earl Kessler of PADCO, Incorporated; Jeff Soule of the American Planning Association; and World Bank consultants John Courtney and David Williams were valuable sources of ideas. In fact, one of my problems with working in Washington was how to exercise enough self-discipline to stay away from a bounty of exciting seminars, workshops, and meetings with interesting people and to instead focus on writing this book.

Finally, the completion of this book is ultimately due to the persistence and patience of my wife, Eleanor, who not only made sure that I kept writing ("How many pages did you write today?") but also read and critiqued each chapter as it was drafted, revised, and rewritten.

Living in downtown Washington between the White House and the U.S. Capitol provided us with a lot of distractions and excitement: museums, restaurants, art galleries, and theaters; a sniper scare that sent nervous people walking in serpentines to avoid becoming easy targets; a blizzard that paralyzed the city for days prompting the mayor to appeal for volunteers to dig out snow-buried fire hydrants; peaceful antiwar demonstrations outside our door that started with "No Blood for Oil" and ended with "Impeach Bush"; a Code Orange terrorist alert causing a run on duct tape and plastic sheets; Black Hawk helicopters hovering overhead at all hours to enforce the no-fly zone; a brace of Humvee-mounted surface-to-air missile launchers stationed just blocks away; and finally, a controversial war with Iraq that heightened the fault lines among Washington's hyperpolitical residents. Yet a day hardly passed during the ten months we spent in Washington that Eleanor did not miss being with our three grandchildren. For those missed moments of bonding, I hope this book proves worthy of her sacrifice of being away from the delightful company of Elizabeth, Maya, and Jackson Daniel, who at the ages of four, two, and one were at their most engaging.

1

From Mega-Cities to Mega-Urban Regions

With the advent of the twenty-first century, the image of Asia has shifted from terraced rice paddies and waving palms to smoke-belching factories and towering skyscrapers. True, Asia has a relatively low level of urbanization (37.5 percent in 2000) compared with Europe (73.4), Oceania (74.1), Latin America and the Caribbean (75.4), or North America (77.4). However, it currently holds twelve of the twenty-two largest cities in the world as well as 60 percent of the global population. Asian mega-cities include the world's largest, Tokyo, with a population of 26.5 million, projected to expand to 27.2 million by 2015. As seen in table 1.1, other large urban agglomerations in Asia are Mumbai (formerly Bombay), with 16.5 million; Kolkata (formerly Calcutta), 13.3 million; Dhaka, 13.2 million; Delhi, 13.0 million; Shanghai, 12.8 million; Jakarta, 11.4 million; Osaka, 11.0 million; Beijing, 10.8 million; Karachi, 10.4 million; Metro Manila, 10.1 million; and Seoul, 10.0 million. By 2015, two other Asian cities are expected to exceed 10 million population: Istanbul, with 11.4 million, and Tianjin, 10.3 million (United Nations 2001).*

---

*Population statistics for large Asian cities should be treated with caution because "urban" is defined by countries in different ways. City population figures are subject to adjustments and the relative rankings of world mega-cities vary through time (see table 1.1). Figures given by the United Nations Population Division in *World Urbanization Prospects: The 2001 Revision* (United Nations 2001) tend to be lower than those in *World Urbanization Prospects: The 1996 Revision* (United Nations 1998b). City rankings by the UN Population Division also differ from those made by the United Nations Center for Human Settlements (Habitat) in *Cities in a Globalizing World: Global Report on Human Settlements, 2001* (UNCHS 2001).

Table 1.1. *Populations of Cities with 10 Million or More Inhabitants, 1950–2015 (millions)*

	1950		1975		2001		2015
City	Population	City	Population	City	Population	City	Population
1. New York	12.3	1. Tokyo	19.8	1. Tokyo	26.5	1. Tokyo	27.2
		2. New York	15.9	2. São Paulo	18.3	2. Dhaka	22.8
		3. Shanghai	11.4	3. Mexico City	18.3	3. Mumbai	22.6
		4. Mexico City	10.7	4. New York	16.8	4. São Paulo	21.2
		5. São Paulo	10.3	5. Mumbai (Bombay)	16.5	5. Delhi	20.9
				6. Los Angeles	13.3	6. Mexico City	20.4
				7. Kolkata (Calcutta)	13.3	7. New York	17.3
				8. Dhaka	13.2	8. Jakarta	17.3
				9. Delhi	13.0	9. Kolkata	16.7
				10. Shanghai	12.8	10. Karachi	16.2
				11. Buenos Aires	12.1	11. Lagos	16.0
				12. Jakarta	11.4	12. Los Angeles	14.5
				13. Osaka	11.0	13. Shanghai	13.6
				14. Beijing	10.8	14. Buenos Aires	13.2
				15. Rio de Janeiro	10.8	15. Metro Manila	12.6
				16. Karachi	10.4	16. Beijing	11.7
				17. Metro Manila	10.1	17. Rio de Janeiro	11.5
				18. Seoul	10.0	18. Cairo	11.5
						19. Istanbul	11.4
						20. Osaka	11.0
						21. Tianjin	10.3
						22. Seoul	10.0

Source: United Nations (2001, 11).

The United Nations defines agglomerations of 10 million or more as mega-cities. Although population size is important, however, it need not be the main factor that determines an agglomeration's status as a mega-city. In this book, which is primarily concerned with the planning and governance of large urban areas, I have taken into consideration other socioeconomic factors in deciding whether to include a city in the study or not. Such factors include (1) demographic variables, such as past, present, and future population growth rates, the changing structure of the population by age, gender, and socioeconomic status, population densities, and the geographic spread of population; (2) financial resources and commercial-industrial structure; (3) the primacy and dominance of a city relative to other cities in the country or region; (4) the city's political role as a national capital or a regional development hub; (5) the administrative and political unity or fragmentation of the city-region; (6) the administrative and political mechanisms that have been used historically for planning and governance; and (7) the relative adequacy or inadequacy of urban services, educational and cultural amenities, and infrastructure to meet the needs of the people.

In the light of these other factors, large cities that by the UN definition did not qualify as mega-cities in 2001—like Bangkok, with 7.3 million people; Guangzhou, 6.7 million; and Hong Kong, 6.8 million—have been included in this study. In cases where interesting events or patterns of development in other Asian cities are worth mentioning (as in Bangalore; Chennai, formerly Madras; Hanoi; and Ho Chi Minh City), I have also noted these in the study.

In 1950, New York, with a population of 12.3 million, was the only mega-city in the world. Fifteen years later, Tokyo, with 19.8 million inhabitants, supplanted New York as the world's largest city; and another Asian city, Shanghai, with 11.4 million, joined the mega-city club. By 2001, the number of world mega-cities had expanded to eighteen, and twelve of these were in Asia. The Asian share of mega-cities has gone up from 40 percent in 1975 to 64 percent in 2001. Of the world's twenty-two mega-cities in 2015, Asia is expected to have fourteen, Latin America four (São Paulo, Mexico City, Buenos Aires, and Rio de Janeiro), Africa two (Lagos and Cairo), and North America two (New York and Los Angeles) (United Nations 2001). The anomaly of using the size of a city's population as the only criterion for defining mega-cities is seen in the fact that by 2015, not a single urban agglomeration in Europe will qualify as a mega-city, despite the obvious status of London, Paris, Berlin, and Rome as great cities of the world.

In the past half-century, many Asian mega-cities have grown rapidly, engulfing the towns and villages on their peripheries, in what some Chinese planners have called the "spreading pancake" pattern. Although the population size and territorial spread of these Asian urban agglomerations are impressive enough, there is some evidence that their fields of influence in economic and social terms are actually much larger. Thus, it may not be accurate to call these large Asian urban agglomerations *mega-cities* anymore. Even the term *metropolis*—denoting a central city with surrounding highly urbanized and rapidly urbanizing communities—may be inadequate. The fact is that some of these Asian urban agglomerations have become so large that they now encompass a number of urban nodes around a central city or a network of urban places that make up an "extended urban region."

Some authors have used the term *extended metropolitan region* to refer to these spread-out settlements (Ginsburg, Koppel, and McGee 1991; McGee and Greenberg 1992; McGee and Robinson 1995). The term *megalopolis,* originally used by Gottmann (1961) to refer to the urbanized North American region stretching from Washington to New York and Boston has also been applied to the "bullet train" corridor made up of Tokyo, Osaka, Kyoto, and Nagoya. Not one of the cities in China's Pearl River Delta (Hong Kong, Guangzhou, Macao, Shenzhen) qualifies as a mega-city by mere size; but considered together, these cities may be seen as a form of multinodal development that make up a *megalopolitan region* (Yeh et al. 2002; Enright et al. 2003).

McGee has coined the term *desakota* region to refer to Asia's sprawling urban settlements, combining the word *desa* (village) and *kota* (city) to highlight the mixed rural/urban character of these agglomerations. Following McGee's lead, a number of researchers have described the process of *desakota* development in city regions like Bangkok, Jakarta, Seoul, Shanghai, and the Pearl River Delta region of China (McGee and Robinson 1995; Dharmapatni and Firman 1995; Marton 1996; Lin 1997). In McGee's view, Asian urbanization is "region-based" rather than "city-based." Urban development has radiated outward from a central city and enveloped densely populated rural areas that also contain a great variety of urban activities. Unlike the usual process, whereby big cities draw migrants from rural areas to a large city, what has been happening in Asia, according to McGee, has been the outward expansion of the city, which has taken over relatively large and dense population centers in situ (McGee 1995, 10).

Friedmann has proposed that the term *city* might refer to a settlement with clearly defined boundaries or to a *city region* that consists of a core city along with its surrounding urban field, which together make up an "integrated/functional economic space." As Friedmann explained:

Urban fields typically extend outward from the core to a distance of more than 100 km; they include the city's airport, new industrial estates, watersheds, recreation areas, water and sewerage treatment facilities, intensive vegetable farms, outlying new urban districts, already existing smaller cities, power plants, petroleum refineries, and so forth, all of which are essential to the city's smooth functioning. City regions on this scale can now have millions of inhabitants, some of them rivaling medium-sized countries. This space of functional/economic relations may fall entirely within a single *political/administrative space.* ... More likely, however, it will cut across and overlap with a number of—in some cases a very large number —of political-administrative spaces of cities, counties, districts, towns, provinces, etc. (Friedmann 1992, 4; emphasis in the original)

The concept of urban field proposed by Friedmann is an excellent way of understanding the emergence of mega-urban regions in Asia. McGee has noted that "a distinguishing feature of recent urbanization in the . . . countries [belonging to the Association of Southeast Asian Nations] is the extension of their mega-cities beyond the city and metropolitan boundaries" (McGee 1995, ix). This urban growth has often spread outward along major transportation routes, forming what has sometimes been called the "palm and extended fingers pattern"—with string developments extending along major transportation routes from an expanding urban core until they link up with other towns and cities on the city-region's periphery:

Extended metropolitan development tends to produce an amorphous and amoeba-like spatial form, with no set boundaries or geographic extent and along regional peripheries; their radii sometimes stretching 75 to 100 km from the urban core. The entire territory—comprising the central city, the developments within the transportation corridors, the satellite towns and other projects in the peri-urban fringe, and the outer zones— is emerging as a single, economically integrated "mega-urban region" or "extended metropolitan region." Within this territory are a large number of individual jurisdictions, both urban and rural, each with its own administrative machinery, laws and regulations. No single authority is responsible for overall planning and management. (McGee 1995, 8)

In this book, I have adopted the concept of "urban field" advanced by Friedmann and the idea of "mega-urban region" advanced by McGee and others in their studies of Asian urbanization. In addition, however, I propose that in a number of Asian countries, mega-cities have greatly expanded to the extent that they now form "systems of cities" linked together functionally in networks of settlements encompassing huge tracts of highly urbanized as well as rural areas.

In focusing on the large urban agglomerations in Asia, I have decided to use *mega-urban region* as a generic term to refer to these very large urban settlements. Strictly speaking, however, mega-urban region may refer to (1) *mega-city-centered extended metropolitan regions* like Bangkok Metropolis, Metro Manila, Jakarta Raya, and the Delhi and Dhaka national capital regions, where development emanates from a dominant urban core and envelopes adjacent settlements; (2) *extended metropolitan regions,* such as the Shanghai-Nanjing-Hangzhou-Suzhou region and the Beijing-Tianjin-Tangshan national capital region, where a number of urban nodes form a regional network; (3) *polynucleated metropolitan regions,* where no one city-region dominates but a number of highly urbanized urban settlements form a system of cities, such as in the Pearl River Delta region in southern China made up of Guangzhou, Shenzhen, Hong Kong, Macao, and Zhuhai; and (4) *true megalopolitan regions,* such as the Tokyo-Nagoya-Osaka bullet train corridor, where several large mega-cities with their own extended metropolitan regions encompass a very large highly urbanized area.

In general, Asian mega-urban regions tend to be fragmented administratively and politically. Some of them cut across traditional provincial and state boundaries and are marked by an absence of unified or coordinated governance structures. Although some urban and regional planners have voiced the need for comprehensive strategic plans that may guide the development of these mega-urban regions, serious problems have confronted and frustrated such attempts. Usually, problems associated with jurisdictional fragmentation, the decentralization of authority and power to autonomous local government units, and the uneven distribution of economic and financial resources among various local units, pose serious issues related to areawide planning and urban governance. The main challenge in Asian mega-urban regions, therefore, is how developments in the mega-city, the extended metropolitan region, and the megalopolitan region can be effectively planned and governed in such a way that these agglomerations can continue to be economically productive, provide gainful employment, meet ever-rising levels of demand for key urban infrastructure and basic urban services, protect and conserve the physical and cultural environment, foster civic involvement and participation of citizens in public affairs, achieve equity and social justice, and ensure the sustained livability of these human settlements.

Because definitions of what constitutes a mega-city, an extended metropolitan region, or a megalopolitan region tend to be fuzzy, it is important to clearly indicate the geographic area and jurisdictional scope of such mega-urban regions. It may be useful, therefore, to try to define the boundaries of these settlements. To illustrate, one may look into the spatial configuration of the national capital region of Japan. The central core of this region is the completely urbanized *mega-city* of Tokyo. Surrounding this densely inhabited core is the Tokyo *metropolitan region,* which includes the prefectures of Tokyo, Saitama, Chiba, and Kanagawa and the cities of Yokohama, Kawasaki, and Chiba. Going farther afield, there is the Tokyo *megalopolitan region,* which includes the cities and prefectures of Nagoya, Kyoto, Osaka, and Kobe. The Tokyo megalopolitan region, therefore, is composed of the interlocking urban fields of at least five city-centered regions that make up the economic, social, and political heartland of Japan (Takahashi and Sugiura 1996, 103).

The emergence of mega-urban regions has also been well marked in China. China's national capital, Beijing, is a mega-city composed of four city districts that make up the urban core (East District, West District, Xuanwu, and Chongwen). The master plan for Beijing, however, encompasses a metropolitan region that includes four inner suburban districts (Haidian, Chaoyang, Fengtian, and Shijingsha), as well as ten counties that have been added to the city's jurisdiction (Tongxian, Changping, Shunyi, Miyun, Yanqing, Pinggu, Daxing, Fangshan, Mentougou, and Huairou). This metropolitan region covers 16,807.8 square kilometers and had a population of 11 million in 2001. In analyzing developments in the Beijing region, however, some planners have proposed that the planned development of China's capital region should include other urban centers in what has been called the Jing-Jin-Tang corridor that includes Beijing, Tianjin, and Tangshan (Ye 1986). This megalopolitan region, which also includes the cities of Langfeng and Qinhuangdao, extends from the northern tip of the Great China plains to the Gulf of Bohai, an area that contains a population of about 36 million (Mao 1996).

The largest mega-city of China, Shanghai, is made up of ten urban districts, four suburban districts, and six suburban counties. The master plan for Shanghai, however, adds seven satellite towns that expand the Shanghai metropolitan region to a territory of 6,340 square kilometers with a population of 12.8 million. As in Beijing, however, some planners have suggested that proper planning for Shanghai should include a megalopolitan region that includes Nanjing and six cities in Jiangsu province as well as another seven cities in Zhejiang province. This would expand the Shanghai megalopolitan region to an area of 100,000 square kilometers with a population of 72.7 million (Shi, Lin, and Liang 1996, 536).

Other urban areas in Asia that may be considered mega-urban regions include (1) the Jakarta region, which comprises the so-called Jabotabek (Jakarta-Bogor-Tangerang-Bekasi) region in West Java; (2) the Metro Manila region, which encompasses the Calabarzon (Cavite-Laguna-Batangas-Rizal-Quezon) region on Luzon Island; (3) the Bangkok region; (4) the Guangzhou–Hong Kong–Macao development triangle, which also includes the special economic zones of Shenzhen and Zhuhai as well as the cities of Zhongshan, Baoan, and Pangyu in the Pearl River Delta of southern China; (5) the National Capital Region of India, which is made up of the city of Delhi and districts in the states of Haryana, Uttar Pradesh, and Rajasthan; (6) the Mumbai-Pune development corridor; (7) the Kolkata region; (8) the Dhaka region; and (9) the Karachi region.

Why This Book?

With the prospect of mega-urban regions dominating the urban landscape in Asia and other parts of the world, it is interesting that although there have been quite a number of analytical studies focused on the emergence of very large urban agglomerations, there has been a dearth of policy-oriented studies dealing with comprehensive planning and governance designed to cope with the many problems faced by these settlements. This book is an attempt to respond to planning and governance needs of mega-urban regions. Essentially, it asks if these extremely large urban agglomerations can remain viable as human settlements, if they can provide the services and amenities required by the tens of millions of people who inhabit them, and if they can ensure their citizens a decent quality of life. Are these mega-urban regions sustainable from an ecological, economic, social, and cultural viewpoint? Will social equity and justice be possible in these large urban city-regions? Can they be planned rationally and comprehensively so that they will be able to strategically respond to both expected and unexpected developments and trends? Are they governable in such a way that public services can be delivered effectively and efficiently? Are there ways by which good leaders can be selected in an open and democratic manner; the costs of government kept within the capacity to pay of the citizens; and all interested citizens, interest groups, and stakeholders be able to participate in decision-making processes that affect their lives? Specifically, the book raises the following issues:

- How did mega-urban regions emerge? What economic, social, geographic, environmental, and historical factors played a role in their growth and development? The various mega-urban regions included in this study represent a wide and complex variety of demographic patterns, levels of economic development, ethnocultural mixes, institutional mechanisms, and systems of planning and governance. What are the unique features as well as the common characteristics that may help to explain their successful or unsuccessful efforts at planning and governance?
- What positive developmental outcomes have resulted from the emergence of mega-urban regions? How have large mega-urban regions influenced the economic, social and political developments of nation-states of which they form a part?
- What problems have been encountered in mega-urban regions? What efforts have been used to solve these problems? How did government policies, programs, and activities contribute directly or indirectly to the rapid growth of mega-urban regions? What lessons have been learned from public, private, and community efforts, and how can these be adapted to varying situations in other countries?
- How can comprehensive and strategic planning approaches be used to make mega-urban regions more livable and sustainable? What governance policies, structures, and mechanisms can be used to help make mega-urban regions more livable and sustainable?

For a detailed overview of the present volume's approach, methodology, and chapter contents, see the section at the end of this chapter titled "About This Book."

Containing the "Exploding Cities"

As early as the mid-1950s, it was proposed that Asian cities were not like Western cities in their historical patterns of development, demographic growth, economic production, labor absorption, and links to industrialization. Analyzing the rapid growth of big cities in Asia, Hauser (1957), concluded that these were "overurbanized," in that the explosive expansion of their populations was not accompanied by the economic and industrial changes that characterized urbanization in Europe and North America. Breese coined the term "subsistence urbanization" to describe the extreme poverty in big Asian cities, "in which the ordinary citizen has only the bare necessities and sometimes not even those for survival in the urban environment" (Breese 1966, 5).

In *The Southeast Asian City,* McGee (1967) coined the term "pseudo urbanization" to refer to a situation where the growth of cities is "unhinged" from processes of economic development and industrialization. Taking off from the observation of Davis and Golden (1955) that it was the "population boom" (arising from natural population growth and internal migration) rather than "true urbanization" (in the sense of "urbanism" as proposed by Wirth 1938) that is responsible for the rapid growth of Asian cities, McGee perceived a pessimistic scenario for Southeast Asian urbanization, characterized by inevitable conflicts between urban elites and the rural masses, growing urban-based centralism and authoritarianism, and a catastrophic shift "from despair to desperation" (McGee 1967, 22).

In 1972, Ginsburg cited four features that made big Asian cities different from their Western counterparts (Ginsburg 1972, 273–74). First, he noted the "indigenous tradition" of urbanism exemplified by ancient cities like Beijing, Delhi, and Tokyo, which historically flourished much earlier than Western cities. During the early phase of development in these cities, according to Ginsburg, they tended to be compact and had densely populated core areas, unlike Western cities that were more spread out because of the influence of economic and technological factors such as industrialization and the wide use of the private automobile.

Second, Ginsburg observed that the vast majority of Asian big cities were the result of "foreign enterprise and/or domination," that took the form of the "colonial city," typified by Jakarta, Karachi, Kolkata, Manila, and Mumbai. Due to their colonial nature, Ginsburg pointed out that these very large cities were not originally designed to serve their contiguous hinterlands but acted more as linkage points between the European countries and their exploited colonies.

Third, Ginsburg noted that big cities were a feature of "dual economies" in most Asian countries, where the modernized sector was reflected in the very big cities while the vast majority of the people lived in tradition-bound rural areas. Fourth, he concluded that big Asian cities were different from Western cities "morphologically and organizationally" because the spatial distribution of . . . population [in Asian cities] is less by so-cio-economic classes than by ethnic, caste, racial, and occupational distinctions. Land uses most frequently are mixed and place of work and place of residence tend to be associated. Suburbanization is relatively slight and . . . such suburbanization as has taken place is associated with lower-income rather than higher-income groups. Even where suburbs in a strict sense are non-existent, given frequent overlapping, settlement on the outskirts of the expanding cities may be associated with squatter settlement. . . . The central business districts are undeveloped and diffuse. Centralization as a principle is clearly not nearly so important [in Asia] as it is in the West. (Ginsburg 1972, 274)

In the decades after World War II, policymakers in many Asian countries—influenced by the negative view of "the exploding cities" that was then pervasive in the urban literature—adopted policy instruments designed to control the growth of big urban agglomerations. In China, strict controls on internal migration through the *hukou* (household registration) program were instituted in the mid-1950s to limit urban growth. Rural industrialization was attempted in the summer of 1958 in the Great Leap Forward campaign, which, combined with the Commune Movement, tried to improve the lives of rural dwellers by accelerating both industrial and agricultural productivity. Unfortunately, both these campaigns had disastrous results that were not helped by the ravages of natural calamities between 1959 and 1961 and the withdrawal of Soviet assistance from China due to ideological differences.

Despite the failure of these two campaigns, China's leaders launched the Great Cultural Revolution between 1966 and 1976. During this period, China instituted programs to decongest big cities like Beijing, Guangzhou, Shanghai, and Tianjin by forcibly moving intellectuals, students, and professionals to the countryside in the so-called *xia fang* movement. The Great Cultural Revolution failed, and many of the "rusticated" persons drifted back to the cities, many as "black" or undocumented migrants. Serious economic and social dislocations caused by the virtual collapse of the government also resulted in an increase in China's population that, combined with uncontrolled migration, greatly expanded the population of big cities.

The launching of economic reforms in 1979 was accompanied by the relaxation of strict controls on internal migration. Officially, however, China to this day still adheres to the policy to "limit the growth of very large cities, rationally plan the development of medium-sized cities, and encourage the growth of small towns." Despite the relaxation of the *hukou* system, some local officials still use it to regulate the inflow of migrants by making it a prime consideration in the allocation of jobs, housing, and other benefits. China's continuing wary attitude toward the rapid growth of very large cities may be partly explained by the realization that something like 450 million people (out of 900 million rural dwellers) are considered redundant in rural areas and that the uncontrolled migration of these people to big cities might create serious problems of unemployment, housing, environmental pollution, crime, and other urban ills.

In other Asian countries, there were similar attempts to limit the growth of big cities with the use of administrative measures. During the early 1960s, Jakarta tried a personal identification system limiting access to urban services to bona fide city residents. Manila also instituted similar measures, where, for example, admission to city schools was confined to official city residents. Some local officials even went to the extent of issuing one-way bus or train tickets to rural–urban migrants to allow them to return to their places of origin. In Indonesia, Malaysia, and the Philippines, government programs for rural development were adopted in the belief that if life in the villages and towns could be improved, people would not flock to big cities. Such programs as the "transmigration" settlements in Indonesia, the federal land development schemes in Malaysia, and the Mindanao resettlement programs in the Philippines were meant not only to develop frontier areas but also to deflect migration away from big cities.

Urban theorists and policy analysts in a number of countries proposed limiting the growth of very large cities by focusing attention on the development of small towns and small cities. In India, Johnson (1970), basing his arguments on the merits of central place theory, proposed that "ten thousand small towns" would effectively service and energize the countryside. Banerjee and Schenk (1984), comparing urbanization trends in China and India, lauded the Chinese government's strategy to limit the growth of very large cities and encourage the development of small towns. After launching economic reforms in 1979, the Chinese authorities resurrected the theories of Fei Xiaotong, which highlighted the developmental role of small towns during the 1930s (Fei 1984). In 1984, Rondinelli wrote persuasively about the economic and social roles of small cities and towns in national development (Rondinelli 1984). Arguing that small town development would achieve "equity with growth," Kammeier and Swan (1984) vigorously supported policies to encourage the growth of "lower level settlements."

Aside from attempting to limit the growth of large cities by encouraging development in rural areas or redirecting development to smaller urban nodes, some authorities in a number of Asian countries decided to tackle big city growth head on. They used planning instruments and zoning codes and regulations to control the outward expansion of big cities. In the mid-1950s, when Seoul was growing at an average annual rate of 7.6 percent, the authorities instituted "greenbelts," wide swaths of green space, around the city; and they prohibited or penalized industrial and housing investments settling outside these belts. These approaches, however, were not very successful because the lure of cheaper land and improved transport facilities simply encouraged investors to "jump the greenbelt" and establish their plants on the urban periphery. South Korean programs to channel public and private investments to growth centers in urban nodes far from Seoul (like Kangjiu, Kyungnam, Pusan, and Taegu) were more successful because these new centers served as "countermagnets" to developments in the capital region.

In India, the government set up "industrial estates" and "new towns" to attract people and discourage them from moving to large cities. Unfortunately, some industrial and new towns were located too close to cities like Kolkata and Mumbai and thus were later engulfed by urban sprawl. In Metro Manila, the government passed a law in 1962 imposing higher taxes and urban service fees on industrial and manufacturing plants built within a 50–kilometer radius from the city center. Instead of limiting urban growth, this law had the effect of increasing urban sprawl as investors took advantage of cheaper land and more accommodating conditions offered by suburban local authorities eager to attract tax-paying concerns to locate in their jurisdictions.

As a whole, past policy efforts in South and Southeast Asia to control the growth of large cities have had very mixed results. In South Asia, annual population growth rates in very large cities declined slightly between 1975 and 2000 but remained high. The exception to this trend was Dhaka, which grew by 6.6 percent a year in the period 1950–75 and by 7.0 percent in 1975–2000. Mumbai grew by 3.1 percent annually in 1975–2000 (down from 3.6 in 1950–75), Delhi by 4.1 percent (down from 4.6), and Karachi by 3.7 percent (down from 5.4). Even as big city populations in South Asia are expected to decline in the future, the United Nations notes that very high growth rates could be expected in medium-sized Indian cities, such as Ghaziabad (which grew by 5.2 percent a year in 2000–15) and Surat (5.2 percent).

In Southeast Asia, the primacy of capital cities like Bangkok, Jakarta, and Metro Manila remains strong, and various programs to encourage rural growth, deflect development to small towns and small cities, set up development nodes in frontier areas, and use planning instruments and zoning regulations to limit big city growth have not met with much success. Although official urban statistics project a reduction in big city population growth rates in 2000–2015, there are indications that some of these declining trends may be due to the statistical "underbounding" of standard metropolitan statistical areas. The populations of inner cities in South and Southeast Asia may not be growing (some core cities are even losing population), but other localities on the urban periphery are growing at annual rates in excess of 8 percent. This growth is not captured in official statistics, which are based on urban boundaries that may be seriously out of date.

The Urban Transition and "Polarization Reversal"

In the early 1970s, the concern about the rapid growth of mega-cities and large urban agglomerations was relieved, somewhat, by an observation that the rates of growth of such settlements had been slowing down. In North America, it was noted that inner-city cores were losing population and even the growth of peripheral areas was slackening. In about 1976, several demographers observed that cities like Buffalo, Cleveland, and Pittsburgh exhibited negative growth rates. Milwaukee, New York, and Saint Louis also had negative growth rates in the 1970s. This decline in big city growth was called "counterurbanization," "reconcentration," or "polarization reversal."

The same tendency toward declining population growth rates was observed in a number of cities in Europe. As early as the 1960s, Liverpool, London, and Manchester had started losing population. Dusseldorf, Essen, Hamburg, and Hanover experienced negative growth rates in the 1970s. So did Florence, Genoa, Milan, Naples, and Rome. London, in particular, lost 853,000 people between 1970 and 1980 (United Nations 1998b).

The decline in the growth rates of cities was also observed in developing countries. The projected population figures for Buenos Aires, Mexico City, Rio de Janeiro, and São Paulo had to be reduced in 1996 because of decreasing growth rates. China and India revised their big city population projections downward in the 1970s. In recent years, however, there has been a perceived increase in the growth rates of very large Chinese cities.

The observed decline in mega-city population growth rates is said to be a key element in the process of "urban transition." It was proposed that large city growth was cyclical, going through at least four phases. The first phase was urbanization, the rapid growth of the urban core. This was followed by suburbanization, rapid growth on the urban periphery. The third phase, counterurbanization, saw declines in population growth both in the core and on the urban periphery. Finally, the fourth phase involved reurbanization, an increasing growth rate in the core followed by slower growth on the urban periphery (United Nations 1998a).

Reading the literature on the perceived decline in the growth rates of mega-cities and mega-urban regions, I was reminded of studies I had conducted in Metro Manila in the early 1960s. At the time, the metropolitan area officially designated as the Philippine national capital region (NCR) was composed of four cities (Manila, Quezon City, Caloocan, and Pasay) and four towns (Malabon, Navotas, San Juan, and Makati). The population figures and other data provided by the Bureau of the Census and Statistics were limited to these local jurisdictions. Because I was interested in comprehensive and strategic planning for Metro Manila at the time, however, I decided to more accurately determine the actual "field" or geographic spread of urban services in the metropolitan area. To do this, I drew up a set of overlay maps on transparent acetate sheets that showed the spatial coverage of the following services:

1. the actual area covered by the service grid of the Manila Electric Company;
2. localities that could be reached by a local call with the Philippine Long Distance Telephone Company;
3. the service coverage of the Metropolitan Waterworks and Sewerage System, including reservoirs, open water sources, and forested watershed areas;
4. localities that could be reached by city buses or jeepneys based on a 50 centavo fare;
5. the residences of workers in a number of government agencies who commuted daily to jobs in the city;
6. localities where city market vendors got their supplies of fruits and vegetables each day;
7. the locations of squatter areas on the urban periphery;
8. the locations of newly established factories and industrial sites;
9. the locations of newly opened housing subdivisions and housing projects; and
10. the locations of open dumps used by city authorities for their solid waste.

By simply putting the overlay maps indicating the geographic coverage of public services in the Metro Manila area on top of each other and shining a naked electric bulb beneath them, I was able to easily determine the actual "field" of economic and social activities that an urban-regional planner needs to consider in formulating a comprehensive plan for the metropolitan area. This rather mechanistic method (the geographic information system had not yet been invented) revealed that instead of the four cities and four towns that supposedly delimited the NCR, the "real" national capital region required the addition of nine other localities that were actively involved in areawide services and economic activities (Valenzuela, Marikina, Taguig, Pasig, Pateros, Mandaluyong, Paranaque, Muntinlupa, and Las Pinas).

Much later, of course, the formal definition of the jurisdiction of the Metro Manila area was revised to encompass all these local government units—although, at present, all but four of the original towns have changed their status to chartered cities. Even with this official adjustment, however, some Philippine planners are already suggesting that the actual field of Metro Manila's development has spread beyond the seventeen local government units affiliated with the Metro Manila Development Authority. With the active economic linkages established between the NCR and the newly created special economic zones at Subic Bay and at the former U.S. Air Force base at Clark, these planners are arguing that a comprehensive development plan for the NCR should encompass these growth nodes and adjacent local government units (HUDCC 1995).

A similar analysis of large urban agglomerations in South and Southeast Asia will probably indicate that the official metropolitan boundaries on which official statistics are based are narrowly underbounded. A significant degree of perceived decline in annual population growth rates in Asian urban agglomerations, therefore, may be due to a statistical artifact. For more effective planning and governance efforts, it may be necessary to adjust the boundaries of city-regions to more accurately reflect actual fields of economic and social influence. The expansion of the mega-urban regions has been so rapid that formal political boundaries have not kept pace with it. The growth rates of the metropolitan area populations (based on formal statistical boundaries) might be declining, but peripheral areas continue to grow. If one considers the rapid population growth rates on the periphery, one may find that such urban agglomerations have not really stopped growing—or, at least, that their perceived declining growth rates may not be as significant as currently stated (Laquian 1994).

Differing Views on Mega-Urban Development

Since the mid-1980s, there has been a shift in perspective about the problematic nature of very large cities and their developmental role. An earlier "antiurban bias" in development policies has been replaced by an appreciation of the economic advantages of cities. The United Nations' *Cities in a Globalizing World: Global Report on Human Settlements, 1996* (UNCHS 1996, xxv) observed that

> urbanization has been an essential part of most nations' development towards a stronger and more stable economy. . . . The countries in the South that urbanized most rapidly in the last 10–20 years are generally those with the most rapid economic growth. Most of the world's largest cities are in the world's largest economies, which is further evidence of this link between economic wealth and cities. Cities and towns also have important roles in social transformation. They are centres of artistic, scientific and technological innovations, of culture and education. The history of cities and towns is inextricably linked to that of civilization in general.

McGee has pointed out that the growth of mega-urban regions has produced some positive results. He specifically cited the increased incomes of people in the region; the fact that such regions often produce 80 percent or more of a country's gross domestic product; the creation of employment opportunities, especially for women; and the great improvements in transportation and communication as well as domestic and international trade and commerce. McGee also noted the modernizing influence of mega-urban development in the spread of planning and governance ideas that enhance more coordinated development.

Hamer, for his part, has cited the positive elements of larger markets, closer integration with the global economy, the attractiveness of working in the region for technically qualified professionals, and the availability of trunk infrastructures and services that make such regions competitive with other countries (Hamer 1994). The global importance of urban growth has, of course, been analyzed by Sassen, who stressed the positive role of cities as centers of producer services, finance, employment, and coordination and control (Sassen 1991).

The rapid and continued growth of mega-cities and their surrounding regions, however, is alarming to many people. The large size of mega-cities and their sprawling mega-urban regions is usually associated with serious problems. Traffic jams in Bangkok and Manila, slums and pavement dwellers in Kolkata and Mumbai, water shortage in Beijing and Tianjin, air pollution in Delhi and Shanghai, and social unrest in Jakarta and Karachi are some of the main concerns of both residents and visitors to these cities. Vast tracts of agricultural land on the periphery of such regions are lost to urban uses every year. The mega-urban regions suffer from water and air pollution. The litany of big city problems goes on and on, and there are few signs that solutions will be found soon.

The poverty, congestion, pollution, and many other problems of mega-cities and their surrounding regions have raised questions about the sustainability of large urban agglomerations. Current production and consumption patterns in these cities prompt many authors to question whether they can continue to grow without adversely affecting the lives of the future generations that will live in them. Many students of development see large city growth as ecologically, economically, and socially unsustainable. Rees and Wackernagel, for example, have argued that big cities are ecologically unsustainable by their very nature. To these researchers, consumption levels, as exemplified in Western cities, do not allow cities and their hinterlands to regenerate resources or dissipate their wastes fast enough. Lacking basic resources themselves, cities draw on an ever-expanding "ecological footprint" to support themselves (Rees and Wackernagel 1996).

A number of economists have argued that cities are the engines of economic growth in most countries of the developing world. As such, these economists argue that the size of cities does not matter. They cite "urbanization economies"—such as those of scale, agglomeration, location, infrastructure efficiencies, labor specialization, and management capabilities—along with other advantages as conducive to positive development. In a provocative article, Hamer argued that "[city] size *per se* is not the issue; instead, it is mismanagement at both the regional and local levels, and wrong-headed national urbanization policies promoted by physical planners with visions of optimal geography and very little sense of economics" (Hamer 1994, 175).

To Hamer, economic development and urbanization "are joint products of a wealth-creating process that generates large urban regions." Concentration in very large cities enhances economic growth. This process of economic growth is accomplished by (1) focusing activity in a small portion of the nation's landscape, which creates agglomeration economies, which in turn creates an inverse relationship between production cost per unit of output and population size; (2) concentrating investments in regional trunk infrastructures for transport, communications, power, and water supply; and (3) gathering in an urban place a large labor force with a wide array of skills, a large number of suppliers, diversified financial and commercial services, venture capital, and access to information on foreign markets and technologies, as well as the amenities needed to attract managerial talent. In mega-cities, the local urban marketplaces concentrated purchasing power at the doorstep of the business community.

The pro-urban arguments of so-called expansionist economists have been questioned by a number of ecological economists in recent years. For instance, a conference convened by the Institute for Research on Environment and the Economy in 1993 concluded that "human beings depend upon a limited range of configurations (stocks and flows) of the Earth's biological, geological, and atmospheric systems for healthy habitat, material and energy resources, and assimilation of wastes." The conference delegates questioned the premise of "expansionist economics" that "while price reflects both values and scarcity, healthy habitat, material/energy resources, and waste assimilation capacity are perpetually available or infinitely substitutable" (IREE 1993, 12).

The conference delegates also contested the claim that "there are no limits to growth." The limits, they argued, are imposed by the fact that economic activities occur in a finite physical world. The limits to growth were listed by environmental economists as (1) *habitat*, that is, human health requires that we maintain the quality of our habitat (the consonance of structure and function that constitutes ecosystem health); (2) *resources*, that is, the rate at which resource inventories are degraded through use (and abuse) should not exceed the rate at which they are regenerated; and (3) *waste*, which should not be generated to either contaminate ecosystems (in the sense that emissions become incapable of being assimilated within the parameters of human and ecosystem health) or to squander resources (i.e., whose loss constitutes the pointless forfeiture of opportunities).

Current development policies (globalization, unhampered economic competition, regional economic integration, trade deregulation, functional specialization, protection of existing business infrastructures, and emphasis on the primacy of material growth), according to Rees, serve to increase the size of high-density settlements. These mega-cities and regions, in turn, appropriate "carrying capacity" from other places and turn their surroundings into sinks for the waste they produce. Pursuing a classical economic doctrine based on the primary importance of growth, very large cities neglect to recognize the fact that they exist in a finite ecological sphere. Wryly responding to the claim that cities are the engines of economic growth, Rees states that "however brilliant its economic star, every city is an ecological black hole drawing on the material resources and productivity of a vast and scattered hinterland many times the size of the city itself (Rees 1992, 49).

From an environmental viewpoint, the growing alarm about the rapid growth of cities and their ecological, economic, and social effects and impact has brought to the fore the age-old debate of whether the Earth is a steady-state economy with built-in limits (Daly and Townsend 1993) or whether market mechanisms, proper pricing, advanced technology, factor substitutability, and human ingenuity will make resources perpetually available or infinitely substitutable, as argued by classical expansionist economics (IRRE 1993). Those who are not too concerned about rapid urban growth argue that cities are the productive engines of national economies and that, in almost all countries, the great bulk of gross domestic product is produced in urban areas. As human beings congregate at very high densities in limited space, urbanism as a way of life grows. Economic forces arising from economies of scale, agglomeration, specialization, and location enhance greater productivity. From the individual to the organizational levels, economic competition in urban areas brings about the survival of the fittest.

Individuals who are worried about the state of cities, however, are concerned about the relationship between the built and the natural environments. Traditionally, it has been proposed that production is a function of land, labor, and capital. According to Marshall (1920), capital is made up of those material things that owe their usefulness to human labor, whereas land (or "natural capital") is made up of things that owe nothing to human labor. Though human beings have no power to create matter, they do create utilities by putting things into useful forms ("cultural capital"). Such utilities can be increased in supply if there is increased demand for them—they have a supply price.

However, there are utilities over which human beings have no control—they are given as a fixed quantity by nature and have no supply price (land). The material things designed, built, and controlled by human beings (capital) have self-organizing properties in accord with market forces. However, they occur within the larger environmental system (land) that, while self-organizing, has finite limits. Cities, as the manifestations of human design, building, and control may function quite well within their human-built spheres. However, because they exist within the finite sphere of the natural ecosystem, there are natural limits to their growth.

In a book published by the Centre for European Studies titled *Sustainable Development and the Future of Cities,* Hamm and Muttagi (1999, 10) noted that "urban areas are by far, the most serious pollutants of our environment. They wrote that

> urban areas have become the functional entities by which humanity organizes its metabolism with nature. The material throughput of the human species is being transformed mostly in cities. Having no natural resources of their own, they import into the urban areas raw materials, capital, and information, which are transformed to emit wastes of all sorts. . . . They have to absorb new technologies, the changing demographic composition of populations, and new and massive migration streams. In the past, the hinterland from where these urban areas received their inputs and to where they expelled their outputs was relatively limited and in close proximity. The hinterland of the urban areas today is the entire globe. . . . With urban population growth, we observe increasing energy consumption and traffic; solid, liquid and gas wastes; decreasing availability of sinks; more pollutant hazards; and degrading technical infrastructures. While tropical rain forest depletion receive much attention . . . the enormous waste of natural and human resources caused in the urban areas of the world remains underestimated.

Clearly, Hamm and Muttagi do not believe that cities and mega-urban and megalopolitan regions in their current state are sustainable. They concluded that "if the present trend in industrialization, pollution, resource depletion, and species extinction continued unchanged, gradually, there will be a breakdown of society and the irreversible disruption of life support systems. This will end in sharpening distributional struggles and eventually in global harakiri" (Hamm and Muttagi 1999, 16).

The Emergence of Mega-Urban Regions in Asia

Asia currently has twelve of the world's largest urban agglomerations (figure 1.1). By 2015, this number may increase to fourteen. Economically and socially, these urban agglomerations already dominate life in many Asian countries. Physically, the growth of some of these agglomerations has been so rapid that the processes of planning and governance have not kept pace with urban expansion. With Asian mega-urban regions becoming so

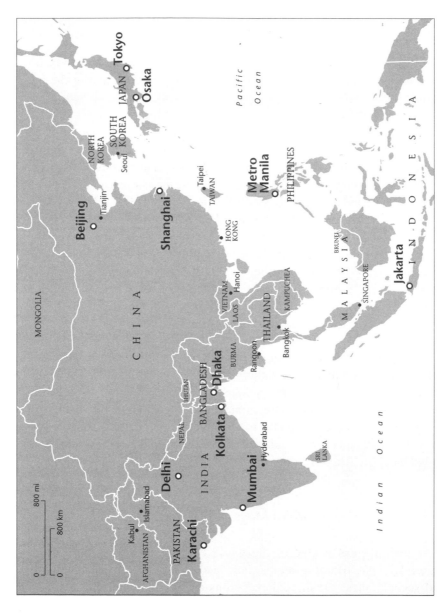

Figure 1.1. Urban Agglomerations in Asia. Istanbul not shown.

important in world urbanization trends, it is necessary to analyze and explain why some of these urban agglomerations continue to grow and others do not, the problems they now have and will continue to face in the future, various approaches that have been used or that may be used to deal with those problems, and some lessons that can be learned by urban agglomerations in other parts of the world faced with the same problems.

Even a cursory examination of the main features of Asian mega-urban regions reveals that they make up a complex mix of varied settlements due to the historical, economic, cultural, and technological factors that have influenced their development. Because of this complexity, it would be a mistake to lump together all the Asian cities in a homogeneous mass. Indiscriminately mixing the dynamics of East Asian and South Asian cities, for example, would most likely obfuscate understanding of the specific conditions in each set of cities. Planning and governance interventions that may be successful in cities like Seoul and Tokyo may not work at all in solving problems in Delhi, Dhaka, Karachi, Kolkata, or Mumbai. Planning mechanisms that have been used in countries in transition from centrally planned economies to more market-oriented systems (China and Vietnam) would probably not be very useful in dealing with problems in more market-dominated countries (India and the Philippines). Political traditions rooted in centralized control and bureaucratic hegemony would probably be ineffectual in managing cities created on the basis of decentralized authority and local autonomy.

Despite the differences among Asian mega-urban regions, however, they do share a number of characteristics, in much the same way that apples and oranges (or mangoes and mangosteens) can all be classified as fruits. The most notable commonality among these urban agglomerations is their population size, which ranges from less than 10 million to more than 26 million (see table 1.2). A second important consideration is the fact that these mega-urban regions have spread outward into adjacent areas, enveloping villages, towns, and cities, and at times linking up with the urban fields of other city-regions. A third common characteristic of Asian mega-urban regions is the economic, social, cultural, and political dominance that they exert on their national or regional hinterlands. Fourth and finally, on the basis of demographic, spatial, economic, political, and administrative features, it is possible to view all the Asian mega-urban regions as commonly following a pattern of organizing economic and social space so that they all have a densely developed mega-city core and an extended metropolitan region—and, some of them, a megalopolitan form as well.

Table 1.2. *Asia's Largest Urban Agglomerations (2000 Rankings)*

Urban Agglomeration	Metropolitan Area (square kilometers)	Population (millions)				Annual Growth Rate	
		2000	2005	2010	2015	1995–2005	2005–2015
1. Tokyo	2,187	26.4	26.4	26.4	27.2	0.3	0.1
2. Mumbai (Bombay)	4,167	18.0	20.9	23.5	26.1	3.2	2.2
3. Kolkata (Calcutta)	1,785	12.9	14.1	15.6	17.2	1.7	2.0
4. Shanghai	6,340	12.8	13.1	13.6	14.5	0.0	1.1
5. Dhaka	1,528	12.3	15.3	18.3	21.1	4.9	3.2
6. Karachi	1,800	11.7	14.0	16.5	19.2	3.7	3.1
7. Delhi	3,182	11.6	13.4	15.1	16.8	3.0	2.2
8. Beijing	16,807	11.0	11.0	11.5	12.2	0.2	1.1
9. Osaka	1,890	11.0	11.0	11.0	11.0	0.0	0.0
10. Jakarta Raya	654	11.0	13.1	15.3	17.2	3.6	2.7
11. Metro Manila	636	10.8	12.4	13.8	14.8	2.9	1.7
12. Istanbul	1,991	9.4	10.8	11.8	12.4	3.1	1.5
13. Tianjin	11,919	9.1	9.4	9.9	10.7	0.5	1.2
14. Seoul	11,718	10.0	9.8	9.8	10.0	−0.4	0.0
15. Bangkok	1,568	7.2	8.0	9.0	10.1	2.1	2.3
16. Hyderabad	217	6.8	8.1	9.3	10.4	4.0	2.5

Source: United Nations (2001, 12).

Taking into consideration the commonalities and differences of the various Asian mega-urban regions included in this study, I have categorized them into four types. First are the *technologically advanced East Asian cities.* Osaka, Tokyo, and Seoul like their counterparts in North America and Europe, have extremely low rates of population growth. After an explosive annual growth rate of 7.6 percent in 1950–75, Seoul is expected to grow at an almost stagnant 0.02 percent in 2000–2015. Similarly, Tokyo grew at 4.2 percent a year between1950 and 1975 but is expected to grow at only 0.19 percent in 2000–2015. Osaka grew at 0.45 percent a year in 1975–2000 and will not grow at all in 2000–2015. Tokyo and Seoul have relatively well-defined administrative and political jurisdictions encompassing highly urbanized areas. They have homogeneous populations, mostly employed in the formal sector. Tokyo has succeeded in curbing the massive environmental pollution that plagued it in the past, and Seoul has managed to deal with its serious housing problem. Both cities have evolved planning and governance mechanisms that adequately meet their demand for basic urban services.

Second are the *mega-cities of China.* Large cities in China, such as Beijing, Guangzhou, Shanghai, and Tianjin, have had low population growth rates as a result of migration and population control policies strictly enforced in the past. Since China's shift from a centrally planned to a more market-oriented economic system in 1979, however, the populations of large Chinese cities have started to grow as a result of in-migration arising from a relaxation of the *hukou* household registration system (the adjusted expansion of metropolitan boundaries has also officially shown an "increase" in city-region populations). Though urban service levels in key Chinese cities are somewhat hard pressed, China's high level of economic growth (an average annual growth of gross domestic product of 8.5 percent since 1979) and a recent boom in infrastructure development are tending to keep services up to meet citizen demand. Administrative reforms that focused on the decentralization of decision-making authority to local government units, land policy adjustments, public finance, and housing provision are also helping to improve urban planning and governance in these city-regions.

Third are the *primate cities of Southeast Asia.* Southeast Asian cities like Bangkok, Jakarta, and Metro Manila currently have moderate rates of population growth, although in 1950–75 they grew at annual rates of 4.8, 4.7, and 4.1 percent respectively. Annual growth rates in these cities are expected to decline in 2000–2015 to 3.0 percent in Jakarta, 2.8 percent in Metro Manila, and 1.9 percent in Bangkok. These cities are very important to national life because of their primacy and their political status as central government capitals. Though they are beset with many problems (inadequate housing, water shortage, congested traffic, environmental pollution), their recent investments in infrastructure (e.g., rapid transit) promise to improve life for city residents. They have also benefited from urban reforms attempting to bring about better urban and regional planning, as well as administrative coordination among local units within city-regions.

And fourth are the *South Asian cities.* Large cities in Bangladesh, India, and Pakistan, such as Dhaka, Delhi, Kolkata, Mumbai, and Karachi, continue to expand at relatively high rates, with population growth only expected to slacken in the 2000–2015 period. Between 1975 and 2000, Dhaka grew annually by 7.0 percent, Delhi by 4.0 percent, Karachi by 3.7 percent, Mumbai by 3.1 percent, and Kolkata by 2.02 percent. Furthermore, other intermediate-sized South Asian cities are also growing rapidly, with annual population growth rates in 2000–2015 projected at 3.1 percent for Lahore, 3.7 percent for Chittagong, 3.4 percent for Pune, and 5.0 percent for Surat (United Nations 2001, 12). The urban agglomerations of South Asia are already plagued with problems such as slums and squatting, inadequate transport, high unemployment rates, and massive levels of environmental pollution. With their continued expansion, they will pose extreme challenges to urban planning and governance.

The vast differences among Asian urban agglomerations demand a more in-depth analysis of their growth patterns, with special emphasis given to the historical factors that have influenced their development. Some Asian cities, such as Beijing, Delhi, and Tokyo, have ancient origins and were the seats of powerful empires. Others, like Jakarta, Karachi, Kolkata, Metro Manila, Mumbai, and Shanghai, trace their roots to the colonial era, when they served mainly as trading and production outposts. The growth and development of Chinese cities was mainly controlled by central government policies focused on population and migration controls. Most Southeast Asian cities prospered because of their dominant roles as national capitals. All these factors are important considerations when attempting to explain the growth and development of each of the Asian mega-urban regions covered in this study.

East Asian Cities

Big cities in East Asia are technologically advanced, having passed through the industrial and even postindustrial developmental stages. *Tokyo* has been the largest city in Japan since the middle of the nineteenth century, when, as Edo, it was the capital of the Shogunate. After the Meiji Restoration of 1868, Edo was renamed Tokyo and became the capital of Japan. Although Tokyo was greatly devastated by the earthquake and fire of 1923 and American carpet bombing during World War II (1941–45), the city was rebuilt and quickly became the dominant center in the country. Tokyo's population, which dropped to 3.5 million in 1945, increased at such a formidable rate that by 1969 it had reached 11.3 million (Royama 1972, 945).

Concerned about the expansion of Tokyo, the Japanese government pursued a policy of decentralizing industries and manufacturing to other urban centers such as Osaka and Nagoya. The structural adjustments of Japan's economy, however—particularly the shift from industrial production to information technology—meant the continued dominance of Tokyo. Although Osaka and Nagoya initially attracted many rural-urban migrants from other parts of Japan, they eventually became out-migration areas for people flocking to the Tokyo metropolitan area. The concentration of people in the Tokyo region became even more marked with its emergence as a global center for finance and other services (Sassen 1991, 1994).

To more effectively manage the growth of Japan's largest city, the national capital region of Tokyo was defined and proclaimed in 1956. This region encompassed Tokyo city proper, the prefectures of Saitama, Kanagawa, and Chiba, and parts of four other prefectures. This new metropolitan region extended from 97 to 124 kilometers from central Tokyo. It was placed under the centralized jurisdiction of the Tokyo Metropolitan Government (Yeung 1990, 72). During the latter half of the 1980s, the Capital Tokyo Metropolitan Area was expanded again to cover eleven prefectures aside from Tokyo itself (Kanagawa, Saitama, Chiba, Ibaragi, Tochigi, Gumma, Fukushima, Niigata, Nagano, Yamanashi, and Shizuoka) to form an extended national capital region (Takahashi and Sugiura 1996, 114).

At present, the official Tokyo national capital region covers 2,187 square kilometers and is run as a self-governing unit encompassing twenty-three wards (*ku*). Aside from the twelve prefectures, it also covers an area containing twenty-six cities, five towns, and one village. This built-up area had a population of 26.5 million in 2001; this is expected to increase to 27.2 million by 2015 (Vogel 2001, 116). The most recent Tokyo Megalopolis Concept Plan seeks to expand this territory, resulting in boundary adjustments that may increase the population of the Tokyo urban agglomeration to 33 million by 2025.

Osaka is the economic and industrial center of the Kansai region, which also includes Kobe, Kyoto, and Nara. Osaka, like Kyoto, is not an ordinary prefecture (*ken*) but an urban prefecture (*fu*). Osaka prefecture covers approximately 1,890 square kilometers and had a population of 11 million in 2001 living in Osaka City, thirty-two other cities, ten towns, and one village. The whole Osaka–Kobe–Kyoto Metropolitan Area, however, had a population of 17 million.

Japanese archeologists claim that humans have inhabited the Osaka area for more than 10,000 years. Osaka became a center of culture around the fifth century A.D., when Chinese cultural influence reached Japan through Korea. During the seventh century, a capital city was set up in the Osaka area that was modeled after the capital of China. Although the Japanese capital was moved to Nara and Kyoto afterward, Osaka continued to flourish as a center of trade and commerce. In 1583, Hideyoshi, who succeeded in unifying Japan, chose Osaka as his base and built Osaka Castle. In the seventeenth century, Japan's capital was moved to Tokyo, but Osaka continued its economic role and became known as the "kitchen of the nation." Japan's modernization under the Meiji Restoration in the nineteenth century undermined the powers of the merchant class that dominated Osaka, but these entrepreneurs soon shifted to industry and manufacturing, reviving the economic vitality of the region. Although Osaka was seriously devastated by repeated air raids during World War II, it was quickly rebuilt and has become the second most important urban center in Japan.

Seoul, the capital of the Republic of Korea, does not qualify as a megacity according to the city-size definition of the United Nations. But it is included in this study because of its important role in the development of the country. The city traces its origins as the capital of the Paekche Dynasty, one of the three ancient kingdoms in Korea. The Koryo Dynasty made Seoul its capital in 1067. With the ascendancy of the Chosun Dynasty in 1392, Seoul became Korea's national capital. The city flourished within and beyond its fortified walls until Korea was occupied by Japan between 1910 and 1945. Seoul was almost completely destroyed during the Korean War, but since 1953 it has been rebuilt and transformed into a manufacturing and industrial base. Starting in 1956, Seoul's population grew explosively, with the annual growth rate reaching 10.8 percent in 1957, 19.2 percent in 1959, 16.8 percent in 1961, and 15.8 percent in 1962. By 1968, Seoul's population had reached 4.3 million and was growing at 8.3 percent a year (Kwon 1972, 256).

At present, the Seoul capital region is made up of the central city of Seoul, eleven suburban districts, and parts of Kyonggi province. It covers a territory of 11,718 square kilometers and had a population of 9.8 million in 2000. In 1995, the Korean government approved the Capital Region Management Plan, which provides the basic direction and guidelines for the location of economic activities as well as the distribution of population. As envisioned by this plan, by 2015 the Seoul national capital region will have a population of 20.2 million and will encompass Seoul, Inchon, Kyonggi province, nineteen cities, and seventeen counties (Kim 1999, 36).

Chinese Cities

China has had very large cities for centuries, with Chang'an (present-day Xi'an) said to have had more than a million inhabitants during the Tang Dynasty (A.D. 618–907), when it was the eastern terminus of the famed Silk Road, the trade route that linked Asia and Europe. China's current capital, *Beijing,* was founded as a military outpost in about 1045 B.C. under the Western Zhao Dynasty (1122–771 B.C.). It became Yanjing, the capital of the state of Yan, during the Spring and Autumn Period (722–481 B.C.) and the Warring States Period (403–221 B.C.). It was expanded by Kublai Khan as Dadu (the Great Capital) in A.D. 1267–1271. By 1949, therefore, when the victorious Communist regime declared Beijing the state capital, the city had been the imperial capital of China for more than 800 years (Wu 1999).

Before 1949, the built-up area of Beijing was only 109 square kilometers. This was expanded to 707 square kilometers (with a population of 1.6 million) after the Communist takeover to make room for economic expansion as Chinese authorities pursued the socialist policy of transforming Beijing from a "consumptive" to a "productive" city. The Beijing master plans encouraged urban development outward—following a "palm and fingers" pattern, where transportation routes made up the fingers extending toward the southern and eastern parts of the region. Despite efforts to control development, however, the fingers around Beijing continued to extend outward, and urban development kept filling up the spaces between the fingers. In 1957, the Beijing master plan expanded the city's territory to 8,860 square kilometers. A master plan prepared in 1982 envisioned that Beijing's population would be kept below 10 million by 2000. This figure was exceeded as early as 1992 (Wu and Mao 1993).

To keep abreast of development, the current master plan for Beijing, which was approved by the State Council in 1993, expanded the municipality's jurisdiction to include four inner-city districts, four nearby suburban districts, two outer suburban districts, and eight counties. The master plan has adopted the "scattered groups" or "urban clusters" strategy designed to turn the capital region into a polynucleated settlement. In this strategy, the central city area would have 6.5 million inhabitants and the rest of the inhabitants would be living in 14 satellite towns and 140 small and medium-sized towns (Mao 1996, 1–4).

Development in the Beijing region has been most rapid along the so-called Jing-Jin-Tang Expressway that connects Beijing with Tianjin and Tanggu Port. Along this main development corridor, nine special economic zones have been constructed: (1) the Beijing Economic and Technical Development Zone; (2) the Yongle Economic Development Zone; (3) the Langfang Economic and Technical Development Zone; (4) the Langfang High-Tech Development Zone; (5) the Yat-sen International Scientific Park; (6) the Wuqi County Development Zone; (7) the Tianjin High-Tech Industrial Park; (8) the Beichen Development Zone; and (9) the Tianjin Economic and Technical Development Zone. In addition to the developments along the Jing-Jin-Tang Expressway, another eight development zones have been established in the region surrounding Beijing. These are (1) the Changping Scientific Park; (2) the Shangdi Information Industrial Base; (3) the Feng-tai Scientific Park; (4) the Liangxiang Development Zone; (5) the Capital International Airport High-Tech Zone; (6) the Shunyi Development Zone; (7) the Yangjiao Development Zone; and (8) the Baigou Development Zone (Wu and Mao 1993).

In effect, therefore, the Beijing megalopolitan region now encompasses a widespread territory with an estimated population of more than 36 million. Within the region are two major cities under the jurisdiction of the central government (Beijing and Tianjin), two intermediate-sized cities (Tangshan and Langfang), and many towns and county seats. The megalopolitan region ranges all the way from the edge of the Great China Plain to the Gulf of Bohai and covers areas within the provinces of Hebei and Shandong. It has been proposed, in fact, that this Beijing megalopolitan region should be planned as a single entity (Ye 1986).

China's largest city, *Shanghai,* owes its development to its coastal location, which has made it a natural center for overseas trade and commerce. After the defeat of China's Qin Dynasty in 1842 by Western powers (in the Opium War), Shanghai became a colonial enclave with separate concessions run by Britain, France, Japan, Germany, the United States, and other powers. Because of Shanghai's "colonial background," the Chinese authorities tended to neglect its development after 1949. Later, Shanghai was turned into an industrial base in accord with Soviet planning concepts favoring the development of heavy industries in big cities.

In 1958, the Shanghai municipality annexed the counties of Baoshan and Jiading, increasing its territory to 5,908 square kilometers. Seven satellite towns were also annexed in 1990, expanding Shanghai's jurisdiction to 6,340 square kilometers. At present, the Shanghai municipality encompasses ten urban districts within the city proper, four suburban districts, and six suburban counties (Yeung and Sung 1965, 5). Economically, however, Shanghai dominates the Yangtze River Delta region that links it with Nanjing, Suzhou, Changzhou, Zhenjiang, Nantong, Yangzhou, and Wuxi in Jiangxu province and with Hangzhou, Jiaxing, Huzhou, Ningbo, Shaoxing, and Zhoushan in Zhejiang province. Shanghai, as the "head of the dragon" in the Yangtze River delta, is now the dominant core of a megalopolitan region covering about 100,000 square kilometers with a population of 72.7 million (Shi, Lin, and Liang 1996, 536).

The Pearl River Delta cities of *Guangzhou, Hong Kong, Shenzhen, Zhuhai, and Macao* have functioned independently until recent times. Lately, however, they have tended to develop in an increasingly coordinated manner because of China's regional development policies. The Pearl River

Delta, at present, has three levels of urban settlements. First, there are the 2 large cities of Guangzhou (6.7 million) and Hong Kong (6.9 million). At a second level are 9 medium-sized cities: Shenzhen, Macao, Zhuhai, Foshan, Jiangmen, Zhongshan, Dongguan, Huizhau, and Zhaoqing. A third tier is made up of 22 small cities that have county status and nearly 300 towns. The Pearl River Delta region, therefore, is a polynucleated megalopolitan region where no one center dominates. It is projected to have a population of 51 million by 2022, 18 percent of which will be in Hong Kong (Enright et al. 2003).

Southeast Asian Cities

Big cities in Southeast Asia are characterized by primacy—the very high concentration of a country's urban population in a single agglomeration. All the Southeast Asian cities included in this study have populations many times larger than the country's next-ranking urban settlement. They are also national capitals that have thrived by serving as the economic, commercial, administrative, and cultural centers of nation-states.

The city of *Manila* was founded in 1571 as the Spanish colonial capital of the Philippines. It thrived on the basis of centralized production of agriculture-based products as well as the main port of the galleon trade that linked the Philippines with Mexico and Spain. When the United States took over the Philippines in 1899, it kept Manila as the national capital. In 1905, pursuant to instructions from Washington, municipal elections were held in Manila to choose Filipino leaders, although actual administrative powers remained in the hands of American officials.

Manila was seriously devastated during World War II, but postwar reconstruction began immediately without the benefit of careful planning. Internal migration—triggered by the push of widespread rural poverty and a communist-led insurgency in other parts of the country on the one hand and the pull of the "bright lights" of Manila on the other—expanded the city's population. By 1960, the four cities and four towns officially designated as parts of Metro Manila had reached a population of 2.1 million and occupied a territory of 362.2 square kilometers.

Since the mid-1970s, the City of Manila proper and the inner core municipality of San Juan have been losing population. The metropolitan population, however, has increased to the point that the jurisdiction of the national capital region has been expanded to cover thirteen cities and four towns. At the same time, towns in the surrounding provinces of Bulacan, Pampanga, Zambales, Rizal, Laguna, Batangas, Cavite, and Quezon have been growing rapidly. The growth of towns located along the arterial roads emanating from Metro Manila has been very fast. So has the population growth rate around areas designated as special economic development zones or high-technology industrial parks.

The rapid expansion of the Manila mega-urban region, in fact, has prompted the government to start formulating a development plan for the whole island of Luzon with Metro Manila as its core. Such a plan includes schemes for the national capital region, the Calabarzon region (made up of the provinces of Cavite, Laguna, Batangas, Rizal, and Quezon), other provinces in the central plains of Luzon, and the two special economic zones established on the former U.S. military bases at Subic Bay and Clark (Laquian 1995).

The capital city of Indonesia, *Jakarta,* was established as the capital of the Dutch colony in the East Indies about 465 years ago. As Batavia, it was planned to mimic a Dutch settlement, complete with a network of canals. The canals, unfortunately, became the breeding place for deadly tropical diseases, and the Dutch colonizers were eventually forced to move to higher grounds. The coastal settlement expanded southward, with the Dutch quarters in the center and the natives settling on the periphery. By 1948, the population of Jakarta had reached about 2 million, living in a built-up area of about 200 square kilometers (including the town of Kebayoran Baru). This population almost doubled to 4 million by 1965, when the built-up area had expanded to 350 square kilometers. The number of city inhabitants increased further to 6.5 million in 1980, when the built-up territory had expanded to 650.4 square kilometers. The 1990 Indonesian census showed that the population of the Special Capital Region of Jakarta (Daerah Khusus Ibukota, or DKI Jakarta, also referred to as Jakarta Raya) had reached 8.2 million.

DKI Jakarta has the status of a province. Surrounding it is the metropolitan region referred to as Jabotabek, which is made up of DKI Jakarta, the municipality of Bogor, the administrative cities (*kota administratif*) of Tangerang and Bekasi, and the regencies (*kabupatens*) of Bogor, Tangerang, and Bekasi. Although Jabotabek is fragmented into local government units, a Joint Development Cooperation Board has been established to coordinate development activities in the region. Planning and governance in Jabotabek, however, is vastly complicated by the fact that many central government agencies exercise authority and power over activities in the region. The local units in the Botabek area are also within the jurisdiction of West Java province, and a number of large private development companies wield considerable clout in public affairs as well.

The United Nations set Jakarta Raya's population at 11.4 million in 2001, projected to increase to 17.3 million by 2015. However, the Jabotabek Metropolitan Development Plan—formulated in 1980 and revised in 1983 as the Jabotabek Structure Plan (1985–2005)—projects a population of 26 million as early as 2005, with more than 18 million people living in the built-up area of DKI Jakarta (Soegijoko 1996, 387). There are even suggestions that for better comprehensive planning, a wider territory that includes the city of Bandung and its surrounding regencies and towns should be taken as the megalopolitan region that actually serves as Indonesia's national capital (Dharmapatni and Firman 1995).

Since the signing of the Bowring Treaty between Britain and Thailand in 1855, *Bangkok* has grown rapidly because of its integration into the world economy. Bangkok's expansion has been fueled by lucrative rice production and exports, the growth of industry, manufacturing and tourism, and the economic boom following the Vietnam War. Late in 1960, the Greater Bangkok Plan 2533 was formulated, designed for a population of 4.5 million on 780 square kilometers of territory by 1990. This plan was later revised by the Greater Bangkok Plan 2000, which projected a population of 6.5 million people occupying 820 square kilometers by the end of the century (Sternstein 1972, 254).

In 1970, Bangkok was combined with Thonburi, across the Chao Phraya River, to form Greater Bangkok, increasing the combined city populations to 2.5 million. Two years later, the Government of Thailand decided to merge the two adjoining provinces of Phra Nakhon and Thonburi into a single city and together with Bangkok created the Bangkok Metropolitan Area (BMA). By 1980, the BMA's population reached 4.7 million. The continued outward expansion of Bangkok has prompted the creation of the Bangkok Metropolitan Region (BMR), encompassing areas in the five provinces of Pathum Thani, Nontaburi, Samut Prakan, Samut Sakhon, and Nakhon Pathom.

Because of the outward adjustments of Bangkok's metropolitan boundaries, in 1988 the BMA's population was said to have "increased" to 5.7 million and the BMR's to 8.5 million (Goldstein 1994, 41). The United Nations, however, has set Bangkok's population at a smaller 7.3 million in 2000, projecting this to reach 9.8 million by 2015. This lower figure is obviously based on a much narrower definition of the metropolitan population and does not consider Bangkok's dominant role in the development of Thailand.

Taking a more expansionist view, the National Economic and Social Development Board (NESDB) estimated in 1990 that the BMR's population had reached 8.9 million and would increase to 12.6 million in twenty years.

Furthermore, the NESDB noted the emergence of an "extended BMR" comprised of the BMR itself and the provinces of Ayutthaya, Saraburi, Chachoengsao, Chon Buri, and Rayong. The total population of this extended BMR is expected to grow from 12 million in 1990 to 17 million by 2010, increasing its share of the national population from 21.5 to 24.3 percent (NESDB 1990, viii).

South Asian Cities

Urbanization in South Asia can trace its ancient roots to the Indus Valley civilization that flourished in preindustrial settlements like Harappa in the Punjab and Mohenjo-daro in the valley of the Indus around 2500 to 1500 B.C. (Sjoberg 1960, 40–41). The origins of India's capital, *Delhi,* have been attributed to the legendary state of Indraphrasta, which is prominently mentioned in the Mahabharata epic. Indian historians have written about the seven cities of Delhi, claiming that the present city is the eighth capital of independent India (Datta and Khosla 1972, 409). The medieval glory of Delhi can still be sensed in the city walls built by the Moghal emperor Shah Jahan during the seventeenth century or the monumental massiveness of the Red Fort.

The modern era in Delhi started with the transfer of India's colonial capital inland from coastal Calcutta (now Kolkata) in 1912. However, city historians indicate that the British colonizers started settlements in the so-called Civil Lines north of the walled city earlier than that date. A well-planned New Delhi was planned and built south of the old city in the 1920s. By 1951, India's capital had grown into a "town group" consisting of two cities, three major towns, and one minor town. All the local government units in the region were amalgamated into a single municipal corporation in 1958, although New Delhi and the Cantonment were allowed to keep their individual identities. In 1961, the Delhi metropolitan population reached 2.65 million for the entire "union territory" that constituted the federal capital of India. This territory was made up of the areas governed by the Municipal Corporation of Delhi (539 square miles with 2.3 million people), the New Delhi Municipal Committee (16.5 square miles with 261,545 people), and the Cantonment Board of Delhi (16.5 square miles with 36,105 people).

Administratively, public services in Delhi before 1958 were managed by four ad hoc authorities: the Delhi State Electricity Board, Delhi Road Transport Authority, Delhi Water and Sewage Board, and the Delhi Improvement Trust. The first three authorities were later merged into the Delhi Municipal Corporation, and the improvement trust was transformed into a development authority under the Delhi Development Act of 1957. The Delhi Development Authority was created as a high-powered body, separate from the municipal corporation, to look after land acquisition and development. It took the leadership in formulating a development plan that came into force in 1962. This master plan envisioned a wider regional context and proposed a ring of towns around the urbanized area (two in Uttar Pradesh, five in Haryana, and one in the union territory itself).

In 2001, Delhi had a population of 13.3 million, occupying a territory of 1,397 square kilometers. At the projected growth rate of 3.4 percent a year (2000–2015), Delhi is expected to reach a population of 20.9 million by 2015. Some Indian planners acknowledge, however, that the current field of influence of Delhi extends way beyond its present territory and should encompass areas in the adjacent states of Uttar Pradesh, Haryana, and Rajasthan to form a larger megalopolitan region.

India's largest city, *Mumbai* (formerly Bombay), is the capital of Maharashtra state and the acknowledged commercial center of India. This port city thrived not only because of manufacturing (particularly cotton and textile) but also with international trade and commerce during the British colonial period. The Bombay Municipal Corporation Act of 1888 specified eight statutory authorities to manage specific activities of the city government—mainly public works, water and sewerage, health, and solid waste disposal. City authorities became so concerned about the heavy industrial pollution in the inner city that they sought to transfer many of the plants to the outskirts early in the city's history.

The first postindependence plans for Mumbai in 1948 proposed the creation of satellite towns north of the city. In 1958, another plan resulted in the establishment of a township across the Thane Creek to draw away population from the crowded inner city. This became New Mumbai in Thane District, which rapidly grew under the guidance and management of the City and Industrial Corporation of Maharashtra state. The New Mumbai Municipal Corporation was established in 1991 and assumed responsibility for nine of the twenty-five urban nodes in New Mumbai. Later, the city was divided into six administrative zones, and the Mumbai Municipal Corporation created sixteen Ward Committees to solve local problems such as water supply, sewage disposal, road repairs, and maintaining streetlights.

At present, the Mumbai Metropolitan Region (MMR) includes Mumbai, New Mumbai, and Thane. Thane, a municipal corporation created in 1982, encompasses Thane District and thirty-two surrounding villages that all fall within the jurisdiction of the Thane Municipal Council. Thane District had a population of 1.2 million in 2001. Also within the MMR are eighteen urban centers located on the periphery of Greater Mumbai. Mumbai City had a population of 11.9 million in 2001, but the whole Mumbai Metropolitan Region had 16.5 million, projected to increase to 22.6 million by 2015.

Kolkata (formerly Calcutta) is the capital of West Bengal state and the second largest city of India. It started as a trading post near the end of the seventeenth century and became the capital of India under the British Empire. In 1912, India's capital was moved to Delhi, but Kolkata continued as an important commercial and industrial center for Eastern India. By 1966, the Kolkata Metropolitan District extended over nearly 490 square miles and contained a population of 7.5 million (KMDA 2004). Within the district, Kolkata City proper covered about 37 square miles and had 3 million inhabitants. Also in the district were thirty-four municipal towns, an almost equal number of nonmunicipal towns, and more than a hundred villages in a built-up area stretching on both sides of the Hooghly River over 20 miles north and 15 miles south of the twin cities of Kolkata and Howrah (Walsh 1969; Ashraf and Green 1972, 301). By 2001, Kolkata City had reached a population of 4.5 million, and the metropolitan area had 13.3 million inhabitants. At an annual growth rate of 2.0 percent, Greater Kolkata is expected to reach a population of 16.7 million by 2015.

Administratively, the Kolkata metropolitan area is divided into three municipal corporations, thirty-four municipalities, and a number of urban localities. The Kolkata Metropolitan Development Authority is responsible for the overall planning of the region and is in charge of large-scale urban infrastructures. The Kolkata Municipal Corporation (KMC) was the first local unit in India to create the mayor-in-council form of urban governance. Under this system, the mayor, deputy mayor, and up to ten elected council members collectively exercise the executive powers of the corporation, functioning as a cabinet. The KMC also administratively decentralized specific responsibility forr certain urban functions to borough committees at the ward level.

Dhaka, the capital of Bangladesh, became an important settlement during the seventeenth century, when it was the Mughal capital of Bengal province (1608–1704). The British took over Dhaka in 1765, and it became the capital of Bengal in 1905. After the partition of British India in 1947, Dhaka became the capital of the Pakistani province of East Bengal and, in 1956, the capital of East Pakistan. In the early 1970s, the Banglee-speaking population of East Pakistan waged a violent rebellion against Pakistan. Dhaka suffered considerable damage during this Bangladeshi war for independence, but it was gradually rebuilt and proclaimed the capital of Bangladesh in 1971.

In 1950, Dhaka had a population of 417,000. But after independence in 1971, it grew at the high annual growth rate of 6.6 percent, so that by 1975 its population had reached 2.1 million. The city currently has a population of 12.5 million, which is projected to increase to 22.8 million by 2015, when it is expected to be the second largest urban agglomeration in the world, second only to Tokyo.

Karachi was settled as a small fishing village and became Pakistan's largest city, with a current population of more than 10 million. In 1843, when the British Army conquered the province of Sindh, the colonizers chose Karachi as a coastal base. When a cholera epidemic ravaged the settlement in 1846, a Conservancy Board was organized, which in turn was upgraded into a Municipal Committee in 1853. In 1933, the City of Karachi Municipal Act was passed, and the Municipality of Karachi was given the status of a municipal corporation. Karachi was made the capital of the new nation-state of Pakistan in 1947 after the partition of the country from India.

By 1950, the population of Karachi had reached more than a million and was growing at 5.4 percent a year. The metropolitan population totaled almost 4 million in 1975. In 1976, the Karachi Municipal Corporation (KMC) was upgraded to a metropolitan corporation. A separate Zonal Municipal Committee was set up in Karachi in 1987, but in 1994 this committee was again merged with the KMC. Five district municipal corporations were also created in the Greater Karachi area in 1996 to adjust to the expansion of the metropolitan area.

The most far-reaching changes in the planning and governance of Karachi occurred on August 14, 2001, when the Government of Pakistan implemented the Devolution Plan creating the City District Government of Karachi (CDGK) as well as 18 town administrations and 178 union councils all over the country. By that date, the population of Karachi exceeded 10 million. Under the devolution scheme, the jurisdiction of the CDGK was extended to 18 towns (Balida, Bin Qasim, Gadap, Gulberg, Gulshan-i-Iqbal, Jamshed, Keamari, Korangi, Landhi, Liaquatabad, Lyari, Malir, New Karachi, North Nazimabad, Orangi, Saddar, Shah Faisal, and a locality called SITE). The new law also introduced a new form of city government. The City Council was headed by the city *nazim,* assisted by the city *naib nazim* and district coordination officers. Each town was headed by a town *nazim,* assisted by a town *naib nazim* and a town municipal officer (CDGK 2004).

The Planning of Asian Mega-Urban Regions

All the mega-urban regions covered in this study have elaborate city and regional development plans. Some of these plans trace their origins to ancient principles derived from religious rites and rituals, quite a number were formulated by colonial administrators, and many were prepared by local planners and international consultants. The plans for Beijing are derived from rituals prescribed in the Zhou Li, which set down explicitly the official rites (including city building) that were practiced during the Zhou Dynasty (1051–403 B.C.) (Nourse 1943, 49; Wright 1977, 47).

Likewise, archaeologists have concluded that the plans for cities in the Indus River Valley, such as Mohenjo-daro and Harappa, reflect cosmological efforts to establish on Earth an idealized notion of the universe (Sjoberg 1960, 40–41). The Khmer cities of Angkor Wat and Angkor Tom (Pym 1968), as well as the centers of Hinduized kingdoms in Indonesia (Borobudur), were also planned along cosmological lines. Chinese cities from Chang'an to Beijing were planned in accordance with classical principles and rituals based on the divine nature of the emperors, the metaphysical influence of wind and water (*feng shui*), and admixtures of Buddhist, Taoist, and other religious traditions (Wu 1986).

Despite the long tradition of Asian city planning, however, the great majority of Asian urban agglomerations were planned and developed in accordance with Western concepts rooted in their colonial backgrounds. The plans for Intramuros (the original walled city of Manila in the Philippines), Batavia (now Jakarta) in Indonesia, Kolkata and Mumbai in India, and Karachi in Pakistan were drawn up respectively by Spanish, Dutch, and British colonial planners. In these settlements, the carefully laid-out grids of city streets and the clearly delineated boundaries of restricted quarters where the colonial officials and their families lived contrasted sharply with the inchoate forms of the "native quarters" occupied by the indigenous populations.

Most plans for colonial cities in Asia were derived from Western planning principles designed to deal with problems of health, sanitation, mobility, and safety. Later, they were also influenced by efforts to achieve the "city beautiful ideal," with its emphasis on parks, open spaces, well-appointed residences, tree-lined boulevards, and other types of controlled land use patterns. Early planners like Howard, Geddes, Lutyens, and Burnham strove for a comprehensive approach to city planning, and some of them tried to apply this approach to Asian cities. Examples of these efforts include the plans of Howard for Bangalore, Lutyens for Delhi, and Burnham for Manila and Baguio (Hall 1988; Mumford 1961).

In general, two planning approaches have exerted a major influence on the development of Asian mega-urban regions: "master planning" and "comprehensive strategic planning." Master planning, the older of the two, has ancient, colonial, and socialist roots. Ancient city master plans, such as those used to establish the imperial cities of China, strictly followed planning principles, such as a rigid north-south orientation, the construction of city walls, how many city gates were to be cut in those walls, the exact number of vertical and horizontal streets that form an urban grid, and the balanced locations of temples and ceremonial altars. These master plans were so rigidly followed that imperial cities were often built in open spaces from scratch or on the razed ruins of conquered settlements.

During the colonial period, master plans applied to Asian cities were mainly copies of those used in the West. The plans for Metro Manila conformed to generic plans used in the Americas that focused on the *plaza mayor* (where the cathedral, city hall, and military barracks were concentrated), neatly laid-out street grids, and the building of city walls. The Dutch plan for Batavia (now Jakarta) featured a network of canals and lanes. In cities like Delhi, Dhaka, Karachi, Kolkata, and Mumbai, colonial master planning was based on British town and country planning traditions, which were mainly concerned with land use, the layout of physical infrastructures, the preservation of green space, and aesthetic urban design.

Such British traditional planning had a strong base in geography—many master plans, in fact, took as a planning unit such geographical configurations as river basins, watershed areas, or mineral resource bases. They tried to use natural science approaches to estimate what people needed and how those needs could be met within an environmentally sustainable system. Often, colonial master planning aspired to achieve aesthetic ideals, as in the garden cities of Bangalore and Singapore.

In the socialist tradition, master planning was based on the "scientific" notion that most things were knowable. There is the assumption that trained professional planners can predict future developments and prepare the physical setting for such developments. Using such tools as statistical analysis, sample surveys, and (sometimes) public consultations, planners believe that they are able to prepare as complete a scenario as possible of future events.

Typically, a socialist master plan would set targets to be achieved at a future date (e.g., the current Hanoi master plan sets the target at 5 million people by 2025). The population target may be based on careful population

projections, or it may reflect a purely political decision (Vietnamese authorities were reputed to have planned for a Hanoi of 5 million people because
they could not accept a capital city that was smaller than Ho Chi Minh City
in the south). From whatever population target is set, other targets are derived
(e.g.: to increase housing floor space area to 12 square meters per person; to
achieve per capita income of $800 per year; to double green space and park
area from what was available in 1995). The resource requirements for implementing the plan are derived from these targeted figures. A typical master
plan places a great deal of stress on the urban infrastructure. The road and rail
network becomes the "backbone" of the plan. Often, the notion of an axis for
development becomes the main feature of the plan. Precisely plotted around
this development axis are carefully demarcated proposed land uses.

In more recent years, a number of Asian mega-urban regions have formulated and adopted comprehensive and strategic plans. In contrast to master planning, strategic planning derives its key ideas from wide-ranging
socioeconomic analysis. Instead of focusing on a desired outcome at the end
of a planning period, strategic planning is more concerned with the process
by which economic and social activities can bring about desired outcomes
at specific points in time. Strategic planning does not assume that complete
knowledge can be attained. Instead, it projects known information up to a
certain point and attempts to anticipate developmental trends so that
planned action can be formulated to deal with those trends. In Asia, strategic planning has been mainly used in countries where the economy is more
influenced by the market than by government intervention. In some countries, such plans are often developed as "indicative plans," which are not formally adopted into law and thereby serve mainly as guides rather than directives for development.

In analyzing planning practices in Asian mega-urban regions, this book
focuses on a number of issues that may help to determine whether or not
the plans formulated and adopted in these city-regions have been able to effectively guide development:

- the extent to which the urban and regional plan reflects or does not
  reflect a developmental vision of the city-region;
- how the plans integrate development schemes for the inner city, the extended metropolitan region, and the megalopolitan region;
- the balancing of cultural and aesthetic conservation with the technological developments arising from rapid globalization; and
- efforts to achieve environmental protection and conservation in the light
  of technological advances and the drive for rapid economic growth.

This book also reviews both urban and regional plans as well as planning processes that have been used in Asian mega-urban regions to determine what approaches have worked and have not worked. In particular, it analyzes (1) detailed plans for the redevelopment of inner cities that often feature cultural heritage conservation, the improvement of deteriorating urban services, and the provision of affordable housing; (2) metropolitan area planning, which is generally focused on basic urban infrastructure, like water and sewerage, drainage, transport systems, traffic management, energy provision, and solid waste collection and disposal; and (3) megalopolitan planning for the effective functioning of polynodal systems of human settlements, including the allocation of open and green space, conservation of agricultural land, balancing of relationships between residence and place of employment, entertainment and basic service centers, and enhancement of environmental sustainability.

In analyzing the role that urban and regional planning has played in the development of Asian mega-urban regions, this study also considers the relationship of planning efficacy to such factors as (1) the population size and spatial extent of the mega-urban region; (2) the level of economic development, as reflected in the gross domestic product, per capita income, and structural composition of the city-region's economy; (3) the relative fragmentation or unified nature of the local government jurisdictions within the mega-urban region; (4) the type of planning approaches used in the mega-urban region (master planning or strategic comprehensive planning); and (5) the jurisdictional scope of the governance mechanism used in the city-region. In other words, do very large cities tend to have urban and regional plans that effectively guide their development, or is planning more productively employed in smaller and intermediate-sized cities? Are mega-urban regions in high-income countries more likely to have more effective planning mechanisms than those in poorer ones? Has the imposition of unified regional governance mechanisms improved the quality of urban plans? What, in effect, constitutes effective urban and regional planning as revealed in the development of Asia's largest mega-urban regions?

The Governance of Mega-Urban Regions

There is common agreement among development theorists that the governance of mega-urban regions is the key to making them more livable. However, there are differences in views on exactly what good governance means. In some cases, urban governance is primarily seen as effective and efficient management of public affairs. In this book, governance is interpreted more broadly to include public processes related to "how a political unit sets its visions and goals of development, translates this vision into policies, selects its leaders, adopts programs and projects, raises and allocates resources, implements programs and projects, resolves conflicts arising from varying decisions and interpretations, enforces accountability on decision makers, evaluates and monitors the effects and impact of programs and projects and then feeds the findings of monitoring and evaluation to policy makers, program implementers, and the general public" (Laquian 2002a, 77).

Broadly, governance may be defined as "the mechanisms, processes and institution through which citizens and groups articulate their interests, exercise their legal rights, meet their obligations and mediate their differences" (Ruble et al. 2001). As an essentially political process, governance encompasses issues of who governs, the just and equitable allocation of benefits and costs, and the relationship of civil society with government (McCarney 1996b, 4).

In December 1998, *Asiaweek* published a special report on the "quality of life" in forty Asian cities. It ranked the "livability" of these cities according to various criteria, such as economic opportunity, environment and sanitation, health care, transportation, personal security, housing costs, and leisure. Among the cities of Asia, the survey ranked Tokyo as number one in livability, despite its problems with affordable housing, garbage disposal, and environmental pollution. Ranked second and third were two other Japanese cities, Fukuoka and Osaka (Choong 1998).

In analyzing the statistics on the cities surveyed, it is interesting to note what correlates most with a city's livability. The data showed that average income per capita was the main factor correlated with a city's ranking. The top ten cities that had the highest per capita income all placed within the top fourteen cities in livability. Tokyo's per capita annual income of $51,374, Osaka's of $39,271, and Fukuoka's of $24,548 clearly outranked the incomes of all other cities. The lowest ranked city according to the income criterion was Yangon (formerly Rangoon), with a per capita annual income of $66. The importance of wealth was also shown in the fact that seven of the cities with the highest per capita levels of expenditures for education ranked among the top ten cities. Hong Kong, which invested $857 per person a year for education, topped this category and ranked seventh overall. The same pattern was seen in rankings according to the number of hospital beds available per 1,000 people. Here again, the seven cities that provided the most hospital beds ranked among the top ten cities overall.

An interesting aspect of the *Asiaweek* survey was the suggestion that a city's size seemed to have mattered in making the city work more effectively, albeit in the opposite direction. Among the top ten cities, only Tokyo and Beijing had populations in excess of 10 million, whereas the seven top-ranked cities were quite small (Georgetown, Malaysia, had just over a million inhabitants, and second-ranked Fukuoka had 1.3 million). Small size, which may make it easier to manage urban affairs may be related to livability. Conversely, it was also suggested that small cities often found it difficult to compete with larger ones in attracting good managers and administrators. They also tended to have a smaller tax base, which limited their ability to mobilize resources. In the qualitative judgment of people interviewed for the survey, therefore, city wealth and size were considered important but not sufficient conditions to make a city more livable. The survey respondents considered effective and efficient governance the key issue in achieving a better quality of life in cities.

The key elements of good governance mentioned in the survey were

1. *the rule of law,* or legal frameworks that are fair, predictable, and equitably enforced;
2. *transparency,* or the free flow of information that enables members of the society to understand and monitor the institutional processes affecting their lives;
3. *effectiveness and efficiency* in meeting needs through the best use of resources;
4. *accountability,* whereby decision makers (in government, the private sector, and citizen groups) answer for their actions to the citizenry;
5. *responsiveness,* the ability and willingness of leaders and administrators to serve the interests of stakeholders;
6. *consensus*, which takes the form of mediating different aspirations through conflict resolution, bargaining, and compromise to reach agreement on what is in the best interests of the community;
7. *equity,* which involves opportunity for all men and women to improve their well-being; and
8. *strategic vision,* a long-term perspective on what is needed for the society to grow and flourish in a sustainable way.

The views expressed in the *Asiaweek* survey confirmed at least two meanings attached to the concept of governance. The first meaning is narrowly administrative and managerial. This is reflected in the first four elements mentioned above, such as reliance on the rule of law as the basis for public decisions, transparency in decision making, effectiveness and efficiency in the use of resources, and accountability for actions by decision makers. These elements are usually what people mean when they refer to urban governance as city management.

The other meaning of governance is more political, which is embodied in these four elements listed above: responsiveness to citizen interests and demands; consensus, the process through which negotiation, accommodation, compromise, and bargaining are used to arrive at common goals; equity, which greatly helps in maintaining the stability of a society by avoiding bitter polarization; and the incorporation of these political outcomes in a strategic vision, on the basis of which citizens elect and select their leaders.

In recent years, the political elements of governance noted above have become widely accepted as key elements of liberal democracy. According to Leftwich (1994), the renewed emphasis on the political aspects of governance since the 1980s can be attributed to (1) the effects and impact of structural adjustments imposed by the World Bank and the International Monetary Fund on the economic and political situations of many developing countries, (2) the dominance of neoconservatism in the West, (3) the collapse of the former Soviet Union and other communist regimes, and (4) the rise of prodemocracy movements in the developing world and elsewhere.

In the mega-urban regions considered in this study, at least three types of governance structures have been used at various times in their history:

- *Autonomous local governments.* Considerable autonomy is given to local government units (cities, towns, municipalities) in a mega-urban region to enable them to independently carry out planning, policymaking, legislation, and the execution of government functions. Examples: Metro Manila between 1945 and 1969; Guangzhou, Hong Kong, Macao, and Shenzhen in the Pearl River Delta.
- *A mixed system of regional governance.* Authority, power, and resources are shared among central, regional, and local government institutions, and responsibilities for public functions are allocated to specific levels of government. Examples: Bangkok, Dhaka, Jakarta, Kolkata, present-day Metro Manila, and Mumbai.
- *Unified regional governance.* A single governance structure plans, manages, finances, supports, and maintains services in an areawide territory, and authority and power are vested in this single unit. Examples: Beijing, Seoul, Shanghai, and Tokyo.

The choice of the governance structure in a specific mega-urban region, of course, depends on the particular historical, cultural, and political characteristics of a country. For example, in Walsh's pioneering work on the administration of urban regions, she has suggested five types of systems: (1) regionally organized systems, (2) comprehensive local government systems, (3) multijurisdictional systems, (4) administrative systems without regional organization, and (5) field administration systems (Walsh 1969). In this book, an attempt is made to go beyond the administrative structures proposed by Walsh to encompass much broader governance systems. I also try to link the type of mega-urban region with the specific governance structure used in a specific city-region. For example, why do mega-urban regions in East Asia tend to have unified metropolitan or regional governments? What is the role of higher levels of government (provincial, state, central) in the creation of such unified areawide structures?

In the case of Southeast Asian cities, mixed regional governance mechanisms have been favored. Such mixed regional governance systems vary, however, from Metro Manila, where strong traditions of local autonomy have created fragmentation among local units, to Bangkok Metropolis, where a more centralist and unified system has been used. In countries in transition from centrally planned to more market-oriented economies (e.g., China and Vietnam), unified governance structures have been widely used. Mixed governance structures, however, have been favored in South Asian cities, largely because of institutional approaches derived from colonial administrations and the complex makeup of urban societies fragmented along ethnic, linguistic, religious, economic, and political lines.

In analyzing the various approaches to governance taken in the mega-urban regions that it covers, this book attempts to identify the key variables that are associated with the outcomes of good governance mentioned above. For example, to what extent does the granting of greater autonomy to local government units achieve democratic goals like popular participation in the selection of leaders and policymaking? Theories of basic democracy propose that local autonomy fosters the responsiveness of leaders to citizen demands and ensures the accountability of power holders to civil society. What has been the experience in Asian mega-urban regions to support or negate these assertions? Has the widespread adoption of decentralization schemes in many countries in Asia resulted in greater transparency in the conduct of public affairs? Have urban citizens in autonomous local units achieved greater consensus in decision making? Are smaller local government units better at achieving political consensus or at integrating the developmental visions of their leaders into policies and programs?

Policy advocates supporting the use of unified regional governance have generally justified the use of this structure from the point of view of efficiency. They have argued that the complex nature of the urban economy, the existence of varied ethnic groups, religions, political cliques, and special interest groups, and the institutional fragmentation of governance structures in mega-urban regions work against cooperative efforts to achieve common welfare. They believe that a number of basic urban infrastructure and services are, by their very nature, best provided at an areawide scale. Among these are integrated water supply, sewerage, drainage and sanitation systems, mass transit and traffic management schemes, energy production and distribution networks, and solid waste collection and disposal.

Unified urban governance systems, these policy advocates have argued, take advantage of economies of scale, agglomeration, and location. Urban problems, such as floods, epidemics, crime, and environmental pollution, do not respect political boundaries and demand unified action. To the fear that unified governance based on a higher metropolitan or regional tier tends to create a barrier between citizens and their governments, supporters of unified governance structures counter that modern information and communication technologies (e.g., newspapers, radio, television, telephones, the Internet) can overcome communication gaps. Metropolitan and regional governments, they believe, tend to elevate people's concerns from purely local issues (street cleaning, traffic calming, school board financing, street crime) to broader issues (reliable energy supply, traffic and mobility, environmental pollution). Unified governance over regional jurisdictions is also seen as a way of increasing financial resources, achieved by a larger and richer tax base and raising the credit rating of the unified metropolitan or regional government that enables it to borrow funds for lumpy infrastructure projects. This basic issue between grassroots democracy and higher levels of citizen participation on the one hand and the search for more efficient and cost-effective delivery of areawide urban services on the other will be explored more fully in chapter 3 and the other sections of the chapters below that touch on governance.

A particularly interesting aspect of governance in Asian mega-urban regions is the huge size of these agglomerations and their evolution into multinodal systems of settlements. In most instances, these regions encompass areas that cut across town, city, municipal, metropolitan, provincial, and state boundaries. This crosscutting tendency has naturally created administrative, political, and institutional fragmentation, which makes cooperative and coordinated action extremely difficult. In this book, the prospects for establishing areawide regional mechanisms in Asian mega-urban regions will be fully explored. By citing experiences in a number of mega-urban regions that have attempted to establish such governance structures, the pros and cons of unified structures will be carefully analyzed.

Another interesting aspect of governance explored in this book is the rapidly increasing role of nongovernmental organizations, people's organizations, and community-based organizations in the business of governance. The emergence of civil society in rapidly changing mega-urban regions is palpable in Southeast Asian and South Asian cities, but it does not seem so apparent in East Asian and Chinese cities. What are the future implications of the expanding role of civil society in mega-urban region governance systems that seek both popular participation and civic involvement on the one hand and more technologically driven and bureaucratic service-provider mechanisms on the other? Can the twin ideals of liberal democracy and efficient delivery of urban services be achieved in the complex and multi-ethnic social structures of Asian mega-urban regions?

About This Book

The primary concern of the present volume is the role played by planning and governance in the development of mega-urban regions in Asia. This objective is based on the premise that, if mega-urban regions play an important role in national economic and social development, more effective and efficient planning and more responsive, transparent, and accountable governance can be used as instruments to enhance that developmental role. The book, therefore, looks at the urban situation in Asia at two levels—at the level of the big city and its hinterland, and at the level of the mega-urban region and its role in national development.

The mega-urban regions considered in this book represent a varied and complex set of urban settlements, ranging from a global city like Tokyo, which wields significant influences on developments beyond its physical boundaries, to a special administrative region like Hong Kong, which with its links to Guangzhou, Macao, Shenzhen, and Zhuhai and aspires to global city status. A key objective of the book is to identify certain common characteristics in the demographic, economic, social, and political growth patterns of these disparate urban settlements in order to explain both their primary urban concerns and also what policymakers, administrators, and civil society groups are doing to effectively deal with those concerns. The book analyzes approaches to planning and governance and attempts to determine what policies and programs work or do not work. By using empirical case studies focused on organized efforts to plan and govern, the book identifies certain lessons learned and rigorously analyzes the circumstances in which these lessons were deemed relevant or not.

An important aspect of this book is the ideological context within which planning and governance functions have been carried out. Four of the original city-regions studied (Beijing, Guangzhou, Ho Chi Minh City, and Shanghai) are in countries in transition from a centrally planned to a more market-oriented system. The other city-regions represent settlements in economic systems that are market dominated. Three are high-income city-regions with ample resources for urban management and governance (Osaka, Seoul, and Tokyo). Another three are medium-income city-regions struggling with problems of urban service delivery (Bangkok, Jakarta, and Metro Manila). The remaining five city-regions (Delhi, Dhaka, Karachi, Kolkata, and Mumbai) are beset with serious problems.

In focusing on the planning process, this book compares and contrasts the basic concepts, processes, and procedures used in "master planning," favored in China and Vietnam, and "comprehensive strategic planning," as practiced in countries adhering to a market orientation. The book describes how these two approaches, though originating in extremely different planning traditions, now seem to be growing closer together as urban officials attempt to deal with very similar problems. The book seeks to explain how planners deal with such concepts as the "rationality" of the planning process, how societal development goals are set, the process of accommodating the varied interests of stakeholders, and how studies and schemes embodied in a plan are translated into binding policies and statues.

As far as governance is concerned, this book uses a structural-functional framework that focuses on how policies are formulated, adopted, executed, and evaluated. It takes an in-depth look at the performance of key public functions devoted to effectively and efficiently providing urban services like water and sewerage, transportation, housing, solid waste collection and disposal, and environmental protection. On the basis of case studies of actual projects, the book cites concrete examples of both successful and unsuccessful efforts. At the same time, it analyzes the specific circumstances in each city-region that accounted for these results.

Methodology

At the conceptual level, this book starts by questioning the tendency in urban studies to view the development of cities and mega-urban regions as a dependent variable. In this approach, the rapid growth of cities is seen as a residual outcome of various influences, such as technological innovations (e.g., the steam engine, the automobile, electrical energy), demographic changes (internal migration, declining death rates), developments in information technology (telegraph and telephone, computers, fiber optics), or processes of capitalist accumulation (transnational capital flows, foreign direct investment, Fordist and non-Fordist production systems).

Moreover, I attempt to regard urbanization as an independent variable in this book. I propose that if a conscious effort is taken to plan, shape, develop, and govern mega-urban regions in a more effective way, it is possible to make them not only more livable and sustainable but to transform them into policy instruments for creating economic and social change in the nation-state and beyond.

In carrying out the field research for the first stage of this book's development, the Asian Urban Research Network (AURN) research teams concentrated on studies at three levels: (1) planning and governance dynamics in the inner-city core, (2) developments in the urban periphery, and (3) the changing situation in the mega-urban region. In examining changes in the inner city, the study concentrated on such aspects as the onset of urban decay in the city core, the physical deterioration of houses and other urban structures, critical shortages of urban services, the migration of poor people to inner-city slums, and the demographic pressures leading to eviction and resettlement of people living in the central city. The research teams also analyzed government programs to redevelop the urban core, the increases in land values resulting from these programs, and the "gentrification" of housing as formerly undesirable areas became more developed.

Shifting to a wider metropolitan scope, this study focuses on both the positive and negative effects and impact of urban sprawl. The locations of basic urban services, radial and circumferential roads, industrial and manufacturing sites, and green space are some of the main concerns of planning in the extended metropolis. In addition, the study analyzes the problems related to the rapid conversion of rich agricultural land to urban uses, the increased costs of extending urban services to outlying towns and villages, and the environmental pollution caused by uncontrolled activities related to agriculture, manufacturing, and industrialization.

A major concern of the study in relation to the formation of mega-urban regions is the search for planning approaches that transcend the formal political and administrative boundaries of urban and rapidly urbanizing areas. In some countries, spatial units such as river basins and deltas, areas with unique microclimates, and those possessing common resource endowments have been used as "natural" planning regions. This book adopts this territorial approach to planning and governance, not only to get over the problems created by administrative and political fragmentation but also to achieve more comprehensive and holistic planning and governance.

By far the most difficult policy issue faced by mega-urban regions of Asia is governance. Historical, constitutional, and ideological conditions have tended to create multifarious jurisdictional units around urban centers. Strong traditions of local autonomy have encouraged the growth of small governance units, such as neighborhood committees, townships or village councils, administrative districts, municipal governments, and special-purpose districts. Although many urban authorities recognize the need for better cooperation and coordination of urban-related activities, the establishment of areawide governance mechanisms has been found to be fraught with difficulties. The search for governance approaches for mega-urban regions, therefore, is one of the main concerns of this book.

Finally, this book identifies and analyzes the various lessons learned in solving mega-urban problems through the use of regional planning and governance approaches. As such, it does not confine its attention to the six mega-urban regions covered in the AURN study but also cites relevant examples of planning and governance interventions that have been used in other Asian cities. This broader approach provides a wider comparative perspective. It also enhances the pragmatic nature of this book's concern—how to cope with problems arising from the rapid growth and expansion of mega-urban regions and to use the development of mega-urban regions as engines of economic growth and social change.

Outline of the Book

This book is composed of ten chapters. Chapter 1 has traced the origins and development of selected mega-urban regions in Asia. It has identified the various types of mega-urban regions and analyzes the historical, economic, political, and social factors that played specific roles in their emergence. The chapter then explained the importance of comprehensive planning and areawide governance not only in making mega-urban regions livable and sustainable but also in enhancing economic and social development at the regional and national levels.

Chapter 2 deals with the planning of mega-urban regions. It analyzes the shift from traditional master planning to comprehensive and strategic planning as practiced in various countries. It describes various approaches to planning and how planning concepts and practices have been influenced by historical and cultural events. It covers the role of infrastructure in the planned development of urban areas, especially the process of integrating transportation, water, sewerage, energy supply, and solid waste collection and disposal in the development of regions.

The governance of mega-urban regions is the theme of chapter 3, which analyzes efforts to find appropriate instruments and mechanisms to implement policies and programs in mega-urban regions. The chapter analyzes governmental functions such as policy setting, program development, project formulation, and project implementation, as well as monitoring and evaluation. The advantages and disadvantages of various types of regional governance structures (e.g., federations of local government units, special functional authorities, unified regional governments) are considered. The case is made for the establishment of governance mechanisms that encompass whole mega-urban regions and ensure both the efficient delivery of urban services and public participation in governmental decision making.

Chapter 4 deals with the economic, environmental, and social aspects of sustainability as a concept and how these relate to the growth and development of mega-urban regions. This chapter accepts that mega-urban regions are not very sustainable in their current state. However, it argues that government, the private sector, and civil society may pursue some policies and programs that may help to improve city-regions' sustainability. Aside from the usual focus on environmental and economic sustainability, special attention is given in this chapter to the development of social sustainability and the role of civil society in city-regions.

Chapter 5 looks into the planning and management of water resources, one of the key elements in the development of mega-urban regions. It describes the problems of water shortages, pollution, and overdependence on groundwater sources and considers various technological and programmatic approaches to deal with these problems. It points to water as an element that naturally takes advantage of the regional nature of resources and proposes a number of planning and management mechanisms to more rationally use scarce water.

Chapter 6 focuses on mobility in urban areas and how transportation can be planned and managed to enhance development in mega-urban regions. It considers transportation not only in its role as a shaper of the mega-urban region's structure but also as a key element of the region's economic and social development. The chapter considers the effects and impact of various transport modes and concludes that in their present stage of development, Asian mega-urban regions will probably benefit the most from mass transit systems.

Chapter 7 is concerned with inner-city redevelopment through programs such as community upgrading, housing, historical conservation, and urban design. It describes efforts in Asia to prevent the deterioration of downtown and to ensure a vibrant inner city. The chapter argues that most Asian mega-urban regions will benefit from redevelopment of inner cities for both regional and national development reasons.

Chapter 8 deals with efforts to develop the urban periphery through programs that include development of small towns, satellite cities, high-technology parks, and special economic zones. Ways to preserve the identities of small towns even as they are engulfed by urban sprawl are analyzed. The chapter also considers the advantages and disadvantages of autonomous development enclaves—such as special economic zones, export-processing zones, and high-technology parks—in developing urban peripheral areas.

Chapter 9 takes an in-depth look at policies that seek to integrate urban poor people in planning and governance through housing and basic urban services programs. The chapter evaluates programs and interventions that seek to make housing accessible to low-income groups in both the inner city and suburban relocation projects. The chapter also deals with other issues, such as housing finance, design, and construction, and it examines unorthodox approaches to housing, such as self-help and mutual aid efforts to operate and maintain housing units.

Finally, chapter 10 poses the theme of the future of Asia's mega-urban regions. On the basis of a historical analysis, it looks at the possible future implications of decentralization, the role of technology (especially information technology), the possible systems of governance, and, of course, the future sustainability of the mega-urban region in an era of globalization.

2

Planning Asia's Mega-Urban Regions

Planning has been defined as "a part of the societal guidance system influencing and controlling the nature and direction of change in a purposeful manner." As applied to urban areas, planning involves "measures that affect, modify, or adapt the sociospatial process of territorial occupation, use and organization, to improve the quality of life of the population." City and regional planning, then, is "the management of change within territorially organized societies" and "that professional practice which specifically seeks to connect forms of knowledge with forms of action in the public domain" (Friedmann 1987, 27). It is an "effort to control, to guide and to accomplish the physical development of towns and cities and thereby to provide for the people who are living and working in them the best possible environment" (Witty 1998). It is also a conscious process to "introduce deliberate changes in the urban spatial form and in civic infrastructure facilities" to improve urban conditions. In the words of Kundu, in his analysis of the planning process in Kolkata (formerly Calcutta):

> Planning stands for clarifying one's objectives and then determining what action shall be taken by whom, when, by what methods and what costs in order to achieve desired goals. In its simplest form, planning is defined as a process for determining appropriate future action through a sequence of choices. Selection of ends, within a general perspective choice of desired objectives and guidance of actions towards projected ends have been accepted as the essential properties of planning. (Kundu 1994, 7)

The key elements in city and regional planning are (1) a future orientation focused on a vision or desired set of conditions for a defined territory at a designated time period or a projected number of periods (short-, medium-, or long-term perspective); (2) a systematized process of choosing various options for the attainment of the desired future conditions on the basis of consultation with interest groups, stakeholders, and the general public as well as technical guidelines from planners and other professionals; (3) an analytical process of defining and evaluating options and prioritizing choices on the basis of benefits and costs to various actors, stakeholders, and society at large; (4) a legal process for adopting plans and prescribing procedures for implementing the plans, including the designation of institutions and adoption of mechanisms for plan implementation (zoning, land use controls, safety and performance standards, etc.); (5) specification of physical, financial, human, organizational, and other resources required for plan execution and ways to mobilize such resources; and (6) processes and procedures for monitoring and evaluating effects and impact of anticipated and unanticipated events and actions and for feeding back the results of such assessments to policymakers, administrators, and planners to effect course corrections while implementing the plans.

It is clear from these six elements that city and regional planning is not a purely administrative or technocratic exercise. It requires the active participation of public officials, political leaders, interest groups, stakeholders, and informed and interested citizens, as well as the technical inputs of planners and other professionals. It involves a comprehensive understanding of the economic, social, cultural, and political elements within a city-region and the coherent integration of all these elements through a process of interest articulation, accommodation, bargaining, conflict resolution, and compromise. As one planning authority has written, planning is essentially "guidance for future action" (Forester 1989, 3). It is a process based on common aspirations, mutually acceptable compromise, and generally accepted procedures. A city and regional plan is not a rigid document, and its provisions are not carved in stone—they can be altered strategically to meet changing circumstances.

City and Regional Planning in Asia

Asia has had a long history of planning cities. A number of ancient city plans in East Asia were based on prescribed rites for the building of imperial capitals (Beijing, Seoul, Tokyo). Other plans were the handiwork of colonial planners (in Dhaka; Karachi; Kolkata; Metro Manila; and Mumbai, formerly Bombay). Some plans for Asian cities were based on utopian ideas that attempted to achieve a balance between natural and human-made elements in an effort to create beautiful "garden cities" (Baguio, Bangalore, Singapore). In some cities in China, urban master plans followed ideology-based approaches that stressed heavy industries, social housing, and monumental architecture (Beijing, Shanghai, Tianjin). A few urban plans in East Asia focused mainly on elements of urban design, paying special attention to street layouts, buildings, squares, parks, and monuments (Jakarta, Osaka).

More recently, urban plans have tended to be more comprehensive, encompassing not only the highly urbanized areas of city-regions but also adjoining rural areas and open spaces (Bangkok, Jakarta, Tokyo). As a whole, the most common urban plans in Asia have been formulated to deal with specific problems, such as the proliferation of slums and squatter areas (Dhaka, Karachi, Kolkata, Mumbai), traffic congestion (Bangkok, Metro Manila), environmental pollution (Mumbai, Seoul, Tokyo), serious health and safety problems (Dhaka, Kolkata), and uncontrolled urban sprawl (Bangkok, Jakarta, Metro Manila, Seoul).

Despite the great number and variety of city and regional planning approaches that have been used in Asia, these can be conceptually divided into four types:

1. *Classical city planning* was formally prescribed in ancient treatises on the establishment of city-shrines or imperial capitals.
2. *Physical urban planning* focused on aesthetic design, monumental and symbolic structures, the formal layout of urban infrastructure, and the development of parks and open spaces in efforts to achieve the "city beautiful" ideal.
3. *Socialist urban planning* combined efforts to achieve economic and industrial production, provide basic necessities for workers, and symbolically glorify the nation-state.
4. *Strategic and comprehensive city and regional planning* integrated economic, social, cultural, and political factors in physical space in an effort to achieve a higher quality of life and environmental sustainability.

In this book, an attempt is made to assess how these four types of planning have influenced the development in Asian cities and mega-urban regions, with special attention given to effects and impact of these plans on the spatial configuration of city-regions, the provision of infrastructure and urban services, the livability of these settlements, and the quality of life of urban residents.

At present, of course, it is extremely difficult to specify individual cities that typify the application of each of these four types of city and regional planning. Throughout their histories, many cities have gone through periods where different types of planning had been used. Beijing, for example, was originally planned in the classical manner, was influenced during the 1930s by physical planning and urban design ideas, was subjected to the rigidity of socialist master planning between 1949 and 1979, and is now embarked on developing comprehensive and strategic socioeconomic plans with environmental conservation elements. Delhi, with its Mughal capital roots, also started with classical city planning, adopted principles of British town and country planning during the colonial period, and has been struggling with comprehensive urban and regional planning since independence. The sixteenth-century plans for Manila featured fortified city walls, those of Jakarta were made up of a system of canals, and Hanoi's plans were focused on the citadel in accordance with classical Chinese planning ideas.

In almost all the cities and mega-urban regions in Asia, urban physical features, population concentrations, the location of economic activities, and patterns of infrastructure and urban services bear the mark of their sequential planning histories. Currently, the various types of planning approaches continue to influence the functioning and structural forms of these mega-urban regions, with positive and negative consequences for livability and human welfare.

Classical City Planning

A number of East and South Asian cities have been planned along cosmological lines that embodied in their urban forms ancient beliefs related to the perceived structure of the universe and the spiritual relationship that existed between a supreme being, a powerful ruler, elite groups, and the common people. In cities and temples influenced by Hinduism—such as Angkor Wat and Angkor Thom in present-day Cambodia and the temple of Borobudur in Indonesia—the main feature of the urban plan was a mound or elevated place, said to represent the sacred mountain or Mount Meru. In Angkor, the center of the city was marked by a monumental structure to house the symbol of the *devaraja,* the god-king. Other structures around this center represented the mandala, the sacred circle, which attempted to physically depict the imagined shape of the heavens (Pym 1968).

Another example of an Asian city initially planned in the classical manner is Delhi. The origins of Delhi have been linked to the city of Indraprastha, the legendary capital of the Pandavas prominently mentioned in the Mahabharata epic. The plans for Delhi were perceived as conforming to the cosmological features of the mandala. The city's location east of the River Jamuna suggested a conscious effort to catch "the cool breeze and morning glory of the rising sun." The exact city center represented the crossing of two mythical roads, precisely where Brahma was supposed to have been situated according to the Vastupurush Mandal. From these features, one author concluded that the ancient plan for Delhi was "a total cosmic symbol" and "a tribute to the Indo-Roman heritage of city design" (Jain 1996b, 77).

In classical Chinese city planning, the centrality of the role of the emperor in the cosmic order of things is seen in the practice of making the imperial palace (the official residence of the "Son of Heaven") the physical center of the whole urban structure. The official name for China, Zhong Guo or the "Middle Kingdom," sees the Earth as the center of the universe, China as the center of the world, the capital city as the center of the country, the imperial palace as the center of the city, and the emperor as the center of the whole society. Aligning the main axis of the city in a plumb north–south direction focused on the North Star symbolized the link between heaven and the emperor. Designating the precise location of sacred places and temples (the earth mound where the emperor made sacrifices to the god of the soil to ensure fertility, the altar of the ancestors, the temple of the sun) ensured balance and harmony designed to preserve the "mandate of Heaven."

For many centuries, these classical ideas of city planning influenced city building in China. According to Wu (1986), Liang (1984, 54), and Wright (1977, 33–73), the original plans for the city of Beijing were derived from rites in the Zhou Li, which chronicled the formal rituals that, among other things, had to be followed in the establishment of an imperial capital. The following quotation from the Zhou Li (Wright 1977, 47) exemplifies the basic ideas behind this classical form of city planning:

Here, where Heaven and Earth are in perfect accord, where the four seasons come together, where the winds and the rains gather, where the forces of ying and yang are harmonized, one builds a royal capital.

More specifically, the key elements of Chinese classical city planning included (1) rigid orientation of the main axis of the city's development to the North Star, on a precise north-south alignment; (2) construction of city walls in the form of a square or rectangle; (3) the use of divination (usually by tortoise shell) in determining the propitious location for a city as well as the time for building it; and (4) articulation of city plans into functional zones or areas (Wright 1977, 45).

In the Beijing classical plan, the main axis of the city's development, going from north to south, ran through the Victory Gate, Coal Hill, the Forbidden City, Tiananmen or the Gate of Heavenly Peace, and Qianmen or the South Gate. Sadly, the ancient city walls of Beijing were dismantled in 1953 as offending reminders of the city's "feudal" origins. In its place, China's communist leaders built a "modern" subway line following the wall's perimeter. After 1979, a replica of a section of the destroyed city wall was built for tourists. As for the use of divination, Beijing's current master plan probably did not have to rely on tortoise shell readings; but here and there, there are still traces of socialist jargon and ideological formulations that form inherent parts of official Chinese documents.

The latest master plan for Beijing may strive for comprehensiveness, but it retains many ancient planning concepts and practices. For example, the division of the city into functional areas in a balanced manner is reminiscent of ancient planning formulas. The rigid north–south orientation of the city' development axis has been maintained, the location of monumental structures respects the city plan's fishbone structure, and even the sites chosen for modern special economic zones and high-technology enclaves continues to be influenced by classical ideals of symmetry and balance. Liang had noted that the imperial palace complex of the Ming Dynasty in Beijing, since its rebuilding five and a half centuries after the Yuan capital visited by Marco Polo was sacked, has remained little changed.

The architecture and city planning practiced during the Qing Dynasty (1644–1912) were mainly continuations of the Ming and older dynastic traditions. Liang traced this rigidity to the official publication of a Qing Dynasty imperial decree on city planning practices in 1734, which effectively stifled any innovation. He concluded that "in the structures built for the emperors throughout the 268 years of the regime, there is a uniformity that no modern totalitarian state could achieve" (Liang 1984, 54).

In other Asian cities, some elements of classical city planning are still used, despite widespread secularization and globalization. The relevance of classical plans is mainly manifested in efforts at cultural revival, particularly in the restoration and redevelopment of inner cities that have tended to deteriorate through the years. In a tourism-oriented city like Bangkok, for example, the classic lines of buildings, streets, gardens, and parks in the zone around the imperial palace and the temple of the Jade Buddha are excellent examples of traditional planning practice. Valiant efforts to maintain structures and forms in the inner city of Beijing—such as attempts to save old courtyard houses (*siheyuan*) in narrow *hutongs* (lanes) and to maintain a lively street life by closing some streets and transforming them into neighborhood markets—are worth noting. The preservation of the lovely and peaceful zones around the Imperial Palace in Tokyo and the maintenance of ancient structures, old trees, narrow streets, and artisan shops around shrines and temples in Kyoto are also clear reminders of good classical planning.

By and large, however, most of the elements of classical city planning have become quite irrelevant in present-day Asian cities. The rigidity and ritualistic approaches inherent in classical city planning have become inappropriate in fast-changing Asian economies and societies.

Planning the "City Beautiful"

During the latter part of the nineteenth century and the first half of the twentieth, city and regional planning in Asia was greatly influenced by traditions associated with attempting to create beautiful cities through landscape planning and urban design. These traditions had their origins in two quite distinct planning approaches. The earlier of these emanated from the "garden city" ideas of Ebenezer Howard and other British planners. The other could be traced to American city planning, which emphasized grand designs featuring monumental structures, wide tree-lined boulevards, broad swaths of open space, and whole systems of verdant parks. Examples of garden city planning could be seen in Bangalore, Delhi, and Singapore. Planning influenced by American "city beautiful" ideas can be seen in Baguio City and Metro Manila in the Philippines.

The inspiration for the planning of New Delhi under the Town Planning Commission, which had Edwin Lutyens, G. S. C. Swinton, and J. A. Brodie as members, was Howard's *Garden Cities of Tomorrow,* published in 1898 (Jain 1996b). Howard designed his ideal garden city as an estate of about 6,000 acres inhabited by a population of 32,000. The city has six boulevards traversing it from center to circumference. The center of the whole city is a beautiful garden, and around it are important public buildings. Next to the buildings is a public park, and spaces along the boulevards are reserved for private homes. Factories, warehouses, and workshops are located on the outer ring of the city, linked to each other by a circular railway. Next to this zone of manufacturing and industry are rich agricultural lands that use the waste from their farm animals and other recyclable refuse as an input to agricultural production (Howard 1965, 54).

The idealized garden city of Howard, of course, could not be directly applied to Delhi, for the city already had too big a population at the time of British colonization and it covered an area that was much larger than was appropriate for a garden city. Lutyens and his colleagues, therefore, ignored the Old City of Delhi and focused their attention on a sparsely populated zone outside the city limits, which was called New Delhi. The plans for New Delhi featured broad avenues lined with trees, residential areas of modern bungalows with ample yards, and a system of parks and public structures. Strict zoning regulations restricted specific urban functions to designated zones in the new city. Functionally, no linkages were established between this new, well-ordered settlement and the indigenous and rather chaotic old city.

In the case of Metro Manila, the planned development of the national capital region began in 1905 with the formulation of a master plan by a team led by the famous Chicago architect Daniel Hudson Burnham. Burnham, who had made his name as part of a team that helped to implement the historic plans of Pierre-Charles L'Enfant for Washington, was invited by the Philippine Commission to prepare a master plan for the capital city and the summer capital in the uplands of Baguio. Not surprisingly, the Burnham plans for Manila were inspired by the expanded L'Enfant plans for Washington as executed by Burnham, Frederick Law Olmsted Jr., and other American planners. They also reflected schemes for building the "city beautiful" popularized in grand events such as the Chicago World's Fair of 1893 and the Saint Louis Exposition of 1904 (Scott 1971, 70–71).

The Manila master plan called for intensive development of the central city, anchored on the Luneta, the Spanish-era open park and promenade on the shores of Manila Bay. To start from that central point, the plan proposed a major thoroughfare lined with monumental Greek- and Roman-style public buildings (the Congress of the Philippines, Legislative Building, Finance Building, City Hall, the Post Office) reminiscent of the grand structures on the Mall in Washington. This main axis of the city's developmental form extended outward and ended at a huge circle in suburban Quezon City, where the massive Quezon Memorial monument was later built. Aside from this axial orientation, the city structure followed a spokes-and-hub pattern (made up of arterial and circumferential roads). The open spaces between these roads were reserved for green areas. An extensive greenbelt located about 50 kilometers from the center of the city was designed by Burnham to limit urban sprawl. A large part of this greenbelt was meant to protect the watershed area and to conserve the rich agricultural lands devoted to the production of rice, vegetables, fruits, poultry, and other food items.

Aside from the aesthetic and urban design influences of British and American planning on the form of South and Southeast Asian cities, a lasting legacy of such approaches has been the emphasis on human welfare, such as those involved in efforts to build affordable housing, provide employment opportunities, and ensure health and sanitation for urban poor people. The Industrial Revolution in England and the boom of manufacturing and industries in the United States produced extreme poverty and the degradation of human life, as exemplified by the teeming slums, crowded tenements, sweatshops, and other urban ills of Western cities during the nineteenth century.

In the United States, the so-called heyday of the city beautiful in the late nineteenth and early twentieth centuries was not confined to the design and building of grandiose cities, the establishment of park systems, or the erecting of monumental structures. The urban reforms during that era also focused on the construction of water and sanitation schemes, low-cost housing projects, slum redevelopment and renewal, improvements in the workplace, protecting the rights of laborers, the care of orphans and the infirm, and other social pursuits.

The health, sanitation, and welfare ideas developed in the West became part and parcel of colonial plans for cities in South and Southeast Asia. In Mumbai, for example, city plans sought to relocate polluting industries from the center of the city to suburban areas. Dutch planners and administrators in Jakarta introduced solid waste collection and disposal, prohibited the throwing of garbage in canals, and dredged silted rivers. In Metro Manila, hospitals and sanitariums were built to deal with tropical diseases such as leprosy, malaria, and tuberculosis. Orphanages and old people's homes were also established, often through the private initiatives of religious groups and civic associations. In many Asian cities, these traditions of caring and nurture that started during the colonial period of city building came in handy after the devastations of World War II and the explosive developments in Asian cities after independence.

A good look at the physical form of a number of South and Southeast Asian cities today reveals the lasting influence of British and American planning approaches. In fact, what little grandeur is left in the urban structures of cities like Delhi, Dhaka, Karachi, Kolkata, and Mumbai can be traced to their colonial planning origins. Even with the serious inner-city decay of Manila, the grand buildings along the main axis built in accordance with the 1905 Burnham plan allow the city to retain its coherent form. The rapid growth of Asian city populations, however, combined with the outward expansion of built-up areas, has frayed the texture of these early plans. The social welfare institutions related to housing, sanitation, employment, and protection of the weak and the infirm were inundated by the massive urban poverty that swept Asian cities in the postwar era.

A major weakness of the colonial planning of Asian cities is that it was essentially elitist. In essence, the aesthetics, rationality, and grandiose nature of the urban designs of cities were meant for the enjoyment of the few colonial administrators, their families, and the wealthy and powerful indigenous classes that collaborated with them. As such, the segments of Asian cities that benefited from these city beautiful plans remained islands of order and efficiency in the midst of the chaos and turbulence of the indigenous city of the masses. To some extent, this elitist approach to city planning is now exemplified by the proliferation of exclusive enclaves and "gated communities" inhabited by the rich and powerful in most of the cities of Asia. In fact, as noted by Akin Mabogunje in Africa, the "modern city" is fast becoming an anachronism in many South and Southeast Asian city plans, and mainstream urban development is represented by the amorphous and sprawling self-built city of poor residents.

Because most government authorities in South and Southeast Asian cities and mega-urban regions today are faced with a host of serious, pressing problems—inadequate income, inefficient and often corrupt bureaucracies, deteriorating urban infrastructure and services, and ever-worsening problems of traffic, slums, squatting, crime, and environmental pollution—they cannot really pay much attention to city beautiful planning ideas. It is all they can do to meet their monthly payrolls, deploy enough police officers on foot patrols, hire street cleaners, and pay their schoolteachers on time.

In wealthy Singapore, and in some parts of Kuala Lumpur, however, city authorities have been able to maintain the shady trees, flowering shrubs, clean streets, and street lights that make for a beautiful city. The shady and cool parks around Hoan Khiem Lake in Hanoi have kept their tranquillity and beauty. Lumpini Park in Bangkok remains a verdant oasis in a noisy and smog-filled metropolis. But in other South and Southeast Asian cities, the colonial grandeur of big cities has eroded. Tree-lined boulevards in Kolkata and Mumbai now shelter pavement dwellers and itinerant peddlers rather than strollers out to enjoy the city air. Delhi's Connaught Place and the Maidan open space in Mumbai are usually dirty and unkempt. The Escolta in the central business district of Manila, which used to be the swankiest shopping center for the elite, is now a run-down area swarming with sidewalk vendors, peddlers of pornographic materials and sex aids, pawnshops, and hole-in-the-wall eateries. The latest controversy in Manila revolves around the plan of the city mayor to cut down the trees in the colonial-era Mehan botanical gardens to make way for an office building and a parking lot. This public debate symbolizes, in more ways than one, the dilemma of city authorities, who are often tempted to sacrifice beauty and nature on the altar of modernity and "progress."

Socialist City Planning

In China and Vietnam, the rigid nature of classical city planning that originally shaped big cities was replaced by socialist planning in the early 1950s. The transition from classical to socialist planning was carried out with apparent ease because the concept of a socialist master plan had great similarities with the key elements of a classical plan. Both types of plans were based on immutable principles prescribed by absolute power holders, with the former owing authority from sacred rites and the latter on the claimed supremacy of "scientific" methods as applied by totalitarian rulers. The great emphasis on urban infrastructure—such as roads, ports, harbors, housing projects, and industrial sites—as the main determinants of the desired physical structure of cities was embodied in both planning approaches.

A review of master plans formulated and adopted for cities like Beijing, Hanoi, Shanghai, and Tianjin reveals the key elements of socialist planning. First, the master plans projected a desired state at a specified point in time (e.g., by 2025, Hanoi will become a city of 5 million people). Second, they set desirable standards, such as an average per capita income of $800, livable housing space of 12 square meters per person, park space of 0.5 square kilometers per person, and similar targets to be achieved at the end of the plan period. From these target figures and standards, socialist planners calculated the material, financial, and institutional requirements to support the full implementation of the plan. The master-planning approach, therefore, assumed that future economic and social conditions in a city were "knowable" and that almost complete information could be gathered on which to base such calculations.

Because this assumption often conflicted with reality, however, sudden unexpected economic, social, and cataclysmic natural changes wreaked havoc on the implementation of these plans. For example, the 1990 master plan for Hanoi absolutely did not anticipate the repercussions of the 1997 Asian economic crisis, which reduced foreign investment in the city to a quarter of the anticipated amounts, and therefore frantic adjustments had to be made to stabilize the economy when the crisis occurred.

In theory, socialist planning had the objective of improving the lives of the urban proletariat and other "exploited" groups in society. This policy of social equity was implemented by schemes, such as massive housing projects, hospitals, educational institutions, and other social amenities. In China, during the height of the communist regime, the concentration of these investments in urban areas made an urban *hukou,* a certificate of urban residential status, most desirable because it guaranteed benefits and privileges, such as extremely low rents for urban housing, subsidized grain supply, educational benefits for children, access to hospitals and clinics, and urban jobs. The government was able to control the internal migration that the wide differences between rural and urban life would have created in an otherwise free society by strictly enforcing the *hukou* system, which denied benefits to persons who did not have urban household registration.

Another key principle of socialist planning pursued in China was the strong emphasis on heavy industries. Thus, in the period between 1952 and 1978, the proportion of heavy industry (steel and iron industry, petrochemicals, heavy machinery) in China's total production was 47.4 percent. With economic reforms in the period 1979–84, heavy industry declined to 30.7 percent but rose again to 39.5 percent between 1985 and 1988 (Wang 1995, 29). The emphasis on heavy industry accelerated the growth of big cities. Thus, in 1958, the boundaries of Beijing were expanded to 8,860 square kilometers, enveloping within the metropolitan area the industrial sites for a steel mill, automobile production, and a petrochemical complex. Similarly, at about the same time, the boundaries of Shanghai were extended to encompass 5,908 square kilometers to make room for industrial expansion. Included in the metropolitan territory were the counties of Baoshan and Jiading, where huge steel and iron as well as petrochemical plants were located.

Chairman Mao Ze Dong—determined to exceed the industrial output of Britain within a period of fifteen years—personally launched the Great Leap Forward in 1958 and urged the people to build backyard furnaces to produce iron and steel. Millions of Chinese workers were withdrawn from agriculture (which was communalized) and were made to work in makeshift industrial plants. Because of primitive technology, however, the millions of tons of iron and steel that were produced were mostly not usable, and China suffered from a lack of food and economic dislocations. These problems were exacerbated by a series of natural calamities between 1959 and 1961, as well as by the Soviet Union's withdrawal of technical and material assistance in 1960 (Houn 1973, 174).

The mistakes of the Great Leap Forward were corrected after 1959, when Chinese development policy began to shift toward light industry and manufacturing. Adjustments were made during the last two years of the Second Five-Year Plan that led to increases in both light industry and agricultural production. Just when China's economic conditions were improving, however, Chairman Mao launched the Great Proletarian Cultural Revolution, which sent Red Guards to factories, mines, and industrial sites to organize workers into "revolutionary rebel committees." Within the next ten years, public order in China virtually collapsed. Most significantly, the implementation of the *hukou* system became sporadic as rampaging Red Guards went all over the country to "make revolution." There were draconian efforts to send young people, students, and intellectuals from big cities to rural areas to make them "learn from the peasants." But by 1976, the chaos created by the Great Proletarian Cultural Revolution had allowed these "rusticated" people to clandestinely return to the cities. The weakening of China's population control program also resulted in a higher birthrate, which, with increased cityward migration, served to expand urban populations.

The thirty years of socialist planning experience in China has shown the limitations of the approach as an effective guide to development. Like classical city planning, socialist planning has left physical traces in the form and structure of some Asian cities. In Beijing and Shanghai, one can still see the monumental Stalinist architecture (Beijing railroad station, Shanghai exhibition hall) that was built to glorify the nation-state and the Communist Party. In many other Chinese cities, huge blocks of government-built tenements showing the same utilitarian drabness of apartments in Moscow still stand. In the Shanghai region, the hollow shells of abandoned industrial plants and the poorly maintained buildings of loss-plagued state-owned enterprises contrast sharply with new factories linked to global companies.

More than the physical manifestations of the failures of socialist planning, however, have been the massive changes in Chinese lives since the abandonment of central planning and its replacement by market-oriented policies. There may be some Chinese citizens at present who deplore the breaking of their "iron rice bowl" and their being abandoned to the random capriciousness of the open market. Others may complain about the high cost of everything, especially housing, and the unaccustomed anxiety arising from having a big mortgage to pay off. However, for most citizens of China, the freedom to move to another place, take on a new job anywhere in the country, own a television set or even a car, buy and own a house in any part of the city, and travel outside the country to study or find work are ample reasons for the abandonment of strict socialist planning. Socialist planning has definitely left its imprint on people in China, and the egalitarian and welfare elements of that planning approach are worth noting. However, in much the same way that market forces are now drastically changing the physical form and structure of Chinese cities, the superstructure of Chinese society is now being rapidly changed by a shift to more comprehensive and strategic planning rooted in market principles.

Comprehensive Strategic Planning

Classical city planning, physical planning for beautiful and well-designed cities, and socialist planning for productive cities all were primarily concerned with the physical form and structure of an urban area. Conceptually, they were based on the assumption that urbanization or the concentration of people in well-defined regions was a dependent variable. Population growth, people's movements, their productive behavior, and their search for leisure and cultural activities determined the shape and geographic extent of the city. Planning, then, was mainly concerned with how the physical infrastructure could be arranged in such a way that what people wanted could be achieved by the layout of streets, location of facilities for production and distribution of potable water, networks and systems for sewerage, sanitation and drainage, location of housing and workplaces, sites for ports and harbors, provision of parks and open spaces, and the like. Master plans defined all these physical structures, and zoning codes, land use controls, and other regulations ensured that the plan guidelines and standards were followed.

Unlike traditional approaches to planning, which tended to have a more limited scope, comprehensive strategic planning views urbanization as an independent variable. It sees urban centers as the engines of economic growth and the facilitators of social and political change. By having their development carefully planned, urban centers could be turned into "transformational agents" that could energize whole countries and societies. To accomplish this, however, the city-region had to be holistically taken as an entity, and economic, social, environmental, and physical development elements could not be treated separately in the plan. What people do to make a living, where they are employed, how they move from home to workplace, and what leisure activities they pursue all have physical and spatial implications. At the same time, the physical structure of the urban area also directly affects people's activities. Physical plans are of limited utility without clear indications of how the resources to implement them can be mobilized. Management and governance mechanisms are needed to ensure that the guidelines embodied in the plans will be followed.

With these realizations, planners have concluded that a comprehensive approach to planning is needed. To be effective, good plans need to integrate economic, social, cultural, administrative, fiscal, and political elements. They have to encompass whole city-regions or even megalopolitan regions, because what happens in each part of a region directly or indirectly affects events and developments in other areas.

Classical, physical, and socialist planning shared the characteristic of being linear. Because these types of planning were based on the assumption that satisfactory data could be marshaled and applied to a master plan, they were poorly designed to cope with unanticipated events and changes. In other words, they did not have a strategic framework that allowed them to respond to changing circumstances. The ideal master plan was meant to be "self-executing"—as soon as the first events laid out in the plan occurred, it was expected that subsequent events would evolve as projected and that the plan would be able to cope with any eventuality. This, of course, was an unrealistic expectation. It was no surprise therefore, that political leaders and other officials chosen by people to lead them usually had serious differences with "expert" planners who believed that their plans, being based on technical and "scientific" considerations, represented the true path to development.

Realizing the limitations of classical, physical, and socialist planning approaches, most urban authorities in Asia have turned to comprehensive strategic planning to guide developments in city-regions. Asian countries whose economies have been influenced more by market forces than by government-mandated interventions were quick to adopt the comprehensive and strategic planning approach (i.e., Indonesia, South Korea, the Philippines, and Thailand). Increasingly, also, countries in transition like China and Vietnam have shifted to comprehensive strategic planning after recognizing the limitations of their master-planning approaches. In these countries, comprehensive plans have often served as elaborations of socioeconomic five-year development plans or as applications of basic principles embodied in those plans. Traditionally, five-year plans were functionally and sectorally divided—with separate sections for industry and manufacturing, agriculture, and social development (i.e., health, education, housing, and social welfare).

In many of the new comprehensive and strategic plans in East Asian city-regions, the intimate linkages between physical plans and socioeconomic development plans are well illustrated. Special attention is now given to the spatial implications of socioeconomic activities, especially because these tend to center on urban clusters and mega-urban regions. The developmental potential of clustering productive activities in urban nodes is also well recognized.

As used in many Asian mega-urban regions, comprehensive strategic planning is characterized by (1) wider areal scope covered by the plans and the incorporation and integration of social, economic, cultural, and environmental elements in the whole plan; (2) the concept of planning as an iterative rather than a linear process, and the incorporation of implementing details in the plan document; and (3) the inclusion of governance and managerial elements in the plan, especially mechanisms for systematically assessing options on the basis of costs and benefits and for monitoring and evaluating effects and impact to ensure self-correction and adjustment to changing circumstances. In comprehensive and strategic planning, the traditional distinction between conceptual plan formulation and political and administrative action is blurred—planning encompasses the whole governance process. It does not mean, of course, that professional planners carry out all the tasks of governance, just that they are informed about what is happening and that the information they gather is used to strategically make adjustments in the plans.

Therefore, the knowledge base and technical skills of comprehensive strategic planners should include economic, demographic, financial, social, cultural, aesthetic, and management aspects. Their expertise should not be limited to the geographic, architectural, physical design, landscape forms, legal, and administrative aspects that primarily concerned traditional planners.

Wider Areal and Substantive Coverage

A good example of a comprehensive plan that encompasses a wider area is the development scheme for the Metro Manila planning region. As shown in figure 2.1, the territorial coverage of the plan goes beyond the confines of the City of Manila, which covers an area of only 38.5 square kilometers and has a population of 1.7 million. It also spreads beyond the territorial juris-

Figure 2.1. Development Plan for the Manila Region

diction of the Metro Manila Development Authority, which encompasses fourteen cities and three towns with a total population of 12.6 million. To comprehensively develop the Manila region, development planners include within the urban area's sphere of influence sixteen towns in the province of Bulacan, fourteen towns in the province of Rizal, seven towns in the province of Laguna, and eleven towns and two chartered cities in the province of Cavite. In fact, some Filipino planners believe that even this areal spread is too limited for a proper development plan for the region. They include in their schemes some towns in the provinces of Pampanga and Zambales, as well as the special economic zones in the former American military bases of Subic and Clark and the cities of Olongapo and Angeles.

The same strategy for the development of central and peripheral areas is reflected in the Tokyo Plan 2000 scheme shown in figure 2.2. In the Tokyo comprehensive plan, the main factor used to guide the development of the city-region is transportation. Thus, expressways have been designed to radiate from the Center Core Area to link up with urban nodes such as Hachioji-Tachikawa-Tama, Urawa-Omiya, Tsuchiura-Tsukuba-Ushiku, Narita Airport, Kisarazu, Yokohama, Atsugi, and Machida-Sagahimara. To facilitate circulation on the edges of the City Core Area, circumferential road systems such as the Tokyo–Gaikan Expressway and the Metropolitan Inter-City Expressway are provided for in the plan. Also included are the airport and waterfront axis routes and the Tokyo Bay shore road.

The scheme for the Hong Kong–Pearl River Delta (HK-PRD) region proposed by the Hong Kong 2022 Foundation (figure 2.3) is an ambitious comprehensive strategic plan that attempts to integrate socioeconomic elements into a spatial development strategy. The proposed plan encompasses the Hong Kong special administrative region (SAR), the Macao SAR, and local government units in Guangdong province (Dongguan, Foshan, Guangzhou, Huizhou, Jiangmen, Shenzhen, Zhaoqing, Zhongshan, and Zhuhai). This whole region includes an area inhabited by about 40 million people.

The main justifications for comprehensively planning the HK-PRD region as a unified entity were as follows (Enright et al. 2002, 8–11):

- The HK-PRD region has become an economic powerhouse with a number of regional clusters of industries. The planned development of the whole region will enhance its economic strength, which will vastly exceed what would be possible if each region acted in isolation.
- The present-day fragmentation of local units in the region is causing a loss of economic opportunities due to barriers that prevent closer economic interaction.

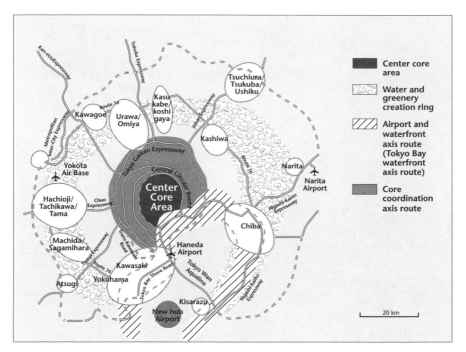

Figure 2.2. The Tokyo Development Scheme

- The "one country, two systems" principle, China's entry into the World Trade Organization, and other national and global developments demand economic cooperation and closer coordination to enhance the competitiveness of the HK-PRD region.
- Hong Kong has evolved into a center for finance, logistics, management, and other activities related to manufacturing, and the PRD region performs a wide range of manufacturing activities. The division of labor among the components of the HK-PRD region needs to be strategically managed to enhance productivity and take advantage of mutually beneficial factors.
- A number of competing activities carried out by local units in the HK-PRD region need better coordination. High-priority areas for coordinated action include the establishment and location of airports, container ports, and other transport hubs, as well as the setting up of industrial estates, high-technology zones, and other production enclaves.
- There are limits to connectivity between development nodes in the HK-PRD region. A coordinated transport plan is needed so that all the main cities in the region will be within the "magic three hours" travel

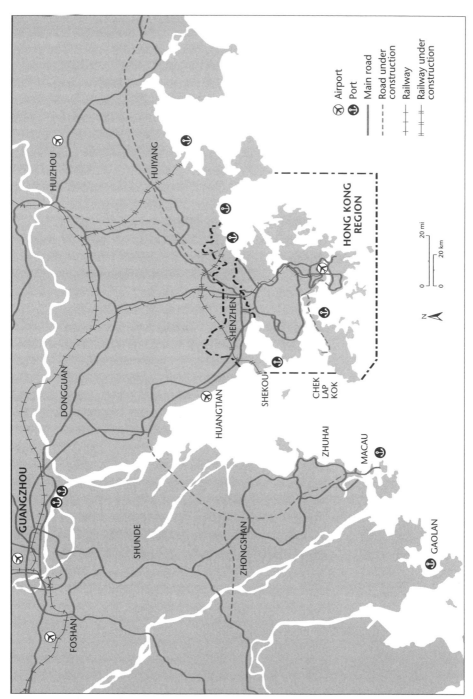

Figure 2.3. The Hong Kong–Pearl River Delta Region

time, which is required for the region's efficient performance of investment, management, service provision, and purchasing activities.

- The business and governmental interactions among actors in the HK-PRD region tend to be among local government and Communist Party officials in the PRD and private business people and administrators in Hong Kong. There is ample opportunity for greater cooperation in activities such as information exchange, trade promotion, investment, financing, and the adoption of governmental rules and regulations.
- Developments in other parts of China and elsewhere—such as the growth of the Yangtze River Delta region, which is focused on Shanghai, and the emergence of growth centers like Bangkok, Singapore, and Taiwan—will provide future competition to the HK-PRD region. If planning for the HK-PRD region's development is not done comprehensively, strategically, and efficiently, the region will lose its competitive edge.

It is clear from the areal and substantive coverage of the HK-PRD comprehensive strategic plan that it does not confine itself to the physical planning approach that has traditionally been the province of city planners. In fact, most of the professionals involved in the preparation of the plan were economists, sociologists, business entrepreneurs, government officials, civic leaders, and other social scientists. They came from different political jurisdictions in the Chinese mainland and various economic and social groups in Hong Kong. The plan they formulated, therefore, represented their various interests and concerns as stakeholders and reflected their understanding that to accomplish their socioeconomic objectives, they had to work out a process of integrating their concerns into a coherent strategy.

If adopted and implemented by the local government units and the central government of China and the Hong Kong and Macao SARs, the HK-PRD comprehensive strategic plan will most likely increase the economic viability of the region and influence its future structural form. This is because the HK-PRD region possesses most of the economic and social factors that have been known to be closely associated with the rapid growth of mega-urban regions. Among the most important of these factors are (1) improved and well-coordinated intraregional and interregional transport facilities, especially ports, airports, expressways, metropolitan transit systems, trunk roads, and local feeder roads; (2) export-processing facilities encouraged by conscious government policies and programs; (3) a competitively priced pool of skilled labor and efficient managers; (4) a critical mass of re-search and development capacity; (5) the ability to access ethnic and lin-guistic ties to outside investors; (6) incentive tax and regulatory schemes that are attractive to investors; and (7) improved "quality of life" amenities, such as good housing, educational institutions, health and medical services, and leisure and cultural activities (Hamer 1995, 9).

What the HK-PRD comprehensive strategic plan still lacks at this time, however, is detailed strategies and development indicators similar to the ones formulated as part of the Tokyo 2000 Plan. This is a daunting task be-cause, up to now, most of the local government units in the PRD have still had a tendency to act autonomously and pursue economic policies compet-itively, without giving careful consideration to the repercussions of their acts for other local units in the region. Most of the initiatives in the com-prehensive strategic planning process are coming from Hong Kong. There are still indications that there are latent suspicions on the part of some main-land Chinese officials and Communist Party members about the motives be-hind such Hong Kong initiatives.

Moreover, from the Hong Kong side, there are some subtle fears about corruption and possibilities of political instability during the difficult process of carrying out "socialism with Chinese characteristics" under the HK-PRD plan. There are also concerns that Chinese leaders may be more interested in enhancing the competitive edge of mainland regions such as Beijing, Shanghai, or the northeast industrial zone (the Shenyang–Dalian corridor). All these concerns have to be resolved before the development vi-sion reflected in the plan can be achieved.

Implementing Details

An example of an approach that goes beyond conceptual plan formulation to specify implementing details is the Tokyo Plan 2000. These details are incorporated in an approach that sets goals, strategies to be followed, and development indicators that may be used for monitoring and evaluating the extent to which the goals are accomplished. All in all, Tokyo Plan 2000 has set sixteen policy goals, thirty-five strategic measures, and sixty policy development indicators to be set in motion over a fifteen-year period. For illustrative purposes, five of the main elements of that strategy that serve as good examples of plan "operationalization" are given in box 2.1.

Box 2.1. *Implementing the Tokyo Plan 2000*

Goal 1: A spacious and comfortable city with a good balance between work sites and residential areas
   Strategy: Encourage more people to live in downtown Tokyo. Reorganize the city block by block and provide open areas and green space for community-focused living. Rehabilitate old buildings instead of tearing them down and building huge apartment blocks.
   Indicator: Percentage of salaried workers and students spending less than one hour each way commuting to downtown Tokyo to be increased from 33.1 percent in 1995 to 38.5 by 2015.

Goal 2: Smooth mobility of people, goods, information, and services
   Strategy: Construct trunk roads, such as Metropolitan Loop 3. Remove traffic bottlenecks by grade separation. Improve public transport systems. Construct depots for large-scale distribution of goods in suburban areas. Expand freight railway network in the national capital region. Expand Haneda Airport and link it more efficiently with other parts of the city.
   Indicator: Increased average speed of motor vehicles during peak hours from 21 kilometers per hour in 1995 to 41 kilometers per hour by 2015.

Goal 3: A green Tokyo with enhanced cultural resources
   Strategy: Create "oases" of green in Central Tokyo. Bury all electric and telephone lines. Convert expressways into underground tunnels and build parks and gardens on open spaces created. Set up wider green space around trunk roads. Encourage more building owners to plant more trees and shrubs on roofs to reduce "heat island" phenomenon.
   Indicator: The proportion of green space in Tokyo will increase from 29 percent in 1995 to 32 percent by 2015.

Goal 4: A safer and more livable Tokyo
   Strategy: Identify areas and houses prone to outbreak of fires and set up firewalls, install more fire hydrants, and provide other safety devices. Identify and improve roads for emergency evacuations. Designate emergency preparedness areas, organize communities, and train people on what to do during emergencies.
   Indicator: Proportion of roads designed for emergency evacuation to be increased from 76 percent in 1996 to 95 percent by 2015.

Goal 5: An economically developed but culturally and environmentally livable Tokyo
   Strategy: Reorganize the physical layout of the Tokyo megalopolitan region and integrate transportation, distribution, disaster prevention, health, and environmental elements into the master plan. Seek the cooperation of seven prefectures and cities and establish a permanent consultative organ for public decision making. Increase revenues of all local government units within the megalopolitan region.
   Indicators: Economic development rates of local government units in the region to increase from 20.3 percent in 1995 to 85 percent by 2015. Increase in the number of foreign tourists visiting Tokyo from 2.5 million in 1998 to 5 million by 2015.
   Source: Tokyo Bureau of City Planning (2003).

Linkage to Governance

From this review of the Tokyo and HK-PRD comprehensive strategic plans, it can be observed that the specification of governance mechanisms is an important part of the planning process. In Tokyo, the governance issue is resolved somewhat by the institution of areawide jurisdiction under the Tokyo Metropolitan Government. The scope of authority and power of the prefectural government structure in Japan also make it possible for a higher level of local government to effect coordination of local activities.

In the case of the HK-PRD plan, however, governance is complicated by political and administrative fragmentation. The Hong Kong and Macao SARs will be independently governed territories for almost half a century under treaty agreements with the United Kingdom and Portugal, respectively. Within the PRD region alone, there are twenty-one cities with a combined population of at least 82.2 million (2000 census) with their own political and administrative structures and often competing developmental aspirations. The largest of these cities, with 9.9 million inhabitants, is Guangzhou, which has been China's main link to the outside world since the Qing Dynasty. Guangzhou's leaders naturally want to maintain the city's lead in industry, manufacturing, retail sales, finance, and the service sector.

The other big city in the PRD region is Shenzhen, which grew explosively from 321,000 inhabitants in 1980 to more than 7 million in 2001. Shenzhen's population currently has the highest average educational level in all of China. Although the initial development of Shenzhen was greatly dependent on Hong Kong investments and entrepreneurial talents, its leaders are now eager to flex their economic muscle and will most likely pursue programs to enhance their own interests. Administrative, political, and other divisive factors, therefore, will in the future make it difficult for the HK-PRD region to achieve its planning goal of "competing together rather than competing against each other."

Decision-Making Framework

An important element of comprehensive strategic planning is setting up a decision-making framework to guide the evaluation of various options for plan implementation. Asian urban and regional planners have used a number of qualitative and quantitative methodologies—such as cost–benefit analysis, cost-effectiveness analysis, and sensitivity analysis—to assess the viability, effectiveness, efficiency, and profitability of various options. Planners have also used tests of potential outcomes, such as possible effects on employment, capital investments, people's movements, and social class formation. Widely used analytical frameworks also include environmental impact and social impact assessments.

A good example of how a decision-making framework functions as an integral part of a comprehensive strategic plan is the case of Dhaka. In this capital city of Bangladesh, the Metropolitan Area Integrated Urban Development Project was faced with the problem of developing a plan to deal with disastrous floods. To do its job, the project staff used scenario building as an analytical framework. The staff came up with three scenarios with different outcomes. Scenario A focused on the extensive development of land immediately adjoining the inner city through heavy investments in flood-protection schemes. Scenario B required the expansion of development at the urban periphery without project support for flood protection. Scenario C involved the expansion of the city into its northern and western peripheral areas, but also without allocating funds for flood protection.

For each of these scenarios, the planners calculated the specific costs of programs and projects, such as land acquisition, flood-protection measures, service provision, and transportation modes. The expected benefits from each scenario were also assessed, including employment creation, improved access to services, agricultural production, and environmental improvement. The relative difficulty or ease involved in pursuing each scenario were analyzed, especially with regard to raising capital for investments, the potential for recovering project costs, technology demands, legal requirements, institutional requirements, and the potential for flexibility in implementing programs. After gathering and analyzing the various positive and negative elements of each scenario, the Dhaka municipal authorities decided that a combination of Scenarios B and C was the most appropriate approach for the planned development of the mega-urban region (United Nations 1987b, 16–17).

Monitoring and Evaluation

In some Asian cities, monitoring and evaluation mechanisms have been incorporated into comprehensive strategic plans to guide plan implementation. In this approach, evaluation has been greatly assisted by anticipating and scheduling individually planned activities within specified periods. In the comprehensive development plan for the HK-PRD region, for example, the whole plan was projected to 2011 but evaluations of development scenarios were built into the plan for the periods 2001–6 and 2006–11 (Campanella et al. 2002, 21).

A good system for monitoring and evaluating how big infrastructure projects are being implemented in the context of an overall plan is the Integrated Urban Infrastructure Development Program (IUIDP) set up by the Government of Indonesia within the National Planning Agency (Bappenas) with the active cooperation of agencies in charge of such functions, such as public works, construction, and housing, as well as local government units. The IUIDP approach identified and consolidated data on urban infrastructure projects such as water supply, solid waste disposal, drainage, sanitation, urban roads and transportation, flood control, and *kampung* (urban village) improvement. The system indicated the financial resources allocated to each project, its source, availability, and extent of utilization. It also arranged the projects in accordance with a set of priorities based on each project's contribution to the achievement of overall development objectives (Soegijoko 1996, 406).

As designed, the IUIDP approach carefully evaluated progress in implementation of each project on the basis of plan-based targets. The system, therefore, took the form of a five-year rolling plan that was updated as annual information came in, was analyzed, and was evaluated to see the extent to which targets were being achieved. The monitoring system, however, went beyond a careful watch over the flow of monetary resources and qualitatively assessed the effects and impact of project activities.

In 1995, for example, the IUIDP system observed that water supply projects in Greater Jakarta were exerting strong pressures on forested areas in the catchment zones of the metropolis. The destruction of vegetation in the watershed was causing soil erosion, flooding, and the siltation of waterways downstream. Groundwater was also being depleted too fast, especially in the northern part of the city, where high levels of fresh water extraction was causing salt water to enter the aquifer. IUIDP monitoring results warned that the piped water system was lagging way behind the spread of populated areas and would not be able to meet industry, manufacturing, and domestic water demand in the near future. The water problem was exacerbated by the poor sanitation and sewerage situation in the city. The majority of the population of Jakarta relied on septic tanks and pit latrines, and a significant portion of poor people living in the *kampung* often threw their human and solid waste into canals, drains, and streams. Jakarta's lack of an integrated drainage plan also adversely affected water management for the whole city-region (Argo 1999).

Problems of Mega-Urban Region Planning in Asia

From a careful review of the planning situation in Asian mega-urban regions, it is clear that the comprehensive strategic planning approach is the current choice of planners in the region. There seems to be wide recognition that narrowly focused physical plans, with their accompanying land use controls, standards, and regulations, are too limited and static to cope with rapidly changing conditions.

However, as more and more Asian mega-urban regions adopt comprehensive strategic approaches, they are encountering a number of problems that pose serious and daunting challenges. Among these problems are (1) the wide gap between planning visions and economic and social realities; (2) the pressing needs for urban infrastructure, housing, and basic services; (3) coping with private-sector activities in the context of strong market forces; and (4) a lack of professionally trained planners. The future development of most Asian mega-urban regions will depend on how urban officials and planners are able to face up to these problems.

Planning Visions and Urban Realities

An assessment of master plans and comprehensive strategic plans in Asian mega-urban regions today reveals the most common vision to be achieving "global city" or "world-class" status. This vision is reflected in the speeches and policy pronouncements of high government officials, business leaders, and civic boosters. It is proclaimed in promotional brochures handed out to guests and sent to potential investors. It is also incorporated into the plan documents themselves.

The vision of a world-class city, for example, is highlighted in the development plan for Shanghai, which focuses on the settlement of Pudong, an instant city of 522 square kilometers built on the eastern banks of the Huangpu River. In April 1990, the Pudong New Area was inaugurated with the stated goal of "transforming Shanghai into one of the leading economic, business and cultural centers of Asia and the world" (Halliday 1995). At the groundbreaking ceremony launching Pudong's development, the vice mayor of Shanghai said he accepted the "historical heavy burden" of developing China's largest metropolis into a world city and promised to do the following:

We will throw ourselves into the great trans-century project with new attitude and new style. . . . We will take the socialist market economy with

Chinese characteristics as a guideline and take the lead, in the Pudong New Area, in setting up a socialist market and the norms of fair competition, integrating with world markets, forming an operational mechanism of positive economic circles, and establishing a new pattern of administrative systems. . . . The reason for our conviction of success is that we have the correct policy of the central government, the correct leadership of Shanghai municipal government, and the sincere support of the people in the whole country and the city. (Pudong New Area Administration 1991)

In literally more concrete terms, Shanghai's world city vision is symbolized by the Pearl TV Tower, which claims the distinction of being the tallest freestanding structure in Asia. It is seen in the plan to build the Shanghai World Financial Center designed by the New York architectural firm Kohn Petersen Fox, which, at 1,624 feet, aspires to be the tallest building in the world by 2007. Pudong's technological ambitions are focused on Zhangjiang Hi-Tech Park, "China's Future Silicon Valley." It is reflected in the area's development strategy, which is titled "Pudong New Area: Facing the World, Facing the 21st Century, and Facing Modernization" (Halliday 1995).

Not too far from Shanghai, the special administrative region of Hong Kong, which is starting to feel the competitive pressure from its coastal city neighbor, has also launched a comprehensive development plan designed to achieve world city status. Even before Hong Kong's incorporation into China in 1997, city authorities had sought to strengthen its linkages to the Pearl River Delta to "compete together" and build upon the economic strengths of Guangzhou, Shenzhen, Zhuhai, and other cities in the region. The new plan builds upon the Territorial Development Strategy (TDS) formulated during the 1980s, a strategy that helped to guide Hong Kong's development until its shift to SAR status. In a revision of the TDS carried out in 1998, the role of Hong Kong as a major node in the development of the whole PRD and other parts of South China was emphasized. Under the revised TDS, development scenarios were formulated for the years up to 2011 and beyond, all designed to make Hong Kong and the PRD a "global city-region" (Campanella et al. 2002, 20–23).

More recently, a multisector Commission on Strategic Development of Hong Kong and the PRD has been engaged in formulating a cross-boundary strategy called "Project 2022." The commission envisions a thriving Hong Kong–centered region by 2022, the halfway point in the SAR's mandated life span of fifty years, under the "one country, two systems" principle. The vision for Hong Kong and the PRD region in this plan was "painted" by one author as follows:

> We see a competitive, vibrant, and prosperous region with blue skies and clean water. Traffic flows across the border as smoothly as a stream. This area bursts with such energy and diversity as to attract millions of admiring tourists and eager businessmen and women. The people of this domain look upon their homes with pride and affection because they inhabit one of the wealthiest, cleanest, most advanced, and most competitive regions in the world. (Fung 2002, 32)

In other parts of Asia, hopeful leaders also pursue the vision of a modern global city. The "Comprehensive Plan for 21st Century Osaka," has for its theme the rebuilding of the urban infrastructure that has, like others in aging Japanese cities, suffered from economic stagnation, population loss, and environmental degradation. The Osaka comprehensive plan looks to increased linkages between the city and the Kansai region and other prefectures and cities in Japan. It pins a great deal of hope on the construction of the Kansai International Airport, which in 2000 already served sixty-seven cities in twenty-seven countries. Osaka, according to this vision, will become an integral part of Kansai, thereby forming a city-region that would be "responsible for playing an important role in the development of a global society in the 21st century" (Osaka Prefectural Government 2000).

Another vision pursued by local leaders in their development plans relates to the role of the city in national development. Realizing the symbolic importance of a great city as the capital of a nation-state, city-region planners focus on the construction of grand buildings, monuments, and other impressive structures that serve to instill greater patriotism. This is the vision in the development plan of Jakarta, which sees the capital with its Merdeka (Independence) monument, grand mosque, and larger-than-life statues of prominent leaders as a unifying symbol in a multiethnic nation that seeks "unity in diversity." It is also the vision embodied in Beijing's Tiananmen Square, with its awe-inspiring Gate of Heavenly Peace, the massive twin buildings of the National People's Congress and National Museum, the monument to the People's Heroes, and Chairman Mao's tomb.

Consistent with this monumental tradition, the 1987 master plan for Beijing set the vision of the capital city as China's "center of politics and culture . . . a city with the most advanced technology, science, education and cultural life in the whole country." To achieve this vision, the plan sought to rehabilitate the inner city, preserve historical buildings, and conserve cultural relics. The plan's vision statement provided that "Old Beijing shall be modernized, with its unique characteristics retained so as to showcase the tremendous achievements made by socialist China, the creativity of its people, and the new look of the nation's capital in the new era of socialism" (Beijing Municipal Government 1987, 5).

From the examples of the vision statements cited above, it is evident that planning for big cities in Asia is not lacking in high ambitions. One problem, however, is that many city-region development plans, like their vision statements, serve more as expressions of hopes and aspirations than as workable and operational planning schemes. They represent the hyperbolic pronouncements of local officials who may not fully appreciate the financial and technical difficulties of achieving these visions. Some vision statements may be no more than the empty boosterism of local business groups hawking the economic attractiveness of their city. Many of the development plans, like their lofty visions, serve mainly as guidelines and not as blueprints for development. In fact, quite a number of plans have not been officially adopted by governments in legislative enactments and therefore lack a legal basis for implementation.

Another indication of the wide gap between lofty visions and operational details is the fact that, with notable exceptions (such as those cited in the previous sections of this chapter), quite a number of comprehensive strategic plans do not have adequate schemes for guiding implementation. They lack careful methodologies for identifying and assessing various options for achieving overall objectives. They do not have systems for setting priorities among competing options. Many lack monitoring and evaluation schemes for determining how the implementation of plan components is faring in terms of achieving planned goals. It is rare to see a comprehensive strategic plan backed up by an appropriate financing scheme.

Most important of all, some comprehensive strategic plans fail to consider governance mechanisms for achieving cooperative and coordinating action among various governmental units. Without these elements, there is a danger that many comprehensive strategic plans for Asian mega-urban regions will not be able to go beyond visions and pipe dreams and will fail to achieve real city-region development.

Increasing Demand for Infrastructure, Housing, and Services

Population growth, which continues to be high in some South and Southeast Asian cities, creates a heavy demand for more infrastructure and services. The Asian Development Bank estimated in 1996 that Asian countries would require about $1.4 trillion in infrastructure projects until 2005. These projects included telecommunications, ports, roads, mass transit, water supplies, drainage, and sanitation (Shah 1996, 15). The planning, implementation, supervision, and evaluation of the projects to be funded by this huge amount called for the services of good planners as well as professional urban administrators.

At present, it is estimated that about 80 percent of new housing in Asian cities is constructed by people themselves (popular housing). The great majority of slum dwellers and squatters have no access to basic services like potable water, sanitation, electricity, and garbage collection and disposal. Projects in slum upgrading and sites and services set up during the 1960s and 1970s in Bangladesh, India, Indonesia, Pakistan, and the Philippines have been overwhelmed by new urban residents. In cities like Bangkok, Dhaka, Jakarta, Karachi, Metro Manila, and Mumbai, serviced land for housing is in extremely short supply. Land scarcity has at times been made worse by supposedly positive programs like land banking that, in some cities, has left land acquired by the government undeveloped while demand has skyrocketed. Land shortages, in turn, have forced poor urban residents to build their shanties on frequently flooded areas (Dhaka, Jakarta), steep ravines (Baguio), or dangerous dumpsites (Payatas in Metro Manila).

In the cities of South and Southeast Asia, land availability is hampered by a strong ideological attachment to private land ownership, constitutional provisions indicating that land can only be alienated on the basis of the exercise of eminent domain, and the legal requirement that land taken by the state should be paid for at fair market value. Even in countries in transition like Vietnam and China, land privatization schemes and the issuance of long-term leases is driving land use regulation and control outside the authority and power of urban authorities. One result has been the uncontrolled conversion of agricultural land to urban uses. In very large megalopolitan regions, such as the Pearl River Delta and the Yangtze River Delta, urban growth has been outstripping formal systems of land use planning and control.

An interesting aspect of the demand for infrastructure and services is the increasing popularity of privatization as a means of funding and managing big projects. In some Southeast Asian cities, transport systems have been set up with private financing through build–operate–transfer and other approaches. In Metro Manila and Greater Jakarta, municipal water and sewerage systems have been privatized (Argo and Laquian 2004). Public-private partnership and domestic-foreign joint ventures have become common approaches in financing and managing urban projects. These developments have put pressure on planning authorities to change their overly bureaucratic ways of doing things and highlighted the need for more efficient and professionally competent planning staffs able to cope with expanding future challenges. The effects and impact of privatization on the lives of urban poor people, however, has rarely been evaluated—although anecdotal evidence suggests that this approach has not always been good for poor and underprivileged residents.

Planning under Market Conditions

Rates of economic growth in Asia have been relatively high (ranging from 4 to 10 percent a year), especially in China and the so-called Asian tigers (Hong Kong, Singapore, South Korea, and Taiwan). These high rates of growth have been maintained despite the adverse effects of global events— such as the 1973 and 1979 oil crises; the 1982 world debt crisis; the 1991 Gulf War; the 1997 East Asian financial crisis; the effects of the September 11, 2001, terrorist attacks in the United States and the war on terrorism; the SARS epidemic; and the 2003 Iraq war. Globalization, which in general fosters policies based on the free interplay of market forces, has had a significant influence on comprehensive strategic planning in Asia.

The supporters of globalization have claimed that unfettered trade and commerce, the free flow of capital, the movement of people across national boundaries, increased foreign direct investment, and full access to information and knowledge have helped to fuel economic growth in a number of Asian countries. Cheaper labor in South Asia and Southeast Asia has attracted foreign investment. The global demand for labor in Europe, the Middle East, and North America has encouraged some countries (Bangladesh, Pakistan, Philippines, Sri Lanka) to adopt "labor export policies" that have increased hard currency remittances to these countries.

The perceived importance of market forces in the economic and social development of Asian countries has brought back old nineteenth-century debates about the relationship of planning to freedom—reflected, for example, in the recent popularity of the economic theories of Friedrich Hayek among Chinese economists. The vaunted resurgence of the Asian tiger economies has been attributed by some to the opening of global markets, free trade, and foreign investment characterized by an open market, and by others to planned government interventions based on currency controls, government investment in government infrastructure and social programs, protecting and supporting agriculture and selected industries, and control over land and other natural resources.

To some extent, the use of comprehensive strategic planning as a tool for policymaking in many Asian countries has resolved some of this debate. Most Asian officials now acknowledge the importance of planning in predictable and sustainable development. They view planning, however, as playing an important role as a mechanism for guiding future action, not as the straitjacket instrument for control that has proved unsuccessful in achieving development in the past.

In a number of cases, city and regional planning in many South and Southeast Asian cities has not succeeded in positively influencing the actions of private business interests. Immediately after the end of World War II in Metro Manila, for example, the fact that the city had been almost completely destroyed by American carpet bombing and Japanese torching of homes and buildings was seen as an opportunity to start planning the city's development with a clean slate. This prompted then-president Manuel Quezon to ask Angel Kayanan, then studying planning at the Massachusetts Institute of Technology, to prepare a master plan for Manila's reconstruction. Before the plan was adopted, however, many property owners started building their plants and homes based on the original plots and street layout of the city. Faced with serious problems of financing reconstruction, the nment had neither the money nor the will to enforce any rational planning to guide the development of the city. The result was that market forces completely thwarted any efforts to use city and regional planning, and the city found itself in a much worse condition than before.

In Bangkok, Dhaka, Jakarta, Karachi, Kolkata, Mumbai, and other cities, planned efforts to control urban sprawl also tended to be frustrated by market forces. Cheaper land on the urban periphery enticed entrepreneurs to locate their plants and housing subdivisions there. When city authorities attempted to obtain land for infrastructure and other development, the high cost of purchasing land at fair market value prevented them from succeeding. Using the constitutional principle of eminent domain to acquire land was too cumbersome and took too long. When some city authorities tried to use police powers to enforce zoning codes and other types of land use regulations, private companies were able to get the services of high-priced lawyers to argue their cases. In any case, a strong tradition of respect for private property rights in the legal systems of many South and Southeast Asian countries invariably overruled the efforts of city authorities to control and regulate land use and other economic activities.

The practice of city and regional planning under market conditions is creating some very interesting results in China. The Chinese Constitution has legalized private enterprise and private ownership of property. The Inheritance Law (1985) allows individuals to inherit private property. Private ownership of property by individuals, enterprises, and other entities is recognized by the General Principles of Civil Law (1986). The Economic Contract Law (1982), Foreign Economic Contract Law (1985), and Civil Procedure Law (1991) all uphold the freedom to make binding contracts and protect contractual rights. Many local governments have enacted rules and regulations for the acquisition, disposal, and protection of land use rights, buildings, patents, copyrights, and even computer software. China has also signed a number of international conventions, including the most important one protecting intellectual property rights.

Despite the passage of so many laws regulating relationships in a market economy, however, many foreign investors in China still complain about the "unbusinesslike" practices of so many officials and private entrepreneurs. Local partners could suddenly ignore contractual obligations. The cost of certain transactions could be arbitrarily raised without adequate explanation. The legal status of land appropriated for physical plants could be questioned. Graft and corruption, politely termed "rent seeking" or "process facilitation," could significantly raise the cost of business ventures. The shift from central planning to market-oriented economic transactions in China, therefore, has not been easy or smooth, and city and regional planning practice has inevitably been affected by the unpredictable developments in the process.

The Lack of Professional Planners

The many problems faced by urban and regional planning in Asia brings to the fore the poor state of the planning profession and the need to strengthen planning capacities. Relative to the critical need for professional planners to guide urban development in the region, Asia has a severe shortage of trained planners. China, for example, with 1.3 billion people, had only 20,000 urban and regional planners in 2003, only 7,000 of whom were certified planners. This compared unfavorably with the situation in the United States, which with a population of 292 million had 33,000 members of the American Planning Association, of which 15,000 were certified planners. Important reasons advanced for planning difficulties in Asia include the low level of technical capabilities, lack of professional identity, and inadequate education and training of future planners (Wu 2000, 371).

In most Asian countries, urban and regional planners have architectural, engineering, and urban design backgrounds. Public functions carried out by planners include the preparation of detailed maps indicating land use and prescribed development zones; formulation of zoning codes and land use control regulations; assessment and approval of building permits and construction schemes; setting up and enforcing health, safety, and building standards; and assessing the environmental and social impact of proposed schemes. The public sees planners as mainly exercising control and regulatory functions. In a few countries, planners engage in the formulation and adoption of comprehensive and strategic development plans. But in most instances, practicing planners are often unprepared or too poorly trained to do these tasks properly.

There are some schools of planning in Asia, but quite a few of these are hampered by inadequately educated and trained faculty members, a lack of equipment, and shortages of books and teaching materials. A serious problem faced by these schools is the lack of agreement on curriculums. There is a tendency in some schools to stick to the architectural and urban design traditions. In others, there are attempts to copy broader curricular offerings from North American and European planning schools.

Furthermore, the education of future planners is complicated by the uncertain professional identity of the graduates of urban and regional planning schools. In countries following the British or Canadian tradition, a planner has to pass an examination to qualify as a planning practitioner. In other countries, graduating with a planning degree qualifies one as a professional planner. This lack of consistency and coherence in the substantive functions, qualification requirements, and professional identity of members of the planning profession in Asia has contributed to the extremely uneven quality of master plans and indicative plans currently in use in the region.

In most instances, the planning literature used in Asia has been based on imported notions arising from control-oriented rules and regulations inherited from colonial administrators. This body of knowledge primarily involved techniques for land use planning and control, the use of zoning codes and subdivision regulations, principles based on architecture and urban design, and the financing and management of housing and basic urban services through government subsidies and special levies. Planning knowledge, because of this background, tended to be regarded as mainly involving the interpretation and application of laws, regulations, and rules. Planning decisions were based more on interpretations of legal concepts than on an empirical analysis of existing situations.

The body of knowledge available for Asian planners is mainly based in educational institutions for planners, of course. In general, the education of future Asian planners reflects the legal, architectural, and urban design tendencies in the field. As noted by Wu, "a traditional planning education program linked closely to its roots in architecture or in landscape architecture often treated planning as merely large-scale design" (Wu 2000, 368). It was only much later that the social sciences were introduced to planning curriculums, with an emphasis on multidisciplinary approaches to decision making, the importance of taking cultural variables into consideration, and linking urban plans to financial schemes and management and governance approaches.

Institutional arrangements for urban and regional planning in most Asian countries have evolved through the years. An excellent example of institutional changes is the situation in China, which has a very long tradition of planning cities. Today, there are essentially three institutions involved in urban planning in the country. First, urban and regional planning is carried out through local urban planning bureaus (*guihua ju*), which are primarily responsible for preparing master plans and approving building permits and architectural design submissions to city authorities. Second, urban planning institutes (*guihua yuan*) are professional organizations that provide technical advice to local officials in accordance with approved master plans. Third, planning commissions (*jihua weyuanhui,* or simply *ji wei*) are local units responsible for the preparation of Five-Year Socioeconomic Development Plans, which are local elaborations of the national Five-Year Plan.

These *ji wei* are concerned with the socioeconomic aspects of planning, but because they also control large infrastructure projects, they are quite powerful and directly influence developments in a city-region. To further complicate the Chinese planning situation, there are also separate agencies in charge of water and sewerage, housing, transportation, railways, and other heavy infrastructure services. And even the national environmental protection agency gets directly involved in urban development through its local units.

Only in recent years has planning in most Asian city-regions become institutionalized as an integral part of urban governance. In general, there has been a rapid transformation of planning structures from control-oriented mechanisms regulating land use to more multidisciplinary bodies focused on comprehensive planning and strategic thinking. Although some Asian cities still produce traditional master plans, quite a few have now formulated comprehensive indicative plans designed to influence economic, political, and administrative decision making. For example, the comprehensive plans for the Beijing region and the plans for the development of the whole Pearl River Delta incorporate demographic, economic, social, and cultural variables. The indicative plans for Greater Jakarta and the plans for Metro Manila are strategic documents designed to influence the patterns of investments in infrastructure, industry, and housing, as well as the allocation of open space for parks and recreational purposes.

To some extent, the difficulties faced by urban and regional planners in Asia can be traced to several factors, including (1) inadequate authority and power vested in planning institutions; (2) the overwhelming force of the market driven strongly by the profit motive; (3) a strong ideological commitment to the sanctity of private property on the part of economic and social elites; (4) weak adherence to the rule of law, with resultant rent seeking, negative bureaucratic behavior, and graft and corruption; and (5) destabilizing economic and social forces related to rapid globalization, such as the oil crisis of 1979 and the Asian economic crisis of 1997.

Key Issues in Mega-Urban Region Planning

A careful reading of the twelve mega-urban region plans covered in this study points to at least four major issues that need to be resolved in a development strategy. These issues include (1) the redevelopment of the inner city, (2) cultural conservation, (3) peripheral area development, and (4) environmental planning.

Inner-City Redevelopment

Most Asian mega-urban regions are faced with the twin problems of decaying inner-city cores and uncontrolled development in suburban and peripheral areas. Although the issue does not have to involve an either/or choice of inner-city versus peripheral area development, because urban authorities are usually confronted with limited resources, they have to set clear priorities to guide their actions. In general, most Asian urban authorities have tended to place greater emphasis on peripheral area or "greenfield" development. However, the redevelopment of inner cities has been pursued in a number of East Asian and Southeast Asian urban regions, especially in older ones where the city core has suffered from extensive decay and deterioration and where the growing importance of tourism demands the conservation of heritage buildings and sites.

As a rule, the cost of inner-city redevelopment tends to be high because conserving, restoring, and maintaining historic buildings costs more than simply demolishing them and putting up new ones. People living in congested inner cities need to be relocated while redevelopment takes place, either temporarily or permanently. The value of inner-city land is usually very high, and if it is privately owned, acquiring it at fair market value becomes very expensive. The legal processes for land acquisition, such as the use of eminent domain, can result in drawn-out and expensive litigation.

In older Asian cities, early industrial and manufacturing enterprises were usually located near ports and harbors that eventually turned into inner cities. The redevelopment of so-called brownfield areas poses tremendous challenges, including the removal of toxic waste from contaminated soils, uprooting abandoned rail lines, and getting rid of outdated machinery and equipment. Problems may arise due to the strict enforcement of laws and regulations designed for the conservation and protection of historic buildings and sites. Organized community groups may sue developers for real or imagined damage arising from the execution of development plans. They may resort to demonstrations and even violently sabotage development schemes. Local politicians usually support local groups for their votes, and they may influence administrators who can delay the issuance of permits and licenses or impose more regulations and requirements, such as environmental impact assessments, social impact assessments, and zoning compliance certificates. Developers may also have to pay "facilitation" fees or "commissions" to grease the administrative process.

Despite the many problems associated with inner-city redevelopment, quite a number of East and Southeast Asian cities have embarked on such ventures. In Beijing, for example, city authorities and housing and land developers have launched a program of "old and dilapidated housing renewal" (Liu 1995). In 1983, the municipal government approved a plan to renovate old housing involving twenty-nine housing renewal areas, 95 percent of which were within the inner-city area that was designated as Zone 1. The first phase of the housing renewal project in Zone 1 was exploratory and "experimental," and it involved three sites in Dongnanyuan, Ju-er Hutong, and Xiaohoucang. These were completed in 1987.

Evaluation studies of the early projects revealed that by building well-designed multistory housing units on the site, more than three-fourths of the families living in congested "courtyard houses" could be accommodated in the same area. The experiment also showed that families that could not be accommodated on the original site were often quite willing to move to more spacious apartments in the suburbs. On the basis of the results of the studies, the Beijing municipal government adopted three official policies: (1) Concentrate housing and other financial investments on redevelopment of inner-city neighborhoods; (2) give the leading role in redevelopment programs to local district governments; and (3) integrate inner-city housing redevelopment with programs related to employment creation, the formation of property markets, and cultural conservation. In accordance with these policies, thirty-seven housing renewal areas covering 340 hectares and involving 1.6 million square kilometers of housing benefiting 50,000 families were completed by 1990 (Zhang Jie 1993, 5).

Zone 2 permitted traditional structures, such as ancient courtyard houses, that could be redeveloped for housing, commercial, and cultural purposes. Industrial and manufacturing activities were prohibited in this zone, and strict controls were imposed on the heights of structures that could be built. Zone 3 allowed a mixture of old traditional housing, multistory buildings, factories, offices, and commercial structures. Zone 4 permitted some old houses that were considered unsafe and marked for demolition or repair. Zone 5 contained deteriorating multistory housing units that were hastily constructed to accommodate poor families, many of which were victims of the Beijing-Tangshan earthquake and other calamities.

A survey in 1990 revealed that about 65 percent of the inner-city people were living in Zones 2 through 4. Proposals were then made to redevelop houses for people living in the zones and to create employment opportunities for them in the same area. The plans indicated that no more than a third of the people in Zones 2 through 4 would be relocated from the sites. Community organization efforts and intensive community development programs were launched to encourage the residents to carry out functions such as street cleaning, the maintenance of parks and playgrounds, regulating local markets, supporting nurseries and kindergartens, and maintaining peace and order.

A full decade after the inner-city redevelopment efforts in Beijing, anecdotal assessments of the project's results suggested that the target of retaining more than 70 percent of original residents was rather optimistic. In some streets, more than half of the original residents moved out and sold their "rights of occupancy" to other families. Employment opportunities in the inner city did not materialize as expected, as developments in manufacturing, industry, and services became concentrated in suburban areas. Owning a home in the central city became so attractive that "development companies" used all sorts of inducements or threats so older residents would move out. There were even newspaper accounts of developers hiring gangs to harass old residents or burn their homes to force them to move out so that new apartments could be built on the sites.

In a number of Southeast Asian cities, the redevelopment of the inner city has meant the demolition of decaying houses and structures in processes that were similar to the "federal bulldozer" urban renewal policies pursued in the United States in the 1950s. During the early 1960s, for example, the city of Manila decided to eradicate squatters from the walled city of Intramuros and resettled them to suburban relocation sites. Residents of a densely populated block in the inner city, known appropriately enough as the Casbah, were forcibly evicted by wrecker crews from City Hall and moved to Carmona, Sapang Palay, and other resettlement sites. In central Jakarta, inner-city *kampung* dwellers were also removed from their homes to make way for modern highways, parks, big buildings, and commercial complexes. As modern highways and structures were built, many poor inner-city residents found that even making a living became more difficult as *betjaks* (tricycles) were banned from major city streets and hawkers and vendors were banned from certain areas. Similar programs to rid inner cities of the nuisance attributed to urban poor people were also launched in South Asian cities like Delhi, Karachi, Kolkata, and Mumbai.

Even as central and local governments attempted to decongest inner cities, however, they had to recognize the fact that the great bulk of the population preferred to live there. In Karachi, for example, local authorities had to recognize during the mid-1980s that the city's economy accounted for 70 percent of the gross domestic product of Sind province and 44 percent of provincial revenue. About three-quarters of the major manufacturing establishments in the whole province were also concentrated in Karachi (United Nations 1988). In recognition of the heavy concentration of people and economic activities in the inner city, the Karachi Development Plan (1974–85) sought to promote intensification of development in a belt extending from North Karachi to the central business district and down to Korangi. A major justification for this inner-city redevelopment strategy was the existence of still underutilized infrastructure (arterial roads, water mains, trunk sewers) in the area. To implement the plan, the city of Karachi, which had only 6 percent of Pakistan's population, got about 70 percent of investment funds approved by the Ministry of Production Investment. It also received 46 percent of the public infrastructure investments included in the central government's Annual Development Plan (United Nations 1988, 15).

Although many serious problems have been faced in planned efforts to redevelop inner cities, quite a number of success stories are worth noting. These include a number of experimental approaches—such as the Ju'er Hutong project in Beijing; the redevelopment of *lilong* or lane housing in Shanghai; the preservation of old city neighborhoods in Tokyo; the preservation of old trees, houses, and traditional shops around Hoang Khiem Lake in Hanoi; the maintenance of quiet neighborhoods around the temples and shrines of Kyoto; the preservation of traditional houses and structures near the Imperial Palace in Bangkok; and recent efforts to refurbish and clean up selected sites in the central business district of Manila. Despite many problems met in redeveloping inner-city zones in Chinese cities, these areas continue to have thriving communities of residents who manage to keep inner-city neighborhoods socially cohesive and productive. Unlike some cities in North America that are abandoned after the close of office hours, Bangladeshi, Chinese, Indian, Pakistani, and Vietnamese cities remain vibrant and alive late into the night.

Planners and city authorities have also discovered that inner-city redevelopment has served as an important policy instrument for cultural conservation. With the growing recognition of the role of international tourism development, more and more city governments are starting to pursue more inner-city development projects. It is useful to look more closely at these initiatives.

Planning for Cultural Conservation

An increasingly important element in development planning in Asia is the desire to conserve and maintain traditional structures, heritage sites, and cultural practices. A key element in Beijing's inner-city development efforts, for example, was the designation of the city as "an important cultural historic city" by China's State Council. In keeping with this designation, the Beijing municipal government issued strict regulations for "conserving the historic landscape while modernizing the city." The city's inner area was divided into five zones, with Zone 1 that had the highest concentration of historic structures given preferential status. In this zone are located culturally important buildings such as the Palace Museum or Forbidden City, Zhongnanhai (the residential enclave for China's national leaders), Tiananmen Square, and most of the *sihejuan* (courtyard houses) built during the Ming Dynasty (1368–1644) and the Qing Dynasty (1644–1911).

With the success of economic reforms after 1979, the Beijing authorities recognized that something had to be done about the deterioration of the city's core. Although the inner city made up only 6.1 percent of the metropolitan territory, it held 82 percent of the people. All of the central and municipal government offices, 90 percent of research institutes, colleges, and universities, and 80 percent of state-owned industries were concentrated in Beijing's inner core (Zhao, Chen, and Zhang 1992, 25). Haphazard planning in the past, including the concentration of industrial and manufacturing plants with their adjacent workers' housing complexes in the inner city, had eroded the cultural makeup of Beijing. The demolition of the old city walls and the conversion of temples and shrines into schools, community centers, factories, or storage places had radically altered the cultural makeup of the city. Rows upon rows of nondescript Soviet-style apartments, though housing most urban residents, were boring and unattractive. During the heyday of Soviet influence, the Chinese authorities built monumental Stalinist structures, such as the offices of Radio Peking, the central exhibition hall, and the massive complexes of central government offices along Chang'an Boulevard and areas adjacent to Tiananmen Square.

In South Asian cities, severe shortages of public funds relegated planning for cultural conservation to something of a luxury. Faced with the critical problems of unemployment, a lack of adequate housing, traffic jams, deteriorating services, and ethnic strife, many South Asian city authorities relegated heritage conservation to the back burner. Historic buildings decayed from lack of maintenance. Verdant parks turned to noisy and dirty spaces as hawkers, vendors, and homeless people took them over. Traditional bazaars spilled over into city streets, causing traffic jams, littering, and problems of waste disposal and sanitation.

In some Southeast Asian cities, similar processes of abandonment and neglect made inner cities dirty, unsightly, and dangerous. In Metro Manila, inner-city decay caused capital flight to suburban areas and, with a dwindling population and tax base, the city simply failed to maintain services in the central business district. The silting up of the city's *esteros* (small streams) due to the indiscriminate throwing of garbage into them and the erection of squatter shanties on stilts right on the water caused destructive floods. In Jakarta, the building of wide streets and boulevards and the establishment of huge commercial and shopping complexes meant the demolition of traditional homes. In both Jakarta and Manila, the increasing use of the private automobile accelerated suburban growth, which in turn resulted in the abandonment of central city areas.

Even in cities that have rediscovered the need for cultural conservation and have the resources to support conservation plans, there seem to be serious problems that are yet to be resolved. A major source of such problems is the difficulty of defining what is culturally relevant and needs to be conserved and what has to be remodeled to keep pace with rapid globalization. In China, for example, some powerful leaders seek to transform major cities into twenty-first-century symbols of economic might and progress. They do not want to see traditional structures and sites that they consider to be backward, old-fashioned, or feudal. This modernist aspiration has resulted in inner cities that seem to represent a "clash of cultures." Thus, between 1980 and 2003, about a third of the old structures in the inner city of Beijing were razed to make way for wider boulevards, shopping centers, and skyscrapers. The number of courtyard houses was reduced from 3,600 in 1980 to 2,000 in 2003 (Yu 2003).

In the areas adjacent to Beijing's Forbidden City, the city authorities have allowed the construction of a massive Hong Kong style mega-mall that stands in jarring contrast to the imperial palace and even the multistyled Beijing hotel. The brand-new National Theater designed by the French architect Paul Andreu in association with ADP Group Ingenierie located next door to the Great Hall of the People and just a stone's throw from Tiananmen Square resembles an alien flying saucer or a giant mushroom that is eerily reminiscent of that Berlin building that some architectural wags have called the "pregnant oyster."

Worse still are the results of the redevelopment of Liulichang Street, the traditional haunt of antique lovers, old book collectors, and calligraphy and art enthusiasts, which has been turned into a tourist trap with gaudy building facades, gold-gilded trim, and oversized window displays. What is reputedly the largest Kentucky Fried Chicken franchise in the world is nested on the southwest corner of Tiananmen Square, and a giant McDonald's concession is located not too far from the famed Beijing Hotel. Quite a number of Chinese architects and critics have spoken loudly against these inner-city developments, but the economic and social forces arising from the global spread of consumerist culture have been too strong and difficult to resist, even in China's historic cultural capital.

In the planning of mega-cities and mega-urban regions, many Asian officials have had to choose between emphasizing culturally relevant urban forms or ultramodern and up-to-date urban development. The pursuit of a global city vision has encouraged many planners to adopt modern city-building ideas. This is seen in the fact that most Asian cities today look the same physically and structurally. They almost universally feature tall buildings made of concrete, steel and glass, spaghetti highways clogged with gas-guzzling cars, blinking neon-lighted billboards advertising Japanese products, air-conditioned shopping malls filled with name-brand stores and boutiques, and ubiquitous suburban strip malls lined with auto repair shops, convenience stores, fast food restaurants, and food courts. It does not matter if one is in Pudong in Shanghai, Makati in Metro Manila, or Shenzhen near Hong Kong—the physical features of new Asian cities look the same. They all appear as rather poor copies of the cityscapes of Chicago, Los Angeles, New York, San Francisco, or Toronto.

In choosing between the old and the new, many Asian urban planners seem to have succeeded mainly in bastardizing the cultural character of their cities. The choices of planners and officials seem limited to preserving old cities as museum-like relics for the edification of tourists or building completely new cities with modern structures that have no aesthetic or functional connections with indigenous culture. There are very few examples of successful planned efforts that effectively blend indigenous and modern urban design. As a whole, the failure to achieve an integration of traditional and modern elements is symbolized by towering skyscrapers topped with the curving roof of a traditional pagoda, a royal crown, or the replica of a temple. The results of such efforts are often neither indigenous nor modern—just ugly and ridiculously inappropriate.

Peripheral Area Development

It has been realized in many Asian cities that confining planning to the highly urbanized sector of an agglomeration does not work. Although local government units may object to the establishment of areawide planning agencies, they usually agree to respect the mandate of such bodies if these are issued by higher levels of government. This exercise of authority and power by these higher levels has had some positive effects in the development of mega-urban regions in Asia because, in general, areawide planning over a whole urban region has brought about better-coordinated development, as well as the more efficient management of urban services.

Probably the most crucial issue faced by city and regional planners in Asian mega-urban regions is peripheral area development. During the past fifty years or so, most Asian urban agglomerations have greatly expanded in both population size and geographic area. This explosive growth has called for regionwide development schemes that integrate inncr-city redevelopment with coordinated efforts to plan and manage peripheral areas.

Many reasons have been advanced for embarking of peripheral area development rather than the redevelopment of inner cities. There is less expensive land and more open space for new development in outlying areas. Private investors are more willing to invest in peripheral areas and build new plants in virgin territories. Local governments in peripheral areas are eager to welcome new developments and are willing to offer many benefits and concessions to investors, such as tax concessions, an assured energy supply, free or cheap land, and even a meek and subservient labor force. They are willing to provide trunk infrastructure, such as main highways, sewers, drains, and water supply lines in urban peripheries. Some private developers also find it more economical and profitable to invest in strip malls along underutilized highways rather than in inner-city "infill" schemes that are more complicated and expensive.

A good example of a scheme that has taken the peripheral area option is the master plan for New Mumbai, a new settlement built across the harbor from Mumbai Island that was proposed by a group of local architects to Indian authorities in the late 1960s. New Mumbai was established in connection with the development of a new modern port in Nava Sheva. The plan was designed to relocate some of the industries and manufacturing enterprises that have been concentrated on the island since colonial times. The plan also was created in the hope that the employment created by the port, the industrial and manufacturing concerns, and housing construction activities in New Mumbai would attract more people and transform it into an effective "countermagnet" to the old city (Jain 1996b).

The development of New Mumbai was an integral part of the comprehensive strategic plan for the Mumbai region. After some initial hesitation, government officers working in Mumbai agreed to be resettled to New Mumbai with the offer of better housing and services. Operators of large agricultural produce markets were also moved from the city center to New Mumbai and provided with better facilities. Most important of all, private manufacturing and industrial plants were attracted to locate in New Mumbai, and their relocation in turn meant that their workers and their families also moved. The new developments, of course, also attracted spontaneous settlements of urban poor people to New Mumbai, where they engaged in petty trading, low-cost transport, and other services (United Nations 1986, 20–21).

Even a highly centralized city like Bangkok has pursued peripheral area development. In Thailand's Fifth National Economic and Social Development Plan (1982–86), it was provided that "the major development issue is how to slow down Bangkok's population growth and lessen its economic dominance." To achieve this goal, "The Structural Plan for the Development of the Bangkok Metropolis and Vicinity Towns" was approved. The plan proposed decentralized development to the five surrounding towns of Samut Prakarn, Pathum Thani, Nontha Buri, Nakhon Pathom, and Samut Sakorn. The towns were to be developed as "planned communities with a high degree of self-sufficiency, thereby ensuring that residents would not need to commute to Bangkok for employment or high-level services" (NESDB 1982).

Parallel to the decentralized development of the five surrounding towns, the Fifth Five-Year Plan proposed the development of the Eastern Seaboard subregion as Thailand's center for heavy industries. To implement this option, the government extended significant incentives to investors, such as lower land prices, the construction of highways opening up the new areas, reduced electricity rates, and financial commissions to persons bringing in new investments. Despite financial difficulties and competition provided by other industrial estates established in other places such as Laem Chabang, Lamphung, and Songkhla, the Eastern Seaboard has grown into one of the most successful development sites outside Bangkok. However, even with this planned decentralized growth, the dominance of the Bangkok region has not been significantly changed. In 1991, it was estimated that this region, with only 10 percent of Thailand's population, contributed more than 50 percent of the country's gross domestic product, and that the per capita income of the region's residents was about nine times greater than that of the Northeast (Kaothien 1991, 1027).

Metro Manila, like other Southeast Asian cities, has expanded way beyond the original national capital region. Three clearly demarcated enclaves have grown in the regional edges of the metropolitan area. In the northwest, there is the special economic zone of Subic Bay, a former base of the U.S. Navy. In the northeast, another economic development zone has been established in the former Clark Base of the U.S. Air Force. In the south, a high-technology zone has been set up in Rosario Cavite. Still farther south, development nodes focused on Batangas City, Cavite City, and San Pablo City. Much of this growth in the peripheral areas of Metro Manila was uncontrolled and was not guided by official city plans.

A factor that makes regional planning extremely difficult in Asian agglomerations, however, is the *fragmentation* of local government units. To some extent, this fragmentation has its origins in the localism of small villages and towns that is common in Asian society, where a person's identity is often rooted in one's place of origin. This localism, in turn, has been enhanced by governmental policies of decentralization, which in turn have been encouraged by international donors and Western countries extolling the virtues of civil society and democracy.

A serious case of jurisdictional fragmentation may be seen in the Jakarta region, or the Jabotabek area (short for the Jakarta-Bogor-Tangerang-Bekasi region). Essentially, there are six identifiable jurisdictions in the region: (1) the Special Region of the National Capital of Indonesia, or DKI Jakarta, which has the status of a provincial government; (2) the municipality (*kotamadya*) of Bogor; (3) municipality of Tangerang; (4) the district (*kabupaten*) of Bogor; (5) the district of Tangerang; and (6) the district of Bekasi. The total population of Jabotabek in 1990 was 14.8 million, of which 86.5 percent was classified as urban and 13.5 percent as rural (Dharmapatni and Firman 1995, 169).

The developments in the Jabotabek region have spread out so rapidly that they are now joining those in the region of Bandung, separated from the national capital by 200 kilometers but linked by a network of roads and railways. In 1990, the Bandung region had a population of 5.26 million, of which 62.7 percent was urban and 37.3 percent rural. In the Bandung metropolitan area, two distinct political units were present: (1) the municipality (*kotamadya*) of Bandung, and (2) the district or regency (*kabupaten*) of Bandung. Although sharing the same name, these are two distinct local government units—the capital of the Bandung district or regency, for example, is the town of Soreang, on the outer fringes of the metropolitan area.

Indonesian planners have proposed that the Jabotabek and Bandung regions should be planned as one unit because of the dominant roles they play in Indonesia's development. For one, nearly half the total domestic and foreign direct investment in Indonesia in the past twenty-five years has been concentrated in these two regions. When oil and gas outputs are excluded, about a third of the total national output in Indonesia's economy also originates in these same regions. Four-fifths of the money circulating in the whole country is concentrated in Jakarta. Major industries in the region include textiles, electrical equipment, cement, plastics, metal and glass products, transport, printing, publishing, chemical industries, and productive services. The Bandung region is recognized as the textile capital of Indonesia, producing about 25 percent of the national total of textiles. It is also the center of aircraft industry, arms production, and telecommunications.

The coordinated planning of economic development in the Jabotabek and Bandung regions is made even more necessary by economic decisions of the national government. In an effort to attract more foreign investment, the Government of Indonesia has simplified many rules and regulations that tended to discourage investors. For example, the Foreign Investment Law of 1967 offered exemption from import duties and sales taxes of equipment and supplies brought in by foreign investors. Tax holidays, accelerated depreciation, guaranteed repatriation of capital and profits, and the carrying forward of losses were also granted. More seriously, regulations related to the conduct of environmental impact assessments and hazard and risk analysis were relaxed. The importation of plant equipment and capital goods was exempted from inspection at points of loading if these were destined for export-processing zones.

Jurisdictional fragmentation in the Jabotabek and Bandung regions was exacerbated even further by the proliferation of special economic zones, particularly after the issuance of Presidential Decree 53/1989 that allowed the private sector to manage its own industrial estates. Since 1989, about 119 private companies have applied for permits to develop industrial estates, 62 percent of which are in West Java, particularly in the Jabotabek-Bandung region. The government of West Java has allocated substantial amounts of land for industrial estates, 70 percent of which are in the Jabotabek-Bandung region. In additional, many investors have applied for the establishment of industries outside the industrial estates. Very large residential subdivisions and "new town" projects have also sprouted in the region. Even the state-owned housing agency, Perum Perumnas, has built a new town in the district of Bekasi. Many of the new towns are designed as "dormitory suburbs" for people who will commute to their jobs in Bandung and Jakarta.

The main problem with the rapid development in the Jabotabek-Bandung region is that its impact does not respect political boundaries. Some of the more serious repercussions of this development have been (1) the conversion of rich agricultural land to urban uses; (2) the depletion of the region's water supply; (3) the displacement of people from traditional residential areas; (4) severe soil erosion, surface run-off, and floods; (5) widespread water, air, and soil pollution; and (6) difficulties related to waste disposal.

At present, a number of comprehensive planning efforts have been carried out in the Jabotabek region to rationally integrate the economic, social, and environmental factors involved in its development. Similar efforts have also been tried in the Bandung region. The problem, however, is the lack of any mechanism to properly coordinate developmental efforts in the two city-regions. This jurisdictional fragmentation takes on a number of levels. First, there is functional fragmentation among central government agencies and ministries devoted to such functions as agriculture, construction, commerce and industry, and the environment that pursue activities in the Jabotabek and Bandung regions. These essentially vertical mandates are supposed to be coordinated at the Cabinet level of the central government, but such coordination does not really work well. Second, the same kind of functional fragmentation exists at the provincial (West Java) and municipal (Jakarta and Bandung) governmental levels, because the Indonesian local government system is essentially a "field administration" structure where the functional differentiation among agencies is just repeated at lower levels. Third, there is the vertical fragmentation at the central, provincial, city, municipal, district, and lower levels of government. Though, in theory, the Indonesian government's ideology of collective decision making (*musjawarah*) is supposed to be adhered to, the natural competition among these units to attract investors and other sectors that might improve their developmental tax base makes such coordination and cooperation difficult.

Dharmapatni and Firman (1995) have advocated the establishment of metropolitan or areawide planning and governance mechanisms to coordinate the planning and management of developments in the Jabotabek and Bandung regions. To date, however, there has been no visible attempt in that direction. In the late 1980s, there were some efforts in the region to set up voluntary mechanisms for coordination that involved municipality and district governments in collaboratively preparing development plans and establishing cooperative management mechanisms. These did not prosper, and many of these mechanisms were abandoned.

There have also been efforts on the part of the West Java provincial government to become more actively involved in planning and administrative coordination in areas within its jurisdiction. Perhaps these efforts may have more potential for success, provided the central government and the more autonomous municipalities agree to cooperate with the province.

The Jabotabek-Bandung case highlights the need for a larger regional framework in the planning of mega-urban regions in Asia. Where economic and environmental factors already reveal the interrelatedness of development efforts, planning authorities have to take a more comprehensive approach to regional development. The tendency to cling to political and administrative particularism has to be overcome. The fragmentation among political and administrative units has to be bridged to arrive at common action. This can be initially overcome through a regional planning framework, which in the future may lead to a regional form of governance.

Environmental Planning

To achieve the vision of becoming a global city, most Asian planners have incorporated aggressive economic development initiatives in their city-region plans. This has especially been the case with planners in China and Vietnam, who saw the socialist city as "a distinct special phenomenon more or less differentiated from the capitalist or market-oriented form" (French and Hamilton 1979, 4). These planners attributed the form of the socialist city to (1) the organization of cities along Marxist principles and premises; (2) the operation of cities as part of a centrally planned economic system that decides capital investment priorities, investment targets, and spatial patterns; and (3) the key role of the state in land ownership, land use, industrialization, capital investments, rents, wages, and the movement of population.

The ideological tenets of the socialist city have been incorporated in the plans for cities like Beijing, Hanoi, Ho Chi Minh City, Shanghai, and Tianjin. In the early 1950s, the victorious Communists in China decided to transform cities from consumption to productive settlements. In the plans for Shanghai, the objective was to transform the "semi-feudal and semi-colonial city" to become the largest "comprehensive industrial city" in the country (Yan 1985, 103). To accomplish this, heavy industries were established in special industrial estates such as Baoshan and Minhang. The socialist emphasis on heavy industries, however, had serious implications for these cities' environmental health. In recent times, many big cities in China have suffered from environmental pollution, especially Shanghai, which with its aging industrial plants, reliance on outmoded production processes, and inefficient and nearly bankrupt state-owned enterprises has turned into the rust belt of China's industrial landscape.

To achieve the goal of rapid economic development, a master plan was drawn up for Beijing in 1956 to transform the city into "a center of production and services for the convenience of the masses" (Dong 1985, 72). The Capital Iron and Steel Company was built within the city as an integrated iron and steel complex, along with the Beijing Nonferrous Metal Industry Plant. The Yanshan Petrochemical Corporation was also established in the early 1960s with a targeted capacity to produce 7 million tons of crude oil per year. Under the Beijing Chemical Industry Corporation, forty enterprises with 620,000 workers producing sixteen categories and 600 types of products were organized. An automobile industry was also set up designed to build 15 percent of all cars produced in the country each year (Sit 1985).

The execution of the master plan transformed Beijing into an economic powerhouse. However, it quickly became apparent that economic development entailed environmental costs. By 1979, Beijing was burning 17 million tons of coal a year, heavily polluting its air. Some 2 million tons of untreated sewage was being dumped into the city's rivers and streams each day, of which about 60 percent came from industrial plants. Because about 11 percent of the inner city was devoted to industrial plants, environmental degradation was particularly severe in the city center. In the early 1980s, about 60 percent of 860 enterprises located in the inner city were classified as serious sources of air, water, noise, and soil pollution.

Worst of all, heavy industrial use had sharply reduced the amount of water available to citizens. In 1980, it was estimated that the average demand for water in Beijing was 5 billion cubic meters per year. However, the municipal water system was only capable of producing 4.5 billion. Experts estimated that if the average water consumption of every Beijing resident was increased from 0.1 to 0.6 cubic meters, an additional 1.4 billion cubic meters of potable water had to be found (Dong 1985, 76).

In more recent times, a number of Asian cities have recognized the environmental costs of industrialization and have decided to emphasize the "software" rather than the "hardware" aspects of development. These "postindustrial cities" have elected to encourage investments in information technology, electronics, financial infrastructure, and trade and commerce (Lin 2002). Hong Kong, for example, has shifted the bulk of its manufacturing enterprises to the Pearl River Delta and shifted its economic structure to finance, information services, management, and other knowledge-based industries. It has invested heavily in the construction of "smart" buildings, requiring that all new structures be wired with fiber optics rather than traditional copper or aluminum wires. Not to be outdone, Shanghai has also aspired to become the financial and cultural center not only of the Yangtze River Delta but also of all East Asia. Bangkok opted for a strategy focused on tourism, as has Osaka, with the construction of its gigantic Kansai International Airport. Most of the plans for Asian cities at present have some sections seeking to make them the New Silicon Valley of the region, aspiring to become what authors have called "the new age boomtown" (Ruble, Tulchin, and Garland 1996, 8).

The growing popularity of more ecologically balanced development plans for mega-urban development is signaling the advent of a postindustrial age. In Asian mega-urban regions, rapid big city growth arising from industrialization has given way to a greater awareness of environmental and social factors that are needed for a better quality of life in urban areas. As Lin has argued in a recent article, the "growth machine" model of urban development energetically pursued in China under Chairman Mao's leadership has lost favor. In its place, the Chinese government has pursued other goals related to a better balance between the development of rural and urban areas, between small towns and very large cities, and between interior and coastal cities. The policies have also shifted from an interventionist to a more enabling style. Rather than blindly pursuing economic development, recent policies now attempt to pursue socially sustainable and ecologically sustainable outcomes. These policies are being applied not to the monocentric development of mega-cities but to more balanced mega-urban regions (Lin 2002, 313).

To sum up, city planning has been practiced in Asia for centuries, but the emergence of very large cities and mega-urban regions has made traditional planning approaches grossly inadequate. The scope of planning has shifted from the physical form and structure of the city to include its socioeconomic and environmental aspects. The scope of planning has also been expanded to include efforts to control the profligate exploitation of natural resources, to limit the negative impact of development on the environment, and to pay more attention to more equitably allocating benefits to such segments of the population as the young, the infirm, and the aged (Sazanami 2000, 6–7).

With the expanded scope of planning activities has also come a change in the nature of the planning profession. In Asia, most traditional planning practitioners came from architectural, surveying, design, and engineering backgrounds. They tended to see urban and regional planning as physical development that needed to be guided by good urban design. They also stressed formal control and regulation mechanisms that demanded strict conformity with plans and implementing details incorporated in zoning codes, land use control measures, building standards, and safety regulations. With the shift to comprehensive strategic planning, more and more planning practitioners are coming from economics, sociology, political science, public administration, and other social sciences. Planning schools are changing their curriculums, and urban research has become much more multidisciplinary. Formal organizations that set standard qualifications for planners have emerged in almost all Asian countries, heralding the emergence of a greater professionalization of planning practice.

The emergence of mega-cities and mega-urban regions in Asia calls for more effective comprehensive strategic planning approaches. Urban and regional planners need to be concerned with issues related to population growth, migration, economic development, social polarization, and environmental degradation. They need to be sensitive to the incorporation of indigenous cultural norms and sense of aesthetics in modern urban plans and designs. Data gathering and analytical methodologies are needed to create adequate informational bases for the formulation and execution of urban and regional plans. More open processes are required to enable various interest groups and stakeholders to get more involved and participate more actively in formulating and implementing plans. Likewise, methods and techniques for accommodating and integrating differing interests, such as mediation and conflict resolution, are needed to ensure inclusiveness and the adequate representation of interests in public decision making.

The future of city and regional planning in Asia will be greatly influenced by three main factors. First, the nation-state in Asia will probably continue to play a very important role in development, despite the suggestion of global city advocates and supporters of decentralization that urban centers and local government units will be the major developmental influences in the future. Although private business and civil society are starting to exert greater influence in urban affairs, the state still lays down the institutional framework within which they act. The state also has the financial resources and constitutional authority to dominate public decision making.

Second, governmental decision making in many Asian countries has shifted from centralized command-and-control models to more transactional modes involving bargaining, accommodation, conflict resolution, and compromise. In some countries, decision making is also influenced by rent-seeking behavior and graft and corruption. This reality sometimes makes the practice of planning in Asia seem like a sharply disjointed enterprise, where plans take the form of "idealized" situations and implementation has to deal with "pragmatic" realities. It is not surprising, therefore, that many urban and regional planners in Asia are often extremely frustrated in their jobs because they feel that their best laid plans are often ignored or violated by politicians and vested interest groups.

Third, the linkages between planning and the workings of free markets will become more and more significant in Asia. With socioeconomic forces emanating from globalization rapidly changing life in city-regions, planners need to expand their horizons to comprehensively understand economic and social realities. They need to be more aware of growing inequality as it exists among social classes and as it is manifested in urban space. They have to see big city urbanization as an independent and not a passively dependent variable. The role of the urban and regional planner in the rapidly changing cities of Asia should not be confined to regulating and controlling the physical environment as it is subjected to economic and social changes. Rather, it is to help create a vision of the good life and to propose dramatic schemes for achieving a decent quality of life.

3

The Governance of Mega-Urban Regions

The concept of governance used in this book encompasses issues of who wields authority and power, how benefits and costs are allocated to stakeholders (who gets what, when, how), and the role of citizens and civil society in public decision making. Governance is much broader than urban management, in the same way that comprehensive strategic planning is broader than physical planning. Operationally, urban governance involves a number of tasks, including:

1. The *articulation* of interests and issues in a free, open, participatory, and inclusive manner. Interest articulation comes into play in selecting leaders through election, appointment, or acclamation, and in choosing among policy options.
2. The *aggregation* of varying interests held by competing groups into specific goals, as well as the *integration* of these interests into policies, programs, and projects.
3. The *mobilization* of resources needed to support policies and programs.
4. The *coordination* and *steering* of policies and programs efficiently and effectively in the course of their implementation.
5. The *adjudication* of competing interests and demands under a system of laws, regulations, and standards.
6. The *monitoring and evaluation* of the output, effects, and impact of program implementation to ensure the responsiveness and accountability of those who govern to their constituents and the general citizenry and to use the results of monitoring and evaluation as inputs to policymaking and programming.

Governance, therefore, is much more than the business of *government,* which is concerned mainly with the functioning of formal institutions. It is much broader and includes "the critical role played by organizations in civil society where formal state structures are weak and unable to provide basic services." Thus, governance is defined as "the *relationship* between civil society and the state, between rulers and the ruled, the government and the governed" and "it is this relation of civil society to the state . . . that distinguishes the study of governance from other studies of government" (McCarney, Alfani, and Rodriguez 1995, 95–96; Laquian 2002b, 77).

Governance, also, goes beyond *urban management,* which is primarily concerned with the delivery of urban services in an effective, efficient, responsive, equitable, transparent, and accountable manner. Perhaps, in an effort to steer clear of the messy business of politics, the World Bank has defined governance as "the manner in which power is exercised in the management of the economic and social resources for development" (World Bank 1993b, 2). However, even the World Bank, in recent years, has recognized the importance of political processes like elections, referenda, and community consultation as key elements in governance. The bank has even raised the issue of graft and corruption (or, more politely, "rent seeking"), which it believes inimical to economic and social development. Figure 3.1, taken from a training manual developed by the World Bank–affiliated Urban Management Program, depicts governance as a system of linkages among governmental as well as nongovernmental sectors.

Figure 3.1 illustrates the key elements in governance. What the diagram does not clearly depict, however, are the various actions and processes that make governance viable. Essentially, these actions include the following:

- Involving the community in identifying people's needs and wants. These actions include activities of individual citizens, communities, interest groups, civic institutions, and nongovernmental organizations as they participate in the process of governance.
- Developing policies and approaches to meet community needs with the involvement of the community, civic institutions, interest groups, academia, and nongovernmental organizations.
- Making sure that all levels of the government system understand their roles and responsibilities. Included in this are actions of local government and national government.
- Ensuring that the allocation of resources among levels of government is fair and equitable, both vertically and horizontally.

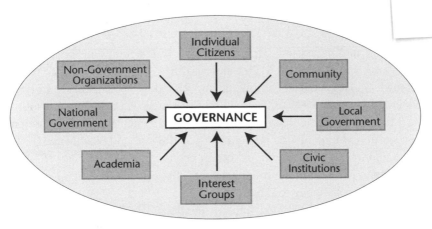

Figure 3.1. Basic Elements of Urban Governance

- Determining ethical standards of behavior for those working within government and monitoring people's performance to make sure that they do meet those standards.

From a traditional political science viewpoint, urban governance focuses on four basic elements: *people,* occupying a specific *territory,* who agree voluntarily to form a *polity* that embodies the people's social contract to subject themselves to a ruling group that represents *sovereignty* in the governance system. These elements are easy enough to understand in the case of a nation-state where all the required elements are clearly discernible. However, the situation in a mega-urban region is a lot more complicated. The size of the population in a mega-urban region (people) expands and contracts, and people constantly change identities and shift political alliances. The spatial extent of the mega-urban boundaries (territory) may change because of central government action or local government realignments. The number and types of citizens involved in political action and public decision making (polity) may also change. With all these spatial, demographic, and political changes, the locus of political authority and power (sovereignty) in mega-urban regions may often be in flux, particularly in the light of statutory and constitutional changes.

A basic issue in mega-urban region governance is the fact that the spatial and functional boundaries of the region are often not well defined. The boundaries of the region may expand or contract, depending on central, state, or provincial government decisions or local patterns of cooperation and conflict. The city-region may be divided into separate political units. In India, for example, Sivaramakrishhnan in 1995 counted 3 public corporations each in Kolkata and Mumbai (formerly Calcutta and Bombay, respectively) and two in Delhi, 29 municipalities in Kolkata, 23 nonmunicipal towns in Delhi and 91 in Kolkata, and 23 village *panchayats* in Kolkata (Sivaramakrishnan 1996, 227). In 2002, Sivaramakrishnan identified within the Mumbai urban agglomeration alone, the Greater Mumbai Municipal Corporation, the municipal corporations of Kalyan, and New Mumbai, 16 municipal towns, 7 nonmunicipal urban centers, and 995 villages (Sivaramakrishnan 2001, 13). The fragmentation of political units, therefore, provides a major challenge to urban governance.

Aside from being divided into formal local government units, many Asian city-regions (particularly those in South and Southeast Asia) are made up of a number of "polities" ranging from large municipal bodies where political parties (some of which are branches of national or regional parties) compete in regular elections to small neighborhoods where factions revolving around local leaders are important and interests are focused on mainly local issues. Many actors and stakeholders advocating specific interests are actively engaged in local politics. The various polities manifest varying states of political cohesion or disintegration. They make up competing enclaves of authority, influence, and power, such as economic sectors, ethnic groups, family-based clans, chambers of commerce, business conglomerates, professional associations, and religious and ideological factions. Within the mega-urban region are found various levels of government, ranging from central ministries and provincial or state administrative departments to local district offices. These vertical lines of authority cut across levels of horizontal jurisdictions, further complicating the interplay of authority and power within the region. The city-region, therefore, is a complex political and administrative unit that may be extremely difficult to govern. As noted by the UN Center for Human Settlements:

Today, governance [of human settlements] involves multiple stakeholders, interdependent resources and actions, shared purposes and blurred boundaries between the public and private, formal and informal, state and civil society sectors, and greater need for coordination, negotiation and building consensus. (UNCHS 2001, 57)

Considering all the various facets of governance cited above, I have decided to define governance, as applied to mega-urban regions, in a specific way. Basically, I define urban governance as the process by which legitimate authority and power are exercised within a political unit. This includes how the polity (1) sets its goals, (2) defines its territorial scope, (3) delineates its substantive functions, (4) selects its leaders, (5) provides for the full articulation and aggregation of interests, (6) specifies and adopts programs, (7) raises and allocates resources, (8) executes programs and projects, (9) adjudicates among conflicting interests based on a system of laws, (10) monitors and evaluates the effects and impact of programs and projects, and (11) feeds back the findings of monitoring and evaluation into the decision-making process (Laquian 1995, 218).

The criterion of *legitimacy* as the foundation for the performance of the eleven functions mentioned above places this discussion in the context of *democratic governance*. The choice of this particular criterion in this book (an explicit ideological bias) recognizes the fact that in analyzing the situation in the mega-urban regions included in this study, some may be regarded as more "democratic" than others. However, despite these differences, governance can be tested in accordance with certain core values. There are, for example, the basic value judgments that human beings are civic equals, that people are the main subject, not objects of government, and that resolving disagreements among people in a complex multi-interest urban environment requires agreement on mutually acceptable ends and means without resorting to violence.

In a democracy, people take a public, not just a private, perspective on the value of binding laws and institutions of governance. Democracy demands citizen participation, and the major challenge to a democratic way of life is how to handle disagreement through conciliation, bargaining, accommodation, and compromise within a system of predictable laws and regulations. Successfully meeting this challenge requires freedom of speech, of the press, association, universal adult suffrage, minority rights, and the freedom of opportunity to convince others without using coercion. It also demands a commitment to basic human values, such as the intrinsic worth of every individual and the need for mutual respect as the basis for living together and resolving disagreements.

Tasks in Mega-Urban Region Governance

Governance of mega-urban regions involves a number of tasks that need to be adjusted to the spatial and structural features of the city-region to make their execution effective and efficient. Carrying out these tasks demands different expertise and skills from those involved in the governance of single cities, metropolitan units, or mega-urban regions. These tasks—which include goal setting, defining territorial scope, allocating substantive functions, and selecting urban leaders—are explained in this section.

Goal Setting

The most important goal in mega-urban region governance is ensuring a high quality of life for people living in the settlement. To Friedmann, this goal is embodied in what he has called "good city outcomes," which include the following (Friedmann 1998, 21):

- A *productive city* where those who work are adequately rewarded for their efforts and those who seek work do not find difficulty in finding it.
- A *sustainable city* that ensures the right to a life-sustaining and life-enhancing natural environment for all citizens, including generations yet to come.
- A *livable city* that guarantees the right to decent housing, public services, and personal safety in neighborhoods of their own choice.
- A *safe city* that ensures each person's right to the physical integrity and security of his or her own body.
- An *actively tolerant city* that protects and promotes citizens' rights to group-specific differences in language, religion, national custom, sexual preference, and similar marks of collective identity so long as these do not invade the rights of others and are consistent with more general human rights.
- A *caring city* that acknowledges the right of the weakest member of the polity to adequate social protection.

There is a tendency in many Asian governance systems where urban officials are elected to look at goal setting as a function of popularly chosen individuals. In these representative systems, there is usually an expectation that an aspirant for elective office would have a vision of what the mega-urban region should be, and he or she may proclaim this during an election campaign. Victory in the election is then interpreted as a mandate for the successful candidate to adopt and execute his or her vision of development. A major problem with this type of goal setting, however, is that city development visions are usually couched in very general terms that are extremely difficult to translate into programs. Some candidates may even avoid talking about their goals ("less talk, less mistakes, no talk, no mistakes") so as not to be pinned down to fulfill their campaign promises.

In countries in transition from central planning to market-oriented systems, mega-urban regions officials are appointed by the central government and are expected to mainly execute centrally set policies and programs. In China, for example, the mayors of cities like Beijing, Shanghai, and Tianjin, which are under the direct control of the central government, primarily exercise authority delegated to them. Even in these centralized systems, however, the magnitude and complexity of issues involved in mega-urban region governance has necessitated the granting of some degree of discretionary powers to local officials. Furthermore, appointed mega-urban region officials often have networks of allies and supporters in the central government that enable them to make important decisions on their own. In the case of Shanghai, for example, much of the municipality's economic growth has been traced to the fact that two former high officials of the city (Jiang Zemin and Zhu Rongji) became top leaders in Beijing. In fact, in recent years, considerable leeway has been given to mayors of big Chinese cities to make autonomous decisions (e.g., they can approve projects costing $50 million or less without first clearing these with Beijing).

In theory, elected representatives to legislative bodies (City or Metropolitan Councils, Urban Commissions) have the duty to set the goals for a mega-urban polity. In a relatively unified city-region, this system may work very well. However, a review of the institutional arrangements for rule-making in some of the mega-urban regions covered in this book reveals serious cases of political fragmentation that makes consensus on urban goals difficult to achieve. In Metro Manila, for example, the policymaking arm of the Metro Manila Development Authority (MMDA) is composed of the fourteen city mayors and three municipal mayors of local government units within the national capital region. A cabinet-level official appointed by the president of the Philippines chairs the MMDA Council. On the basis of an analysis of the deliberations of the council, it is quite obvious that most of the local executives are often more interested in pursuing goals that will benefit their own political units rather than the whole metropolitan area.

In February 2003, for example, the MMDA chair attempted to make traffic in the region flow more smoothly by conducting an experiment involving "number coding" of vehicles (vehicles with plate numbers ending in an odd number can be used only on odd-numbered days). The mayors of

Makati City and Mandaluyong City refused to join the experiment, creating massive traffic bottlenecks. Similar conflicts of local government versus metropolitan government in the past had involved setting up sanitary landfills and open dumps (no local unit wanted garbage in its backyard), jurisdictional disputes over local police forces, sharing tax revenue, and the automatic transfer of budgetary contributions of the local units to the coffers of the MMDA.

Another example of institutional problems in goal setting is the situation in Mumbai, India's largest city. The historical center of the Mumbai region is the island city, covering only 438 square kilometers but holding a population of 10 million. Mumbai City is divided into seven wards for administrative purposes, with each ward having its own set of officials. Surrounding the core city are the western suburbs and the eastern suburbs, which are also divided into wards. In total, Greater Mumbai covers an area of 4,167 square kilometers and has a population of more than 18 million (MMRDA 2002), but most policies and programs adopted by local government units are designed to benefit only the residents of their specific units rather than the mega-urban region as a whole.

Exercising jurisdiction over metropolitan Mumbai is the Municipal Corporation of Greater Mumbai (MCGM), which was established in 1888 and has a council made up of elected representatives. It has responsibility for a range of civic services, such as water supply and sewerage, bus transport, electricity, health and medical services, solid waste collection, education, roads, traffic control, and slum improvement. However, along with the MCGM, the State of Maharashtra has created the Thana Municipal Corporation (1982) and the Kalyan Municipal Corporation (1983) to carry out specific functions in their respective territories.

Although these corporate entities are integral parts of Greater Mumbai, their autonomous nature creates a number of difficulties for coordination. The State of Maharashtra's Department of Urban Development has also set up the Mumbai Metropolitan Regional Development Authority, which technically has authority over the whole Mumbai urban agglomeration and has the responsibility for the general direction of urban development and urban transport in the Mumbai region; in practice, however, it also has limited powers (United Nations 1986, 22).

Further complicating the governance situation in Greater Mumbai is the presence of branch offices of the Government of India. These central government agencies exercise authority over specific functions, such as central planning, public works, and environmental protection and control. They monitor developments in the city-region to ensure that the decisions of metropolitan, municipal, and ward units meet certain central government standards. There are also specialized central government agencies, such as India Railways, which manage and control special functions in the city-region. As a whole, therefore, the presence of so many administrative entities and local government units in the Mumbai mega-urban region has complicated decision making and made it difficult for goal setting to be coherent and consistent.

From a review of goal-setting activities in a number of Asian mega-urban regions, it is not easy to identify factors that are significantly associated with the ability to set coherent and doable goals and policies. Still, there are certain factors associated with effective goal setting. In East Asian mega-urban regions, for example, central government direction seems closely associated with the adoption of coherent objectives. In Chinese cities, the delegation of authority to appointed big city mayors, coupled with their network of influence (*guanxi*) among top leaders in Beijing, make for the adoption and execution of effective programs and projects. The same seems to be true in Vietnam, where the mayors of Hanoi and Ho Chi Minh City are able to set and implement coherent policies for the cities' development that have the full support of central government authorities.

In other Asian mega-urban regions, the presence of a subnational higher level of government (state, province) may also be associated with the ability to set coherent and doable policies and programs. In Japan, for example, the prefectural government system around Osaka and Tokyo provides both authority and additional resources that make it possible for areawide objectives and programs to be achieved. In South Asian mega-urban regions, state governments have wielded authority and power to reorganize local governments within the regions to bring about coordinated action. The influence of these subnational authorities in South Asia is remarkably similar to the situation in Canada and the United States, where provinces and states have played a key role in reorganizing mega-urban regions and setting up areawide governance structures.

Interestingly, the role of civil society in setting coherent and doable goals and policies in mega-urban regions is not yet clear in the cases included in this study. The situation in Metro Manila, where civil society groups (supported by religious and military allies) have been credited with the overthrow of the Marcos regime in 1986 and the ousting from office of former president Joseph Estrada in 2001, presents a mixed bag. It is acknowledged that civil society groups, through their use of "people power," have brought about major changes in national politics. At the local level, however, they seem to have had rather limited success. Civil society environmental activists were active in the passage of the Clean Air Act that banned incinerators and established a system to enforce emission standards on vehicles. Their efforts to establish recycling and composting programs for solid waste, however, have had only a limited impact. They have also been unsuccessful in their advocacy of poverty alleviation measures, such as more land and housing for urban poor people, protecting street children, limiting the sex trade, preventing exploitation of sex workers, and creating more employment opportunities for poor people.

Some analysts have attributed the problems of civil society in Metro Manila to the fact that most members of civil society groups belong to the educated middle and upper classes (referred to in public opinion polls as the A, B, and C groups). At times, some of their policy concerns seem to have been focused more on issues that were of little relevance to the needs of the masses (e.g., preventing the MMDA chair from cutting down old trees lining Katipunan Avenue, and fighting to keep the mayor of Manila from turning the botanical garden into a parking lot). There have even been cases where the policies advocated by civil society groups have been perceived as being against the welfare of urban poor people, such as in supporting the MMDA chair in his campaign to rid streets and sidewalks of hawkers and vendors (so that the upper and middle classes can travel unimpeded in their air-conditioned cars?) and the banning of jeepneys and tricycles (the main transport mode of poor people) from major city streets.

Despite these civil society limitations, quite a number of Filipinos take pride in the open, confrontational, and rambunctious nature of their "democratic" system. As far as the contribution of civil society to more effective and efficient urban governance is concerned, however, the evidence is still too murky to arrive at a firm conclusion.

Defining Territorial Scope

There are a number of processes by which the territorial scope of a mega-urban region can be defined. Legislation may fix the boundaries of a city, but as the city expands, central, provincial, or state governments may redefine these official boundaries. In Shanghai, for example, the expanded boundaries of the municipality were set by a series of central government edicts. In Metro Manila, the boundary of the metropolitan structure was established by an act of Congress and later approved in a plebiscite, as required by the Philippine Constitution. In some cases, local government units have quietly acquiesced to their absorption into a metropolitan body. Many other local units, however, have resisted being absorbed into a metropolitan structure, arguing that a second-tier government structure undermined local autonomy.

For example, partly due to political pressures exerted on the framers of the 1987 Philippine Constitution by local officials whose authority was greatly diminished by the creation of a Metro Manila Commission during the Marcos regime, a specific provision in the Constitution was passed specifying that in the course of creating metropolitan political subdivisions, "the component cities and municipalities shall retain their basic autonomy and shall be entitled to their own local executives and legislative assemblies. The jurisdiction of the metropolitan authority that will hereby be created shall be limited to basic services requiring coordination" (Article X, section 13, of the 1987 Constitution of the Philippines).

Considering the vast differences in the sizes, governance structures, management processes, and political traditions of Asian mega-urban regions, it is extremely difficult to determine the best territorial scope for effective governance. One can only conclude that the issue of territorial scope is primarily based on value judgments. For example, it is intuitively desirable to set up a distinct governmental entity that is wide enough to allow adequate performance of a number of urban functions in an integrated manner and to realize economies of scale. However, it is also important that the activities within a political unit are accessible to and controllable by its residents, allowing for maximum citizen participation in public affairs as well as accountability of decision makers to the people.

What is called for, then, is delimitation of territorial scope that provides a balance between efficiency in the delivery of urban services and optimization of economic development activities on the one hand and citizen participation and political accountability to the people on the other. Achieving this balance depends very much on existing economic, social, political, and cultural conditions in a specific mega-urban region.

The search for balance between efficiency and popular participation in mega-urban region governance has often taken the form of choosing between a single unified governance structure and a multijurisdictional one. This is an issue that is familiar to analysts of metropolitan governance in North America and Europe. During the debates on the possibility of establishing a metropolitan form of government in Metro Manila, considerable attention was focused on the experience of Metropolitan Toronto. In 1967, a proposal was made to amalgamate the thirteen municipalities in the Toronto region into a single metropolitan government. The Royal Commission on Metropolitan Toronto and the Provincial Government of Ontario rejected this proposal. Instead, the Provincial Government decided to consolidate the thirteen local units into six reconstituted municipalities and six coterminous school boards. The argument used for defining this territorial scope of Metro Toronto was similar to the one used in the reorganization of the Greater London Council in 1963 that justified the council's boundaries in terms of the ability to permit "wide participation and control by electors and, at the same time, the efficient discharge of its responsibilities" (Forstall and Jones 1970, 52).

In Asian mega-urban regions that serve as national capitals, there has been a tendency to set up unified systems of governance. For example, national capitals like Bangkok, Delhi, Dhaka, Jakarta, and Seoul are governed by unified metropolitan structures. Regionally important mega-urban regions, like Karachi, Mumbai, and Shanghai, also have some type of unified systems. The existence of these unified structures does not mean, however, that all authority and power is vested in them. In fact, quite a number of central government agencies, public corporations, and private concerns providing urban services in the region exercise considerable autonomy in the exercise of their functions. The actual form of governance structure set up for mega-urban regions varies based on the economic, political, and cultural condition in each area. What is important, however, is the realization that in the choice of structures for mega-urban region governance, there is a need to find a balance between efficiency and democratic people's participation.

In reviewing variables that seem associated with desirable territorial scope, the wealth and stage of technological development in a particular mega-urban region appears to be significant. In Japan, for example, Osaka and Tokyo have wider territorial coverages that are associated with more extensive transportation networks, efficient communication facilities, good professional managers, and the more closely integrated structure of the economies in the city-regions. However, it should be noted that although some mega-urban regions in China, like Beijing and Shanghai, have administrative systems covering wide metropolitan jurisdictions, they do not have extensive and efficient transport networks, their managers are not as highly qualified, and their economic structures are not well integrated.

Finding an appropriate governance structure for mega-urban regions in Asia is complicated by the trend toward polynucleated urban agglomerations. Because of the influence of market forces or planned administrative interventions, Asian countries are increasingly seeing the emergence of several urban nodes around a central city as a preferred settlement form. Coordination of efforts in a city-centered configuration is hard enough—and it becomes more vastly complicated in the case of a polynucleated region where no one settlement dominates, as in the Hong Kong–Pearl River Delta region.

A comprehensive strategic plan proposed by the Hong Kong 2022 Foundation has clearly indicated the economic, social, trade, communication, and cultural linkages among the various governmental units in the Hong Kong–Pearl River Delta region. The plan proposed the adoption of an integrated approach to development reflected in the slogan "Competing together, not against each other." The plan, however, found it extremely difficult to suggest an overall governance mechanism to coordinate public and private activities in the region. To begin with, there was the problem of political fragmentation—both Hong Kong and Macao were autonomous special administrative regions whose territories were fixed by international treaties. The special economic zones of Shenzhen and Zhuhai had strictly demarcated boundaries that separated them from the jurisdiction of Guangdong Province as ordered by the State Council.

In addition, Chinese authorities had set up three "bonded areas" within the Hong Kong–Pearl River Delta region (in Guangzhou, Futian, and Shatoujiao) that also enjoyed autonomous status. All these special political-administrative units were designed not to have close economic relationships with their hinterlands. Encompassing them within a cohesive governance unit, therefore, was virtually impossible.

Allocating Substantive Functions

Within Asian mega-urban regions, allocation of functional responsibility is usually done in a hierarchical manner. The highest and most powerful agencies of the central government, the ministries, carry out such functions as economic planning, construction, agriculture, transport, communication, regulation of commerce, manufacturing, and industry. Government-owned or -controlled corporations, often with authority over whole regions, deliver water and sewerage, drainage and flood control, and solid waste disposal. Private concerns may provide electricity, telephone, cable, gas, and other services, subject to oversight by central regulatory agencies. Central agencies also set national policies and standards, allocate funds, provide technical assistance, and monitor and evaluate local government and private activities to make sure that standards of performance are met.

In a number of mega-urban regions, regional or metropolitan structures have been established to look after specific functions. The Metropolitan Waterworks and Sewerage System in Metro Manila, for example, is charged with overseeing water and sewerage in the city-region, despite the fact that actual production and distribution of potable water has been privatized to Manila Water and Maynilad Water Company. Setting up these areawide agencies has been justified in terms of the need to coordinate local efforts and take advantage of economies of scale. It has been argued that functions such as bulk purchasing and general service and maintenance contracts can be arranged as integral parts of large contracts. When a metrowide department consolidates its purchases, it may be able to get lower prices and better terms than individual local government units.

In the survey of public functions provided within mega-urban regions conducted for this book, four modalities were used. These are (1) provided mainly by the central government, (2) provided by regional or metropolitan structures, (3) shared between regional and local structures, and (4) provided by local government structures. A general breakdown of the allocation of functions in twelve mega-urban regions is given in table 3.1.

It can be seen from the table that central government agencies play a dominant role in the process of setting overall policies for the governance of mega-urban regions. After having set those policies (and setting standards), many of the activities carried out by central agencies have mainly involved monitoring and evaluation to make sure that the policies and standards are followed. Central agencies also play an important role in financing local programs and projects through such mechanisms as the direct allocation of budgetary funds for large infrastructure projects, grants-in-aid, and allowing local units to borrow locally or internationally. In the Philippines, local governments are entitled to a share of national internal revenue taxes collected within their jurisdictions, but in the past, the release of their shares was subject to central government discretion. The Local Government Code of 1991 stipulated that the share of local units in internal revenue taxes should be released automatically upon approval of the budget and certification by the national treasurer that funds were available. This has made it possible for local units in metropolitan areas to budget their funds more rationally as the flow of funds has become more predictable.

Table 3.1. *Allocation of Responsibilities for Urban Functions*

Function	Central Government	Regional-Metro Government	Shared Regional-Local Government	Purely Local Government
Electricity	P	P&M	M	
Water and sewerage	P&F	P&M	M	M
Transport and traffic		P&M	M	
Housing and services	P&F	P&M	M	M
Garbage collection				M
Garbage disposal	P	P&M	M	
Education	P&F	M&F	M	M
Health	P&F	M	M	M
Police and security		P&M	M	M
Fire protection		P&M	M	
Environmental protection		P&M	M	M

Legend: P: policy-setting function, including setting standards. P&F: policy setting and financing. P&M: planning and management. M: management.

In many Asian mega-urban regions, metropolitan authorities have been given such functions as water and sewerage (including drainage and flood control), traffic management, solid waste disposal, public parks and open space, and urban and regional planning. Private entities have also been made responsible for such functions as water and sewerage, transport systems, solid waste collection, electric generation and distribution, telephone, and gas. Public–private partnerships, usually involving very large multinational corporations and local entrepreneurs, have taken over the management of water and sewerage systems in Jakarta and Metro Manila and rapid transit systems in Bangkok, Hong Kong, and Metro Manila.

The key issue in governing mega-urban regions is how to achieve efficiency in delivering urban services and at the same time give all interest groups the chance to participate in decision making. It has been argued by supporters of unified metropolitan governance that allocating urban functions that are, "of their very nature," areawide adds to efficiency because it facilitates coordination. They propose that areawide services should be vested in metropolitan or regional authorities to achieve economies of scale and management efficiency.

Conversely, opponents of unified metropolitan governance express the fear that a larger metropolitan structure erodes citizen participation because it tends to become bureaucratized and remote as it deals with issues at a distance from the grassroots. They also claim that setting up another governmental structure between local units and the provincial or central government can cause delays. In practice, quite a number of Asian mega-urban regions have tried to strike a balance in assigning services at the metropolitan or local levels. Some functions—such as the cleaning and maintenance of local roads, operation of nurseries and kindergartens, maintenance of local parks, and garbage collection—have been left to local units.

It is obvious from a review of practices in the mega-urban regions in Asia that there is no "one best way" for allocating functions. In Metro Manila, police services have been assigned, at one time or another, to local, metropolitan, and central government agencies. Local mayors and council members have argued that the police function should be managed at the city or municipal level because local police forces know the local situation much better and they enjoy better cooperation with local citizens. The central government has argued, conversely, that police services should be regionalized or even nationalized to achieve high quality and standards of performance, limit petty corruption, and prevent local political leaders from using the police as their private armies. An effort has been made in Metro Manila to set up a metropolitan police force, but this has failed to satisfy local officials. As of January 2004, local mayors were still clamoring for authority to have their own police forces.

An interesting consideration in allocating urban functions to different levels of government is the possibility of sharing responsibility for specific activities within each function. For example, in the case of solid waste management, responsibility for garbage collection in Jakarta is vested in local groups at the street or community level. Private contractors under contracts with the city or municipal governments take the solid waste to sorting areas, where private recycling groups recover useful items. The remaining garbage is then taken to open dumps or sanitary landfills managed by metropolitan authorities. Theoretically, city, municipal, or metropolitan-level activities related to solid waste management have to conform to environmental policies and standards set by the central government. But in many South and Southeast Asian cities, such policies and standards tend to be ignored.

Despite a strong policy commitment toward decentralization, many governments in Asia still refrain from delegating full responsibility over functions to purely local bodies. Some municipalities and cities have their own police departments. The building and maintenance of local roads, maintenance of local parks, enforcement of zoning codes, subdivision regulations and building standards, and the operation of local fire fighting vested in local units.

In many Asian mega-urban regions, however, there is a tendency to distrust local units. Metropolitan and local governments argue that fragmentation of responsibility in the management of urban functions makes coordination difficult. They point out that local units usually do not have the financial and organizationally capabilities to do their tasks well. In some cases, there is a strong suspicion that local political leaders use their authority and power to engage in local graft and corruption.

The allocation of urban functions to various levels of government, of course, is heavily influenced by the size of the mega-urban region, its financial and organizational resources, ideological factors, and traditional ways of doing things. There have been attempts to put forward general principles that can be used to guide the allocation of functions, but it has been generally accepted that these essentially involve culturally based value judgments. In a democratic system, for example, it has been suggested that the allocation of urban functions should be based on the following criteria:

1. The governmental jurisdiction responsible for providing any service should be large enough to enable the benefits from that service to be consumed primarily within the jurisdiction.
2. The unit of government should be large enough to permit realization of the economies of scale.
3. The unit of government carrying on a function should encompass a geographical area adequate for effective performance.
4. The unit of government performing a function should have the legal and administrative ability to perform the services assigned to it.
5. Every unit of government should be responsible for a sufficient number of functions so that it provides a forum for the resolution of conflicting interests, with significant responsibility for balancing government needs and resources.
6. The performance of functions by a unit of government should remain controllable and accessible to its residents.
7. Functions should be assigned to that level of government that maximizes the conditions and opportunities for active citizen participation and still permits adequate performance.

The United States Advisory Commission on Intergovernmental Relations set the seven criteria mentioned above in 1963 (Forstall and Jones

1970, 52). They represented a set of value judgments made by a group of officials attempting to arrive at balanced decisions when faced with inconsistent and contradictory tendencies in the allocation of functions among local units. The judgments were based on the political realities of American federalism in the early 1960s, but it is interesting that they still have some relevance to the governance of mega-urban regions in Asia in 2004. A similar effort in Asia at present will have to deal with the contradictions and inconsistencies noted above, but it may be useful in guiding allocation of urban functions to various governance structures in mega-urban regions.

Selecting Urban Leaders

Leadership in Asian mega-urban region governance may take the following forms: (1) officials appointed by central governments, (2) officials elected indirectly by local councils or boards, and (3) officials elected directly by the people. Centrally appointed officials may include governors, mayors, commissioners, and other executives, heads of special authorities in charge of specific services, or professional managers. Ministers who head central government agencies with important activities in the mega-urban region play important leadership roles. Heads of special urban authorities are particularly powerful, such as those in charge of port authorities or other areawide services. Increasingly, as a number of major urban services are privatized, the chief executive officers of enterprises are becoming important local leaders. For that matter, the heads of major private corporations, including transnationals, exercise considerable leadership in urban affairs with their control over employment, taxes, construction, and investments.

The importance of mega-urban regions in national life makes urban leaders natural candidates for national positions. The mayors or governors of mega-cities like Bangkok, Jakarta, Karachi, Manila, and Seoul have traditionally been considered natural contenders for president or premier. The top leaders of Beijing, Shanghai, and Tianjin, in fact, are central government officials. A former president of the Philippines (Joseph Estrada) and premier of China (Jiang Zemin) were former mayors (of San Juan and Shanghai, respectively). At the same time, however, some individuals consider leadership in a mega-city as more important than national office. As the late Manila mayor Arsenio Lacson once said (paraphrasing Mayor Fiorello la Guardia of New York), "Who wants to be president of the Philippines when one can be mayor of Manila?"

The political dynamics in mega-urban regions is complicated by the observation that in countries where top leaders are elected, the influence of mega-urban region political leaders in national affairs tends to be reduced by the perceived "oppositionist" stance of big urban area electorates. This oppositionist nature is attributed to the fact that people in urban areas tend to be better informed than those in rural areas because they have higher levels of education, better access to the mass media, and a stronger interest in public affairs (governmental actions tend to affect their lives more directly), and because there are more civil society groups that articulate their views and mobilize resources to pursue specific causes. In many Asian mega-urban regions, residents tend to complain that rural area voters dominate national politics and that people living in inner-city areas, compared with suburban dwellers, tend to be proportionately underrepresented in metropolitan legislatures.

In general, increased decentralization of authority to local governments in many Asian countries has given the voting public the right to elect their own leaders. There are exceptions, of course, as in China and Vietnam, where the central government appoints key local officials. However, even in China, officials at the lowest local government levels began to be elected in 2003, with people allowed to put up candidates other than those chosen by the local Communist Party branches. Elsewhere in Asia, the top–down influence of national leaders and political parties has been diminishing as local parties and civil society groups, concentrating mainly on local issues, are starting to flex their muscles and manage to elect leaders of their own persuasion.

Where elections are conducted in Asian mega-urban regions, there is an obvious need for electoral reforms to ensure that the "best" candidates are chosen by the people. Unfortunately, the conduct of local elections in a number of Asian cities does not seem to guarantee that the best leaders win. In Philippine cities, for example, there is a common belief that elections are mainly won with the use of "gold, guns, and goons." With limits on how much candidates can spend on elections set by law but ignored in practice, only candidates with the most money tend to win. Thus, candidates who have no money of their own rely on supporters who are really "investors." Once their candidates win, the supporters collect on their "investments" by getting special favors through corrupt deals. The concentration of political and economic power in the hands of dynastic families has also made local politics very undemocratic.

In the Asian mega-urban regions included in this study, success in governance seems to be significantly correlated with a number of leadership factors such as (1) strong linkages to the central government; (2) metropolitan or regional scope of leadership; (3) commitment of urban citizens to wider issues; and (4) more generalized public support, often from civil society groups. In general, mega-urban-region leaders with strong linkages to central governments tend to be more successful in pursuing economic development programs and delivering urban services. This is because central government resources are very important in supporting "big ticket" projects, such as water and sewerage systems, transport networks, ports and harbors, and energy generation and distribution systems. In mega-urban regions that serve as national capitals, the residence of central government officials in the area inevitably results in their direct involvement in local affairs, and their support for local officials is a big factor in making these officials more effective.

The ability of local leaders in mega-urban regions to get their act together and pursue common objectives at a metropolitan or regional level also tends to make them more effective. Areawide cooperation and coordination are particularly useful in the field of taxation and levying of local charges. Investors can manipulate fragmented local government units to get particularistic deals through a system of "divide and conquer." By cooperating, local leaders can even out differences in appraised values of properties, tax rates, and the tax burden to residents. By binding together to form metropolitan structures, they can increase their credit ratings and borrow larger amounts to support big projects. Most important of all, urban leaders who cooperate tend to have stronger bargaining powers when dealing with central governments.

Local autonomy advocates committed to grassroots democracy in Asia have been reluctant to support metropolitan or regional structures because they are afraid that the bureaucratization of these units tends to deflect citizen attention from local issues. Local leaders are concerned that the distancing of popular discourse from local issues will decrease citizen participation and create apathy. Recent developments in North American cities, however, seem to contradict this apprehension. In January 1998, for example, the Regional Municipality of Metropolitan Toronto was joined with six other surrounding constituencies to create the New City of Toronto. The amalgamation reduced the number of elected officials in Metro Toronto from 106 to 58. A mayor, deputy mayor, and 56 councilors were elected. A 30 percent cut in the number of senior administrative positions was carried out, with 1,400 positions simply eliminated. The New City bureaucratic structure was reorganized into four "clusters," and the number of collective agreements with government personnel was reduced from 55 to only 7 contracts.

Although the situation in Metro Toronto might be very different from that in many Asian mega-urban regions, the results of Toronto's reorganization efforts may provide some insights that may be of some interest to Asian officials. The Toronto New City was justified by arguing that it would reduce the squabbling among local leaders and enhance their commitment to common goals. The new structure would standardize tax rates, result in the adoption of common assessment and collection procedures, lower tax rates, and reduce inequalities among tax payers. The metropolitan structure would lower costs because of the reduction in the number of offices and officials.

An evaluation of effects and impact of the New City of Toronto reorganization conducted three years after its creation indicated that the new structure has achieved all these positive results. Interestingly, the feared reduction in popular participation because of amalgamation did not materialize. In fact, in the elections of 1998, the voting turnout increased to 48.6 percent, compared with 35.2 percent in 1996. It was suggested by analysts that the election of a mayor for the whole metropolitan area aroused greater interest among voters. It was also argued that the policy issues raised by metropolitan governance—such as achieving higher efficiency in running areawide services, lowering the tax burden, acquiring a higher credit rating and bringing about a more equitable distribution of the tax burden—aroused greater citizen interest and actually generated higher levels of popular participation.

Emphasis on the role of people's organizations (POs) and nongovernmental organizations (NGOs) in urban governance is starting to bring about institutional innovations in a number of Asian countries. In the Philippines, for example, the Local Government Code of 1991 provided that a specified proportion of metropolitan and city councils should be filled with leaders from the civil society sector. Local leaders were also appointed to commissions and boards that ran public services to represent the popular sector. In India, Indonesia, and Thailand, civil society groups are also becoming very active in public issues such as poverty alleviation, environmental protection, women's rights, and civil liberties.

In countries in transition such as China and Vietnam, however, there is very little evidence to date that civil society groups are becoming more active in urban governance. In fact, it is extremely difficult to regard so-called NGOs in these countries as civil society groups, because most of their members are extensions of the Communist Party or auxiliary groups such as Women's Federations or Youth Leagues. In Vietnam, war veterans, women's groups, and patriotic youth associations pursue policies and programs set by the central government and receive financial and other forms of support from it. In China, it is still too early to tell if the local elections that began in 2003 will help bring into leadership positions individuals who are not formally affiliated with the Communist Party or its auxiliary arms. It need to be noted that such elections have been conducted at the neighborhood or village levels, where developmental resources are extremely limited. Leaders in towns, cities, and metropolitan governments are yet to be elected, and there are no indications when legislation will be adopted to make electing these officials a reality.

Articulating and Aggregating Public Interests

Democratic theory considers articulation of public interests as the key to good governance, and leaders are expected to be responsive to citizen demands. In the Asian mega-urban regions covered in this study, interest articulation and aggregation are carried out through (1) the activities of interest groups and various stakeholders, (2) the mass media, (c) political parties and factions, and (d) the policy pronouncements of political leaders. It is expected that the various stakeholders would articulate their interests, advocate specific policies and programs, and mobilize their followers in support of common causes.

In 1996, Kokpol suggested that Thailand, a parliamentary democracy that is highly centralized, is slowly becoming more "democratic." He attributed this to (1) the democratic atmosphere, indicated by the 1992 elections that saw the active participation of NGOs, activists, and ordinary citizens in public affairs; (2) the agitation of civil society for more influence and power in decision making; and (3) the recognition that centralized administration and weak local units serve as the main constraints to development (Kokpol 1996, 135). In the Philippines, the "people power" revolution that toppled the Marcos dictatorship in 1986 is said to have triggered the proliferation of people's organizations, NGOs, and cause-oriented groups. The fall of the authoritarian rule of former president Suharto in Indonesia in 1998 has been taken as an indicator of more responsive democratic governance. The impeachment of former president Estrada of the Philippines and his incarceration in 2001 is also widely attributed to the agitation of civil society groups (supported by the military and some traditional politicians).

The adoption of the policy of *doi moi* in Vietnam in 1986 is said to be ushering in more democratization and popular participation in local governance. The transition to a more market-oriented system in Vietnam, however, is being ushered in gradually by the central government. In Ho Chi Minh City, for example, all social organizations are placed under the leadership of the Fatherland Front. Organizations made up of youth, women, veterans, laborers, and the like work in parallel with government agencies and are under the "guidance" of these agencies as well as the Communist Party.

In some poor communities in Ho Chi Minh City, a number of grassroots organizations have been formed to cooperatively get access to clean water, electricity, and other basic services. These groups, however, operate within the traditional sphere of party procedures. They have used acceptable organizations—such as the Women's Union, Youth Union, Veterans Union, and Council of Elderly Citizens—to press for their needs. In the rare instances when outside groups, such as international NGOs, have been allowed to work with local NGOs, the reaction of the government has been predictably negative. Local leaders working with these outside groups have been branded as "troublemakers," and people have been discouraged from working with them.

Similar negative reactions have also been met in China in connection with the activities of NGOs. As in Vietnam, so-called people's organizations in China are basically extensions of the Communist Party and various popular front organizations. The All China Women's Federation is one of the key mobilizing forces in China's population and family planning program, the Young Pioneers and Youth Brigades carry out the party's policies, and privileged groups such as veterans and old revolutionaries are active at the community level to uphold party policies. People's organizations are most effective at the neighborhood or street level, where committees look after activities such as street cleaning; controlling petty crimes; operating day care centers, nurseries, and kindergartens; and enforcing family planning quotas.

Interestingly, some people at the community level do not see their organizations as simply following dictates from above. They argue that observing one's obligation to people's communal welfare is often as important as insisting on one's rights and entitlements. To many of them, the needs of China's huge population cannot be met if each person becomes "too selfish" and pursues only his or her demands. The pragmatic need for cooperation at the local level, therefore, has become a strong legitimizing force in urban governance.

The Philippines has the most active and certainly the most vocal civil society groups in Asia at present. In 1997, it was estimated that there were more than 58,000 sectoral organizations registered with the Securities and Exchange Commission, and thousands more were probably operating without formally incorporating themselves. These civil society groups have been involved in practically all aspects of governance at the national, provincial, regional, municipal, and local levels. The participation of sectoral groups in governance was incorporated in the revised 1987 Constitution of the Philippines, which provided for the membership of such groups in the organs of government. In the Local Government Code of 1991, it was provided that at least 25 percent of members in local development councils at the *barangay,* municipal, city, and provincial levels should represent POs and NGOs.

In addition to this legislated mandate, other mechanisms for direct people's participation were prescribed. For example, major changes in a local government unit (e.g., the conversion of a town into a city or the inclusion of a local government unit into a metropolitan area) have to be approved by a plebiscite. If a local council is not acting on a measure deemed important by NGOs and POs, it can be forced to consider this through an *initiative,* usually carried out through a signature campaign. Finally, local people, by using the power of *recall,* can replace an elected official found to be corrupt, incompetent, or incapable of managing public affairs. (Tapales 1996, 217).

In a number of Asian mega-urban regions, NGOs and POs have become important elements in governance by articulating specific interests. The advantages of such grassroots organizations have been summarized as follows (Morato 1991):

- NGOs deliver services effectively and efficiently because of their small size, manageability, and freedom from bureaucratic rigidity.
- NGOs understand local realities better and mobilize local resources more effectively than government agencies.
- NGOs can complement governmental programs and supplement public resources with voluntary efforts and organizational capabilities.
- NGOs are often managed by individuals who sacrifice pay and family to serve others, thereby eliminating the need to maintain an expensive organizational overhead.
- In cases where government agencies are corrupt, inefficient, or ineffective, the work of NGOs provides a contrast or even a model of how things should be done, thereby putting the pressures on government to improve performance.

Even as the merits of NGOs and POs as an aid to governance are widely recognized, four shortcomings have also been cited. First, many NGOs operate with scanty resources and have limited institutional capabilities. This makes them overly dependent on outside help—the government, private enterprises, or bilateral and multilateral donors—which may undermine their capacity for independent action. Second, some NGOs have alienated government authorities because of their ideological stand or confrontational style, thereby limiting chances for cooperation with government.

Third, NGOs are good for starting small projects, but they often fail to follow through. When their activities expand, they evolve from small voluntary activities to full-time management of sizable programs, requiring fully paid managers and bureaucratic procedures, thereby losing flexibility, adaptability, and responsiveness. After raising people's expectations, many NGOs may run out of steam and create frustrations and cynicism. Fourth, some NGOs have been co-opted by government, private business, or international donor agencies. There have even been cases where charges have been leveled against NGOs for engaging in corruption, as in a 2002 case in Metro Manila in which the leading NGO group in the country was alleged to have conspired with government authorities in a bond issue that netted it millions of pesos in transaction fees.

Formulating and Adopting Policies

It is customary in traditional political science to attribute the process of policy formulation and adoption to formally constituted government bodies, such as central government executives, city or regional councils, governors, and mayors. In the complex world of mega-urban regions, however, it is often extremely difficult to pinpoint the responsibility for policymaking. A local government committed to responding to "market forces" that gives concessions to a transnational corporation and provides free or cheap land, tax cuts, cheap energy, and a docile nonunionized labor force may not actually be exercising authority and power autonomously.

Similarly, an "autonomous" local government completely dependent on grants-in-aid from the central government may be vested with policymaking authority in a decentralization law, but it does not really set policies if senior government officials just tell it what to do. The real test of policymaking then, is the capacity of the local unit to make final decisions.

In mega-urban regions where many economic and social interest groups pursuing different (and often conflicting) objectives actively participate in the formulation and adoption of policies and programs, it becomes difficult to achieve compatibility and coherence. Processes of conflict resolution, bargaining, accommodation, and compromise takes time. Often, mega-urban regions in which policies are formulated, adopted, and funded at higher governmental levels are carried out more effectively and efficiently. In China, for example, policies adopted immediately after the pronouncement of former premier Deng Xiaoping that it was all right to be rich and that some people could become rich earlier than others quickly reshaped governance patterns in mega-urban regions. In Japan and South Korea, industrialization policies backed up with central government funding also exerted deep influence on planning and governance in mega-urban regions.

In South and Southeast Asian mega-urban regions, a major issue in urban governance is the fact that in many of these, a significant proportion of basic urban services, such as affordable housing, sanitation, and garbage collection, are actually provided by poor people. The United Nations and other international development agencies have proposed "enabling strategies" designed to encourage these people-based efforts, in recognition of the fact that governments are usually too poor themselves to provide these services. The real financial and institutional costs of adopting and implementing these enabling strategies, however, are usually underestimated. Poor people, even in their traditional communities, need to be organized. Local leaders have to be trained in processes of problem identification, strategic planning, resource mobilization, organization and management, conflict resolution, and other skills—and all of these cost money.

Effective mechanisms for formulating and adopting policies and programs in Asian mega-urban regions have generally been associated with top-level bodies that have adequate authority, resources, and power to actually implement decisions. Often, these have taken the form of regional or metropolitan structures led by strong executives supported by officials representing areawide rather than fragmented autonomous local units. These decision-making structures employ methodical approaches for assessing and evaluating the costs and benefits of various options, often relying on research groups to provide them with accurate information. Legislation clearly vesting authority and power to formulate and adopt policies and specifying areas where these decision-making structures can operate legitimately greatly enhances their efficacy. Popular support, as manifested in the activities of civil society groups, is an important but not a sufficient condition for effective governance. Often, the ability to use accommodation, bargaining, and compromise, backed up by strong support from central governments in the form of legitimate authority and ample resources, is the key to effective policy setting and program adoption.

Mobilizing Resources

Despite the concentration of economic activities and wealth in mega-urban regions, those in Asia show a marked dependence on the central government for financial resources. A review of municipal and regional or metropolitan agency budgets reveals that in most instances, a significant proportion of resources comes from shares of national taxes, grants-in-aid, and international assistance. If one makes a distinction between capital investments and current operating expenditures, studies show that mega-urban regions tend to depend more on external sources (central governments, foreign direct investment, the private sector) for the former and on internal resources for the latter. Because, proportionally, current operating expenditures are much smaller than capital investments, the dependence of local units on external resources is highlighted by this observation.

The main goals of mega-urban regions in mobilizing resources are *efficiency* and *equity.* Taxes and other governmental revenues need to be collected with minimal inputs, relying on simple and easily understood procedures. Efficiency in resource mobilization can be enhanced by accurate assessments, up-to-date lists of taxpayers (assisted by computerization of tax rolls), adequate personnel training, and disseminating accurate information about tax procedures to avoid bureaucratic arbitrariness and corruption. In Shanghai, for example, income from real estate taxes were significantly increased by the application of geographic information systems and satellite data for defining plots and using the plot identities as the basis for property assessment and taxation. In other cities, computerization of real estate property rolls has made it possible to identify those that have benefited from public improvements (roads, sewers, trunk lines) and "recovering" some of the benefits by increased assessments and higher tax rates on these properties.

Faced by the need to raise resources, many Asian urban governments are tending to rely more on service fees and service charges to pay for infrastructure. In this regard, the need to price public services properly is proving to be most important. The "pay as you go" principle is particularly applicable to services that are more intensively used by some people and not by others—such as roads, bridges, and tunnels—that can be funded by tolls or services that can be billed according to the amount used, like water, electricity, and solid waste disposal. In most Asian mega-urban regions, services and amenities tend to be priced considerably below the cost needed to deliver them to the people. A proper price for urban services might not only improve the financial situation of local units; it might also have positive environmental effects, in that higher fees would probably discourage waste, which in turn would reduce environmental pollution.

The large numbers of poor people in Asian mega-urban regions make it imperative that self-help and mutual aid schemes are included in resource mobilization programs. In low-cost infrastructure and housing projects, "sweat equity" has been used as a means of resource mobilization. By requiring project beneficiaries to donate their labor, skills, and organizational abilities in community-based projects, real costs can be reduced. An important side effect of such voluntary schemes is the feeling of commitment and ownership that it generates. Where urban services and infrastructures are built with the active participation of beneficiaries, it has been found that they tend to value these and to keep them well ordered and maintained. In the long run, this sense of ownership translates into lower costs and more efficient management.

In Asia and other urban areas around the world, there is increasing concern about the state of urban infrastructure, including roads and highways, sewage and water treatment plants, solid waste disposal facilities, electricity, and telecommunication facilities. All these items require sizable investments beyond the capacity of individual local government units to finance. In a number of cities, it has been suggested that the private sector may be the right entity for financing, constructing, operating, and maintaining these services. The main argument used is that the private sector has the resources, technical capacity, and professional managers and technicians to properly manage public services. Public enterprises have proven to be incapable of delivering urban services efficiently, and dissatisfied clients see privatization as a way of dealing with service problems.

One of the most dramatic changes in resource mobilization in Asia has been the rapid emergence of private enterprise in China. With the launching of economic reforms after 1979, new Chinese policies—such as the production responsibility system, the State Council 1981 regulations on *geti* or individual business ventures, and the 1988 revision of the Constitution—legitimized the existence of private enterprise. A further constitutional change in 1999 changed the legal status of the private sector from merely a "supplementary" part of the state economy to "an important component" of the socialist market economy. In his speech celebrating the eightieth anniversary of the Communist Party in 2001, President Jiang Zemin praised private entrepreneurs as "outstanding elements" of society, and he later named them as one of the pillars of Chinese society (Sun and Wong 2002, 68–69).

Booming private enterprises have played an important role in financing major infrastructure and development projects in Chinese cities. During the 1980s, China decentralized responsibilities for urban services to local governments. While "downloading" these responsibilities to local units, the central government adopted tax measures in 1994 that increased the share of the center in tax proceeds. These actions put tremendous financial pressures on local units and forced them to depend on private enterprises for investments in urban projects such as housing, energy production and distribution, roads, and transport networks.

The privatization of urban infrastructure has also been widely accepted in other Asian countries. Some services, such as electricity, telephone, gas, and transportation, seem to have no problem being privatized—these are mostly in private hands in Bangkok, Jakarta, and Metro Manila. In Jakarta and Metro Manila, the water and sewerage systems have been privatized. With the construction of toll roads, transportation has also been privatized in sections of Bangkok, Jakarta, and Metro Manila. Public conveyances in these cities, such as buses, jeepneys, and taxis, have traditionally been provided by the private sector, usually by small-scale entrepreneurs.

An approach that has been used in some Asian mega-urban regions is the public-private partnership (PPP), whereby specific functions in infrastructure provision are shared by the government and private enterprises. This partnership may range all the way from project planning and initiation to construction, operation, ownership, financing, management, and maintenance. A number of options have been used to take advantage of private funds and management efficiencies, including build-operate-transfer (BOT) schemes, lease-purchase, and "turnkey" approaches.

In the BOT approach, a private contractor finances, designs, builds, and operates an infrastructure, usually on publicly owned land leased on a long-term basis. Upon completion of the project, it is turned over to the government for an agreed-upon price. In the case of infrastructures where users are willing to pay an economic price for the service, some private firms may be willing to enter into a build-operate-own-manage approach. In some cities, for example, solid waste or toxic waste disposal services can be established through this modality. The government may, in some instances, sweeten the deal for private enterprise by offering certain incentives, such as free land, tax incentives, subsidies, and other benefits. If the risks involved in such enterprises are acceptable to investors, they may be encouraged to invest.

Although PPP approaches have been used to finance projects in some Asian mega-urban regions, a number of problems have been encountered in their application. Where foreign partners are used—as they usually are in very large projects requiring big investments—the fact that loans have to be repaid in hard currencies may become problematical in developing countries with unstable currencies. An event such as the 1997 Asian economic crisis may suddenly increase the foreign exchange costs of such projects. Foreign partners may also be forced to withdraw because of unexpected circumstances (e.g., large PPP projects in Vietnam that were to be jointly carried out with Indonesian investors had to be canceled or severely cut back when the Suharto government failed because the investors were linked to the former president's family). PPP projects for the building of major expressways in Metro Manila were also scaled down for the same reason.

Program or Project Implementation

Central, provincial, or city governments can usually implement projects and programs effectively if the responsibility for implementation is clearly indicated and lines of authority are well defined. The situation, however, is more complicated in the case of programs and projects at the mega-urban region level that require cooperative and coordinated action of several levels of government and a functionally differentiated set of agencies. Despite careful efforts of system planners to define and clarify specific responsibilities, duties, and lines of authority, many mega-urban often get bogged down in coordination failures.

Experience in Asia has shown that while it is tempting to focus attention on the formulation and implementation of single large projects (e.g., rapid transit, metropolitan water and sewerage, ports and harbors), such a project-oriented approach does not work too well. In most instances, city-region development is too complex, and focusing on a single project, no matter how large, is not enough. City-region governance involves the interests of many sectors, politically active groups, and stakeholders. These interests have to be taken into consideration if regionwide efforts are to be successful. An overly technocratic approach that sees governance mainly in terms of urban management will most likely fail, because it is often isolated from the larger picture of elections and the political processes involved in policymaking and program implementation.

The budgeting process is a crucial element in program or project implementation. Asian countries, however, have been rather slow in adopting innovative techniques, such as the "participatory budgeting" process that has become quite popular in Latin America, especially in Brazil. Early budgeting approaches—such as performance budgeting, which has been used in Philippine city and municipal governments for more than three decades—have greatly improved program implementation. Unlike line-item budgeting, which puts monetary figures opposite specific expenditure items (salaries and wages, building materials, transportation, etc.), performance budgeting breaks planned objectives into targets, and specific programs are formulated to hit each target. The inputs of money, materials, and methods are then calculated and incorporated into the budget. In this way, performance budgeting allows managers to measure whether they are achieving their targets or not, which particular inputs are helping or not to achieve good performance, and how long the process is taking. Aside from being an excellent management tool, therefore, performance budgeting also facilitates monitoring and evaluation.

The lack of adequately trained managers and administrators in many Asian mega-urban regions is a serious barrier to effective program implementation. In general, city-regions like Osaka, Seoul, and Tokyo that have professional managers and efficient and adequately paid administrators perform much better in governance. The use of advanced management techniques incorporated in generally accepted processes and procedures also aids in achieving bureaucratic efficiency. In South and Southeast Asian cities, problems in program or project implementation are generally associated with low salaries and benefits of local officers and personnel, crowded and poorly maintained offices, old and dilapidated equipment, outmoded procedures and red tape, and other factors that combine to create low morale. When combined with petty graft and corruption, these unsatisfactory conditions are serious impediments to program implementation.

Monitoring and Evaluation

In a number of Asian city-regions, coordinating mechanisms for monitoring and evaluating programs and projects have been set up to improve regionwide program management. In the Philippines, more efficient monitoring of infrastructure projects has been by using the Capital Investment Folio (CIF), which is basically an orderly list of infrastructure projects approved by the authorities for funding. Approval is based on thorough analysis of each project's technical, financial, and managerial viability, augmented by an exhaustive assessment of its environmental and social impact.

The CIF projects are reviewed annually by a committee composed of national, regional, city, and municipal officials from units within the metropolitan area. In years where there are adequate funds, the pace of project execution is accelerated. When there is less money, the CIF uses a priority-setting formula for deciding which projects will be finished first and which ones are to be postponed until more funds are available. Each project decision is made on the basis of predetermined, often quantifiable criteria. By using this approach, there is less political interference in the implementation of projects.

A similar monitoring and evaluation system has been used in Indonesia, called the Integrated Urban Infrastructure Development Program. In Greater Jakarta, all large-scale infrastructure projects are listed in this program, together with their physical location, annual budgets, schedule of implementation, the name of the responsible agency or agencies, and specific output indicator measures (e.g., the number of kilometers to be built per year, number of tons to be moved). A committee composed of national, provincial, and local officials monitors the implementation of each project regularly. Projects that are behind schedule are investigated to find the reasons for their delays. Budgetary allocations are also adjusted according to the pace and rate of development. The program's budget is a rolling one. It has a system of priorities that are carefully adjusted in accordance with the progress achieved or not achieved for each project.

Urban managers have found that "built-in" monitoring and evaluation components in projects are an excellent way of improving performance. This process is relatively easy to do in big infrastructure projects where outputs can be quantified. However, in the case of social development programs, such as poverty alleviation, it is not that easy to set up quantitative and qualitative indicators. In these cases, the close attention paid by policymakers and political officials to qualitative outputs is needed.

Globalization and Urban Governance

Globalization has a direct impact on urbanization because cities act as the aggregating and articulating devices for demographic, economic, social, political, and informational changes. It is in cities where the concentration of people at very high densities effects significant changes. It is also from cities that economic, social, political, and cultural influences are disseminated to other areas. Large cities, especially those that have attained global city status, can be the "growth machines" that can energize the other parts of nation-states. Conversely, they may also "harbor important movements of political opposition to the party or regime in power at the center" (Stren 2001, 4).

Turning to the mega-urban regions in Asia, I believe that a number of interrelated factors are tremendously important in analyzing their developmental roles. First, there is the process of *social transformation* that underlies most of city-region growth. Foremost among these is the process of *urban transition,* where the demographic changes such as population growth and internal and international migration influence the growth of cities. The *environmental effects* and impact of urban concentration and dispersal are also of great significance. Another key issue is the process of the *institutionalization* of factors that are related to the decentralization of authority and power and the impact of market forces on urban growth. Finally, the growing importance of *transnational corporations* has significant effects on urban development patterns.

The massive changes occurring in Asian mega-urban regions are easily discernible in the expansion of built-up areas. In most Asian urban agglomerations, rural–urban migration seems to have slackened, but some mega-urban regions in South and Southeast Asia continue to have high population growth levels in their peri-urban zones. In South Asian countries like Bangladesh, India, and Pakistan, there has been a shift from primary industries to secondary ones, and employment in services, especially in the informal sector, has risen tremendously. Although East Asian cities like Seoul and Tokyo seem to have effectively dealt with urban problems like air, water, and noise pollution, those in South and Southeast Asia continue to suffer from these urban ills.

To respond to the changes occurring in Asian mega-urban regions, government institutions have attempted to come up with innovative strategies. Here, the increasing linkages of urban agglomerations with international markets and capital flows are posing new problems. Proponents of globalization have argued that increased economic engagement through trade promotes accelerated economic growth and is more conducive to citizen empowerment, democracy, and increased personal freedom. Yet many Asian leaders are arguing that their weak economic situation vis-à-vis technologically advanced countries, and their lack of cohesion in the face of unified efforts of those pushing global policies, makes them vulnerable to negative economic and social influences.

As has been pointed out by McCarney, "the increasing role of transnational corporations, construction of new trading blocks, globalization of economic and socio-cultural development spheres and the persistence of international debt all find expression in the city" (McCarney 1996a, 7). As international trade, global finance flows, cross-border manufacturing, offshore industrial investments, outsourcing of production inputs, and the use of advanced information technology encompass more and more countries, urban centers have become important development nodes. They have turned into crucial hubs of development in a global network of settlements, even as they have remained important engines of economic growth in national development.

The issue of good governance as a key element in achieving development has its ideological underpinnings, of course. The argument for democracy advocated by conservative ideologues that is, in turn, pushed by those who believe in globalization has an antistate bias. It has been described as "formal, constitutional . . . a form of democracy that separates politics from the structures of power in the economy. . . . Harking back to Lockean theory, but with a more modern Thatcherite patina, democracy here is understood simply as 'less government'" (Rocamora 2002, 83).

A particularly disturbing effect of globalization in many cities in Asia has been the resurgence of particularistic movements based on religion and on cultural and ethnic identities. Globalization—with its emphasis on spread of information, free trade, the movement of financial resources, technological innovation, and less constricted movement of people across national boundaries—is supposed to erode primordial loyalty and identification with family, clan, tribe, linguistic group, or religion. This is supposed to occur more rapidly in cities that are more exposed to globalization.

Even a quick look at what is happening in many Asian mega-urban regions reveals, however, that religious fundamentalism and identification with ethnic enclaves are on the rise. Violent clashes between Hindus and Muslim occur frequently in Indian and Pakistani cities. Bombing of bus depots, airports, resorts, and shopping centers have caused deaths and serious injury in Indonesia and the Philippines. Racially linked riots and violent demonstrations have broken out in Indian, Indonesian, Malaysian, and Pakistani cities. Random acts of terror—burned into the global consciousness after the September 11, 2001, terrorist attacks on New York and Washington, and sustained by color-coded terrorism alerts and the worrisome travel advisories associated with the American-led war on terrorism—have become integral parts of the global picture.

With worsening poverty and an increasing sense of helplessness among the poor residents of many Asian cities, people have started to turn to alternative social structures for help. Thus, in some squatter settlements in Metro Manila, drug lords and their violent gangs have become more effective enforcers of "peace and order" than the national police force. Some of these drug lords have even provided food, medicine, and other types of assistance to poor people in their communities. In Pakistan, the Lashkar-e-Taiba, an organization condemned by the government as terrorist, has provided educational and health facilities. In some cities, certain activities that on the surface look like usual urban occurrences, such as the eviction of squatters in Mumbai, have been linked to religious strife (Roy 2002, 41). All these developments have significant implications for governance because they contribute to fragmentation and limit the capacity of formal governance mechanisms to bring about cooperative and coordinated action.

It is worth noting that governance issues have become more prominent since the collapse of former socialist regimes and the widespread adoption of what has been called the "Washington consensus," which highlights the role of democracy, free markets, unconstrained global trade, privatization, and less government intervention in economic affairs. Since the collapse of socialism, the "victorious" Free World countries and the international donor agencies they strongly support have stressed "democratic governance" as an element in their developmental assistance programs. Terms such as "enablement," "empowerment," "democratization," "popular participation," and "civil society" have become key code words for the dominant philosophy in the development literature. Even the catchy phrase "socialism with Chinese characteristics" may be viewed as a euphemism acknowledging that China, the world's largest country, has adopted market-oriented philosophies. With the "triumph" of democracy over socialism, belief in the benefits arising from the unhindered play of free market forces has strengthened. Democracy advocates have argued that government intervention in developing countries needs to be reduced, and that a market economy encourages people to work hard and to take risks if they are allowed to keep most of the fruits of their labor.

After a decade or so of pursuing free-market policies, however, it has become quite clear that mechanically applying approaches such as free trade, foreign direct investment, and unhindered flow of capital to developing-country situations does not necessarily result in higher economic growth or reduced inequality among people and sectors. Rodrik, for one, has argued that most of the higher economic growth rates in Asia have been achieved in China, Singapore, Taiwan, and Vietnam—countries not particularly known as great believers in the unhindered play of market forces or the practice of popular democracy. On the contrary, higher economic growth rates in these countries have been attributed to strong governmental influence and direct intervention in socioeconomic affairs, which included social subsidies, human resource development schemes, and poverty alleviation programs (Rodrik 1994). China, for one, has chosen to open up to the outside world in a methodically gradual manner, allowing market forces to play a bigger role in the economy while at the same time maintaining central control. A similar approach has been used in Vietnam, where a delicate balancing between the economic dynamism enhanced by globalization and its potentially destabilizing effects arising from rising social inequalities can be discerned in development policies.

Increasingly, the role of a "strong state" in providing political stability and social order is cited as a prerequisite to a more efficient working of the market. The predictability of public and private actions based on a system of institutionalized laws and standards has a positive effect on development. Some authors have noted that "an effective and transparent government, operating within a framework of civil liberties and good governance, is vital for sustained welfare gains and poverty alleviation" (Thomas et al. 2000, 136). Others have argued that if people are to achieve economic progress, a strong state must ensure social justice, equity, and environmental sustainability through better governance. Popular participation and the responsiveness of government to people's needs are seen as key elements in attaining true development (Frischtak 1994).

Among international agencies, the World Bank was one of the earliest to address the issue of good governance. In 1989, the bank highlighted the need for good governance to achieve sustained development in African countries. In its report on the "East Asian economic miracle" in 1993, the bank acknowledged the role of government intervention in enhancing economic development even as it stressed that "correct economic fundamentals" are the linchpins of development. These fundamentals included the importance of increased savings, a stronger role for the private sector, lifting tariff and nontariff barriers to trade, the need for increasing government revenues, more investments in public infrastructure, increased allocations to human resources development (especially education, health, and welfare), and achieving efficiency in delivering public services (World Bank 1993a).

In recent years, the World Bank has given special emphasis to good governance and the need for more transparency and accountability in public affairs. Since Breton Woods, the bank had scrupulously tried to keep within purely economic realms and steer away from political issues. However, the bank's new leaders have issued pronouncements and adopted policies to encourage good governance, even going to the extent of mentioning the need to control if not eradicate corruption. Other international bodies have followed suit. At the United Nations International Conference on Financing for Development held in Monterrey, Mexico, in March 2002, the participants gave highest priority to the need to "fight corruption at all levels" (Jauregui-Rojas 2002, 19).

The secretary general of the United Nations, Kofi A. Annan, has declared that "good governance is perhaps the single most important factor in eradicating poverty and promoting development" (UNDP 2002). Echoing this pronouncement, good governance has been cited by the World Bank and other international financial institutions as a key element in the fight against poverty and social inequality. The Millennium Development Goals, adopted in 2002, set the target that by 2015, global poverty would be cut by half and child mortality by two-thirds, and that every child would be given the chance to finish primary education. The goals also seek to reduce the proportion of people in low- to middle-income countries living under the poverty line from 29 percent in 1990 to 14.5 percent by 2015. The lives of 100,000 urban poor people would be "significantly improved" by 2015.

In Monterrey, the United States and the European Union pledged an extra $12 billion a year in aid, starting in 2006, to support education, health, and antipoverty programs. The Monterrey Consensus provided that "good governance is essential for sustainable development. Sound economic policies, solid democratic institutions responsive to the needs of the people and improved infrastructure are the basis for sustained economic growth, poverty eradication and employment creation" (World Bank 2002b, 53). As a follow up to Monterrey, the Millennium Challenge Account (MCA) was set up in 2004 to provide development assistance to countries that "rule justly, invest in their people, and encourage economic freedom." The U.S. Congress approved $1 billion in initial funding for fiscal 2004 for the MCA, with promises of an increase to $5 billion by 2005. Sixteen developing countries, ranging from Armenia to Vanuatu, were targeted for MCA assistance. In addition, a number of "threshold countries" were identified for potential assistance, provided they committed themselves to governance reforms (MCC 2004).

Despite the hope that globalization and economic development would narrow the gap between rich and poor people, however, studies have shown that there are quite a number of developing countries where this has not happened. The "balance sheet" cited in the United Nations Development Program's (UNDP's) *Human Development Report 2002* indicated that the richest 5 percent of the world's people had incomes that were 114 times higher than those of the poorest 5 percent. The World Bank estimated that the total number of people subsisting on less than $1.00 a day had risen from 1.2 billion in 1987 to 1.5 billion in 2000. It projected the number of people who would be living below the poverty line to increase to 1.9 billion by 2015.

It is interesting to note that, in recent years, the World Bank has started to support more projects in urban areas. This rediscovery of the urban field is helped tremendously, of course, by the realization that by about 2005, more than half of the world's total population would be living in urban places. In many countries, also, poverty in urban areas, as seen in the persistent growth of slum and squatter communities, continues to worsen. All these factors have been serving to highlight the importance of cities in development and of good urban governance as a global issue.

On their part, the UN Center for Human Settlements (Habitat) and UNDP have reemphasized the role of local governments in achieving development. These agencies see local governments not as builders and suppliers of urban infrastructure but as "enablers," "facilitators," and "enhancers" of local capacity in the provision of public services. This indicates a broader view that regards governments as supporters and motivators of private-sector and civil society efforts. The importance of local governance was highlighted in the 1996 Second International Conference on Human Settlements (Habitat II) in Istanbul, where governments were encouraged to include city mayors, NGO leaders, private-sector representatives, and civil society leaders in their official delegations. Renewed interest in good urban governance has also brought about multiagency international efforts, such as the Healthy Cities Project and the Metropolitan Environmental Improvement Program.

Alongside the policy shifts among international development agencies noted above, there has also been growing recognition of the importance of city-regions as venues for development. As the Institute for Research on Public Policy (IRPP) has indicated "city-regions are key transmission points in the global economy. They are home to skilled labor, extensive communications and transportation networks and the most supple and innovative of firms" (Sancton 1994, 1). The IRPP has noted that city-region governance is needed to deal with the problem of local government fragmentation. It observed that local government structures tended to be unwieldy, and because of this capabilities to raise taxes and other resources were woefully low. Local taxation and financial transfer systems were out of sync with modern city-region economies. Central government programs were often sector-specific and did not adequately address the particular problems of cities. The IRPP, therefore, saw city-region governance as a key solution to worsening urban problems in developing countries (Sancton 1994).

Governance Problems in Mega-Urban Regions

There is widespread recognition that urban governance reforms are needed if the hoped-for developmental role of cities in developing countries is to be realized. The problems of mega-urban regions most frequently cited in the literature as possibly amenable to improved governance solutions are (1) fragmentation and jurisdictional conflicts, (2) inappropriate decentralization schemes, (3) a lack of financial capacity, and (4) issues related to transparency and accountability.

Fragmentation and Jurisdictional Conflicts

The most serious problem faced by many Asian mega-urban regions is political and administrative fragmentation. Typically, a mega-urban region is made up of a central city and adjacent municipalities, towns, districts, wards, or villages that compete against each other for resources. Some of these units may have organically evolved from indigenous settlements, such as the Philippine *barangay,* the Indian *panchayat,* or the Indonesian *kampung.* Others may trace their origins from colonial legal structures, such as municipal corporations, military cantonments, special service wards, development trusts, or chartered cities. A common feature of these local organizational units is a strong adherence to local autonomy and an antagonism to the powers and prerogatives of higher-level governments.

In a city-region that serves as a nation's capital, the dominant power of the central government might be able to avoid the negative effects of fragmentation. This is shown in cases like Bangkok, Beijing, Delhi, Jakarta, or Seoul, where a central-government-delineated national capital district or territory has been able to overcome local government particularism. However, even in such territory-wide political-administrative jurisdictions, problems of fragmentation may continue because of sectorally defined responsibilities. Central government ministries and departments may engage in turf wars as they exercise authority over specific functions. There may also be vertical administrative fragmentation in cases where the territory is divided into national, provincial, district, municipal, ward, township, or village-level authorities.

The complex and confusing interrelationships among various agencies in a mega-urban region is seen in Mumbai, even in a relatively narrow field like transport. A 2001 World Bank study revealed that although the Mumbai Metropolitan Regional Development Authority (MMRDA) is formally charged with coordinating transport in the region, it actually has little influence on the planning and provision of this important service. For one, jurisdiction over the suburban rail service rests with India Railways, a specialized central government agency. Two zonal railway systems in the Mumbai suburbs are also run by independent agencies that pursue their separate policies and activities without any significant efforts at service integration. The allocation of financial resources to support the building and operation of rail-based transport requires the approval of the Central Planning Commission. The planning and construction of roads and major trunk lines are vested in the Public Works Department of the State of Maharashtra. Maintenance of roads is the responsibility of the Municipal Corporation of Greater Mumbai as is the planning and implementation of traffic management. The Brihan Mumbai Electricity and Transport (BEST) organization, a quasi-autonomous entity supported by the government, provides bus service in Mumbai (World Bank 2002a).

A number of policy analysts have recommended closer integration and areawide governance for the Mumbai city-region to rationally manage transport services. The World Bank, for example, has recommended the strengthening of the MMRDA as a regional planning and coordinating authority that would manage the implementation of the Mumbai urban transport project. A Project Management Unit headed by a project director was set up within MMRDA to plan and implement specific project components. To enhance coordination further, the Government of India had also established the Mumbai Rail Vikas Corporation, a joint venture of the Government of Maharashtra and India Railways to manage the implementation of the Mumbai Urban Transport Project and other rail-based projects in the region. Yet though the results of these specific interventions might have improved the management and coordination of the transport project, they have not adequately dealt with the larger territory-wide issues faced by the Mumbai region.

The Perils of Decentralization

As the international donor community pursues "good governance" as a theme in its development efforts, the strengthening of "the capacity of all countries to implement the principles and practices of democracy" has been set as a global millennium goal. In general, democratization is viewed as requiring greater people's participation in public affairs. Participation, in turn, is seen as being maximized by the decentralization of authority and responsibility to local government units.

Conceptually, there are two types of decentralization. There is, first of all, the process of *delegation* of authority and responsibility from the central government to field units to enable these units to carry out specific functions. The Government of Thailand, for example, appoints governors and district officers who are essentially functionaries of the central government, though they operate at the local level. Mayors of municipalities under the direct supervision and control of the central government in China (Beijing, Chongqing, Shanghai, and Tianjin) are appointed by the center. Though authority is delegated to these officials, it is never lost to the central government, because the delegating officials retain inherent powers of supervision and control.

The other meaning of decentralization is *devolution,* which is the transfer of both responsibility and authority to local government units from the central government. This is exemplified by the Philippine Local Government Code of 1991, which devolved key functions—such as health, social welfare, agriculture, environmental protection, and local public works and highways—to provinces, cities, and municipalities. The scope of decentralized authority granted under the code depended on governmental levels—responsibility for health, for example, was devolved to provincial and city hospitals. Even the lowest level of governance, the *barangay* or village council, was given authority and responsibility to run day care centers (Tapales 1993).

A special form of decentralization is *privatization,* which is the transfer of authority to nongovernment entities. This may take the form of special franchises or the outright sale of public enterprises to private companies to make them responsible for supplying basic services such as electricity, telephone, and gas. It may also mean the transfer of responsibility and authority to civil society groups, such as NGOs, which may carry out research, training, information dissemination, community organization, and other functions on behalf of the government.

Decentralization also has a spatial dimension in the process of *decon-centration,* which involves the hiving off of activities and structures from a central or core area to other areas. Deconcentration may be effected either through administrative delegation of authority and responsibility or through devolution of functions to local government units. Its main function is the physical allocation of structures and functions in space. It is particularly important in the formulation and implementation of national urban strategies that suggest the location of specific governmental and nongovernmental activities.

Many arguments have been advanced in favor of decentralization; four can be readily cited. First, it has been argued that the people themselves are best qualified to understand and define their needs. They are most familiar with local conditions so that, when it comes to choosing policy options, they have the objectives facts on which to base their decisions. Second, the people who are best informed about local conditions will be more willing to support programs that will redound to their own welfare. They would be more willing to pay taxes and raise revenues to support local programs, provided they see the actual impact of these programs on their lives.

Third, local people know the potentials and capabilities of their leaders. They can elect and choose individuals who can best serve the community. At the same time, these leaders will be directly accountable to the people for their actions. They need to be transparent in their official and personal actions, because doing otherwise would make them lose public support. Fourth, it has even been argued that decentralization is good because if graft and corruption occur at the local level, their ill effects can be confined to a small area, compared with at the central government level, where their negative effects would be spread more widely.

The move to decentralize authority to local governments has been reflected in major constitutional revisions and legislative enactments in a number of countries. Indonesia, the Philippines, Sri Lanka, and Thailand have passed decentralization measures. In India, the Seventy-Fourth Amendment to the Constitution, approved in 1992, defined "municipalities as fully representative institutions" (Mathur 1996, 121). The amendment took away the power of state governments to dissolve municipalities indefinitely (dissolved municipalities must be reconstituted within a period of six months after the date of dissolution). The amendment vested in municipalities key tasks such as planning for economic and social development and poverty alleviation. More important, the amendment provided a mechanism for fiscal management between states and municipalities, including clarification of the authority to impose taxes, duties, tolls, and levies, and the allocation of grants-in-aid to local units.

The Local Government Code of 1991 in the Philippines drastically altered the centralist tendencies in governance (Tapales 1996, 212). The act transferred key governmental functions to local units. It devolved important fiscal powers to local governments, including the authority to impose taxes, levies, and fines on citizens. Local governments were allowed to float bonds, issue various debt instruments, or borrow from banks to finance local projects. The code provided for the representation of NGOs, sectoral representatives, and civil society groups in local councils. As in India, the law defined the fiscal relationships between the central government and local units, even going to the extent of instructing central government authorities to automatically release the share of local units in national taxes and other revenues, thus taking away from central government officials a vital instrument for administrative and political control.

Despite the experience with decentralization in a number of Asian countries and the seemingly logical arguments for decentralization noted above, a number of pitfalls serve to dampen enthusiasm for granting autonomy to local units. Foremost among these is the fact that the factors directly or indirectly affecting the lives of local people might actually come from outside the community instead of being the product of local political dynamics. People's information about these external influences might be very limited, making it extremely difficult for them to arrive at rational local action. Local political leaders, who may be privy to information coming from outside as "gatekeepers," might then be able to manipulate information to pursue their own selfish goals.

The argument has been made that because decentralization will bring government closer to the people, local leaders will be more willing to take on full responsibility for local development. However, this may not always be the case. Some local leaders may find it an onerous task to tax their constituencies. Because some of them may get into positions of power by their ability to extract resources from higher levels of government, they may find this preferable to taxing their constituents. Instead of fostering self-reliance, therefore, such local leaders may create dependence on central governments. They may trade the local votes they mobilize for personal or community favors, setting up "political machines" to do this. Such an arrangement is hardly conducive to grassroots democracy.

Simply mandating devolution of powers to local units by law does not mean that people who wield power at the center will automatically relinquish those powers. National politicians who derive their powers from local bailiwicks will resist local autonomy. Private business groups that usually exert influence through such politicians will also use their resources to undermine and emasculate decentralization efforts. Central government bureaucrats who have gotten used to wielding tremendous powers will fight decentralization. In the Philippines, for example, central government officials lobbied mightily to stop the government from implementing the Local Government Code of 1991. They argued that transferring them to local government jurisdictions would disrupt their career ladders in the national civil service, place them under the control and supervision of local officials less qualified than them, expose them to the pernicious pressures of local politics, and reduce their salaries and benefits. It took a number of years for these objections to be resolved, and there are still periodic campaigns by former public servants (especially health personnel) to reverse the provisions of the decentralization law.

In a number of instances, the very philosophy of decentralization as the means for achieving grassroots democracy has been a major cause of problems. A romanticized notion of basic democracy has prompted some governments to decentralize authority to the lowest level of governance. Using an idealized image of the Athenian polis or the New England town meeting, decentralization advocates have devolved authority to the smallest villages and towns.

Examples of such basic democracy efforts include the Barrio Council Law in the Philippines, the *kampung* governance scheme in Indonesia, and the *panchayat*-based community development movement in India. Under the first, the Philippine government devolved authority for specific functions such as agriculture, peace and order, rural roads, and social welfare to village-level barrio councils, each of which was headed by a *capitan del barrio* (barrio captain) supported by functional *kagawads* (council members) directly elected by eligible voters in annual elections (Abueva 1959). The elected village-level officials did not receive any salaries but were expected to lead the community in both economic and democratic development efforts.

Although noble in its intentions, the law did not match the responsibility given to barrio councils with commensurate authority needed to carry out their tasks. For example, the councils were given very limited revenue-raising powers—the authority to impose taxes, fees, and fines was defined as an inherent right of the central government, and only "enumerated taxing powers," such as the authority to collect fees from vendors in periodic markets or impose a tax on game cocks, were included in the law. The central government, therefore, managed to have its cake and eat it too—it appeared democratic in decentralizing authority to local units but continued to keep its most important powers to tax and to ration out public funds. Not surprisingly, the Barrio Council Law neither improved democracy nor fostered economic development in Philippine villages.

The Local Government Code of 1991 sought to correct many of the mistakes in the Barrio Council Law. Although the code has strengthened local governments in the Philippines somewhat, it has not been able to bring about areawide cooperation and coordination in rapidly expanding urban agglomerations. In Metro Manila, for example, the strengthened cities and municipalities raised many objections to the actions of the Metro Manila Development Authority. Municipalities lobbied hard for central government legislation to transform themselves into cities to gain greater autonomy. Some cities refused to turn over to the MMDA portions of their annual tax revenues as mandated by law. In September 2002—in response to soaring crime rates and to widespread suspicion that some corrupt officers in the Philippine National Police were in fact linked to the activities of drug lords and kidnap-for-ransom gangs—the local government units in Metro Manila regained their control over local police forces.

In fighting for their autonomy, the local units have found support in the 1987 Philippine Constitution that limited the creation of metropolitan governance structures. Article 10, section 11, of the Philippine Constitution allowed the creation of metropolitan governance structures, provided their creation was upheld by a plebiscite. It stipulated: "The jurisdiction of the metropolitan authority that will be created shall be limited to basic services requiring coordination." It also ruled: "The component cities and municipalities shall retain their basic autonomy and shall be entitled to their own local executives and legislative assemblies." In essence, the Local Government Code of 1991 continued the approach of the Barrio Council Law of the 1950s that decentralized authority to traditional local units.

The main lesson learned from the Philippine situation is that decentralizing authority and power to small local government units—based on the argument that they are closest to the people and that, therefore, empowering these units will enhance democracy—is not necessarily a good thing. For decentralization to work, authority and power must be devolved to a political unit large enough and financially capable enough to take on the responsibilities of good governance. The Philippine move failed to recognize the importance of big cities and metropolitan areas as viable units of governance. It failed to decentralize authority and power to the metropolitan unit with the financial, organizational, and leadership capabilities to deal with areawide problems.

Reviewing the situation in Latin America and elsewhere, Campbell arrived at the same conclusion that decentralization has to be carried out selectively. He observed that "decentralization laws and administrative reforms in most countries have treated all municipalities alike, irrespective of size, experience and installed capacity . . . municipalities the size of mega-cities were mixed indiscriminately with tiny hamlets. . . . An important lesson . . . is that governments should discriminate not just by size, but by readiness to undertake the new burden of local autonomy." To deal with problems of premature decentralization, Campbell proposed measures such as establishment of performance standards that local governments have to meet before being granted decentralized powers, classification of cities by size and administrative capability, and the phasing in of decentralized powers in stages to allow local governments to develop their capacities first before graduating to higher levels of decentralized autonomy (Campbell 2002, 129).

Lack of Financial Capacity

In a survey of forty-six countries conducted in 1997, it was found that about 82.5 percent of governmental income went to central governments, 4.5 percent to subnational units, and 13.0 percent to local governments (Ebel and Vaillancourt 2001, 158–59). Local government incomes ranged from less than 1 percent to about 50 percent of government revenues. To carry out their functions, therefore, local units rely very heavily on allotments of tax revenue from central governments, grants-in-aid, political "pork barrel" allocations, and other types of assistance. This is true even for highly urbanized local government units with rich tax bases and incomes from operations.

Typically, local governments in rich urban areas are required to turn over the great bulk of their tax collections to central government coffers. They are then forced to beg central authorities for their share of revenue allotments. Many big city officials lament that they get only a very small percentage of the taxes they collect because, in effect, they subsidize the central government, which assists poorer local units through "income-sharing" and "income-equalization" payments.

In view of the weak capacity of local governments to raise revenue, some researchers have suggested decentralizing fiscal authority to local government units. Ebel and Vaillancourt have advanced three economic arguments for fiscal decentralization. They argue that fiscal decentralization enhances economic efficiency because "that set of governments closest to the citizens can adjust budgets [costs] to local preferences in a manner that best leads to the delivery of a bundle of public services that is responsive to community preferences." They also proposed that decentralization improves resource mobilization because well-functioning local units can access tax bases more readily than the central government (e.g., they can use user charges, sales taxes, and real property taxes). Finally, Ebel and Vaillancourt have argued that local governments are best able to price public services accurately, thus making it possible to arrive at the correct size of a local government jurisdiction for carrying out such services (Ebel and Vaillancourt 2001, 158–59).

Other researchers have advocated a "demand-driven" approach to the financing of urban services like water and electricity. They have proposed that "tariff structure and rates need to be designed to ensure that the full capital, operation and maintenance costs can be recovered," arguing that user fees "will help to reduce wasteful consumption and curtail excess demand that arises when a valued good is provided free" (Gulyani 2001, 186). If utilities like water, electricity, solid waste collection and disposal, and other basic services have adequate revenues, they will not be a burden to local government units. The problem with this approach, however, is that the administrative mechanisms for cost recovery in most developing-country cities are often inefficient and ineffective. User charges, when strictly enforced, tend to penalize urban poor people, who in most instances are already paying more for lower-quality services than their well-to-do neighbors. Existing urban services structures traditionally subsidize better-off members of society while poor urban residents benefit only marginally. Doing away with the subsidies will deny urban poor people even the marginal benefits they manage to enjoy.

A key issue in fiscal decentralization is the authority of local government units to borrow from domestic or international markets, especially for financing large infrastructure projects. As a rule, central governments are leery of granting authority to borrow to local units for fear of irresponsible local borrowing that might lead to uncontrolled inflation and other fiscal dislocations. However, experience in China, the Philippines, and other Asian countries has shown that local leaders—especially those managing megacities that have the financial and organizational capabilities to run their own affairs—have proven to be trustworthy borrowers. Mega-urban regions, in fact, have shown that they can get excellent credit ratings when they pool their local resources and cooperatively raise funds from borrowings to finance areawide services.

Another way of improving the financial capability of local government units is by privatizing the provision of urban services. Traditional economists have looked to competitive market mechanisms as a way to improve efficiency in service delivery. They have argued that the public ownership of service enterprises increases the financial burden for local units, results in gross inefficiency as monopolistic public enterprises become subject to political and partisan interference, creates misallocation of services to people who really do not need it, and contributes to the wastage of public funds (Batley 2001, 201).

The experience with privatization in Asian cities, so far, has not been too encouraging. Pursuing higher profits, private enterprises have increased rates without a corresponding improvement of service levels. They have tended to ignore disadvantaged sectors of urban society, such as urban poor people living in uncontrolled settlements, because such residents have little or no capacity to pay. They have used corruption to get franchises and contracts and recouped their losses due to corrupt practices by increasing rates. The expected benefits in efficiency supposedly emanating from privatization, therefore, have not materialized, and urban authorities are increasingly becoming leery of privatization schemes, despite the insistence of donor agencies and international financial institutions that they should try these approaches.

On the basis of the analysis of fiscal management in the Asian megacities in this study, the proper jurisdiction for the governance of rapidly changing urban agglomerations seems to be the mega-urban region. For one, the study shows that the fragmentation of urban areas into competing local units hampers the capacity to raise revenue. A municipality eager to attract an investor to its jurisdiction might offer a tax moratorium or lower tax rates. Investors, in turn, play local officials against each other to get the best concessions. Local taxpayers shop around and travel to jurisdictions where there are no sales or value-added taxes.

Taking a regional approach serves to rationalize taxation and avoids the unequal allocation of the tax burden among residents of the city-region. It will certainly reduce the harmful competition among local government units. The larger and richer economic base of a whole city-region may increase the creditworthiness of the urban government units. Such an improved financial situation may allow the city-region to access national and even international financial sources to finance long-term projects and large infrastructure investments.

Transparency, Accountability, and Corruption

City-regions usually require investments in urban services, such as transit systems, water and sewerage, energy supply, roads, ports, harbors, and other high-priced items. The large amounts involved and profits that can be gained from these projects provide opportunities for graft and corruption. Unless governmental processes can be instituted to ensure transparency and accountability in public transactions, inefficiency, waste, and moral decay could afflict urban governance.

The problem in almost all of Asia's mega-urban regions, however, is that the cultural, institutional, and behavioral aspects of urban life usually make it difficult for anticorruption measures to succeed. There are at least three reasons advanced for this. First, as Lee has observed based on a comparative study of corruption in six Asian countries, the notion of corruption may be culture-bound: "An act that may be corrupt in one society may be normal in another society or in the same society at another time." Most traditional Asian societies have "folk conceptions" of what is right and what is wrong, and these do not necessarily correspond to the legal norms of conduct that are officially defined as corruption (Lee 1986, 71).

Second, corruption may be regarded as just a form of market-oriented deal making, with bribes considered a normal price for rendering of services in a situation ruled by supply and demand. An official considers holding an office as a way of maximizing gains, a process of economic rent seeking. Because he or she invests in acquiring a public office, it is only natural that adequate returns should be obtained from that investment. This was the conception of public office during imperial and colonial times, and it continues because of cultural inertia.

Third, urban societies are highly differentiated and pluralistic, and specific groups compete against each other for private gain. Ruling elite groups attempt to hold on to power and use whatever means they have to do this. Countervailing elite groups also use all sorts of methods to gain power. In many Asian cities, the most likely instrument for gaining and holding onto power involves corrupt practices.

Most Asian governments define corruption as "an act that violates or deviates from the formal rules of a public office for the sake of private-regarding gains" (Lee 1981, 6). Corrupt acts involve "purposive behavior which may be a deviation from an expected norm but is undertaken nevertheless with a view to attain material or other rewards" (Carino 1986, 29).

Corruption means "charging an illicit price for a service or using the power of office to further illicit gains" (Klitgaard, Maclean-Abaroa, and Parris 2000, 2). Typical examples of corrupt acts include

- *graft,* which refers to embezzlement or illegal appropriation of public funds and properties, usually carried out by an individual officeholder or a group of officials;
- *nepotism,* which refers to granting of special favors to individuals (hiring, promotion, allocation of duties and responsibilities, rendering of services) on the basis of particularistic considerations such as kinship, friendship, or regional or ethnic ties rather than on merit; and
- *bribery,* which refers to demanding, offering, accepting, or receiving valued items (money, properties, gifts) that are not legally provided for, so as to induce officials to deviate from their legal public duties.

In the Philippines, the Anti-Graft and Corrupt Practices Act (Republic Act 3019, August 1960) provided very specific definitions of corrupt acts. Thus, a public official was prohibited from accepting any gift that was "manifestly excessive" (set at 200 pesos in 1970) from any person who was not a relative (up to the fourth degree of consanguinity). Accepting employment in a private enterprise that had pending official business with an officer's office was illegal (this included accepting employment from a relative). Delaying action on certain decisions to receive pecuniary or material benefits or advantages was corrupt. Even the failure of a government official to file a correct statement of assets and liabilities was punishable by one year in jail and a fine. Despite these very specific definitions of corrupt practices in the law, however, graft and corruption remains a fact of life in the Philippines, as reflected in the fact that the country has been ranked as one of the ten most corrupt in Asia by Transparency International.

The extent to which corrupt practices are practiced is well known in most Asian urban societies. There have been estimates of the economic and social costs of corruption, and the negative consequences of corrupt acts have been well studied (Coronel 1998, 2000; Carino 1986). In general, circumstances in governance that have been found conducive to corruption have been identified. They include (1) very low salaries and benefits in the government; (2) monopolistic powers lodged in powerful agencies; (3) too many administrative steps and requirements in government transactions, where each step is an opportunity for corruption; (4) lack of clarity in governmental procedures; (5) lack of clear punishment for corrupt acts and uncertainty in the application of punishments; and (6) widespread public cynicism based on the belief that corruption is systematic, it is only natural, everyone is doing it, and nothing can be done about it.

A number of measures have been used in Asian mega-cities to limit, if not eradicate, corruption. Some of these measures have achieved significant success and have been used as models by other governments seeking to deal effectively with corruption, including:

- *Anticorruption agencies.* Special high-powered agencies have been set up by governments to deal with corruption. An excellent example of an agency that has achieved a great deal of success in combating corruption, especially in the police department, is the Independent Commission Against Corruption (ICAC) set up in Hong Kong in the early 1970s. Having been granted considerable "stop and search" powers and reporting only to the governor, the ICAC managed to bring 218 prosecutions in 1975 and 259 prosecutions in 1976, effectively curbing corruption in the city.
- *Anticorruption laws.* Governments have passed special legislation to deal with corruption. Such laws clearly define corrupt acts and levy specific punishments for such acts. Good examples of anticorruption laws are the Prevention of Corruption Act and the Prevention of Corruption Ordinance in Singapore.
- *Letting the public know.* In many instances, corruption thrives because people who need government services do not know what is required by regular procedures. Just putting up posters on correct procedures, and letting people know that each step can be done without bribing anyone or asking an influential person to intercede, can cut down corruption. Exposure of corrupt acts, such as those carried out by investigative journalists, and wide coverage in the media shaming corrupt individuals have been used as effective deterrents to corruption.
- *Streamlining administrative procedures.* In cities where corruption is common, the steps required in governmental transactions are often multiplied because each one provides an opportunity for bribes. A recent study found, for example, that getting a construction permit takes two months in Hong Kong and Singapore, eight months in Tokyo, twenty-eight months in Jakarta, and thirty-six months in Delhi. It was proposed that the number of months needed correlated directly with levels of urban corruption (Klitgaard, Maclean-Abaroa, and Parris 2000, 3). Simplifying and streamlining procedures, such as those re-

lated to procurement, revenue raising, granting of permits, and licenses and contracts, can reduce corruption.

Governmental efforts to achieve responsiveness, transparency, and accountability in governance in many Asian mega-urban regions have not met with much success. Graft and corruption continue to be a fact of life in Asian urban societies. Here and there, as in Hong Kong and Singapore, there have been successful efforts to make urban governance more efficient and less corrupt. In general, however, corruption thrives in most Asian mega-urban regions.

In the light of these conditions, some people advocate that, perhaps, reducing rather than eradicating corruption should be a primary goal in urban governance. A more modest objective may encourage reformers to achieve success slowly but surely. Reformers may be able to understand the systemic roots of corruption and use this greater understanding in formulating workable measures to reduce it. In the meantime, corruption will continue to thwart good governance efforts, and public officials just have to learn to live with it.

Types of Mega-Urban Region Governance

In Asia, essentially three approaches to mega-urban region governance are reflected in the types of institutions currently in use: (1) autonomous local government systems, (2) mixed regional governance approaches, and (3) unified governance systems. This typology is conceptual in that it is based on the political and administrative structures that perform specific public functions. In reality, it is not easy to find empirical examples that precisely conform to each of these categories.

In the first type, governmental functions are carried out by a host of local government units with jurisdictions over their specific territories. Governance structures are fragmented, and there is poor coordination in delivering basic services. In the mixed regional governance approach, both central and local governments play a role in public affairs. For example, key services such as construction, health, and education might be handled by central government agencies; certain areawide functions like planning, water, electricity, and solid waste disposal might be managed by regional entities; and mainly local functions like police, fire, traffic, and waste collection might be the responsibility of lower-level units. In central-government-dominated systems, most functions are managed by ministries or special development authorities. These are essentially field administration systems rather than local governance arrangements.

Autonomous Local Governance

Metro Manila before 1963 was a good example of autonomous local governance. Four cities and four towns made up the metropolitan area. Each of these local government units had its own municipal or city charter where the mayor–council form of government was enshrined. There were few cases of intermunicipal cooperation, for elected mayors and council members often belonged to warring political parties. If a fire broke out in one municipality, the fire department in another would not come to help. A main thoroughfare emanating from one city might suddenly end at the boundary, and there would be no effort to connect it to another road in the other jurisdiction. This chaotic situation was ended in 1963 by the creation of the Metropolitan Manila Commission, which placed the whole metropolitan area under the authority of a governor. Unfortunately, that governor was the wife of the president, and her abuses of authority have resulted in a profound suspicion of areawide governance in Manila ever since she and her dictator husband were thrown out of power.

In the Philippines, the American reformers who governed the country from 1899 to 1935 championed local autonomy as a manifestation of "direct democracy" patterned after an idealized version of the New England town meeting. In theory, small local governments would be responsive to local needs. Decision making would be directly influenced by the wishes and demands of the citizenry. People would be more willing to pay taxes and other government charges because they would see the benefits arising from the use of these resources much more immediately. Voters would know candidates more and be able to choose the best leaders. They would be directly knowledgeable about local issues and made their decisions more rationally. Leaders would be more responsive to people's needs.

In practice, however, local autonomy did not exactly achieve worthy results. Local communities tended to be dominated by local elites, who usually used the resources of government to amass wealth and power. Authority and power made these leaders unresponsive to people's wishes. Sensing that they had no influence at all, people lost interest in government and often did not bother to vote or participate in public affairs at all. Believing that the taxes they paid only went to the pockets of the elite, the people became reluctant to pay taxes. Worse of all, many local government units became the private fiefdom of "family dynasties," who perpetuated themselves in power. Because they mainly pursued their private interests, local leaders did not cooperate with those from other local governments, making regionwide cooperation and coordination difficult if not impossible.

At present, the Metro Manila Development Authority has tended to regionalize more authority and power compared with the old Metro Manila Commission. Despite the policies embodied in the Local Government Code of 1991, municipal and city governments in Metro Manila have lost their control over such functions as regional planning, traffic management, police, and solid waste disposal (garbage collection remains a local function). Where before, the chair of the MMDA was elected by rotation among the mayors that made up the commission, he or she is now appointed by the president of the Philippines. The situation in Metro Manila, therefore, is shifting toward a mixed form of regional governance.

Mixed Regional Governance

Jakarta Raya, or the Special Capital City District of Jakarta (Daerah Khusus Ibukota Jakarta, or DKI), is an example of regional governance (although its jurisdiction is smaller than the extended urban area of Greater Jakarta). In the Indonesian system, Jakarta Raya has the status of a province, which is considered a Level 1 administrative unit. The president of Indonesia appoints the governor of DKI, although the governor reports to and is under the supervision and control of the minister of internal affairs. The Jakarta Raya territory is divided into five administrative zones (Level 2 units, called *wilayah kota*), each one headed by a mayor (*walikota*). Each district is in turn subdivided into subdistricts (*kecamatan*), headed by a *camat*. The *kecamatan* is divided into local units called *kelurahan,* each headed by a *lurah.* Below the *kerurahan* are two more local units, the *rukun warga* and the *rukun tetanga.* These lowest-level bodies function at the neighborhood and street levels (Leaf 1995, 21;Widianto 1993, 46).

In the review of governance mechanisms conducted for this study, mixed regional governance systems appear to have had some success in delivering public services to the people. This may be partly due to the allocation of urban functions to appropriate bodies at the central, regional or metropolitan, and municipal, town, or city levels. In a mixed system, functions requiring national standards or massive funding, such as education, health, sanitation, and public works, are usually under central government units. Some areawide functions, like regional planning, transport and traffic, water, electricity, telephone, and public transit, may be managed at the regional-level tier. Issues of local concern are handled at the lowest levels.

In some instances, a specific function may be broken down into components. For example, garbage sorting and collection could be made a purely local function. The collection and disposal of solid waste through incineration, sanitary landfill, or composting could be done at a regional level. The setting up of environmental standards and the adoption of implementation measures that would provide incentives to nonpolluters and penalties to polluters could be looked after at the national level. The most important thing is the determination of what factors make it logical for a specific aspect of the whole function to be managed at what level.

Despite the relative success of the mixed governance system, some problems have been encountered in its use. Foremost among these is the difficulty of achieving effective coordination. In South Asian mega-urban regions, for example, the use of specialized agencies of the state or central government to manage specific functions such as transport or land use control creates problems for local government authorities. Funding continues to be a source of friction among levels of government. In China, legislation passed by the central government in 1994 tightened Beijing's control on tax collection and raised the share of the central government in revenue. At the same time, under the policy of *fangquan rangli* (administrative decentralization), the center devolved a number of functions to local units.

Unified Regional Governance

To cope more effectively with fragmentation problems in mega-urban regions, unified governance systems have been adopted in a number of Asian countries. Examples of such unified systems include the Bangkok Metropolitan Administration (BMA), the Tokyo Metropolitan Government, and the "municipalities" of Beijing, Shanghai, and Tianjin. The governance systems in the mega-urban regions mentioned above had jurisdiction over the metropolitan territory. However, some areas on the urban periphery that also have close economic and social linkages with the metropolis are often not included in the jurisdiction of the unified structure.

The BMA was formed in 1972 by the merger of Bangkok and Thonburi municipalities, and it was headed by an elected governor. However, in 1978, the election provisions in the BMA law were abrogated by decree, and the governor had to be appointed by the minister of the interior. Election of the governor was restored in 1985, and a popular official was elected (Sivara-makrishnan and Green 1986). Since 1985, the BMA has become more autonomous and has assumed more and more responsibilities in managing urban affairs in Bangkok, including the newly built sky train system.

Despite the growing autonomy of BMA, some urban services in Bangkok continue to be managed by central government enterprises, such as the Electricity Authority, the Water Authority, and the National Housing Authority. Construction in the metropolitan area is carried out under the supervision of the Ministry of the Interior, which provides public works, police services, and town planning. Central government ministries control programs in education, health, and communications. The fact that most important government functions in Bangkok are run by central government agencies or special authorities does not mean that coordination in the delivery of services is assured.

In reality, the persistence of substantive specialization makes coordination difficult. On one hand, there is the advantage in a city like Bangkok of getting a significant share of national revenues. On the other hand, Bangkok still has to compete with other local governments all over the country for central resources. It also becomes more difficult for the municipal government to convince local citizens to pay more taxes or accept higher service charges because it is easier to rely on the central government.

The cities of Beijing, Shanghai, and Tianjin in China also have unified governance structures that have authority and power over other local government units within their jurisdictions. As in Thailand, however, there are a number of specialized agencies that operate within the municipalities that have considerable authority and power of their own. The fact that the municipalities are under the direct control of the central government, however, gives their governing authorities considerable powers. As such, coordination of activities within their unified fields of influence is often efficiently carried out.

In some mega-urban regions, problems have arisen because of the lag between the spread of economic development on the urban periphery and the inclusion of such zones under the jurisdiction of the unified governance structure. The reverse problem has also been encountered, where the areal extent of the unified jurisdiction has been extended too far from the core, encompassing still largely rural areas that have not yet established linkages with the center. This, for example, has been the case in Chongqing municipality, which was carved out of the territory of Sichuan province and placed under central government control. Although some villages and towns within the municipality are formally within the jurisdiction of the unified governance structure, they really have very little to do with the center and are managed autonomously.

One of the issues raised against unified regional governance is the fear that the big bureaucracies needed to govern the mega-urban regions may become unresponsive to citizen demands. It has to be noted that the samples of unified governance structures in this study are all in highly centralized governmental systems. From an evaluation of the performance of these unified governance structures, however, it is quite apparent that the biggest challenge that they face is the need to efficiently coordinate the various hierarchically arranged and horizontally differentiated agencies that operate within their jurisdictions. In this, the positive outputs that they achieve are testimonies to their effectiveness and efficiency.

4

Are Mega-Urban Regions Sustainable?

To some people, a sustainable city is an oxymoron. They believe that a city, by its very nature, is a center of consumption that extracts food, water, and energy from its hinterland and then despoils it with waste. As observed by Rees and his colleagues, "as a result of high population densities, the rapid rise in per capita energy and material consumption, and the growing dependence on trade (all of which are facilitated by technology), the ecological locations of human settlements no longer coincide with their geographic locations. Modern cities and industrial regions are dependent for survival and growth on a vast and increasingly global hinterland of ecologically productive landscapes." Cities are incapable of renewing themselves. Once they exceed their "carrying capacity" and go beyond their "ecological footprint" (the land/water area required to support the flows of energy and matter in a specific settlement), they cease to be sustainable (Rees and Wackernagel 1996, 29).

Part of the problem in attempting to analyze a sustainable city is the concept of sustainability itself. As pointed out in an editorial in a popular journal, "the term 'sustainable city' like the term 'sustainable development' from which it comes, can be interpreted in many different ways. Since there is no agreement on the term's meaning, it can be used to legitimize virtually any interest relating to environment or development in urban areas" (*Environment and Urbanization* 1999, 3).

The most quoted definition of sustainability is the one used in the report of the World Commission on Environment and Development (WCED), popularly known as the Brundtland Commission, which defined it as "development that meets the needs of the present without compromising the ability of future generations to meet theirs" (WCED 1987). The commission noted that the "major urban crisis" in large cities in the developing world was a problem, but it concluded that if developing-country cities followed the development patterns of cities in technologically advanced countries, they might be able to achieve sustainability. In this, the commission pinned its hopes on "more rapid economic growth" as the main approach to sustainability. It proposed that sustainability could be achieved by "a five- to ten-fold increase in world industrial output," which it anticipated could be reached "by the time world population stabilizes some time in the next century" (WCED 1987, 8).

As pointed out by Rees, however, there was an internal contradiction in the Brundtland Commission's idea of sustainability. The commission sought to uplift the living standards of people to industrial-country levels by using current approaches of technology and social organization. However, Rees noted that it was these very same "historic patterns of material growth [that were] responsible for present unsustainable levels of ecological disintegration" in the first place (Rees 1994, 2). In other words, in trying to achieve sustainable development through economic growth that did not consider limits set by the finite environment, the Brundtland Commission wanted to bake its cake, eat it, and still have slices left over for future generations.

Current understanding of sustainability focuses on three components: economic, social, and ecological. Economic sustainability addresses the proper and full valuation of natural resources, the maintenance of capital stock, the promotion of growth with equity, poverty reduction, and the internalization of the impact of economic activities that most economic models treat as externalities. Social sustainability requires consideration of "social capital," which includes factors that enhance the capabilities of human beings (education, health, skills training)—human dynamics that make possible social mobility, the empowerment of disadvantaged groups, poverty alleviation, and the prevention of the disintegration of societies. Ecological sustainability addresses ecosystem integrity, habitat conservation, the interaction of species and their preservation, and consideration of the carrying capacity of ecological systems (Serageldin 1995, 111).

From an ecological perspective, the sustainability of a city is based on its "carrying capacity," which is defined as "the population of a given species that can be supported indefinitely in a given habitat without permanently damaging the ecosystem upon which it depends" (Reader and Croze 1977, 14). To reduce the concept to its most basic elements, Reader and Croze, using the African savanna as an example, estimated that 1 square mile of grass can provide sufficient food for 100 gazelles, which in turn can keep one lion adequately fed indefinitely. If more lions enter the picture or more gazelles are introduced to eat more grass (or if droughts, grassfires, or other calamities destroy the vegetation), the carrying capacity of the ecosystem will be exceeded and "nature's fearful symmetry" will be unhinged. Reader and Croze observed that there is a pyramid in nature, with plants that convert the energy of the sun into edible form as its foundation. Herbivores (eaters of plants) form the second "trophic," or nourishment level, in the food chain. These, in turn, are eaten by carnivores (eaters of flesh), which form the third trophic level. Of all the organisms in nature, human beings are the biggest threat to sustainability because they consume most everything and, with their technology, have the ability to alter the basic order of life.

Believers in the power of technology could argue, of course, that fertilization, irrigation systems, the development of hardier and faster growing varieties of grass, or other innovations can expand the carrying capacity of the ecological territory. Chemical supplements to the diet of gazelles or the lion could reduce their food consumption rates. The fertility of gazelles can be enhanced, enabling them to produce more offspring. Other animals that do not depend on grass can be introduced into the ecosystem, and these can supplement the lion's diet. In other words, human creativity and ingenuity can be used to alter ecological relationships for the better. Extending this analogy, because cities represent the best products of human technology, they can also be made more sustainable.

Ecologists, of course, do not share this faith in human technological wizardry. To Overby (1985, 12), "the city is a node of pure consumption existing parasitically on an extensive external resource base." Likewise, Rees believes that "the maximum rate of resource consumption and waste discharge that can be sustained indefinitely in a given region without progressively impairing the functional integrity and productivity of relevant ecosystems" has already been exceeded many times, especially in cities of technologically advanced countries (Rees 1992, 125). Rees and his associates have calculated that the lifestyle of the average urban North American needs the equivalent of four to five hectares of land to continuously provide the resource inputs and assimilate the waste outputs of one person. By thus defining the "ecological footprint" of individuals, they estimate that the more than 6 billion people on earth, if they are to have the same lifestyle as North Americans, will require 24 billion hectares of land. Because there are only 8.8 billion hectares of land on Earth, Rees calculates that two additional Earths would be needed to sustain the world population at current North American urban consumption levels (Rees 1994).

It may be possible, of course, that not all human beings on earth will ever achieve the lifestyles of North Americans. Crops like rice, cassava, potatoes, and plantains, which are the staples in less developed countries, may not require as much land, water, fertilizer, and other inputs as the wheat, meat, dairy products, fruits, and vegetables that make up the bulk of the average North American diet. Miracle rice, genetically modified corn, and other technological breakthroughs promise to keep the human population adequately fed. Population control programs are reducing human pressures on natural resources. In many cities all over the world, innovations in transportation, water and sanitation, solid waste collection and disposal, recycling, and other environmentally friendly activities are being adopted. These technological advances should greatly expand the carrying capacity of cities.

The current situation in the cities of the developing world, however, does not allow for much optimism. Even the well-planned and efficiently governed city-state of Singapore, which is 100 percent urban, relies on Johore Bahru in Malaysia for its water supply and on Riau and Batam Island in Indonesia for food, industrial and manufacturing sites, sports, and leisure. The special administrative region of Hong Kong is heavily dependent on adjacent Guangdong province for water, food, energy, manufacturing and industrial space, waste disposal, and an assured supply of laborers, professionals, managers, entrepreneurs, and service providers. The other city-regions of Asia do not have the advantages of Hong Kong and Singapore, which are politically and administratively separate from their rural hinterlands. As such, these other city-regions are even less able to achieve self-sufficiency and sustainability, because they are so intimately linked to other parts of the nation-state that depend on them.

Similar problems confront mega-urban regions that aspire for social sustainability. To be sustainable, a city-region needs *social organization*—it must be able to achieve social cohesion and to bring together all actors and stakeholders in urban life into constructive debates and mutually advantageous actions to achieve the common good. As Friedmann stated, "Political communities come into existence as a result of voluntary decision by the members of a territory-based social group to peacefully resolve problems that rise to public attention." He likens this process to the "contract theory" of political community, whereby citizens need to agree to civilly deal with each other within acceptable "rules of the game" if they are to avoid the brutish nastiness of a Hobbesian world (Friedmann 1992, 74).

Some researchers argue that cities are not sustainable socially because they are not self-organizing units. Cities bring millions of people from varied backgrounds together and pack them at high densities within limited physical space. Living at such high densities brings about qualitative changes in social life that may have positive or negative effects. On the positive side, urbanism may erode primordial identities and weaken ties to institutions like the family, clan, or religious group, turning the individual into a free citizen and releasing him or her from selfish particularistic interests. This is what Aristotle meant when he said "City air makes man free." Conversely, by eroding these primary identities, urbanism may atomize an individual, drive him or her to a state of anomie, and create pressures that may cause personal and social disorganization. In place of the family, clan, or community, the city sets up bureaucratic structures—such as the police, law courts, counseling services, and welfare departments—that may efficiently provide basic services and impose social order.

However, these formal bureaucracies may treat individuals in impersonal and dehumanizing ways, causing antisocial tendencies and conflicts. Certainly, the positive and negative effects of urbanism are observable in the multiethnic and complex urban societies in Asia. The challenge to those who plan and govern cities is how to make sure that the positive rather than the negative aspects of urbanism predominate (Laquian 1994, 1996).

Friedmann attempts to deal with the issue of social sustainability by differentiating between what he calls *life space* and *political/administrative space.* The former is the "space of everyday domesticity, of residential households in their social relations with neighbors, friends, family and basic service providers." To Friedmann, it is the *primary space of social reproduction.* Political/administrative space, conversely, is the *primary space of governance.* It is usually a territory-based entity where economic activities, the operations of urban infrastructure, and governmental service provision occur. The secret to achieving social sustainability lies in merging these two spaces within what he calls "the city as a polity" (Friedmann 1998, 17).

Another dimension of sustainability focuses on the city as an *economic unit* of production and consumption. A number of researchers have proposed that a major problem in this area is the "dematerialization" of economic life and the separation of economic processes from physical realities. The new subdiscipline of ecological economics argues that the human economy depends on the finite biological, geological, and atmospheric processes on Earth. It proposes three main rules:

1. Human health requires that the quality of the habitat is maintained.
2. The rate at which resource inventories are degraded through use or abuse should not exceed the rate at which they are regenerated.
3. Wastes that contaminate ecosystems and squander resources should be limited or not generated at all.

In other words, economic activities in urban areas, despite the high productive capabilities possible within them, should be significantly limited. There are limits to growth. City economies that do not recognize the limits imposed by their physical and material environments will not be sustainable (Institute for Research on Environment and the Economy 1993, 13).

The main thing to remember in planning for the sustainability of human settlements is that environmental, economic, social, and political factors are all closely interlinked in the urban setting. Urban development is not linear; it occurs within a natural and human-built loop with finite boundaries set by the physical environment. As pointed out by Rees and Roseland, "strong sustainability has serious implications for the urban form, for the material basis of urban life, and for community social relationships that must be expressed as practical measures in planning" (Rees and Roseland 1998, 203). This calls for "proactive planning" and "positive governance" measures that will overcome the sociopolitical barriers to sustainable development and eventually make possible "an ecologically habitable, economically viable and politically secure world in the 21st century" (Rees 1998, 39).

Environmental Sustainability

The environmental sustainability of cities depends on a holistic approach that views a human settlement as a coherently integrated unit made up of people living in physical space, occupying a specific niche in nature, pursuing productive and consumptive activities, dealing effectively with the waste created by their activities, and achieving a harmonious way of life by ensuring equity, respecting human rights, and upholding social justice. As such, planning for a sustainable city requires a combination of policies dealing with agriculture and green space, land use, transport, water, sewerage and drainage, energy use and conservation, solid waste collection and disposal, and pollution control.

Although most Asian cities have policies and programs in each of these areas, it is not usual to find a comprehensive strategy that considers all these elements in a coherent way. There is a tendency to ignore the social need to maintain cooperation and harmony in social relationships in human settlements, creating social polarization that thwarts environmental policies. Also, in some cases, cities have formal statements incorporating strategies but do not have the capabilities to implement them. Often, there is confusion regarding what policies have to be carried out, what level of government will do what, where the resources will come from, and who will manage and coordinate the programs and projects.

Urban Agriculture, Greenbelts, and Open Space

The mega-urban regions of Asia contain vast tracts of open space on their peripheries devoted to natural habitat, forests, marshland, agricultural production, and nature reserves. Often, greenbelts have been used to limit the sprawl of the built-up area and to ensure that the city-region would have "lungs" for generating oxygen and absorbing the air pollution and other environmental degradation created by urban living. Watershed areas are being maintained to ensure sources of raw water, and wetlands and marshes are left undeveloped as recharge zones for rain and storm water runoff. Though the traditional planning approach is to keep the green space unspoiled and forested, some planners also consider agricultural areas as part of the green zone, because when fields are not paved over for urban uses they serve to absorb excess water and even urban waste.

As Asia's most markedly primate city, Bangkok has tried to control the urban sprawl that has been rapidly eating up rice-growing areas, vegetable plots, and orchards on the urban periphery. To achieve this, the Bangkok authorities proposed a development plan aimed at achieving a polynucleated urban region. The plan was never adopted or implemented, but it reflected key ideas and values that were dominant during the 1980s. As seen in figure 4.1, a horseshoe-shaped greenbelt had been drawn around the city's built-up area. The idea was to confine intensive urban development schemes within the greenbelt. In addition, the plan targeted development into densely populated urban nodes in Nakorn Pathom, Orm Noi, Bang Pakong, and Chachoengsao. It was hoped that concentrating development in the central city and these peri-urban areas would preserve the surrounding open space and conserve agricultural land. Despite this public effort to limit urban sprawl in Bangkok, however, urban development in the peri-urban areas has not been effectively controlled.

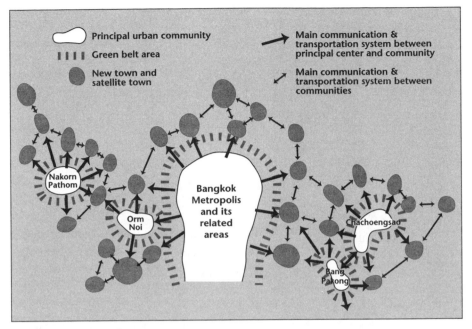

Figure 4.1. Spatial Strategy for Bangkok Metropolis
Source: NESDB (1991).

In the planning of big Chinese cities, it was common practice during the 1950s to encompass within the city-region agricultural areas that were designed to serve as the "food base" for the urban population. This socialist approach to urban planning, which was also practiced in Vietnam by the Viet Cong and in Laos by the Pathet Lao, saw guerrillas that conquered a city immediately setting up garden plots and food production activities, usually in peri-urban areas. In keeping with this approach, significant proportions of the populations of cities like Beijing, Guangzhou, Shanghai, and Tianjin were officially designated as agricultural. In these agricultural areas, perishable food items such as fresh vegetables and fruits, as well as poultry, meat, dairy, and other products, were produced and often brought directly to city markets by the farmers themselves. Fish, eels, turtles, and other food products were also produced in ponds or caught in nearby lakes and rivers.

During the 1990s, fourteen out of the fifteen largest cities in China were designated "eco-cities," which had their own farm belts and were largely self-sufficient in food. These cities were purposely zoned so that only 20 to

40 percent of their land area was actually built on and the rest was devoted to agriculture and open space. By keeping the city core compact, devoting the peri-urban areas to agriculture, and using the waste of the city as an input to agricultural production, China's eco-cities were designed to enhance economic and ecological sustainability (Ray 1998, 180).

In almost all Asian cities, the loss of agricultural land to urban uses has been a major problem. In China, the loss of agricultural land was particularly serious in the Yangtze River and Pearl River Delta regions. For example, a study using geographic information systems revealed that Dongguan, near Guangzhou in Guangdong province, lost 35 percent of its cropland to urban uses between 1988 and 1993 (Yeh and Li 1996, 195–222). The loss of agricultural land around Guangzhou is expected to accelerate if the Comprehensive City Plan for the metropolitan area formulated in 1994 is implemented. This plan projects that the urbanized area of the metropolis will expand from 335 square kilometers in 2000 to 555 square kilometers in 2010, based on the estimate that each permanent resident of the city-region would require 90 square meters and every temporary migrant would need 70 square meters for living and productive space. The additional space needed by this urban expansion will most likely come from agricultural land. Between 1980 and 1990, from 75 to 100 percent of the land requisitioned by the Guangzhou Municipal Government for urban use was former agricultural land (Taubmann 2002, 80–81; Yeh and Wu 1996, 333).

Similarly, in the Suzhou-Wuxi-Changzhou region in the Yangtze River Delta not too far from Shanghai, about 25,000 hectares of land were taken up by urban development between 1954 and 1988. Because of the "development zone fever" that swept the region in the early 1990s, 110 of the 116 townships in the region built industrial zones and high-technology parks. The water needs of these industrial developments greatly aggravated environmental problems. The excessive extraction of groundwater in the area has resulted in ground subsidence, estimated at about 1 meter since the 1950s. Also, about 23 percent of the cultivated land in the Tai Lake area has been polluted by industrial waste (Cui 1995, 252).

To control loss of agricultural land, many Chinese urban authorities have passed strict regulations limiting the conversion of agricultural land to urban uses. However, there have been frequent violations of such control measures, because land is practically the only resource that local officials can use to attract foreign and domestic investors. In some regions, the central government has imposed restrictions on the use of soil and the wanton cutting of trees for fuelwood for making earthen bricks. The practice continues, however, because China's massive construction boom has created high demand for bricks.

In the coastal regions of China, the temptation has been very strong to make money legitimately through land development schemes and illegitimately through the unauthorized conversion of agricultural land to urban uses. In these coastal areas, local officials have engaged in land speculation, withdrawing cropland from agricultural use, putting in some roads and drains, and then declaring the zones as commercial and industrial tracts. The loss of agricultural productivity from such schemes has been significant in Guangdong, Jiangsu, and Zhejiang provinces. Land conversion in these provinces has also created flooding problems as the cementing and paving over of agricultural land has resulted in massive runoff and insufficient storm water drainage.

Despite many difficulties, a number of city-region authorities in Asia have pursued successful programs to preserve green space and agricultural land to help achieve environmental sustainability. In the Beijing region, for example, a massive campaign started during the 1960s by the New People's Army, the Young Pioneers, and local volunteers to reforest the area using soft poplar, pine, willows, and other quick-growing tree varieties has created the "Green Great Wall," which has helped to reduce the massive dust storms that have plagued the country's capital for centuries.

The authorities have also improved agricultural practices in the Beijing region by allowing farmers, under the "production responsibility system," to plant what they consider to be appropriate crops, instead of blindly following the quotas that used to be imposed under the old commune system. Irrigation in the area has been vastly improved by lining irrigation canals with concrete and by using pipes and culverts to prevent the massive loss of water from seepage and evaporation. The use of greenhouses to produce vegetables during the winter season has enhanced agricultural productivity. At the same time, plastic-covered greenhouses have helped to reduce pressures on open agricultural land because they could be set up in infertile plots or hard-to-till hilly and rocky areas.

In other cities, various methods have been used to increase agricultural productivity and limit the conversion of agricultural land to urban uses. Traditional practices that used "night soil" as fertilizer have been revived in intensive agriculture areas in the Pearl River Delta to dispose of a leading source of environmental pollution and, at the same time, increase agricultural productivity. In Hanoi, the city's sewage has been used to fertilize rice fields. In Kolkata (formerly Calcutta), the sewage system also feeds into fishponds that provide city residents with a source of protein. In Bangkok, Dhaka, and Metro Manila, the composting of organic urban waste is a common source of agricultural fertilizer. The goal of most of these measures, of course, is the development of an integrated system whereby sustainability is enhanced by the use of urban waste as an input to urban agriculture.

One of the most challenging aspects of urban agriculture is how to use the waste of the city as an input to agricultural production. In most Southeast Asian mega-urban regions, in contrast to the technologically advanced cities of East Asia like Osaka, Seoul, and Tokyo, the solid waste from individual households tends to be "wet garbage" that includes fruit peelings, vegetable cuttings, and other kitchen waste. This type of garbage is well suited for composting. A very successful experimental project in Metro Manila carried out in the town of Marilao used the so-called NURTURE (Networking for Urban Renewal Through Urban Ecology) approach to encourage composting. As box 4.1 shows, success was made possible by cooperation between local citizens, who were helped by nongovernmental organizations and local government units.

One of the main problems faced by advocates of urban agriculture is the fact that many urban and regional planning approaches do not have a place for it, even in the formulation of comprehensive development plans. This is mainly due to the sharp conceptual distinction between urban and rural areas in traditional planning. The experience in Asia has shown that in the few cases that urban agriculture has been included in mega-urban regions' plans, it has usually been due to (1) the need to respond to food shortage emergencies, such as during wartime; (2) augmenting the income of poor residents living as squatters in peri-urban areas; (3) encouraging "grow and green" activities in city beautification campaigns; and (4) using solid waste as an input to urban agriculture.

It is interesting that during World War II, many urban dwellers in Metro Manila copied the "Victory Gardens" projects in the United States and planted vegetables in vacant city lots. The Chinese Communist Party, the Khmer Rouge in Cambodia, the Viet Cong in Vietnam, and the Pathet Lao in Laos all encouraged soldiers and partisans to plant vegetables and raise animals for food in the cities. When China sent engineers and laborers to Africa to build the Tanzania–Zambia railway, one of their most lasting contributions to the development of human settlements was the transformation

---

Box 4.1. *The NURTURE Project*

One of the most serious problems of Metro Manila is garbage disposal. The town of Marilao in Bulacan province, located near Metro Manila, has 15,000 households and 850 business firms that generate a lot of waste. However, almost all the garbage dumps in the Manila metropolitan area became full, and the residents of Marilao could not get rid of their garbage properly because officials in other local government units adamantly refused to open new dumps. In 1996, the citizens of Marilao, under the leadership of environmental nongovernmental organizations (NGOs) and with the support of the municipal government, launched the Networking for Urban Renewal Through Urban Ecology (NURTURE) project, which encouraged people to compost garbage and use it as fertilizer.

The NURTURE project was carried out by the Marilao Federation of Service Organizations, a network of seventy-five community-based organizations composed of religious groups, women's associations, labor organizations, and youth clubs. The NURTURE organizers decided to do things step by step. First, 500 households were approached to participate in the project. The NGOs and municipal officials conducted seminars and training programs on how to collect, sort, and compost garbage. After three months, another 400 households were included. Six months later, the number of participating households had increased to 2,000. In a year, all the 15,000 households in the municipality were actively involved in the project.

The main incentive provided by the municipal government and the NGOs was that people who sorted and put out their garbage in clearly marked containers would have their trash collected regularly at no cost to them. Useful items like plastics and glass were collected and sold separately. "Wet garbage" was taken to composting sites, where it was mixed with layers of agricultural by-products (hay, rice, and corn husks), and the resulting compost was sold to farmers.

The NURTURE project in Marilao has become a model for similar garbage composting efforts in the Philippines. The main lesson learned from the project is that the municipal government can tap the support of citizens, NGOs, and environmental activists in solving an environmental problem. The NURTURE project is an integral part of the development plan formulated and implemented by the Municipal Development Planning Council of Marilao. It also has the full support of the municipal government and the business sector.

Source: Duran (2001, 40–42).

---

of railway workstations into centers for vegetable production and pig- and poultry-raising projects.

A common feature of onsite slum-upgrading projects in Asian cities during the 1960s was vegetable gardening as a source of food for family consumption or for sale. In Bangkok, Jakarta, and Metro Manila, where urban space is at a premium, people have been encouraged to grow vegetables and other edible crops in pots, empty cans, and other containers. There are also projects that focus on raising ornamental plants, such as orchids, bonsai, and flowers, that command a higher price. At best, however, many of these efforts have only marginally improved the incomes of poor urban families. Besides, except in peri-urban squatter relocation sites, space for urban agriculture has been extremely limited, and even in these areas water shortages have been common, making vegetable gardening difficult.

The future challenge facing Asian mega-urban regions is how to make urban agriculture and green space integral parts of comprehensive urban and regional planning efforts. Happily, because of increased awareness among leaders and government officials of the need for environmental sustainability, planners are now becoming more amenable to including urban agriculture and conserving open space in urban development plans. Big metropolitan areas need watershed zones to ensure predictable water supply. Wetlands, marshes, and other water-absorbing places are needed to prevent flooding and allow for the recharging of groundwater aquifers. The need to make the city more beautiful and green certainly helps. The argument that urban agriculture augments the income of poor urban residents is a powerful one. The role of urban agriculture as a way of reusing and recycling urban waste as an input to agriculture makes scientific and ecological sense. Efforts to combine all these arguments within a sustainability program are achieving some degree of success in a number of Asian cities, but a great deal still has to be done to make planners and policymakers more aware of the need to include urban agriculture as a key element in planned sustainable development.

Energy

Asian mega-urban regions are prodigious consumers of energy for their production, consumption, transport, and leisure activities. Unlike their counterparts in Europe and North America, however, many Asian cities, particularly those in South Asia, do not use as much energy for industrial production or manufacturing. For example, a survey of energy use in Delhi between 1980 and 1990 showed that cooking food was the dominant area of energy use among low-income groups. About 47 percent of the total per capita energy consumed each year by low-income residents was for cooking. The majority of poor urban residents relied on wood, charcoal, and even dried cow dung for cooking.

These three sources of energy did not only have a low level of efficiency (about 52 percent); they also contributed to environmental pollution in the form of smoke, ashes, and harmful gases. Burning animal dung also de-

stroyed a good source of fertilizer. The reliance on fuelwood as a m
ergy source in Delhi has had a negative effect on the forest cover
cent areas. Satellite images showed that the forest cover within a 1Ou-kilo-
meter radius of Delhi was reduced by 60 percent between 1972 and 1982.
This loss was largely attributed to the use of fuelwood by urban poor people.
Burning wood and charcoal is also an important contributor to air pollution
in the city (Pachauri and Sen 1998, 169).

Among middle- and higher-income households where kerosene, liquid
petroleum gas, or electricity have been the main energy sources used for
cooking, energy efficiency has risen to about 63 percent. Though less
harmful to the environment than burning wood and charcoal, these "modern" sources of energy are relatively expensive. In shantytowns and slum
areas, these energy sources have also caused destructive fires. Other activities that consumed considerable amounts of energy among middle- and
higher-income households included lighting (17 percent), space cooling
(10 percent), water heating (5 percent), space heating (1 percent), and others (19 percent).

As the socioeconomic status of households goes up, the proportion of energy used for these activities also goes up. However, Indian urban authorities have adopted various measures to make energy use more efficient. For
example, shifting to fluorescent bulbs from incandescent bulbs could cut
electricity consumption. A typical 60-watt bulb could be replaced by a 20-
watt fluorescent bulb, saving electricity amounting to around 43 percent.
Using ceiling fans instead of air conditioners could mean a gain of more
than 17 percent. Refrigerators used in India have high energy consumption
and poor efficiency (a typical 165-liter Indian fridge consumes 540 kilowatt-hours per year, whereas a 200-liter Korean model consumes only 240
kilowatt-hours per year). Improving the quality of Indian-made refrigerators, therefore, would save a lot of energy (Pachauri and Sen 1998, 170).

As cities become larger in many Asian cities, they demand more and
more electrical energy. The main methods for generating electricity in many
Asian cities depend on fossil fuels, especially coal. Like Western industrial
cities before them that also relied on coal earlier in their development, many
Asian cities suffer from air pollution in the form of smoke haze and smog.
Smog produced by the burning of coal is often sulfurous and produces acid
rain, which contaminates lakes and rivers. Acid rain has also been associated with the loss of soil fertility because the acid rain's high concentration
of hydrogen ions accelerates the leaching of essential nutrients, making
them less available for plant use (Goude 1990, 299).

Although large hydroelectric projects that combine power generation, flood control, navigation, irrigation, and agricultural production have been criticized by many environmentalists, some Asian countries rely on them for energy generation. For example, China has gone ahead with the Three Gorges Dam project, which when finished in 2009 at an estimated cost of $24.6 billion (critics say the cost will most likely be in excess of $75 billion) will be the biggest such project in the world. The project is designed to generate 84 billion kilowatts of electricity a year when all its twenty-six 700-megawatt turbine generators are operational. Supporters of the dam claim that this will be the equivalent of the power generated by burning 36 million tons of coal, which would otherwise cause serious pollution in China. The project's reservoir (one and half miles wide, 600 feet high, holding 22.1 billion cubic meters of water) will "drown" more than 100 towns and 1,300 archaeological sites and force the resettlement of more than 1.2 million people. However, the official Three Gorges Web site claims that the project will provide about one-ninth of China's electrical production and will meet the industrial, manufacturing, and domestic power needs of more than 15 million people living in cities and towns along the Yangtze River.

Another source of energy that has been used to meet the needs of Asian mega-urban regions is nuclear generation. Part of the electricity for cities like Osaka, Seoul, and Tokyo comes from nuclear generation plants. Nuclear plants, however, are extremely expensive to build and operate. There have been very serious concerns about the safety of nuclear power plants, particularly after the Chernobyl and Three Mile Island incidents. Countries using nuclear generation plants have found it difficult to safely dispose of the plants' spent fuel rods, which are a definite environmental hazard. Also, after the September, 11, 2001, terrorist attacks on the United States and the widespread fear of global terrorism, deep concerns have been expressed about the security of nuclear generation plants.

To meet their energy needs, some Asian countries have explored alternative energy sources, such as natural gas, solar cells, volcanic geothermal plants, windmills, ethanol, hydrogen, methane, and small-scale hydroelectric plants. Metro Manila authorities have expressed great optimism for the development of the Malampaya Sound natural gas fields to provide energy for the Philippine capital region. The Philippine National Oil Company operates 60 percent of installed geothermal capacity all over the country and, through its Energy Development Corporation, plans to set up 40-megawatt wind farms in Northern Luzon. Innovative schemes have been proposed in China to manufacture more efficient solar panels as sources of electricity and for water-heating purposes (a joint-venture company in Shenzhen is using advanced research and development techniques to try to make solar more cost-competitive). Japanese carmakers have produced prototypes of electric vehicles and cars using hybrid engines.

In the past, in China's attempt to achieve economic development by developing energy sources of its own, nationwide campaigns were launched to set up small-scale hydroelectric projects and biogas digesters. Small-scale hydroelectric plants capable of generating 10,000 to 30,000 kilowatts were more manageable than large projects that took too long to build and were prone to cost overruns. Biogas digesters that relied on the controlled fermentation of plant and animal matter (i.e., crop residues, animal waste, and even excrement) in airtight pits became popular in China during the Great Cultural Revolution (1966–76). The digesters produced methane gas, which was used for cooking, lighting, and even running buses and farm vehicles at about half the cost of energy generated by small-scale hydroelectric plants. Digesters also had the additional benefits of not taking significant nutrients from the ecological cycle and of safely disposing of the harmful parasites found in human and animal waste (McDowell 1993, 191–92).

In general, many of the alternative sources of energy discussed in this section are suitable mainly for small-scale, autonomous, and decentralized urban settlements. Because they lack scale economies, they are not very practical as energy sources for large mega-urban regions. Because most Asian mega-urban regions have smaller urban nodes in peri-urban areas, however, these alternative energy sources may be able to play a role in a comprehensive energy strategy. If the mega-urban regions of Asia continue to develop in polynucleated patterns, local government units may find that these alternative fuel resources have a very important role.

Transportation

The transport sector exerts a significant influence on sustainability because it is a big user of energy as well as a major contributor to air and water pollution. A survey of energy use in thirty-eight countries (in the 1970s–90s) showed that the transport sector accounted for 29 percent of energy used, up from 24 percent in 1970. In terms of petroleum use, transportation took up 55 percent of total demand. Interestingly, the study showed that energy consumption per vehicle in Asian countries was significantly higher compared with consumption in North America. This was because Asia had wider use of low fuel-efficient vehicles, poor vehicle maintenance, small and narrow roads that contributed to traffic jams, inefficient traffic management, longer hours spent by vehicles in traffic, and higher road congestion (Foo 1998, 67).

To enhance sustainability by introducing improvements in the transport sector, Asian mega-urban regions have tried a number of measures, including (1) limiting the use of the private automobile, (2) the use of rapid transit systems, (3) planned concentrated development, (4) trip reduction and traffic regulation, (5) emission controls, and (6) encouraging walking and bicycle use.

Limiting Automobile Use

The private automobile has been blamed for encouraging urban sprawl, worsening traffic congestion, and increasing air and water pollution. One effective approach has been to make ownership and operation of cars very expensive. In 1974, Hong Kong introduced a first registration tax on the purchase of a private car and set the tax at 15 percent of the cost-insurance-freight (CIF) value. The annual license fee to operate a car was also increased threefold.

In December 1975, the Hong Kong government doubled the first registration tax on private vehicles. Before that date, the vehicle registration tax was not imposed on taxis and goods vehicles—these were now taxed at the same high rate. Despite these measures, however, car ownership in Hong Kong continued to increase because affluent citizens could afford expensive cars and car ownership was considered important for status and prestige. In 1982, therefore, the government raised the first registration tax to 70 to 90 percent of CIF value, depending on the type and price of the vehicle. It also tripled the annual license fee and doubled the tax on gasoline. These measures served to cut car ownership in Hong Kong somewhat—it was not until 1990 that car ownership exceeded the peak level set in 1982 (Hau 2001, 140).

Aside from imposing high taxes on car ownership and operation, the Hong Kong government tried an "area-licensing" scheme in 1983, similar to the one that had been used in Singapore between 1975 and 1998. In this system, entry into the central business district was allowed only upon payment of a significant fee. Later, Hong Kong decided to automate the system by introducing an experimental electronic road-pricing scheme in 1983–85. The experiment involved installing an electronic transponder in 2,500 vehicles that permitted radio wave communication, with electronic loops embedded below the road surface. Roadside microcomputers installed at selected charging points relayed the vehicle's identification code to a computer center, and the car owner was billed every month for the actual time spent on the road. Higher charges for road usage were imposed during peak morning and evening hours in three selected high-usage zones.

Despite the clear advantages of this road-pricing scheme, however, it was rejected by the Hong Kong public for three main reasons. First, people charged that the scheme was primarily designed to maximize the collection of revenue rather than reduce traffic congestion or prevent pollution. Second, the scheme was only applied to private cars, which brought about charges of class discrimination. Third, critics of the system were wary about the invasion of people's privacy, because the built-in transponders could be used to track and monitor people's movements. This third objection, however, was later dealt with by replacing the transponders with "smart cards" that stored specified amounts of money that were then used to automatically pay the electronic charges.

Rapid Transit Systems

One of the key issues in environmental sustainability is how to plan rationally for *urban density*. Studies have shown that "compact cities," where there is strong concentration of urban jobs in the city center, use relatively less energy. An efficient rapid transit system linking the central city to the suburbs discouraged commuting by car and resulted in reduced energy use. In European cities, 25 percent of all passenger travel was by public transport; 21 percent of people used bicycles or walked to work, 44 percent used cars, and the rest used other means (Hall 1994). Studies have found that European cities that rely more on rapid transit than the private automobile used less than one-fourth of the gasoline burned in North American cities (Newman and Kenworthy 1989).

The comprehensive transport strategy of Hong Kong places heavy rail transport at the top of preferred transport options because of the system's high capacity for moving people, low adverse effects on the environment, and efficiency of operation. In 2000, the Hong Kong government decided to invest HK$200 billion in a railway project over a fifteen-year period and set as specific goals putting 70 percent of the population and 80 percent of employment sites within walking distance of a rail station. The plan estimated that the share of rail in public transport patronage would increase from 30 percent in 2000 to 45 percent by 2015 (Yeh, Hills, and Ng 2001, 12).

In China, the government has also adopted a policy establishing public transport as the country's dominant transport mode. Rapid transit systems have been set up in Beijing, Shanghai, Guangzhou, and Tianjin. At the same time, however, China has embarked on massive highway construction, especially in the rapidly growing coastal provinces (total road traffic in Guangdong has grown at an average rate of 20 to 30 percent a year since 1980). However, while road building in China has grown at the rate of 12 percent a year, the number of vehicles has been growing annually by 15 percent. The domestic automobile industry in China has been encouraged by government incentives. Though the Chinese automobile industry produced only 129,000 cars and trucks in 1979, it is estimated that by 2015, the Chinese vehicle fleet will reach 70 million motorcycles, 30 million trucks, and 100 million cars (Yin and Wang 2000).

At the United Nations Conference on Environment and Development held in Rio de Janeiro on June 13 and 14, 1992, China agreed to abide by the Rio Declaration, especially Agenda 21, which is a comprehensive plan of action to be taken at the global and national government levels. Every year, each country that has agreed to the plan submits information to the UN Commission on Sustainable Development on how it is implementing Agenda 21. In China's 2002 submission, it indicated that it could not afford to import large quantities of oil or allocate more land to build more highways if it was to achieve sustainable development.

In spite of the increasing use of rapid transit in a number of Asian cities, the sustainability of large mega-urban regions is far from assured. In Bangkok, the launching of Skytrain service in 1999 did not really significantly reduce heavy reliance on private automobiles. A major reason for this is the fact that the transit lines do not yet extend to the main suburban residential areas and there is limited parking space near the stations to encourage "park-and-ride" commuting. Many Bangkok Skytrain riders also think the fares are too high. The elderly and the infirm complain that many stations do not have escalators and elevators. Thus, a significant number of Bangkok people still rely on the two-stroke gasoline-powered *tuk tuks* to get around, especially in narrow lanes. There has also been a proliferation of motorcycle taxis, despite the fact that they emit more than ten times the amount of fine particulate matter per kilometer than a modern car and only a little less than a light diesel truck (World Bank 2002b).

Concentrated Development and Densification

One approach that has been found to enhance environmental sustainability in Asian cities is to concentrate people's residences, jobs, civic functions, entertainment, and lcisure activities in reasonably self-contained compact areas. During the 1950s and 1960s, Chinese work units (*danwei*) provided housing, schools, health clinics, and other services in compounds adjacent to the workplace. In case there was not enough room for housing within the work compound, a planning rule of thumb was that a worker should not live more than 30 minutes away by walking or taking a bicycle. After 1979, when many factories were moved to suburban areas, housing was also provided close to the workplace. In cases where jobs had to remain in the inner city, workers were fetched by bus from suburban apartment complexes that were designed to have community centers, shopping areas, and entertainment venues.

Concentration and densification were also followed in the establishment of industrial and housing estates in Hong Kong, Kuala Lumpur, Singapore, and southern China. The design of these industrial and residential enclaves has given a great deal of attention to self-containment and autonomy. Although the industrial and residential estates were often connected to the central city and other urban places by transit systems, the majority of their residents could live comfortably within the enclaves. In Bangkok and Hong Kong also, transit authorities have concentrated residential, commercial, and manufacturing activities around rapid transit stations. In this way, when residents have to go outside their communities, they can use the rapid transit system instead of private cars.

Some Asian planners have noted that, in general, there has been reduced commuting between suburbs and the central city in North America. The problem, however, is that the number of trips between suburban centers has tended to increase and most of these trips have been by automobile. Another problem is that people are also taking more non-work-related trips (for shopping, entertainment, leisure), and most of these are being made by car (Hall 1992). Asian urban and regional planners, therefore, have been advocating the use of rapid transit linking the central city to suburbs. They have also proposed building densely populated regional town centers, where people could work, live, and have direct access to shopping, services, and entertainment and not have to commute to the central city.

Trip Reduction and Other Regulations

Direct methods to reduce the number of urban trips that people take and to change traveling patterns and behavior have been used in Asian mega-urban regions to minimize air pollution. In Metro Manila, a system of "number coding" private vehicles has been introduced, whereby vehicles with license plates ending in an even number are allowed only on certain days and those ending in an odd number on other days. Despite the efforts of some car owners to foil this system (rich people just bought at least two cars and made sure each one had the right-numbered license plate), the measure did cut the volume of traffic.

In Bangkok and Manila, the volume of traffic, which tended to get really jammed during "zero hours" (6:00 to 9:00 AM; 4:00 to 7:00 PM), was reduced by various measures. Offices, banks, and schools were asked to introduce "flexible hours," whereby employees and laborers were given the opportunity to travel outside the heavy traffic time zones. Movie theaters, shopping centers, and markets were also asked to open at different times of the day so as to stagger trips and not concentrate travel during rush hours.

In Singapore, vehicle entry into the inner city has been restricted. Vehicle owners who wanted to enter the inner city had to pay a hefty sum for a license. Parking for vehicles in the inner city was also limited, with the few parking spaces available charging heavy fees. These restrictive regulations were softened a bit by the urban authorities providing suburban park-and-ride facilities, where suburban commuters could leave their vehicles and take free buses into the inner city. Singapore is also well served by taxis, buses, and other forms of transit.

Emission Controls

The Philippine government passed the Clean Air Act of 1999, and the law's provisions on emission controls went into effect in February 2003. Under the law, all vehicles operating in city streets have to be tested in Air Care Centers, and they must show certificates that their emissions are within legal limits. Similar laws had been in force in Hong Kong and Singapore for years. In fact, during the 1970s, Singapore banned the use of eight-cylinder cars on its roads, effectively storing one of the highest concentrations of Rolls-Royce cars on the planet in luxury garages.

The Use of Bicycles

Chinese cities like Beijing, Guangzhou, Shanghai, and Tianjin relied heavily on the bicycle during the 1950s and 1960s as an efficient and environmentally friendly mode of transport. To encourage people to use bicycles, the government, with the support of employers and work units, provided sizable subsidies to make these vehicles affordable. Special bicycle lanes were marked on city streets. Inexpensive and well-managed bicycle parking places were maintained in specific zones. There were even community-run repair facilities operated on a voluntary basis to help people keep their bicycles in good operating condition. The government entered into joint ventures with foreign bicycle manufacturing companies like Raleigh to improve the quality of local bicycles.

Despite these efforts to encourage the use of bicycles, however, there has been a steady decline in bicycle use in most big Chinese cities. As urbanites become more affluent, they are aspiring to own a car, or at least a motorcycle. Chinese urban authorities, unlike their Vietnamese counterparts, have managed to limit the number of motorcycles licensed to operate on city streets. However, the demand for private cars is increasing. The rate of car ownership in China is still low, about ten per 1,000 persons in 1999, but of the vehicles sold in the country in that year, about half were for private use, compared with only 10 percent in 1998 (Yin and Wang 2000, 165).

Certain approaches now used in North American and European cities, however, can be adapted to Asian conditions to encourage people to use bicycles. These include (1) designation of bicycle lanes in city streets; (2) providing secure places for bicycle parking; (3) making it possible for bicycle riders to take their bikes on buses and rapid transit vehicles; (4) introducing "pay-and-ride" schemes (as in Copenhagen), whereby individuals can use public bicycles in specified zones for a modest fee; (5) encouraging private industry to manufacture more efficient bicycles, as well as helmets, clothes, reflectors, and other accessories that make bicycle riding safe; and (6) encouraging workplaces to install shower facilities for staff members using their bikes. Public information and mass media campaigns can be used to highlight the positive environmental and health effects of bicycle use. Planners can also encourage more people to ride bicycles by designing more compact cities where workplaces and service sites are more accessible to cyclists.

Industry and Manufacturing

A major source of environmental sustainability problems are the manufacturing and industrial processes in many Asian cities. The location of industrial sites, types of technology used, the lack of environmental control enforcement measures, and patterns of energy use all have a direct impact on the environment. In China, for example, an old policy to transform consumption-oriented cities to productive ones has encouraged the growth of heavy industries within city boundaries. Since the return to consumption orientation after the launching of economic reforms in 1979, there have been more efforts to locate industry and manufacturing to peri-urban areas and to redevelop inner-city zones for offices, financial services, trade and commerce, residence, and leisure and entertainment.

The development of Shanghai illustrates the environmental impact of industrial and manufacturing policies. At the time the Communists took over China in 1949, about 86.4 percent of Shanghai's gross industrial output (GIO) was contributed by textiles and other types of light industry. Only 13.6 percent came from heavy industries like iron and steel. Between 1958 and 1960, during the disastrous Great Leap Forward campaign, about 60.2 percent of GIO in Shanghai was contributed by heavy industries and only 39.8 by light industries. The failure of the Great Leap Forward resulted in a reduction of investments in heavy industries, but during the Great Cultural Revolution (1966–76), investment in heavy industries went up again, to account for 53.4 percent of GIO. When China's economic reforms were launched in 1979, urban authorities found that Shanghai had become the "rust belt" of Chinese industry, with technologically outmoded machinery and processes, decaying buildings, poorly trained workers and managers, and inadequate transportation and communication facilities. The worst conditions were found in state-owned enterprises, many of which were later allowed to go bankrupt (Mok 1996, 200–205).

Of the major contributors to environmental pollution in Shanghai, the most important one was industry, which in 1993 contributed 90 percent of gaseous emissions and 60 percent of liquid discharges. Coal used to be the main source of energy in industrial production, and the volume used increased at 10 percent per year. Industries in Shanghai, as a result, contribute 81 percent of total sulfur dioxide and 78 percent of particulate emissions a year. Heavy industry is also a significant contributor to water pollution, because only 85 percent of effluent is treated before being pumped into rivers and streams (Lam and Tao 1996, 474–75).

One of the measures used by Shanghai authorities to help make the city more sustainable was the rejuvenation of its industrial and manufacturing base. Under the First Five-Year Plan (1953–57), heavy industries were concentrated in four industrial satellite cities (Beixinjing, Pengpu, Qingningshi, and Zhoujiadu). In 1958, twelve more industrial satellite cities were built on the urban periphery. After 1979, the Chinese government set up four special economic zones (SEZs) in the Shanghai region: (1) the Minhang

Economic and Technological Development Zone, devoted to light industry; (2) the Hongqiao Economic and Technological Development Zone, focused on financial services, hotels, foreign residences, retail services, and tourism; (3) the Caohejing New Technology Zone, devoted to electronics, fiber-optic communication, biochemical industries, and computer software; and (4) the Pudong New Area, made up of four subzones devoted to high-technology industries, free trade, port facilities, and financial services. In these development schemes, the Shanghai authorities drastically changed the nature of manufacturing and industry in the city-region. More important, they also located the industrial enclaves in SEZs that were designed to be environmentally sustainable (Lam and Tao 1996, 478–79).

Solid Waste Management

Urban activities create waste, defined as materials left over after productive use or things that could no longer be utilized for the purpose for which they were meant. The authorities traditionally classify waste as domestic or household, institutional, commercial, industrial, or hospital/clinical. It could also be classified as organic (biodegradable) or inorganic, dry, or wet. For example, classified according to source, municipal solid waste in Dhaka was found to be 49.1 percent residential, 20.8 percent commercial, 23.8 percent industrial, and 7.2 percent hospital/clinical. By composition, about 59.9 percent of the waste was food and vegetable matter; 17.6 percent was plastic, rubber, wood, or leather; 11.2 percent was paper; 8.7 percent was garden cuttings; 2.3 percent was rock, dirt, and debris; and 0.15 percent was metal (Islam and Shafi 2004).

Most Asian cities have both formal and informal waste collection and disposal systems. However, many of these systems are woefully inadequate. For example, Metropolitan Jakarta produces about 21,894 cubic meters of solid waste per day. This waste is about 73.9 percent organic matter and 26.1 percent inorganic. Only 17,874 cubic meters of waste per day (82 percent) is hauled away to three dumpsites and sanitary landfill sites. The remaining waste ends up in rivers and canals, in empty lots, or on the roadside.

A number of systems have been used to collect and dispose of urban solid waste. In Japanese cities, households are required to sort their garbage before sending it out for disposal. Materials are separated according to specific categories, and transparent plastic bags are used to enforce household-level sorting. Garbage is divided into (1) combustible items (to go to the incinerator; e.g., soiled paper, kitchen waste, filmy plastic, and unusable wood);

(2) recyclables (glass, metal, paper); (3) hazardous waste (batteries and items containing mercury or cadmium); or (4) landfill materials (broken ceramic items, construction debris). The collection of solid waste is either done house-to-house by the municipal sanitation service or people take it to collection stations. Voluntary groups collect recyclable materials and sell these to dealers. About 68 percent of combustible waste is incinerated, and only 10 to 20 percent is sent to landfill sites. However, the residue from incinerators, which has a high content of toxic waste, has to be disposed of in concrete boxes that have to be buried elsewhere. Sanitary landfills are used for raw waste materials, and these are lined with impermeable materials to prevent leaching into the soil or water aquifers.

In many Asian cities, organized groups of scavengers sort out the garbage and collect useful items. These scavengers can be classified into three specific types. First, there are itinerant waste buyers, who go from house to house to buy items like old newspapers, empty bottles, aluminum cans, and pieces of metals. Second, there are pushcart scavengers, who recover useful things from roadside garbage bins. Third, there are organized waste pickers, who work in alliance with municipal sanitation personnel, who sort out items at the temporary garbage station or the city dump. All these scavengers and recyclers sell their recovered items to retailers and wholesalers, who then bring them to manufacturers, bottlers, and other users.

Despite this degree of organization, the collection and disposal of solid waste in many Asian cities leads to many unsustainable practices. For one, the collection of waste from low-income areas is often a huge problem. Most of these communities are not accessible by road, so the garbage trucks have to collect the waste on the area's periphery. Rather than take their garbage to the temporary waste collection station, many people simply throw it anywhere. Because many low-income communities are located near rivers and canals, these places become the dumps for the residents. In a study of solid waste disposal in low-income settlements in Bandung and Jakarta, it was found that although the municipal waste collection agencies provided garbage containers on the edge of the communities, many *kampung* dwellers found it too cumbersome to take their garbage to these collection points. They also objected to the garbage collection charges imposed by the companies and the city (Argo 1999).

Even in communities served by garbage collection services on accessible streets, people engage in traditional practices that lead to unsanitary conditions. Households take out their garbage in uncovered receptacles or untied bundles, allowing stray animals to scatter them about. Even in the exclusive subdivisions of Makati City in Metro Manila, the city government found it difficult to sell the color-coded garbage bags that were meant to sort garbage by type. In other communities, people do not sort out their garbage, so even human and animal waste, dead animals, and other smelly and dangerous items are dumped into the garbage bins. Though some cities have rules and regulations imposing fines for illegally disposing of garbage, these are rarely enforced. Municipal garbage trucks are often old and dilapidated and, when they break down, garbage collection schedules go awry. There is also considerable corruption in the handing out of garbage collection contracts to private entrepreneurs, leading to inefficient services. Finally, most garbage dumps are unlined or untreated, thus becoming a source of soil and groundwater pollution.

There are plans in a number of Asian cities to install recycling and composting facilities that will make solid waste collection and disposal more sustainable. However, the high cost of such facilities hinders their implementation. Surprisingly, however, a number of municipal governments have shown deep interest in integrated incineration equipment, which would also generate electricity, produce landfill materials, and heat buildings. In some instances, this interest may be generated more by the commissions and kickbacks that foreign suppliers will give to local officials than the effectiveness or efficiency of the systems.

Economic Sustainability

Much of the rapid growth of mega-urban regions in Asia is based on progress in industry, manufacturing, financial markets, and infrastructure investments. Typically, investments are concentrated in already-congested urban centers. The ideology and policies that govern investments are influenced by unequal access to and control over financial and natural resources. Basically, a small urban elite has a disproportionate share of these resources. They naturally concentrate investments in one or a limited number of urban places that they dominate.

During the colonial period and immediately after achieving independence, most Asian countries depended on agriculture and extractive industries for their prosperity. Primary industries like timber, mining, oil, and the export of cash crops thrived. The profits from these enterprises made urban-based elites rich and powerful. The economic elites exercised monopolies and other schemes to concentrate authority and power within their hands.

In time, however, the industrial client countries found cheaper substitutes or the exploited resources ran out.

In the 1950s, most urban industrial investments went to "import-substitution" industries that were often little more than repackaging plants for imported goods. The policies governing these investments made privileged members of the elite even richer, because the important element in the system was not what items were to be produced but who could get access to scarce foreign funds (e.g., interest-free loans, war damage reparations). Other aspects of the program (duty-free import privileges, tax exemptions, import quotas, export licenses) were also concentrated in the hands of a few in a system that has been called "crony capitalism."

Because the economic enterprises thrived not because of the dictates of the market but on acquired privileges, many of the Asian companies set up during the 1950s were very inefficient. Many "infant industries," classified variously as "new and necessary" or "protected enterprises," paid little attention to plant location, technological innovations, managerial improvements, or labor relations. These were unnecessary, because high profits were assured by the simple fact of access to privilege. Naturally, when the era of high levels of international assistance ended, most of these industries went bankrupt, and the cities they were located in faced extremely hard times.

In the 1960s, sources of investments in industry and manufacturing in Asia shifted from North America and Europe alone to also include the more technologically advanced countries in the region, such as Japan, Singapore, South Korea, and Taiwan. Most of these investments went to very big cities because of their need for professional and technical personnel, better communication and information facilities, good safety and security for expatriate staff, and an emphasis on more comfortable lifestyles. In some instances, enterprises were established outside the metropolitan areas because of a desire to be close to raw material sources, better energy supplies, more efficient transport facilities, and the like. Of particular importance were special economic zones, export-processing zones, and high-technology parks, which were set up 50 to 100 kilometers from large metropolitan areas.

The information revolution that now influences urban growth patterns in Asia has made possible the building of regional cities. Investment in such cities had been tried in the past in efforts to create "growth centers" or "growth poles," but the heavy costs of infrastructure, the centralized nature of government bureaucracies, and difficulties related to keeping highly trained staff and their families in small cities far from the metropolis led to many failures. Now, concentrating investments in special economic zones is producing positive economic results.

Unfortunately, in China, because special economic zones are strictly separated from provincial or municipal jurisdictions, they are having limited beneficial impact on adjacent areas. Managers and workers in SEZs are provided with good housing and amenities inside the zones, but the "floating population" attracted to the zones live in makeshift dwellings outside the SEZ perimeters, and they sometimes engage in illegal activities such as gambling and prostitution.

In the former American military bases of Clark and Subic Bay in the Philippines, which have been turned into exclusive SEZs, the thousands of workers that commute daily from their homes in Olongapo City and nearby towns have to fend for themselves while foreign investors and their families live in well-serviced communities inside the former bases. The hotels and restaurants inside the SEZ prefer to buy their meat, poultry, dairy products, and fruits and vegetables from California and other parts of the United States, instead of encouraging Filipino farmers to produce them in nearby areas. As in the olden days, when the SEZs were military bases, the sex industry in the towns and cities near the bases has flourished.

In her study of global cities, Sassen attributed the growth of very large urban agglomerations to the altered nature of the world economy, the accelerated industrialization of a number of countries in the developing world, and the rapid internationalization of the financial industry into a worldwide network of transactions. Because of these changes, Sassen has argued that the role of major cities has changed. Whereas such cities were once primarily centers for industry, manufacturing, international trade, and banking, they have now become (1) command points in the organization of the world economy; (2) key locations for finance and specialized service firms; (3) sites of production, including the production of innovations; and (4) markets for the products and innovations produced (Sassen 1991, 3–4). These economic changes, in turn, have altered the spatial organization and social structure of large cities as well as their governmental structures and functions.

Future changes in the size and shape of Asian mega-cities will probably take the form of expanded mega-urban regions. Interestingly, even as the global importance of the mega-city will probably lead to a greater concentration of authority and power in the hands of a few, innovations in the information technology field will make it possible for decision points to be decentralized. Manufacturing and industrial production processes will be driven to peri-urban areas or, in the case of Hong Kong and Singapore, even to zones outside the formal political boundaries of the country. Japan and South Korea, in fact, have tended to invest more in offshore enterprises because of higher land costs at home, expensive labor, strict pollution abatement and control measures, more efficient transportation and communication facilities, and other factors.

There are those who believe that the sustainability of mega-urban regions may be enhanced by this tendency toward decentralization. If the main element in planning and management is the communication of ideas and the making of quick decisions (so-called just-in-time delivery), then the increasingly digitized world of information technology will make dependence on a specific place less important. Mega-urban regions can be planned as multiple nodes linked together by communication networks. Communication between citizens and officials can be made efficiently, enhancing dialogue and greater participation in decision making. The need to move ideas rather than objects around will make the mega-urban region less subject to problems of pollution and congestion as frictionless planning and governance becomes possible. In the brave new world of the third millennium, the tyranny of place will be conquered, and mega-urban regions will become the natural pollution-free habitat of urban citizens.

The dark shadow that looms over the brave new world of Asian cities, however, is made up of millions and millions of poor citizens who share the mega-urban regions with urban elites. The economic shifts from primary, secondary, and tertiary industries do not necessarily denote improvements in the economic life of cities. Growing alongside these shifts has been the rapid expansion of the so-called popular sector, which is made up of petty trading, unskilled physical labor, paratransit enterprises, and a variety of semilegal or even illegal activities in cities, such as those in South Asia. In Jakarta and Manila, for example, more than three-fourths of the food consumed by people daily is said to be channeled through hawkers, vendors, and itinerant peddlers. In Delhi, Dhaka, Mumbai (formerly Bombay), and Karachi, many commuters depend on two- or three-wheeled paratransit vehicles operated by individuals who can barely keep their vehicles properly maintained. After the Chinese government relaxed rules on internal migration in 1984, more than 100 million peasants moved to cities and found jobs as noodle vendors, shoe repairers, carpenters, barbers, manicurists, domestics, and others in the so-called informal sector. The economic sustainability of mega-urban regions in East, South, and Southeast Asia, therefore, will be strongly determined by the extent to which these poor people can be absorbed into the labor force and allowed to earn a decent living.

Social Sustainability

The big city brings together a large number of people with their ethnic, religious, linguistic, racial, educational, social class, and occupational identities. Living at high densities, these people compete or cooperate with each other, singly or in groups, to achieve their personal or communal objectives. As social animals, they learn to interact with each other and control the tensions and animosities that competition creates. They establish social institutions for group decision making (neighborhood committees, community councils, city governments). They create instruments for social control (neighborhood watch associations, local police forces). They arrive at the conclusion that an urban polity will be sustainable only to the extent that it enjoys the continued support of its citizens.

In theory, urbanism as a way of life supports and accelerates this sense of social cohesion and solidarity in large cities. The separation of residence and workplace in the city erodes the customary autonomy of family life that has been a feature of rural life for millennia. A person's separation from nature in the human-built city also erodes autonomy. People need to get along well—in fact, they have to cooperate well with each other to survive amid the growing anonymity of urban society. In the process of "becoming urban," most formerly rural people naturally coalesce into primary-group communities to ease their transition to city life. This is the basis of the strong spirit of cooperation among the residents of *kampungs, barangays, panchayats,* and *hutongs* in Asian cities.

In many Asian cities, policymakers and administrators have consciously used the ethnic heterogeneity of big city populations as a way of molding an urban image that is larger than individual ethnic identities. For example, Greater Jakarta and Metro Manila have mini–theme parks extolling the ethnic mix that make up their metropolitan populations. Xi'an, China's old Tang Dynasty capital, has a vibrant Muslim community focused on an ancient mosque. Metro Manila has a Muslim village, Singapore has an Arab Street, and practically all the big Asian cities have their ubiquitous Chinatowns. With a few exceptions, big cities in Asia manage to maintain social harmony. They have attempted to bridge ethnic differences in their efforts at economic modernization, political mobilization, consensus seeking, and nation building (Laquian 1996, 43).

As a city grows very large, however, it tends to become more complex and, at the same time, more centralized. Municipal or city bureaucracies are created to deal with urban problems—such as access to clean water, improved mobility, collecting and disposing of solid waste, and so on—that little communities are not able to provide for themselves. As Friedmann has observed, however, political and administrative centralization creates social problems such as communication overload, long response times, and the distortion of information—"administrative pathologies" that get in the way of efficient decision making. Officials of centralized structures also tend to become less responsive to local demands because they do not want to be bothered with particularistic pressures that they tend to see as overly selfish. They may also start regarding local requests as political threats to their authority and power. They may eventually resort to repression or use brute force, which inevitably results in a loss of legitimacy and social sustainability (Friedmann 1992, 81).

Another threat to social sustainability is the growing polarization between a small economic and social elite and the great masses of poor urban citizens. The big and increasingly widening gap between the elite and mass populations of Asian mega-urban regions at present poses the most important challenge to urban sustainability. In Delhi, Dhaka, Jakarta, Karachi, Kolkata, Manila, and Mumbai, the elites reside in exclusive, well-guarded "gated communities," where they enjoy a lifestyle not too different from that of North American or European cities. These enclaves of luxury, however, exist as isolated islands in a sea of slums and squatter shanties that make up from a quarter to more than half of the total housing stock.

Studies have shown that the residents of these poor urban communities are not revolutionaries—in fact, they aspire to the same lifestyles as the rich for themselves or their children. They use their numbers to exact services from the government, especially during elections. They sacrifice to give their children an education in the hope that this will serve as the escalator to upward mobility. They see the burgeoning city and dream about their future role in it. Increasingly, the sustainability of Asian cities will depend on whether those dreams are realized or not.

In almost all Asian mega-urban regions at present, decentralization programs have been introduced. In some cases, decentralization was a condition under the "structural adjustment" regimes that the World Bank and other international financial agencies imposed on debt-ridden developing countries. In others, it was the result of genuine efforts on the part of neoliberal leaders desirous of achieving a democratic way of life. A common fault of many decentralization schemes, however, is the tendency to delegate authority and power to the lowest levels of government. In the Philippines, for example, this would be the *barangay;* in Thailand, the *tambon;*

and in Indonesia, the *kampung*. The *barangay* is a community of roughly a hundred families occupying a street or neighborhood. Under Philippine legislation, it is charged with setting up livelihood projects, maintaining health, supporting nursery and primary schools, helping to maintain peace and order, and the like.

To enable it to do these tasks, the *barangay* council receives a share of internal revenue allotments from the central government and is also allowed to impose local taxes, impose charges and fines, solicit voluntary contributions, and collect charges for services rendered. As worthwhile as these legislative mandates are, experience has shown that the powers of the *barangay* officials are virtually useless because the small social unit just does not have the resources to sustain its existence. The same situation has been found to be true in Indonesian *kampungs*. Here, the situation is made even worse by the further subdivision of the *kampung* into smaller units, such as the *rukun warga* and the *rukun tetanga*. The main usefulness of these smaller units lies in their role as venues for discussing public issues and in mobilizing community resources in support of mutual-help activities pursuant to the traditional practice of *gotong royong*. They serve as excellent instruments for mobilizing local labor or for financing local efforts. But in the long run, they tend to elicit more resources from the people rather than serve as vehicles for receiving resources from higher levels of government.

Civil Society and Social Sustainability

One of the fastest growing elements of the urban political and governance processes in many Asian cities are nongovernmental organizations (NGOs). The rise of these organizations had originally been rooted in the efforts of poor people to gain access to housing and basic urban services; in the struggle to achieve social equity and social justice; in efforts to protect the rights of groups like women, children, poor urban residents, and refugees; and in work to conserve and protect the environment. It is interesting to note that the number of NGOs in a country rapidly increases during times of political turmoil. In Thailand, for example, the student uprising in 1973 and the May 1992 revolution saw the birth of many people's organizations, including a number of radical ones. In the Philippines, the two decades of dictatorship under the late President Ferdinand Marcos witnessed the birth of many NGOs as well.

Many efforts to strengthen NGOs have been supported by international programs. In the Philippines, 40 percent of the total assistance of the Canadian International Development Agency was earmarked for NGOs. In many other countries, international assistance to NGOs has been motivated by democratic objectives and good governance. In others, international donors have preferred to channel their assistance through NGOs because of widespread corruption in the government. This practice, of course, has not endeared NGOs to government agencies, because they are seen as critical, confrontational, challenging, or even subversively threatening to government sovereignty.

One of the key issues in urban social sustainability is the extent to which NGOs and various community-based organizations may be able to organize so that they can translate their numbers into organized action. During the 1998 presidential elections in the Philippines, a conscious effort was made by supporters of President Joseph Ejercito Estrada to mobilize poor people. Estrada's political party, the Partido ng Masang Pilipino (Party of the Philippine Masses), used an unabashedly "propoor" strategy during the campaign. Alongside the party, a mass movement called JEEP (Movement for Justice, Economy, Environment, and Peace) brought together activist cause-oriented groups, civic associations, community organizations, youth clubs, women's groups, and others. Though it cannot be said that the participation of NGOs and community-based organizations was responsible for the electoral victory of Estrada, it cannot be denied that they helped tremendously in the campaign. It is worth noting also that, when the abuses of the Estrada administration became apparent, civil society groups played a key role in throwing him out of office in 2001 (Laquian and Laquian 2002).

In South Asian cities, civil society groups, such as the Self-Employed Women's Association in India, have been active in poverty alleviation programs, and in carrying out projects involving microcredit schemes, environmental conservation, solid waste recycling, and the like. In the Philippines, an NGO supported by an international network belonging to Couples for Christ has launched housing projects for urban poor people. Organized groups such as the Asian Coalition on Housing Rights have been active at the local and international levels for years, advocating projects that benefit urban poor people. All these efforts have played important roles in enhancing social sustainability in Asian cities.

Analysts of political development in Asia pin their hopes on the emergence of a middle class that might challenge the extremes of elite rule on the one hand and the mass-based "tyranny of the majority" on the other that seem to characterize Asian urban politics. They look to civil society to spearhead such a development. They are hoping that a civil society–led middle class might be able to influence elections so that more qualified leaders can be elected to political office.

However, with possible exceptions, such as the Asian tiger economies and China, economic development in Asia is moderate at best. Labor-exporting countries like Bangladesh, Pakistan, the Philippines, and Sri Lanka are losing potential members of the middle class to emigration. Even in China, with its continuing high rates of economic growth, there is a danger that an underclass of people made up mainly of rural–urban migrants who have joined the "floating population" converging on areas of rapid growth is emerging. Therefore, the emergence in Asian cities of a civil society–led middle class that can help achieve social sustainability might take a long time.

Achieving Sustainability through "Smart Growth"

While many planners agree that mega-urban regions in Asia are not sustainable under current patterns of energy use, resource consumption, and lifestyles, they aspire to make city-regions sustainable by adhering to policy recommendations that parallel those made by so-called smart growth advocates in North America. The policy recommendations encompassed by smart growth include (1) concentrating developments in selected areas at very high densities; (2) preserving open space, farmland, natural beauty, and critical environmental areas; (3) setting up polynucleated or multinodal human settlements in a regional context; (4) providing a variety of transport options; and (5) involving citizens, civil society groups, the private business sector, and governmental agencies in the formulation, adoption, and implementation of smart growth policies and strategies (Smart Growth Network 2003).

Many Asian cities have already concentrated urban development in high-density nodes. The inner cities of Bangkok, Delhi, Hong Kong, and Mumbai have some of the highest densities in the world. High-density living has achieved a great deal of efficiency in energy use. It has cut down on the need for travel by locating people's residences close to their places of work, shopping, and entertainment. The planning of such high-density urban centers has favored mixed land uses, resulting in more social interaction and a stronger sense of community. Planning has also been characterized by greater flexibility and a more responsive use of zoning codes, planning regulations, land use control laws, and the application of building standards.

Most important of all, despite their huge populations, many Asian cities have been able to plan at the proper human scale both from the point of view of urban design and for political and administrative purposes.

A serious problem for inner cities, however, is the deterioration of old houses, physical structures, and infrastructure systems. Happily, in the cities of China, Vietnam, and other countries, the redevelopment of inner-city areas is not taking the form of "destroy-and-build" urban renewal that dislocates people and separates their residences from their workplaces. Though a proportion of inner-city residents has been relocated to the suburban areas of Beijing and Shanghai, for example, these mega-cities' redevelopment plans provide for keeping the housing stock for residents in the inner city. There are also serious efforts in cities like Bangkok, Hanoi, Kyoto, and Seoul to preserve the cultural and urban design character of the inner city.

Establishing urban nodes or "regional town centers" in the midst of green zones and open space has also been pursued in Asian mega-urban regions. Though it is recognized by urban planners that densities in such centers in peri-urban areas cannot be as high as in the inner city, there are successful efforts to integrate housing, employment, infrastructure, and commercial and trade services to enable residents to more or less lead self-sufficient lives within their communities. An important achievement in the establishment of these compact peri-urban nodes is the conservation of agricultural land. Urban agriculture has flourished around Asian cities, and there are a number of successful efforts to use the waste of the city as an input to production. The preservation of open green space for the urban watershed has been attempted to ensure a reliable source of water. The maintenance of marshy places, low-lying floodplains, and bogs and ponds has helped to ensure that excess water from rain and storms is absorbed and returned to the aquifer. These green areas have helped mega-urban regions to generate oxygen and absorb carbon dioxide and other gases.

Asian mega-urban regions have had less success in their efforts to link together the urban nodes with nonpolluting transport systems. Though most countries have approved policies advocating less reliance on the private automobile, rates of car ownership are increasing, especially in economically robust East and Southeast Asian cities, where a significant number of people are able to afford a car. In some East Asian cities, where bicycles used to be the main mode of transport, motorcycles and even cars are replacing them. Heavy rail and light rail transit systems have been constructed in cities like Bangkok, Beijing, Delhi, Guangzhou, Metro Manila, and Shanghai, but most of these systems do not yet reach outlying suburban areas. There are also complaints that the fares in these systems are too high, especially for poor residents who have been used to the low fares of paratransit systems.

Where many Asian mega-urban regions excel in pursuing smart growth principles is in the maintenance of a strong sense of community among urban residents. For ethnic and cultural reasons, most urban communities in Asian cities are small enough to make it possible to carry out fully participative consultative planning, service provision, and governance. Community life is enhanced by traditional activities, such as festivals, religious rituals, civic events, and night markets. A downside of strong community ties, however, is the particularism that can take the form of ethnic discrimination or religion-inspired violence. The emergence of nongovernmental organizations, community-based associations, and people's organizations in many Asian cities might help to limit the misunderstandings among social enclaves. Some civil society groups have succeeded in involving people in economic, social, and political activities at the community level. They have been able to draw on the knowledge and skills of local people to carry out more effective and efficient planning and governance.

In their current socioeconomic state, it must be admitted that Asia's mega-urban regions still have far to go before achieving a satisfactory level of economic, environmental, and social sustainability. It is likely that the best that Asian mega-urban regions can hope for, at present, is to minimize the negative impact on the environment of their production and consumption activities. In energy use, transportation, the management of manufacturing and industry, and solid waste management, quite a number of positive measures have been tried, and some progress has been achieved. However, a great deal more still must be accomplished to really help achieve sustainability.

The areawide approaches in planning and governance that have been used in a number of Asian mega-urban regions offer some leads on how sustainability can be enhanced. The concentration of dense enclaves of productive and consumptive activities in certain areas and the preservation of open green space between these nodes may help in attempting to find a balance between the human-built and natural elements of the environment. The interconnection of these urban nodes by efficient, nonpolluting, and environmentally friendly transport modes may help reduce the negative impact on the air, water, and land. The shift in production from heavy industry to cleaner high-technology industries and services might also reduce pollution. The efforts to encourage urban agriculture to feed urban residents and to use the wastes produced by those residents as an input to agricultural production may also help reduce negative environmental impact.

More important, the heightened awareness of urban residents of the negative environmental impact of their activities carries with it the hope that city-regions may become more sustainable. Certainly, the reduced consumption of nonrenewable resources such as fossil fuels would go a long way in reducing negative environmental impact. A greater awareness of economic and social inequalities might help to reduce urban tensions, which are already being exacerbated into violent and terrorist acts. With greater awareness, urban citizens might participate more in their local affairs and become more demanding and discriminating in selecting their leaders, policy options, and programs of action.

5

Planning and the Management of Water Resources

A lack of potable water is one of the most serious problems in Asian mega-urban regions. As table 5.1 shows, the proportion of people with access to clean water has run as low as 35 percent in Greater Jakarta and 65 percent in Dhaka. In the mid-1990s, piped potable water was available only four hours a day in Karachi, six hours in Dhaka, and seven hours in Delhi. The municipal water systems could produce less than 1 cubic meter per person per day in Dhaka and Jakarta. More than half of the water delivered by the municipal system could not be accounted for in Dhaka, Manila, and Jakarta due to leakage, pilferage, unauthorized water use, nonpayment of water charges, or faulty reporting of consumption. Worst of all, piped water has been very expensive, costing as much as $4.72 per cubic meter in Bangkok, $5.29 in Seoul, and $7.60 in Jakarta.

The water situation in Asian mega-urban regions is made worse by the fact that the water supply system is often not well integrated with the sewerage, drainage, storm water, and flood control systems. In Bangkok, only 2 percent of households were connected to the city's sewerage system, 25 percent relied on septic tanks, and the rest used pit latrines and other means for disposing of human waste and gray water. These patterns have increased the risk of water contamination from leaking septic tanks and simple pit latrines. In Jakarta, 35 percent of the city's households had direct water connections, 47 percent relied on shallow wells, and 18 percent had deep wells. About 90 percent of shallow wells in Jakarta provided water that was contaminated by coliform bacteria. In Chennai (formerly Madras), although 31 percent of households were served by the city's sewer system, poor maintenance allowed raw sewage to seep into the area's groundwater sources (World Health Organization 1992, 124–25).

Table 5.1. *Indicators of the Water Resources Situation in Selected Asian Cities*

Indicator	Delhi	Dhaka	Karachi	Bangkok	Jakarta	Manila	Beijing	Seoul
Population (millions)	13.0	13.2	10.4	7.2	11.4	12.6	10.8	10.0
Water coverage (percent)	69	65	83	75	35	70	95	100
Water service (hours/day)	7	6	4	24	19	16	24	24
Production (millions of cubic meters per day)	2.3	0.7	1.6	2.9	0.9	2.5	1.8	5.0
Unaccounted-for water (percent)	40	50	n.a.	37	52	58	7	38
Outlets metered (percent)	53	68	1	100	100	100	99	100
Liters used per day per person	145	120	124	240	157	116	190	198
Cost per cubic meter (dollars)	0.49	2.46	n.a.	4.72	7.60	3.70	1.64	5.29

Note: n.a. = not available.
Sources: Laquian (2004); Argo (1999); *Beijing Statistical Yearbook,* 1997; Landingin (2003); Villanueva (2002); Easter and Fedder (1997); World Bank (1995); Asian Development Bank (1993).

Water problems in Asian mega-urban regions are also exacerbated by inadequate protection of viable water sources. In January 2004, for example, residents of Metro Manila braced themselves for a 5 percent reduction (projected to 20 percent in April) in the water supplied by the Metropolitan Waterworks and Sewerage System (MWSS), because the water level in the Angat reservoir that supplied 97 percent of water in Metro Manila had dropped to dangerously low levels. Blame for the water shortage was placed on the Department of the Environment and Natural Resources for allowing logging in the Marikina watershed reservation and on the National Water Resources Board for delaying approval of a scheme to tap water from the Wawa dam. With denudation of the forest cover in the watershed area and the lack of rainfall limiting the supply of raw water, the residents of Metro Manila faced a critical water problem during the summer months (*Philippine Daily Inquirer,* January 20, 2004).

To supplement surface water sources that feed into their municipal water supply systems, some Asian city-regions draw upon groundwater aquifers. Beijing, for example, gets 85 percent of its water supply from ground sources. However, groundwater extraction results in serious problems of subsidence (Bangkok; Beijing; Dhaka; Jakarta; Kolkata, formerly Calcutta; and Metro Manila are also sinking because of excessive groundwater extraction). In Jakarta, the pumping out of groundwater causes the intrusion of saltwater into the aquifer. It also results in the contamination of groundwater from leaking sewage pipes, pit latrines, open wells, unlined solid waste dumps, oxidation ponds, and other sources of pollution (World Health Organization 1992, 110).

In some Asian cities, an abundance of water rather than a water shortage has become a critical problem as well. Bangkok, Jakarta, and Metro Manila are coastal communities served by networks of canals and streams (*klongs* and *esteros*). Because these cities are barely a meter above sea level, they get frequently flooded during the monsoon season, especially when heavy rains coincide with high tide. The adverse effects of frequent floods in Manila are made worse by the fact that the city's storm water drainage and sewerage systems are combined, resulting in surface water and groundwater contamination during heavy rains.

Canals and streams in Bangkok, Ho Chi Minh City, Jakarta, and Metro Manila are so badly silted and clogged with garbage that they easily overflow their banks. In addition, so much of the cities' surface areas (including marshes and wetlands) have been paved over that rainwater does not get absorbed into the ground but simply runs off, overloading drainage pipes, canals, and streams, and greatly adding to the volume of flood waters. Flooding is also a serious problem in Dhaka, especially during the cyclone season. Low-lying parts of Hanoi get flooded even when it is not raining in the city itself, because heavy rains upriver cause the water level of the Mekong River to rise rapidly. In Metro Manila and Ho Chi Minh City, squatter shanties on stilts have been built on top of streams and canals, hindering the flow of floodwaters and making periodic cleaning and dredging difficult.

Reasons for Poor Water System Management

The serious water supply problems in Asian mega-urban regions may be traced to a number of factors. First, there is the attitude of people toward the *value* of water. Where people view water as a free gift from nature, they do not appreciate its economic value and tend to waste it. Among recent rural–urban migrants who are not too far removed from an agricultural way of life, water is regarded as a natural resource, like rain. Studies in low-income communities in Jakarta and Metro Manila, for example, have noted the lack of concern among residents about the water supply. Even when public faucets are dripping and artesian wells are broken, residents do not repair them because they consider these facilities to be the responsibility of the government. In socialist cities like Beijing and Hanoi, access to water is considered a basic public service. As a result, what people pay for water in these cities is not even enough to cover maintenance costs.

Another attitudinal factor that adds to the ineffectiveness of water supply systems is the low expectation of people about the performance of metropolitan waterworks organizations. Most urban citizens seem quite content with inefficient systems, provided these charge low water rates and are not too strict in going after pilferers. This attitude is particularly prevalent in cities where inhabitants have gotten used to augmenting the meager and unreliable supply from the municipal water system with water from shallow wells, artesian wells, and rivers and streams. In these places, as long as people do not encounter serious water shortages or suffer from epidemics because of contaminated water, they do not seem to clamor for piped potable water.

Most residents of Asian mega-cities have a high tolerance for inadequate urban water supply systems because they can use "creative" means to get water. In Metro Manila, people get water from illegally opened fire hydrants or public standpipes, especially during the summer months. Some squatter communities tap into water mains illegally, resulting not only in a loss of revenue by the municipal water system but also in the contamination of water mains. In Bandung and Jakarta, people use unsafe water from shallow wells for bathing and washing, although they may boil it for drinking. Urban households in squatter areas may share the cost of water with neighbors lucky or politically influential enough to have piped water connections to their homes. These water "entrepreneurs," in turn, tamper with water meters so they will not have to pay normal water charges or bribe water inspectors to look the other way. By resorting to these various methods, urban poor people are somehow able to meet their water needs, though at times they actually pay more per unit of water than their richer neighbors living in gated communities.

Second, there is inefficiency and ineffectiveness of institutional water providers. In general, government institutions at the local, metropolitan, or regional levels charged with water provision encounter severe difficulties in operating, maintaining, and financing the system. Some water systems are very old—Metro Manila's waterworks system was built in 1878 by Spanish colonialists and was designed for a city of 300,000. Jakarta's water system was constructed by the Dutch about the end of the nineteenth century. Faced with a lack of funds, waterworks authorities have not been able to upgrade the systems. They have relied on low-grade or outmoded technologies for collecting, purifying, and distributing water. They are unable to attract good managers or personnel with the low salaries and benefits they offer. A great deal of the problem faced by water system administrators arises from the reluctance of water consumers to pay for a reliable water supply. With the costs of producing water generally higher than the amounts collected from water charges, administrators are unable to expand the coverage of the system or improve the quality of service.

Third, the intrusion of politics in the management of water supply systems in some Asian city-regions makes water management inefficient and ineffective. For example, the board of directors of MWSS in Metro Manila is composed of political appointees. The career advancement of water system managers appointed by higher levels of government is usually influenced by political connections. Administrators have to accommodate the demands and pressures of politicians by hiring political protégés, providing "special services" to people living in political bailiwicks, granting concessions or contracts to favored enterprises, or giving in to the rent-seeking demands of corrupt officials. These are hardly activities that can make water systems effective and efficient.

Fourth, the sorry situation of Asian municipal water systems may be traced to the very nature of these systems themselves. In general, the systems tend to be very large, covering whole regions, in which there are many jurisdictions wielding their own authority and power. Though some local government units may be able to prevent the invasion of watershed areas by squatters, others may tend to accommodate them. Responsibility for water may be vested in various central and local government agencies.

In Metro Manila, for example, MWSS is supposed to manage the water and sewerage system for the metropolitan region, but many other agencies are also involved in the function. The National Power Corporation has jurisdiction over the Angat dam hydroelectric power plant, and it can decide how much water should be held in or released from the reservoir. The National Irrigation Administration has call on water from the Angat River and the reservoir for the use of farmers. The National Water Resources Board controls the public and private use of water by issuing or not issuing water permits. The Department of the Environment and Natural Resources can approve logging and other activities within the watershed area and requires environmental impact assessments before any activities can be carried out in the area. The National Economic and Development Authority checks if proposed activities are in accordance with the government's plans. If foreign funds are needed for water-related activities, it passes upon the use of such funds. The provincial governments around the national capital region and the fourteen cities and three towns in the region all have a say in water management. Finally, since the privatization of Metro Manila's water and sewerage system into two sectors in 1997, two private companies linked to their international partners are now also involved in water services management. The fragmentation of authority and power arising from so many agencies makes cooperative coordination of water-related activities extremely difficult in Metro Manila.

Metropolitan water services, of course, benefit greatly from economies of scale and economies of density. Because they serve high concentrations of people, increasing the volume of water available and the number of households connected to the system reduces the network's average costs. Because of this, retail competition among several suppliers may be hard to justify, and the water system becomes peculiarly prone to monopolistic practices. Waterworks systems also demand huge capital investments and involve lumpy "sunk costs" that are difficult to recover within a short period of time. In Asia, some municipal water development efforts involve foreign partners that have the technological, financial, and managerial capabilities to plan and operate large water schemes.

Finally, a key factor in municipal water management is the fact that water is a commodity that is prone to massive consumption. The greater the volume of water that is made available, the greater is the tendency of consumers to use more of it. Rationing water through administrative means is costly and cumbersome. Setting an appropriate price for water becomes quite difficult, especially in urban societies characterized by a high proportion of poor households, where the persistent view of water as a social benefit creates pressures for heavy subsidies (Spiller and Savedoff 1999, 6–7).

Policy Measures for Urban Water Provision

The primary reality faced by policymakers in relation to water is that while planet Earth has an ample supply of water (estimated at 1.36 billion cubic kilometers), 97.2 percent of that is in the oceans, 2 percent is frozen in glaciers, and only 0.8 percent is in all the streams, rivers, lakes, swamps, ponds, the atmosphere, and underground (Monroe and Wicander 1997, 281). The world's supply of water is also being used rapidly—by the beginning of the 1990s, about 44 percent of the world's supply of fresh water in terms of reliable runoff had been utilized through the construction of dams, reservoirs, and conveyance structures (Clark 1993, x).

Another issue faced by people who want to improve urban water systems is that governmental and private efforts in water management tend to be politically and spatially fragmented. This reality was pointed out in 2000 by a program on Integrated Water Resources Management (IWRM) supported by the World Bank and the Government of the Netherlands. The IWRM program is based on the premise that many of the problems related to water provision are comprehensive and cut across functional boundaries. The program supports water projects in a set of "windows" focused on dam planning and management, river basin management, watershed management, wastewater management, groundwater management, and flood management (see figure 5.1). As stated in the IWRM brochure:

> The program's action-oriented approach supports specific efforts through the individual windows. Each window is a sub-component of a broad framework that embraces comprehensive, cross-sectoral water management; water user participation; transparent and efficient institutions; the treatment of water as a social and economic resource; the importance of water to the natural environment; and the link between water management and poverty alleviation. (World Bank–Netherlands Water Partnership Program 2002, 6)

Although water managers have to focus attention on individual areas or windows for action, these managers also have to be keenly aware of the fact that any action they take in one area has repercussions in other areas. For example, the building of dams directly affects river basin management, the availability of irrigation water downstream, flood prevention, and the possible extinction of species directly affected by changes in the volume, flow, temperature, and other characteristics of water. Wastewater management has direct effects on surface water and groundwater pollution. On a sociopolitical basis, the allocation of water to various productive uses—industry, agriculture, commerce, domestic households—also affects questions of access to water of various income groups as well as the residents of specific geographical areas. Increasingly, in fact, access to water is becoming one of the most common causes of "water wars" and other conflicts among local government units and even among nations.

In policy debates related to the provision of water to large urban areas, two quite divergent approaches have evolved through the years (Swyngedouw 1996, 399–401). One approach, which is essentially technological and engineering oriented, focuses on the large-scale impounding, diversion,

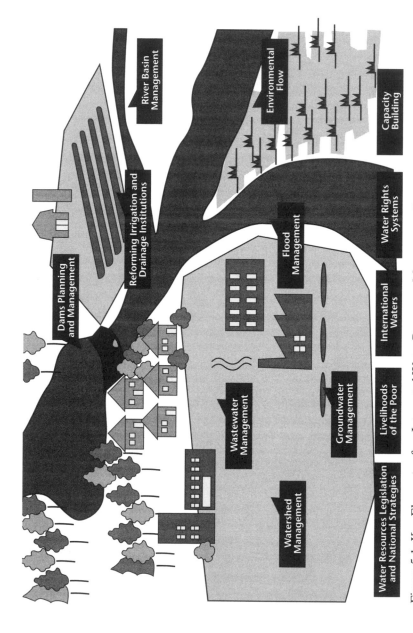

Figure 5.1. Key Elements of an Integrated Water Resources Management Program

Source: World Bank—Netherlands Water Partnership Program (2002, 7).

Labels within figure:
- River Basin Management
- Environmental Flow
- Capacity Building
- Dams Planning and Management
- Reforming Irrigation and Drainage Institutions
- Flood Management
- Water Rights Systems
- Wastewater Management
- Groundwater Management
- International Waters
- Livelihoods of the Poor
- Water Resources Legislation and National Strategies
- Watershed Management

purification, and distribution of water. Often, it favors centralized monopolistic agencies for managing water systems and depends very heavily on international financing. Such technological-engineering approaches often link water provision to power generation, drainage, flood control, irrigation, sewerage, and wastewater treatment and disposal.

The scale of some technological-engineering water projects pursued in some Asian countries is daunting, as evidenced by the controversial Three Gorges Dam in China. The Three Gorges project is designed to meet the power and water needs of a vast industrial and agricultural region in China with an estimated 30 million inhabitants. When finished, the 1.4-mile-long barrier will be more than five times the length of the Hoover Dam. Behind the barrier will be a reservoir extending over 365 miles with the water level rising up to 578 feet, submerging 312 million square feet of land. The project is designed to produce 84.7 billion kilowatts of electricity a year for cities as far as Shanghai at the mouth of the Yangtze River. It will make it possible for oceangoing vessels of up to 10,000 tons to travel to China's interior. It is also expected to control the annual flooding of the Yangtze River, which has killed more than 300,000 people in the past century and destroyed property and crops worth billions of dollars.

When finished in 2009, the Three Gorges project will submerge 2 cities, 11 county seats, and 1,352 villages. It will require the resettlement of about 1.3 million people. Some ecologists predict that it will make the river dolphin extinct because of the massive changes in its habitat. There are also fears that the dam may fail and cause a massive disaster, that heavy silt will make the project eventually ineffective, and that the massive reservoir created by the dam will become a cesspool in about fifty years because of the heavy industrial, domestic, and agricultural pollutants dumped by residents of urban and rural settlements along the Yangtze River.

Other controversial big water projects in Asia include the Tehri and Narmada dam projects in India and the Pak Mun Dam project in northeastern Thailand. Critics of the Tehri Dam in northern Uttar Pradesh charge that it will threaten the fragile Himalayan ecology and way of life of hill-dwelling people in the Gahrwal area. Like the Three Gorges Dam, the Tehri Dam will displace many people (estimated at 100,000), and it will also submerge some of the most productive farmland in the region. The Narmada Valley project in Gujarat, Madhya Pradesh, and Maharashtra states in India is one of the largest hydroelectric and irrigation projects in the world. Jurisdictional disputes among the three states have complicated planning for the project. The World Bank and the Government of India have been widely criticized for pursuing Narmada because of its potential to cause social disruption and environmental damage (Howard 1993, 7).

The other policy approach to water provision is conservationist and holistic, viewing water as a limited economic resource that has to be used efficiently and wisely to maximize its benefits for the whole society. This approach places an emphasis not just on the production but also on the consumption of water, seeking a more equitable distribution of water among various sectors. It pays special attention to the careful management of water resources, stressing less water consumption, and paying greater attention to water recycling, reasonable water pricing, and water conservation. Often, water schemes adhering to this approach depend on local revenue rather than on international financing. Where the private sector gets involved in schemes within this approach, it tends to be community based and focused on limited functions such as small-scale water production and local distribution management.

Interestingly, the global tendency in recent decades has been to use the technological-engineering approach. The water systems of Osaka, Seoul, and Tokyo are centralized municipal systems covering the major portions of the city-regions. The internationally planned and constructed water systems for Bangkok, Jakarta, and Metro Manila have been expanded and updated into centralized technological-engineering systems. With a few exceptions, these metropolis-wide water and sewerage systems have been regarded as quite successful at delivering potable water, getting rid of wastewater and sewage, preventing floods, and limiting health hazards.

A number of researchers have been critical of the technological-engineering approach. They have argued that such large systems have often failed to meet demand in large mega-urban regions. They have been accused of being inefficient, as indicated by the fact that an estimated 50 percent or more of clean water that enters the piped distribution system in many cities is unaccounted for or classified as "nonrevenue water." Potable water in large urban systems is also often inequitably distributed, with poor residents in underserved communities paying a great deal more for drinking water than people living in areas connected to municipal water systems (Serageldin 1994, 11; Rosegrant and Meinzein-Dick 1997, 40).

An increasingly important element in the urban water debate is the widespread view of water as a "commodity." During the 1990s, at the end of the International Drinking Water Supply and Sanitation Decade (1981–90), the United Nations stressed policies treating water as an "economic good," a resource that is subject to conditions of abundance or scarcity and therefore amenable to the effects of market mechanisms. The role of the government in providing water, pursuant to this perception, was deemed to be somewhat excessive.

This new policy looked with disfavor at highly subsidized public programs that delivered potable water directly to citizens. It favored programs that confined the government's role to policy setting, establishing and ensuring the implementation of health, safety and environmental standards, ensuring more equitable access to water of all social sectors, regulating the price of water, and enabling other actors in the water economy to efficiently deliver clean water and dispose of wastewater and effluents in the context of an open market (Stokke 1997, 438–39). Direct management by the government of water production and distribution systems was regarded as ineffective and inefficient. Often, there was fear that governmental management of water programs invited political intervention, favoritism, and graft and corruption.

Advocates of the conservationist-holistic approach to water management believe that the scarcity value of water does not only rest on its economic value but also on the ecological fact that the supply of water on earth is finite. They view a city-region as an ecosystem dependent on large areas outside it for energy, food, fiber, water, and other materials. The city-region's water resources are part of a hydrological system with specific inputs, throughputs, and outputs. In the view of Rees and Wackernagel (1996), a city is typically characterized by intense metabolism per unit area, large requirements of material inputs, particularly water, and a large toxic output of waste. As human beings spend more of their lives in cities, they lose track of their intimate connection with nature. Treating water as a simple commodity subject to the vagaries of markets and financing schemes creates a disjuncture between economic processes and physical reality. Rees and Wackernagel concluded that "since most of us spend our lives in cities and consume goods imported from all over the world, we tend to experience nature merely as a collection of commodities or a place for recreation, rather than the very source of our lives and well being" (Rees and Wackernagel 1996, 7).

The conservationist-holistic approach argues that large technological-engineering systems in big cities tend to encourage the overconsumption of clean water and overgeneration of waste. They favor smaller, more decentralized systems where people become more aware of the direct impact of their water and sanitation practices on the environment. In the Orangi Pilot Project (OPP) in Karachi, for example, people have set up sewerage systems themselves and then connected these to the larger municipal system.

According to the OPP model, the "internal" parts of the system that the people were responsible for building were a sanitary latrine in the house, an underground sewer in the lane, and a neighborhood collector sewer. The government, in turn, was responsible for the "external" part, involving a trunk sewer and a sewage treatment plant, to which the community-built facility was connected. The OPP model had been replicated in a number of "scaling up" operations in various parts of Pakistan. An assessment of the viability of the model in 2002 revealed that out of thirteen such schemes, five were considered failures, two were remarkably successful, four were showing signs of promise, and two were still undetermined (Hasan 2002, 206). An analysis of the reasons for success included the following:

1. The presence of an activist leader who could establish linkages between the community and local government officials.
2. The development of a technical-cum-social organization team trained from people in the community. This involves training by the OPP Research and Training Institute and continued linkages with the project for advice, training, and documentation.
3. The availability of funds for staff, administration, and credit for developing collector sewers.
4. The development of community organization processes, such as regular weekly meetings for reviewing progress, assigning responsibilities, identifying weaknesses, and determining how to solve problems. This includes consultation with local government officials and other organizations.
5. Transparency in account keeping and the accountability of the project leaders and staff to the people.

It is interesting to note that an evaluation of the five unsuccessful projects revealed that the reasons for failure in using the OPP model involved not only the inability to carry out the items mentioned above but also three important elements: (1) the acceptance of large sums of money for expansion, (2) subsidies for lane development; and (3) a lack of patience. As pointed out by Hasan, small-scale, community-based efforts require a great deal of patience. Attempting to accelerate the development process through the infusion of large sums of money or subsidizing activities that people themselves are expected to carry out undermines people's initiative and creates dependency and undue reliance on the government. This dilemma of how to work out the transition from voluntary community efforts at the level of the community and scale these up to effectively link them to the bureaucratized efforts of the local government is the main challenge faced by small-scale water and sanitation efforts.

In other countries, projects based on the conservationist-holistic approach have included minihydroelectric systems that integrate water impounding, electricity generation, flood control, and potable water production at the community level. Such systems were popular in China during the mid-1960s and early 1970s, but they have been largely abandoned, perhaps because they were pursued as governmental "campaigns" that became too associated with initiatives from Beijing. At the household level, the conservationist-holistic approach explored the use of waterless composting toilets; the reuse of gray water for flushing, washing, and gardening; and other approaches that minimized the use, and wastage, of water.

The problem with these approaches, of course, was that they failed to achieve economies of scale. They have been found effective and efficient in small, autonomous, low-density urban settlements but have been considered inappropriate for very large cities with high population densities. Some other technologies used by small-scale systems, such as ozonation and desalination, are also still too expensive and mainly used in high-technology zones with highly specialized waste disposal needs. More traditional approaches, such as oxidation ponds for wastewater disposal, tend to suffer from undesirable smells and other disadvantages.

Faced with the two policy approaches to water provision noted above, mega-urban region authorities have to consider the benefits and disadvantages of alternative water systems very carefully. Essentially, they have to rely on good planning and management in choosing specific policy interventions. The key areas they have to consider include (1) the development of a reliable water supply, (2) safeguarding water safety, (3) demand regulation and management, (4) wastewater reuse and recycling, and (5) water quality management and pollution control.

The Development of Water Supply Systems

In planning the development of water supply systems for mega-urban regions, it is useful to view the city-region as being made up of an "inner system" consisting of the densely populated built-up area or areas and an "outer system" where the raw water comes from and where wastewater can be disposed of. Sources of water in the hydrological cycle are basically precipitation (rain, snow), surface water (rivers, lakes), groundwater (deep and shallow wells), and wastewater (gray water, sewage, effluents). Most of these water sources (except wastewater) are in the outer system. The main activities in the outer system are the collection and impounding of raw water, purification and treatment, and the protection of the watershed from green-cover destruction and chemical or pathogenic contamination.

The mega-urban region's inner system is where the most intensive users of water are located—mainly households, manufacturing concerns, industries, public institutions, and the like. Raw water from the outer system is impounded, purified, brought in, used, and then discarded as waste. The main concerns in the inner system focus on the distribution of clean water to users, the efficient allocation of water among competing groups of consumers, the maintenance of water purity standards, the cost-effectiveness of use, the affordability of water, and the equitable allocation of water among social groups and classes. These concerns also include the possible reuse and recycling of water, water conservation, the collection of appropriate water charges, and ensuring that wastewater does not pollute outside sources.

The experiences of Asian mega-urban regions highlight the fact that *planning for a city-region's water system is most effective when it encompasses a much wider geographical area than just the city's built-up zone.* Typically, this zone will cover both the inner and outer systems. In many cases, the source of water for a city-region is located a great distance from the city center. The protected green area or watershed feeding the water source may cover an even larger area. Even if the watershed and sources of water belong to separate local government jurisdictions, water resources planning requires establishing firm jurisdiction over the whole region to facilitate cooperative and coordinated action.

A case study of effective water resources planning for Jakarta, for example, revealed that the region covered by the plan went way beyond the 652 square kilometers that made up the built-up area of Jakarta Raya (Argo 1999, 28). For protection of the watershed, the plan encompassed territories in the entire river basins of the Citarum and the Cisadane Rivers. These areas were under the political jurisdictions of regencies such as Bandung, Bekasi, Bogor, Cianjur, Tangerang, and Purwakarta in the province of West Java, and the authorities for these places were included as stakeholders in the planning process. In addition to the watershed area, the plan covered the surface water sources, mainly made up of the two rivers running through the districts of Bogor, Cianjur, and Tangerang. Finally, the plan focused on the areas of water demand, where residences, manufacturing, industry, government, and trade and commerce were concentrated, within the built-up areas of Jakarta City itself, as well as the urban municipalities within the surrounding regencies and districts. Policymakers, administrators, actors, and stakeholders from these local government units and economic and social sectors were also consulted and involved in the planning process.

Another example of water supply development planning is the so-called Middle China Water Transfer project, which proposes to pump water from the Yangtze River to Beijing and Tianjin. Tapping water from the Danjiangkou Reservoir and then piping it about 1,600 kilometers to Beijing and Tianjin has been estimated to cost about $5 billion. The project would cross 219 rivers and take more than six years to complete. In the plans for this project, the watershed areas, the source of water, and the route of the massive pipes have been clearly demarcated. Protective measures have also been proposed to ensure that the project will have a minimal negative environmental impact on the areas it affects. Like the Three Gorges project, the Middle China Water Transfer project has been criticized by environmentalists and other activists because of its huge cost, the significant environmental impact of the construction and other activities it requires, its displacement of people and communities in affected areas, and the fear that it will generate overconsumption and waste in the Beijing region.

The Chinese government insists, however, that Beijing needs the water and other sources of water in the region have almost all been fully tapped. Heavy pumping of groundwater in the Beijing region has already caused subsidence in various parts of the city. The small rivers and streams in the Beijing area are almost all dead from pollution. Bringing in water from the Yangtze River will ease the water shortage in Beijing and Tianjin, though it will also create serious problems of wastewater disposal. China has the financial resources, technological capabilities, technical skills, and professional management capabilities to set up an effective and efficient water and sewerage system befitting the nation's capital, and it has decided to upgrade the country's water and waste disposal system.

A major issue in the planned development of urban water systems is cost. In villages and small towns, it has been found that "appropriate technology" measures—such as artesian wells, the conversion of springs into piped water systems, and minihydroelectric projects integrating energy generation with potable water supply and flood control—worked efficiently. These projects were particularly effective when carried out with maximum participation from local residents and innovative community action.

In contrast to these low-technology and people-centered approaches, however, the favored approach in very large cities is to undertake large standardized civil engineering projects that require dams and reservoirs, chemical treatment plants, purification and aeration facilities, piped distribution systems, metered consumption, and professional and technical management. The high costs of such projects have inhibited many developing countries from developing water supply projects. Thus, at the end of the International Drinking Water Supply and Sanitation Decade, the World Bank found that Asia's mega-cities had been able to raise their clean water targets by only 4 percent. A survey in 1994 found that at least 170 million urban dwellers worldwide lacked a source of potable water near their homes and another 350 million lacked access to basic sanitation (World Bank 1995, 12).

The main factors that need to be considered in the establishment of large waterworks and sanitation systems include (1) construction costs, (2) mitigation costs, (3) environmental costs, (4) resettlement costs, and (5) development and management costs. Construction costs involve capital, labor, technology, and financial borrowings. These tend to be very large and lumpy and are likely to be sourced from international investors. Mitigation costs will entail paying for the project's negative impacts on the environment. They are extremely difficult to determine because the effects and impact of water development activities might take a long time before they become apparent. The environmental costs include both the direct negative effects (e.g., flooding rich agricultural lands for the building of dams and reservoirs) and indirect costs (e.g., the spread of waterborne diseases because of water impoundment and the redirection of water flows).

Moreover, big waterworks projects usually require the resettlement of people from areas that would be adversely affected, entailing heavy costs for transportation, land development, job creation, and housing for the people affected. The projects also involve massive costs for organizational management and operation because they require coordinated action among a number of public and private agencies.

The high direct and indirect costs of developing water supply systems are the main arguments used for questioning the technological-engineering approach that continues to be the preferred option among water system planners. In some ways, the magnitude of the water needs of mega-urban regions makes the technological-engineering solution preferable. Economists point to economies of scale and density economies that are palpably high in these technologically based systems.

Despite arguments favoring large municipal water systems, advocates of the conservationist-holistic approach to water systems development contend that it is possible to design a number of smaller systems for large mega-urban regions. Such systems can be more easily funded because they do not require lumpy financing, they can be managed more efficiently, they can be made more responsive to people's demands, their impact on the environment can be reduced, and they encourage people to see how closely their lifestyle is linked to nature, making for a more responsible attitude toward the environment.

On the basis of the experience in Asian human settlements, a combination of large municipal systems and smaller autonomous systems may be the best solutions in mega-urban regions. An areawide municipal system may be best for the densely built up city center and surrounding areas to take advantage of economies of scale and other benefits arising from comprehensive management approaches. However, within the mega-urban region, smaller urban nodes may use autonomous water and sewerage systems that, with greater community involvement and support, might become more responsive to local community needs.

If the situation warrants, linkages may be established between the municipal water and sewerage system and the local systems. The experience in the Orangi Pilot Project in Karachi, for example, shows that such linkages and complementarities are possible in the design and operation of a sewage disposal system that is more in keeping with the technical and management capabilities of local people and is amenable to scaling up and upgrading once linked to the larger municipal system (Orangi Pilot Project 1998).

Protecting Water Safety

Unsafe water is a serious problem in most Asian mega-cities. An inadequate water supply, for example, threatens Kolkata's 12.9 million people. Early in Kolkata's history, an Indian planner described the city as "an undrained swamp in the vicinity of malarious jungle" (Jain 1996a, 39). Little in the way of water safety has changed since that comment was made, except that the health situation in the city has become much worse. The explosion of the city's population, particularly after Partition in 1947, has severely strained the city's water supply. Epidemics, such as the deadly cholera outbreak of 1958, remain a serious threat. In the 1960s, Kolkata could barely supply 20 gallons of water per person a day to residents. The city's piped water system—which had one set of pipes for potable water and another for untreated water for toilet flushing, fire fighting, gardening, and street cleaning—has become so inadequate that people were sometimes forced to use the untreated water for washing, cooking, and drinking, resulting in serious illnesses.

The pollution of water sources is also a serious problem in other Asian mega-cities. The Pasig River in Metro Manila is effectively dead. The city's ancient sewerage system pumps effluents into Manila Bay with only rudimentary treatment and, as a result, serious cases of "red tide" disease breaks out each summer and the Health Department has banned the consumption of oysters, clams, mussels, and other shellfish from the bay. The Yamuna River that cuts through Delhi receives nearly 200 million liters of untreated sewage each day. The Hooghly estuary in Kolkata receives untreated industrial waste from more than 150 major factories, and raw sewage is dumped into the river from 361 municipal outfalls. In Karachi, Pakistan's largest industrial city, raw sewage and untreated industrial effluents are dumped in the Lyari River from about 300 major industries and textile mills. About 75 percent of water contamination in Jakarta is said to come from domestic sources, such as untreated sewage, gray water, storm water drainage, and solid waste, whereas 25 percent comes from manufacturing and industrial enterprises (World Bank 1994, 69).

The water pollution situation is not much better in China. About 3.4 million cubic meters of industrial and domestic waste a year pour into Suzhou Creek and the Huangpu River in Shanghai. The Huangpu has been essentially dead since 1980. This is because less than 5 percent of the wastewater from the city that is dumped into the river is treated. In addition, industrial plants have significantly polluted Shanghai's groundwater with toxic waste, contaminating deep wells that are increasingly being tapped as a major source for the city's water supply.

The relationship between water and sanitation services and the prevalence of diseases in developing-country cities is clear. The World Health Organization estimates that 80 percent of all sickness and disease in the world is attributable to inadequate water and sanitation (World Health Organization 1988). The Canadian International Development Agency has cited water-related diseases as responsible for between 10 to 25 million deaths per year worldwide. As developing countries urbanize, their capacity to bring in clean and safe water to city dwellers and to take out dirty and contaminated water from urban areas is not growing accordingly. As a result, most mega-cities and mega-urban regions chronically suffer from lack of water and sanitation facilities. Unfortunately, it is vulnerable members of urban society—infants and young children, the poor, the infirm, and the elderly—who suffer the most from inadequate water and sanitation.

Health authorities know that most of the disease agents that contaminate water come from human and animal feces. They include viruses, bacteria, protozoa, and various types of worms. These are ingested, multiply in the alimentary tract, and then are excreted with feces. Without proper sanitation or good personal hygiene, they get into water and are ingested through food or drink or enter the body through the skin.

Communicable diseases may be classified as waterborne, water washed, water based, or water related (Cairncross and Feachem 1983). Waterborne diseases include cholera, typhoid, infectious hepatitis, dysentery, and diarrhea. They spread through ingesting water that contains the pathogenic organisms that cause the disease. Water-washed diseases, such as scabies, ringworm, yaws, trachoma, and conjunctivitis, are associated with a lack of personal hygiene due to shortages of water. Water-based diseases, such as schistosomiasis, filariasis, and guinea worm, are caused by parasites that spend parts of their natural life cycles in water. Vector-transmitted diseases like malaria, yellow fever, and dengue are spread by insects carrying the disease-causing agents (mosquitoes) that breed in stagnant water.

The management of urban water systems involves the use of a number of measures that require an adequate supply of clean water and the disposal of dirty water to ensure good health. Table 5.2 shows a number of preventive measures to deal with water and sanitation-related diseases (Grekel 1995, 24). As indicated in the table, adequate water supply and the provision of sanitation facilities—including excreta removal, wastewater disposal, and drainage—are important factors in preventing diseases. At the same time, of course, simply providing clean water and sanitation facilities does not automatically result in improved human health. There must be key interventions in changing human attitudes and behavior within the family, in schools, and in communities. In fact, some studies have shown that hygiene-related interventions are often more effective in influencing behavior related to water and sanitation than citing impact studies tracing the relationships between water supply and health (UNICEF 1993).

Cultural beliefs related to water may profoundly affect how people react to disease prevention. It is important to analyze and understand these perceptions, attitudes, and behavior if one is to effectively manage water resources in an area. Some of the key aspects of these belief and behavior systems include the following:

Table 5.2. *Measures for Preventing Water-Related and Sanitation-Related Diseases*

Type of Disease	Food Hygiene	Personal Hygiene	Home Hygiene	Water Hygiene	Excreta Disposal	Wastewater Disposal
Diarrhea, dysentery, typhoid	•	•	•	•	•	
Roundworm, hookworm, tapeworm	•	•	•		•	
Scabies, ringworm, yaws		•	•			
Malaria, yellow fever	•					•
Bilharzia, filariasis			•		•	•

Sources: Grekel (1995); UNICEF 1993.

- *The use and protection of water sources.* These are influenced by (1) people's access to sources of clean water (wells, open streams, rivers, municipal water system); (2) means used for collecting and transporting water (jugs, water skins, jerry cans, water trucks, pipes); (3) wastewater disposal and drainage; (4) water treatment (boiling, filtering, chemical treatment); (5) the prevention of contamination of bodies of water; (f) garbage disposal in bodies of water; and (6) conserving water supply sources.
- *Water and personal hygiene.* These include beliefs and rituals related to (1) the washing of hands, face, feet, and other body parts; (2) hygiene after defecation; (3) the washing and use of clothes; and (4) personal hygiene during menstruation and illness, and in dealing with death.
- *Disposing of feces.* These include factors such as (1) the choice of place for defecation; (2) hand washing and anal cleansing; (3) disposing of cleansing material; (4) the cleaning and maintenance of toilets; and (5) the use of feces as fertilizer and fish feed, and animals eating feces.
- *Food hygiene.* These factors include (1) washing and peeling raw food and fresh fruits and vegetables; (2) the temperature used in cooking; (3) food and water used for feeding babies; and (4) washing cooking and eating utensils.
- *Domestic and environmental hygiene.* Important factors are (1) wastewater disposal and drainage; (2) cleaning the house, yard, streets, and public places; (3) the control of animals and household pets, and the safe disposal of animal feces; (4) solid waste collection and disposal; and (5) insect control, especially of mosquitoes and other vectors.

The five areas of intervention mentioned above demand changes in the attitudes, perceptions, and behavior of urban residents in relation to water, sanitation, and diseases. In general, without a proper understanding of the linkages among these three elements, it is extremely difficult to effect behavioral changes.

In many Asian mega-urban regions, the use of the formal school system for creating an awareness of the importance of hygiene in dealing with diseases has gained some notable achievements. In Metro Manila schools, teachers have used educational modules focused on "Health through Knowledge and Habits" at the primary school level to develop good habits and practices related to health. In Beijing, community schools have used educational materials that are based on a clear understanding of the relationships between water, sanitation, and health. In particular, teaching good habits to preschool children, such as washing hands with soap and water frequently, has yielded excellent results.

In their efforts to ensure the safety of water for municipal water systems, a number of measures that have been used in Asian mega-urban regions have been found to be effective. Foremost among these have been prevention mechanisms against the contamination of water supplies. In almost all city-regions in this study, serious attempts are being made to treat sewerage before it is discharged into bodies of water.

Another key effective measure is the management of transportation systems to prevent the generation of pollutants responsible for acid rain that is despoiling surface water sources. Campaigns have been waged against smoke-belching vehicles and emission control regulations have been passed and implemented in cities like Bangkok, Delhi, and Metro Manila to cut down air pollution, which is mainly responsible for acid rain. In other cities, solid waste collection and disposal systems are also being improved to prevent the dumping of garbage in canals, rivers, and streams.

Because many municipal water systems in Asia are old and based on outmoded technology, modern efforts are being used to detect pipe leakages that contaminate water supply. In Singapore, a Water Service and Operations Center is open 24 hours so that citizens can report pipe leakages. Leakage detection night tests are carried out for the entire distribution network eleven months of the year, leaving one month for retesting leak-prone regions. When leaks are detected in a region, it is isolated by shutting off all strategic boundary valves and individual services valves. Regular tests using stethoscopes, geophones, electronic leak detectors, and leak noise correlators have been used effectively to reduce the amount of water lost through leakage (Arlosoroff 1998, 37).

Considerable investments are being made in large municipal water systems that employ filtering, chlorination, aeration, and other methods of purifying water before its distribution to consumers. Though many of these approaches are very expensive, better physical design and water system management are showing that they could be cost-effective in ensuring the safety of the water supply. In smaller and more autonomous water systems, traditional filtering through pebbles and sand has proven effective, especially when combined with the use of activated charcoal. Ozonation has been used on a smaller scale for high-technology water systems. Reverse osmosis has also been proven effective in filtering impurities as part of the growing industry of providing bottled drinking water in many Asian mega-cities. In general, however, these sophisticated and small-scale systems for ensuring water safety are beyond the financial capabilities of local government units in Asian mega-urban regions.

Demand Regulation and Management

As indicated in the case of the Beijing water transfer project described above, most municipal authorities first think of increasing the water supply rather than regulating and managing demand as a solution to water problems. Actually, a number of authorities in water management recommend a shift from water supply provision to water demand management as a desirable strategy (Nickum and Easter 1994; Brandon and Rawankutty 1993). Demand-oriented interventions include the allocation of water supply among various users based on a system of priorities, rationing of water according to quotas, and appropriate pricing of water.

Water Allocation

Urban authorities have a choice on where to more cost-effectively allocate water—to agriculture, domestic use, manufacturing, industry, or leisure. It is interesting that in a number of Asian mega-cities, a considerable amount of water is allocated to agricultural uses. In Jakarta, for example, about 90 percent of the water from Jatiluhur Dam, which gets its water from the Cisadane and Ciliwung Rivers, is allocated to irrigating about 230,000 hectares of double-cropped rice fields. The water is provided free to farmers. Unfortunately, it has been found that the irrigation systems used by farmers are quite inefficient, resulting in massive water losses from both seepage and evaporation. Furthermore, agriculture has polluted the surface water sources with fertilizers, pesticides, fungicides, and herbicides, as well as organic waste. In 1994, it was estimated that about 30 percent of the pollution in the Citarum River was attributed to agriculture (Bukit 1995, 3; Argo 1999, 109).

In China, quite a number of urban authorities still adhere to the planning principle that an urban area should have its own food base. Large sections of cities like Beijing, Guangzhou, Shanghai, and Tianjin therefore are designated as agricultural zones devoted to vegetable, dairy, orchards, poultry, and fish-farming enterprises. Many Chinese planners have criticized these projects as inefficient users of water. Some studies have shown that the use of water for irrigation in agricultural production has an efficiency rate of about 10 percent, compared with 30 percent in Japan and 80 percent in Israel.

The use of unlined irrigation canals in urban agriculture causes much leakage, the open canals result in loss from evaporation, and inefficiencies in pumping and water diversion and use create much wastage. It has been suggested that a simple shift from furrow irrigation—with an efficiency rate of 0.6 percent—to sprinkler or drip irrigation in China would achieve effectiveness rates of 0.8 and 0.9 percent respectively.

Other policy interventions that have been suggested to better manage the use of water in agriculture include (1) reducing the size of irrigated areas; (2) changing the crop mix and planting crops that use less water; (3) increasing the efficiency of irrigation systems; and (4) reallocating water from irrigation to rural industry, such as township and village enterprises (Nickum and Easter 1994).

A large consumer of water in Asian mega-cities, of course, is manufacturing and industry. In China, the principle that cities should be productive rather than consumptive means that city authorities favor heavy industry and manufacturing to other uses. In the case of Beijing, for example, urban authorities have set up a large steel mill, big automobile assembly plants, and other heavy industries within the city confines. The heavy use of water for manufacturing and industry by state-owned enterprises has added to the water authorities' woes, because almost all these firms have been losing money and have not been able to pay their water bills. Using outmoded manufacturing and industrial processes, these state-owned enterprises have also added to water pollution in urban areas.

The use of water in manufacturing and industry can be managed more effectively through the adoption of water-efficient industrial technology.

For example, the use of water for cooling may be reduced dramatically by shifting to more efficient technologies. The reuse and recycling of water can also be more aggressively pursued. In some instances, the industrial mix in a city can be changed so that processes that require less water can be used. Aged, inefficient, and outmoded machines need to be replaced with more efficient ones to reduce water wastage.

Typically, domestic use takes up about a quarter of water use in a city. The volume of water used in households can be reduced by the introduction of water-saving devices, such as flush toilets that use less water, faucets that automatically shut off when not in use, and sprinklers that aerate water into mists. Leakage reduction through better plumbing practices can save much water. Educational campaigns that teach people how to reuse, conserve, and recycle water have also achieved excellent results in reducing water consumption. In Hong Kong, a two-system approach to water has been used, whereby pure water for drinking (which requires expensive technologies to purify) is piped through one system and raw water primarily meant for toilet flushing, fire fighting, cooling, and other purposes is piped in another. This approach, though entailing higher costs for distribution, has been found to be more cost-effective in the long run because of the savings in water purification and treatment.

Faced with serious water shortages, some Asian mega-cities have tried rationing water to different parts of the city by shutting off supply at certain hours of the day or night. Though some water savings have been achieved through this approach, a number of problems have also been encountered. In Metro Manila, for example, shutting off water at certain times of the day or night drastically changes water pressure in the pipes, resulting in the entry of dirty water and other polluting elements into the water supply system. In other Asian cities, where some of the pipe distribution systems are centuries old, the closing and opening of water supply contributes to the deterioration of the system. In systems that combine the drainage and the sewerage system, the danger of contamination is even worse because leakage from the combined system gets into the aquifer and then pollutes the weakened water distribution network.

Water Pricing

A most effective policy tool in water management, of course, is pricing. This is based on the commonsense argument that if people have to pay for water, they will be inhibited from using too much of it or wasting it. However, this economic rationale flies in the face of the concept of water as a public good and the argument that people should be entitled to it because water is an essential ingredient of life. In almost all the cities of Asia, therefore, the process of supplying potable water is subsidized. It has been estimated that water charges to consumers in Asian cities cover only 35 percent of the cost of supplying it (Easter and Feder 1997, 268).

To price water appropriately, it is necessary to find out the actual cost of producing and delivering potable water to consumers and to use this as the basis for user charges. It will be necessary to set up a metering system for measuring actual use, and establishing a mechanism for charging water users and collecting payments. Water may be priced on the basis of a flat rate (say, per cubic meter consumed) or on the basis of an escalating scale, where charges go up as the amount of water used increases.

Under normal circumstances, an economic enterprise usually prices its goods and services in such a way that the more units are purchased, the lower will be the price demanded. In the case of water, however, the situation is quite the reverse. In Bangkok, Beijing, Ho Chi Minh City, Hong Kong, Karachi, Kuala Lumpur, Manila, Seoul, and Singapore, entities using more volumes of water are charged more per unit than those that consume less. This approach is a tacit recognition of the fact that water is a scarce and limited resource. It also represents a welfare-oriented strategy that considers water an essential element in achieving a good quality of life and recognizes that poorer segments of the urban population should have access to water at a price they can afford. In Jakarta, for example, a study found that each public faucet installed in a low-income community serves, on the average, about 250 people, whereas one directly connected to a house serves only seven. Likewise, every piped connection to a commercial enterprise uses 3 cubic meters of water a day, whereas each industrial connection uses 14 cubic meters a day (World Bank 1993b, 34).

Despite a long-standing tradition of free or subsidized water in most Asian mega-urban regions, many urban authorities are now instituting appropriate systems for pricing water closer to its true economic cost. This is most apparent in cities like Jakarta and Metro Manila, for example, where private enterprise has taken over management of the water system and water charges have been repeatedly jacked up. Despite an adverse reaction from the public, strongly supported by civil society groups, the idea that clean water has a value and that people should pay for having access to it is rapidly spreading. Interestingly, this changing point of view seems to be shared more and more by poor urban residents, who have effectively been paying a lot more for drinking water bought from vendors compared with their richer neighbors, who have enjoyed the privilege of having water piped into their homes for some time.

Wastewater Use and Reuse

An increasingly popular approach in water demand management is the use and reuse of wastewater for various uses. In city-regions where urban agriculture is practiced, wastewater reuse has been known for centuries. Because water for irrigation does not require purification, some authorities have advocated the use of wastewater in watering and fertilizing crops. Farmers in Beijing, Guangzhou, Shanghai, and Tianjin have used municipal wastewater for irrigation for many decades. Such water has not only been used to water crops—in the Pearl River Delta in China's Guangdong province, the Red River Delta around Hanoi, and the Mekong River Delta around Ho Chi Minh City, wastewater has been used to fertilize rice fields and to raise fish in ponds.

In recent times, however, it has been found that municipal wastewater in most cities contains a lot of pathogens and toxic materials that pose threats to public health. A study of wastewater quality in Beijing and Tianjin has revealed that half the water samples drawn from the Hai and Luan Rivers do not meet the lowest quality standard set for irrigation use (World Bank 1995). The problem is that municipal wastewater is currently used to irrigate about 150,000 hectares of crops in Tianjin and 88,600 hectares in Beijing. There is a need, therefore, to either reduce the use of wastewater for irrigation or improve the quality of the water before it is used for agricultural purposes.

Certain manufacturing and industrial purposes do not require potable water (e.g., for cooling, flushing, and cleaning). This means that wastewater, with some form of treatment, can be used for these purposes. This approach has been used in Beijing with excellent results. In the past fifteen years, industrial output in Beijing had increased by 650 percent, but total water use for industrial purposes had increased by only 57.5 percent. In 1996, the average recycling rate for industrial wastewater in Beijing had reached 91.4 percent.

Using treated wastewater for industrial processes has proven to be cost-effective. It has been estimated that it costs about 1.20 yuan to purify 1 cubic meter of tap water. However, the cost of treating wastewater to make it appropriate for industrial use is only 0.50 yuan per cubic meter. Even secondary treatment entails a cost of only 0.77 yuan per cubic meter. At these rates, it would be cost-effective to use treated wastewater even for certain domestic uses, such as flushing toilets, watering vegetable gardens and lawns, and cleaning (World Bank 1995).

Water Quality Management and Pollution Control

Controlling pollution and preventing water contamination in Asian cities is a difficult job. Sources of pollution, such as agriculture, manufacturing, industry, and households, are often outside the jurisdiction of water agencies. In many cities, the inefficient collection and disposal of solid waste is a big problem. In Jakarta, for example, a 1998 study found that 1,350 metric tons of garbage were produced in the city each day and that only 25 percent of this was disposed of in sanitary land fills and open dumps. About 28 percent was thrown into canals and rivers, and 42 percent was disposed of at sea (Argo 1999).

Contributing to Jakarta's water problem was the fact that only 9 percent of households were connected to the municipal sewage system. A World Bank review found that the system served only 500,000 users and used a mechanical-biological treatment plant that discharged effluents into the Banjir Canal and an oxidation pond. More than 60 percent of Jakarta's households relied on septic tanks with leaching fields, 17 percent on pit latrines, and 6 percent on public toilets. Most of these facilities were old and tended to leak and pollute surface water and groundwater (World Bank 1993b, 26).

There is widespread agreement among experts that regulatory measures alone will make it extremely difficult to maintain water quality in large cities. Market forces must play a major role in dealing with water use, particularly with regard to controlling the pollution of water sources. All over the world, many municipal authorities have imposed pollution charges not only to meet the costs of mitigation but also to finance investments to deal with pollution in a more lasting way. The "polluter pays" principle has been applied in many cases.

Another innovation in dealing with pollution is the use of "tradable permits of pollution charges." In this system, enterprises will be subjected to environmental audits that determine their levels of water pollution. An industry that exceeds permissible pollution levels can "buy" allowable pollution permits from one that more than meets pollution standards. In this way, the total pollution levels in a city or region will not be exceeded while productivity will be achieved.

The Privatization of Water Systems

Some Asian mega-urban regions, like Jakarta and Metro Manila, have turned over the management of their water systems to private enterprise. The main arguments for privatization are rooted in the view that although water is a public good, providing it to consumers entails considerable production and distribution costs and these should be reflected in the real economic price of water. As a scarce resource, water should be allocated in accordance with its highest value use as determined by market forces. It is argued that subsidizing potable water encourages wasteful use. The private sector may earn profits from managing water, but the costs of these profits may be offset by their managerial efficiency (it is claimed that private firms can be more efficient than government agencies because they have to be competitive and are less vulnerable to political pressures, nepotism, and corruption). Private entrepreneurs may also be made more responsive to public demands and accountable to public regulatory agencies if the government establishes performance standards and monitoring and evaluation mechanisms to oversee their activities.

The huge capital requirement of urban waterworks systems has been used as a justification for the increasing role of giant international conglomerates that favor privatization. Very few urban governments in developing countries can afford to build and support such systems from tax proceeds or user charges. Private companies can provide the capital as well as the technology and expertise needed to build and manage large systems. They are also able to get support from the World Bank and the Asian Development Bank; the World Bank approved more than $20 billion in loans between 1990 and 1992 for 276 waterworks systems all over the world, and 30 percent of the schemes required privatization. The World Bank has also teamed up with the United Nations to set up the World Water Council and the Global Water Partnership—two international bodies that favor privatization.

The privatization of urban water systems does not get unanimous support, however. Some people view the provision of potable water as an essential service designed to guarantee public health, welfare, security, and safety— desirable goals that merit government support. Turning over water services to the private sector may lead to inequity because concessionaires may serve only communities that can pay for water. Private water providers, acting as monopolies, may charge exorbitant rates that urban poor people may not be able to afford (Hardoy and Schusterman 2000, 67). The profit motive may make private water concessionaires less responsive to public demand, because of "the displacement of one set of managers entrusted by the shareholders—the citizens—with another set of managers who may answer to a very different set of shareholders" (Goodman and Loveman 1991, 28).

Critics of privatization are also concerned about the dangers of monopolistic practices that the sheer size of municipal waterworks systems may invite. They have pointed out that three gigantic private international conglomerates already dominate the world urban waterworks field and that these three firms will probably control 65 to 75 percent of these systems in the next fifteen years. These are the French firm, Suez Lyonnaise des Eaux, which with its major subsidiaries Ondeo and United Water Resources currently controls water systems in 130 countries that serve 115 million customers; Vivendi Universal, with projects in 100 countries serving 110 million; and Thames Water of the United Kingdom, owned by the German conglomerate RWE, which has projects all over the world serving 70 million people. In addition to these three conglomerates, three other large international firms are also active in the water supply field: Bechtel, with six current and former subsidiaries; the Saur of Bouygues, with twenty; and United Utilities, with twenty-four (Landingin 2003).

In response to the fear that private enterprise may provide inequitable service by charging an exorbitant price for water to maximize profit, some privatization supporters have argued that it would be extremely difficult for them to do this because private water suppliers cannot set their price too high or consumers will reduce consumption or seek water from other sources (e.g., artesian wells, deep wells). Private water suppliers can withhold their product from the market only up to a certain point, because doing this would require very large storage facilities. They can exclude nonpaying customers only if the cost of exclusion (e.g., controlling pilferage) is lower than the revenue generated by inclusion. In many cases, it may be too expensive to go after nonpayers. The government may also demand that private enterprise should provide water at an affordable price to urban poor people, in keeping with its philosophy of fostering social equity (Anderson and Snyder 1997, 50–52; Dowding et al. 1995, 274).

An analysis of the results of privatization can be made based on what has happened in Jakarta and Metro Manila, where the waterworks systems were both privatized in 1997. In Jakarta, the privatization scheme was carried out by Thames Water Overseas Limited, which entered into a partnership with Sigit Harjojudanto, the son of former president Suharto; and Suez Lyonnaise des Eaux, which partnered with Anthony Salim, the chief executive of the Salim Group, owned by a close friend of Suharto. Greater Jakarta was divided into two water zones, one under a new company called PT Kekar Thames Airindo, owned 80 percent by Thames and 20 percent by Sigit, and another under PT Garuda Dipta Semesta, owned 40 percent by Suez and 60 percent by the Salim Group (Argo and Laquian 2004).

The privatization of water activities was not new in Jakarta. In the past, the government agency in charge of water, the Perusahaan Air Minum Jaya (PAM Jaya), turned over to a private agency, PT Belmanda Lestari, the activities of reading water meters, issuing water bills, and collecting water charges for an initial period of ten years. Later, PAM Jaya entered into contracts with PT Ciburial Aqua Mineral for the management of one of the agency's treatment facilities in North Jakarta. Pam Jaya signed a private contract with members of AKAINDO, an association of private contractors, for the installation of new water pipes to expand the network. The main justifications for these uses of private-sector services were the hopes that privatization would increase the rate of collection of water charges, reduce cases of "leakage" in revenue flows, and lower the price of water for the average consumer (Argo 1999, 253).

The division of Greater Jakarta into two privatized waterworks systems, however, was an entirely different arrangement. The contracts turned over the entire water system—the raw water supply sources, treatment plants, delivery system, metering, billing, and even the offices of Pam Jaya—to the concessionaires. The water concessions were to be for twenty-five years, and the arrangements turned the public agency, PAM Jaya, into a powerless entity that could not even see the private companies' financial reports. The contract also forced private businesses and homes to shut down private wells, a significant imposition, because about 70 percent of the water consumed in Jakarta in 1997came from private wells.

The Greater Jakarta waterworks arrangements collapsed in May 1998 when Suharto resigned amid riots that reputedly saw more than 2,500 killed in the city. Executives of Thames and Suez fled to Singapore but returned as soon as calm was restored. The Indonesian government tried to cancel the privatization contracts but withdrew when the foreign companies threatened to sue. The contracts were renegotiated in 2001, and Thames and Suez each got 95 percent interest in the private companies, with the remaining interests given to Indonesian subcontractors.

The privatization of the water system in Metro Manila paralleled that in Greater Jakarta. Metro Manila was also divided into two zones and twenty-five-year concessions were awarded to private companies. The eastern zone concession was awarded to Manila Water Company, Incorporated (MWCI), and the western zone to the Maynilad Water Services, Incorporated (MWSI). Manila Water was 60 percent owned by the Ayala Corporation, with the remaining 40 percent interest taken over by United Utilities Limited of the United Kingdom and Bechtel Corporation of the United States. Maynilad Water Services was a consortium led by the Lopez group with Ondeo, a subsidiary of Suez Lyonnaise des Eaux, as the foreign partner. The eastern zone serviced a population of 6.2 million people, though in 1997 only 4.3 million of those were connected to the system. The western zone had 4.5 million people, with 3 million connected to the system. Both private concessionaires promised that by 2006, from 94 to 97 percent of all people in their respective areas would have potable running water, with Maynilad promising to lower rates by 44 percent and Manila Water by 74 percent (Gaylican and Donato 2002; Villanueva 2002; Landingin 2003).

Before the privatization venture, the 11 million residents of Metro Manila had long suffered from critical water shortages. As a government corporation with a monopoly over the metropolitan area's water supply, the Metropolitan Waterworks and Sewerage System served only two-thirds of Metro Manila residents, leaving 3.6 million people without running water. The system admitted that more than half the water it produced was unaccounted for, through leakage and pilferage. MWSS was notorious for inefficiency and corruption and was overstaffed with political protégés. Petty corruption was rampant, ranging from bill collectors who did not report meter tampering or illegal connections because they were bribed to top MWSS officials getting kickbacks on anomalous service contracts. People who favored privatization of MWSS argued that letting the private sector manage Metro Manila's water system would bring about efficiency, responsiveness, transparency, and accountability. They hoped that privatization would make potable water more readily available to citizens at a fair and reasonable price.

Five years after the privatization of Metro Manila's water system, however, the whole scheme started unraveling. In December 2002, Benpres, the Lopez family firm responsible for the MWSI, defaulted on its debt-servicing obligations. To make matters worse for the Lopez clan, their other enterprises also experienced financial strains. The Supreme Court of the Philippines ruled that Meralco, the flagship company in the Benpres group that provided electricity to Metro Manila, should refund its customers 28 billion pesos in billing overcharges. Rockwell Towers, the Lopez-owned luxury condominium project, was put up for sale. The construction of the north diversion toll road system, another Benpres venture, lagged behind schedule. Most critical of all, subscribers to MWSI were up in arms in hastily convened "public consultations," filing vocal objections against increases in water rates (*Manila Bulletin,* December 3, 2002).

The Lopez-owned MWSI tried to explain that in five years, it had invested more than $428 million in the project—$143 million in equity financing, $120 million in a performance bond, and $165 million in commercial debts. The consortium had expected that the Asian Development Bank and six private commercial banks would lend it about $350 million for the venture, but these funds had not materialized. In mid-December, Benpres asked the government to allow it to raise water rates from 15.46 pesos per cubic meter to 31.30 pesos. The government approved a raise of 26.00 pesos. Because of this decision, MWSI said it was returning its franchise to MWSS. The government raised the issue for mediation with the Singapore-based International Chamber of Commerce for resolution.

A major reason behind MWSI's financial woes was the fact that, in its contract, it had failed to put in an automatic currency exchange adjustment that would have protected it against currency fluctuations. When the privatization agreement was signed in February 1997, the Philippine currency was valued at 26 pesos to the dollar. In August 1997, however, the Asian financial crisis hit with the devaluation of the Thai baht, and the value of the peso declined precipitously. The peso went down to 53.60 pesos to $1.00 in December 2002, in effect doubling the foreign exchange obligations of MWSI. It slid further to 58.92 pesos to $1.00 in January 2004, making the situation for Benpres much worse.

In its eagerness to land the MWSS contract, MWSI grossly underestimated the cost of rebuilding and streamlining the metropolitan water system. It ignored the fact that the system's basic infrastructure had been built 120 years earlier during the Spanish colonial period. Many of the old pipes had collapsed or were leaking, broken, or corroded. More than a century of neglect and a lack of maintenance had seriously damaged a system that had been originally designed to serve fewer than a million people but was now expected to serve more than 11 million.

Added to the basic problems of the metropolitan water system was the precarious financial condition of MWSS. To keep the water system running, MWSS had embarked on piecemeal engineering interventions funded by international loans. These included water diversion projects that tapped the Umiray River, additional filtration facilities at its Balara site, and thousands of kilometers of new distribution pipes. At the time MWSI took over part of the system, the foreign indebtedness of MWSS amounted to $800 million. MWSI agreed to absorb 90 percent of that debt, while MWCI absorbed 10 percent. To add to its woes, MWSS had huge unpaid bills from government agencies. MWSS also admitted that 67 percent of the water it supplied was "unaccounted for," classified as nonrevenue water.

A complicating factor for MWSI was the fact that a full third of the population of Metro Manila lives in slum and squatter areas, most of which were on the western side of the metropolis. Most of these poor urban families were not formally served by the waterworks system—they got their water from illegal connections, opened fire hydrants, or water vendors. Because it was concerned about the political backlash that a drastic stopping of these practices would create, MWSI decided to expand connections to the poor urban communities but proposed a stepped system of water charges. For poor urban households getting their water supply from shared sources, the proposed charge was 10.18 pesos per cubic meter. People getting their water from metered standpipes would pay 30 pesos per cubic meter, and those with water piped into their homes would be charged 150 pesos per cubic meter. With this innovation, MWSI hoped to encourage poor people to recognize the need to pay for water. With this and other innovations, it hoped that the proportion of nonrevenue water in the system could be reduced from 67 to 48 percent.

An analysis of the Metro Manila water privatization scheme points out that simply transferring control of a facility to private hands without fully considering the shortcomings of the publicly owned system would not solve deep-seated problems. As the private concessionaires found out, it was extremely difficult to change people's attitudes and values. Poor households who had become used to not paying for water found it hard to accept the additional costs. Public officials, who had traditionally used public corporations as dumping grounds for their political protégés, tried to continue the practice. More important, privatization raised people's expectations; and when improvements did not occur, they complained vociferously.

More specifically, some of the problems encountered in privatization schemes such as the ones used in Metro Manila and Greater Jakarta include

(1) the economic uncertainties arising from international financing, (2) local and international political considerations in privatization schemes, (3) the high cost of metropolitan waterworks systems, and (4) difficulties in efforts to make water provision fair and equitable.

In an era of rapid globalization, big-ticket projects, such as the privatization of metropolitan water systems, are usually affected by international financial changes. As a result of the 1997 Asian financial crisis, Maynilad found it extremely difficult to raise capital funds. It had hoped to borrow $238 million in long-term money by 2001, but it was able to raise only $16.7 million. A $350 million long-term loan from a group of banks stalled in 1999 and was abandoned. As a result of these financial difficulties, Maynilad's capital expenditures of $82 million between 1997 and 2001 were less than half the $170 million it had promised to spend under its contract. Manila Water was also not able to meet its contractual obligations, allocating $30 million for physical plant, property, and equipment, compared with $42 million promised in the contract.

The Asian financial crisis, coupled with the toppling of the Suharto regime, also made the financing of the Greater Jakarta privatization scheme difficult. Indonesian plans to abrogate the contracts were withdrawn because of fear that prolonged litigation would scare away other foreign investors. After the renegotiation of the contracts and signing of agreements in 2001, the expected financing from the foreign concessionaires did not fully materialize. According to the contracts, Thames Water and Suez were supposed to allocate $318 million to the projects by 2002—but they actually spent only $100 million.

The hope that involving large international conglomerates in waterworks projects would increase transparency and limit political manipulations was not fulfilled in either Jakarta or Metro Manila. In Jakarta, Thames Water chose as a partner one of the sons of Suharto, a known gambler with no experience in the water business, whereas Suez chose the son of a Suharto crony. One critic of the arrangement observed that the Indonesian partners got shares in the venture "without putting up any money, just their political influence." A World Bank official, asked why he supported the privatization arrangement despite these shady deals, said: "You cannot expect the private sector not to be in a mess in a messy environment" (Harsono 2003).

In Metro Manila, the foreign concessionaires also chose as their partners powerful and well-connected families like the Lopezes and the Ayalas. To lay the groundwork for the privatization scheme, former president Fidel Ramos declared a "water crisis" in 1995, and the Philippine Congress passed the "Water Crisis Act" giving the president legal powers to privatize MWSS. The president allowed MWSS to increase water rates by 38 percent in August 1996, six months before the bidding on the project. This enabled the bidding consortia to set rates in their bids that looked considerably lower than the existing ones (Landingin 2003).

Accounts of how the Metro Manila projects were set up revealed, in fact, that the international financiers and, perhaps, the donor agencies themselves were capable of making questionable moves. When the privatization of the Metro Manila water systems was being discussed, the World Bank paid for the visit of a number of Filipino officials, politicians, and labor leaders to take a look at a project in Buenos Aires—a project chosen to show the merits of a privatized scheme. Later that year, the French government gave the Philippine government a grant of $1 million to hire a consultant, which turned out to be the French company SOGREAH, which, not surprisingly strongly recommended privatization. The International Finance Corporation, the World Bank's private-sector affiliate, was also contracted to draft the concession agreement, and it designed the bidding process for selecting the two international partners for the scheme. Critics of the process charged that the International Finance Corporation had vested interest in assuring that the privatization process was successful because a clause in its contract would award it at least $1 million if the privatization bidding process was successful.

The primary reality of large-scale privatization of metropolitan water systems, of course, is that these are very expensive. Furthermore, private international concessionaires will usually not assume responsibility for key functions that do not create revenue. For example, protecting the watershed is basically a government function, but it is very important because if it is denuded, the supply of raw water will be inadequate. Building dams and reservoirs to hold water is also very expensive. Thus, the Philippine government allocated $200 million for the Umiray-Angat Transbasin Project in 2000 to increase Metro Manila's supply of raw water by up to 800 million liters a day. PAM Jaya in Jakarta said that the foreign companies just took over the water sources, the production and purification facilities, the whole distribution network, and the water installations and no proper valuation had been made of the costs of all these facilities. The international concessionaires, however, were less interested in the sewerage, drainage, and wastewater treatment aspects of the system because it was more difficult to make money from these components.

A major complaint against international water concessionaires in both Metro Manila and Jakarta was the high cost of their services. In the case of

Manila Water, for example, almost 70 percent of capital expenditures in the project went to fees for consultants, and experts from abroad accounted for a major share of company costs. In Jakarta, local PAM Jaya officials complained that top executives of the foreign companies were paid $150,000 to $200,000 a year, while their Indonesian counterparts were paid less than $25,000. The foreign executives and consultants also set up offices in posh buildings in downtown Jakarta, refusing to stay in PAM Jaya's buildings. Consultants also stayed in luxury hotels, and foreign executives lived in exclusive subdivisions, with all their costs charged to the waterworks projects.

One of the hopes in privatizing metropolitan waterworks systems is that it would improve people's access to potable water. The Metro Manila case showed that, at least initially, privatization did increase the amount of water that flowed to communities. The two concessionaires claimed that in the five years after the system was privatized, some 2 million persons were connected to the network. However, these figures were contested by analysts, who explained that the foreign concessionaires estimated water coverage by employing a ratio of 9.2 individuals served by each connection. French consultants set this ratio when the privatization scheme was initiated, but MWSS questioned the results by citing census population figures. For example, the Maynilad concessionaire claimed that it had served 1.7 million people in its area by 2001 based on 184,782 connections. MWSS said the census showed that there were only 1.4 million people in the area. Similarly, Manila Water, using its 9.2 per connection ratio, claimed that it had served 450,000 people in the city of Makati based on 47,178 connections, but MWSS pointed out that there were only 250,000 potential customers in the city (Landingin 2003).

Privatization was also supposed to improve access to water on the part of urban poor people. The two concessionaires in Metro Manila claimed that of the 238,000 new water connections they made from 1997 to 2001, 128,000 or 54 percent were in poor urban communities. However, an evaluation of the project showed that in these communities, the concessionaires installed metered water connections only near the water mains. Because access to densely populated neighborhoods was extremely difficult, private contractors entered into agreements with organized poor urban groups to extend the pipes to individual houses or corner standpipes. The poor urban communities had to pay for these special arrangements themselves, which increased costs to at least three times per cubic meter of water compared with what better-off families were paying.

The increased cost was also due to the fact that water charges were set progressively—consumption of the first 20 cubic meters was charged at

1.60 pesos, whereas consumption above 100 cubic meters was charged at 6.00 pesos. Because many more household connections were connected to each metered outlet in poor urban communities, poor residents usually paid a lot more. These inequitable rates were made worse by the fact that poor people tended to get less water than their wealthy neighbors. The National Water Resources Board estimated in 2004 that each resident of a poor area got only 4 cubic meters of water per day, whereas a person in an exclusive subdivision got 80 to 120 cubic meters. The higher water consumption was for watering the lawn, washing the car, swimming pools, bathtubs, and flushing toilets (*Manila Times,* January 23, 2004).

In Jakarta, Suez and its Indonesian counterpart stated that they had increased water connections by 50 percent, from 200,000 in 1997 to 300,000 in 2001. Thames also claimed that it had increased connections from 268,000 to 320,000 in 2001. The combined connections of 620,000 of both companies, however, were still below their original projection of 711,000 set in 1997. Also, a significant portion of the new connections were to wealthy neighborhoods like Menteng and Pondok Indah, where many households that used to pump their own water from deep wells could now get it piped into their homes. Suez claimed that it had increased connections to poor neighborhoods from 9,000 in 1997 to 35,000 in 2001. Some critics of Suez disputed this figure, because the company defined connection in terms of the installation of new water meters, which did not necessarily mean that more water flowed through those metered connections.

To sum up, privatization in Jakarta and Metro Manila did expand the supply of water in both systems, and more connections to households and business enterprises were made. The price for delivered water increased significantly, however—although ironically, poor urban residents, while being charged more than their wealthier neighbors, actually found the water cheaper compared with the exorbitant amounts they used to pay to water vendors. Privatization did not make access to water more equitable—in fact, in both Jakarta and Metro Manila, poor residents tended to pay more for less water because of the way connections were set up in their communities and the progressive rates imposed on the volume of water consumed.

The 1997 Asian financial crisis adversely affected the privatization schemes because it raised the foreign exchange costs of the projects. Six years after the privatization of the systems, the schemes were struggling—with at least one, the Maynilad project, on the brink of bankruptcy. Although the international financial conglomerates were supposed to have massive capital resources to finance privatization schemes, they relied very heavily on World Bank and Asian Development Bank loans. The fact that these loans were made in hard currencies affected the projects adversely when the financial crisis devalued local currencies.

The Jakarta and Metro Manila schemes revealed that private concessionaires, in their efforts to gain higher profits, seemed more interested in expanding water connections to businesses and households rather than in dealing with systemic problems, such as reducing unaccounted-for water. They also preferred to extend services to middle-income and high-income households in exclusive gated communities rather than to communities of poor people. This was because they could earn more from increased connections and could pass the cost of unaccounted-for water to customers by raising water rates. They were also unable or unwilling to finance some elements of waterworks systems, such as the protection of the watershed, the construction of dams and reservoirs, and piping raw water into these reservoirs. It was true that the private concessionaires were able to introduce efficient methods of metering, distributing, and collecting water charges. However, the efficiencies achieved were offset by their higher costs of operations and their inability to deliver water more equitably to all segments of the urban population.

6

Managing Mobility in Mega-Urban Regions

From a physical-planning perspective, the skeletal form of a mega-urban region is defined by the roads, railroad tracks, rapid transit lines, streets, paths, and lanes that make up its transport network. On maps of city-regions, the familiar outlines of ring roads delimit the extent of the metropolis. The arterial loop roads around Tokyo Metropolis, for example, have reorganized the urban structure of Japan's capital region into a central core and four suburban nodes forming a ring-shaped cluster of cities. The Jing-Jin-Tang Expressway linking Beijing, Tianjin, and Tanggu forms the developmental axis of China's national capital region. Some city regions, such as Bangkok, Jakarta, and Metro Manila, take a fan-shaped, palm-and-fingers pattern, with string developments stretching along arterial highways radiating from the city center. Others, like Mumbai (formerly Bombay), conform to a fishbone outline with a major road and railway making up the spine and secondary roads forming the spurs emanating from it.

Far more important than the physical form provided by a transport network, however, is the role of barrier-free mobility in ensuring the economic vitality of a mega-urban region. Transport activity is the bloodstream that dictates if a mega-urban region pulses with economic energy or stagnates because of blocked arteries or congested pathways. Food, raw materials, and other productive inputs are brought into the city daily while finished products and wastes come out. People dash from their homes to their workplaces and back, and then they go out for leisure and entertainment. Parents take children to and from school, or they go marketing or shopping. The time people spend tied up in traffic greatly influences their productivity and level of comfort or frustration. The type of transport mode used in the city-region is an excellent indicator of how much pollution is generated, which

239

is measurable by the ill effects of pollution on people's health and the environment. The number of people traveling each day, of course, exerts pressures on the transport network.

On average, it has been estimated that an additional 1 million people in a developing country city would generate an extra 350,000 to 400,000 public transport trips each day. Wealthier cities, where more people can afford to drive private automobiles, will also tend to have more daily trips. Other factors—such as the extent of urban sprawl, the locations of job sites relative to residences, the cost of public transport, traffic volume, and the types of vehicles used—also influence the frequency of daily trips.

The primary objective of a transport system is "an acceptable level of mobility for both passenger and freight in order to satisfy the transport demand generated by economic growth and urban development in a territory" (Yeh, Hills, and Ng 2001, 7). An acceptable transport system should be safe, predictable, affordable, comfortable, flexible, responsive, and accessible, and it should not create excessive noise, air, water, and soil pollution. A comprehensive strategic transport plan for a mega-urban region, to be effective, requires the integration of land use, economic, and social activities, transport modes, information systems, and a full consideration of the economic, social, and environmental effects of the type of transport chosen. It must respond to the travel needs of all income and cultural groups, especially urban poor people, who usually makes up the bulk of the traveling public (Wang and Chan 2004).

Typically, transport policy may focus on supply-side elements, such as the construction of roads, rail lines, water routes, bridges, tunnels, ports, harbors, and airports, and the improvement and maintenance of various transport modes. In many Asian city-regions faced with problems of congested traffic and environmental pollution, however, transport planners and urban authorities are realizing that the "predict and provide" approach to transport planning has become inadequate ("more roads attract more traffic"). They are finding that this approach has to be complemented by demand-side regulation policies that make the external costs of transport more transparent and thus enable vehicle users to make more informed decisions when they plan to own or operate a vehicle.

These demand-side interventions include the control of vehicle ownership by licensing, imposing quotas on vehicles, taxation, road pricing, fare setting, and enforcing emission standards and control regulations. Some authorities have also used transport management instruments, such as intelligent transport systems for electronic traffic control and surveillance, automatic toll collection, smart cards, and real-time information signs to inform drivers about road and traffic conditions.

The main determinants of what type of transport system is appropriate for a mega-urban region are (1) the income level of residents; (2) the role of government in public affairs; and (3) the size, population density, and physical configuration of the city-region. As far as income is concerned, studies have shown that, other things being equal, high income is directly correlated with private vehicle ownership. High-income countries like Australia, Austria, Canada, Germany, New Zealand, Switzerland, and the United States all have on average more than forty-five cars per 100 persons. However, as the adverse environmental and health effects of widespread automobile use have become more evident in these countries, urban authorities have started introducing policies to limit car use and offer alternative transport modes.

In other cities, where the bulk of the people have low incomes, residents tend to do more walking, use bicycles or motorbikes, take the bus, or rely on paratransit systems composed of two- or three-wheeled vehicles powered by two-stroke engines. Interestingly, because of worsening environmental pollution problems, urban authorities in high-income cities have started adopting programs that encourage more walking and bicycling, mobility modes more associated with cities with low-income residents.

In Asian mega-urban regions, the role of government in transport ranges from a relatively relaxed view that considers the government to be mainly concerned with setting basic policies and conditions for private-sector initiatives to a more dominant role that directly involves the government in financing, constructing, maintaining, providing, and managing transport systems. In most South Asian cities, transport is mostly provided by private modes. In Delhi, for example, 63.6 percent of the vehicles on the streets are privately owned two-wheelers (Iyer 2002). Similarly, in Karachi, 72 percent of all commuters take privately owned and operated minibuses (Sohail 2000). Dhaka residents rely on about 10,000 "baby taxis" and "tempos" financed by private moneylenders and owned by shadowy operators.

In Metro Manila, 66.4 percent of vehicles for hire are privately owned—composed of 39.1 percent jeepneys, 14.9 percent buses, and 12.4 percent tricycles. In contrast to the conditions in the cities mentioned above, in the Chinese cities of Beijing, Guangzhou, Shanghai, and Tianjin, the government owns and controls the urban transport system (i.e., buses, subways, mass transit), although in recent years, the number of private vehicles in these cities has increased significantly. In Osaka, Seoul, and Tokyo, more than half of daily trips taken by people are on publicly operated mass transit systems. Private car ownership in these cities, however, is relatively high, because of residents' average high income.

The size, population density, and shape of a mega-urban region also greatly influence the type of transport system. In general, cities with small areas that have very high population densities will tend to have fewer vehicles in proportion to population. For example, Hong Kong and Singapore, with respective densities of 5,924 and 5,476 persons per square kilometer, have a high per capita gross domestic product, but their rate of car ownership is quite low (respectively 5.2 and 11.6 cars per 100 persons). Hong Kong, because of its small size, has the most crowded road network in the world, measured by the number of vehicles per unit of road length, but it has low private vehicle ownership (Hau 2001, 131; Wang and Chan 2004).

Conversely, cities like Osaka, Seoul, and Tokyo have high population densities but also larger land areas. Furthermore, they have also developed into multinodal settlements, with the various nodes well connected by rapid transit. Authorities in these high-income cities have the resources to finance subways and rapid transit systems. The governments of these cities have also exercised their authority and power to enforce demand-related transport policies that have attempted to limit car ownership.

Transport Modes

The transport situation in Asian mega-urban regions is best illustrated by the type of transport mode taken by people on their daily trips (the so-called mode split). In the past fifteen years or so, the shifts in travel modes have been very rapid in many Asian mega-urban regions as some Southeast Asian cities have cut down on the use of paratransit systems and bus fleets and embarked on building heavy rail and light rail transit systems. The mode split in Asian city-regions is seen in table 6.1, which shows that the choice of transport modes varies sharply according to a city's income, size, population density, and level of technological development.

Table 6.1 shows that majority of the poor population of Southeast Asian cities relies on paratransit vehicles for daily trips, including motorized *betjaks* (Jakarta), jeepneys (Manila), and *samlors, silors,* or *tuktuks* (Bangkok). The bulk of residents of South Asian cities, like Delhi, Dhaka, and Karachi, use two- and three-wheeled vehicles such as minibuses, tempos, and baby taxis. Many residents of these cities also walk or take their daily trips using

Table 6.1. *Modal Shares of Urban Transport Trips in Asian Mega-Urban Regions (percent)*

Region	Walking	Nonmotorized Vehicles	Paratransit	Public Transit	Motorcycles, Motorbikes	Private Automobiles
Tokyo	8			53	17	22
Osaka	24	10		38	8	20
Seoul	5			75	5	15
Bangkok	1	5	5	40	17	32
Jakarta	23	2	3	25	13	34
Metro Manila	12	3	39	13	3	30
Beijing	12	48	6	20	2	12
Shanghai	31	33		25	6	5
Tianjin	14	64		12		10
Kolkata (Calcutta)	15	9	40	6	10	20
Delhi	20	12	53	8		7
Dhaka	40	20	8	20	4	8
Mumbai (Bombay)	15	3	28	9	20	25

Note: Nonmotorized vehicles include bicycles, rickshaws, tricycles, and pedal-powered *betjaks.* Para-transit includes motorized vehicles such as "baby taxis," tempos, jeepneys, auto-rickshaws, motorized tricycles, *helijaks, tuktuks, samlors,* and various types of two-, three-, or four-wheeled vehicles. Public transit includes buses, trams, heavy rail transit, light rail transit, subways, commuter rail, and bus rapid transit systems. Motorcycles and motorbikes include motorized two-wheeled private vehicles. Private automobiles include taxis, rental cars, and limousines.

Sources: Figures for Delhi are from Badami, Tiwari, and Mohan (2004). Dhaka data are for 2002 and from the World Bank report on the Dhaka Urban Transport Project. Data for Tokyo, Beijing, and Tianjin are from World Bank (2000). Data for Osaka are from Osaka Prefectural Government (2002). Seoul data are from "Seoul's Urban Transportation Policy and Rail Transit Plan, Present and Future," *Japan Railway and Transport Review,* October 2000. Additional data for Delhi are from Delhi Traffic Police, Ministry of Surface Transport (http://www.teriin.org/urban/delhi.htm). Metro Manila data are from Roth (2000). Data for all other city regions are from Asian Development Bank (1989).

nonmotorized transport such as bicycles and rickshaws. A significant number of travelers rely on private buses, which are often extremely crowded, poorly maintained, do not follow predictable schedules, and suffer from frequent breakdowns.

The mode-split patterns noted above reveal that many people in richer Asian mega-urban regions rely on public transit. For example, 75 percent of trips in Seoul and 53 percent in Tokyo are by rail-based transport. In these cities, the polynucleated shape of the city-region is made possible by public transit networks that allow daily commuting between suburban homes and workplaces in the inner city. In medium-income city regions, however, paratransit vehicles are still used by most people. Still, in some cities like Bangkok and Metro Manila, the newly built mass transit systems are starting to become popular despite their relatively high fares. The Bangkok Sky-train started operating in 1999 with a design capacity to carry 500,000 passengers a day. In 2002, it claimed to have carried 93.5 million person-trips, a 24 percent increase from 74 person-trips in 2001. On Valentine's Day, February 14, 2003, the Skytrain was said to have carried a record 400,000 persons. In addition to Skytrain, a new Bangkok subway system involving an investment of $2.7 billion was to be inaugurated in August 2004. The metro was projected to be able to carry 631,000 persons a day when it became fully operational (*South China Morning Post,* November 2, 2003).

Chinese cities have traditionally encouraged the use of the bicycle, and many people still use them. In 2002, Beijing had 8 million bicycles and 1.3 million motorcycles. The city's subway system, which ran for 50 kilometers, transported roughly 10 percent of the city's population, and the bus system carried another 15 percent. For the 2008 Olympics, however, Beijing plans to expand its subway system to 150 kilometers. It is expected that with the construction of the new subway segments and the increase in the number of private cars (which were growing at 40 percent a year), fewer people in Beijing would be using bicycles (*China Daily,* September 30, 2003). A bus rapid transit system with dedicated bus corridors, multidoor buses, modern bus stations, and a ticketing system fully integrated with the subway system is also under construction in Beijing (Sustainable Urban Transport Project, Bangkok, http://www.sutp.org).

Big cities in South Asia rely very heavily on paratransit systems made up of two-, three-, or four-wheeled vehicles powered by two- to four-stroke engines. In Delhi, there were 2,261,132 two- or three-wheeled vehicles in operation, 960,799 four-wheelers, 86,985 auto rickshaws, 38,481 taxis, 47,085 buses, and 161,022 goods vehicles (Duggal and Pandey 2002). High levels of pollution in the city have been attributed to these vehicles. Indian authorities have calculated that two- and three-wheeled vehicles powered by two-stroke engines contributed 61 percent of hydrocarbon pollution and 35 percent of particulate-matter pollution in Delhi (Iyer 2002). To combat pollution, the Delhi authorities had mandated the use of natural gas as fuel for two- and three-wheelers by order of the Supreme Court. This action is said to have cut air pollution levels in the city by 25 percent (Badami, Tiwari, and Mohan 2004).

Public transit in Karachi is mainly composed of private buses—in 2001, it was reported that there were 14,854 intracity and 513 intercity buses operating in the city-region. The Karachi Transit Corporation used to have 800 buses, but the company was closed down for reasons of mismanagement and corruption. According to the Regional Transport Authority, 72 percent of all commuters in Karachi used minibuses. These vehicles were blamed for the city's chaotic traffic, because 43 percent of the minibuses did not have any route permits. The minibuses were privately owned, and the owners had formed the Minibus Drivers Association, which was rumored to have much influence on transport authorities. There were also rumors that many of the real owners of minibuses were on the police force.

It is interesting that high levels of private car use in Asia are found in cities like Bangkok and Jakarta that already suffer from traffic congestion. In Osaka, Seoul, and Tokyo, where there are many residents with high incomes, car ownership has been controlled by measures such as high taxes, registration fees, licensing, and parking fees, as well as the high cost of fuel, insurance, and vehicle maintenance. The governments of Indonesia and Thailand have started to use demand management policies as well, but the desire to own a car among upwardly mobile individuals is very high. Car ownership is also expected to rise in Chinese cities because of growing affluence and the rapid growth of a domestic car-manufacturing industry. However, in Hong Kong, car ownership is being controlled by a combination of policy measures making it very expensive to own and offering an alternative transport mode in the form of an efficient mass transit system.

To sum up, the transport modal shares noted above suggest the following contradictions: (1) Many low-income city-regions are going for expensive transport modes like road-based private vehicles and rapid transit systems, but the great majority of citizens, especially poor residents, cannot afford these; (2) walking as a healthy and environmentally conserving mobility mode is rarely included in city-region transport plans; (3) low-income city-regions are banning nonmotorized modes like bicycles while high-income ones are encouraging people to use them; (4) in low- and medium-income city regions, where paratransit modes are used by most people (especially poor people), there are very few practical proposals to improve these; and (5) though high-income city-regions have started curtailing the ownership and use of private automobiles, the authorities in lower- and medium-income ones are continuing to encourage private car use. Most important of all, many Asian city-regions still have to see the direct link between comprehensive and strategic development plans and the role of transport in the efficient functioning of those plans. They fail to appreciate the importance of locating residences closer to jobs, services, shopping, and entertainment. They still pursue rigid zoning codes and subdivision regulations that prevent mixed land uses. They also do not respond to the transport needs of the great majority of their people but choose modes that favor the elite.

Transport Problems in Asian Mega-Urban Regions

Transport-related problems in very large Asian city-regions differ markedly from those in smaller urban settlements. In smaller cities, many people can usually walk to work or rely on nonmotorized transport modes like bicycles and rickshaws. As cities become larger, however, the distance between trip origins and destinations become longer and people have to use motorized transport. They also use motorized vehicles to transport freight and trade goods.

In comparison with transport conditions in mega-urban regions in North America and Europe, those in Asia are quite different in transport modes used. With the exception of Osaka, Seoul, and Tokyo, private car ownership in Asian mega-urban regions is still relatively low. In 1994, Asia's population made up 60 percent of the world's total, but the region accounted for only 10 percent of the world's automobiles and more than 25 percent of its trucks and buses (Midgley 1994, 14). Private vehicle ownership in some Asian cities, however, has increased since 1994, especially where some people have become affluent enough to afford a car, as in Bangkok, Jakarta, and Metro Manila. The 1997 Asian financial crisis, urban pollution, and the adoption of restrictive legislative and administrative measures have somehow slowed down private car ownership. Since the crisis, however, continued high rates of economic growth in some countries have generated a higher demand for cars, especially in China, where a domestic car manufacturing industry has joined with international firms to meet growing car demand.

In South and Southeast Asian cities, the dominant form of transport is privately owned two- and three-wheeled vehicles powered by two-stroke engines. In Delhi, about 66 percent of the for-hire vehicles on the road in 2002 were two-wheelers and another 28.3 percent were four-wheelers (Duggal and Pandey 2002). Most residents of Dhaka, especially poor people, depend on more than 10,000 baby taxis and tempos and about 500,000 rickshaws to get around. When baby taxis were banned from major streets in 2003 because they were blamed for air pollution, many people objected because it was claimed that about half of these paratransit vehicles would be taken off the roads (*BBC News Online,* May 15, 2003). A major source of serious traffic problems in Southeast Asian cities has been the rapid increase in the number of motorcycles, mopeds, and motorbikes. Ho Chi Minh City is estimated to have more than 2 million motorbikes, and these vehicles are also the dominant mode of transport in Hanoi.

In general, the most serious mobility problems in Asian city-regions include (1) traffic congestion; (2) environmental pollution; (3) overloaded public transport systems; (4) unsatisfactory conditions for pedestrians and cyclists; and (5) a lack of funds and managerial and institutional resources for the construction, operation, and maintenance of transport systems. The types of problem faced by each particular city-region, of course, depend on many socioeconomic and political factors, and not all Asian mega-urban regions suffer from each problem to the same degree. The efforts to solve those problems also differ in strategic emphasis, resource allocation, transport modes of choice, and social class or groups benefiting or disadvantaged by the specific policies adopted.

Traffic Congestion

It is paradoxical that many mega-urban regions in Asia have lower rates of motor vehicle ownership compared with those in North America and Europe but suffer more from traffic congestion. The most important reason for this is the large number of people using a great variety of vehicles on narrow and poorly maintained streets. It is not uncommon in Asian cities to find bicycles, tricycles, push carts, rickshaws, ox carts, horse-drawn carriages, and other slow-moving vehicles competing for road space with motorcycles, scooters, mopeds, buses, trams, minibuses, trucks, taxis, and private cars. This mix of transport modes results in greatly reduced mobility because the slow-moving vehicles set the pace and flow of traffic on urban roads.

Poor road design and inadequate traffic management add to these problems. In cities like Beijing, Guangzhou, Hanoi, Ho Chi Minh City, and Shanghai, where multilane expressways have been constructed in recent years, traffic is often slowed down (and made very dangerous) by bicycle riders, ox carts, farm tractors, pedestrians, and the occasional cow or water buffalo sharing the same road space or crossing at poorly marked intersections. In densely populated cities like Bangkok, Dhaka, Kolkata (formerly Calcutta), Metro Manila, and Mumbai, inner-city traffic is also constricted by hawkers, vendors, peddlers, and pavement dwellers who take over the sidewalks and push pedestrians into the streets, where they then block the passage of vehicles.

Because of traffic congestion, the journey to work each day in most Asian mega-cities is taking longer and longer. In the Greater Tokyo area, for example, where an extensive mass transit system is already in place, a survey revealed that 31.9 percent of office and commercial workers spent up to 30 minutes a day, one way, commuting between home and office; 33.2 percent spent more than 30 minutes to 1 hour; 32.3 percent spent 1 to 2 hours; and 2.6 percent spent 2 hours or more (Tokyo Metropolitan Government 2003). Aside from the long hours spent commuting, passengers are subjected to serious discomfort and indignities. The congestion in Tokyo subways and commuter trains is so bad that some commuter lines have had to run women-only trains at night because of complaints about groping by male passengers.

Most Asian mega-cities have inadequate road space to meet the mobility demands of people. Road network densities in the early 1990s, measured in meters per 1,000 inhabitants, were 600 in Metro Manila, 400 in Jakarta, and 230 in Hong Kong (Midgley 1994, 26). Densities have become higher since then because of the increase in number of vehicles. Another problem is caused by the fact that urban roads are not well integrated with each other—main thoroughfares are often blocked at intersections without grade separations, traffic circles, or well-coordinated systems of traffic lights. Many roads are not well maintained. Potholes not only slow down traffic and cause accidents; they also cause considerable damage to vehicles. Accidents create huge traffic jams, especially because the police usually take a long time to investigate and the vehicles involved are not promptly moved to clear the flow of vehicles.

The rapidly increasing use of motorcycles, motorbikes, scooters, and mopeds in Asian mega-urban regions has greatly added to traffic congestion. It has been estimated that with the exception of Japan and South Korea, from 60 to 80 percent of the vehicle fleets in Asian cities is made up of two- or three-wheeled vehicles powered by two-stroke engines (Iyer 2002). Though two-wheeled vehicles occupy smaller road space per unit than cars, they travel fast and their drivers are more likely to weave in and out of traffic lanes, often causing serious accidents. Accidents are particularly bad in cities where helmets for motorcycle riders are not required and where riders do not always follow traffic rules and regulations. When motorcycles are attached to passenger cabs, as in the motorized tricycles of Metro Manila or the *helijaks* of Jakarta and Surabaya, they do not only slow down traffic— the extra passenger load strains the engines and contributes to air and noise pollution.

To sum up, the various complicating factors that add to traffic congestion in Asian mega-urban regions include road conditions, sidewalk and street invasion, poor traffic control, grade separation, designated vehicle stops, designated traffic lanes, traffic rules and regulations, vehicle maintenance, road repairs, calamities and emergencies, uncoordinated traffic plans, expressways and bypass highways, mass transit systems, and traditional ceremonies. Before moving on, it is helpful to examine these factors in more detail.

Road Conditions

Streets in many South and Southeast Asian cities are usually narrow, twisting, potholed, and poorly maintained. They are designed more for walking and slower vehicles than for motorized transport (*calesas,* horse-drawn rigs, are still used in inner-city neighborhoods of Manila). Circulation in inner-city areas—such as the *bastis* (slums) of Mumbai, the *chawls* (poor neighborhoods) of Delhi, the *katchi abadi* (uncontrolled settlements) of Karachi, the *barrios* (slums) of Manila, and the *kampungs* (urban villages) of Jakarta—is severely limited. There are dead-end streets, like the *sois* in the middle of superblocks in Bangkok or the *looban* ("interior") communities in Metro Manila, that are inaccessible even to police, fire, and emergency vehicles. Self-built squatter communities on the metropolitan periphery also have very narrow and poorly maintained lanes that only tricycles, bicycles, and motorcycles are able to negotiate.

Sidewalk and Street Invasion

Road space in many South and Southeast Asian cities is often limited because of sidewalk invasion by hawkers, vendors, and pavement dwellers that push people and activities into the streets. There are about 800,000 pavement dwellers occupying sidewalks and other urban space in Mumbai. In Dhaka, one of the solutions used by the World Bank–financed Dhaka Urban Transport Project was the forced removal of hawkers and vendors from major traffic corridors to facilitate traffic flow. Traffic in Metro Manila is usually slowed by young boys and girls who jump in and out of public vehicles to sell candy, peanuts, chewing gum, and cigarettes, endangering themselves and others as they try to make a precarious living. The Metro Manila Development Authority has waged periodic campaigns against sidewalk vendors and street food sellers, but it has achieved only limited results in easing traffic congestion because many people patronize these peddlers, enforcement officers look the other way because they have been bribed, and many of the vendors are organized as effective lobbying groups that enjoy the support of local politicians.

Poor Traffic Control

Many cities lack appropriate traffic signals to control traffic. Computer-coordinated traffic signals have been installed in some Asian mega-urban regions, but their operation has often been disrupted by electricity brownouts, poor maintenance, typhoons, and even sabotage by operators. Police forces and traffic enforcers augment their income by tolerating illegal parking, loading and unloading passengers in restricted zones, or accepting bribes instead of issuing traffic tickets. They also sometimes enforce traffic regulations selectively, favoring the cars of political figures and influential people and exploiting private vehicle operators.

Grade Separation

A lack of grade separation results in traffic bottlenecks at intersections. Many cities have found that it is extremely expensive to build bridges or underground channels in existing and heavily used roads. Delays in construction also disrupt traffic flows. Some pedestrian underpasses and overpasses have been constructed in a number of cities, but these have tended to be poorly maintained and quite a few have become congested by vendors.

Designated Vehicle Stops

Lack of designated vehicle stops where passengers can get on or off is a serious problem in Asian cities. Traffic on Metro Manila streets, especially on heavily traveled Epifanio de los Santos Avenue, tends to be clogged by buses and jeepneys stopping anywhere so passengers can get on or off. In Dhaka, designated "slip lanes" for buses and other vehicles have been set up at regular intervals, but enforcement of traffic rules has been sporadic because drivers of public conveyance vehicles easily bribe police and traffic officials to escape arrest or fines. Passengers also fail to line up to board public vehicles, causing delays and congestion.

Designated Travel Lanes

Many Asian urban streets lack designated travel lanes to separate slow-moving from fast-moving vehicles. Some cities, like Bangkok, Manila, Hong Kong, and Jakarta, have introduced special lanes for public buses or high-occupancy vehicles. Beijing, Shanghai, and Tianjin have special bicycle lanes. The enforcement of rules on the use of designated lanes, however, has been rather sporadic. Metro Manila has instituted traffic violation ordinances that penalize drivers who shift from one lane to another, but the enforcement of these rules has been ineffectual.

Traffic Rules and Regulations

The enforcement of traffic rules and regulations is usually poor because drivers have not been properly trained and enforcement officials can be corrupted. Many Asian urban authorities have adopted formal laws and regulations on how to get a driver's license, register a motor vehicle, submit a vehicle for a certificate of roadworthiness, require regular emission checks, and the like. However, most of these rules are frequently circumvented as people find it easier and cheaper to bribe an official than to conform to the laws and rules. Many private transport operators, such as bus and jeepney drivers in Metro Manila, use the "boundary system," whereby their daily earnings depend on a sum of money (the "boundary") that they have to pay the vehicle owner each day. To earn money beyond the set boundary, drivers often have to speed, weave in and out of traffic, pick up and let off passengers in illegal areas, and bribe traffic officers when caught. Drivers of baby taxis and tempos in Dhaka also have to meet daily payments to operators and moneylenders, so they try all sorts of techniques, including illegal ones, to earn enough to make these payments.

Vehicle Maintenance

It is quite common for urban roads in Asian city-regions to be blocked by stalled motorized vehicles that are old and lack proper maintenance. Technically, vehicles need to pass inspection and need a certificate of public conveyance before being allowed on public roads. However, poor enforcement of these rules adds to the number of disabled vehicles that block traffic in many city streets. Often, drivers and operators drive their vehicles into the ground to earn as much money as possible, neglecting preventive maintenance.

Road Repairs

Frequent public works road repair and construction jobs close important thoroughfares or force vehicles to detour to side streets. There is poor coordination among the public and private agencies in charge of water supply, drainage, sewerage, electricity, telephones, gas, and the like that use the streets for their pipes and distribution systems. Digs and construction jobs may be done on the same spot at different times by these companies, requiring detours, street closings, and slowed traffic. Poor construction methods, inferior road building materials, and a lack of government funds also contribute to poor road maintenance and frequent repairs.

Calamities and Emergencies

Natural calamities, such as typhoons, cyclones, fires, and floods, often disrupt traffic in Asian cities. Mega-urban regions like Bangkok, Dhaka, Hanoi, Ho Chi Minh City, and Metro Manila are frequently subjected to floods, high winds, and other calamities that disrupt movement of people and goods. Fires that often burn down uncontrolled human settlements also disrupt traffic. Unfortunately, many of these Asian cities do not have adequate disaster preparedness and emergency plans for dealing with these problems.

Uncoordinated Traffic Plans

The fragmentation of local government units in Asian city-regions makes coordinated traffic action difficult. Some mega-urban regions have comprehensive traffic plans, but their enforcement is decentralized to local government units. In Metro Manila, rich cities like Makati and Mandaluyong can afford to have paved and well-maintained streets, but roads in neighboring cities like Paranaque and Pasay tend to be full of potholes. Designation of one-way streets may also be messed up by local officials responding to local pressures. In some exclusive "villages" in Metro Manila, traffic is absolutely restricted to vehicles bearing special permits. Special subdivisions in peri-urban areas also refuse public conveyances to pass through their private enclaves.

Expressways and Bypass Highways

Many Asian cities lack limited access highways and expressways for by-passing congested urban centers. Many mega-urban regions have found the construction of bypass highways expensive. Interprovincial vehicles often have to drive through inner cities, greatly clogging their streets.

Mass Transit Systems

Some Asian mega-urban regions have set up mass rapid transit systems, but many cannot afford them. A number of Asian mega-urban regions have built rapid transit systems at great expense. But others, like Karachi and Mumbai, have had to delay or cut down their mass transit plans because of a lack of funds.

Traditional Ceremonies

In some Asian mega-cities, traffic is blocked or slowed down by traditional ceremonies and observances—such as funeral processions, periodic market days, fiestas, and fairs—that clog city streets. It is also quite customary for top government officials, visiting dignitaries, and other important people to travel very fast, accompanied by motorcycle escorts and other vehicles that stop regular traffic and disrupt traffic flow.

Environmental Pollution

The dominance of road-based transport—especially diesel-powered automobile, buses, freight trucks, and goods vehicles, and also two- or three-wheelers using two-stroke engines—has been a major source of environmental pollution in many Asian mega-urban regions. Incomplete combustion and a lack of state-of-the-art catalytic converters in vehicles raise the level of gases responsible for the so-called greenhouse effect. The hydrocarbons that build up in the soil, animal feed, and food crops pose serious dangers to human health because of their known carcinogenic effects. High concentrations of nitrogen oxide arising from the oxidation of compounds in fuel additives result in acid rain, erosion, and weathering, and also have morphological effects on people's respiratory systems. Particulates and soot from incomplete fuel combustion damage people's respiratory systems and result in dirty buildings. Carbon monoxide is dangerous to health and is linked to ozone formation in the atmosphere. Road-based transport also contributes a great deal to human noise, which is not only a nuisance but also adds to health risks (Button and Rotherngatter 1993, 30).

On the basis of the results of a number of studies, the environmental pollution in Asian mega-cities is considered very serious by global standards. The levels of lead in the air breathed by residents of Jakarta and Metro Manila are far above the guidelines set by the World Health Organization, although the situation in these cities has improved since the banning of leaded gasoline. The amount of suspended particulates in all cities except Tokyo, however, is considered serious. The air quality in Bangkok, Beijing, Jakarta, Metro Manila, and Shanghai is significantly below standard because of concentrations of sulfur dioxide, carbon monoxide, and ozone-depleting gases.

A World Bank study in 2002 concluded that the Philippines has spent or wasted more than $1.5 billion a year because of air pollution. This huge amount, representing about 2 percent of the country's gross domestic product, was measured in terms of lost productivity, lost wages, premature loss of life, and medical costs. The study estimated that every Filipino spent about $400 a year for treatment of illnesses caused by air pollution, such as 9,000 cases of bronchitis and pneumonia and 2,000 premature deaths from tuberculosis in big cities like Cebu, Davao, and Manila (*Philippine Daily Inquirer,* March 23, 2003). The health effects of pollution in other Asian cities are also alarming—the Hong Kong Environmental Protection Department estimated that the air pollution level in Hong Kong accounted for at least 2,000 premature deaths a year, and it blamed the pollution on the use of diesel-powered vehicles. The department warned people, especially those with respiratory illnesses, to avoid prolonged exposure to air in designated "black spots," that is, areas with heavy traffic congestion.

In Dhaka, air pollution is mainly blamed on the number of two- and three-wheeled vehicles that are the main transport modes of poor residents. In 1998, the Department of the Environment stated that the amount of suspended particulate matter (SPM) in the city ranged from 1,000 to 2,000 micrograms per cubic meter of air, four to five times higher than the acceptable levels set by the World Health Organization. The acceptable level for sulfur dioxide is 60 micrograms per cubic meter, and recorded readings in Dhaka range from 300 to 500 micrograms. The Bangladesh Atomic Energy Commission also reported that each day vehicles in Dhaka emitted 100 kilograms of lead, 3.5 tons of SPM, 1.5 tons of sulfur dioxide, 14 tons of hydrocarbons, and 60 tons of carbon monoxide.

The major polluters in Dhaka were three-wheeled vehicles powered by two-stroke engines, locally known as baby taxis and tempos. The baby taxis were said to contribute 64.5 percent of SPM, 49.5 percent of carbon monoxide, and 38.6 percent of nitrogen oxide pollution in the city. Larger buses also contributed 51.4 percent and trucks 30.4 percent of SPM pollution. Buses were also responsible for 36.4 percent of hydrocarbon emissions, followed by trucks at 21.4 percent.

All Asian mega-urban regions have adopted environmental laws and regulations to combat air pollution. However, the implementation of these statutory enactments in some cities has been ineffective because of a lack of trained personnel and appropriate equipment, easily circumvented procedures, and the willingness of enforcement officers to exempt some violators because of personal and kinship ties and bribes. Some progress has been achieved in controlling pollution from transport in some cities (Osaka, Seoul, Singapore, and Tokyo are good examples), but in general, conditions are most likely to become worse before they get better in many Asian cities.

A somewhat encouraging situation is emerging in New Delhi, where the conversion of three- and four-wheelers, taxis, and buses to compressed natural gas by order of the Supreme Court and the adoption of a vehicle inspection system have started to reduce air pollution. New Delhi's proposed dedicated high-capacity bus lane system with designated stops, coupled with special lanes for bicycles and nonmotorized transport, also promises to reduce congestion and ease mobility (Tiwari 2002, 217).

Inadequate Public Transport

In view of their large sizes, high population densities, and low incomes of their residents, many Asian mega-urban regions have inadequate transport systems and thereby suffer from congestion, delays, and pollution. Some cities, notably those in South Asia like Delhi, Kolkata, and Mumbai, are mainly dependent on paratransit systems, although they also have publicly managed bus and commuter rail systems. Others, like Hanoi and Ho Chi Minh City, rely mainly on motorbikes.

In Chinese cities like Beijing, Guangzhou, Shanghai, and Tianjin, the bicycle used to be the main mode of transport. During the mid-1980s, Beijing had more than 8 million bicycles and only 2,500 automobiles. Traffic was light because people lived close to their work units. City streets had dedicated bike lanes that helped maintain safety for bicycle riders. The price of bicycles, even of the highly coveted "Flying Pigeon" brand, was affordable because the government subsidized bicycle manufacturers. The few automobiles on the road were mainly for the use of top government officials and the diplomatic personnel in the city. By 1990, however, the number of bicycles in Beijing had gone down to 6.2 million. At the same time, the number of cars had jumped to 380,000, buses to 5,267, and trolley buses to 514 (Zhao, Chen, and Zhang 1992, 18). By 2,000, there were 2.5 million automobiles in Beijing, and traffic in the city had become a lot worse.

The number of private automobiles has increased even faster in other Asian cities. In Greater Jakarta, privately owned cars increased at an average rate of 15 percent a year during the 1970s. By 1984, 85 percent of motor vehicles in the city were private cars. In an effort to cut automobile use, the government encouraged the local production of minibuses and light pickup trucks as trade vehicles. However, because these vehicles were so cheap, people bought them and used them as private vehicles, contributing to the city's already bad traffic congestion. Bowing to the inevitable, the Jakarta Master Plan formulated in 1982 projected that the city-region would have 2.1 million automobiles by 2005, an increase of 255 percent (United Nations 1989, 35).

Although Jakarta's wealthy families traveled around in private cars, about 60 percent of the population relied on private buses. The problem, however, was that the buses were mostly old and poorly maintained and did not keep to a regular schedule. Bus fares were kept relatively low because of a gasoline subsidy provided by the government. However, management of the bus fleets was in the hands of private entrepreneurs motivated primarily by profit. Many of the bus operators had been withdrawing from the business because of low profitability. Jakarta's master plan projected that by 2005, the proportion of trips on buses will decline from 52 to 30 percent, and trips by private automobile are expected to increase accordingly (DKI Jakarta 1984).

The deterioration in bus service has made the lives of poor people in Jakarta even worse, because in the early 1980s the government banned the operation of *betjaks* (three-wheeled bicycle rickshaws) from Jakarta's main streets. By 1984, there were less than 25,000 *betjaks* in Jakarta, and some of these were motorized *bajajas* (refitted motorcycles). Because each *betjak* had been known to provide inexpensive transport to an estimated sixty persons daily, the loss of mobility to poor residents was considerable. Banning the *betjaks* from main streets eased traffic congestion somewhat for car-riding residents, but this had negative effects on the lives of poor citizens.

Buses have also been the main transport mode in Kolkata, Mumbai, Delhi, and Karachi. The Kolkata Metropolitan Development Authority estimated that the total capacity of public transport in the city was 2.8 million trips a day but the total passenger demand was 6.8 million. In Mumbai, the bus and rail system accounted for 90 percent of all person-trips. More than half of daily trips in Delhi were by bus. However, all the bus companies providing transport service in these South Asian cities had suffered great losses. The Karachi Transport Corporation, which ran more than half of Karachi's buses, had suffered heavy losses because of low bus fares, pilferage, and fare jumping. Some of the losses had been offset by a government subsidy, but this had to be curtailed because of poor economic conditions.

Because of the inadequate service from buses, South Asian cities have seen a proliferation of paratransit systems. During the mid-1980s, the number of minibuses and metered taxis rapidly increased in Karachi, but they contributed so much to air pollution (and to the high incidence of traffic accidents) that their use was later also limited. The situation was even worse in Dhaka, where it was estimated that about 80 percent of the population could barely afford to pay for normal transport costs and patronized rickshaws and auto rickshaws. The possibility of setting up full-blown mass rapid transit systems for Delhi, Karachi, and Kolkata has been discussed in recent years, but poor economic conditions are barring their realization.

A bus system has satisfactorily met Seoul's transport needs since the 1980s, when ninety private companies carried more than 90 percent of person-trips in the city. Since that time, however, the rate of private car ownership in Seoul has rapidly increased because of the rise in people's income. In 1984, private automobiles carried only 8 percent of all passengers but made up 85 percent of all vehicles in the city. To solve Seoul's transport problem, the government has embarked on building a subway network, both to solve congestion and to encourage the growth of the city toward the periphery.

Light rail transit (LRT) systems have been constructed in a number of Asian mega-urban regions to solve transport problems. In Metro Manila, a Light Rail Transit Authority was created in 1980 and, with the help of a thirty-year interest-free loan from the Belgian government, it set up a 16.8-kilometer rapid transit line in 1984 and 1985. The system was upgraded in the period 1992–99 to increase its passenger capacity to 27,000 persons an hour at peak periods. Phase 2 of the system was opened in 2003 and extended the line another 5.5 kilometers. In addition, two separate transit lines managed by Metro Rail Transit Corporation were also built to extend the system—Line 3, an eastern orbital line covering 17 kilometers, and another line to the north, adding 5.5 kilometers. A proposed Line 2 called the Megatren, an east–west line of 13.8 kilometers, is expected to be inaugurated in 2004. That system will have eleven stations (for more information, see http://www.railway-technology.com/projects/manila).

Early assessments of the effects and impact of the LRT system in Metro Manila have shown mixed results. The first line, after auspicious beginnings, suffered from equipment breakdowns, a lack of maintenance, and unpredictable service. Construction of the new lines has been delayed by a lack of funds and by investigations of alleged mismanagement and corruption. Complaints against the lack of escalators and elevators to take passengers to the platforms have been aired. The construction of the elevated structures has darkened city streets and ruined the central business district of Manila. Most important of all, there have been many complaints that the fares charged by the new lines have been too high. As a result, many people have continued to use the more affordable jeepneys and buses, which have continued to operate along the same routes taken by the rapid transit systems.

In 1992, Bangkok started construction of Skytrain. After seven years, the project was finished at a cost of $1.2 billion. The system currently maintains two lines and runs for 23.5 kilometers, along Sukhumvit and Silom Roads. In 2002, Skytrain claimed to have accounted for 93.5 million person-trips, an increase of 24 percent over the 74 million person-trips in 2001. On Valentine's Day, February 14, 2003, Skytrain carried a peak load of 400,000 passengers. In addition to Skytrain, Bangkok is also expected to inaugurate a subway system in August 2004 that is expected to carry 237,000 passengers a day.

Although rapid transit systems are being built or planned in many other Asian cities, a number of questions have been raised, particularly about the costs of such systems and whether the rates they charge are affordable by poor people. It has been noted, for example, that bus rapid transit (BRT) systems can cost 20 to 200 times less than rail-based systems, depending on the technology chosen. Dedicated bus lines cost less to build than elevated rapid transit lines and are not as intrusive or as expensive as subways. BRTs can also use buses that are powered by less-polluting fuels like natural gas. In fact, BRT systems are already in operation in Jakarta and Kunming, a line is under construction in Beijing, another line is about to be inaugurated in Metro Manila, and a line is proposed for Bangkok (Sustainable Urban Transport in Developing Asian Cities 2003; http://www.sutp.org).

As a whole, the main dilemma in Asian mega-urban regions, as elsewhere in the world, is the economic and social effects of policy choices among transport modes. As residents of city-regions become more affluent, they have a tendency to prefer the private automobile for reasons of comfort, flexibility, independence, and others that may not be directly related to achieving better mobility at all, such as the status and prestige that owning a car entails. Policymakers and those who benefit from the car industry (manufacturers, oil companies, and road-building enterprises) respond to higher car demand by adopting supply-side policies.

This policy choice, however, has implications not only for the environment but also for social sustainability. The private automobile effectively separates wealthy from poor people, because the former have a wide range of choices as to where they could live, work, shop, or be entertained. Car owners are cocooned in their comfortable cars and, when granted the privilege to drive along limited access highways and freeways made possible by government subsidies, they do not even see their poor neighbors. This dualism has severe negative implications for social sustainability in Asian mega-urban regions, a phenomenon already happening in cities of more developed countries (Polese 2000, 316–20).

Furthermore, as noted by Downs, if transport systems in Asia and other developing countries follow trends in the United States, traffic congestion will be a permanent feature of life in very big cities. Downs asserts that expanding road capacity to accommodate more vehicles will not work, because as soon as a new route is opened, many people will rush to use it until it gets congested. Building rapid transit in nine American metropolitan areas saw only 17 percent of commuters shifting to this mode by 2000—expanding transit capacity three times, according to Downs, would raise morning peak-hour transit travel by 11 percent but would only reduce private vehicle trips by 8 percent. In view of these trends, Downs has concluded that "peak-hour traffic congestion in almost all large and growing metropolitan regions around the world is here to stay. In fact, it is almost certain to get worse during at least the next few decades, mainly because of rising populations and wealth. This will be true no matter what public and private policies are adopted to combat congestion" (Downs 2004, 8).

Pedestrians, Cyclists, and Other Nonmotorized Travelers

In densely populated Asian cities, various efforts have been made to encourage people to walk rather than take motorized vehicles. In Hong Kong, for example, conscious efforts have been made to construct elevated walkways both outdoors and indoors to allow people to walk from one point to another. Elevated walkways have also been constructed in the "Greenbelt" section of Makati City in Metro Manila, where the planting of shade trees, shrubs, and flowering plants along urban paths has encouraged people to walk. Less environmentally friendly but supportive of pedestrian travel just the same is the traffic-free redevelopment of parts of Nanjing Road in Shanghai, which is lined with shops, offices, restaurants, and entertainment venues.

Despite these successful attempts at pedestrianization, some city officials and transport planners have misgivings about such schemes. It is argued that pedestrianization causes congestion and hinders the flow of traffic in adjacent areas. Pedestrian-only streets attract hawkers, make cleanliness and refuse collection a serious problem, and can result in higher crime rates because service and police vehicles do not have access to the areas.

The experiences of Hong Kong and other densely populated Asian cities show, however, that encouraging pedestrianization is sound economically, socially, and environmentally. What is needed is careful planning—such as the location of rapid transit stations close to the pedestrian-only zones; the introduction of escalators, elevators, ramps, and other facilities to help handicapped and incapacitated people as well as the elderly; the provision of services, such as shops, cafes, pubs, markets, and other amenities, that facilitate social interaction; and carefully laying out paths to destination points and installing clear signs to guide walkers (Brown 2001, 190–91).

Considering that up to a third of daily trips in some Asian mega-urban regions are by walking, and that an almost similar proportion of travelers use bicycles, tricycles, and other nonmotorized modes to get around, the conditions faced by pedestrians, cyclists, and other users of nonmotorized modes in such city-regions are very unsatisfactory and even dangerous. In South Asian cities, people often have to walk long distances because of inadequate motorized transport modes. They have to negotiate wide and busy streets and rush at the crowded street corners where pedestrian-crossing lanes are located because the streets are designed as barrier-free channels for fast-moving cars and trucks. Here and there, urban authorities have built overpasses and underpasses for pedestrians, but in general, crossing the streets is limited to designated spots. Police forces also enforce jaywalking rules very strictly or demand bribes from violators.

Chinese cities have designated special lanes for bicycle riders, but other Asian cities have not followed suit. As a result, accident rates are high. In collisions between bicycles and cars or buses, cyclists are invariably on the losing end. In Ho Chi Minh City, there are also frequent accidents between pedestrians and riders of motorcycles, mopeds, and scooters. In many Asian cities, there are clearly marked pedestrian crosswalks, but speeding drivers do not always obey traffic regulations and accidents occur quite frequently.

Because pedestrians and cyclists are directly exposed to air pollution, they are more likely to suffer from illnesses such as asthma, bronchitis, lung cancer, and lead poisoning. Noise pollution is also a serious problem. Health officials consider a noise level in excess of 65 decibels as injurious to health, but this level is often exceeded in many Asian cities. High levels of noise have been known to contribute to physiological and psychological disorders, cardiovascular disease, and hearing loss. A study of noise levels in Bangkok showed that more than 75 percent of buses, 60 percent of trucks, and 25 percent of minibuses used in the city emitted noise levels in excess of 100 decibels at a distance of 0.5 meters (Midgley 1994, 19).

It is ironic that urban authorities in technologically advanced countries are encouraging people to walk more or use bicycles but that in Asian mega-cities, where a lot of people walk and use bicycles, many government policies and programs actually discourage these means of getting around. With the exception of Chinese cities, where bicycle use has been encouraged by public policies in the past (but is declining because people see it as "backward" and local governments have started banning it from streets with high traffic volumes), very few urban authorities in Asia are doing this. The trend in many Asian cities is to encourage more motorized vehicles by building multilane highways, lowering the prices of fossil fuels, importing luxury vehicles, and lowering taxes on vehicles, fuel, and oil. There are very few measures designed to make the lives of pedestrians and cyclists safer and more comfortable, with the result that as more people take motorized transport, the streets get more clogged and the atmosphere gets more polluted.

A Lack of Resources

Most Asian mega-urban regions habitually cite a lack of funds as an explanation for their inability to deal with their transportation woes. In many instances, however, a lack of funds is only a generalized excuse that hides other problems such as (1) misallocating or mistargeting resources when deciding what sectors or groups are to be subsidized, (2) an unwillingness to charge local constituents the full economic costs of transport services, (3) overreliance on tax shares and grants-in-aid from the central government for transport improvement, and (4) avoiding transparency and accountability in the use of public resources for transport services.

One of the most common reasons given by local officials for their inability to set up efficient transport networks is that travelers and riders have a low capacity to pay. They thus justify the need for subsidies, either direct or hidden, to help urban poor people. However, in many Asian mega-urban regions, the private sector has often been able to provide relatively inexpensive transport to the public. Jeepneys and buses in Metro Manila are run by the private sector. The two- and three-wheeled vehicles in Delhi, Dhaka, Karachi, Kolkata, and Mumbai are also private.

Of course, roads, bridges, and highway networks are provided by the government and can be considered public subsidies. Other subsidies take the form of keeping the price of gasoline low, encouraging the easy importation of automobiles, not charging for environmental pollution costs, and the like. Yet the problem with these types of subsidies is that they end up benefiting rich instead of poor people. A World Bank study reported that "although energy subsidies in developing countries are often justified as protecting the poor, evidence suggests that the non-poor capture up to 90 percent of subsidies" (World Bank 2002a, 21).

Some economists have argued that subsidies, in general, have a number of serious negative effects. First, because consumers do not pay the full cost of the service they enjoy, they tend to overconsume or waste it. Second, overconsumption and waste leads to serious environmental pollution, which in turn affects people negatively, especially poor citizens. Third, the inability of government to collect the full price for the public service places it in a situation of chronic financial insolvency, which then translates into a greater incapacity to provide more services. Thus, the replicability and sustainability of projects are negated.

In the case of transport, the issue does not seem to be the nature of subsidies as such but rather the fact that the benefits from subsidies do not usually go to poor people. This happens because of *leakage,* or the enjoyment of the benefits by nonpoor people, and *improper targeting,* or the failure of poor people to actually benefit from the subsidy because they do not have access to it. For example, subsidies to keep the price of gasoline artificially low because of lobbies and threatened riots by bus and paratransit owners and operators actually benefit private automobile owners more. Not charging tolls for superhighways also does not help poor people because such limited-access highways are used more by rich car owners than the bus- or paratransit-riding public.

Solving Mega-Urban Transport Problems

The worsening transport problems in most Asian mega-urban regions is generating a number of planning and management efforts to deal with the most severe aspects of traffic jams, high economic costs, people's discomfort, and environmental pollution. From a review of policies and programs devoted to solving mega-urban transport problems in Asia, these approaches seem to offer the best chances for success: (1) improving paratransit systems and integrating these into comprehensive strategic planning and management schemes; (2) the construction, operation, and maintenance of road-based transport systems; (3) the provision of mass transit systems; (4) regulatory and control measures based on transport demand management; and (5) formulating and implementing truly comprehensive strategic transport schemes. Of course, the effectiveness of each approach will depend on the circumstances in each mega-urban region. This section examines each approach in turn.

Improving Nonmotorized and Paratransit Systems

With the exception of cities like Hong Kong, Osaka, Seoul, and Tokyo, many residents of Asian mega-urban regions rely on walking, bicycles, and paratransit systems, such as baby taxis and tempos in Dhaka; minibuses in Karachi; two- and three-wheeled vehicles in Delhi; jeepneys in Metro Manila; motorized *betjaks* in Jakarta; and *samlors, silors,* and *tuk-tuks* in Bangkok. These transport modes are mainly used by poor residents, who make up the great bulk of urban populations—people who usually cannot afford to pay for other modes. They are also the source of livelihood of tens of thousands of poor families.

Transport planners and government officials, however, often consider paratransit vehicles undesirable—blaming them for chaotic traffic, charging them with willful violation of traffic rules and regulations, and holding them responsible for air, water, soil, and noise pollution. Therefore, paratransit vehicles have been banned from major city streets, harassed by police and traffic enforcement officers, and threatened with outright abolition. However, they continue to be used because they meet the need for an inexpensive and responsive transport system for poor people and they provide employment for many individuals.

To solve the pollution problem attributed to paratransit vehicles, urban authorities in other Asian city-regions might well consider the decisions taken in Delhi, which established clear emission standards for two- and three-wheeled vehicles and has enforced them with strict emission testing and regular inspections. The introduction of improved two-stroke lubricating oil, such as the mandatory dispensing of 2-T oil in Delhi, drastically cut pollution from two- and three-stroke engines. The Delhi authorities also promoted the use of compressed natural gas (CNG) as an alternative fuel for two- and three-wheelers. As a result of these actions, Delhi has become "the world's largest user of CNG as automotive fuel," a move that was enhanced by a mandatory ruling of the Supreme Court of India banning the use of polluting fuels. These measures—which focused on improving fuel quality, stopping the use of leaded gasoline, enforcing emission standards, and phasing out old two-wheelers—has resulted in a 25 percent reduction in the pollution load in the city-region (Duggal and Pandey 2002).

As for the use of human-powered vehicles, such as tricycles, *betjaks,* and rickshaws, some transport planners consider them undesirable and even inhuman because they "exploit" the labor of human beings. They have been banned from major streets because they slow down automobiles and trucks and cause traffic congestion. As an analyst of the Dhaka Transport Project from the World Bank observed, however, "non-motorized transport is remarkably efficient and does not adversely affect the environment—but it is threatened by the attitude of planners that regard it as 'backwards.' The problem is how to integrate non-motorized transport with other modes" (Khan 2003). In Dhaka, it was recommended that nonmotorized transport vehicles be used as "feeders," which will take people from narrow lanes and interior communities to transport junctions, where they can access faster transport modes.

Because of the very important role played by nonmotorized and paratransit systems in many South and Southeast Asian cities, it is important that authorities in these cities consider the appropriateness of policies and programs that rationalize these systems' role and integrate their activities into metropolis-wide transport systems. For example, in designing the rapid transit systems of Bangkok and Metro Manila, planners have conceived of a "hierarchy" of transport modes, whereby people living in inner-city neighborhoods and narrow lanes could walk or take motorcycles, *samlors,* and *tuk-tuks* to rapid transit stations. In suburban areas in Metro Manila, tricycles and jeepneys could act as "collectors" and bring travelers from villages and communities to the main transport junctions. This pragmatic approach not only facilitates mobility—it does not take away jobs from drivers, mechanics, conductors, and other people who depend on paratransit for their livelihood.

Planning and Managing Road-Based Transport

Most transport systems in Asian mega-urban regions are road-based, although water transport and heavy rail are still used for hauling heavy cargo, and light rail transit and bus rapid transit are starting to gain popularity for moving people. An important reason for the prevalence of road-based transport in many Asian cities is their ancient origin; these cities have seen the historical evolution of transport from walking, to human- or animal-drawn vehicles (palanquins, rickshaws, ox carts, horse-drawn wagons, carriages), and later to motorized vehicles (cars, buses, motorcycles, two- and three-wheeled vehicles). Indicative of this evolution is the fact that the inner-city layouts of old cities like Beijing, Delhi, Osaka, and Tokyo are made up of tiny lanes and paths poorly suited to motorized travel. Although cars, buses, trams, commuter rail, and mass rapid transit have been introduced to most Asian mega-urban regions, their inner-city road networks have not changed enough to suit these transport modes.

The use of roads has greatly facilitated the development of Asian mega-urban regions. Streets provided not only greater mobility but also valued space for economic activities and social interaction. They served as important means for escape during natural or human-made disasters and calamities. In many cases, streets improved the aesthetic character of urban settlements with their arches, monuments, and tree-lined sidewalks. They supplied edges to city areas and clearly demarcated territorial boundaries. They also provided a coherent sense of spatial identity to residents of urban neighborhoods.

Although building more roads or widening and improving existing ones in central cities will most likely not help to relieve traffic congestion, it has been found that mobility can be enhanced if new roads are built that efficiently link densely inhabited urban nodes with each other and with the central city. For example, the Greater Jakarta Master Plan (2005) focused mainly on developing new communities in the peri-urban area and constructing an extensive road network to serve these communities. Government Decree 678/1994, one of the enabling pieces of legislation for implementing the plan, extended incentives to developers of commercial areas around urban nodes and promised to build roads that would link these to the inner city. Government Regulation 20/1994 sought to facilitate infrastructure development by providing incentives to local and foreign investors interested in financing roads, ports, railways, and the like under public–private partnership schemes (Bray 1996, 217).

The construction of the Jakarta outer ring road, a 58-kilometer toll road connecting the northwestern and northeastern ends of the Harbor Toll Road, has significantly changed the shape of the Jakarta region. The increased accessibility has encouraged the setting up of commercial, industrial, and residential enclaves on the urban periphery. The transport plan had also enhanced clustered development focused on self-contained communities located beyond the outer ring road. It has been estimated that the increased acquisition of land for infrastructure and property development has significantly increased land values on the urban periphery by more than a third. Greater Jakarta's local authorities have been preparing legislation to "capture" the increases in land values by reassessing land parcels benefiting from road construction as closely as possible to their fair-market value and using these reassessment results as the basis for new real estate taxes.

Establishing new urban nodes and building roads, of course, is not enough to ensure rational development. In the Jakarta case, it was found that not enough attention had been given to the secondary road network that would feed into the major toll roads. Because of this, land development (and increased land values) had been mainly focused on the outer-city areas directly linked to the toll roads, leaving potentially valuable land closer to the city undeveloped. This may eventually lead to potentially uncontrolled urban sprawl, especially if not enough secondary roads, feeders, and connectors are linked to the major toll roads (Bray 1996, 217).

As in Jakarta, road construction and other types of road-based transport efforts have created many problems in other Asian cities. The extensive road-building programs pursued by many urban authorities have encouraged the use of the private automobile, especially in cities where an increasingly affluent population could afford to buy cars. Automobiles are more comfortable, faster, more private, more convenient for timing trips, more flexible, and, in status-conscious Asian societies, they impart higher status and prestige. The building of more roads to accommodate more cars, of course, takes up very valuable land. Roads are extremely expensive to design, construct, and maintain. They can have negative social and environmental effects, as when superhighways cut off segments of neighborhoods or result in paving over farmlands, marshy areas, or fragile wildlife habitats. Most important of all, where governments have invested heavily in road networks, they have found it extremely difficult to allocate public funds to other transport systems (e.g., rapid transit), irrevocably committing themselves to an environmentally unsustainable transport system.

To deal with these issues and other problems arising from road-based programs, transport planners and urban authorities may consider three approaches that have been found successful in a number of Asian mega-urban regions. The first approach is *road-pricing schemes*. The government and private entrepreneurs who build roads may recoup some of their investments and limit the number of vehicles using the roads by charging tolls. Toll charges may vary according to size, weight, and type of vehicle. Higher tolls may be charged during peak hours. Cities may also charge vehicles entering the inner city, as in Hong Kong and Singapore. To counter the inequitable effects of charging hefty amounts for vehicle owners entering the central business district, cities may provide "park-and-ride" facilities that allow people to leave their vehicles in suburban stations and use a transfer service to bring them to their inner-city destinations.

The second approach is *limiting the number of road-using vehicles*. Because traffic congestion is directly related to the number of vehicles allowed on the roads, it stands to reason that limiting the number of vehicles in a city will help ease traffic problems. Some Asian countries have used quotas that limit the number and types of vehicles licensed to operate in cities. Vehicle registration taxes and annual license fees have been charged, with some cities earmarking proceeds from these revenue sources for road maintenance. Other measures that have been used to limit the number of vehicles include imposing high taxes on gasoline, oil, spare parts, and other items needed for vehicle operation. Fees have also been charged for annually inspecting the roadworthiness of vehicles and for regularly checking emission standards. Compulsory insurance for vehicles, with premiums determined by the age of the driver and other factors, also serve as limiting factors on vehicle ownership. Parking subsidies and other benefits that encourage car ownership can also be abolished to discourage more vehicles on the road. Government offices, private businesses, banks, schools, and other institutions have been requested to allow their employees, staffs, and students to work or go to school on "flexible hours" to spread out the number of travelers beyond the peak hours. Leisure and entertainment venues like movie houses, restaurants, cafes, and shopping malls have also been requested to open early or late, to stagger the time when people would travel to get to them.

In some cities, heavy trucks and freight vehicles are allowed to enter the city only at night. An approach that has been discussed in North America but that does not appear to have been used in Asian mega-urban regions extensively is telecommuting or encouraging people to work at home using advanced information technology, such as the computer and other means. In theory, if ideas rather than human bodies are allowed to travel, the number of vehicles on the road will be reduced.

The third approach is *improving the efficiency of road use.* Building more roads in a city-region, aside from being prohibitively expensive, will not really improve the efficiency of road use because the rate of growth of vehicle ownership is invariably higher than the ability of the government to build more roads. Transport authorities in Asian mega-urban regions, therefore, can use various approaches that improve the efficiency of road use. Response teams may move stalled vehicles and clear those involved in accidents quickly. High-occupancy vehicle lanes have been introduced in a number of cities to allow faster travel. Intelligent transportation system devices have also been used to speed traffic flows.

Dealing with Pollution Problems

The use of gasoline and diesel as the main fuel for road-using vehicles is the main contributor to air pollution in Asian mega-urban regions. To solve the pollution problem, a number of measures have been used in these regions: (1) requiring the use of lead-free gasoline for motor vehicles; (2) encouraging the use of alternative fuels, vehicles that use hybrid engines, or electric cars; and (3) using regulatory measures such as banning the operation of polluting vehicles, limiting the use of motorized vehicles, and requiring emission tests.

At present, all the mega-urban regions in Asia require the use of unleaded gasoline. However, in almost all South Asian cities, two-stroke engines that are known to contribute heavily to air pollution are still widely used for paratransit systems. Diesel engines are also the main motors used for heavy trucks and buses and, when not properly maintained (which is usually the case in Asia), they tend to be heavy polluters. In Metro Manila, a significant amount of air pollution has been traced to the use of secondhand diesel engines from Japan, South Korea, and other countries, which have been imported by the government at concessional rates and then installed in city and suburban buses. Periodic campaigns are waged to get rid of these "gas guzzlers" and "smoke belchers," but every time the campaigns relax, the offending vehicles return to the roads.

The use of alternative fuels has significantly reduced the level of pollution in some Asian mega-urban regions. Electric cars, hybrid cars, and the highly touted hydrogen-powered car are still at experimental stages. In Chinese cities, methane from biogas digesters had been used for long-distance buses, but this is rarely seen today. A promising fuel is compressed natural gas, which has been used in Delhi to power notoriously polluting two- and three-wheeled vehicles. In Metro Manila, the government had announced that at least 100 buses fueled by CNG were plying routes along Epifanio de los Santos Avenue in October 2003. The prospects for more widespread use of CNG as a vehicle fuel are bright because it has been estimated that the Malampaya Sound natural gas reserves in Palawan can yield as much as 3.4 trillion square feet of natural gas for the next twenty years (*Manila Bulletin,* August 13, 2003).

Some Asian urban authorities have had more success with regulatory measures to control pollution. In Hong Kong and Singapore, the operation of eight-cylinder cars had been prohibited, virtually consigning some of the world's most expensive Rolls-Royces, Bentleys, and Mercedes-Benz limousines to garages. In Metro Manila, diesel-powered buses have been banned from city streets. The Clean Air Act of 1999 required that all motorized vehicles should pass an emissions test before being issued a license.

Metro Manila authorities have also tried to limit the number of vehicles on the road, using a "number-coding" system stipulating that vehicles with a license plate number ending in an odd number can be used only on odd-numbered days and those with even numbers on even-numbered days. When introduced in 1996, traffic planners had hoped that the system would reduce vehicular volume in Metro Manila by 20 percent. The pollution prevention scheme was supported by the Asian Development Bank with a $700 million loan, which was earmarked for (1) the setting up of private emission-testing centers; (2) the procurement of gas analyzers and opacity meters for the use of the Land Transportation Organization; and (3) the establishment of a motor vehicles inspection system. In 2002, the Asian Development Bank was told that franchises for the operation of private emission-testing centers had been issued to as many concessionaires. The opacity meters had also been purchased by the Land Transportation Organization and were ready to be used.

By 2003, however, an evaluation of the number coding scheme revealed that it had managed to reduce the volume of motor vehicle emissions by only 4.5 percent. The study found that many people had succeeded in beating the system by simply buying extra cars for use when their primary vehicles were not allowed on the road. Strong pressures from car owners to lift the ban forced the temporary lifting of the scheme, despite the complaint of many people that the scheme had only been in place for a short time and that it should be allowed to remain operational for a longer period. However, because of insistent lobbying by private car owners, the scheme was temporarily lifted for three months in early 2003.

To reduce pollution from vehicles, some Asian cities have decided to limit the number of vehicles on the road by taxation and other charges. The issue has been raised as to whether subsidies to public road-based transport are progressive or regressive. Studies on this issue have not been conclusive, but in Australia it has been suggested that public subsidies are regressive. In other countries, it has been found that public transport subsidies can sometimes benefit urban poor people, at least, initially. For example, in Metro Manila, the government allowed the importation of secondhand buses from Japan and South Korea and allocated these to private bus operators. The availability of the reconditioned buses, combined with the designation of special bus lanes and designated places where passengers could be picked up and dropped off, eased the city's notorious traffic for a while. Later, however, poor vehicle maintenance resulted in increased air pollution, noise, and other problems. All these externalities have been imposed on poor residents and not on middle-class riders, who use air-conditioned buses, or on the wealthy elite, who drive luxury cars.

Mass Transit Systems

Almost all mega-cities in Asia have set up some form of rapid transit, which is defined as "a public transport system which can carry large numbers of people and which uses a dedicated fixed track" (Bray 1996, 219). Examples of rapid transit systems are the light rail transit schemes in Kuala Lumpur and Metro Manila, the subways in Shanghai and Beijing, and the rail commuter line in Kolkata. Metro systems have also been set up in Hong Kong and Singapore. A proposal to construct a busway in Bangkok similar to the ones found in Adelaide, Curitiba, and Ottawa has also been made (Asian Engineering Consultants 1994). A bus rapid transit system has just been inaugurated in Metro Manila, and a similar one has been operating in Kunming, China.

The main issue with rapid transit systems is the heavy financial investment required. It has been estimated that a light rail transit system that can carry from 20,000 to 50,000 persons an hour in one direction can cost from $25 to $75 million per route kilometer. A bus rapid transit system on dedicated bus lines or guided tracks that can carry up to 20,000 persons an hour per direction can cost from $10 to $15 million per kilometer. These investments will most likely require government financing. It has been argued that under the conditions that exist in most Asian cities, the private sector will find rapid transit systems commercially viable (Fouracre et al. 1996).

In Hong Kong, part of the costs of the rapid transit system was covered by major land development schemes around transit stations. Even here, however, only about 15 percent of total revenues came from these land schemes and, as observed by Bray, "very few cities have sufficiently high land prices and severe enough congestion to emulate the Hong Kong experience" (Bray 1996, 220).

Despite the high cost of rapid transit systems, really congested cities such as Metro Manila have decided to invest in them. The Manila LRT, which cost about $170 million to build (at 1986 prices) commenced operations in December 1984 along a 15-kilometer route on the city's Taft Avenue. From the start, the system enjoyed a high utilization rate, with passengers increasing from 191,400 in 1985 to 355,700 in 1993. Although the fare box rate was relatively low (6.00 pesos, or $0.22 in 1991), the fare box ratio (gross revenue divided by direct operation costs) was a relatively high 1.5. The main problem, however, was the extremely high capitalization cost of the project, which, because it came mainly from bilateral foreign loans, increased even more because of foreign exchange fluctuations. As a result, the debt-to-equity ratio of the Light Rail Transit Authority increased from 5:1 in 1989 to 10:1 in 1991. The authority, therefore, has found it difficult to service its debt burden and to keep its system functioning and well maintained (Esguerra 1994).

At present, it has been estimated that about half the person-trips in Asian cities are taken on public transport systems, compared with about 10 percent in technologically advanced countries. In very large cities, therefore, there are good arguments for setting up LRT systems, despite their high costs. In planning the Shanghai rapid transit system, designers calculated that the physical space needed by a person being moved from one place to another is very small, compared with other transport modes. If the space needed by a person riding an LRT was set at an index of 1.0, a person walking would require 3.0, a bicycle rider 5.0, and a car rider from 15 to 25, depending on size, speed, and the driver's ability (Shanghai Institute of Comprehensive Urban Transport Planning 1994, 53).

Studies have estimated that a relatively efficient LRT system can accommodate from about 15 to 20 percent of total passenger trips in a city-region. Most of those trips would be by individuals who formerly took buses and paratransit systems. The trouble with this scenario is that, even with the shift from other transport modes to LRT systems, from 40 to 50 percent of trips in a large Asian city would still be relying on road-based transportation for at least part of their journey. Rapid transit systems, therefore, often have to be justified by factors other than physical space requirements, funding, ease and comfort, and so on. Other factors have to be considered, such as easing road space requirements for other transport modes, cutting down on air pollution, encouraging real estate development in certain desirable locations, and capturing increased land and property values along transport routes. All these factors point to the need for government involvement and intervention, because LRT systems cannot be justified from a purely economic rationale alone.

Transport Demand Management

Experience in the Asian mega-urban regions covered in this study has elicited the conclusion that traffic congestion and other problems related to road-based transport cannot be solved by supply-side measures, such as building more roads and wholly or partly subsidizing their operation and maintenance. In this regard, traffic demand management has been widely used in a number of Asian mega-urban regions to deal with problems of urban congestion, environmental degradation, and high traffic accident rates. In general, five components of traffic demand management can be used in a synergistic way:

- economic instruments, such as road pricing, road user charges, and the levying of licensing and operating fees on vehicles and owners;
- regulatory measures, such as deregulation, traffic management, privatization, and land use controls;
- physical restraints, such as closing certain streets to vehicles and designating them as solely for pedestrian traffic; and
- planning provisions, such as setting up telework communities and high-density settlements where the time and distance between residence and workplace is reduced.

Economic Instruments

The system of high fees charged by Singapore and Hong Kong for vehicles allowed to enter the inner city is a good example of effective road pricing that limits vehicle trips. The Singapore area licensing scheme, which has been used since 1975, has worked remarkably well. Recently, the system was elevated to a fully automated electronic road pricing scheme that has added to its efficiency. A number of factors has facilitated the Singapore scheme: the small size of the inner city, relatively few thoroughfares leading to and from the inner city that are easily controlled, and the high incomes of vehicle owners, who are quite willing to pay the fees. Singapore has also enhanced public acceptance of the scheme by providing alternative ways of entering the inner city, such as park-and-ride facilities where commuters can leave their cars on the urban periphery and take subsidized vehicles into the city center. The ready availability of buses and taxis has also eased mobility for people who do not want to pay the exorbitant rates charged by the area licensing scheme.

The increasing popularity of toll roads, many of which are increasingly run by private concessionaires, has also exacted a more economic price for road infrastructure. Many of these toll roads, such as those in Bangkok, Jakarta, and Metro Manila, are manually operated. Others, however, like the ones in Beijing, Shanghai, and Hong Kong, use "smart cards" that automatically charge the accounts of vehicle owners. While the technology costs of automating toll road collection are high, some private concessionaires are finding these useful because they reduce delays at tollbooths and increase the efficiency of financial transactions.

Economic instruments such as road pricing and toll roads have certain advantages for both concessionaires and consumers. They have certainly improved traffic flow and road use efficiency. They have offered vehicle owners and operators a better choice for travel decisions and, where they have been used extensively, they have reduced congestion in city streets. On the negative side, however, economic instruments currently used in Asian mega-urban regions are inherently regressive—they favor wealthy owners and operators of private vehicles but do not improve the mobility of poor residents. Because most of the profits from these schemes go to private concessionaires, they are not available for transport schemes that benefit poor people.

Regulatory Measures

The use of laws, rules, and regulations has been the traditional approach to traffic management. In general, urban authorities can deal with problems of congestion by setting the maximum and minimum speeds that vehicles can travel at, designating the places where they can stop to pick up or unload passengers, opening or closing certain streets, ruling whether streets should be one way or two ways, and the like. Traffic controls constitute the largest bulk of regulatory measures, and they can be used to solve transport problems. Examples of regulatory measures include

- Instituting traffic circulation measures, such as designating one-way streets that can make vehicles go faster or traffic rerouting schemes (detours) that can avoid congested or dangerous areas.
- Devising segregation schemes, such as separating slower- from faster-moving vehicles, setting aside special lanes for high-occupancy vehicles, buses, bicycles, and so on. These also include grade separation to make traffic flow faster or setting up special pedestrian crossing lanes and underground or overhead footbridges for pedestrians.
- Setting maximum and minimum speed limits on certain roads and expressways to speed up and regularize traffic.
- Making junction improvements, such as the provision of turning lanes, installation of traffic islands, and setting up of electronic or computerized traffic signals.
- Providing information for road users, such as traffic signs, road markings, electronic signals for open and cross lanes, and billboards and early warning systems.

An important element in vehicle regulation is the provision or banning of parking in specific areas. This may include the installation of parking meters, the designation of space for parking lots, the amounts charged for parking privileges, the employment of parking enforcers, and the passing of ordinances requiring the setting up of parking standards (e.g., how many parking spaces have to be installed for every 1,000 square meters of living space?). As a rule, many Asian urban authorities discourage providing free or cheap parking in urban centers. There are also guidelines set for private companies or government offices regarding their support or subsidy for parking privileges.

Physical Restraints

The most common type of physical restraint used in Asian mega-urban regions is the designation of certain areas as no-vehicle zones. For example, some streets may be closed to motorized traffic on certain days (e.g., the

Ginza in Tokyo is transformed into a pedestrian mall on Sundays; and some streets in Jakarta, Kuala Lumpur, and Singapore are closed for night markets, *pasar malams*).

To slow down the speed of vehicles, "traffic-calming" measures have also been used. In exclusive villages in Jakarta, Kuala Lumpur, Manila, and other cities, for example, humps are placed on city streets to force drivers to slow down. In some cities, traffic collars are also used, whereby the space on roads where vehicles are allowed to travel is limited by the setting up of traffic cones.

Traffic regulators in some Asian cities have used their powers to ban certain types of vehicles from city streets at certain hours. For example, in Metro Manila, big cargo trucks and trailers are not allowed to enter the city during daylight hours. Provincial buses are also not allowed to enter the city—they can only go directly to bus terminals located outside the city boundaries. So-called smoke-belching vehicles are banned on city streets. Left-hand-drive vehicles have also been banned, because it has been found that drivers using these vehicles on streets designed for right-hand driving have a higher rate of accidents. In Bandung and Jakarta, pedal-powered or motor-powered *betjaks* have been banned from main thoroughfares but are allowed as feeders to take people living in congested *kampung* areas to main highways, where they can take public transport (Soegijoko 1981).

Planning Instruments

Comprehensive and strategic planning is an effective instrument for solving problems related to transportation. The main policy tool used by planners is deciding on the location of specific urban activities so that they become easily accessible through the transport network. A good example of planned intervention is the location of wholesale markets in the Tokyo megalopolitan area. The Tokyo Municipal Government, in formulating and approving the Basic Policy on the Improvement of Physical Distribution Facilities in the Tokyo Metropolis, decided to locate ten wholesale markets and four branch markets in ward areas that were easily accessible to people and transport modes.

Another creative intervention is the designation of certain areas in the mega-urban region as special sites for information technology industries that enable people to work where they live (telecommuting). In a few Asian cities (Hong Kong, Osaka, Tokyo), a number of zones have been planned where major fiber-optic networks are provided for and buildings are designed for working at home. For example, the new Tokyo master plan sees the Shibuya subcenter as "a fashionable city that transmits lifestyle information" and provides for rapid development of information technology facilities there. The Osaki subcenter is also designed as "the site for the technological development industry that will lead Tokyo's industries in the 21st century." As such, a new rail line has been opened to the Osaki subcenter, and facilities for research and development have been provided.

Comprehensive Transport Planning and Management

A good lesson from transport-related policies and programs used in Asian mega-urban regions is the need to take the whole region as the basic unit of planning and management instead of the traditional approach of looking at transport as a purely sectoral phenomenon requiring technological, financing, and management approaches. Because of the territorial fragmentation of local government units within mega-urban regions, individual cities or municipalities are not able to solve transport problems that are directly or indirectly affected by events and decisions outside their boundaries. The functional separation of authority and responsibility among central or provincial/state administrative departments also works against better management coordination. To get over these problems, some city-region authorities in Asia have used comprehensive planning and management approaches to deal with transport issues. Foremost among them have been the Tokyo Megalopolis and the Pearl River Delta regional development effort.

The Tokyo Megalopolis Concept Plan has proposed to develop the Tokyo region by focusing attention on a regional transport system. The plan projects a population of 33 million for the Tokyo Megalopolis by 2025. It aims to turn Tokyo into a global center of economic and cultural prominence and, at the same time, ensure a high quality of life for its residents. The Tokyo City Planning Bureau hopes to achieve these goals by building a "circular megalopolis structure" (Tokyo Metropolitan Government 2003).

The Circular Megalopolis Structure for the Tokyo city-region focuses on a Center Core Area, from which radiate seven arterial expressways. These expressways link the city core to four urban nodes in the northern (Urama-Umiya-Saitama New Urban Center), eastern (Chiba-Makuhari New City), southern (Kawasaki-Yokohama), and western sectors of the region (Hachioji–Tachikawa–Tama New Town). A special Tokyo Bay Ring Road and a Tokyo Aqualine are designed to develop the Tokyo Bay area, eventually linking up to the Tokyo Bay Waterfront City. A new hub airport is also planned on reclaimed land along Tokyo Bay to supplement Haneda and Narita airports.

The main justification for the Tokyo transport plan focused on correcting these problems: (1) the overconcentration of population, goods, and information in Tokyo, which has caused traffic jams, commuter congestion, transport bottlenecks, and a costly loss of time; (2) excessive fuel conception of vehicles because of traffic congestion; (3) massive air and water pollution from vehicular exhaust fumes, which causes health and other ills; (4) uncontrolled and disorderly sprawl of manufacturing, industrial, and other urban activities into the surrounding areas, resulting in landscape degradation and a loss of green space; and (5) inappropriate structure and layout of the city-region transport system for dealing with disasters and other calamities.

In the Tokyo Action Plan prepared by the Tokyo Metropolitan Government, these measures were proposed:

- Development of regional trunk roads and urban expressways linking the Greater Tokyo Metropolitan Area with peripheral area cities and establishing ties between radial arterial roads and loop roads, such as the National Capital Region Central Loop Road, the Outer Loop Road, and the Dai-ni Tokyo Bayshore Road. All in all, eighteen routes with a total length of 217 kilometers have been planned, of which fourteen routes of approximately 178 kilometers had been completed by April 2000.
- Construction and improvement of public transportation systems to ease congestion on the subway and rail commuter systems. The Rinkai Line of the Tokyo Rinkai Kosoku Railway will be extended to the Japan Railways Osaki station. Better coordination will be worked out among the various railway systems operating in the city-region.
- Improvement of the bus service through the installation of dedicated bus lines, giving priority to buses at intersections, and the direct linkage of bus services with the metro rail system by constructing integrated terminals and stations.
- Improvement of airports, ports, and harbors to facilitate movement of people and cargo and more efficient linkage of these transport hubs with the rail, bus, and other public transport facilities. This includes the proposed expansion of Haneda as an international airport, negotiations with the U.S. military for the use of Yokota Air Base by commercial aircraft, and the possible construction of a new hub airport in Tokyo Bay.

Aside from the largely physical interventions noted above, the transport plans for the Tokyo Megalopolis contain provisions for improving parking facilities, the installation of elevators and escalators in transport stations, the design of terminal platforms so people can easily move from one transport mode to another, and the provision of easy access facilities for elderly and handicapped residents. In addition, careful consideration has been given in the plan for noise abatement, planting trees and shrubs along highways to serve as buffers and greenbelts, and the designation of certain scenic paths for pedestrians. As indicated in the Tokyo transport plan, "Roads not only facilitate traffic but also act as precious urban space to accommodate various important public facilities, perform functions for disaster prevention, and landscape creation, and provide place for people's interactions. It is necessary, therefore, to construct roads taking these diversified aspects into consideration" (Tokyo Metropolitan Government 2003, 3).

Another example of a comprehensive transport strategy is the scheme integrated into the Hong Kong–Pearl River Delta [HK-PRD] Development Plan for 2000–25. The HK-PRD plan proposes a regional transport scheme that links Guangzhou, Hong Kong, Macao, Shenzhen, Zhuhai, and other urban settlements in the region into one network. The key issues in the planning and management of the PRD's transport system are (1) the location of airports, ports, and harbors; (2) the construction of trunk roads and rail lines; and (3) the regulation of cross-border traffic. Closely related to these issues are the maintenance of the economic viability and competitiveness of the region and ensuring the protection of the physical environment.

Planners of the HK-PRD region view the area as a single regional economy despite its political division into the mainland and the two special administrative regions (SARs) of Hong Kong and Macao, as well as the separate jurisdictions of cities, municipalities, and special economic zones in Guangdong province. A major issue in the development of the HK-PRD region has been the construction of at least five big international airports within a radius of 100 kilometers from each other. A great deal of criticism has been aired about the overcapacity of these airports. In 1998, the total actual traffic for the airports at Guangzhou (Baiyun), Hong Kong (Chek Lap Kok), Macao (Macao International), Shenzhen (Huangtian), and Zhuhai (Sanzao) was 45.5 million passengers and 2.16 million tons of cargo. However, the estimated total design capacity of these airports was 90 million passengers and 4.15 million tons of cargo, indicating unused capacity (Wang and Ho 2002, 120). Some of the airports have been grossly underutilized, with Zhuhai, for example, functioning at only 5 percent of its rated capacity. To add to the complication, another six local airports within the PRD have been put into the long-term development plan of the region.

The trend toward overcapacity and potentially harmful competition among transport nodes is also seen in the building of ports and harbors in the HK-PRD region. For decades, the port of Hong Kong has dominated international and domestic freight traffic in the region. In 2000, Hong Kong port handled 174.6 million tons of cargo, including 18.1 twenty-foot equivalent units (TEUs) of container cargo (Fong 2002, 121). Between 1998 and 2000, however, four container ports in Shenzhen (Chiwan, Mawan, Shekou, and Yantian) became operational and began to compete with the Hong Kong port, increasing their cargo handling from 2 million TEUs in 1998 to 4 million TEUs in 2000. To improve its competitiveness, Hong Kong has built a river port terminal in Tuen Mun and a container port terminal in Tsing Yi. These development plans were based on the expectation that the volume of containerized cargo from Guangdong province would continue to increase to about 22 or 24 million TEUs by 2005 and that 80 percent of that cargo would be shipped through Hong Kong. Although these optimistic projections justified increased investment in port development in Hong Kong, the fact that more and more mainland ports are handling Chinese cargo and the decreasing role of Hong Kong as a transshipment hub for global trade has started to worry Hong Kong authorities.

To solve the problems noted above, the HK-PRD authorities have formulated an integrated transport network plan composed of air, sea, water, and land-based transport (highways, railways, depots, terminals) (Pearl River Delta Economic Zone Planning Committee 1996). As seen in figure 6.1, key elements of the development plan include (1) railway transport; (2) a network of expressways, state highways, and provincial highways; (3) airports; and (4) ports. Railway lines that run mainly north and south connect Guangzhou, Hong Kong, and Shenzhen to Beijing, and the east–west Guangzhou–Sanshui–Maoming line connects the PRD with southwest China. Limitations of the railway network, such as the lack of linkage to Zhuhai and the flourishing cities of Nanhai, Shunde, and Zhongshan in Guangdong province, are being seriously considered in the plan.

Complementing the railway system is a vast network of highways projected to run to 33,000 kilometers by 2010, including more than 1,583 kilometers of expressways and 3,500 kilometers of first-grade multilane highways. The Guangzhou–Shaoguan expressway and the Guangzhou–Qingyuan expressway have already been completed, while other expressways linking Guangzhou to Zhanjiang and the Western Coastal Expressway

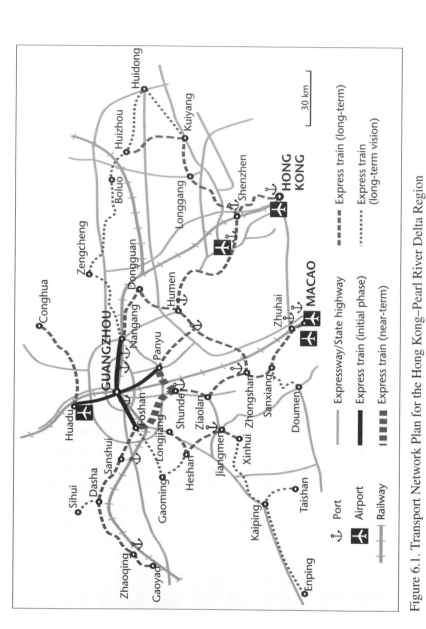

Figure 6.1. Transport Network Plan for the Hong Kong–Pearl River Delta Region

Source: Xu and Xu (2002, 131).

are well under way. However, PRD planners are quite conscious of the fact that the road-based transport system does not reach inland areas yet, and the Guangzhou–Zhuhai expressway is still in the planning stage (Xu and Xu 2002, 130).

Because the SARs of Hong Kong and Macao are still, technically, politically separate units, cross-border travel between these enclaves and the mainland constitutes a unique transport problem. Since 1991, traffic volume in three border crossing points between Hong Kong and PRD has grown at 9 percent a year. In 2000, 30,721 vehicles crossed these points, with 84 percent of the vehicles carrying freight, 12 percent being private cars, and 4 percent being passenger buses and coaches (Ng 2002, 273).

The pattern of cross-border crossings between Hong Kong and Guangdong shows a very asymmetric relationship. The flow is heavily dominated by Hong Kong residents traveling to the mainland, at about 1.3 million in a two-week period in October–November 1999, which contrasted sharply with only 110,000 mainland visitors going to Hong Kong. The most common reasons for these Hong Kong–to–mainland trips were business (29 percent), visiting relatives and friends (23 percent), shopping/leisure (20 percent), and sightseeing (17 percent). Interestingly, the 1999 survey showed that about 51,000 Hong Kong people lived on the mainland. In addition, another survey conducted in April 2000 showed that more than 1 million Hong Kong residents had thought of moving to Shenzhen to live there and that another 375,000 may consider buying property in Shenzhen (Ng 2002, 275).

Despite the conceptual comprehensiveness of the HK-PRD transport strategy, the Hong Kong and Guangdong authorities recognize several difficulties in implementing it. The most obvious problem is the political and administrative fragmentation of local government units in the region. Although the authorities say that they are committed to the slogan of "competing together, working together," the fact remains that there are economic rivalries between Hong Kong and Guangzhou and, in the future, between Hong Kong and rapidly growing Shanghai to the northeast. The uncoordinated overbuilding of airports and maritime ports in the HK-PRD region is only a small indication of this competitive rivalry.

There is also a mismatch between transport modes preferred in different parts of the HK-PRD region. Most of the transport investments in the Pearl River Delta are focused on roads, whereas Hong Kong is in favor of rail-based transport. These differences are a reflection of the fact that Hong

Kong has one of the highest urban population densities in the world and thus can justify rail-based transit, but many of the urban nodes in the PRD region are too small and are best reached by roads.

A far deeper difference between Hong Kong and Guangdong decision makers that cannot be wished away by the "one country, two systems" principle is the fact that urban authorities on the mainland rely heavily on government measures while Hong Kong decision makers are mainly market oriented. Some Hong Kong entrepreneurs interested in transport investments feel that the HK-PRD region is not a level playing field because their counterparts on the mainland can call on government policies and direct or indirect subsidies, whereas they have to use their own capital without much support from the SAR government to achieve an acceptable level of profit. There are also Hong Kong investors who say they face extreme difficulties in getting decisions of a regional nature from the Guangdong local government officials, who have been given considerable local autonomy by Beijing and tend to favor actions that only benefit their own particular bailiwicks (Cheung 2002, 52–53).

As shown in the case of the HK-PRD region, a major issue in transport provision in Asian mega-urban regions is the role of the government and the private sector in planning, financing, operating, and managing transport systems. In general, many economists believe that the provision of transport in cities should be the responsibility of the private business sector because they believe that responding to market forces ensures efficient and appropriate services. Believers in the market argue that, in the case of transport management, the government should come in only in case of "market failure." Examples of market failure that may justify government intervention include the following (Roth 1987, 31–32):

- When markets get distorted by a *monopoly* arising from the dominance by one supplier.
- Where there are insufficient *economies of scale,* whereby the investment requirements of public transport become too lumpy for the private sector, or whereby a private provider may not be able to recover costs within a reasonable time.
- The presence of *externalities,* costs that are not borne by the service provider but are instead passed on to third parties. These include negative externalities, such as noise and air pollution. Governments may deal with these externalities by regulation, taxation, subsidies, and imposing fines and user charges.

• The need to provide *public goods*. Some goods and services are of value to the community and not just to individuals. Street lighting and the construction of pathways that open up new areas are public goods, in that their enjoyment by one person does not diminish their usefulness to others. It is also extremely difficult to charge individual users for the benefits from these public goods.

Aside from dealing with cases of market failure, many authorities consider it the responsibility of the government to take a broader and longer view of the transport needs of a city and its region and to provide the policy context for the realization of that vision. The government must clearly indicate the pace and direction of future urban development. Once development thrusts are defined, the government may, for example, acquire and protect public lands for future transport corridors to prevent speculation. Land banking may be used to achieve this goal. The government may support innovative transport approaches that the private sector may not be able or willing to pursue. It can influence transport prices through taxation and regulation.

Most important of all, the government must provide the conditions under which the private sector might be able to provide transport. This can be done by explicitly stating transport plans and strategies as well as policies and programs that give private investors the certainty and predictability they needed to make appropriate decisions.

A major challenge in big cities of South and Southeast Asia is how to ensure that government and private business act in complementary ways. This issue is of special relevance to the need to formulate comprehensive metropolitan transport plans that specify clear roles for walking, bicycling, paratransit systems, buses, and rapid transit systems. At present, in most South Asian cities, privately owned and managed paratransit systems are not integrated with overall transport schemes. Some cities even ban the use of these vehicles or force them to operate only on side streets. Special efforts, therefore, are needed to integrate these private transport modes into an appropriate regional and metropolitan system so as to serve the large segment of the urban population that uses them.

To sum up, considering the importance of transport in the development of mega-urban regions in Asia, one expects that the use of policy instruments to solve transport-related problems would have higher success rates. With the exception of cities like Hong Kong, Osaka, Seoul, Singapore, and Tokyo, however, most urban authorities in Asia seem unable to deal with the transport problems adequately. Because of the small geographic sizes and unique city-state statuses of Hong Kong and Singapore, however, some of the policy instruments they have used successfully might not be applicable to the conditions in other Asian mega-urban regions. Many other Asian mega-urban regions also do not have the high incomes or the level of technological development of Japanese and South Korean cities.

The experiences of Asian mega-urban regions indicate that piecemeal tinkering with transport issues may achieve some results but will not be sufficient unless policy interventions are carried out in the context of a comprehensive plan covering a whole mega-urban region. The experiences of all the mega-urban regions covered in this book show that the location of developmental nodes in the city-region and the linking of these nodes together through an effective and efficient transport network is a vital component of a comprehensive transport plan. Various measures—such as what type of transport mode to favor, what financing scheme to use, whether to charge full economic costs or subsidize, or whether the government or the private sector should play the leading role in the transport scheme—need to be integrated into this comprehensive development plan.

7

Inner-City Redevelopment

Unlike North American inner cities, which become ominously quiet after dark, Asian inner cities are teeming beehives of activities. In hot and humid climates, inner-city dwellers carry out most of their daily activities outdoors. In Delhi, Dhaka, Jakarta, Kolkata (formerly Calcutta), and Metro Manila, small inner-city lanes are alive with the cries of itinerant peddlers, toting their wares to people's doorsteps. The sidewalks of Bangkok, Ho Chi Minh City, and Hong Kong are usually filled with shoppers haggling with sidewalk vendors over a great variety of goods and food items. Beijing's silk alley and Bandung's jeans alley are great places for bargains for tourists and locals alike. In Jakarta and Kuala Lumpur, streets are closed to make room for *pasar malams* (night markets), where people stroll around and enjoy street food. In most Asian cities, therefore, the central business district is not the empty "doughnut hole" that it so often is in the cities of North America—instead, downtown is a bustling, thriving, and frenetic center of human activity all day and late into the night.

In the United States, Garreau has described three waves of development that have seen people, commerce, and jobs move from the city center to periurban areas. First, there was the movement of people to the suburbs, made possible by the automobile, which enabled people to live in outlying areas and commute to work or shop in the central city. This was followed by the move of the marketplace to the suburbs, in the form of mega-malls, "big box" stores, and entertainment centers. The third wave was the movement of jobs to the suburbs, creating the so-called edge city, a clustered complex of offices, malls, entertainment centers, and other urban facilities built to the "automobile scale." Such edge cities are identifiable by their tall buildings, covered malls, and leisure centers, which sprouted in formerly vacant lands on the urban periphery (Garreau 1991).

Interestingly, although some Asian cities have reached a level of affluence that enables residents to own a private car, edge cities have not developed in Asia. Metropolitan regions like Osaka, Seoul, and Tokyo have suburban communities but no real edge cities. In Bangkok, Jakarta, and Metro Manila, where a segment of the population owns cars, the rich live in exclusive suburban gated communities and shop in mega-malls. However, these places do not conform to the main features of an edge city— described by Garreau as a "single end" destination with ample office and retail space that has grown out of nowhere in a very short time.

A noteworthy thing about a number of Asian cities is that though buildings, houses, and other structures in inner cities may be old, they are usually clean and well maintained. Because development traditionally started in the city core, government offices, monuments, museums, theaters, and markets are found there. Special places for public ceremonies, rituals, and entertainment abound in large plazas, parks, and public squares. People flock downtown for entertainment, shopping, business transactions, and public services. Lovers walk hand in hand in Bangkok's Lumpini Park, Manila's Luneta, or along the Bund in Shanghai. Shoppers congregate on Beijing's Wangfuching Street, and antique lovers flock to Jakarta's Jalan Surabaya. On Sundays, bargain hunters go to Chandi Chawk in Delhi or the Ginza in Tokyo. On national holidays and special occasions, one can sense a palpable sense of civic pride and patriotism among the many people attracted to these commemorative events in the center of Asian cities.

In cities that have grown organically from small traditional settlements, the development of the urban core was often not consciously planned. In Tokyo, for example, houses in inner-city neighborhoods tended to be small and made of wood because earthquakes discouraged the building of large permanent structures. Roads in what was then the capital city of Edo were narrow and designed for walking, because horses and carriages were not used until after the Meiji Revolution (1868). Thus, as noted by Fukami, "Japanese cities grew by building one house after another around city nuclei, e.g., street junctions, temples, shrines, and the castle. As a result, a sprawling built-up area has emerged. . . . Japanese cities did not have to prepare positive plans" (Fukami 2000, 278). In other words, Japanese cities grew as self-organizing communities where people clustered around the core of the urban area.

In Chinese cities, the planned development of the inner city historically reached a high level of development quite early. An excellent example of a well-planned city core is that of Beijing. The focal point of the city is the Gugong (the Palace Museum), more popularly known as the Forbidden City. The area around the Forbidden City is made up of thousands of courtyard houses (*siheyuan*) built during the Ming (1368–1644) and Qing (1644–1911) Dynasties. Even after more than forty years of Communist efforts to erase Beijing's "feudal" past and the demolition of some courtyard houses after the adoption of economic reforms in 1979, a number of inner-city neighborhoods in Beijing still retain the features of traditional city life. The houses along narrow lanes (*hutongs*) are packed with families, sometimes ten to a courtyard, sharing one or two standpipes and communal toilets.

Life in these Beijing lanes is vibrant, with people buying things from itinerant vendors or hawkers clogging the sidewalks. Periodic markets are held on certain days, when streets are closed and converted into bustling marketplaces. Bird fanciers gather on weekends in specific parks to buy and sell rare birds or simply listen to bird songs. Some narrow lanes in Beijing open to wide boulevards lined with persimmon, gingko, and other trees maintained by neighborhood committees. Highly organized neighborhood committees manage and control community life, looking after street sweeping, nurseries and kindergartens, the cleaning of communal toilets, and beautification.

The inner-city neighborhoods of Shanghai are not as old as Beijing's, but the residents of *lilong* (small lanes) housing have strong attachment to their dwellings, which were mainly built during the 1920s and 1930s. By the early 1990s, the *lilong* houses had become very congested—a 1992 survey showed that the average per capita living space in an inner-city neighborhood within Luwan District was 6.6 square meters. The city government estimated that about 3.65 million square meters of housing in the city could be classified as "old, dangerous and dilapidated" (Bao 1992, 58). However, despite the poor conditions of the houses and the severe congestion, most of the *lilong* residents said they were very happy with their life. Two illustrations made by the Tongji University researchers capture the people's satisfaction with life in the small lanes (figure 7.1). This warm feeling about life in the community was described in the following way:

In the old lanes and alleys, the dwellers have lived together for a very long time, perhaps, since their grandparents' childhood. Therefore, a quite special and intimate relationship has been established between neighbors [and people referred to each other as] "old sister," "younger sister," "old fellow" or "young fellow." It is very easy to find a person in these alleys because everyone knows each other [and everyone is known by] the policeman in charge of household registration. . . . Apart from the structural characteristics of the lanes . . . the most recommendable aspect is the people's way of life. . . . The residential buildings were made of two, three, or four-story apartments so the dwellers contact each other through "horizontal communication." The *lilong* apartments were sometimes called "shaking hands" houses or "exchanging food" houses as neighbors could literally reach out to each other by opening their windows. (Bao 1992, 68)

Another example of serene inner-city life is that of Hanoi. The district known as the "Thirty-Six Ancient Streets" around Hoan Khiem Lake currently holds almost a million people. In accord with the Hanoi master plan, approved by the Office of the Prime Minister in 1998, the inner city is to be kept as a residential, cultural, commercial, and public affairs center. No highrise buildings are allowed in the city core. The old streets with their mature trees are preserved. The unique "tube houses," which serve as both residences and commercial venues, are classified as cultural treasures. They cannot be demolished without the city government's approval. When these structures become too old and dilapidated, they are upgraded, but strict cultural preservation rules stipulate that their facades should not be changed and as many of the older building materials that can be saved should be reused.

Despite global pressures for the establishment of modern hotels and shopping centers in Hanoi, the city authorities have resisted such developments. The Hanoi authorities realize, however, that there are too many people living in the city center, and the city's master plan provides for resettling some of the residents and keeping only about 600,000 people in the inner city. The authorities have encountered a great deal of difficulty in decongesting the inner city, however, because very few people want to leave their home communities.

Bangkok, the "city of angels," has also been able to preserve the unique character of its old Ratanakosin quarter, with its Royal Palace and complex of temples and pagodas on the banks of the Chao Phraya River. Because the public authorities are conscious of the importance of tourism in the country's development, they have adopted a master plan for the cultural preservation of Ratanakosin so that its physical structures and people's activities will continue to reflect Thai cultural characteristics. Skyscrapers and other modern structures have not been allowed to intrude into this old neighbor-

Figure 7.1. Traditional Way of Life in *Lilong* (Lane) Neighborhoods of Shanghai.

hood. Although the center of economic and social life in Bangkok has moved elsewhere, Ratanakosin has been kept as a reminder of the essence of Thai culture.

Unlike Beijing, Hanoi, and Bangkok, however, other Asian mega-cities have not been too successful in preserving the unique features of their inner cities. In Metro Manila, American bombing in World War II practically destroyed all the structures in the old city. After the war, the government passed a law that, for cultural reasons, all buildings and structures built within the Walled City of Intramuros should follow Spanish architectural designs. Building heights were also limited so as not to spoil the skyline, marked by the spires of the national cathedral and many churches. These cultural preservation rules greatly delayed reconstruction in Intramuros. In the meantime, the old walls and wrecked buildings attracted thousands of squatters, who made construction even more difficult, especially in the light of a new law that forbids forced evictions without the government first providing acceptable housing for the former squatters.

In some cases, as in Jakarta, an intense drive to achieve modernism has also altered the city's urban core. After achieving independence in 1949, Indonesia's nationalistic leaders embarked on a frenzy of construction that has almost completely gutted the residential sections of the inner city. Traditional *kampung* houses were demolished to make way for multilane boulevards like Jalan Thamrin and Jalan Surabaya, which quickly got clogged with automobiles, buses, and other vehicles, jostling out the lowly *betjaks* and getting these banned from major boulevards. Monumental structures were built, such as a mosque and an independence tower in the middle of a grand plaza. High-rise buildings, mega-malls, five-star hotels, air-conditioned shopping centers, and huge office blocks were built downtown, pushing out old-time residents. The main result of this intense drive for modernism is a city that conforms to a Western model: congested and vibrant during the day but abandoned by office workers and laborers at night. It is also a city whose streets are clogged with traffic during "zero [rush] hours" each morning and afternoon, whose fetid air is polluted by dust and particulates, whose rivers and canals are strewn with garbage, and whose solid waste often festers uncollected on street corners for days.

Inner-City Decay

Inner-city conditions in Asian cities, of course, do not conform to just one pattern. In some cities, such as Metro Manila, inner-city deterioration has followed the same pattern as that of cities in North America, in which people and their capital moved to the suburbs and left the central city with decaying structures and a weak tax base. In other cities, such as Delhi and Mumbai (formerly Bombay), inner-city slums have grown and become greatly congested, even as rural–urban migrants have set up squatter colonies on the urban periphery. Shanghai and Guangzhou, where city authorities seem to have had less sentiment for preserving historical structures compared with those in Beijing, have practically gutted their inner cities to make room for more office buildings, shopping centers, offices, and luxury housing. In Ho Chi Minh City, squatters have occupied public land, including space along railroad tracks and highways, at the same time that thousands of them have also built makeshift houses on the banks of rivers and streams and in old cemeteries. In Kolkata and Mumbai, tens of thousands of pavement dwellers have appropriated the sidewalks for their living space. Millions more live in overcrowded *bastis* and densely packed neighborhoods.

In Metro Manila, the central business district, focused on the old Escolta, has decayed rapidly as land developers have opened up new areas in Makati, Quezon City, Mandaluyong, and other suburban areas. The old office and commercial area in the central business district has turned into a wretched zone of pawnshops, bedbug-infested movie houses, dollar exchange cubbyholes, and sidewalk stalls selling everything from sex aids to illegal drugs. Close to the Escolta, the inner-city districts of Quiapo, Santa Cruz, and Binondo also show signs of physical deterioration. Chinatown, focused on Ongpin Street, has been losing population as upwardly mobile Chinese families have moved to the rich neighborhoods of New Manila and exclusive villages in Makati and Mandaluyong. The entertainment centers along Azcarraga, C. M. Recto, and Quezon Boulevards used to be dirty, run down and decayed, but recent efforts by the city mayor have attempted to beautify these places. The construction of the light rail transit ramps along Rizal Avenue has turned that once glittering street of movie houses, department stores, bookshops, and restaurants into a dark alley.

Recent efforts of the city authorities to redevelop this once proud center of Manila by painting the light rail transit concrete posts and removing illegal structures under the platforms have helped to improve the city core, but traffic congestion still prevents a lot of people from going downtown. The mega-malls of Makati and Mandaluyong, with their super bargains, frenzied food courts, and air-conditioned comfort are much more attractive to people than the old city area.

The inner core of South Asian mega-cities reflects even serious problems of housing and congestion. Mumbai, for example, has more than 144 slum areas occupying 877 acres inhabited by more than 425,000 people. The largest of these is Dharvi, about 160 hectares of marshy land where more than 53,000 households live. In other parts of the city, poor people live in clusters of single-room dwellings called *chawls*. A five- or seven-story *chawl* may house as many as 300 families. Often, the residents of these tenements get water from only a few faucets and have to share communal toilets. Most *chawls* in Mumbai are more than sixty years old and are seriously dilapidated.

In Kolkata, three-fourths of its 12.6 million people lives in *bastis* (slum and squatter settlements). Of these, two-thirds of the families lives in *kutcha,* or temporary makeshift structures. Many of these shanties are located in frequently flooded areas. Because only a part of Kolkata is served by the sewerage system, most people dispose of their human and solid waste in marshy places. The lack of sanitation has subjected Kolkata to periodic cholera epidemics.

The old part of Delhi still shows traces of the glorious city built by Shah Jahan when he shifted his capital from Agra to old Delhi in 1638. After the British conquest in 1803, the colonizers decided to build an entirely new city in New Delhi, leaving the inner city to congestion and decay. Partition in 1947 saw tens of thousands of migrants moving into Delhi's center. In 1958, the government had formulated a plan to move out about 48 percent of these poor inner-city dwellers, but resources for carrying out this ambitious plan were lacking. Only about 4,000 dilapidated dwellings were cleared. At the same time, about 20,000 dwelling units and 100 commercial shops were provided. By 1991, about 500 acres of land in Delhi were cleared, but only 50 acres were used for slum rehousing schemes. Because about 616,000 people lived in the area (there were 607,000 in 1958), the plan to decongest the inner core of Delhi obviously failed (Jain 1996b, 85).

The inner-city section of Ho Chi Minh City is only 800 hectares (about 7 percent of the city's total land area), but it holds more than a quarter of a million inhabitants. Located within the compact city core are thousands of small industrial and manufacturing enterprises that severely pollute the rivers and streams threading through the area. In a housing survey in 1993, about 4,000 dilapidated housing units were enumerated within the zone. Many of these were located on the banks or on top of the Nhieu Loc-Thi Nghe Canal, which runs through five of the city's main districts. Along its length, in 1996 the canal was lined with houses on stilts, home to about 13,000 households or roughly 70,000 people (Nguyen Quang Vinh 1996).

The main issue in redeveloping Ho Chi Minh City's inner core is what to do with the tens of thousands of poor families packed within the zone. At present, more than 60 percent of all projects in the city funded by foreign direct investment are seeking to locate within this zone, to be close to markets and have access to infrastructure and urban services that are too expensive to build de novo in peri-urban areas. Accommodating these investors in the central city would require the resettlement of inner-city dwellers. The Ho Chi Minh City People's Committee, through its Town Planning Institute, estimates that relocating the "excess" people from the inner city will require the renovation or partial reconstruction of about 1,446 houses and the relocation of 2,746 families that formally do not have any residence permits to stay in the city. The problem, then, is how to achieve the economic and cultural reinvigoration of the inner city and at the same time ensure that the poor people who currently live in the zone are not too adversely affected.

Inner-city decay in Asian mega-urban regions, then, is a function of the deterioration of old houses, buildings, and other urban infrastructure, the overstraining of basic urban services because of the great number of people concentrated in the inner city, and the outward movement of people, jobs, commercial activities, and entertainment facilities to suburban areas. Unlike in some North American cities, however, the physical deterioration of Asian inner-city zones (with some exceptions, e.g., the area around Shinjuku Station in Tokyo) has usually not been accompanied by social pathologies such as drugs, homelessness, and crime. In Beijing, in fact, inner-city redevelopment has been focused on the rehabilitation of "old and dilapidated housing" and not "slum clearance," implying that social life in the inner city has not been adversely affected by physical deterioration and that most inner-city neighborhoods remain coherent, cooperative, and well-functioning communities.

Strategies for Inner-City Redevelopment

Strategies for redeveloping the inner city vary according to the economic, cultural, and historical conditions in each city. In general, the issues revolve around a number of questions. For example, should land values be the main determinant of what physical structures, types of economic activities, and class of people will be allowed to be located downtown? What types of functions would be encouraged in the inner city? What importance should be given to the preservation and maintenance of historic buildings and relics? How many people should be allowed to live permanently in the inner city? What emphasis should be given to community organization and the participation of people in inner-city redevelopment? These and other questions become the basis for the formulation of strategies for inner-city redevelopment.

In general, authorities in Asian cities have taken several approaches to solve inner-city problems, including (1) accommodating inner-city residents in city centers, (2) rejuvenating the economy of the inner city, (c) the eviction and resettlement of inner-city residents to peripheral urban areas, (d) repairing and maintaining infrastructure and services in the inner city, and (e) improving the inner city for tourism and the conservation of historic and cultural structures. Many cities, of course, have combined several of these approaches in their comprehensive plans. Some have left the formulation and implementation of these plans to bureaucratic organizations, whereas others have encouraged more participation by local people.

Accommodating People in the Inner City

Many Asian cities have found it easier to accommodate people at inner-city sites, and there are many successful projects using in situ development. Community upgrading has been used in many low-income communities in Bandung, Bangkok, Delhi, Jakarta, Kolkata, Metro Manila, and Mumbai. In this approach, simple improvements—such as providing pathways, drainage canals, artesian wells, community toilets, garbage collection, community centers, and playgrounds—have been pursued, usually through communal efforts and aided self-help initiatives. During the 1970s, the World Bank supported projects such as the Kampung Improvement Program in Bandung, Jakarta, and Surabaya; the Zonal Improvement Project in Metro Manila; and the Slum Improvement and Renewal efforts in Cebu and Davao. A detailed evaluation of the effects of such projects on the lives of urban poor people showed that, in general, the incomes of the project beneficiaries went up, their health improved, houses became consolidated and changed from makeshift to more permanent construction materials, and people developed a stronger sense of community by being allowed to remain in their old communities (Laquian 1983a; Van Horen 2004).

Onsite development has been found successful in many Asian cities but it is also faced with five main problems. First, inner-city communities are often too densely populated, and projects cannot accommodate all the original residents at the site. Some resettlement and dislocation of people, therefore, must occur. Second, the physical structures in the inner city may be too dilapidated to renew, improve, or rebuild, raising project costs considerably. Third, land values in the inner city are very high, and there are probably more economically efficient ways of using the land than for housing and services to accommodate the original residents (although the use of high-rise apartments may make inner-city housing viable). Fourth, a significant proportion of inner-city residents are very poor and would not be able to afford housing and urban services in the inner city, especially if standards and prices were raised. Fifth, other people would desire to move into the improved inner city, thereby creating the process of gentrification.

These five issues have been encountered in the planned development of the central part of Seoul. To comprehensively deal with all these issues, the city planners in South Korea's capital decided to divide the inner city into five zones: (1) the Relocation Promotion Area, (2) the Development Promotion Area, (3) the Growth Management Area, (4) the Environmental Preservation Area, and (5) the Development Preservation Area. As the names of the zones suggest, the Relocation Promotion and Growth Management Areas were designed to absorb factories, industries, and workers and their families transferred from the inner city. The Development Preservation Area and the Environmental Preservation Area were not to be turned over to urban uses. Strict rules were promulgated to control the process of resettlement. Thus, government offices, universities and colleges, and training institutions were not permitted to be located in the Relocation Promotion Area, but teaching institutions were allowed in the Growth Management, Development Promotion, and Development Preservation Areas. The implementation of the rules and regulations was also monitored by the Ministry of Construction (Sung 1996, 172).

A good example of planned inner-city redevelopment is the Old and Dilapidated Housing Renewal program in Beijing, which focused on inner-city districts such as Chaoyangmen Nei, Guanyuan, and Nanchizi. In a study of redevelopment in Chaoyangmen Nei and Nanchizi Districts, a researcher observed that a major source of problems was the use of standards suited more for "green field sites" (housing on the city outskirts) rather than for traditional inner-city neighborhoods. When old and dilapidated houses in the inner city are demolished and replaced by high-rise apartments, one positive effect is the increase in livable space. Before the housing reforms, average living space in Chaoyangmen Nei was about 5.77 square meters per person. After the reforms, this increased to 6.67 square meters per person in low-rise schemes and 7.23 square meters per person in mid-rise schemes.

A negative effect of these improved standards, of course, was the fact that fewer people could now be accommodated in new housing (Liu 1995).

Another negative effect of the housing redevelopment was a reduction in the number of small shops and stores serving the neighborhood. Before the housing renewal project, there were 5.77 small shops per 100 households in Chaoyangmen Nei and 5.71 in Xiohoucang. The number of shops went down to 4.35 per 100 households in Dongnanyuan after the reform and to 3.35 in Huaibaishu. In the desire of the housing redevelopers to "rationally" plan the communities, shops were allowed only in the main streets. This meant that the old neighborhood shops that conveniently served residents of a lane (*hutong*) had to make a special trip to the main street to buy everyday necessities. In some areas, some apartment units had been partly converted into stores. The building authorities classified these innovations as an "illegal" and unauthorized use of housing space, but they encountered many objections from residents, who blamed the designers for not anticipating the shopping needs of people. As a result, many housing authorities just turned a blind eye to these "illegal activities." A negative side effect of the reduction in the number of shops was that the remaining stores tended to charge higher prices because of reduced competition.

An approach that has been used to suit the lifestyles of inner-city people is the regularization and rationalization of street markets, hawking, and vending. A large proportion of inner-city residents derive their income from so-called informal-sector activities that are labor intensive, require small capital, involve the labor of family members and relatives, rely on indigenous resources and technology, and thrive within unregulated and unregulated markets (International Labor Organization 1995; Tinker 1997). A study of employment in the Industri Dalam project in Bandung, for example, found that the majority of the residents in the onsite apartment project earned their living by selling food and other items from pushcarts. The fact that these vendors could live within walking distance of the streetcorners where they sold their wares (and that the apartments were designed to provide secure space for their pushcarts on the ground floor) greatly improved their chances of making a decent living (Karyoedi 1995).

In general, municipal government officials are often critical of street markets in the inner city. They see them as causing traffic jams, especially when streets are closed or vendors take over sidewalks to sell their wares. Those who sell food are accused of spreading disease such as hepatitis, dysentery, and cholera. Formal, tax-paying businesses complain about the competition from hawkers and vendors. Officials say that vendors encourage corruption as they bribe police and sanitation officials, so they will not enforce the law, they bribe market officials and tax collectors, and they may even deal in stolen goods. Some officials also complain that the vendors and street markets make the city dirty and ugly—ignoring the fact that many tourists love going to these markets for bargains, the general hustle and bustle, and the local color.

In the street markets of Beijing, policies of accommodation or repressive control depended on the level of government. In general, higher-level local units tended to be more control oriented. They viewed street markets as nuisances that added to congestion. The vendors produced garbage and waste and were charged with corrupting local officials. Ideologues among higher-level officials viewed petty trading as "capitalist-roading" that violated socialist principles. Lower-level governments, however, favored the street markets as a ready source of local revenue (in the form of business licenses, fees for use of government-built stalls, and local taxes). They argued that the markets employed many individuals and responded to the basic needs of people. The problems cited by other officials could be dealt with by providing the vendors with specific services: clean water to wash their goods and utensils, garbage bins, stalls where they could display their wares, portable toilets for the use of the public, and police and street patrols to direct traffic and maintain peace and order. Many lower local government units in Beijing, therefore, have chosen specific streets as market sites, provided services to these places, and continued to encourage hawking and vending.

In some cities, there have been successful "accommodationist" projects combining onsite development with relocation. In these projects, the families moved out of the old sites because of improved standards are moved to areas not too far from where they used to live. For example, in the Tondo–Dagat-dagatan project supported by the World Bank in Manila, community upgrading was carried out in Tondo and new relocation plots were found in reclaimed land in Dagat-dagatan about two kilometers away. At the Tondo site, roads were straightened, drainage ditches and canals were dug, potable water was supplied, and a piped sewerage system was installed. Individual house plots were sold to residents at concessional rates. At the relocation site in Dagat-dagatan, water and sewer connections were also installed and individual plots were allocated to relocated families. These were basic serviced units that allowed the families to build their own homes. Some of the relocated families constructed houses right away, using the old materials they had salvaged from their original homes in Tondo. Others took longer to build, preferring to buy new materials, such as cement hollow blocks, timber, and galvanized iron, to construct more solid houses. The Dagat-dagatan project was strongly criticized by some people because it initially resembled an instant slum. Over time, however, both the Tondo and the Dagat-dagatan residents consolidated their homes and eventually came up with strong, well-built structures (Laquian 1971).

Pressures to integrate poor people into inner-city areas may be strengthened by the political power exercised by poor residents themselves. With the championing of their cause by some politicians and nongovernmental organizations, many poor urban groups are able to resist and fight evictions. In some societies, appeals to basic human rights are used. In others, the outright use of "force of numbers" and the mobilized voting capacity of poor people have been effective instruments for avoiding evictions. It is worth noting that the "people power" movement in Metro Manila—which has exerted such a strong influence on national political life—actually had its origins in the activism of poor urban groups clamoring for specific benefits, such as being provided with water and other basic services and being allowed to stay where they lived instead of being forcibly evicted (Constantino-David 1998).

Accommodating as many original residents as possible by housing them downtown has proven to be an excellent way of ensuring the vibrancy and livability of the city's inner core. After 1979, for example, the Chinese government decided that Shanghai should be turned into an international economic, financial, and trade center. Between 1984 and 1990, 64.2 million square meters of housing were constructed in the city, 3.5 times more than the total amount of housing built in the previous twenty-nine years. Between 1990 and 2003, more than 38 million square meters of old housing, mainly in the central city, was torn down in an "urban renewal" program that largely focused on old *lilong* (lane) houses that made up about 40 percent of the total dwellings in the old section of Shanghai. The Shanghai Housing and Land Administrative Bureau claimed that about 800,000 households were provided with larger apartments as the average per capita living space in the city expanded from 6.6 square meters in 1990 to 13.1 square meters in 2003. Among the households benefiting were 120,000 that had less than 4 square meters per person of living space and that were now provided with housing costing less than 3,500 yuan per square meter. Before the urban renewal program, most households had to share toilets and kitchens. But in 2003, 90 percent of the local residents were said to have individual toilets and kitchens in their units (*China Daily,* September 8, 2003).

A far more impressive accomplishment in Shanghai housing, however, has been the accommodation of families in suburban apartment units. In 1983, about 138,000 households were relocated from twenty-three districts in the inner city. And between 1986 and 1990, another 117,000 households were moved out of central Shanghai after the demolition of 4.08 million square meters of old buildings. The relocation and rehousing of inner-city dwellers in suburban housing was mostly handled by district-level housing agencies, which used the funds from redeveloped inner-city properties to build new housing in the suburbs. For example, in April 1992, the Real Estate Administration of Huangpu District leased valuable properties in Block 71 of Beijing Dong Road. With the lease proceeds, it built apartments on 5.6 hectares of land in Linjia Long District in Pudong, and the relocated households were moved there.

Efforts to accommodate people in the inner cities of Asian mega-urban regions have shown the need to strike a balance between relying on market forces and more interventionist policies that seek to achieve equity and cultural preservation. Supporters of a market-oriented system argue that land in the inner city should be devoted to high-value investments such as offices, commercial ventures, financial institutions, and high-end shopping. Critics of this approach, however, point to the situation in North American cities, where the inner city is abandoned after the close of office hours—an abandonment that encourages crime, drug dealing, prostitution and other social ills. Socially concerned policy advocates assert that inner cities in Asia are usually inhabited by thousands of poor people who live in well-organized communities and give life to downtown. They feel that instead of evicting these people, destroying their homes, and building offices and commercial structures, as many of these people as can be accommodated in multistory housing should be allowed to stay living where they are. In this way, inner cities become human habitations rather than mere physical structures.

The Economic Rejuvenation of the Urban Core

The main economic asset in the inner city is land, the value of which is determined by land use plans and zoning regulations, the availability of infrastructure and urban services, and accessibility to transport lines. In recent years, quite a number of Chinese planners have expressed the view that land uses in the inner city were not maximizing benefits. In Shanghai, for example, it has been argued that too much of the land in the city's core is devoted to residential uses. A 1995 survey of Fuzhou Road in Shanghai, stretching from the Huangpu River to Xichang Zong Road in the west, revealed that 70.0 percent of land was devoted to residential homes, 8.9 percent to public buildings, 15.6 percent to roads and rights of way, 5.2 percent to trade and commerce, and only 0.3 percent to parks and green space. The planners who did the survey concluded that there was a need to change land uses "by optimizing land distribution and using the land for the tertiary industries so as to give full play to the functions of limited space in urban, social and economic activities" (Yu and Shai 1995, 1).

Following a similar perspective, urban planners in the Chaoyangmen Nei urban renewal area in Beijing decided that to make the area more productive, about 54 percent of the existing residential areas should be used for large commercial buildings, public areas, and new roads. This more productive land use would mean the relocation of 8,800 residents (out of a population of 23,000). In addition, the developers thought that the housing standards for the neighborhood needed to be upgraded to attract more affluent people (the high-standard new homes would average 140 square meters per unit, as against the old actual average of 28 square meters). Though this upgrading of standards would benefit a number of families, it would adversely affect 6,800 individuals who would have to be moved from the area. As a Tsinghua University professor observed: "After renewal, Chaoyangmen Nei will have a lower population density and a higher level of amenities— but the effect on the city overall may be a net decrease in environmental quality as more people will spend more time commuting and will lose their access to amenities they currently enjoy" Liu (1995, 51).

In other parts of Beijing, inner-city redevelopment and affordable housing has been achieved through a system of cross-subsidies. In these schemes, the redeveloped land was devoted to different uses: office buildings, commercial sites, entertainment centers, and shopping places. The profits from these various uses were used to cross-subsidize the cost of housing for local residents. Thus, in the Dongnanyuan project in Beijing, the funds borrowed for the housing project were repaid from the sale of 800 square meters of commercial space along the main street, rental income from 1,000 square meters of underground space for parking, and the sale of apartments to new residents. In Xiaohoucang, the housing subsidies for former residents were recouped through the sale of 3,100 square meters of office space. In Huaibaishu, the housing project was financed mainly by the sale of 8,000 square meters of commercial space on the main road and 10,000 square meters of commodity housing (Tan 1994, 55).

The use of land to finance inner-city projects has been quite common in Japan. In Tokyo, the urban authorities have successfully used the Land Readjustment System (LRS) in pursuing development schemes. Very simply, LRS involves the government's purchase of a piece of congested inner-city land to be developed by an agency such as the Japan Housing and Urban Development Corporation (JHUDC). A portion of the land is earmarked for high-end development, such as a high-technology factory, offices, or a shopping complex. Another portion is set aside for high-density housing to accommodate as many of the community residents as possible. The new housing units, usually high-rise apartment blocks requiring less land space, are allocated to original community residents at affordable prices, because the units are cross-subsidized by the higher values created by the commercially developed land.

In a case study of the redevelopment of a parcel of land in Kamiya District of Kita Ward in Tokyo, for example, the site owned by an old metal manufacturing company was purchased by JHUDC. The old factory was transferred to a suburban industrial site, and the cleared site was divided into three zones: a site for smaller-scale factories, a housing complex for company personnel, and an affordable housing zone for a model housing community. Old houses at the site were demolished, roads and lanes were built, parks and open space were provided, and new model houses were constructed. Seven new factories decided to move into the improved site, and 275 new houses and apartment units were constructed. The government, through JHUDC, subsidized 50 percent of the project cost, which was justified by the physical and civic improvements, increased property values, and new tax revenues created by the whole scheme (Fukami 2000, 289–91). The LRS approach has been rather successful in Japan, where many people trust the government and housing agencies are able to resist political pressures. It may not be as useful in other Asian countries, where citizens are distrustful of government agencies and many projects fail because of political interference or outright graft and corruption.

A serious problem faced by Shanghai and other Chinese cities where inner-city housing has been improved is the increased demand for such housing as the inner city develops. Surveys of people who have agreed to be relocated to suburban apartments in Shanghai revealed that quite a number of them want to return to their old neighborhoods because they did not have to travel far to go shopping, see a movie, or go to work. It is almost inevitable, therefore, that a process of gentrification will occur as inner-city redevelopment proceeds. Chinese housing authorities are generally instructed by the government to accommodate as many households as possible in the redeveloped inner-city projects. However, in time, families originally allocated units in the projects sell their units or, where this practice is prohibited, their "rights of occupancy" to such units.

Probably the most important economic issue in rejuvenating inner-city housing is the high value of land. Urban economists have argued that accommodating low-income residents on the most expensive real estate in the city is an unwise use of resources. Public officials want a more robust tax base in the inner city, and thus they prefer to build offices, hotels, shopping centers, and entertainment venues there. If housing is to be built at all, it should be luxury high-rise apartments for high-income people. In many Asian cities, therefore, old and dilapidated houses have been razed and high-price apartments have replaced them. In most instances, this new housing has dramatically changed the demographic and social character of downtown. It has also drastically changed the physical design of the inner city, not always for the better.

The introduction of economic housing in Beijing, for example, has had rather mixed results. With the introduction of housing reform, collective-owned semiprivate developers launched economic housing projects in the inner city. They demolished old and dilapidated houses and put up more expensive multistory apartments. In 2001, the price of a 60-square-meter apartment unit had risen to 6,000 yuan or $720 per square meter, which was about twenty times the average family income in Beijing. It was no wonder that for some time quite a number of housing schemes had many vacant units in the city because not too many people could afford to buy them.

A factor that helped to raise the price of housing in the inner city has been the practice of some wealthy *danwei* (work units) purchasing high-priced apartments at government-subsidized rates. Public agencies like the Ministry of Public Security, People's High Court, State Property Management Bureau, and Ministry of Foreign Trade and Economic Cooperation have been able to buy six-story apartments at the concessional rate of 3,000 to 6,000 yuan per square meter. These units have then been rented out to key officials in these agencies at the standard rent of 0.55 yuan per square meter (Tan 1994, 45). This practice has helped to change the character of the inner-city communities as privileged government officials and their families have replaced poor courtyard dwellers in housing projects.

An unfortunate aspect of housing renewal in Beijing was the fact that many developers did not have any regard for the historical and cultural importance of the *siheyuan* (courtyard housing) that had been the main housing type in the city for centuries. Many courtyard houses were demolished and replaced with rows upon rows of look-alike glass and concrete apartments. Some developers even went to the extent of harassing and intimidating residents of courtyard houses to move out so they could demolish them and build apartments (*People's Daily,* August 7, 2001).

Eviction and Resettlement

In many Asian urban regions, inner cities are congested and lack even basic services. In Chinese cities like Beijing, Guangzhou, Shanghai, and Tianjin, for example, as many as 100,000 persons per square kilometer were packed in shared old houses or multistory apartments before the 1979 economic reforms were launched and more housing units were built. In some Beijing apartments built during the Great Cultural Revolution (1966–76), when the emphasis was on communal living, families were allocated small sleeping quarters but required to eat in communal dining rooms, share bathrooms, and attend daily ideological meetings in crowded halls.

In Shanghai, one *lilong* (small lane) house originally designed for a single family could accommodate as many as ten families. Living rooms in such houses were partitioned into small units separated by flimsy walls or, at times, even by cloth curtains. Even attics, stair landings, and foyers were converted into dwelling areas. Many families shared a single water tap, a toilet, and a kitchen. In good weather, most domestic activities in the overcrowded lanes were held outdoors so inner-city residents could escape the congestion of their homes.

One of the most common approaches to inner-city redevelopment in Asia has been the forced eviction and resettlement of residents. This policy, for example, was the method of choice in Seoul during the late 1950s, by the aptly named Mayor "Bulldozer" Kim. Taking his cues from American urban renewal programs, Kim demolished old houses and moved the residents to hastily built "citizen apartments." In other Asian cities like Metro Manila and Jakarta, the people relocated from the inner city were not even given housing options; they were simply dumped at relocation sites that were far from their jobs and did not have basic services like water and sanitation. It was no wonder, then, that many of those resettled people abandoned these sites and filtered back into other low-income areas of the inner city.

In general, a number of factors served to influence decisions to evict and relocate inner-city dwellers. These factors were reflected in such policy approaches as (1) measures to deal with urban blight, (2) efforts to economically develop the inner city, (3) programs to enforce the law and to uphold and protect the right of private property, and (4) projects to develop new areas on the urban periphery (Khan 1992).

As Asian countries actively pursued programs of economic development, they were constantly reminded of their plight by the congestion, decay, and deterioration of their inner cities. In South and Southeast Asia, the "shame of the cities" was an all too visible reflection of the failure to improve the lives of poor people. In parts of Delhi and Mumbai, slum dwellers occupied what had once been the large homes of the elite. In Ho Chi Minh City, Jakarta, and Metro Manila, squatter shanties lined riverbanks, canals, road rights-of-way, and railroad tracks. In many Asian urban regions, upper-class families and tourists avoided inner cities characterized by high crime rates, gambling, prostitution, and other urban ills. Government officials, who mostly came from the elite classes, proposed and implemented "urban renewal" policies that were often simply slum eradication and resettlement schemes.

Even in socialist China, where housing was ideologically considered a basic human right that was supposed to be guaranteed by the state, inner-city deterioration has been viewed as requiring eviction and resettlement of inner-city residents. In Beijing, the inner-city problem was regarded as a physical condition involving "old, unsafe, and dilapidated housing." Living conditions where individuals had less than 4 square meters of living space each; shared water taps, toilets, and kitchens; and were in real physical danger from possible collapse of dilapidated houses were not acceptable to public officials. The obvious solution to these problems was decongestion of these places through eviction and resettlement (Tan 1994; Liu 1995).

In Asian countries where market forces are the main determinants of public decision making, many city administrators uphold the importance of property rights and consider it their duty to enforce the rule of law. The eviction of squatters, therefore, is easily justified, because they are regarded as guilty of violating other people's property rights. Some squatter eviction programs have been aimed at so-called professional squatters, who are accused of extorting money from private landowners before moving out of invaded properties. Some government officials have even justified the eviction of squatters as efforts to save them from dangerous circumstances. In many Southeast Asian cities, squatters have been moved from dangerous areas such as steep hillsides, frequently flooded riverbanks, and toxic garbage dumps.

The attitudes and views of a city's citizenry and officialdom have direct effects on evictions and resettlement programs. In South Asian societies that are based on elite/mass distinctions, such as those that adhere to the caste system, government authorities may find no trouble justifying evictions of poor residents from inner cities. They may blame inner-city squatters and slum dwellers for problems like floods and epidemics because they clog open waterways, throw their human and solid waste into rivers and canals, and pollute their immediate surroundings. By casting negative attributes on urban poor people, it becomes easier to justify evicting them from the inner city.

The experience with eviction and relocation in many Asian cities has not been positive as far as the living conditions of urban poor people were concerned. In Metro Manila, many people relocated to suburban sites like Carmona, San Pedro Tunasan, and Sapang Palay abandoned them and returned to the city (Laquian 1966; Van Horen 2004). Similar failed projects have been seen in Bangkok, Delhi, Dhaka, Karachi, and Mumbai.

There were many reasons for the failure of eviction and relocation efforts. Too often, there were no employment opportunities or ways to make a living at the new sites. There were inadequate services, such as water, sanitation, drainage, electricity, and garbage collection and disposal. There were no schools, health centers, community halls, or social welfare stations, although some religious and civil society groups tried to provide these facilities on a voluntary basis. Transportation to and from the city was difficult and expensive. Building materials were rarely provided in the relocation schemes, and it took a long time before the relocated families could afford to build a livable home. Security at the relocation site was bad—building materials, valuables, and personal items were often stolen. There were conflicts involving property boundaries because of the haphazard surveys carried out by project staff. There were fights among children and personal disputes among neighbors, but policing was insufficient to deal with these. The members of relocated families had to live apart—employed members rented bed space near their place of work in the city and joined their families on weekends if they could afford it. Sometimes, this led to broken homes, as the commuting members established new families in the city center.

Thus the failure of many eviction and resettlement schemes in Asian cities has been mainly due to poor planning and indifferent management. However, quite a number of eviction and resettlement schemes have achieved positive results. In Beijing, Guangzhou, Shanghai, Tianjin, and other Chinese cities, public housing authorities have set up housing projects in suburban areas after the launching of economic reforms in 1979. Apartments in these projects were purchased by Chinese work units that formerly provided housing for their workers adjacent to their inner-city factories. The work units rented the suburban apartments to their employees and either awarded transportation allowances to pay for commuting costs or provided buses to pick them up and take them home every day. In later years, many employees have been allowed to buy their suburban apartments at subsidized rates using private savings, contributions to provident funds, and loans from relatives and, at times, even from banks.

In-depth studies of relocated residents in Beijing, Guangzhou, and Shanghai conducted by the Asian Urban Research Network teams between 1991 and 1995 revealed, in general, that many relocated families were satisfied with their new housing arrangements. The most important reason for satisfaction was the much larger sizes of the suburban apartments. Relocated families were pleased with better amenities, such as their own bathrooms and kitchens and the availability of balconies where they could dry their clothes. They were happy with the reliable supply of electricity, gas, and heating, as well as access to telephones and other amenities. They enjoyed the playgrounds for their children and marveled at the cleaner air and more open spaces available to them in the suburbs. There were some complaints about the extra time spent commuting, but work units often provided free bus services and many of the housing sites were along bus routes. Some residents also felt bad about losing friends in the old neighborhood, but they formed new bonds with their new neighbors, who often worked in the same work units.

Even people not belonging to work units who were relocated from inner-city sites tended to be satisfied with their new life. A survey of 130 families that have been resettled to the new residential district of Zhong Yun on the outskirts of Shanghai (conducted by Tongji University researchers in 1994) revealed general satisfaction with the move. The families had been resettled because the land they were occupying was needed for the construction of a new bridge. A survey was made before the people were moved from their inner-city neighborhood, and another was conducted a year after their eviction and relocation. The families were asked about their opinions regarding their living conditions at the old site and their reactions to the move and their current living conditions (Yu and Shai 1995).

In general, the study showed that the relocated people were happy with the move. They were most happy with the larger apartments. Before relocation, about 14.6 percent of the families had less than 4 square meters of living space per person. After relocation, 70.6 percent had more than 8 square meters. Not a single family at the new site had living space of less than 4 square meters per person—the smallest units had 6 square meters per person, occupied by 8.3 percent of the surveyed families. Not surprisingly, 52.4 percent of the families surveyed said the amount of living space they had in the new apartments was "good" and 47.6 percent said it was "average." Not a single family rated its new living space "poor." In contrast, before relocation, not a single family said its living space was "good," 64.4 percent said it was "average," and 35.6 percent said it was "poor" (Yu and Shai 1995).

With regard to the advantages and disadvantages of life in the old and the new neighborhoods, the survey found that, in general, people saw more advantages in the new site. They cited as clear advantages more parks and green space, better sanitation facilities, less noise, reduced air pollution, more playgrounds, easier access to schools, better medical facilities, and improved security. They were less happy about the increase in the time needed to travel between home and work (72 percent complained about increased travel time) and the greater commuting expense (76.7 percent said they have to spend more for transport). There was also some dissatisfaction about separation from relatives and friends, especially more elderly family members who had elected to stay in the inner city. Some respondents wistfully longed for the Chinese ideal of "three generations living under one roof." The size of families at the relocation site had become significantly smaller—before relocation, almost 10 percent of families had more than six members; but at the relocation site, not a single family had more than six members.

In the case of Beijing, the city authorities were initially not in favor of resettling inner-city residents and ruled that in projects where resettlement was required, at least 30 percent of new housing units built to replace old and dilapidated houses should be reserved for the original residents. Implementing this rule, however, caused some difficulties even for households allocated housing units. First, the residents needed to find their own accommodations at their own expense while the new houses were being built (a period of about one to two years). Then, they had to buy the new apartments—even at a subsidized price that was roughly one-tenth of the market value of the units, many families could still not afford to buy the units, especially because they also had to pay for any living space beyond what they originally had at the prevailing market rates. In the Chaoyanmen Nei housing project, the values of apartments per square meter rose from 350 yuan to 600–800 yuan in just one year. Faced with the difficulties of paying for housing and tempted by the higher market values of their units, quite a number of the original residents sold their "rights" to their units.

Studies of the relocation of families from the inner-city zones of Ho Chi Minh City had shown that these projects were generally successful. A 1996 sample survey of 2,711 families evicted because of the cleaning up and dredging of the Nhieu Loc-Thi Nghe Canal revealed that most of the evicted people did not have to move too far from their old neighborhoods. About 41.4 percent of evicted households purchased apartments in one of Ho Chi Minh City's five districts located from 1 to 5 kilometers away from their original homes, whereas 58.6 percent agreed to receive payment in cash and decided to find alternative lodging farther away. It is interesting that of the families that purchased apartments, 38.2 percent paid for the dwellings in one lump sum (from the government compensation and personal savings) and 59.1 percent paid by installments. Only 2.7 percent of the respondents said they were unable to meet payments and were renting their units, hoping that the government would agree to apply their rental payments to the purchase cost at a later date (Nguyen Quang Vinh 1996, 33).

When asked about the general level of satisfaction with their apartments in the relocation sites, 22 percent of the Ho Chi Minh City residents interviewed said they were fully satisfied, 64 percent said they were generally satisfied but were quite concerned about how they would meet installment payments for the unit, 9 percent said they were not that happy but because they had already bought the unit would stay in it, 2 percent said they were unhappy and would probably find ways of selling their unit, and 3 percent had no answer. Among the positive factors accounting for satisfaction, the most frequently mentioned was that the apartments were "more refreshing," "better lit," "had a steady supply of electricity," and "had steady supply of water." Some of the unsatisfactory factors noted were: apartments inconveniently located for the place of work, poor quality of construction of the apartments (leaking roofs, cracking walls), and inconvenience for elderly people (the five-story apartments had no elevators).

An interesting survey finding was the higher proportion of women who expressed dissatisfaction. Most of their complaints centered on a lack of facilities to care for their children and elderly family members. Despite these complaints, however, the general satisfaction with the new housing among all relocated residents was very high. In fact, almost immediately after moving into their homes, most households started making renovations, such as enlarging kitchens and toilets, putting in mezzanine floors for additional sleeping space, replacing windows and doors, and applying new coats of paint.

Among families who agreed to receive payment for moving out of the canal area, the survey found that 48.8 percent doubled up in homes of their relatives and friends, 24.4 percent bought another house in the city, and 26.8 percent returned to their province of origin. The Ho Chi Minh City Research Team traced some of the families that had moved to another part of the city and found that they also had a relatively high level of satisfaction. Most of the families that bought new houses had moved to "higher-income" districts, supplementing the funds received as compensation with personal savings or loans from friends and relatives. Some of those who moved in with relatives and friends eventually also bought their own unit. It proved extremely difficult to trace the families that had returned to their provinces of origin. Many of these families had no official registration in the city to begin with and would have encountered many difficulties in finding a niche in the big city.

An evaluation of projects conducted for this study revealed that where relocation has been successful, it has often involved provision of high-standard houses with adequate services in relocation areas. There has been careful planning to provide not only housing and services but also employment opportunities. Considerable investments have been made in physical infrastructure and social amenities. The problem, however, is that for many South and Southeast Asian countries, these inputs are often too expensive. Even when international financing—such as loans from the World Bank and Asian Development Bank—have been provided, many of these projects have faced difficulties because of a lack of funds, poor planning, inefficient management, bureaucratic red tape, and corruption.

Providing Infrastructure and Basic Urban Services

Living in the center of an Asian city is usually based on a rational process of weighing pros and cons. Inner-city communities may be crowded, noisy and, at times unsafe, but there are many attractive aspects of inner-city life as well. For example, a study of residents of Wangjia Harbor in Nanshi District of Shanghai (conducted by researchers from Tongji University in May 1995) asked a sample of residents what they "liked most" in their communities. The responses, as shown in table 7.1, had proximity to shopping and markets, the convenience of not having to fight traffic jams, and good neighborly relations as the three most important features liked by the residents.

Despite the congestion in Nanshi District, residents still could go to parks and squares and enjoy the outdoors. The neighborhood was quiet, it had good schools, and people felt safe and secure living there. Interestingly, when the residents were asked where they would like to move if they were

Table 7.1. *Results of Nanshi District Survey on Items Liked Most about the Inner-City Neighborhood*

Item Liked Most about the Neighborhood	Number of Responses	Percent
Convenience of shopping, proximity to markets	140	30.1
Do not have to spend too much time in traffic, close to everything	130	27.9
Excellent relations with neighbors, strong sense of community	113	24.3
Easy access to parks, public square, lots of sunshine, old trees	30	6.5
Presence of old buildings, temples, old houses in community	23	4.9
Feeling of safety and security in old neighborhood	18	3.9
Presence of good primary and middle schools	7	1.5
Love quiet neighborhood, people know each other very well	4	0.9
Total responses	465	100.0

Source: Tongji University (1995).

relocated from Nanshi, 59.3 percent of them just said they hoped to stay in the community and did not want to be relocated. Even when they were given a list of potential relocation sites, many of the Nanshi residents refused to indicate where they would like to be relocated (Tongji University 1996).

Other studies conducted by Tongji Universtity for the Asian Urban Research Network revealed that people have a deep attachment to their communities. This emotional attachment was particularly strong in the *lilong* houses located in central Shanghai. These lane houses were built immediately after the Opium War, after the forced opening of Shanghai as a trading port by Western powers. They were built to accommodate the millions of people who flocked to Shanghai because of the settlements opened up by the British, French, American, Japanese, and other colonizers. The traditional *lilong* house was originally patterned after the *siheyuan* or courtyard house, which had four sides (each independent residence was known as a *li*). These courtyard houses were built along narrow lanes or *long,* giving rise to the term *lilong* house. Each Shanghai *li* had one entrance gate, usually richly decorated with carvings and other embellishments.

As more and more *lilong* houses were built, the decorations were abandoned and the residences became plain and boxlike. The *lilong* apartments became really congested after 1949, when many were simply taken over by the people who flocked to Shanghai. Much later, despite the decay and dilapidation of the *lilong* houses, many inner-city residents preferred them to the modern apartments offered to them in the suburbs (Qian 1996).

Although there are many studies indicating that old-time inner-city residents in Asian city-regions are happy to live where they are, most Asian governments are bent on relocating these people and converting inner cities to "more productive" purposes. Most large Asian cities serve as national or regional capitals. Because they represent dominant government authority, there is a strong desire on the part of the authorities to keep improving them as a symbol of national or regional pride. In the age of globalization, there is intense competition among Asian cities to build the highest buildings in the world (Petronas Towers in Kuala Lumpur, China Financial Center in Shanghai), to stage the most dramatic spectacles (the staging of Turandot in Beijing's Forbidden City), or to show the world athletic prowess and accomplishments (the Seoul and Beijing Olympics). Tourism is a good incentive for improving the inner city. Attracting international investments is another motivation. To do all this, Asian cities compete with each other in setting up special economic development and high-technology zones, as in Shanghai's Pudong District or the Shenzhen Special Economic Zone in Guangdong province. Hong Kong styles itself a "smart city," where all new buildings are wired with fiber optics to connect them more efficiently to the wired electronic world.

In China, investing in the inner city used to be the primary responsibility of the central and local governments. Since the launching of urban reforms in 1979, however, other entities have devoted resources to urban improvement. The first to start redevelopment projects were state-owned enterprises, which were focused not only on production but also on improving housing and other benefits for their workforces. These work units invested in housing close to their inner-city plants or bought housing for their workers in peripheral areas.

Another source of investments in urban improvement is the cooperative. In China, cooperatives are social groups that raise their own resources to pursue productive projects. They raise their own funds, manage their own affairs, and share the benefits and profits with their members. In some cases, cooperatives receive assistance from the government or from work units. They may also borrow funds from banks and other institutions to finance their productive and service activities.

In recent years, development corporations have sprouted in Chinese cities. Some of them have grown out of the construction bureaus of local governments, and others originated in housing departments. These development corporations usually receive considerable loans and grants from cities or provinces. They invest these in land development and housing schemes, paying back the local governments for their loans and grants.

Whatever development instruments are used, it has been made clear by recent experience that the state of infrastructure in a city is a key influence on the decision of both domestic and local investors to locate in a particular urban area. As noted by a World Bank economist, international investors usually have a wide number of options when deciding where to locate. A World Bank survey indicated that one of the most important things investors were looking for was the adequacy of infrastructure and services. The survey showed, for example, that many international investors preferred to put up their plants in Shanghai rather than Delhi, Karachi, or Kolkata, because of the fact that firms located in Shanghai reported losing less than 1.5 percent of sales due to power failure, compared with 6 percent in South Asian cities. There were also fewer transportation breakdowns in Shanghai, and public services there were more predictable and efficient because there were fewer bureaucratic delays and very little corruption (Dollar 2004).

Many Asian authorities are finding that the success or failure of their efforts to redevelop inner cities is usually dependent on the resources and efforts of the people whose lives are directly affected by projects. In some countries, like Indonesia and the Philippines, this lesson is driven home by the confrontational position taken by poor urban groups that resist government efforts to evict them from their communities. To some Filipino urban authorities, one of the main sources of problems in assembling land for urban infrastructure and other development projects has been legislation (the so-called Lina law) stipulating that no squatter or slum dweller can be moved without providing adequate and acceptable housing and services for them in the relocation area. Quite a number of road-building projects have been delayed because people refuse to move before they are provided with an acceptable relocation site. This policy has also been followed in projects funded by the World Bank and the Asian Development Bank, and it has been identified as a key factor in the unsatisfactory execution of infrastructure projects.

Conversely, the ability of poor inner-city households to help in the planning of their communities and the implementation of project activities has been proven in the Indonesian Kampung Improvement Program, the Slum Improvement Program, and the Zonal Improvement Program in the Philippines. In the Tondo Foreshore redevelopment project in Metro Manila funded by the World Bank, community activists belonging to the Zone One Tondo Organization insisted on being involved in planning their community from the very start. They contributed their labor and other resources through "sweat equity" arrangements with the National Housing Authority. They managed the tasks of identifying the bona fide beneficiaries in the project, decided which families were to remain in the community or be moved to the nearby Dagat-dagatan "sites-and-services" project, and actively participated in the relocation of houses required by rationalizing the street grid of the community. At present, the Tondo project is still largely managed by locally elected officials at the *barangay* or neighborhood level. Under the Local Government Code of 1991, *barangay* units were given authority to raise their own funds, manage their own affairs, and serve as the basic unit for democratic life in the Philippines.

Participation in local-level planning and governance in Indonesian cities is also greatly facilitated by the traditional philosophy of *musjawarah* and the communal decision-making process of *gotong royong*. The former requires that all decisions of people at the community level should be arrived at by consensus. Until the full agreement of all parties is achieved, community stakeholders and decision makers in Indonesian local units have to continue discussions. The tradition of *gotong royong,* or communal self-help and mutual aid, is stressed in pursuing activities such as cleaning up canals, pathways, and surroundings; digging community wells; the construction of public latrines; and the sorting and collection of solid waste. Many Indonesian communities also have communal fundraising systems to support community activities such as neighborhood libraries, local health clinics, primary schools, mosques, and temples.

In general, therefore, the vitality of inner-city neighborhoods in many Asian cities may be due to the careful attention given to public participation in community affairs. In some cases (e.g., during the time of the Marcos dictatorship in the Philippines or the authoritarian rule of Suharto in Indonesia), there were attempts to co-opt traditional participatory practices by the government. These attempts failed miserably because of the strength of traditional cooperative practices. Many Asian governments, therefore, seem to have accepted the importance of community participation in urban redevelopment and have formulated programs to make this a regular feature of city planning and governance. There are some exceptions, of course. In China and Vietnam, government authorities still wield a great deal of power and influence to plan and implement projects with little or no community participation. This seems to be changing in some big cities, where organized groups—such as those advocating environmental protection or a more equitable distribution of economic and social benefits among social groups—are becoming more active.

Cultural Conservation and Tourism

In redeveloping inner cities, Asian urban authorities are faced with three main options. First, they could decide to do nothing about current trends, allowing the inner city to decay and deteriorate while economic and social development occurs in the suburbs and on the urban periphery. Second, they could plan the inner city as the modern symbol of their aspirations for nationhood, clear out the old and decaying inner-city structures, and rebuild the central business district as a center for business and finance, governance, commerce, entertainment, tourism, and cultural activities. Third, they could engage in serious heritage and cultural preservation, restoring palaces, temples, colonial offices, and culturally significant buildings, sometimes justifying these actions as necessary elements in the development of tourism. This cultural conservation approach may include keeping spatial elements of the inner city, such as plazas, squares, and parks, and the continued operation of traditional centers of economic activity, such as markets and bazaars.

In the Asian city-regions included in this study, very few urban authorities have resigned themselves to doing nothing about current inner-city situations, despite the many economic and political difficulties that they have been facing. As a whole, the choices have been either to vigorously pursue urban renewal and modernization policies or to embark on cultural conservation and tourism programs. In some cases, as in Beijing and Shanghai, the drive for economic development has drastically altered the nature of the central business district, not always in aesthetically pleasing ways. In others, as in Jakarta, inner-city redevelopment has almost succeeded in the complete destruction of the cultural character of downtown. In a number of cases, however, as in Bangkok and Hanoi, urban authorities have managed to achieve a fine balance between economic modernization and maintaining the cultural and historical character of the inner city in a process that has been called "contextual adaptability" (Ikaputra, Narumi, and Hisa 2000, 298).

As a whole, therefore, Asian mega-urban regions have been reasonably successful in renovating and redeveloping their inner cities and to keep these zones culturally vibrant and socially alive. In many cases, the fact that mega-cities are the focal point of national life encourages inner-city redevelopment. Tourism is also a very strong incentive to maintain the historic cultural heritage of the inner city. The most important element of inner-city redevelopment in Asian city-regions, however, is the continued residence of people in the inner city. Even when these inner-city residents are poor, they give the city core the social energy that makes for good community life. This social cohesiveness provides the foundation for the viability of inner-city life in Asian mega-urban regions.

8

Developing the Urban Periphery

Historically, many great cities in Asia owed their origins to the powers of supreme rulers. In China, emperors planned and built their capitals from scratch or on the ruins of conquered cities (Wu 1986). Indian rulers built mighty walled cities and graceful monuments to their loved ones (Jain 1996b). Feudal lords in Japan constructed great castles that became the centers of cities. In Indonesia, it was suggested that it was not the city that created the center of social and political power but the ruler in the palace. Tracing the early development of Bangkok, Korff held the view that the city's national dominance was at succeeding stages "personal, communal and hierarchical." Personal power emanated from the king, ruling from the capital with the help of loyal administrators. Bangkok was simply a shell, its physical form shaped by social stratification and kingly powers (Korff 1989, 12).

From their centralist beginnings, Asian mega-cities expanded outward, often randomly and haphazardly. This was especially true of colonial cities, which progressed from the wealth created by monopolistic trade. Manufacturing enterprises initially focused on the processing of agricultural products near port areas eventually built factories outside the city to take advantage of cheap land and labor. Heavy industries, with their noise, soot, and polluting wastes, also had to be located on the urban periphery. As employment opportunities became available in manufacturing and industrial enterprises, the people followed, and residential areas clustered around these enclaves. These new settlers joined villagers in a process of uncontrolled urban sprawl.

Improvements in transport systems accelerated the outward expansion of mega-cities. As roads and highways fanned out into the countryside, string developments followed. Housing projects, seeking cheaper land, were pushed to the outer limits of suburbia. Rich agricultural land was destroyed to make way for urban construction. The costs of extending basic services like water and sewerage to outlying areas soared. Authorities had to go farther and farther from the city to tap new sources of raw water. They also found it hard to find open areas where they could safely dispose of their solid waste. In time, many cities felt the acute adverse effects of uncontrolled expansion. Faced with worsening problems, Asian urban authorities sought effective policy measures to properly plan and manage urban peripheral areas.

From a review of policies designed to plan and manage urban peripheral areas in the Asian mega-cities covered in this study, six distinct approaches have been identified: (1) peri-urban agriculture, (2) small town development, (3) satellite cities, (4) innovation centers and high-technology parks, (5) special economic zones, and (6) open coastal regions. In most countries, there have been attempts to integrate these policy measures into comprehensive strategic plans that serve to link central cities with their rural and urbanizing hinterlands. But local government fragmentation continues, and the gap between small towns and big cities has persisted despite these efforts.

Peri-Urban Agriculture

Market forces and policy interventions have been rapidly transforming the peri-urban areas of Asian cities into a complex mix of urban and rural activities. Urban agriculture—defined as "the production for domestic consumption or sale of food grains, tree crops, fresh horticultural produce, fish and animal products within an urban area"—has flourished in most urban settlements (Koc et al. 1999, 13). Traditionally, many urban households have planted vegetables and fruit trees or grown chickens and pigs in peri-urban areas to augment their food supply or sell their surplus for extra income. In Dhaka, for example, a 1999 survey involving 400 individuals engaged in peri-urban agriculture found that, on average, each person earned only about $1.50 per day, barely keeping them above the poverty line (Remenyi 2000). In other countries, however, growing crops and raising animals in peri-urban areas has become a major source of employment and income, and some peri-urban agricultural enterprises have even applied advanced technologies like hydroponics and climate-controlled sterile greenhouses in their production efforts.

Peri-urban agriculture has many advantages aside from augmenting food supply and increasing a family's income. The commercial production of food items in peri-urban areas ensures that they are fresh when they reach city customers. Elaborate and expensive storage, preservation, and packaging of agricultural products are often unnecessary because the distance between farm and market is short and products can be delivered more quickly. Lower transport costs can reduce the price of agricultural products for urban consumers. Lands on the urban periphery planted with orchards, grain, and vegetables serve as greenbelts that act as the lungs of big cities. Such open areas can be used for leisure activities and tourism. In some cities, there have been successful efforts to use urban waste as an input to agricultural production, helping to make urban settlements more sustainable.

In China, the intensive production of agricultural products in peri-urban areas has been practiced for many years. In Shanghai, for example, about 3.6 million farmers supply 40 percent of wheat, 90 percent of eggs, and 100 percent of milk needed by the city. In addition, forty-three flower-growing concerns produce 290 million tons of cut flowers a year, about a third of total flower production in all of China. In Beijing, between 1970 and 1990, about 70 percent of the nonstaple food in the city-region was produced in open fields and plastic-covered greenhouses in the suburbs (Cai 2000).

Since 1979, peri-urban agriculture in Chinese cities has been undergoing very rapid changes. There has been a shift from family-based small-scale agricultural production to larger and more sophisticated enterprises. This shift has been caused by the increasing value of land, which in turn is due to the conversion of significant amounts of arable land to urban uses. In Metropolitan Shanghai, arable land decreased from 360,000 to 290,000 hectares between 1979 and 1995. As a result, land close to the central city has become too expensive for traditional urban agriculture to remain profitable, and about 75 percent of new agriculture farms are now located more than 10 kilometers from the city (the rest are located 30–60 kilometers away). Increasingly, peri-urban agriculture has been shifting from small-scale production to more technologically advanced enterprises. About 26.7 percent of vegetables in Shanghai are currently grown in climate-controlled greenhouses, including 10 very large commercial enterprises and 200 medium-sized farms. In addition, in 1998, there were 547 large pig farms, 88 of which had a capacity to produce 10,000 pigs a day; 100 broiler chicken farms that could produce 100,000 birds each a day; 120 egg-producing enterprises with more than 10,000 hens each; and 150 dairy farms, with 100 head of cattle each. These large firms are vertically integrated and pursue activities from production to processing, packaging, distribution, research, product line development, and marketing (Cai 2000).

A veritable show window of the tremendous progress that has been achieved in peri-urban agriculture in China is the Xiaotongshan urban agriculture complex outside Beijing. This center is made up of Xiaotongshan town, three adjacent towns, and 45 villages covering an area of 112 square kilometers and holding a population of 40,000. Within the complex are eight zones: (1) the Agricultural Production zone, where experimental approaches have succeeded in increasing crop yields from 18 to 30 percent; (b) the Flower Producing Zone, which is capable of turning out 6 million flowering plants a year in Asia's largest flower nursery; (3) the Tree Nursery, which covers 156 hectares and grows 2 million young trees a year; (4) the Aquaculture Zone, which involves experimenting with various ways of growing fish in ponds and other bodies of water; (5) the Lamb Raising Zone, covering 67 hectares and raising about 800,000 lambs a year; (6) the Seed Zone, which produces good-quality seeds for both flowering plants and vegetables; (7) the Agricultural Processing Zone, which engages in varied processing techniques for food items as well as packaging the produce from the experimental farm; and (8) the Agritourism Zone, which is complete with hotels, conference rooms, and flower and vegetable gardens and trails. From this account, it is apparent that Xiaotongshan is not only an experimental peri-urban farm and a tourism site, it is also an ongoing production and research center that, as of 2003, had already attracted 51 enterprises to locate within its complex (Cai 2000).

A particularly significant element in peri-urban agriculture is the prospect of using the waste of the city as an input to agriculture. The traditional use of "night soil" as a fertilizer has been known in China, Vietnam, and other countries. More recently, the "wet garbage" of urban households has been used to produce compost as fertilizer in Bangkok, Dhaka, Jakarta, Metro Manila, and other cities. Fish farms in Kolkata (formerly Calcutta) have been linked to sewage systems. And in Hanoi, a combined system of growing rice and raising fresh water fish in paddies "fertilized" by sewage has been used for centuries. The main drawback in using urban sewage and waste for agriculture, of course, has been the high level of pathogens in waste (i.e., fecal coliform bacteria, worm eggs) that pose serious health hazards.

However, some studies have shown that simple techniques can be used to use waste as a fertilizer without expensive chemical waste treatment. For example, a study in Haroonabad—a peri-urban town in Pakistan where untreated sewage has been used for irrigation for the past thirty-five years—showed that farmers who worked in the area had a high incidence of hookworms and other helminthes. However, a simple method of mixing one part of sewage effluent to two parts of fresh water in irrigation canals served to make the nutrient-rich water safe for irrigation. Laboratory analysis in sewage-enriched farms in Haroonabad showed that the resultant irrigation water was high in macronutrients like nitrogen, phosphorus, and potassium that were good for the plants and that had low levels of heavy metals. The proper mixture of sewage effluent and fresh water met water quality standards for agriculture set by the Pakistan Environmental Protection Ordinance (Ensink et al. 2002).

If urban agriculture trends in more technologically advanced countries are an indication, more and more mega-urban regions in developing countries will most likely see more efforts at food production in peri-urban areas. Technological approaches for the production and processing of agricultural products are being adopted in many cities, and a number of centers in industrial countries, such as City Farmer in Canada and the Urban Agriculture Network in New York, are disseminating more information on the subject. Studies such as those carried out at the Asia Pacific Research Center at Stanford University on peri-urban development are shedding more light on policies and programs that work and those that do not.

In some Asian mega-urban regions, urban agriculture has become big business. It provides an adequate, reliable, and affordable food supply for urban residents. It has helped to increase income, and in some cases it has been a way to utilize urban waste as an input to agricultural production. If the problems of local jurisdictional fragmentation, inadequate infrastructure systems (especially roads and water provision), and lacks of technical and managerial skills in peri-urban areas are solved, peri-urban agriculture can become an even more effective instrument for the planned development of Asian mega-urban regions.

Small Town Development

Many countries in Asia have sought balanced development that combines the benefits of urbanization with the idylls of rural life. During the 1960s and 1970s, a number of authors proposed that this balance could be achieved by the development of small towns closely linked to rural villages (Johnson 1970; Lipton 1977; Kammeier and Swan 1984). Small urban settlements were supposed to spark modernization and development in rural places while avoiding the problems of congested mega-cities. They were meant to act as administrative centers and provide much needed services, such as schools, health clinics, rural banks, and other credit facilities to rural dwellers. Advocates of small town development hoped that they would serve as ready markets for farm products. They were expected to offer employment opportunities in the secondary and tertiary sectors. If located on the periphery of large cities, small towns could absorb large numbers of rural–urban migrants and serve as new sites for relocated inner-city dwellers. They could also provide ample room for the expansion of factories and industrial enterprises.

Experiences with approaches such as integrated rural development and other schemes have shown, however, that the high expectations regarding the development roles of small towns were rather unrealistic. Studies revealed that small towns lacked the economies of scale to support sustained development. They could not attract the capital or the professional and managerial resources necessary for development programs. Moreover, the hope that economic and social progress in small towns would help to discourage movement to larger cities was not realized. In fact, migration studies showed that it was precisely the individuals whose lives had improved in rural areas who had the highest propensity to move to bigger cities.

Between 1949 and 1979, China effectively controlled rural–urban migration through the *hukou* (household registration) system. After the launching of economic reforms in 1979, the *hukou* system was relaxed, and rural dwellers were allowed to move to small towns and some cities provided they did not rely on the state for their grain supply. By 2002, more than 100 million people had moved from rural areas to towns and cities, and 50 million of these were registered as "temporary migrants" (*Xinhua,* February 25, 2002). Many analysts suspected that these figures were most probably underestimated because many migrants did not reveal their *hukou* status and most employers, especially in small enterprises, did not care to check this status because they were no longer responsible for the benefits and welfare of the migrants. In 2002, it was also estimated that there were 124 million "surplus" workers in rural areas, and their numbers were projected to increase to 200 million by 2000. Recent estimates set this at about 450 million out of China's 900 million rural residents.

The *hukou* system has been criticized by some quarters and has been called "the equivalent of an apartheid system between rural and urban residents" (*China Labor Bulletin,* February 25, 2002). However, the Ministry of Public Security has continued to justify the *hukou* system as an instrument for keeping public order (the ministry said it allowed the police to track down criminals more easily) and for providing demographic data for planning and program formulation. In continuing the use of the *hukou,* the more restrictive aspects of the system—such as linking residence, employment, education, and medical care to a person's *hukou* status—have been officially dropped. However, some local government officials continue to use the *hukou* as the basis for the power to provide or deny such benefits that gives them an opportunity to indulge in petty corruption.

The *hukou* system was an important factor in the growth of small towns in China. In the Chinese development scheme, small towns were designated as "growth points" that would effect the modernization of rural areas. At the same time, they were considered as "key bridging points" that served to link cities with villages. Small towns were designated as growth nodes in regional systems that formed a "network development pattern." They constituted the lowest tier in a hierarchy of urban settlements designed to achieve balanced growth.

In the master plan for the Shanghai mega-urban region, four different types of towns were marked for development:

- *Auxiliary towns* are large urban settlements with populations of more than 250,000 designated as industrial production sites and reception areas for residents resettled from the inner city. The town of Baoshan, for example, holds one of China's largest steel-manufacturing complexes. Minxin is made up of Minhang, designed as a key production base for the chemical industry, and Xinzhuang, an important transport hub and an economic and cultural center in the Yangtze River Delta.
- *Secondary towns* are settlements with populations ranging from 50,000 to 250,000 designed to absorb people who are attracted to the Shanghai region. Most of these towns are the urbanized centers of prefectures and act as administrative, political, commercial, and cultural hubs for surrounding areas.
- *Small towns* are planned to have 30,000 to 50,000 inhabitants. They act as administrative centers at the county level and as market towns.
- *Townships* are rural settlements with populations of 5,000 to 10,000. They are usually large villages that have been designated as townships.

The small town development policies adopted in China after 1979 were actually a revival of development schemes proposed by the sociologist Fei Xiaotong, who based his theories on intensive studies he conducted in Wujiang County of Jiangsu province in the mid-1930s. From his studies, Fei noted the contributions of nonagricultural enterprises in small towns to the rapid development of the countryside. He therefore recommended that the government should support small-scale enterprises focused on the processing of agricultural products, sericulture, handicrafts, furniture making, and other ventures (Fei 1984). Fei's proposals initially ran counter to policies advocated by Chairman Mao Zedong, who during the Great Leap Forward (1958–60) pushed for rural industrialization. It was not until after Deng Xiaoping gained ascendancy in China and launched his economic reforms that the proposals of Fei were adopted as official policy by the Government of China.

Before the adoption of the small town development strategy, there were only 2,786 small towns in China with a total population of 62.3 million people. By 1985, the number of small towns had increased to 7,511, with a combined population of 166.3 million. In 1990, there were more than 12,000 small towns all over China (Ebanks and Cheng 1990). This jumped to 55,000 in 1994, 16,702 of which were classified as rural "organic towns," 31,463 proclaimed as the seats of township governments, and 6,835 designated as small towns for the management of state farms, mining towns, and other sites for specialized activities. The First Agricultural Census conducted in 1996 enumerated residents of 16,124 "rural towns," which accounted for 37.4 percent of the total number of townships and towns all over the country. On average, each of these rural towns covered an area of 2.42 square kilometers and had a population of 4,520, of which 2,072 (45.8 percent) was registered as having nonagricultural *hukou* status (Agricultural Census Communiqué 4, March 31, 2002). By the end of 2002, China had 660 officially certified cities and 20,601 officially certified towns, with the total urban population reaching 502 million and the urbanization level standing at 39 percent (Ministry of Construction, China 2004, 6).

To enhance the development of small towns, the Chinese government encouraged the setting up of township and village enterprises (TVEs). In 1985, most of the old commune and brigade enterprises were transformed into TVEs, and many of these were turned into collectives. Some were even privatized. The TVE approach was first tried in fourteen selected pilot project areas and later greatly expanded. In 1992, the National Plan Committee of the Chinese Government launched a program of "small town experimental units," whereby 100 small towns with high population densities, good natural resources, and appropriate agricultural and industrial potentials were awarded loans of 1 million yuan each for infrastructure and other construction projects. In Guangdong province, for example, the town of Renhe was chosen as one of these experimental units. Renhe had grown rapidly because of investments from Chinese compatriots living abroad (about 20,000 of the town's 65,900 population had relatives in Hong Kong, Malaysia, Singapore, and other places). The town's strategic location close to Guangzhou and Hong Kong was also a primary consideration in its choice as an experimental project site (Yan 1995a).

An intensive case study of Renhe's development carried out by the Asian Urban Research Network team from Zhongshan University between 1991 and 1995 revealed that industries organized in the town fell into four categories. First, there were *state enterprises* owned by the city of Guangzhou, including an umbrella-making factory and another turning out compressors for a refrigerator factory. These large firms were fully capitalized with public funds and managed by city officials. Second, there were *foreign enterprises* owned by foreign investors or joint-venture companies, primarily geared to the export market. Third, there were *collectives,* which were formerly commune- and brigade-level enterprises mainly engaged in manufacturing clothes and toys, food production, and processing leather and fur products. These constituted the largest number of enterprises (about 72.9 percent), supported by pooled capital from village and town units. Finally, there were *private enterprises,* which were often very small and were owned by either one or a group of families. Many of these private ventures provided personal services (e.g., barber shops, beauty parlors) and others included karaoke bars, coffee shops, and small eateries (Xue 1996, 4).

In encouraging the growth of TVEs the Chinese authorities had to institute basic reforms. Foremost among these was the clarification of individual and collective property rights, especially those connected with land tenure and the buying and selling of fixed assets. In addition, government agencies offered small-scale credit to TVEs, conducted training programs in production techniques, improved regulations for accounting and basic financial management, and expanded information services and technical assistance to local entrepreneurs. Some small town governments offered serviced sites for the new enterprises, and others even built physical plants and provided essential services. Local units set up local labor offices to regulate the employment and residency status of rural–urban migrants who found jobs in TVEs. Rules and regulations were also instituted to facilitate the collection of local fees and taxes, enforce environmental regulations and standards, and curb petty corruption.

The pilot project approach enabled the Chinese authorities to experiment with a variety of production approaches to improve the performance of TVEs. For example, in Wenzhou municipality, Zhejiang province, the experimental approach focused on the development of private for-profit enterprises rather than collectives or cooperatives. In Fuyang prefecture, Anhui province, experiments were conducted on the relative costs and benefits of shifting from agricultural to nonagricultural enterprises. In Zhoucun district, Zibo municipality, Shandong province, the experiment involved the formation of cooperatives to manage TVEs. By carefully monitoring these and similar pilot projects, local authorities were able to develop appropriate institutional approaches to manage TVEs (Wickramanayake and Hu 1993).

Yet after a great deal of fanfare had been focused on TVEs, the Chinese authorities encountered several difficulties that resulted in a virtual abandonment of the program. The most important problem was the environmental pollution caused by TVEs. Because of a lack of capital and limited knowledge of the environmental consequences of their actions, many TVEs engaged in production processes that emptied organic wastes, toxic chemicals, used oils, dyes, and effluents into canals, streams, and drainage systems. In the Pearl River Delta and the Yangtze River Delta, surface water became so polluted that people could only raise eels and turtles instead of carp and other fish. In other areas, groundwater was also polluted from the waste created by TVEs. The widespread burning of coal for energy added to serious air pollution. Although China had adopted national pollution control laws, most of the TVEs were too small and underfinanced to abide by environmental regulations.

The decentralization of authority and power to local government officials also contributed to problems associated with TVEs because many officials, some of whom were associated with TVE enterprises, were not able to control their activities. Although small towns and other urban places in China were required to have master plans and zoning codes that regulated land use, TVEs were allowed to be established in ecologically sensitive zones. Agricultural land was taken over by TVEs, sometimes with the connivance of local officials. Some local officials were found to be only too willing to ignore environmental laws, rules, and regulations for a price.

Although the development of small towns was encouraged all over China, the greatest success achieved by the approach occurred on the peripheries of large metropolitan areas. A special study conducted by Tongji University for the Asian Urban Research Network project (1991–96) monitored developments in the town of Hongmiao, located on the outskirts of Shanghai (Tongji University 1996). A survey of TVEs in this town revealed productive linkages between enterprises in both the town and the city along the following lines:

- *Capital investments.* Big enterprises in Shanghai opened up branch operations in Hongmiao town to take advantage of less expensive land, cheaper labor, better housing for workers, and tax incentives offered by the town administrators. In some instances, the Shanghai firms simply bought out existing TVEs engaged in similar production lines. In others, the metropolitan firms entered into local "joint ventures" in what were called "horizontal economic alliances."

- *Subcomponent manufacturing.* TVEs in Hongmiao entered into contracts with Shanghai-based enterprises to produce subcomponents for consumer products. For example, 90 percent of the output of the Phoenix Bicycle Parts Factory in Hongmiao went to the Shanghai Phoenix Bicycle Factory, and only 10 percent was sold to other manufacturers in the open market.

- *Technical assistance.* Shanghai-based enterprises provided technical assistance to their town partners in such technical areas as product design, production techniques, quality control, and financial management. For example, although the Hongmiao Weaving Mill that manufactured ladies underwear was regarded as an independent enterprise, it had strong linkages with the Shanghai Xinguang Underwear Weaving and Dyeing Mill for technical assistance. Similarly, the Weili Shoemaking Factory in Hongmiao was greatly assisted by the Shanghai Sports Footwear Company. Through such technical assistance arrangements, the Shanghai enterprises were able to "let out" and subcontract some of their production activities to the township company while being assured of the quality of the products made for them.

- *Leisure and recreation.* Because they were pressed for space in their central city locations, many big enterprises in Shanghai set up leisure and recreation centers on the urban periphery for their employees. Thus, the Jiangong Architectural and Engineering Group set up the Kunming Lake Holiday Camp in Hongmiao. The Shanghai Yuyuan Limited Liability Corporation even established a Tourist and Business Center in the town. These town-centered ventures, which were initially designed to serve city employees and their families, later expanded and became independent enterprises that served the leisure and recreational needs of other people.

The planned development of small towns around Shanghai strongly complemented policies that had been in place for many years. In fact, during China's First Five-Year Plan period (1953–57), the Shanghai government had built four industrial satellite towns located about 3 to 5 kilometers from the city's built-up area (Pengpu, Zhoujiadu, Beixinjing and Qingningshi). In 1958, twelve additional industrial satellite towns were constructed (Anting, Changjiao, Gaoqiao, Jiading, Jinshanwei, Minhang, Songjiang, Taopu, Wujiaochang, Wujing, and Wusong). These industrial satellite towns were classified into two types: (1) comprehensive industrial satellite towns, such as Jiading and Songjiang, which were larger and had well-developed economic and cultural bases, and (2) specialized industrial districts, which were smaller and were designed to concentrate on specific activities. For example, the specialized industrial district of Jinshanwei concentrated on the petrochemical industry, Minhang on electrical engineering, Changjiao on building materials, and Wusong on iron and steel (Yan 1985, 115).

To manage and control the expansion of the Shanghai mega-urban region, the municipal government integrated small town development into its master plan and passed zoning codes and regulations to guide the implementation of the plan. Interestingly, these codes and regulations abandoned the restrictive single-function zoning approaches that had been borrowed by the Chinese from Russian urban planning. The new plans provided for mixed-use development. They took into consideration economic and social linkages between residence and workplace, the need to form coherent and stable communities, better management of basic urban services, and the creation of a strong sense of community among residents. Most important of all, the new zoning codes and regulations were more responsive and flexible, having been formulated with an eye to economic and social realities rather than the need for strict administrative and bureaucratic control.

In general, China's small town development strategy had worked quite well, especially in developing urban peripheral areas and improving economic and social linkages between the towns and their rural surroundings. One of the problems caused by peripheral area development in many cities had been the transformation of suburban towns into "bedroom communities" for commuters. The Chinese solved the problem by locating residences near job sites. In the areas adjacent to the small towns, they instituted the policy of "leaving the land but not the village," simultaneously dealing with the twin issues of nonagricultural employment and housing.

The small town development strategy also drastically changed the pattern of employment on the urban periphery. The case study of Hongmiao town monitored the shifts in employment between 1986 and 1995 and showed a significant change from primary- to tertiary-sector production. At the beginning of the period, 76.1 percent of the labor force in Hongmiao was engaged in agriculture. This proportion dropped to 30.5 percent in 1989 and 26.9 percent in 1995. In contrast, employment in manufacturing and other enterprises increased from 20.2 percent in 1986 to 51.5 percent in 1995. Most important, employment in the tertiary sector (small-scale enterprises and personal services) increased from 3.7 percent in 1986 to 22.6 percent in 1995 (Tongji University 1996).

To say that the small town development strategy in China has been generally successful does not mean, however, that it has been free from problems. One criticism leveled at the policy has been that some of the towns selected for development were too small and were not able to take advantage of economies of scale, location, and agglomeration. As the saying went, "Every village lights a fire, smoke goes up everywhere, but real development is not sparked." A number of analysts argued that focusing attention on small and intermediate-sized cities rather than small towns would probably have achieved greater results in the development of China. Developing small towns close to large cities as integral parts of mega-urban regions would have also accomplished a great deal more, as is shown in the cases of Beijing, Guangzhou, Hong Kong, and Shanghai.

A second problem attributed to China's small town development policy has been the social polarization of classes in small towns, resulting in a large and widening gap between a very tiny wealthy and powerful local elite and a great mass of rural–urban migrants that dangerously portends the emergence of an impoverished underclass. A Zhongshan University study of small towns in the vicinity of Shenzhen, a special economic zone in Guangdong province, estimated that 0.4 percent of the residents were wealthy Hong Kong entrepreneurs; 20 percent were equally rich local leaders, party functionaries, and town officials; and 79.6 percent were poor migrant workers and laborers.

Most of these migrant workers, dubbed the *liudong renkou* or floating population, were poorly educated individuals from the interior provinces of Anhui, Sichuan, and Hunan and from the Guangzi Zhuang Autonomous Region who were willing to accept any jobs available in the towns. Because most of them had "temporary" or even illegal migrant status, they were denied access to public services. Female migrants, who formed the great majority of factory workers, were especially vulnerable. They worked long hours and received low pay. Some were housed in barracks-type accommodations, but those who had to work in the informal sector usually had to find housing in congested and squalid slums (Yan 1995b).

The living and working conditions of rural–urban migrants was revealed in a study of Nanhai, where it was found that the number of migrants increased at the rate of 13.2 percent a year. The survey found that about 71.9 percent of workers in textile factories in Nanhai were females. On average, migrant workers got paid 300 yuan a month, about half the average wages of permanent workers. Migrants also worked about 10 hours a day or 300 hours a month, compared with regular workers who worked for 8 hours a day or 240 hours a month (Yan 1995b). Interestingly, the Nanhai survey revealed that not too many of the migrants expressed dissatisfaction with their life in the small towns (more than 85 percent of the workers interviewed said that compared with their parents, their living conditions had significantly improved). When a female factory worker was asked if she felt exploited in a Taiwanese shoe factory that paid low salaries and required long working hours, she said that working conditions were hard but it was much better than "working knee deep in mud planting rice in our village in Anhui."

A third problem associated with small town development was environmental degradation. A study of nineteen small towns in Baoan County, for example, found that about 128 square kilometers of land converted to urban uses suffered from erosion. It was estimated that 960,000 tons of topsoil were being lost from this developed area each year. Aside from the loss of agricultural productivity, the soil erosion resulted in the silting up of rivers and streams, causing destructive floods (Meng 1995).

A fourth problem arising from the small town development strategy was the loss of agricultural land to intensified urban development policies. In small towns around Shenzhen, for example, fewer than 22,000 hectares of farmland remained in 1986, compared with the 35,000 hectares that were available in 1979 (Yee 1992, 141). A survey of Baoan and Longgang Counties found that arable land in the study area decreased from 28,600 to 4,300 hectares within a fifteen-year period before 1995. As a result, grain production in the area decreased from 110,000 tons in 1980 to 5,100 tons in 1995 (Meng 1995). For Guangdong province as a whole, a total of 327,800 acres of cultivated land within the delta was lost to nonagricultural uses between 1980 and 1990. The existing cultivated land within the delta decreased from 2.58 to 2.25 million acres. The size of cultivated land per capita also dropped from 0.15 to 0.11 acres within the same period.

The rate of loss of agricultural land was highest in the designated towns, 214 of which were created in the delta between 1980 and 1986 alone. Between those years, the Pearl River Delta lost an average of 77.32 square kilometers of cultivated land per year to nonagricultural uses (Lin 1997, 113–15). More recent data indicate that the loss of agricultural land all over China has reduced the average size of arable land per capita to 0.1 hectares,

an area about 104 feet by 104 feet. The rate of arable land loss was estimated at 1 percent a year, and if this trend continues, the per capita arable
land in China will drop to 0.07 hectares (87 feet by 87 feet) when the country's population hits 1.6 billion by 2030 (Frick 2000).

Arable land was also often withdrawn from cultivation because of the
miscalculation of town officials who had hoped that by converting farmland
to industrial sites or housing projects they would attract investment from
Hong Kong, Taiwan, and other places. These ambitious officials engaged in
land speculation, setting up subdivisions or industrial sites by putting in
roads, drainage, and other rudimentary services in demarcated plots, hoping that if they built these, investors would come. In many instances, however, these officials did not conduct careful feasibility studies for these projects, and they found that investors did not come. In the meantime, however,
valuable land had been taken out of cultivation and had become extremely
difficult to bring back to a productive state.

As a result of these speculative practices, large tracts of land on the urban peripheries in China were withdrawn from agricultural production. In
the winter and spring of 1992–93, for example, one-quarter of the total
farmland in Zhejiang province was not being cultivated. In Guangdong
province, about 455,000 acres of grain fields were taken out of cultivation.
Land earmarked for urban development in Hainan province was being
sold and resold to "developers," but no construction was being done on it.
In 1992, only 18.9 percent of total leased land in the province was built
on or was under construction; the rest was idle. The problems arising from
land speculation in China became so severe that in 1993 the State Council imposed tighter controls over the leasing of land by local governments.
Bank loans for land development were frozen. A special committee
headed by China's premier was set up to investigate abuses in withdrawing land from production. The negative practices were reduced, but in
more remote parts of China, local officials with grand dreams continued
to try to use land to attract greatly sought after foreign investment (Hsing
1998, 156–57).

Despite the problems noted here, it is possible to conclude that, as a
whole, China's small town development strategy has helped to develop peripheral areas in a balanced manner. The small towns helped to transform
rural folk into urban citizens, easing their transition from agricultural to
nonagricultural employment. They deflected millions of migrants from going directly to big cities by absorbing them in secondary- and tertiary-sector jobs on the urban periphery. They reduced pressure on basic urban serv-

ices for inner cities. They also provided a temporary way station in the inevitable trek of rural folks toward urban centers.

Unless the small town development strategy is pursued in the context of a comprehensive regional planning and governance scheme, however, the temporary gains from it will probably be lost. With the continued relaxation of internal migration controls, people who moved to small towns will probably not stop there but instead follow the stepwise migration toward small, intermediate-sized, and very large cities that has been the pattern in other countries. Some of the small towns, therefore, need to be encouraged to grow into large enough countermagnets to hold on to increasing numbers of people. Close attention needs to be paid to linking residences to job sites, public services, leisure, and recreation centers. Efficient transport linkages that are nonpolluting and affordable are needed. A whole network of urban places, made up of settlements of varying sizes, has to be created in such a way that they are linked together to respond to the changing needs of people. Eventually, therefore, the main contribution of the small town development strategy could be realized in the context of the mega-urban region.

New Towns and Satellite Cities

Taking their cues from British town and country planning, urban authorities in India and Pakistan have set up new towns on the outskirts of cities to manage growth in city regions. New towns were established around Delhi, Kolkata, Mumbai (formerly Bombay), and other Indian cities. Conceptually, these new towns attempted a balance between a pleasant natural environment and productive urban development. They were designed to provide employment, housing, mobility, energy, and basic urban services to residents in a parklike setting reminiscent of the garden city ideal proposed by Ebenezer Howard and other urban visionaries.

In reality, however, many of the new towns in India were prompted by a need to accommodate poor residents resettled from the central cities. For example, the Kolkata Urban Development Program provided for the establishment of the Baishnabghata-Patuli township to house about 40,000 people, two-thirds of whom were classified as poor families. After the enactment of the Town and Country Planning Act of 1979, the Kolkata Metropolitan Development Authority (KMDA) set up the East Kolkata Township, located about 9 kilometers from the central business district, to absorb more poor families. The KMDA also launched the East Kolkata Extension

Project for 20,000 inhabitants and the West Howrah Development project, which included 8,580 dwellings, mainly in low-cost housing projects (Jain 1996b, 55). As interesting as these programs were, they were very small and inadequate efforts compared with the needs in these mega-urban regions.

The 1962 Delhi master plan envisioned the development of a ring of new towns, which included Bahadurgarh, Ballabhgarh, Faridabad, Gargaon, Ghaziabad, Loni, and Narela. These new towns were designed as industrial sites and housing estates to absorb more people, particularly those who were going to be resettled from the city core. They were supposed to be served by infrastructure and basic urban services that would be separate from the already stressed institutions in Old and New Delhi. However, it soon became apparent that the new towns were located too close to the city. An evaluation of the new towns came to the conclusion that "rather than relieving or deflecting population from Delhi, on the contrary, [the new towns] created more pressures on its services and amenities" (Jain 1996b, 82).

In Metro Manila, there were early efforts to design and build new towns that would serve as "transitional reception sites" for rural–urban migrants. The main justification for these new towns was the need to ease the transition of rural migrants to city life. The idea was to "catch" the migrants before they got to central city areas. In the new towns, they would be provided with housing, basic services, and amenities. For a period of two to five years, the migrants were to be trained in the practical skills that would prepare them for jobs in an urban setting. Though the new towns seemed attractive and innovative at the time, they did not really flourish. For one, there was a shortage of resources to provide the housing, services, and trainers needed by the scheme. Also, because of dissatisfaction with the program, many of the migrants left the town prematurely and moved to the city as squatters and slum dwellers. The people who stayed at the site got attached to their plots and refused to move after the experimental period (Laquian 1966; Van Horen 2004).

In anticipation of the rapid growth of the Jakarta region, the Indonesian government encouraged private developers to set up new towns in surrounding regencies. In the *kabupaten* (regency) of Bekasi, for example, 241 private developers proposed the establishment of a settlement that would contain 490,000 housing units within 8,100 hectares of prime land. Bekasi Integrated New Town was to cover 1,300 hectares; Cikarang Baru New Town, 5,400 hectares; Bekasi New Town, 2,000 hectares; Lippo City, 2,000 hectares; Legend City, 2,000 hectares; and Bekasi New City, 3,000 hectares. Similar developments were also proposed for the regency of Tangerang, made up of Bumi Serpong Damai New Town (6,000 hectares), Tigaraksa New Town (3,000 hectares), and Lippo Village (500 hectares). New projects were also proposed for Citraland New Town and the Serpong Gading New Town.

The 1997 Asian economic crisis and the unraveling of the Suharto regime aborted the ambitious new town schemes for Jakarta. In hindsight, some Indonesian planners felt that this was a blessing, because it had become apparent that many of the schemes were merely land speculation schemes. If the new towns had been built, the amount of agricultural land around the capital city would have been drastically reduced. The environmental impact of the new towns would have also been serious, because the sites proposed for development were in the watershed and natural recharge areas of Jakarta's water supply system (Argo 1999).

The negative impact of the new town schemes became apparent even with the limited realization of some of the projects. For example, in the initial construction of Bekasi New Town, about 16,500 farmers had to be evicted from the site. Another 12,000 agricultural laborers were also forced to move out. For the families who moved into the newly built housing projects, the time, money, and effort involved in commuting daily from their jobs in Jakarta became a heavy burden. By the late 1980s, about 300,000 persons were commuting daily from Bogor, Tangerang, and Bekasi. Although the government had allowed private developers to build limited access highways for the commuters, the expensive tolls that these concessionaires charged became an extra burden.

In China, early planning approaches were heavily influenced by socialist ideas that borrowed heavily from Soviet industrial strategies. During the First Five-Year Plan (1953–57), it was decided that Shanghai would be developed as an industrial base. Heavy industries were located in twelve satellite cities that were developed as bases for petrochemical production, electrical engineering, and iron and steel complexes. Later, these satellite cities in Caohejing, Hongqiao, and Minhang were vastly overshadowed by the development of the Pudong New Area, a 552-square-kilometer site located east of the Huangpu River that was divided into four subzones devoted to high-technology industry, port facilities, free trade, and financial services.

A similar plan to establish satellite cities was prepared by Chinese authorities for Beijing. On the city's periphery, four satellite cities were built, each one zoned for a specific industrial function. For example, the satellite city of Dagang was designed for petroleum processing, Dananhe for textiles, and Mixian for tourism development. The satellite city of Langfang located between Beijing and Tianjin was also developed as a food production center and a transportation hub linking the capital to its all-important port city.

The experience in Asian cities has shown that new towns and satellite cities could be used effectively as instruments for developing urban peripheral areas. However, the effectiveness of the new town and satellite cities approach depended on three main factors. First, new towns and satellite cities needed to be planned and managed as more or less self-contained settlements where residents would be employed, housed, and provided with commercial, leisure, and entertainment services in situ. Their transformation into bedroom communities for workers in the central city has serious implications for the degradation of the environment. This means that new towns and satellite cities have to be on a large enough scale to make a certain amount of autonomy possible. This also indicates that single-purpose zoning and subdivision regulations that restrict new towns and satellite cities to specific functions (e.g., industrial development, housing for poor people) are not appropriate.

Second, the location of new towns and satellite cities in relation to the central city is important. If these settlements are located too close to the city, they are likely to be absorbed by urban sprawl. Though the new towns and satellite cities need to be linked to the central city by appropriate transport modes, they must be far enough from the city to function autonomously.

Third, new towns and satellite cities need to be effectively linked to their immediate hinterlands. Because of their specific functions, many new towns and satellite cities in the past had been isolated from their environs. By conscious planning and design, new towns and satellite cities must serve as administrative, political, and cultural centers. They should be energizing nodes to spark rural development. As such, they should be seen as key elements of a coherent and comprehensive regional plan arranged hierarchically from the dominant central city to the smallest villages.

Innovation Centers and High-Technology Parks

The global information revolution has influenced mega-urban development in Asia in a most significant way, evidenced largely by the rapid emergence of innovation centers and high-technology parks on urban peripheries. Historically, the establishment of innovation centers and high-technology parks has originated in so-called high-tech regions, "technology-oriented complexes," or "technopoli" that blossomed in the United States, England, Japan, and other technologically advanced countries during the 1960s. Models of such centers were Silicon Valley in Santa Clara County, California, the Route 128 phenomenon in Greater Boston, the M-4 development corridor outside London, and Tsukuba Science City outside Tokyo.

The high-tech zones in industrial countries were seen as "incubators" or "seedbeds" for innovations that could be commercialized and brought into the development mainstream in the quickest possible way. Their growth was attributed to agglomeration economies that attracted complementary firms to the zone and concentrated technical, entrepreneurial, financial, and management expertise in the area and took advantage of the synergistic relationships emanating from physical propinquity. As observed by Saxenian, who based her conclusions on an in-depth study of Cambridge, the high-tech zones were rooted in a belief in the "neo-classical economic model of free markets in which perfectly competitive firms and unimpeded, frictionless flows of capital, labor, technology and information automatically maximize economic efficiency and wealth creation" (Saxenian 1989, 449). Many Asian governments sought to realize this model in their countries.

At least five factors made high-tech zones very attractive to Asian policymakers. First, these zones depended on "clean" technological processes that were in sharp contrast to the heavily polluting manufacturing and industrial enterprises that were popular in the past. Second, the zones complemented the intellectual expertise that was available in local universities and research centers. Setting up the zones encouraged academics and technically trained people to stay in the country instead of joining the brain drain. The zones also provided bright career prospects for young graduates and technically trained school leavers. Third, zones encouraged important linkages with foreign institutions and enterprises, with resulting increases in foreign direct investment, technical licensing arrangements, access to advanced information, and mutual learning opportunities. Fourth, the zones encouraged public–private partnerships, with the government providing the planned physical and institutional setting and private businesses making the capital, human resource, institutional, and managerial inputs. Fifth, the zones required relatively modest inputs of infrastructure, energy, public works construction, and basic urban services, which were often within the limited financial capabilities of local governments.

In general, five important factors have been identified as key elements in the development of high-tech zones: (1) the availability of scientific and technological expertise; (2) access to venture capital; (3) forward and backward linkages with other sectors of the economy; (4) opportunities for economic spin-offs; (5) adequate communication and transportation infrastructure; and (6) a quality of life that is attractive to highly technical people, engineers, and scientists (Glasmeier 1988, 288; Saxenian 1989).

Since 1988 when China embarked on the establishment of high-tech zones, more than 120 high-tech parks have been set up all over the country. About 60 percent of these parks are located in super large mega-urban regions, 17 percent in big cities, 16 percent in medium-sized cities, and 7 percent in small cities and towns. The high-tech parks are classified into three types:

- *Comprehensive high-tech parks,* usually linked with key universities and research institutes, industrial parks, export-processing enclaves, and special economic zones.
- *Torch parks,* located in small and medium-sized cities, which are designed to help accelerate the development of regions around these urban settlements.
- *Spark parks,* located in remote, backward, and lagging areas, have been established to develop these areas through the introduction of high-tech approaches.

One of the most prominent high-tech parks in China is located in the Haidian District of Bejing, which is strategically located close to important sources of technical and scientific expertise, such as Tsinghua University, Peking University, People's University, the China Academy of Sciences, and other research and teaching institutions. About 2,800 high-tech firms are clustered within this area of 1.8 square kilometers. These firms are engaged in such fields as electronics, biotechnology, computer science, information control systems, and related fields. Most of the high-tech firms grew out of the application of the results of basic research projects and experimentation by experts. In 1992, it was estimated that within the zone occupied by the Haidian High-Tech Park, no less than 1,300 scientific and technological "research achievements" had been registered with the government by experts. Many of the technicians and scientists responsible for these achievements wasted no time in transforming these research results into productive and profitable ventures (Wu and Mao 1993).

Another high-tech enclave in Beijing is the Beijing Economic and Technological Development Zone, located close to the Beijing–Tianjin superhighway. Within this 30-square-kilometer zone, a number of companies have been established to produce computer screens and motherboards, machine tools, medical instruments, and chemical products. At the other end of the superhighway, not too far from Tianjin, the authorities have set up the Tanggu High-Tech Park, which almost immediately upon its opening in 1993 attracted 202 corporations, 52 of which were supported by foreign investors.

An important reason for the success of the Beijing high-tech park has been the infusion of venture capital that helped to rapidly bring innovations to the market by financing research and development ventures and the quick production of prototypes and mainstream products. In some instances, as in the establishment of the high-tech park outside the campus of the University of the Philippines in Metro Manila, the financing came from foreign sources; in this case, it came from wealthy expatriate Filipinos who had achieved success in Silicon Valley ventures. In others, such as the High-Tech Park at the former U.S. Navy base in Subic Bay, the conventional capital came from Hong Kong, Japan, South Korea, and Taiwan. Computer companies in these countries invested in the Philippine high-tech parks to ensure themselves a reliable and steady supply of computer chips and motherboards. Aside from these backward linkages, they also linked forward to Philippine manufacturers of radios, television sets, and other appliances that used advanced electronics circuitry.

Opportunities for economic spin-offs have been a very important element of the establishment of high-tech parks. Many of the high-tech ventures in the Pearl River Delta started out as subcontractors of foreign enterprises in Hong Kong, Japan, and South Korea. However, as technology was transferred to these local firms, the Chinese companies started turning out other products for the domestic and international markets. Many firms in the Pearl River Delta, such as those in the Tianhe High-Tech Park and the Zhongshan District High-Tech Park, were closely linked to companies in the special economic zones of Shenzhen and Zhuhai. Eventually, the productivity of many of these enterprises reached such a volume that they became independent of the foreign companies that had helped them get started.

Because of their close ties to global technological developments, enterprises in high-tech parks need good information and communication linkages. Architects and engineers designing buildings in these parks, therefore, have routinely installed fiber optics instead of copper or aluminum wires in new structures. Zoning codes and building standards in Guangzhou, Hong Kong, Shanghai, and Shenzhen now require fiber optics in all new construction to transform these settlements into "smart" cities.

A most important ingredient in successful high-tech parks in Asia has been the maintenance of a good quality of life for the highly educated and trained individuals that supply the creative energies to these enclaves. Designers of high-tech parks have learned to provide comfortable homes, good schools, modern health facilities, and creative leisure and recreational facilities to keep experts and their families happy. Often, high-tech parks offer ample parkland and green space, golf courses, jogging trails and tennis courts, high-class restaurants and pubs, access to good shopping and other facilities, and other amenities required for a safe and comfortable life. Because people attracted to work in high-tech parks are drawn from the ablest and the best from all over the world, the firms that employ them try their best to provide them with a high quality of life. They know that in a borderless world linked by instant communication, the productivity of their high-tech experts depends on ensuring such a setting.

Although innovation centers and high-tech parks have been effectively used to help develop urban peripheral areas, their very specialized nature has limited their ability to maximize the "spread effects" of their developmental thrusts. As a whole, high-tech parks have become isolated enclaves in suburban and exurban areas. They have provided only limited employment and service opportunities to rural people, who have often been resettled elsewhere to make room for the high-end structures required by the parks. In some areas, as in the Haidian district in Beijing, high-tech firms have become integrated quite well with educational institutions and their thousands of students and faculty members. In other places, however, high-tech parks have become "gated communities" for intellectual elites who pursue a global lifestyle far removed from their immediate neighbors.

Yet it should not be denied that the shift from industry and manufacturing to less space sensitive "knowledge-based industries" in the pursuit of regional development has significantly influenced patterns of peri-urban development in many Asian cities. Because of the concentration of information and communication facilities in high-technology zones and the growing importance of circulation and producer services, these new settlements are changing the nature of the urban landscape. Regional development in the future might become less concentrated in dominant central cities and might shift to smaller but more intensely developed urban places. As pointed out by Moulaert and Swyngedouw (1989, 334):

The transition from Fordism to post-Fordism has brought rapid and revolutionary technological and organizational change . . . the traditional urban hierarchy based on manufacturing industry and social and personal services is increasingly being replaced by a hierarchy strongly determined by the location of circulation and producer services. . . . The growth of high-tech industrial complexes tends to turn the traditional urban hierarchy upside down. Smaller and more remote cities, which until recently were only low ranking manufacturing centers, manage to attract a substantial piece of the pie.

Industrial Cities and Growth Poles

One of the most successful efforts to rationally plan a city-region by concentrating development in new industrial cities and growth poles in the urban periphery is found in Seoul. During the 1960s and 1970s, the South Korean authorities became concerned about the extremely high population growth rates and uncontrolled development of the Seoul national capital region. They pursued two strategies to deal with this problem: setting up new industrial cities and growth poles within the metropolitan area, and establishing growth poles far enough from Seoul (in Pusan and Taegu) to act as "countermagnets" to the capital city's development.

Korean planners established new industrial cities in Banweo, located within the Seoul metropolitan area, and in Anjung, Balan, and Joam, farther south. They also set up growth poles in Pyeongteg and in Yicheon, also in the southern part of the metropolis. Strictly speaking, the term "growth pole" did not really apply to these development enclaves, which were located within the city-region. Nevertheless, the objective in setting up these growth poles was to redirect development away from the inner core area of Seoul and from the existing cities of Incheon, Sungnam, and Suweon within the metropolitan area.

The planned development of the Seoul city-region was made possible by the central government's control over land; the technical capabilities of professional planners; the central government's command over investments in infrastructure, such as roads, energy, water and sewerage and waste disposal; and the use of central government funds. It was also greatly enhanced by the close working relationship between the large industrial enterprises producing automobiles, electronic products, and telecommunication equipment and the South Korean government. These enterprises were on such a scale that their physical plants and labor forces could be located in an area to spark industrial development. They could, therefore, encourage development in urban clusters that could be more or less self-sufficient. By linking these clusters to each other and to the central city with efficient transport, the Seoul metropolitan authorities have been able to achieve planned and controlled growth.

Special Economic Zones

The key ideas for the establishment of special economic zones (SEZs) evolved from early ventures, such as the Shannon Export Free Zone in Ireland, which was first established in 1959. Basically, an SEZ was designed as a production enclave where foreign and domestic investors were allowed to set up their enterprises under favorable terms, provided they sold the bulk of their products in international markets. Within the zones, the government provided incentives—such as duty exemptions on the importation of production machinery and material inputs, assured supplies of reliable energy, good housing, reliable infrastructure, efficient information and communication linkages, access to professionally trained and highly disciplined workforces and top-level managers, the free repatriation of profits, and full security for personnel and staff. Most investors in the SEZs brought in capital and technical know-how, new product designs and prototypes, raw materials, and new technology and processes. The SEZ provided energy, labor, services, and management, and logistical services.

In China, an SEZ was defined as "a small area demarcated within a country's territory and suitably insulated for adopting special and flexible policies to attract and encourage foreign investment in industrial and other economic activities" (Yee 1992). The main purpose of an SEZ was "to expand exports, to utilize foreign capital, to introduce foreign technology and to develop the economy" (Mayor Liang Shang of Shenzhen, quoted by Yee 1992).

The most widely known SEZs in China are Shantou, Shenzhen, and Zhuhai in Guangdong province and Xiamen in Fujian province. Of these, Shenzhen has been the most successful. Before 1970, Shenzhen was the seat of Baoan County and had a population of less than 20,000 occupying an urban area of less than 3 square kilometers. When Shenzhen was declared an SEZ in 1979, it absorbed Baoan County and Shenzhen municipality, increasing its population to 70,000 and expanding its territory to 1,800 square kilometers, 350 of which were defined as urban and the rest as rural.

By 1988, the population of Shenzhen had reached 800,000, and its gross domestic product (GDP) had increased from 60 million yuan in 1979 to more than 8.8 billion yuan (Wang 1990, 394; Yee 1992, 237). In December 2003, Shenzhen's territory covered 2,020 square kilometers, and the city had a population estimated at 7 million, 95 percent of whom were migrants. On February 18, 2004, Shenzhen was said to have become the first city in China without rural areas, as 270,000 residents with agricultural *hukou* status were given nonagricultural *hukou*s and the municipal government agreed to provide them with retirement benefits, pensions, medical insurance, and funeral benefits that were the same as those extended to employees of city enterprises (see http://www.china.org.cn).

In comparison with Shenzhen, Zhuhai had an area of only 15.2 square kilometers. Its proximity to Macao served as a good justification for setting it up as an SEZ. Xiamen SEZ was about 131 square kilometers. It had a deep natural harbor and the advantage of being close to Taiwan. Shantou SEZ, located near the mouth of the Rong River in Guangdong province, was 52.6 square kilometers. It was designed to encourage development in the areas between Shenzhen and Xiamen in the southeastern coastal region of China (Wang 1990, 394).

The original plans for the Shenzhen SEZ required the construction of 360,500 housing units and provision of 17,000 hotel rooms between 1985 and 2000. Electricity supply would be increased from 125,000 kilowatts in 1985 to 400,000 by 2000. A grand total of 2,239 factory buildings would be constructed. The total capital construction investment was estimated to climb from 3 billion yuan in 1985 to 21 billion yuan by 2000 (Yee 1992, 116–17). In reality, these initial targets turned out to be exceedingly modest. Shenzhen's population, targeted to reach 800,000 by 2000, actually reached more than 2 million in 1989 (1.1 million for the SEZ). By 1999, the city's population had jumped to 4.05 million, a growth rate of 13.6 percent a year.

Between 1989 and 1999, the built-up area of the zone increased from 3 to 320.3 square kilometers. Shenzhen's GDP rocketed from RMB 196 million to RMB 143.6 billion, ranked sixth among the large and medium-sized cities in the whole of China. Per capita GDP increased from RMB 606 to 35,908, 5.5 times higher than the per capita GDP for the whole country. Fixed asset investment in Shenzhen amounted to RMB 56.8 billion in 1999, and the value of exported goods amounted to $28.2 billion, having grown at an average rate of 42 percent a year (Shiu and Yang 2002, 247–48). In 2000, per capita GDP in Shenzhen had reached RMB 39,700, and this was projected to increase to RMB 63,100 ($7,602) by 2005. At an expected growth rate of 12 percent a year, Shenzhen's GDP is expected to reach RMB 300 billion ($36.1 billion) by 2005. The city will also expand its territory by building seven new towns outside the SEZ within the next five years. This will add another 500,000 people to the city's population (*News Guangdong*, February 8, 2004).

Shenzhen's fantastic progress, however, has come at a very high price. During the first ten years of its development, Shenzhen received ten times the amount of per capita investment in infrastructure compared with other localities in Guangdong province. In 1989, Shenzhen spent RMB 5.0 billion on infrastructure projects, accounting for 34 percent of the total capital construction expenditures in the province. Interestingly, in contrast to SEZs in other countries that relied heavily on foreign investments, the funds for Shenzhen's development came mainly from local sources. In their desire to rapidly transform the SEZ into a world-class city, Chinese authorities relied heavily on money that could be raised from land, drew on tax revenues, borrowed heavily from local banks, and took out loans fully guaranteed by the government. Even some of the highly publicized "foreign" investments supposedly coming from Hong Kong actually came from mainland firms located within that city. Among these Chinese firms stationed in Hong Kong investing in Shenzhen were the Chinese Merchants Steam Navigation Company, Limited, which funded the first projects in the port of Shekou that initially triggered Shenzhen's development; Everbright; China Resources; and China Travel Services (Yee 1992, 94).

Instead of following the Shenzhen model and developing SEZs from scratch at very high cost, the Philippines has chosen to build upon existing urban facilities. The turnover to the Philippines of the United States of the military facilities in the Naval Base in Subic Bay and the Air Force Base in Clark provided the opportunity to set up two important SEZs in already-serviced enclaves. In 1992, the Subic Bay Freeport and Special Economic Zone was established in accordance with the provisions of the Bases Conversion and Development Act. The law provided for the creation of the Subic Bay Metropolitan Authority to operate and manage the SEZ. By 1995, the SEZ had attracted 169 domestic and international companies that invested $1.2 billion in projects.

Two years later, more than 42,000 Filipinos were employed in the SEZ in enterprises that included computer chip manufacturing, textiles, shoes, heavy machinery, duty free shops, hotels, and casinos. The SEZ also revived the economy of the adjoining city of Olongapo and provided employment in surrounding towns. Despite some initial problems, the Philippine authorities have expressed bright hopes for the SEZ. It has been projected that by 2020, the combined population of Olongapo and the Subic SEZ would reach about 769,000 and that the rapidly growing urban settlement would become a key node in the development of the Manila region (Wardrop Engineering 1995).

The experience with SEZs as instruments for developing urban peripheries in China, the Philippines, Indonesia, Thailand and elsewhere has been a positive one. These development enclaves have enabled Asian countries to directly link to the global economy through SEZs that have brought in foreign direct investment, advanced technology, managerial talents, and innovative ideas while allowing these countries to gain access to global markets. By concentrating investments in infrastructure and services in SEZs, governments have been able to rapidly modernize physical plants and use energy more efficiently. The same concentration of expertise, talents, and skills in SEZs also has given Asian countries the cutting edge necessary to participate in the global economy (it had been estimated that in 1995, 10 percent of the Ph.D.s in China worked in Shenzhen and that in 2003, there were 8,060 college-educated individuals for every 100,000 residents in Shenzhen municipality).

One criticism of SEZs as regional development mechanisms, however, arises from their autonomous nature in relation to their rural and urban hinterlands. Typically, SEZs are completely separate enclaves. Items produced in the SEZs are meant primarily for export, which justifies the tax-free importation of machinery and raw material inputs. Public authorities have taken strict measures to prevent the "leakage" of items produced in the SEZs into local markets. They have also controlled the recruitment and hiring of SEZ personnel to prevent the inundation of the zones with untrained and unskilled migrants. The isolation of the SEZs from their hinterland, however, has greatly limited their developmental influence. The main local benefit they have created is employment. However, many SEZs do not provide enough housing and basic urban services to the people employed within the enclaves, thereby "offloading" responsibility for these responsibilities to surrounding local governments.

In the Subic Bay and Clark SEZs in the Philippines, for example, thousands of local workers commute daily from their homes in nearby cities and towns. Their presence has created a massive housing shortage, huge traffic jams, a lack of water, an inadequate electricity supply, overcrowded schools, and poor health service facilities—all of which local government units are hard pressed to alleviate. Outside the high walls of the Shenzhen SEZ, congested uncontrolled communities have grown, and some illegal shanties have even been constructed along dangerous railroad tracks. Attracted by the SEZs, temporary and illegal migrants flock to these uncontrolled settlements. Many local governments have their hands full dealing with the problems caused by these settlements, such as crime, drugs, prostitution, epidemics, and other urban ills.

If SEZs are to be effective elements in mega-urban development, therefore, their links to their hinterland have to be strengthened so that they can become the subnuclei of development in a multinodal regional system. This approach is particularly relevant to the Subic and Clark SEZs in the Philippines, which are isolated from their surrounding areas. A far more effective approach to the establishment of SEZs is the Shenzhen model, whereby development has been designed to spread outside the limited confines of the original SEZ and expanded to include the districts of Baoan and Longgang. At present, 2,000 villages in Shenzhen municipality are sharing in the SEZ's progress because their residents are granted nonagricultural *hukou* status. The planned inclusion of 7 new satellite towns adjacent to the SEZ in three to five years will further spread the effects of Shenzhen, turning the original SEZ into a true developmental node in the Hong Kong–Pearl River Delta region.

Coastal Open Cities and Open Economic Regions

When China decided to open its economy and society to the outside world after 1979, it decided to concentrate development efforts in priority development areas, which included SEZs and fourteen open coastal cities (figure 8.1). Most of the open cities were on the coast, ranging from Dalian in Liaoning province to Zhanjiang in Guangdong. Aside from SEZs and open cities, China also set up "open economic regions" in the Pearl River Delta in Guangdong, the Yangtze River Delta around Shanghai, and the Minnan Delta Economic Region in Fujian province. The only inland priority development area was the North China Industrial Energy Zone, which included the ancient city of Xian. Aside from establishing the Shanghai Economic Region in 1983, the State Council also made Shanghai an "open coastal city" in 1984. Under this designation, Shanghai was allowed to attract foreign and domestic investors by setting up economic and high-technology zones, offering tax incentives, and extending special land use rights. Finally, in 1986, the State Council designated the whole Yangtze River Delta an open economic region (Yeh 1995, 155).

China's northeast region (the Liaodong Peninsula), made up of the provinces of Liaoning, Jilin, and Heilongjiang, was an old industrial area

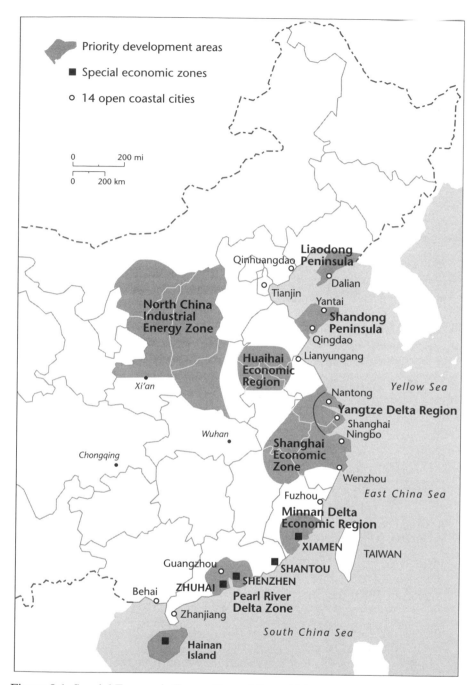

Figure 8.1. Special Economic Zones, Coastal Open Cities, and Open Economic Regions in China

that was developed by the Japanese before World War II, when it was known as Manchuria. The two cities of Shenyang and Dalian form the cores of its development. The region is rich in energy (the Daqing oil fields account for 40 percent of China's crude oil production, and coal mines in the region produce 15 percent of national output). The Songliao plain has also produced about 60 percent of the region's agricultural output.

Unfortunately, the industrial base of the northeast is mainly made up of old, outmoded, and badly managed state-owned enterprises that could barely compete with firms in other regions in China. After being designated a special priority area, the northeast zone started developing rapidly. By 1993, massive investments in infrastructure and the establishment of new industrial plants had energized the region. Trade ties were established with Japan and South Korea. In 1994, the Chinese government expanded its support for "pillar industries" in the region, such as automobile manufacturing. The First Auto Works in Jilin, a joint venture with Volkswagen AG, received a $450 million loan for technological renovation that enabled it to produce 25,000 Audi models, 18,000 Jetta models, and 120,000 trucks. Anshan Steel in Liaoning province, the second largest steel producer in China, also produced 8.12 million tons of steel, about one-twelfth of the country's total steel output (Asian Technology Information Program, November 11, 1995).

In the southern parts of China, development was focused on the Pearl River Delta region. In 1985, part of Guangdong province was designated as an "open economic region." Included within this region were four cities (Dongguan, Foshan, Jiangmen, and Zhongshan) and twelve counties (Baoan, Doumen, Enping, Gaoming, Heshan, Kaiping, Nanhai, Panyu, Shunde, Taishan, Xinhui, and Zhengcheng). With the addition of Sanshui to the region in 1986, the open economic region (referred to as the "Inner Delta," covered 22,700 square kilometers. In December 1987, the Pearl River Delta open economic region was expanded to include an additional seven cities and twenty-one counties covering 45,005 square kilometers. This newly enlarged open economic zone ("the Greater Delta") had a population of more than 20 million (Lin 1997, 80; Ng 2000, 73).

In 1992, China's president and general secretary of the Communist Party, Jiang Zemin, a former mayor of Shanghai, designated the city as the "dragon head" that would encourage the development of the Yangtze River Delta open economic region. With its population of 17 million, Shanghai was chosen to lead the economic development of a region estimated to have a population of almost 200 million (living in the provinces of Zhejiang, Anhui, and Jiangsu). As noted by Olds (1995), this region's economy was 11 percent larger than that of Thailand, 132 percent larger than that of Malaysia, and only 4 percent smaller than that of Indonesia (Olds 1995, 237).

In some ways, the creation of open economic regions has addressed the problem of isolation that is caused by SEZs and other developmental enclaves. By creating areawide planning that is coterminous with a natural setting (e.g., a river basin), an open economic region makes it possible to properly consider ecological, topographical, and other factors. The regional perspective also allows the authorities to determine the specific function of each urban settlement within a hierarchy of settlements. By linking the settlements into a network of transport and communication modes, it becomes possible to optimize the economic productivity of the whole region.

A regional perspective also enhances the designation of green space for both agricultural and environmental purposes. Strict land use controls can limit the overutilization of forested and agricultural land. They can facilitate the wise use of surface water bodies for production as well as prevent pollution from agricultural runoff and industrial uses. Setting up an open economic region makes it possible to establish economic linkages among various types and sizes of urban settlements. This is shown, for example, in the close economic relationships that have been established among the settlements in the Pearl River Delta and Hong Kong.

Among the cities in the Pearl River Delta, the best linkages have been created between Dongguan and Hong Kong. A study of such linkages revealed that Dongguan residents had at least 650,000 relatives in Hong Kong and Macao. Even during the Maoist period, when China worried about "capitalist contamination" from Hong Kong, these kinship ties made it possible for Hong Kong residents to help refugees sneak into the British colony and send remittances to relatives on the mainland. After 1979, the economic ties between Dongguan and Hong Kong grew stronger. A special office in Dongguan was opened to look after the needs of Hong Kong investors. Economic relationships took the form of export-processing enterprises, joint ventures, "letting-out" arrangements, subcontracting, and cooperative ventures. By 1991, a study showed that 10,586 contracts had been signed between enterprises in Dongguan and manufacturers in Hong Kong. Most of these contracts involved the processing of materials imported from Hong Kong, assembling parts supplied by Hong Kong manufacturers, or executing models and prototypes. More than 70 percent of the industrial labor force in Dongguan was engaged in export-processing enterprises by the end of the 1990s (Lin 1997, 175).

As the cost of land and labor rose in Hong Kong, many enterprises decided to relocate their factories to Dongguan, Baoan, and other parts of the

Pearl River Delta. Many of these ventures were small scale and did not require heavy machinery. They required processes that were simple and repetitive and skills that could be learned with minimal training. A 1991 survey in Dongguan showed that among 2,931 enterprises, the average size of a factory was 147 workers for joint ventures and 105 for trading companies. Because of the modest size of these enterprises, they tended to be widely distributed in the delta rather than concentrated in key urban places. Perceiving this danger, the delta's planners and administrators decided to concentrate infrastructure and urban service investments in the highly urbanized cores of Dongguan, Baoan, and other cities. In this way, economies of scale, location, and agglomeration could be achieved in the concentrated settlements (Lin 1997, 176).

Open economic regions have greatly helped in developing peripheral urban areas, but they have also caused a number of problems. The problem of the administrative and political fragmentation of governmental units within these regions remains a serious one. For instance, in the Pearl River Delta, the hierarchy of local units runs from the county (*xian*), township (*zhen*), administrative district (*guanli qu*), village (*cun*), to the village community (*cunmin weiyuanhui*). Officials at the county level have the highest authority for managing local affairs, with powers to impose and collect taxes, appoint personnel, approve budgets, and allocate funds. Townships have been created to replace the rural communes that existed in China from 1958 to 1984. Typically, a township would have an urbanized "county seat," accorded a "designated town" status, and a largely rural area. The administrative districts were created in 1984 to replace the rural brigades. They were composed of a number of villages, with each village corresponding to the old production team. The village communities have very little economic significance because they are mainly used for census and household registration purposes.

The dispersed economic growth in open economic regions, even those that are centered on large cities, can result in uncontrolled urban sprawl. In planning very large mega-urban regions, therefore, a prime consideration should be to create a comprehensive strategy that considers the hierarchy of mega-cities, intermediate-sized, and small cities. An open economic region, such as the Pearl River Delta or the Yangtze River Delta, may become too large for coordinated development, especially in the light of decentralization tendencies. It may be more manageable to concentrate development in mega-urban regions made up of nucleated peri-urban settlements that are effectively linked together by transport and informational networks.

9

Housing and Basic Urban Services

The term "marginal settlements" is hardly used in the planning literature anymore, but the slum and squatter communities it refers to continue to grow in many mega-urban regions, especially in South and Southeast Asia. On average, a fourth to more than half of families in South and Southeast Asian cities live in inadequate or poorly serviced homes. More than 40 percent of Metro Manila's 12.6 million people live in slum or squatter areas. In Jakarta, vendors use ambulatory stores as both homes and workplaces. In Mumbai (formerly Bombay), about 800,000 pavement dwellers have no homes at all. Even in Beijing, where the government proudly claims that there are no slums, 13.6 million square meters of structures in the inner city are classified as "dangerous and dilapidated housing." There are homeless people around Shinjuku Station in the rich metropolis of Tokyo. In many South and Southeast Asian cities, the bulk of the additions to the housing stock each year are produced by squatters, slum dwellers, and "illegal developers" who build housing without paying attention to building codes and regulations.

The acute housing problem of urban poor people does not involve shelter alone. It includes access to clean water, sanitation, electricity, cooking fuel, garbage collection and disposal, and other services needed for a comfortable and healthy urban life. It means freedom from fear—from criminals, local gangs, drug lords, corrupt police officials, and from calamities like fire, typhoons, epidemics, and floods. It involves a sense of personal worth, of being included in public decision making, of having the opportunity to actively participate in community affairs. Most important of all, it means a sense of security, that a person's home cannot be demolished or one's family cannot be arbitrarily evicted and resettled elsewhere without a legitimate reason.

348

The term *slum* has a pejorative meaning; but as used in this book, it simply refers to a wide range of low-income settlements that are physically dilapidated and lack basic services and whose inhabitants do not have secure tenure. Slums take the form of congested inner-city districts, where people occupy old houses at very high densities. Slums are found in peri-urban areas where people have very little or no access to water, sanitation, and other basic services. Slums are shanties on the banks of rivers and streams, which are in constant danger of being washed away during floods and typhoons. They are houses on stilts in tidal basins or shallow waters. Slum dwellers are people living along the railroad trucks or communities of refuse gatherers and recyclers, living at the base of mountainous garbage dumps. Some slum dwellers are squatters, people who occupy lands and buildings without the explicit consent of the owners. However, not all squatters are slum dwellers because some squatter houses are built of strong materials and have access to public services.

At times, the slum problem may take more pathological forms. In cities like Bangkok and Metro Manila, gambling, prostitution, drugs, and human trafficking have dominated the lives of people in slums. In these communities, drug lords and gambling bosses have taken over functions such as employment creation, personal protection, maintaining peace and order, security, social welfare, and conflict resolution. Government programs have failed to penetrate these communities, so illegal structures have simply taken over by default.

A major part of urban activities devoted to housing and basic urban services in Asian cities occurs in the *informal sector,* that part of the economy and society outside the realm of governance. As noted by Van Horen, "One of the primary defining characteristics of informal settlements is that the land occupation process, the shelter construction process, and continued existence of such settlements takes place outside of the boundaries of any statutory planning or administrative frameworks" (Van Horen 1996, 7).

A key policy issue in Asian cities, therefore, is how to "formalize the informal," or how to bring about a transition from de facto housing and livelihood arrangements to de jure status. The challenge is to incorporate social norms and structures that have evolved largely outside the formal planning and governance processes into political and administrative structures, thereby regularizing them. As such, this "regularization may include a gradation of strategies that legitimize and integrate aspects of de facto institutions into the planning process, thereby also contributing to a legal regulatory framework" (Van Horen 1996, 22). Regularization might mean the elimination of norms and structures previously prevalent in the informal sector, their amendment into more legally acceptable forms, and their integration into planning and governance mechanisms in the formal sector. It also involves the process of "scaling up" individual and community efforts to link them with institutional approaches led by the government, the private sector, or organized civil society groups (Van Horen 2004).

The important role of housing in mega-urban planning and governance rests on the *location* of homes and service structures in the mega-urban region. The proximity of residences to workplaces, schools, playgrounds, places of worship, hospitals and clinics, and other institutions determines the value of housing to homeowners and renters. Commuting long distances entails additional costs to individuals, social costs to the community, and external costs to the environment in the form of time lost and the adverse health effects of pollution. The time wasted in traffic jams and the amount of air and water pollution caused by vehicular exhaust can be avoided by well-located housing. Providing appropriate housing in regularized communities can also reduce crime and juvenile delinquency.

Ideally, investments in housing can be used to positively influence the shape of the mega-urban region. A dense and vibrant downtown can be achieved by redeveloping inner-city housing and upgrading aging services and amenities. Opening up densely populated and compact housing estates on the urban periphery can result in well-planned decentralized development if these are located close to employment sites, are provided with adequate commercial and leisure facilities, are designed at the proper scale, and are linked together by efficient transport systems. Locating housing projects in self-contained clusters around stations in a mass transit system eases mobility. Resettling poor urban families to suburban places may work if—aside from housing and basic urban services—the resettlement sites will also provide employment, shopping, schools, health, entertainment, and leisure facilities. The planned location of housing on the urban periphery can prevent uncontrolled urban sprawl.

The positive role that housing can play in the effective planning and governance of mega-urban regions, however, is significantly negated by the fact that, in many South and Southeast Asian cities, housing activities occur outside the formal sector. To date, a significant portion of housing in cities like Delhi, Karachi, Kolkata (formerly Calcutta), and Metro Manila has been self-built. This housing is located in areas not zoned for residences. It is constructed of makeshift materials that do not conform to safety standards, built without the benefit of architectural design or engineering blueprints, and paid for by resources outside the formal financial system. Often, the services in poor urban settlements are obtained informally and even illegally. Jobs in such settlements are also largely in the informal sector, where issues like payrolls, taxes, insurance, health benefits, and other features of official employment are rarely considered.

To solve the problem of how to provide housing and basic urban services in Asian mega-urban regions, it is important to recognize that there are four major housing types needing urgent attention. The first type, the *old stock of housing* in the inner city, is marked by physical deterioration, a lack of water and sanitation, infestation by pests and vermin, and inadequate access to public services. Examples of this type of housing are the *bastis* in Delhi, Kolkata, and Mumbai; the slums inside the walled city of Intramuros in Manila; the "tube houses" in central Hanoi; the congested *lilong* (lane) housing in Shanghai; and the "courtyard houses without courtyards" in the center of Beijing. These old and dilapidated structures are subject to dangers of fire, earthquakes, floods, and other calamities, and they are a source of serious health hazards. Urban economists also see them as examples of the questionable use of very expensive land in city centers, land that could be devoted to high-value and tax-generating structures such as offices, hotels, banks, shopping centers, and luxury condominiums.

Second, there is *makeshift housing* in both the inner city and the surrounding areas. Aside from lacking basic services, this housing is also often located in dangerous areas, such as riverbanks, canals, garbage dumps, flood zones, and road and railway rights-of-way. Examples of this type of housing are found in Bangkok, Dhaka, Jakarta, Karachi, and Metro Manila. Despite the great danger to themselves and their properties, the occupants of these shanties resist eviction and persist in living in these dangerous areas, quickly rebuilding their communities after each disaster.

The third type is *squatter housing* on the urban periphery, most of it self-built or provided by illegal "subdivision developers" and almost always also lacking in basic services. There are large communities of illegal subdivisions surrounding factories in Greater Bangkok and Jakarta, along railroad tracks in Bandung, Kolkata, Manila, and Mumbai, and on private and public land in other cities.

Fourth, there is *rural housing* on the urban periphery, where the main problem is spatial isolation and a lack of access to basic services. In Chinese cities, where internal migration used to be strictly controlled, recent migrants without urban household registration have rented bed spaces in farmhouses or built temporary shelter on the urban periphery. In Bangkok,

Ho Chi Minh City, and Greater Manila, communities have sprouted on the edges of rice fields and along the banks of rivers and canals. The people who occupy these houses are usually not engaged in agriculture but instead are trying to find employment in the city. They have very little incentive to improve their dwellings, because they hope that once they find employment in the city, they will be able to move out.

Public officials and administrators usually view the housing problem of the mega-urban region in at least three ways. First, poor housing is seen as an issue of *health and safety*. People living in slum and squatter communities, lacking rudimentary services like water and sanitation, are blamed for epidemics and other health hazards. The makeshift shanties of urban poor people are fire hazards. Squatters are blamed for floods and other calamities, especially when they build their shanties along rivers and streams and carelessly throw garbage into them. Slums are associated with high crime rates involving drugs, gambling, prostitution, and physical violence. People who live in slums and squatter communities are also regarded as threats to public health.

Second, housing by squatters is viewed as a *legal* issue, because it entails the appropriation or use of land or physical structures without the consent of owners. Because most squatters do not pay for the use of land or buildings, many landowners (public or private) feel they are denied the benefits from their assets and complain about the violation of their property rights. Squatters do not pay real estate or other taxes, they do not obtain building permits, and they often violate zoning codes and subdivision regulations. Therefore, landowners fear that tolerating squatting will contribute to lawlessness because it shows the inability or unwillingness of the government to enforce the law. Many projects in mega-urban regions, in fact, cannot be implemented or suffer long delays because squatters refuse to vacate needed sites. Some local politicians are blamed for "coddling" squatters to get their votes. There are also accusations that the housing problem in some Asian cities is due to "professional squatters," who make a living by setting up squatter colonies and then extorting money from landowners before they move out.

Third, housing is seen as an issue of *equity* and basic human rights. A number of governments consider adequate housing an integral part of the welfare function. To respond to the need of poor urban citizens, some governments have provided socialized housing and pursued "enabling" strategies involving such approaches as "self-help," "mutual aid," and various forms of housing subsidies.

Through the years, a number of policies and programs have been implemented in Asian cities to deal with the housing problem, including (1) slum clearance and resettlement; (2) public housing; (3) slum upgrading and the provision of basic services; (4) sites and services; and (5) private-sector housing, including subsidies, credit schemes, tax breaks, land allocation, and infrastructure provision. Despite the allocation of billions of dollars by governments, international donors, and the private sector, however, in many Asian mega-cities the problem of housing and basic urban services is far from being solved. In fact, as mega-cities continue to grow and spread to peripheral areas, this problem seems to be getting worse.

Slum Clearance and Resettlement

In the years immediately after World War II, many Asian governments did not quite know what to do with the millions of people who moved to big cities—invading public and private lands, setting up shantytowns, and using up public services without paying for them. The initial literature on slums reflected Western attitudes toward urban decay, seeing low-income communities as being composed of people suffering from personal and social disorganization, the social dropouts unable to compete in a Darwinian world. The view of squatters was even more negative. Squatters were seen as the "human flotsam and jetsam" who inhabited "tin can cities" (*bidonvilles*) and willfully violated the property rights of others.

Policymakers saw the colonies of urban poor people as a "cancerous growth" on the city. They branded squatters and slum dwellers as social misfits involved in crime, gambling, alcoholism, prostitution, and other urban ills. The solution to the problem of slums and squatters, therefore, was to surgically excise these cancerous growths by tearing down shantytowns and resettling slum residents at far-off relocation sites. Some officials justified slum clearance and resettlement as a way of getting rid of the criminal activities of "syndicates of professional squatters" (Dwyer 1974, 1975).

Many slum clearance and resettlement activities were carried out to create space for urban infrastructure projects like roads, hospitals, schools, and government offices. Some were done to make cities look clean and beautiful, such as the massive cleanup of shanties in Metro Manila on the occasion of the Pope John Paul II's visit to the country or the hosting of the annual meetings of the World Bank and the International Monetary Fund. Squatters and slum dwellers fought eviction and resettlement, of course—often with violent confrontations that cost a number of lives. One big issue was the fact that poor residents were dumped at relocation sites located far from the city. These sites were not accessible by public transport, lacked employment opportunities, and did not have basic services such as water, sanitation, and drainage. Not surprisingly, many slum clearance and relocation schemes failed because, eventually, most of the resettled people returned to the city to squat somewhere else (Laquian 1966, 1969).

Because of insistent complaints and lobbying by poor urban groups and their supporters, many Asian governments have been dissuaded from indiscriminately using the resettlement approach. In the Philippines, it was mandated by law that people can be moved from a site only if (1) they are staying in dangerous places such as riverbanks, steep slopes, along railroad tracks, or near toxic waste dumps; (2) the occupied land is needed for an infrastructure project that is required for the general welfare; or (3) an occupant is in clear violation of another person's property rights. The so-called Lina law stipulated that persons cannot be removed from slums or squatter sites without alternative housing and basic services acceptable to them being provided at a new site by the person or institution initiating the move. Projects supported by the World Bank and the Asian Development Bank also provide that eviction can occur only after appropriate measures have been taken to ensure the welfare of the people affected.

Similar arrangements governing resettlement have been instituted in both China and Vietnam, where revised regulations on resettlement have made it more difficult for the government to simply move people from one place to another. However, they have also made it difficult for planning and construction authorities to pursue housing and other development projects (except in China, where land is owned by the state and housing provision is regarded a responsibility of the state and work units). In a number of cities like Bangkok, Hanoi, Ho Chi Minh City, Jakarta, and Metro Manila, many projects have been delayed because the cost of relocating people from the site needed was extremely high.

In Indonesia, Malaysia, and the Philippines, the government has attempted in the past to relocate people from urban peripheries to frontier zones. Volunteers were given the opportunity to move to frontier areas through the *transmigrasi* program in Indonesia, the Federal Land Development Authority (FELDA) scheme in Malaysia, and the homesteading program in the Philippines. Though these resettlement programs were mainly focused on rural dwellers, some urban residents joined them as well. Evaluations of such programs revealed, however, that they did not succeed too well in the case of former urban residents, for three reasons. First, most of the urban dwellers had lost their farming skills and could not make a living in the frontier zone. Second, life on the frontier was very hard, and some of the returned settlers complained of a lack of medical facilities in areas that were infested with malaria and other diseases.

The third reason for the programs' lack of success was that products from the frontier areas could not be marketed because there were no roads or accessible markets. The main exception was the FELDA scheme in Malaysia, which concentrated on the production of cash crops like rubber and palm oil in well-managed estates. Because the estates were well planned, had full services for settlers, and ensured the marketing of products, many of the re-settled families stayed and became committed to the schemes. Even here, however, the projects encountered so-called second-generation problems, whereby the children of the original settlers had become dissatisfied with life on the frontier and wanted to move to cities and towns.

Experience in Asia has clearly shown that in many instances resettlement does not really solve the housing problem of urban poor people—it merely transfers the problem to other sites. Such schemes as transitional reception areas, clustered sites, and relocation sites have not worked, mainly because they have lacked even the most basic services to make life in these new areas viable. The lack of employment opportunities at the new sites has been a key issue—and when this lack of employment is combined with the lack of basic services, the high cost of transport because of the sites' isolation, the failure to instill a sense of community among relocated families, and bureaucratic delays in carrying out plot surveys and allocating land titles, it almost ensures the failure of these projects.

Therefore, because of the negative experience with resettlement, only a few governments still use this approach, instead preferring sites-and-services and community upgrading approaches. For instance, in the recent eviction of squatters and slum dwellers along the Pasig River in Metro Manila required by infrastructure projects financed by the Asian Development Bank, there have been serious attempts at consultation and participatory planning, although the process has been marked by confrontation and there has been some delay in implementation.

Public Housing

The traditional governmental solution to the housing problem is the construction of public housing. Early public housing programs were meant to benefit civil servants, military personnel, and special groups. These programs were justified as partial benefits to augment low salaries or to reward individuals like war veterans (in South Korea), old revolutionaries (China), or war widows (Vietnam). Some housing schemes were simply continuations of programs that provided housing for colonial civil servants (Bangladesh, India, Malaysia, Pakistan). Others were constructed and allocated to partisans as a part of political patronage (Indonesia, Philippines, Thailand).

After World War II, a number of Asian governments tried to provide low-cost housing programs for poor urban residents, especially squatters and slum dwellers relocated from sites that were required for public works and economic development projects. Bilateral and multilateral donor agencies funded many of these housing public projects, for example, the Bagong Barangay Housing Project in Manila funded by the U.S. Agency for International Development. In this project, five-story walkup apartments were built near bus routes in Pandacan, a working-class district. The units were raffled off to low-salaried employees of the Manila City government. Rents for the units were set at no more than 10 percent of monthly income.

An evaluation of the Bagong Barangay project conducted ten years after its establishment revealed that about one-third of its residents were not original unit recipients. Newcomers had bought "rights of occupancy" from the original tenants, an illegal transaction prohibited by the original lease terms. Many apartment units had also been physically altered by the addition of "mezzanine" sleeping quarters or overhanging balconies. These "illegal constructions" had been tolerated by housing managers who had been bribed (Laquian 1966).

In some Asian countries, governments have heavily subsidized public housing. In Indonesia, for example, the National Urban Development Corporation (Perumnas) had built about 24,000 housing units per year in urban areas. In the Jakarta area, most of the public housing units were reserved for civil servants, national bank employees, and the military. Some units were offered for sale to the public, but because these were located on the urban periphery and were too costly, there were not that many takers.

In Bangkok, the National Housing Authority launched an ambitious program in 1973 to construct 120,000 housing units, mainly in the Bangkok metropolitan area. Despite the housing authority's incurring of a huge deficit, it absorbed all the construction costs and interest charges on capital to build the multistory housing units. About 6,000 to 7,000 units of housing were built each year. In view of the fact that the housing demand was for an estimated 300,000 units, the scarcity value of these units made them favorite items of illegal transfer or "key money" transactions, which eventually benefited not the low-income target families but higher-income people. Many of these units are now occupied as city apartments of senior civil servants. This was in spite of the fact that the quality of construction of the apartments was often quite poor (United Nations 1987a).

In general, the experience with public housing in many Asian countries has not been positive. Many public housing projects failed because (1) they were too expensive and the low-income beneficiaries could not afford them; (2) not enough units were built, creating a premium market price based on scarcity value, thereby encouraging those allocated the housing units to sell their "rights of occupancy"; (3) housing units were allocated on the basis of political patronage rather than housing need, leading to corruption; (4) some units were built far from workplaces, which increased actual costs to residents and led to abandonment or secret sales; and (5) units were poorly designed, badly constructed, and/or inefficiently maintained, leading to rapid deterioration of the housing stock.

Because of these failures, public housing efforts in Asia have been easily dismissed as ineffective. However, the experiences of Singapore and Hong Kong show that adequate public housing can be provided by the government. In these geographically small cities, where in-migration could be controlled and where the government had ample resources, high-density housing has been built to meet housing demand. At present, more than half of Hong Kong's housing stock is public housing, whereas in Singapore the proportion is about 85 percent. Both cities have committed themselves to housing policies that make up for imperfections of the market. Housing is regarded as an instrument for enhancing productivity as well as a way of improving the lives of residents (Yeh 1975; Wong 1996). These successful housing programs have influenced and shaped the whole mega-urban region. Thus, housing programs in Hong Kong and Singapore have shown that a mega-urban region can be turned into a livable settlement if housing is integrated with comprehensive planning, linked to and efficiently serviced by transport and other infrastructure, provided with basic urban services and amenities, and the location of housing projects is integrated with employment opportunities.

It is interesting to note that Hong Kong and Singapore plan housing estates in the context of developmental goals. The location, level of utilities and services, transportation linkages, social amenities, and occupancy selection schemes of each housing project are fully considered from both the employment and residence perspectives. In Singapore, "flatted factories" suitable for small-scale industries have been built on housing estates to provide employment for people close to where they live, thus minimizing traffic. Factory sites on the estates have been leased at concessional terms to investors to encourage them to open up productive enterprises and jobs to project residents. Similar efforts have been carried out in Hong Kong as part of its resettlement schemes. Inner-city families have been relocated to suburban sites where housing and employment have been fully integrated (Yeh and Laquian 1979).

The Hong Kong and Singapore situations, of course, have been heavily influenced by their small territorial space, which requires them to build at very high densities. The overall urbanized area of Hong Kong, where the great bulk of its 6 million residents live, takes up only 15,000 hectares, or less than 15 percent of the 110,000 hectares that make up the whole territory. The gross residential area—places actually occupied by housing—is only 6 percent of the territory (Wong 1996, 7).

Building at such density levels (about 300 to 400 persons per hectare in Hong Kong, as against 25 persons per hectare in many North American cities) makes considerable savings in energy and building materials possible. For example, Wong has concluded that per capita energy use in Hong Kong is about 15 percent of that in a North American city like Chicago. Each Hong Kong resident uses about 220 liters of water a day, which is about half that of an average North American city. Per capita building material use for construction in high-rise dwellings is less than half of the material cost per person of North American single-family dwellings. In general, this may be due to the high-occupancy density (the average Hong Kong resident has only 15 to 20 square meters of floor area), which is about a quarter of North American standards (Wong 1996, 121).

The revolutionary changes in housing development in China have seen a dramatic shift from public housing provision (started in 1949) to private housing (after the launching of economic reforms in 1979). In 2002, it was estimated that 94 percent of households in China owned some form of accommodation and that more than 80 percent of China's public housing had been sold to local residents. During the first half of 2003, China sold houses worth $25.4 billion with a total floor area of 86.7 million square meters, with 74.0 square meters of that (95.7 percent) bought by individuals. In the same period, houses with a combined floor area of 775.8 million square meters were under construction, and 604.1 million square meters of those were residential (*People's Daily On Line,* July 24, 2003).

After the 1949 communist revolution, housing was made accessible to most Chinese families by the state simply taking over privately owned houses and redistributing it to needy families. In Beijing, for example, the privately owned housing stock declined from 70 percent in 1949 to 5 percent in 1985 (Li 1997, 35). City authorities also engaged in large-scale housing construction. In most Chinese cities, responsibility for housing was vested in the *danwei* (work unit). Work-unit housing was made up of five- to six-story apartments with no elevators within a 30-minute walking or bicycling distance from the workplace. Up to 1994, work units owned 62 percent of the total housing stock in Beijing. Added to the 18 percent of housing owned by the municipal government, this meant that 80 percent of housing in the city was publicly owned.

Since 1979, the Chinese government has shifted from a "socialized" to a "commodity" view of housing. The Beijing 1992 Comprehensive Plan for Housing System Reform indicated that housing should be regarded as a "commodity," even as a certain segment of the housing stock should be "socialized." What this meant was that the bulk of public housing should be sold to individuals according to the private market's prices as determined by supply and demand. However, for certain families who could not afford market-rate housing, the government should still provide affordable dwellings and basic services.

China's Ninth Five-Year Plan (1996–2000), set these housing targets for the city of Beijing:

- Increase public housing rent to a level where the state would fully recover the cost of depreciation of the housing stock, maintenance, management, interest on the housing investment, and the property tax.
- Each housing beneficiary household should contribute at least 10 percent of its annual income to housing.
- The average per capita living space for housing should be at least 9.5 square meters. At least 80 percent of housing units should be self-contained, meaning that they would not have to share toilets, kitchens, or other amenities.
- By 1997, there would be no more "housing poor families," defined as those who were homeless or lived in "dangerous and dilapidated dwellings."

Because of the 1997 Asian economic crisis, which hit China quite badly, there was some uncertainty as to whether the targets in the Ninth Five-Year Plan could be achieved, for four reasons. First, many Chinese work units, especially state-owned enterprises, were seriously in the red and could not afford to meet their housing obligations. Privatizing housing did not only reduce their financial burden; it actually gave them new income by using some of their assets, especially land, for housing. Second, an increasing number of Chinese workers were self-employed and had to find housing in the open market. Third, serious inequalities had occurred between rich work units that could provide good housing for their workers and poorer ones that could not, resulting in considerable social tension. Fourth, the relaxation of rules governing internal migration (the household registration system) had flooded the cities with temporary migrants (the "floating population"), and these migrants had exerted heavy pressure on housing demand.

In 1980, real estate development corporations (REDCs) were established to build housing in Beijing. These were essentially of three types: (1) companies under the administration of the construction committees belonging to municipal or district governments, (2) companies associated with work units, and (3) joint-venture companies. REDCs belonging to municipal or district governments were formed in pursuance of government policy that separated the administrative functions of local government units from their business functions. Formerly, these companies merely built housing and then transferred these to the local government unit for operation and management. After the change, these REDCs acted like private developers, which were required under the "production responsibility system" to become financially self-sufficient. As such, REDCs carried out all the functions related to land assembly, housing design, construction, finance, operation, maintenance, and management. Because many of these companies enjoyed the backing of local governments, they usually got the big and lucrative development contracts. They also thrived because they were allowed to sell housing units at "comprehensive cost prices," which included a comfortable profit margin. By the end of 1993, there were 444 REDCs in Beijing, and 292 of these were joint ventures involving foreign investors.

During the housing construction boom period in Beijing around 1993, more than 100 work units decided to set up their own companies to construct, sell, and/or rent out housing units. Although these companies initially got their investment capital from the work unit, most of their projects later had to be financed with bank loans. In theory, these companies were not obligated to allocate the housing units they constructed to their work units. However, many of these companies responded to the housing needs of work-unit members, especially top managers, even as they sold housing units to private individuals.

Joint ventures belonged to municipal and district governmental units or were associated with work units. The main difference was that their capitalization involved investment from foreign sources. Aside from acquiring foreign capital, these companies also introduced new building techniques, modern building materials, creative financing methods, and efficient management systems. In 1993, there were 297 joint-venture companies operating in Beijing, most of them with Hong Kong and Singaporean partners. Interestingly, some of the joint ventures expanded from housing construction to engage in estate management, financing, and maintenance.

In effect, public housing programs in China came to an end during the late 1990s, when at the Ninth National People's Congress (March 1998), the new prime minister, Zhu Rongji, announced that housing reform was one of the major tasks of the state. The government announced that it would eliminate the in-kind welfare housing it had provided in the past and declared "home purchase" as the major thrust of housing reform. After the announcement of this policy, individual local governments set up their own housing programs. Guangzhou Municipality actually beat the central government by launching its "Housing Allowance Scheme" in January 1998. Under this program, civil servants who joined the government after September 30, 1997, were not given housing units by the government. Instead, they were granted a housing allowance that depended on their rank, seniority, and length of service over a twenty-year period. Such allowances could be used as a down payment on a house, and the predictable flow of funds could be used as collateral for a housing loan from a bank. By 2000, more than 2,000 civil servants were receiving housing allowances and buying houses at market prices (Wong and Hui 2000).

In general, public housing in many Asian cities will not probably play a major role in making housing accessible to most people, especially poor urban residents. Most governments, with the exception of Hong Kong and Singapore, just do not have the capital to invest in public housing, despite the known multiplier effects and economic development impact of the housing sector. Joint ventures involving the government and private developers are building housing, but such housing is generally priced beyond the capacity to pay of the urban poor people. In Malaysia and Thailand, the private sector has been able to build housing for workers, but one has to have gainful employment and a predictable income to buy or rent these units.

In the Philippines, it has been hoped that more credit made available to individual homeowners would encourage the private sector to go into housing. However, a program of granting land titles to squatters and slum dwellers—prompted by the advice of Peruvian economist Hernando de Soto to the government—has not taken off after almost three years of hopeful pronouncements. The procedural problems involved in legitimizing squatters' de facto "ownership" of land that they have occupied have been grossly underestimated. Doubts have also been raised about the willingness of private banks to grant housing loans on the basis of land titles awarded to former squatters, because even middle-income families find it difficult to get housing loans from private banks, which have many much more lucrative opportunities for investing their funds.

In some instances, public housing might be used to direct developments in self-contained clusters on the periphery of the mega-urban region. This may be an effective policy instrument to achieve decentralized growth if the housing is combined with employment opportunities, infrastructure, services, and amenities. Housing by itself, however, is not a good enough incentive for people to locate in high-density nodes in suburban areas. Even when the price of suburban housing becomes affordable to individual homeowners, suburban housing will entail long commuting times, and the environmental pollution costs passed on to the larger society does not make it sustainable.

Slum Upgrading and the Provision of Basic Services

Slum upgrading is based on the theories that gained a great deal of popularity during the 1960s that urban poor people have the capabilities to effectively deal with their own housing problems. According to these theories, poor people know their own needs and, given the appropriate support to "empower" them, could be "enabled" to meet these needs themselves. What was required was to discard overly controlling rules and regulations, such as unnecessarily high standards of urban housing and infrastructure, and to allow poor people to develop at their own pace ("gradualist development"). Given such assurances as security of land tenure, low interest loans, appropriate building materials, and some technical assistance, poor residents would build their own homes and avail themselves of the right services (Abrams 1964; Turner 1965, 1968, 1976; Mangin 1970; Peattie, 1968, 1982; Turner and Fichter 1972).

In its simplest form, slum upgrading assists urban poor people in situ by providing potable water, toilets, roads and pathways, storm water drainage, refuse removal, and sometimes electricity. Slum-upgrading projects are usually carried out with the full participation of the slum dwellers themselves. In other projects, designers attempt to enhance the "consolidation" of target communities by including components such as the regularization of land tenure, introducing small-scale credit schemes to support local enterprises, extending building materials loans, organizing and training community leaders to facilitate planning and decision making, and promoting health and sanitation schemes. Examples of slum-upgrading schemes in Asian cities are the Tondo Foreshore project in Manila (Laquian 1969; Reforma 1977), the Ashok Nagar project in Chennai (formerly Madras) (Robben 1987), the Orangi pilot project in Karachi (Brockman and Williams 1996; Hasan 2002), and the Kampung Improvement Program in Indonesia (Silas 1984, 1989, 1994; Taylor 1987).

Indonesia's Kampung Improvement Program (KIP) is a noteworthy example of slum upgrading because it has been expanded into a nationwide effort covering many cities in the country—the only example of a program of significant scale in Asia. Essentially, KIP upgraded existing low-income communities by improving roads and footpaths, drainage, flood control, water supply, communal toilets, and garbage collection and disposal. Although KIP was managed by the Housing Directorate of the Department of Public Works, it had no provision for housing construction. Rather, the program sought to encourage people to improve their own homes by supporting their voluntary efforts to uplift basic services in the community. By making physical improvements relevant to the lifestyle of the people in the *kampungs*, KIP avoided the problem of "pricing poor people" out of their improved communities. This approach seems to have worked well, because many *kampung* residents have generally continued living in their communities (Koswara 1997, 185).

Another good example of slum upgrading is the Orangi Pilot Project (OPP), which was organized in the largest *katchi abadi* (unplanned settlement) in Karachi. The project included improving water, sanitation, and sewerage facilities through voluntary community action. About 1 million people benefited from the project. And having been inspired by OPP, four autonomous community organizations have carried out similar projects in Karachi. The initial emphasis on sanitation and sewerage improvement has been expanded to include building materials provision, small-scale credit, and livelihood improvement. These projects have also provided training, community organization, and other forms of assistance to residents of low-income communities all over Pakistan (Brockman and Williams 1996, 20).

It should be noted, however, that efforts to "export" the OPP model to other cities and countries have had rather mixed results. Of thirteen attempts at replicating the OPP approach by nongovernmental organizations (NGOs) and community-based organizations (CBOs), two were successful, five were failures, and four "showed signs of promise" (Hasan 2002, 206). In the case of the failures, the connections of self-built sewerage systems to the municipal networks were not adequately provided for. The CBOs and NGOs were too small and did not have the financial and managerial resources to successfully carry out the projects. Interestingly, in some cases, the infusion of large amounts of money from foreign donors was an important element in project failure, because it undermined community cooperation and created a sense of dependence instead of self-reliance on the part of project participants.

An important issue in slum upgrading is the need to "decongest" slum and squatter communities. Because houses, footpaths, and other structures in a spontaneous low-income settlement are usually built without any formal planning, any attempt to rationalize the layouts of these structures through community upgrading will require moving people either inside or outside the community. In the Tondo Foreshore project in Metro Manila, for example, about a quarter of the original families living in the uncontrolled settlement had to be moved out. Streets and footpaths in the area had to be straightened and widened to allow fire trucks, ambulances, police cars, and other vehicles to enter the community. Space was also needed for community centers, health clinics, police stations, parks and playgrounds, and other public uses. A process of "reblocking" houses within a grid street layout had to be used, involving the people in deciding where streets should go, what space to allocate to public uses, which houses have to be moved in accordance with the street grid, which families would have to move, and so on.

Happily, in the case of the Tondo project, a reclaimed piece of land in Dagat-dagatan, about a kilometer from the original site, was found to resettle some of the families. At this new site, serviced plots were allocated to the resettled families, a building materials loan made new materials available, and the city authorities provided vehicles to facilitate the residents' moves. In this way, the slum-upgrading program was carried out without any hitch (Laquian 1983a, 17).

A most important ingredient in upgrading programs is assuring low-income families that they will have secure tenure in their community. Security of tenure can be achieved by selling the land to the families outright, through long-term leases, long-term contracts, or a public announcement by city authorities that residents will not be forcefully evicted from their place of residence. Without any assurance about security of tenure, people will be very hesitant to invest time, money, materials, and effort in upgrading their homes. This is the reason that many low-income settlements remain in such a poor and dilapidated condition. It does not make sense for low-income residents to invest more money in houses that may be in danger of being dismantled and bulldozed by the authorities.

While the conventional approach to community upgrading involves reliance on community resources and efforts to improve conditions, it is possible to upgrade a community by introducing public housing. In the Industri Dalam project in Bandung, for example, the construction of four-story apartments in a vacant lot within the community started the process of upgrading. As soon as the apartments were finished, selected families occupying makeshift shanties nearby were allocated units. In turn, they had to agree that their shanties would be dismantled as soon as they had moved to the apartments. On the cleared sites, another four-story apartment was built. When it was finished, families moved in, vacating their old house sites. In this way, it was possible to improve the whole community by using up less than a quarter of the land. The freed land, in turn, was devoted to commercial uses that brought in considerable money for the city government (Karyoedi 1995).

Combining medium-rise housing with community upgrading has been tried in Chennai, the fourth largest city in India, with a population of 6.5 million. Projects by the Tamil Nadu Slum Clearance Board erected multistory buildings on the slum sites, complete with basic services and amenities. However, the actual buildings constructed met only a fraction of the housing demand, so many beneficiaries sold their rights of occupancy to others. The government, therefore, ended up subsidizing housing for families that could afford to pay in the open market. The high cost of this housing approach had encouraged the government to use community upgrading, sites and services, and resettlement as the main approaches to deal with the housing problem.

Although community upgrading has become the most popular approach to housing in South and Southeast Asian mega-urban regions, it is, at best, a temporary palliative. Even the most successful projects—such as KIP in Jakarta, the Zonal Improvement Project in Metro Manila, and the National Housing Authority schemes in Bangkok—do not adequately meet the housing and basic services needs of poor people. Although investments in community upgrading are relatively low, cost recovery is extremely difficult, because the actual benefits to individual households are difficult to identity. The supply of water in upgraded communities, for example, is often good for only a couple of hours a day. It is provided through public standpipes and is considered a free service by the people. Electricity, though it can be metered, is subject to meter tampering and theft, practices that are not only illegal but also increase the danger of fire. Physical structures in the upgraded communities continue to be dilapidated even after many years of housing consolidation. The densities of makeshift dwellings are extremely high, making fire an ever-present danger. Toilets are often communal, smelly, hard to keep clean, and often serve as a source of health hazards. And garbage collection is very difficult to do in communities served only by wooden plank bridges and footpaths.

Worst of all, because many upgraded communities are inaccessible to regular municipal services, they tend to deteriorate even when joint government–community partnerships are instituted to enable communities to look after their own needs. In some instances, in fact, governments have used so-called enabling strategies as an excuse for not doing anything for low-income communities because promising announcements, sloganeering, and the well-promoted launchings of future projects take the place of actual improvements.

Sites and Services

The sites-and-services approach involves "the opening up of new land and its subdivision into serviced plots" (Laquian 1976; 1983a, 18). Land may be located in the central city or on the periphery. Often, it has been found that successful sites-and-services projects are located not too far from community-upgrading projects, to catch the "overspill" of households that have to be moved from the upgraded site and resettle them at locations that are not too far from the original communities being upgraded.

The size of sites-and-services plots varies—from about 35 square meters in Chennai and 45 square meters in the Tondo project in Metro Manila to as high as 80 square meters in Delhi. The house plots are arranged along roads and pathways usually in a grid pattern. In some projects, the plot is serviced by piped water and a water-sealed toilet (a "sanitary core"), as in the World Bank–funded Dagat-dagatan project in Tondo. In others, communal toilets and standpipes for every five houses are provided. In a number of projects, a "core house" made up of four posts and a roof over a compacted floor might be built to give immediate shelter to project participants. Others do not have any structures at all, and participants are expected to build their own structures.

Sites-and-services schemes located on the outskirts of a city have been justified because they extend serviced land into the urban periphery. Their relatively lower costs have also been used as justification—typically, about 85 percent of project costs go to infrastructure, such as water supply, sanitation, drainage, and roads. Because few or no funds are allocated to housing (which is the responsibility of project participants), sites-and-services projects are seen as low-cost solutions to expanding services.

One of the main problems faced by sites-and-services projects involves the setting of housing and service standards through municipal legislation. In most cities, such standards are set at too high a level. In some cases, therefore, projects have been ruled illegal or substandard by city authorities, delaying the occupancy of units by project participants. In others, projects have been allowed to operate by the expedient of establishing "spot zoning" regulations that exempted the projects from the formal standards. There have even been projects that defined their structures as "makeshift and temporary" and therefore not required to comply with housing standards.

A frequent issue in standards setting is the size of house plots. Using formal zoning and subdivision regulations—many of which were inherited from colonial planners and administrators, who simply brought their codebooks with them from their mother countries—the small plots in sites-and-services schemes were considered too dense. In comparison with the original densities in the slum or squatter areas where the project participants came from, the project densities were really quite low. However, in the eyes of formalistic planners and administrators, the sites-and-services schemes had all the potentials of "planned slums," and they did not consider these acceptable.

To avoid the emergence of "planned slums," some city authorities have allocated additional funds to sites-and-services projects to build finished houses. In the Tondo project, for example, a building materials loan was extended to project participants so that they could use "strong materials"—such as timber, cement hollow blocks, steel reinforcement bars, and galvanized iron sheets—in building a "starter house." When the project was inaugurated, rows upon rows of finished houses were displayed for the media. However, as soon as the project participants moved in, the first thing they did was to dismantle the finished houses, which they considered too small. They wanted to build their houses in accordance with their own cir-

cumstances (e.g., family size, need to do work at home) as well as their capacity to pay. The money used to build the original starter homes was
wasted, because the government had not considered people's wants and
needs in insisting on sticking to housing standards.

Another issue involving standards is related to the time needed to finish
the houses in a project. Because most participants in sites-and-services
schemes have low incomes, they usually build a modest core shelter first,
which they can move into right away. Then they can improve the structure
as their incomes allow. To formalistic administrators, however, a project is
not considered finished until the house structure is complete. Thus, they try
to pressure project participants to accelerate the process of "housing
consolidation," which may result in the allocation of a larger proportion of
family income to housing, which in turn leads to malnutrition, children
dropping out of school, and other negative effects. Evaluations of sites-and-
services schemes have revealed that, in time, project participants are able to
consolidate and improve their homes. However, the time varies, and pres-
suring them to conform to formal standards of housing completion may lead
to undesirable results, such as a high abandonment rate.

During the 1970s, the World Bank supported sites-and-services and
slum-upgrading projects all over the world. However, after a decade of such
efforts, the bank shifted to more institutional approaches, such as the en-
couragement of financing institutions in an attempt to pursue a "wholesale"
rather than a "retail" approach to housing and urban services. Interestingly,
quite a number of governments in South and Southeast Asia, often complemented by civil society support, have continued to pursue upgrading and
slum redevelopment projects. There is a feeling among urban development
advocates that the lessons from these continuing efforts need to be analyzed
more closely, because they may reveal factors that might help to improve
the living conditions of urban poor people in many Asian countries.

Private-Sector Housing

During the mid-1970s, Angel analyzed the housing situation in Bangkok
and identified six types of housing suppliers: (1) low-income people living
in slum and squatter areas who provided their own housing; (2) landowners
who allowed low-income people to temporarily build houses on their property for a fee; (3) private developers and contractors that built houses for
those who could afford them for rent or for sale; (4) employers that provided

housing as part of employee benefits; (5) governments that built public housing; and (6) NGOs and charitable institutions that provided financial, organizational, and technical advice, as well as other forms of assistance, to low-income people (Angel 1977).

At the time, it was estimated that the private for-profit sector was capable of meeting less than 10 percent of the housing need in a city, the public sector another 10 percent, and the popular sector the remaining 80 percent. Later, an analysis of World Bank–financed low-cost housing schemes concluded that the bottom 20 percent of participants in slum-upgrading and sites-and-services projects could not afford even the most basic housing options and required government or other types of subsidies (Laquian 1983b).

Because most Asian governments did not have the resources to provide housing to citizens, some tried to encourage the private sector to construct more housing by offering incentives such as inexpensive land, opening up infrastructure in new areas, tax breaks, easy-credit financing, or relaxing building codes and housing standards. In general, however, even with these incentives, the private sector was not able to construct adequate housing because of a lack of capital and the limited capacity to pay of many urban dwellers. Studies of people in slum and squatter communities found that poor residents were too busy finding or keeping a job to worry too much about housing. These studies also revealed that housing, per se, was not the most important problem in low-income areas—the most basic needs were for potable water, sanitation, drainage, electricity, garbage collection and disposal, health and personal security.

The main challenge in private-sector housing is affordability. In poor urban communities where 40 percent or more of the residents live on $1.00 a day or less, a family of four would be hard pressed to pay $40 a month for housing and amenities. Added to this lack of capacity to pay is the high cost that some poor urban families have to pay for services. For example, before the World Bank set up a slum-upgrading and sites-and-services project in the Tondo Foreshore squatter area in Metro Manila, a survey revealed that low-income people had to buy drinking water from vendors and paid more than seven times what families with water directly piped into their homes paid. If the rule of thumb that a household should not spend more than a third of its income for housing is used as a test of affordability, more than three-fourths of households in low-income communities of Asian mega-urban regions would probably not be able to pay for adequate housing and basic services.

Without financial subsidies, tax breaks, infrastructure support, and other benefits extended by governments and donors, it would be extremely difficult for the private sector to make a profit from low-cost housing. In Indonesia, the Philippines, and other Asian countries, the private sector has primarily been involved in designing and constructing housing projects for the government. Even in such countries, however, some contractors have met the need to make a profit by cutting down on standards. In some instances, private builders had been known to use substandard materials like smaller steel reinforcement bars, poorer quality cement, or substandard timber to make enough profits and recoup money used to pay bribes to corrupt officials. Crooked inspectors certified that houses conformed to government standards for a fee. As a result of these corrupt practices, some privately built housing units in a number of Asian cities have turned out to be substandard, and some have been actually unsafe and dangerous.

The most successful private housing efforts in Asia to date have been those in China. As noted above, housing in China was considered a government responsibility by the Communist Party leaders. At present, however, 94 percent of housing is privately owned. Seven types of policy measures have been used to bring about this dramatic transition. The first type is *economic rents*. The traditional practice of charging minimal rents by work units was rapidly phased out in 1997. For example, in Shenzhen, rents in 1988 were increased from RMB 0.14 to 2.06 per square meter. However, under the so-called three-categories approach, "welfare housing" with low rents was still made available to workers with low incomes, "low profit housing" could be sold to workers in state-owned enterprises, and "commodity housing" could be bought by anyone with money.

The second type of policy measure is *housing accumulation funds*. In 1994, government units set up housing accumulation funds, into which employees deposited 5 percent of their monthly wages and work units contributed an equal amount each month. When enough funds had been accumulated by an employee, these funds were used as a down payment on a housing unit. Employees could also use the accumulated housing fund as a collateral for a bank loan. By 2002, it was estimated that about 65 million Chinese had set up housing accumulation funds, and 20 million of these had bought their homes. The total accumulated housing funds amounted to $49.9 billion, and about $18.3 billion had been used to buy homes.

The third type of policy measure is *subsidized housing*. Aside from commodity housing sold by developers for profit, the government also offered "inexpensive but comfortable apartments" that could be bought at affordable prices. For example, in Beijing, such an apartment sold for $150 per square meter; in 2001, 60 percent of these units were sold on the open market.

The fourth type of policy measure is *assistance to developers*. Private developers were encouraged to go into housing construction by granting them exemptions from twenty-one types of taxes, as long as their profit margins did not exceed 3 percent. Land was also made available to developers at concessional rates, and infrastructure and services were extended to developer-initiated housing projects.

The fifth type of policy measure is *compensation to homeowners*. Owners and residents of "old and dilapidated housing" in inner cities were compensated for giving up their houses, which had to be demolished by developers building multistory housing. These homeowners then used these funds as collateral for loans from private banks to enable them to buy their own homes.

The sixth type of policy measure is *housing allowance schemes*. In Guangzhou, civil servants were given housing allowances instead of being provided with housing by their work units. These housing allowances were to be paid over a twenty-year period. They could be used for a down payment on a housing unit or as collateral for housing loans from commercial banks.

The seventh type of policy measure is *the development of a mortgage market*. With the advice of the World Bank, China has opened up a market for mortgages and mortgage-backed securities. Commercial banks have been allowed to participate in this mortgage market and to open up new channels for housing loans. In March 1998, the People's Bank of China lifted restrictions on loans for Comfortable Housing Projects. Banks have been allowed to provide loans to housing development companies if these companies have at least 60 percent of construction funds in hand, encouraging private developers to go into the comfortable housing development market.

Yet despite China's dramatic success in privatizing its housing, it has faced a number of problems in recent years—the most important being the "overheated" housing market. In early 2003, the People's Bank of China issued rules and regulations restricting bank loans to developers by stipulating that developers should have assets equivalent to at least 30 percent of the cost of the project. Individual homebuyers were also allowed to borrow only up to 80 percent of the house price. It was revealed that domestic banks had issued $24 billion worth of loans to real estate firms and 750 billion yuan to individual homebuyers. This was considered dangerous, because the average ratio of debts to assets among domestic real estate companies ranged from 72 to 94 percent.

Another housing problem was the overconcentration on high-end luxury housing in certain cities. In Beijing, a housing analyst said that there was a surplus of luxury housing costing more than $734 per square meter in 2002, at a time when only one-fifth of economic housing targets were being met. Moreover, overbuilding was also shown by the fact that the average vacancy rate for housing averaged 19 percent, compared with 10 and 15 percent the previous year.

Finally, China's privatization of housing has shown serious inefficiencies in the property management field. In Beijing, 63 percent of 3,127 residential communities had contracted out the management of their properties to private companies. Because these management companies had a virtual monopoly in the field, there have been many reports of mismanagement and even corruption. The Beijing Consumers Association reported that it received many complaints about poor services, high charges, and scams. As a result, Beijing Municipality had passed legislation setting standards and rules to be followed by property management companies. But it has taken some time to have these rules and regulations effectively implemented.

Housing Finance

It is widely recognized in Asian mega-urban regions that the private banking sector can meet the housing needs of only a segment of the population. Interest charged by banks for a home mortgage generally ranges around 18 percent or more a year with full collateral. At these rates, only wealthy families can afford to buy homes in the private sector. Housing surveys consistently reveal that the bottom 20 percent of households in poor urban settlements cannot afford even the cheapest option provided by public or private agencies.

Because of the lack of financial capacity on the part of urban poor people, some housing programs in the past depended on contributions "in kind" to support projects. Thus, in Indonesia and the Philippines, World Bank–financed projects in slum upgrading and sites and services accepted "sweat equity" contributions from project beneficiaries, in the form of voluntary labor for digging ditches, preparing house foundations, and other forms of labor. The monetary value of such labor contributions was at times accepted as a down payment for a housing loan. In the Community Mortgage Program in the Philippines, self-help construction was recognized as an important element in housing consolidation, and a detailed estimation of the capacity of the household to provide this was included in feasibility studies.

Housing authorities generally expect that a household should not spend more than 30 percent of its income for housing and basic services. Studies have shown, however, that in the case of really poor people ("the poorest of the poor"), devoting that much to housing and services would mean severe cutbacks on food, medicine, education of children, and other more immediate survival needs. This is the reason why very poor people live in squatter areas, where they do not have to pay for housing, or in slum areas, where cheap rents are available.

Slum and squatter areas enable poor people to survive by using such strategies as doubling up with family members and friends, buying things in small amounts on informal credit, not paying any rent, relying on community water taps or illegally opened fire hydrants for water, using illegal "jumpers" to steal electricity from live lines, and buying cheap stolen goods. Even with these survival techniques, however, most poor people are not able to save enough to consider making a down payment on a house or taking out a house loan, a fact that many formal housing-finance institutions often fail to appreciate.

The costs of urban housing and services are influenced by a number of factors, including (1) land and land development, (2) basic urban services, (3) capital, (4) construction, and (5) operation and maintenance. The government, private entrepreneurs, and/or the homebuyers themselves may pay for these costs. The key to housing policy is how to allocate the incidence of such costs—whether the government will absorb most of these costs or pass them on to homeowners.

As far as land costs are concerned, many Asian governments use their ownership of land or the authority to regulate land use as key instruments in housing policy. They may use the proper valuation of public lands as an instrument for executing an effective housing program. In China, land has been the main asset of many local governments in supporting housing projects. By making land available to developers, local authorities have been able to lower the cost of housing and make it affordable even to poor urban residents. They have also influenced the location of housing projects by deciding where developers could build. Other countries that did not have China's state control over land have had more difficulties in using it as an input to housing. Some have relied on the principle of "eminent domain"—the right of the state to take over land for the public's welfare—but such efforts have often been hampered by legal tangles and bureaucratic delays, making the use of land more costly.

A major problem in many South and Southeast Asian cities is the taking over of land by squatters. Because most countries require the government to provide alternative housing and services for people who must be relocated from a project site, this adds significantly to the cost of land. In Indonesia, the Philippines, and Thailand, evicting squatters from project sites has at times turned into bloody confrontations with the police. It is not uncommon for large infrastructure projects to remain unfinished because of the refusal of squatters and slum dwellers to move out. In some countries, cultural features, such as communal ownership of land under *adat* laws, have also complicated efforts to effectively use land as an input to housing.

Using land on the urban periphery for housing may initially entail lower land acquisition costs. But in the long run, the costs of extending services to these sites may become much higher. This is especially the case when public services are designed as parts of large-scale metropolitan systems. Increasingly, some Asian governments are setting up small-scale autonomous service systems for self-contained projects. For instance, a suburban housing project might have its own water supply, drainage, sanitation, and waste disposal system (e.g., using groundwater sources, septic tanks, and composting facilities). Such smaller systems are proving to be easier to construct, operate, and maintain compared with massive metropolitan-wide systems, which require much capital, higher-level technologies, and large-scale management systems.

As far as the cost of capital is concerned, a country needs a well-developed banking and financial system to support a housing program. For most households, housing is the largest financial cost, and usually only a few are able to save enough to pay for the cost of housing outright. Unfortunately, in most Asian countries, the banking system is usually not geared for housing finance. The banking sector can make more money in high-risk ventures, and the returns from housing investments are often considered too low. Even where mortgages are available at very high interest rates, poor urban households—which usually do not have collateral or good credit track records—will be hard put to qualify for them.

In some countries, special finance institutions have been set up to support housing. The Provident Fund of Singapore, for example, was established to help finance projects of the Housing and Development Board. In the Philippines, pension funds such as the Government Service Insurance System and the Social Security System have been mandated to devote parts of their fund portfolios for housing. In general, however, financial institutions in South and Southeast Asian countries tend not to be very active in financing housing. The exceptions are in China, Hong Kong, and Singapore.

Since the launching of economic reforms in 1979, housing finance in China has changed dramatically—with the result that about 94 percent of all Chinese families now own some form of housing. The Chinese government started to reform housing finance in the mid-1980s by separating the operational and the business aspects of work units, which had been mainly responsible for housing workers. So-called three-track programs were launched to accommodate low-income people in low-rent apartments, provide middle-income people with cheaper housing, and sell luxury houses at market prices to those who could afford to buy them. The Provident Fund was also established, in which contributions from employees and their employers were accumulated for use as down payments or collateral for housing loans.

Most important of all, the People's Bank of China authorized domestic banks to extend housing loans to qualified households. In 2002, housing loans issued by domestic financial institutions in China totaled $80 billion. The People's Bank announced that the housing loans from domestic banks increased by 32.5 times compared with those made in 1997. Studies also showed that loans were being taken out not just to own a home for the first time—about 67 percent of buyers of public housing said they wanted to improve their units, and 48 percent among these were planning to swap houses or buy new and better homes (Xinhua News Agency, August 12, 2002).

Aside from housing banks and conventional commercial banks, there have been efforts in some countries to organize secondary financial institutions to support housing. For example, the Housing Finance and Mortgage Corporation in the Philippines was established to focus especially on housing. The Housing Finance Guaranty Corporation was also set up to help raise more capital for housing. There have been efforts to organize secondary mortgage markets to raise more money for housing. Most of these efforts, however, have not been very successful because of people's low savings rates and the lack of resources of housing finance institutions.

There has been considerable innovation in construction technology to reduce the cost of housing. Such innovations, however, have tended to follow Western efforts to achieve efficiency in housing construction by using such approaches as prefabrication, modular coordination, the use of heavy machinery, and high-technology materials. Many of these approaches are not relevant to conditions in many Asian mega-urban regions, where unemployment rates are very high; the importation of high-technology materials, machines, and processes is too expensive; people have traditional construction skills using local tools; and there is a shortage of capital to pay for imported technology and materials.

As far as the operation and maintenance of housing projects is concerned, many problems in South and Southeast Asian cities arise from the lack of professionals and trained personnel to manage real estate. Housing projects tend to be owned or managed by the government, and they therefore suffer from overly bureaucratic practices as well as graft and corruption. Where the proceeds from rents and sales of housing are low, maintenance tends to be neglected. Even cooperative management can be expensive, because it requires well-trained community organizers and facilitators. The hidden costs of housing management usually make it extremely difficult for public housing agencies to run projects well.

There have been efforts in many Asian countries to obtain international financing for housing. The World Bank, the Asian Development Bank, the U.S. Agency for International Development's Housing Guarantee Loan Program, and other bilateral and multilateral schemes have been tapped for housing. Although many of these programs provide housing finance at low and concessional rates, the fact that all financial transactions are in hard currencies eventually makes housing money quite expensive. The Asian financial crisis in 1997 showed that currency volatility could stop the flow of housing finance almost overnight. Even when governments are willing to guarantee external housing loans, some lenders are often unwilling to make such funds available because of the high risks involved.

Housing Design and Construction

In traditional Asian settlements, housing design and construction techniques were heavily influenced by the local climate and the culture. For instance, in the humid tropics, rural houses were built of timber, bamboo, grass or palm thatch, and other light materials. In more temperate zones, compacted earth, wattle and daub, timber, fired bricks, and roof tiles were extensively used. In the past, carpenters, artisans, and other craft practitioners built houses, sometimes under the supervision of master builders. People used simple tools, which usually belonged to each household. In most instances, the homeowners themselves took an active part in house construction, for they often had the knowledge and skills to do this. There were no formal architectural plans, no zoning codes, and no building standards to follow—people just knew how to build houses using techniques that had been passed on from generation to generation.

In the modern Asian city, however, most traditional design and construction approaches are no longer applicable. Building materials like timber, bamboo, and palm thatch have become too expensive. Light materials are a fire hazard. The cost of land makes small individual houses on separate plots uneconomical. Getting clean water, obtaining a source of energy for cooking, getting rid of human waste, and disposing of garbage become real problems. And yet traditional housing design, construction techniques, and daily routines that were suitable for rural areas and smaller settlements persist in some slum and squatter areas in a number of Asian mega-cities.

It is true that squatters and slum dwellers today use recycled lumber, rusty galvanized iron sheets, cardboard, plastic, and other discarded and recycled materials instead of timber, bamboo, and palm thatch. Yet in these poor urban communities, houses are still constructed without architectural plans, building a house is still pretty much a cooperative and communal occasion, and homeowners usually engage in self-building and mutual aid practices.

In the past, there was a big debate among housing advocates in Asia about the merits and demerits of multiple-unit housing (e.g., townhouses, multistory apartments). Some sociologists argued that most Asians, especially urban poor people, did not like to live in multistory apartments. Reasons advanced for this included the people's love for and attachment to the soil, their desire to plant vegetables or flowers in garden plots, the need to take care of animals (fattening pigs for the market, raising fighting cocks), or the fear that children would fall from high-rise buildings. More pragmatic reasons revolved around the idea of land as an item for speculation and the ownership of land as a traditional symbol of wealth.

Some people, however, argued that urban densities in Asian cities required multistory dwellings. Land costs, especially in central cities, required more intensive uses. Insisting on the single detached house-and-lot approach meant that most housing would have to be located on the urban periphery. If jobs continued to be located in the inner city and people lived in the suburbs, the transport costs and the costs of pollution would be exorbitant, not only for individual commuters but also for the environment and society as a whole. Even when housing was clustered around suburban development nodes where employment, housing, and public services were made available, single detached housing would still result in urban sprawl.

There is some evidence from research that it may not be so much the height of buildings as the lack of services and amenities that make people hesitant to live in multistory apartments. In Bangkok, Jakarta, Metro Manila, and Mumbai, water pressure is so low that apartment dwellers usually do not get enough water. Fetching water and bringing it up several stories is a difficult job. Electrical brownouts affect apartment dwellers more, especially if they have to rely on elevators, electric pumps for their water supply, refrigerators and freezers to keep their food fresh, and air conditioners to keep them comfortable.

Certainly, the experience in Hong Kong, Singapore, and the high-income enclaves of Kuala Lumpur, Metro Manila, and Mumbai, where people live in luxury condominiums that are adequately serviced, prove that the issue is not the physical height or form of buildings. The high price of condominiums, in fact, is driving home the point that physical property, not just land, can be an item for asset value accumulation and speculation. In due time, the myth that Asian cultural norms preclude living in multistory apartments might be dispelled, and housing design and construction might give more importance to multiple-unit dwellings.

Institutional Arrangements and Housing Management

The immediate reaction of many Asian governments to the need for better housing management was to create specialized agencies, such as the National Housing Authority of the Philippines or of Thailand, the Housing and Development Board in Singapore, and the National Urban Development Corporation (Perumnas) of Indonesia. This institutional approach was based on the idea that housing is not just a commodity that needs to be delivered by the government.

Yet because housing is also an economic investment that benefits owners, it was recognized that the role of government is not necessarily that of house builder and service provider. In recognition of the fact that people's lack of funds to invest in housing is the main problem, many governments set up financial institutions, such as the House Building Finance Corporation in Pakistan, the Korea Housing Bank and the National Housing Fund in South Korea, the Housing and Urban Development Corporation in India, and the Home Mortgage Finance Corporation in the Philippines.

In South Asian cities, there were institutional attempts to deliver houses directly to the people. For example, in Dhaka, the Housing and Settlement Directorate of the Public Works Ministry developed serviced lots for individual home construction. In Kolkata, the Kolkata Improvement Trust and the Housing Board build houses and allocate these to beneficiaries. The Delhi Development Authority constructs conventional housing for middle- and higher-income groups, along with attempting to upgrade slums.

Soon after the launching of economic reforms in China, the municipal governments of Beijing, Guangzhou, and Shanghai also attempted to deliver housing directly to the people. In Beijing, the Municipal Housing and Property Management Bureau, which was hierarchically organized at the district, county, and local housing office levels, had overall authority over housing. In particular, it carried out such functions as (1) raising the funds to support housing construction, operation, and maintenance; (2) building or contracting to build public housing; (3) allocating finished housing units to local residents; (4) setting standards for housing and rent levels; (5) collecting rents and other incomes; (6) maintaining and repairing the housing stock; (7) managing the registration records of all urban housing beneficiaries; (8) organizing and arranging housing swaps or exchanges; and (9) managing land leases and transfers.

With the rapid changes brought about by housing reforms in China, the Housing and Property Management Bureaus have lost most of their functions. Housing has been mainly privatized, and individual homeowners and housing finance institutions now make the key decisions related to housing. Still, local government units maintain institutions to help coordinate activities related to housing.

For example, in Shenzhen Municipality, the Shenzhen Housing Bureau is in charge of overseeing transactions involved in welfare housing and low-profit housing (but not commodity housing). The bureau directly manages the Center for Housing Sales, which coordinates programs of low-profit housing (for civil servants) and welfare housing (for low-income households). The center evaluates the qualifications of applicants for these two types of subsidized housing programs, prepares a list of qualified families, and signs housing contracts. It acts as a mediator between the government and potential buyers of housing units. It is the central agency in the city for the allocation of welfare housing to poor recipients. In effect, the center has taken over all the functions related to welfare housing and low-profit housing from individual work units, and it effectively coordinates all social housing activities in the city (Wong and Hui 2000).

In other Asian cities, the problems encountered by central government agencies directly charged with delivering public services such as housing have encouraged decentralization measures. In the field of housing and basic urban services provision, only a few local government units have assumed full responsibility, despite their having been given legislatively mandated powers. One reason might just be inertia—the central government has looked after housing problems in the past. Another reason for the reluctance of local governments to look after housing is the lack of financial resources and management capabilities.

A World Bank assessment of urban management capabilities in Thailand, for example, has come up with the conclusion that "very few Thai cities are bankable." The bank observed that most local government units were highly dependent on the central government. Local officials lacked ownership of investment decisions, and at the same time did not widely consult with the private sector and civil society leaders. As a result, the bank observed that grant financing from the central government translated into an inefficient allocation of resources and poor investments (World Bank 2002a).

A basic reason for the reluctance of local units to go into housing and basic urban services is their lack of financial capacity. In many South and Southeast Asian cities, about half or more of a local government's income comes from its share of centrally collected taxes and from grants-in-aid. Although most local government units have been given the power to borrow money, they are often reluctant to do so. This is especially true of borrowing from abroad because of fears that future economic downturns would adversely affect local finances.

Asian governments have pinned a great deal of hope on the "enabling approach" to providing housing and basic urban services. With the great bulk of housing being built by the popular sector, such enabling strategies that depend on people's efforts do seem to make a lot of sense. Experience has shown that urban poor people do have the human and organizational capabilities to provide housing and services themselves, as long as the government does not block their efforts with unnecessarily restrictive rules and regulations, inappropriate standards, and punitive measures.

The enabling approach to housing and basic services provision can be seen, essentially, as a transitional stage. Providing security of tenure to low-income people encourages housing consolidation, self-help, and mutual aid. Leaving people alone to deal with their own problems encourages the growth of NGOs and other elements of civil society that empower people to look after their own concerns. In the long run, however, many of the temporary and makeshift approaches encouraged by the enabling approach will have to be replaced with more stable and institutionalized mechanisms. It can be hoped that, by that time, people's income, education, and civic awareness will have matured enough to make possible more ordered housing management.

10

Toward Viable Mega-Urban
Regions in Asia

Mega-urban regions in Asia have been showing significant signs of viability in the past couple of decades. Tokyo which once had oxygen inhalation stations at street corners for people overcome by air pollution has evolved into one of the least polluted cities in the world. The high population growth rates of Seoul have been checked, and its primacy among urban settlements in South Korea has been reduced. Shanghai's role as the economic motive power of the Yangtze River Delta has been revitalized, and Beijing is planning a massive facelift as it gears up for the 2008 Olympics. Hong Kong continues to strive to maintain its role as the finance and service center of Southeast Asia and is strengthening its ties with Guangzhou, Shenzhen, Zhuhai, and other settlements in the Pearl River Delta. Even the noxious traffic fumes in Bangkok and Metro Manila are showing signs of improvement as light rail transit systems have started operating.

The review of developments in the largest mega-urban regions in Asia carried out for this book indicates the importance of adopting policies and programs that directly affect the size, shape, internal structure, functioning, and future growth patterns of these sprawling city-regions. It has tried to identify policies and programs that have worked and those that have not been too successful. Mainly, this review has suggested that innovations in planning and governance are needed to enable mega-urban regions to become more viable. In this final chapter, I analyze some of those policies and programs, derive some lessons learned from their application, and make a number of recommendations on how Asian mega-urban regions can fulfill their potentials as energizers of economic and social development.

In analyzing developments in Asia's mega-urban regions, it is important to keep in mind the differing levels of economic and social development found in each urban agglomeration. In general, policies and programs that may work in one type of city-region may not necessarily prove successful in others. Differing historical backgrounds, cultural values, and patterns of social organization exert important influences on the operation and impact of chosen policies and programs. Still, because big city urbanization is basically a matter of large numbers of people living together in a defined place at very high densities—a process that generates socioeconomic changes reflected in urbanism as a way of life—a number of policy measures might have general application among different mega-urban regions.

Policies and Programs That Work

This review of policies and programs used in Asian mega-urban regions to plan and govern city-regions has identified those that seem to be effective in enhancing development. Among the more successful interventions are (1) the development of polynucleated mega-urban regions; (2) the use of comprehensive and strategic regional planning approaches; (3) the formulation and adoption of integrated mass transit systems; (4) the use of comprehensive and integrated water, sewerage, and sanitation systems; (5) the adoption of housing and basic services programs, including inner-city renewal and redevelopment; (6) financing schemes for urban development; and (7) unified regional governance. In discussing these policy measures, I have contrasted them with others that have been tried but somehow did not manage to achieve the desired developmental effects.

The Development of Polynucleated Regions

One major conclusion in this study is that the most viable mega-urban settlements in Asia are those that have been planned and managed as polynucleated regions. Such city-regions have taken the form of central city cores surrounded by urban nodes (Greater Shanghai, Tokyo Metropolis). They also include a regional system of cities linked together economically and socially in a coherently integrated network (the Hong Kong–Guangzhou–Macao development triangle). In the former configuration, a number of compact and densely populated urban nodes that are more or less self-sufficient in employment, housing, and urban services surround the central city. In the latter, no one urban center dominates, but symbiotic relationships exist among a number of urban nodes to create a coherent city-region. In all cases, residents of the urban nodes lead the great part of their daily lives within their communities. However, when they need to go to the central core or to other nodes, they can avail themselves of efficient transport, including mass transit systems. The areas between the central city and the densely settled urban nodes are devoted to open space, parks, green areas, and peri-urban agriculture.

Allowing a monocentric settlement to grow in an uncontrolled and haphazard manner is a recipe for disaster. In a sprawling city-region, it becomes extremely expensive to extend basic urban services to all urban residents in the peri-urban area. Waterworks systems have to go farther to tap new sources for raw water supply. Getting rid of sewage and gray water becomes difficult. Appropriate sites for solid waste disposal will be hard to find. Moving people, goods, and services will be extremely costly as roads and other transport networks get stretched to the agglomeration's outer limits. Such a settlement may find it extremely difficult to feed itself as more and more agricultural land is converted to urban uses.

The Asian experience shows that urban agriculture can help to make city-regions viable for achieving economic production as well as ecological balance in well-planned polynucleated regions. Around Guangzhou, Hong Kong, Shenzhen, and other city-regions in the Pearl River Delta, designated green areas are not just devoted to parks and forested zones; they are also used to produce vegetables, fruits, dairy products, poultry, and other food items that can be easily transported to the cities. In Dhaka, Hong Kong, Jakarta, and Metro Manila, peri-urban agriculture has been enriched by the use of urban waste as fertilizer through composting and human waste treatment schemes. Fish have been successfully raised in wastewater ponds on the outskirts of Kolkata (formerly Calcutta) and Guangzhou, and sewage has been used to fertilize rice paddies in Hanoi and Karachi. In many Asian mega-urban regions, increasing environmental awareness is encouraging people to find ways and means of using urban waste as an input to agricultural production. There are even some experimental efforts to generate energy from solid waste, as in the methane-generation plants set up in the Payatas garbage dump in Metro Manila or the biogas digesters outside Chengdu in China's Sichuan province.

Although most Asian mega-urban regions still have low rates of private car ownership (Osaka, Seoul, and Tokyo are notable exceptions), private vehicle increase in others is a serious concern. The private car and individual motorized transport modes like motorcycles, scooters, motorbikes, and mopeds lead to the "hollowing out" of the city-region, as those who can afford these vehicles seek homes in suburban areas. This process has been evident in Greater Bangkok, Jakarta, and Metro Manila, where residents have abandoned downtown areas as car-led suburban growth has accelerated; it is not surprising that despite recent improvements, these three city-regions still have some of the worst traffic jams and environmental pollution levels in the Asian region. They also have significant proportions of their urban populations living in slum and squatter communities that are poorly served with basic services and transport modes.

As evidenced by the Asian situation, the emergence of a polynucleated mega-urban region may be the result of geographical, historical, technological, and ideological influences. The emergence of urban nodes in the Pearl River Delta adjacent to Hong Kong, for example, was influence by the island colony's limited and hilly territory, as well as by private investment decisions based on perceptions of trends in Chinese–British discussions about the former colony's fate. The establishment of satellite cities for industrial production around Shanghai was largely the product of Soviet-type urban and regional planning models. The polycentric structure of Osaka and Tokyo might be related to transportation technologies that allowed easier commuting between the city center and suburban communities, the high cost of inner-city land, and the structural shift from industry and manufacturing to more footloose knowledge-based enterprises and urban services.

In recent years, however, a number of Asian mega-urban regions have consciously planned the structure of their settlements by applying explicit policies and programs designed to achieve a polynucleated regional form. In China and Vietnam, positive measures linked to the state ownership of land and land use control measures adopted by the government have enabled many metropolitan authorities to establish satellite cities, high-technology zones, and special economic development zones that have served as viable peri-urban nodes.

The use of such measures warrants close scrutiny as these formerly socialist countries are being rapidly transformed into market-oriented economies. As the price of land becomes a major determinant of where development will occur, big cities in China and Vietnam are also starting to experience urban sprawl. Accelerating private car ownership in China and the increased use of motorcycles and scooters in Vietnam are creating traffic jams and serious levels of air pollution. The high demand for factory sites and housing estates on the urban periphery is encouraging the conversion of agricultural land to urban uses. Most serious of all, the rapid abandonment of state support for social safety nets and the frenzied drive to achieve higher profits are creating a widening gap between rich and poor residents. This social polarization is reflected in the emergence of urban enclaves composed of gated communities for the elite on the one hand and impoverished shantytowns for migrants and temporary residents on the other.

As Asian urban authorities have applied policies and programs for the planned development of polynucleated city-regions, they have also identified measures that do not work. For example, traditional efforts to limit urban sprawl by setting up greenbelts and prohibiting developments in areas designated as open space have, at times, had the opposite effect. Discouraged from investing near the city, investors simply "jump the greenbelt" and build their factories and housing estates in peri-urban areas. Land banking measures, whereby the government purchased raw land and reserved it for public uses, have also had the same unexpected effect because they limited the amount of land available in the market and led to rampant land speculation. The forced eviction of low-income squatters and slum dwellers from inner cities without providing them with adequately serviced alternative sites tended to cause land invasions in the urban periphery. In some cases, forced evictions have pushed urban poor people to dangerous areas like deep ravines, steep riverbanks, railroad rights-of-way, toxic garbage dumps, and frequently flooded tidal flats, wetlands, and marshes. The social costs of forced evictions, in real terms, have been very high—measured in lost lives, epidemics, riots, and other forms of social upheaval.

In Bangladesh, India, Indonesia, and Pakistan, the establishment of "new towns" and "satellite cities" on the urban periphery has generally failed to achieve the desired polynucleated regional form. The reasons for this failure have not been difficult to ascertain. First, the new towns and satellite cities were too small to be viable settlements. Residents did not have adequate employment opportunities, housing, urban services, shopping, and entertainment and cultural facilities. Second, many of the new towns and satellite cities were located too close to the central city. As a result, they were simply transformed into "bedroom communities" for people who commuted to the central city to work. Finally, the new towns and satellite cities were not integrated with their rural hinterlands. They became clumped enclaves of urban-oriented residents whose lives were directly linked to events in the central city.

A major challenge that needs to be addressed in relation to the emergence of polynucleated agglomerations in Asia is the search for coordinated management and governance mechanisms for these very large city-regions.

Conceptually, it is quite easy to understand that areawide urban functions like water and sanitation, transport, solid waste disposal, and controlling of environmental pollution have to be planned and managed in a comprehensive and strategic manner. The use of metropolitan and regional planning processes and metropolitan management structures in Bangkok, Metro Manila, Osaka, Seoul, and Tokyo is worth noting, although in some of these city-regions, considerable resistance has come from local government units that jealously guard their local autonomy. From a civic perspective, it can be appreciated that leaders who uphold the interests of all citizens in a city-region rather than those who pursue the particularistic demands of specific areas or groups should be selected.

However, this review of mega-urban development in Asian countries reveals that there are many impediments to areawide planning and governance. It has been extremely difficult for authorities in Asian mega-urban regions to find the proper balance between measures that efficiently and effectively manage urban services on one hand and processes that ensure popular participation, civic involvement, and active interest articulation and aggregation on the other.

From Master Plans to Strategic Plans

In general, the formulation, adoption, and implementation of some comprehensive strategic plans have helped to transform a number of Asian mega-urban regions into polynucleated settlements. These plans have indicated what types of productive developments would occur, where they would be located, how they would be financed, and the manner in which they would be operated, managed, serviced, and maintained. In a few cases, some of these polynucleated mega-urban regions have also been able to establish effective mechanisms energized by good leadership and guided by appropriate institutional mechanisms for good governance.

Most Asian mega-urban regions have abandoned top–down physical master plans and adopted comprehensive and strategic planning approaches. Many planners have realized that rigid formulaic approaches were grossly inadequate for dealing with the complex and rapidly changing situations in city-regions. The future development of urban settlements is not a question of providing physical infrastructure or formulating aesthetic urban designs. New urban plans need to focus on systems of human settlements rather than individual cities. They have to recognize the natural geographic features of urban and rural territories, the integrated nature of biore-gions, the economic forces that provide productive impetus, and the ethnic and cultural mixes that make for a cooperative and harmonious urban soci-ety. In turn, urban plans need to be based on a proper understanding of how socioeconomic relationships are manifested in geographic space.

Alongside the focus on territorial comprehensiveness in strategic plan-ning lies the need for social and economic inclusiveness. Citizens, includ-ing local leaders and organized groups, have to be actively involved and consulted in the planning process. The interests of political actors and stake-holders need to be carefully considered in the formulation and adoption of plans. Successful planning in Asian mega-urban regions should be consul-tative, open, participatory, and consensus based. To achieve this type of planning, planners have to develop proficiency in finding out what people really want (through data gathering and analysis). They have to learn to sort out and synthesize group interests, how to resolve conflicts, and how to bring about a workable consensus through democratic means.

There is a price to be paid, of course, for widespread participation in pub-lic decision making. The experience in Metro Manila—where civil society groups have been very active in interest articulation, aggregation, and mobi-lization—has shown that decision making can be seriously delayed, bitter confrontation can fragment the polity, and special interests can gain the up-per hand in public debates. It is only natural that those who actively partici-pate in public decision making will be stakeholders that seek to maximize their own special interests. Civil society activism cannot guarantee that the general welfare will always be upheld. As one observer of political processes in Metro Manila has asked, "How do you expect any group in a messy soci-ety to be untouched by the mess?" Some civil society leaders can be co-opted by power elites and even corrupted. They can be transformed from cause-oriented activists into traditional politicos as they get more deeply involved in public decision making. (Filipinos use the derogatory term *trapo*—liter-ally, "dirty rags"—to refer to people who "live off" politics.)

In some cities where urban authorities have continued to use traditional master plans, they have discovered that they sometimes achieved exactly the opposite of what they had intended. For example, in China, some planners have pursued what has been called the "rabbits don't eat grass near the bur-row" philosophy (Zhang Jinggan 1993, 12). They passed strict regulations conserving agricultural land and green open space. At the same time, they set up housing subdivisions, industrial estates, high-technology zones, and factory sites as far from the city center as possible. In their effort to limit the size of the city and preserve green space, they merely succeeded in expanding the territorial scope of the city and added to urban sprawl.

Because changing management and governance structures to transform fragmented local government units into coherent metropolitan or regional bodies can be difficult, it may be possible to start the process by first introducing comprehensive strategic planning. In this approach, provincial or state-level authorities may initiate the formulation of comprehensive strategic plans that link together the central city with other settlements within the region. In the case of the planning of the Hong Kong–Pearl River Delta region, for example, the proponents of areawide comprehensive planning started with analytical studies and surveys that identified problems and shortcomings in the existing situation. On the basis of the research findings, the Hong Kong 2022 Foundation initiated the process that came up with a proposal for a comprehensive strategic plan. The comprehensive plan focused on the interdependence of economic and social activities carried out in all the various settlements in the region. It illustrated the close linkages among the various sectoral areas and functional services that were being provided. From the substantive research findings, the planning group advocated the adoption of governance mechanisms for achieving coordinated action in the whole city-region (Enright et al. 2003).

One major advantage of comprehensive regional plans is that they make it possible to identify urban services that are naturally regionwide, as well as those that are best carried out at the local or community level. On the basis of the experiences of the Asian mega-urban regions considered in this study, it is apparent that services like water and sewerage, drainage and flood control, transportation, health and sanitation, electricity, solid waste collection and disposal, and pollution control are best planned on an areawide and regional scale.

Conversely, street cleaning and maintenance, garbage collection, community beautification, and running preschool programs, kindergartens, and well-baby clinics are mainly local functions. Very large urban settlements need a lot of clean water, and a reliable water system requires a large enough watershed area to ensure an adequate supply from surface water sources, aquifers, and recharge areas. This vast territorial expanse usually includes areas lying outside the city-region's political boundaries. Similarly, drainage and flood control plans are based more on natural topographical features, soil types, natural bodies of water like streams and rivers, wetlands and marshy areas than on formal municipal or metropolitan boundaries.

Planning for these water-related services, therefore, requires areawide approaches that cover wide areas and transcend artificial political or administrative jurisdictions.

Detailed planning for urban services, of course, makes it possible to sort out specific activities in the delivery of services that can be carried out at different levels. For example, in many Asian mega-urban regions, solid waste is collected at the local level and brought to municipal facilities for sorting and separation at the municipal level. There are some communities where local centers operated by nongovernmental organizations recover useful items like plastics, aluminum and tin cans, glass, and metals and then sell them to recyclers. There are also communities where kitchen or wet garbage is placed in backyard or neighborhood composting facilities and later used as fertilizer. The large-scale sorting and disposal of solid waste, however, may best be handled at the regional level through the use of sanitary landfills or incineration plants. This latter approach to solid waste disposal requires planning at the regional level, because the location of landfills and incinerators is usually resisted by local units because of the smell, noxious gases, health hazards, and noise of the vehicles bringing the garbage to the facility (Maclaren 2004).

Although most urban authorities in Asia now appreciate the importance of comprehensive, strategic, and areawide planning, the effectiveness of this approach is sometimes hampered by the special interests of local leaders and interest groups. In the light of the all-but-inevitable expansion of mega-urban regions in Asia, more effective planning mechanisms are obviously needed to bring about cooperation and coordination among various levels of government. An inability to bring about such cooperative megalopolis-level actions will create serious problems.

In the Pearl River Delta region of China, for example, the construction of international airports in Guangzhou, Hong Kong, Shenzhen, Zhongshan, and Zhuhai has already resulted in duplication and costly underutilization of these grossly expensive facilities. In Metro Manila, the not-in-my-backyard attitudes of local government units that have refused to accept the planned location of sanitary landfills within their territories have created health and environmental hazards arising from the piling up of stinking garbage on the city streets. The inability to control destructive floods in the Dhaka region is partly due to lack of agreement on a megalopolis-wide emergency preparedness plan acceptable to all local government units and socioeconomic sectors. All these problems are clear indicators of the need for cooperative action through planning at the mega-urban level.

The Politics of Planning

In some Asian mega-urban regions, planning is seen as a technical, value-neutral, and "rational" process carried out by professionally trained and technically qualified experts capable of determining what people want and indicating the various ways and means of satisfying those wants. There is a belief that once political leaders set development goals, the planning process can start in a purely technical manner. Population projection methods can be used to determine the size of the city at a future point in time. The needs of people in terms of living space per capita, liters of potable water needed, number of persons per hospital bed required, teacher/student ratios, amount of solid waste to be disposed of, and so on, can be estimated. Requirements for infrastructure, basic services, housing, and the like can be calculated. An urban and regional plan can then be formulated, and its implementation can be translated in terms of the usual planning instruments—zoning codes, building codes, subdivision regulations, transportation networks, water and sewerage systems, resource requirements, taxation regimes, land use plans, and all the traditional tools used by planners in their profession. If possible, a self-executing plan may be developed, strategically adjusting plan components in response to changing circumstances in both the planning-implementation-monitoring-evaluation-feedback loops and the economic and social situation of the mega-urban region.

This technocratic approach to planning, however, has not worked too well in most Asian mega-urban regions. The goals of political leaders are not always explicitly stated, and they are rarely quantifiable. As politically derived decisions, they are subject to significant changes because of accommodation, bargaining, trade-offs, and compromise. The participation of many stakeholders pursuing individual interests causes sudden shifts in objectives and priorities. Often, the wishes of large groups of unorganized citizens, especially urban poor people, are poorly articulated. Finally, planning methods are often imprecise, because many social and economic data on which they are based are often extremely difficult to quantify.

The rationality of the planning process is sometimes hailed, even when government units fail to officially approve the plan and give it statutory legitimacy. It is believed that a plan that is not officially approved can still guide mega-urban region development because of the "authority of ideas" embedded in the plan. The experience in Asia shows, however, that this approach rarely works. It is often difficult enough to get local governments, private entrepreneurs, professional groups, and civil society advocates to arrive at a consensus on specific policy issues when attempting to implement formally approved master plans. The task becomes doubly harder when the plans serve mainly as guides and conceptual approaches to solving specific problems.

One of the most common complaints of planners in the Asian mega-urban regions covered in this book is "there is too much politics" in city or metropolitan affairs. Many planners argue that with local officials, party leaders, community groups, and even civil society activists pushing only their own individual interests, urban governance loses a larger vision that reflects policies resulting in the common good. Those who advocate areawide planning and governance, therefore, argue that what is needed is more participation that focuses on the common welfare.

What the real situation in the mega-urban regions of Asia indicates, however, is that, indeed, the planning process is inextricably intertwined with the political process. This is especially true in cases of extreme local government fragmentation and central government agency competition and rivalry, which are the norm in most Asian countries. Specific interest groups and power blocs often dictate the developmental options embodied in the plan. Land use provisions often depend on the location of economic interests of powerful elites, land ownership, and political bailiwicks. Planners who believe that they can independently determine what economic sectors are to be encouraged in the plan, where developmental activities are to be sited, what types of infrastructure services should be built, and which geographic areas will benefit are setting themselves up for frustration and failure. These issues are essentially political ones, and they will be determined by the interplay of political forces.

The politics of planning in Asian mega-urban regions is made a great deal more complicated by the current emphasis on the decentralization of authority to local government units. Though decentralization and local autonomy programs have helped to make people more aware of public issues (and encouraged them to participate more actively in local affairs), such participation has tended to be mainly confined to purely local issues directly relevant to people's daily lives. People are able to deal with such local issues effectively, especially when they are encouraged and mobilized by civil society groups and they have the resources to meet local costs.

However, when the issues become complex and involve problems that slip over normal municipal boundaries, decentralization programs encounter severe difficulties. Though one can idealistically hope that local government officials and citizens will be able to rise above their particularistic interests and commit themselves to policies seeking the common good, it is more common for them to resist broad-gauged actions. One of the most common objections to the amalgamation of local government units to form metropolitan or regional governments, for example, is the loss of local identity.

Another serious problem of decentralization schemes has been the devolution of authority and responsibility to small local government units under a system of grassroots democracy designed to bring the administrative units as close to the people as possible. In Mumbai, for example, the Government of Maharashtra had implemented the Seventy-Fourth Amendment to the Indian Constitution by decentralizing political authority to elected ward committees and delegating administrative authority to appointed "beat officers" designated as "nodal officers for citizens' grievance redressal" at the beat level. An amendment to the Mumbai Municipal Corporation Act of 1888 gave statutory status to the ward committee. The revised act empowered ward committees to grant administrative and financial approval to public works projects amounting up to Rs 500,000. The beat officers could also provide speedy redressal to citizen grievances related to municipal services like water, drainage, sanitation, and storm water disposal. Mumbai (formerly Bombay) even approved a "Citizens' Charter" detailing the types of decisions that could be made by local officials and the processes for redressing grievances.

This new system in Mumbai has supposedly simplified procedures, delicensed a number of activities, and done away with cumbersome clearances that used to be controlled by municipal departments. However, it has not reduced the tendency to resort to local politics—it actually increased local political interference in some instances.

Another example of how decentralization to the smallest local units can create problems is the implementation of the Local Government Code of 1991 in the Philippines. The code set up *barangay* councils in the lowest tier of local governments in the country. The implementing details for the law promulgated by the Department of the Interior and Local Government specified the powers of councils and the *barangay* heads. For example, although the code did not specifically mention that the *barangay* government had the power to require permits for setting up businesses and other enterprises in the community, the implementing details specified that if technical issues were raised in such matters, the decision should be always done "in favor of the individual *barangay.*" The implementing details even gave *barangay* councils the authority to levy a fine of up to 1,000 pesos for any person or entity that operates a local enterprise without a permit. The result of this provision has been widespread graft and corruption among *barangay* councils in various parts of the country. Before, bribes for the issuance of permits were only demanded by municipal councils and mayors, but the decentralization of powers to local *barangay*s had multiplied the practice significantly.

A major problem with the decentralization schemes typified by wards and beats in Mumbai and *barangay* councils in Metro Manila is the lack of technical capabilities in planning and governance of officials at the lowest local government levels. In Mumbai, for example, a typical ward would occupy a territory of two square kilometers with a population of about 20,000 people; in Metro Manila, by contrast, a *barangay* would have 100 to 500 families. Such small units do not have the resources to support themselves adequately with much-needed services.

In fact, as actually organized, the main function of the ward committees and beat officers in Mumbai seems to have been to provide an easier way of raising complaints to metropolitan government officials. A telephone-based complaint registration system, whereby any local citizen could complain to Mumbai officials simply by dialing 1916, was instituted in December 2000, and a "One Window System" for demanding local services was set up in August 2001. The decentralization efforts, therefore, seem to have been primarily designed to give ordinary citizens a chance to bring problems to the attention of the Mumbai Municipal Government, not to empower the local wards to undertake planning to solve the problems themselves. In Metro Manila, the *barangay* councils served mainly as local units of political parties and became energized mainly during election time.

To enable urban authorities to effectively solve their many problems in the future, decentralization schemes should devolve authority to large metropolitan or mega-urban structures that have the resources and capabilities to actually carry out their responsibilities. For example, the decision of the Chinese government to decentralize more authority to the municipal or provincial governments of Beijing, Guangzhou, and Shanghai has achieved positive results. Municipalities and cities in China now formulate and adopt their own development plans. Armed with adequate powers, city officials have been able to respond to investment proposals very quickly, a fact that has encouraged more foreign direct investment.

In this regard, one of the major challenges to urban governance is how to "scale up" local efforts to provide reliable services and infrastructure not just to small localities but also to the whole urban area. In most developing-country cities, poor communities are aware of their specific problems (e.g., a lack of water, crime, the danger of fires) but they are usually not too concerned about the problems of the larger city or metropolitan area. They may be able to raise enough financial resources to deal with their local problems but are unable or unwilling to contribute to citywide efforts. Similarly, when they bring their problems to city or metropolitan authorities, they often find these officials uninterested and unsympathetic to their plight.

The very formal structures and processes for urban development might even be used to thwart poor residents' own efforts to deal with their problems. City authorities, for example, might refuse to prepare plans for slum areas and uncontrolled settlements because to do so might be misconstrued as legitimizing the illegal tenure of the squatters. There may also be official fears that expanding services to help poor residents will just encourage potential migrants to move to the city. The private sector, which usually has the capability to invest in urban services, is sometimes discouraged from doing so by governmental disincentives. In some countries, nongovernmental organizations (NGOs) and people's organizations engage in scaling up project efforts, but they also usually suffer from inadequate financial resources, untrained leadership, and inadequate organizational capacities to scale up local efforts to higher levels (Van Horen 2004).

Getting Around in Polynucleated Regions

It is interesting that despite their huge size and high population densities, some Asian mega-urban regions are somehow succeeding in achieving better mobility through the use of various transport modes. Using road networks and the main spurs of heavy rail systems as developmental axes, Asian urban authorities have created polynucleated systems of settlements. A significant portion of daily travels in Osaka, Seoul, and Tokyo is taken on mass transport modes. In Bangkok and Hong Kong, there are future plans to expand mass transit systems to nodes on the metropolitan periphery. In the meantime, in the Hong Kong system, concentrations of trade, commerce, shopping, entertainment, and residences have been planned and established around transit stations to enhance mobility.

Policy measures to improve mobility in Asian mega-urban regions and to limit the environmental impact of vehicles mainly focus on four types of interventions. First, almost all cities with populations of 10 million or more have built mass transit systems, and those that already have such systems are improving and expanding them. The systems are heavy rail commuter systems, such as those in Osaka, Seoul and Tokyo, or light rail rapid transit systems, such as those recently built in Bangkok and Metro Manila. These systems are mostly publicly owned and operated, but the Asian experience seems to suggest that private enterprise could also run these systems efficiently and profitably.

Second, there are serious efforts to limit private automobile ownership as well as the operation of buses, trucks, trade goods vehicles, motorcycles, scooters, and mopeds in some Asian mega-urban regions. Although not all these efforts are achieving significant success, many citizens and urban authorities are starting to recognize the health and other hazards of the pollution caused by these transport modes. Metro Manila has limited the number of smoke-belching vehicles on major thoroughfares. Beijing controls the number of motorcycles and scooters by strict licensing quotas. Singapore has made the ownership of private cars prohibitively expensive by subjecting it to public bidding. In South Asian cities, the use of leaded gasoline has been banned, and there have been efforts to reduce the number of two- and three-wheeled vehicles, encourage the use of less polluting oil additives, and promote the conversion of two-stroke engines to less polluting four-stroke engines.

Environmental pollution and its attendant health dangers have been influencing authorities in Asian cities to limit the use of the private car and other vehicles using fossil fuels. Some of the measures used to do this are (1) imposing licenses and fees for access to inner cities, (2) charging tolls for use of limited access highways, (3) requiring tests for emissions and charging fees for these tests, (4) prohibiting the use of fuel-guzzling and smoke-belching vehicles, and (5) limiting the number of vehicles allowed on the streets by using color-coding systems. Alongside efforts to limit car use, some urban authorities have encouraged the use of alternative transport modes.

Third, traffic demand management is achieving considerable success in some Asian mega-urban regions in dealing with urban congestion, environmental degradation, high accident rates, and vehicle-caused environmental pollution. Traffic demand management involves the use of economic instruments like road pricing, licensing, and the imposition of user charges for roads and public services. It includes regulatory measures, such as traffic management, and the imposition of physical constraints, such as closing certain streets and designating them as pedestrian-only pathways. It may also take the form of intelligent transport systems that electronically provide real-time information to drivers on traffic bottlenecks, the least congested roads, and the best routes for getting to their destinations. The residents of many Asian mega-urban regions are learning to accept these policy measures as they realize the high social and economic costs of traffic-induced pollution.

Fourth, planning instruments are being used in Asian cities to encourage people to live as close as possible to their places of employment, leisure, entertainment, and sites for public services. In this regard, the planned development of self-contained urban nodes on the urban periphery is helping to ease commuting. Building homes and apartments close to workplaces facilitates walking or bicycling to work. Where commuting to the inner city still becomes necessary, the location of residences close to mass transit stations helps to facilitate mobility. In some cities, networked communities are being planned where people can work from their homes.

In general, the main hope for improving mobility and reducing pollution in Asian mega-urban regions rests on planned communities where people do not have to go too far from their homes to work, shop, avail themselves of public services, or be entertained. In Asia, as in North America and Europe, an increasing awareness of the principles of the "new urbanism" is influencing the planning of urban communities. Compact settlements where people have ready access to what they need are being established. The human scale of such communities makes interpersonal communication and active participation in public decision making possible. The proximity of workplace to residence, of course, eases the travel burden.

Alongside the establishment of compact communities runs the use of comprehensive and functionally integrated transport systems that assign specific roles for individual transport modes. In such an integrated system, individuals walk or ride bicycles from their residences to destinations that take less than half an hour to negotiate. For longer distances, they may take small two- or three-wheeled vehicles to a point where they can take a public bus. For other destinations, the bus may take the rider to a mass rapid transit station for a fast, smooth, and affordable trip. By carefully planning the physical linkages among these transport modes, working out coordinated trip schedules and vehicular time tables on the basis of demand, designing stations and terminals for quick transfers, and charging appropriately affordable fares, areawide transport systems in the future may vastly improve mobility and reduce environmental damage.

As the transport situations of most Asian mega-urban regions show signs of improving, it is pertinent to ask if recent scientific breakthroughs related to the invention of the electric car, the hybrid car, and the hydrogen-fueled car will help to reduce pollution in Asian cities. Discussions with transport planners in Asian cities raise some doubts that these inventions will help in making mega-urban regions viable, even if the high prices of these cars, currently beyond the capacity to pay of most people, can be lowered. This is because of the fact that although these individual cars will be less polluting, they will still require the network of highways and streets, parking facilities, traffic management, and road signs that take up a great deal of space in urban areas. They will also continue to encourage automobile-dependent developments such as suburban housing, strip developments, shopping malls, and perhaps even edge cities—developments that North American experience has shown to be unsustainable.

Future hopes for improving mobility and reducing pollution in very large city-regions are pinned on four technological areas: (1) vehicles that do not rely on fossil fuels, (2) the use of alternative fuels, (3) innovative mass transit systems, and (4) information technologies that make it possible to transport ideas rather than people and physical objects. Though scientific breakthroughs in these fields promise to improve mobility in mega-urban regions, they also bring with them a host of technical and managerial problems.

Electric cars, hybrid cars, and hydrogen-fuel-cell cars have the great merit of not contributing to environmental pollution. However, old Asian cities have narrow lanes and street networks designed more for walking and bicycling than driving, and they are not suitable for cars. Even nonpolluting cars require the network of roads, bridges, tunnels, flyovers, highways, and expressways that eat up a lot of land and make cities so unsightly. Cars demand parking spaces, traffic control devices, traffic enforcers, traffic signs, drivers' education, traffic regulations, insurance schemes, and other elements of transport management. The widespread use of private cars contributes to suburbanization, strip malls, and traffic congestion that waste time and contribute to psychological stress. And, of course, the availability of cars will most likely deter people from walking, bicycling, or taking public transit.

The increasing use of new less polluting fuels—such as ethanol from sugarcane, cereals, and other products, methane from animal waste and other biomass sources, natural gas, or hydrogen fuel cells—has the same disadvantages of electric and other less polluting vehicles. They suffer from the same problem that vehicles driven by these alternative fuels will still require expensive networks of roads and highways. They will not solve the problems of traffic congestion, wasted time on the highways, high rates of motor vehicle accidents, spaghetti overpasses, cloverleaves, and uncontrolled suburbanization. Though new cars and new fuels will greatly reduce environmental pollution in very large cities, they will not significantly change the physical configuration of mega-urban regions for the better.

It is in the field of mass transit that the new technological innovations hold a great deal more hope for better managing mobility and pollution reduction in mega-urban regions. The recently introduced locomotives powered by turbine engines promise to make rapid transit more efficient. Faster magnetic levitation trains, if technical glitches can be solved, may prove their worth in intercity transport, whereas light rail elevated trains are good for intracity systems. In some cities, less expensive systems such as bus rapid transit on dedicated bus tracks (Adelaide, Curitiba, Ottawa) have been efficiently used, and these are now being set up in Beijing, Metro Manila, and New Delhi. Even simple dedicated lanes in which public buses can travel faster have proved their worth in some cities. These mass transit innovations will certainly be more influential in changing the shape, scope, and sustainability of mega-urban regions compared with those focused on less polluting cars using nonfossil fuels.

Some planning experts are proposing that the most far-reaching interventions that will affect the development of future mega-urban regions are those that will make it possible to move ideas and images rather than people and physical goods. The computer and the Internet have already significantly changed human behavior by allowing people to work where they are instead of being placed in fixed offices, factories, or other work sites. More advances in the field of nanotechnology will probably make machines and appliances in the home and office more efficient. Robots or robotized equipment will do most precise and repetitive work. People will communicate with each other instantaneously in real time. In the future, therefore, the shape of "urban areas" may not be determined by physical objects like roads, bridges, and vehicles but by the abstract flows of data in information and communication highways.

At this time, however, it is still too early to tell if the advent of the virtual city will physically alter the size, scope, and shape of the Asian mega-urban region. Initial indications suggest, however, that people engaged in information technology and e-business are not really as footloose and space-independent as originally expected. In the "smart city" enclaves of Hong Kong, Shanghai's Pudong, Shenzhen, and Tsukuba City, urban planners are finding that people engaged in high-technology activities still prefer to live and work in communities where they can transact business face-to-face, press the flesh, network, and socialize. Communities inhabited by information specialists in Bangalore, Beijing's Haidian High-Tech Zone, and Metro Manila's mini-version of Silicon Valley, feature high-class hotels and luxury homes, country clubs, swanky restaurants, pubs, excellent schools, golf courses, tennis courts, and other centers for human interactions. These features suggest that the information revolution may not significantly contribute to uncontrolled urban sprawl where people will be working from isolated areas communing only with their notebook computers. In the era of the new urbanism, they may still yearn for the social comfort of community life and continue to live in urban nodes.

Water for Thirsty Cities

With some notable exceptions, many Asian mega-urban regions suffer from water, sanitation, and sewerage problems. These include inadequate water supply, poor drainage, frequent floods, the contamination of surface water and groundwater sources, high levels of unaccounted-for water, inappropriate water pricing, and an inequitable distribution of water among social groups and classes. These water-related problems are likely to get worse in the future, especially in South and Southeast Asian cities. However, the adoption of a number of positive policy instruments and the allocation of more resources to the water sector promise significant future improvements.

In general, Asian mega-urban region authorities can choose between two water policy approaches. In high-income, technologically advanced city-regions such as Hong Kong, Osaka, Seoul, and Tokyo, authorities are already committed to using technological and engineering-oriented systems based on the large-scale production and distribution of piped water to individual households and industrial, manufacturing, commercial, and institutional entities. These mega-urban regions have to go farther and farther from the urban core to tap additional sources of water. They invest huge sums of money to set up systems for impounding, purifying, storing, distributing, and ensuring water quality for their clients.

The viability of such high-technology approaches to water provision, however, depends on the realization that sources of raw water are not limitless. Systems have to be instituted to reduce water use, price water appropriately, monitor actual consumption by metering, reduce levels of unaccounted-for water, and recycle water. It is also important for cities using high-technology systems to integrate water provision with sewerage and sanitation, link drainage and storm water runoffs with sewer systems, preserve wetlands and water recharge areas, and understand the effects and impact of water extraction and disposal on the environment.

As centralized municipal water systems reach gargantuan scales in the future, it is likely that diseconomies of scale will hamper their effectiveness. In this regard, the planned development of polynucleated mega-urban regions will most likely encourage the decentralization of water systems. Thus, a centralized municipal system might continue to be used for the densely inhabited core city area and trunk lines might be extended to smaller networks that are integrated with the main waterworks systems. By using this approach, individual water systems might become more manageable. Their negative impacts on the physical environment might also be reduced.

In less technologically advanced mega-urban regions like Delhi, Dhaka, Karachi, Kolkata, and Mumbai, past efforts to rely on technology-based engineering systems for water provision have proven severely inadequate. In these mega-urban regions, authorities may consider policies that would be less centralized and rely more on a variety of options, such as district-level or community-based water systems. People served by municipal systems will have to be educated and trained in water use reduction, water reuse, recycling, and conservation. New devices—such as waterless composting toilets, self-shutting faucets, and spray-type shower heads—need to be introduced and popularized. More efforts also need to be made in the area of community organization, stressing the real economic value of water, the need to pay appropriate water fees, ways and means of reducing water wastage, and how to protect water sources against contamination and pollution.

It is in mega-urban regions that have a choice between high-technology engineering systems and independent decentralized systems that water policies will probably generate a great deal of debate. In mega-urban regions like Bangkok, Beijing, Guangzhou, and Shanghai, some degree of success has been achieved in running municipal water systems. However, water demand in these city-regions has been increasing rapidly. The capacity of municipal water systems to supply more potable water is being rapidly eroded. In these middle-income mega-urban regions, it may be possible to adopt mixed water provision strategies that would operate and maintain centralized municipal systems for the built-up inner city and more decentralized systems on the periphery. When new development enclaves, such as housing subdivisions, suburban shopping complexes, and high-technology industrial sites are constructed on the metropolitan periphery, setting up autonomous water supply, sanitation, and sewerage systems that will not overburden the already stretched capacities of centralized municipal systems might be a more efficient and environmentally appropriate approach. This approach, of course, will depend on the scale of the system. It can be tried in cases where economies of scale and agglomeration are possible and where management and financial resources are available.

This mixed water provision approach may also make sense in the case of polynucleated city-regions. For each urban node in the regional system, an independent water provision, sewerage and sanitation, drainage, flood control, and water recharge system can be set up. Each independent system will not be directly linked to the central municipal system, unless there are specific topographic, hydrological, and seismological factors that make this linkage necessary. The central municipal system and independent peripheral node systems will be separately managed, but all the managers will be made cognizant of the environmental and other factors that holistically affect their individual jurisdictions.

A potentially important factor in the establishment of smaller and more autonomous water systems is the possible use of desalination plants. Although desalination has been tremendously expensive in the past, recent technological breakthroughs based on pushing salt water at high pressure through plastic membranes that filter out and remove salt molecules are making it more cost-competitive. Desalination has the advantage of having ample water supply, because almost 97 percent of water on earth is in the oceans. In California, where desalination may supply from 10 to 20 percent of water needs within the next two decades, it is now possible to produce an acre-foot of fresh water (about 326,000 gallons) for about $800, plus another $100 per acre-foot for new pipes and pumps. This is more costly than buying fresh water (about $250 per acre-foot), but desalination will not require dams, reservoirs, wells, and recycling plants that account for a great deal of the costs of municipal water systems (Booth 2003, A3). In the Middle East, quite a number of urban areas are already using desalination plants. Even in a less wealthy Asian city like Metro Manila, a desalination plant had been used to augment the metropolitan water supply during the water crisis in January 2004 (Ibon Foundation 2004).

An interesting issue facing mega-urban regions in the future is the privatization of water systems. The experience with privatization in Metro Manila and Jakarta to date does not make for too much optimism about this approach. In both these city-regions, the immediate effects of privatization have been rapid increases in water charges and little significant improvement in water services. In Metro Manila, in fact, one of the private concessionaires has decided to withdraw from the contract because of the refusal of the government to allow it to increase water rates to help it compensate for foreign exchange losses arising from the devaluation of the peso. Privatization has also improved water services to zones inhabited by wealthy families, but water provision in low-income areas has not improved at all.

Perhaps, in the future, water authorities may find it more useful to privatize specific functions (e.g., metering and collecting water fees) rather than the whole system. It may also be easier for private companies to take over smaller decentralized water systems for urban centers on the mega-urban region periphery rather than comprehensive municipal systems that require huge capital investments and a bureaucratic machinery.

A Home of One's Own

Access to shelter and basic urban services in Asian mega-urban regions depends very much on their stages of development. In city-regions like Osaka, Seoul, and Tokyo, the government and the private sector offer adequate (albeit expensive) housing with individual water, electricity, gas, and other connections. Residents of big cities in China and Vietnam have bought their houses in the open market with various types of subsidies. It is in cities in South and Southeast Asia that access to shelter and basic urban services on the part of urban poor people still remains a serious problem. In cities where squatters and slum dwellers make up from a fifth to more than half of households, affordable shelter and services like water, sanitation, electricity, and solid waste collection and disposal continue to be a problem, because these items are way beyond the capacity to pay of poor residents.

In mega-urban regions where space is at a premium (Beijing, Guangzhou, Hong Kong, Osaka, Seoul, Shanghai, Singapore, Tokyo), smaller dwelling units in high-rise structures have been constructed to meet housing demand. The average Hong Kong resident lives on 20 square meters of floor space, which is about one-fourth of the space used by the average urban American. If future trends in some Asian cities will follow the Hong Kong example, the predominant housing forms will be high-rise buildings located in densely populated urban nodes. This may not necessarily be bad, because cities like Hong Kong, Osaka, Singapore, and Tokyo, along with other vertically oriented cities, have achieved considerable savings in building materials and amount of energy used. Comparative studies have shown that per capita building materials used per square meter in high-rise construction in Hong Kong are less than half of those used in single-family dwellings in North American cities. Per capita water use in Hong Kong is also about half of that in American cities. Energy use is also only about 15 percent in Hong Kong, compared with comparable buildings in North American cities (Wong 1996, 121).

In South and Southeast Asian mega-urban regions with sizable segments of the population lacking adequate shelter and basic urban services, the challenge in the immediate future is how to "scale up" self-help housing programs. Housing authorities are hoping that mutual aid and community-based efforts can be effectively linked to formal credit schemes and other public and private institutional approaches. Initiatives like the Kampung Improvement Program in Jakarta and the Community Mortgage Program in Metro Manila indicate that poor residents can be organized and mobilized to combine self-help efforts with public assistance to gain access to shelter and basic urban services. Such initiatives become even more successful when supported by civil society groups like NGOs and community-based organizations (CBOs) that provide training, community organization, and program management support.

The possibility of linking community-based efforts to municipal services has been shown in the Orangi Pilot Project in Karachi. In Orangi, the largest *katchi abadi* (informal settlement) in the city, the 1.8 million inhabitants have constructed 405 secondary sewer lines in 5,987 lanes serving 90,596 houses. The people had invested Rs 78.79 million in these projects. It has been estimated that if these low-cost sewer lines had been built by the government, they would have cost more than six times this amount (Hasan 2002).

When the Karachi municipal government obtained a loan from the Asian Development Bank to improve the sewerage system for the city, the Orangi project officials suggested that the low-cost sanitation facilities they had already constructed should be "upscaled" to effectively link these to the municipal system. Instead of constructing a separate high-technology sewerage system as originally proposed by engineers, the government and the Asian Development Bank agreed to the scaling up approach. A total of 120,983 running feet of sewer lines were constructed, to which over 23,000 houses in 1,093 lanes were connected. The revised project did not only cost much less than the original high-technology one but also did not waste the considerable investment of the poor people in their own self-built sewer system (Hasan 2002).

The main issue in housing in Asia's mega-urban regions is affordability, which is best measured as the ratio of the price of an average home to years of annual household income. It is interesting to note that this ratio is lowest in cities like Jakarta, where the average home costs only 2 years of annual income; in Metro Manila, 7.6 years; and in Bangkok, 10 years. The ratio of house price to years of annual household income in Chinese cities is also relatively low, although it is rising rapidly; in Shanghai, 21 years; in Beijing, 22 years. The most serious affordability problems are in South Asian cities, where, for example, the ratio in Karachi is 52 years, in Dhaka is 60 years, and in Mumbai is 109 years. In these mega-urban regions, the price of housing has risen way beyond the capacity to pay of the average citizen, and many poor households do not have any choice except to live in uncontrolled settlements (*Asiaweek* 2000).

Going Back Downtown

As Asian urban authorities in low-income cities have attempted to plan and develop polynucleated mega-urban regions, they have become more aware of the deterioration of the inner city. In many city-regions, the decay of downtown areas has driven people and businesses out, sharply reducing tax revenues. With a reduction of city income, city governments have been less able to effectively solve their problems. The inability to provide services and maintain basic infrastructure push more people away, resulting in a negative downward spiral leading to more serious deterioration.

The obvious solution to inner-city deterioration is encouraging more investment in the central city. This is akin to what Zhang called the strategy of "clenching the fist tightly" in his proposal to solve inner-city problems in Beijing. To encourage the redevelopment of China's capital, Zhang recommended concentrating investments in the inner city and in only one or two satellite towns instead of pursuing the strategy of "blossoming everywhere" that creates urban sprawl. As Zhang noted, "Major construction of the city as a whole cannot be over scattered and much can be accomplished only when there is high concentration of investments" (Zhang Jinggan 1993, 12).

The four main forces responsible for the deterioration of inner cities are well known. First, the high cost of land and of building anything in the urban core encourages investors to move their activities to suburban areas. Second, this same high cost of land fosters investments in offices, commercial centers, entertainment facilities, and institutional structures rather than residences, actions that lead to the depopulation of the inner city. This out-migration is greatly facilitated by transport developments, such as the wider use of the private automobile, that make it possible to live in the suburbs and work in the city. Third, the moving out of people and economic activities weakens the ability of inner-city governments to pursue development efforts. With an eroding tax base, inner-city local governments barely have enough income to maintain services and facilities.

Fourth, the rapidly aging and decaying structures of the inner city become attractive to poor migrants. The concentration of poor people in the inner city increases the service and welfare burdens of inner-city governments at the same time that their resources are dwindling. Caught in this vicious circle of increasing demand for welfare services, the out-migration of people and businesses, the deterioration of inner-city structures, services and amenities, in-migration of poorer people, and declining incomes, inner-city governments are not able to stop or reverse inner-city deterioration. It is not until governments and citizens realize that areawide action is needed to comprehensively solve mega-urban problems that central and local government authorities will start pursuing programs for inner-city redevelopment.

A key issue in inner-city redevelopment is a choice between "destroy and build" and "conserve and redevelop" approaches. In many Chinese cities, such as Guangzhou, Shanghai, and Tianjin, governments have used the "urban renewal" approach, whereby "old and dilapidated" structures in the inner city have been razed and new structures have replaced these. The same "destroy-and-build" approach has been used in Seoul, especially during the administration of the aptly named mayor, Bulldozer Kim. Even in Beijing, with its abundance of heritage treasures and culturally important buildings, large sections of the inner city have been destroyed and replaced with "modern" structures. The old city walls have been dismantled, courtyard houses dating back to the Ming and Sung Dynasties have been demolished, monuments considered unwanted relics of a feudal past have been torn down, and temples and monasteries have been converted into factories, warehouses, and public offices. The folly of these actions has been revealed in the recent decision of the Beijing authorities to build a replica of the city walls for the tourists.

In a number of Asian city-regions, programs to "conserve and redevelop" inner cities have been successfully pursued by urban authorities. In some cities, historical conservation has been motivated by a need for cultural symbols to assist in fostering national identity and nation-building efforts. It has also been heavily influenced by tourism, especially the need for historical and cultural structures that highlights the development of the city or the nation. Unfortunately, some of these tourism-inspired inner-city redevelopment efforts have created too many false gilt-and-glitz structures that neither reflects the authentic symbols of a country's cultural heritage nor an attractive site for discerning tourists.

An excellent example of successful inner-city redevelopment is found in Tokyo, where crafts people, designers and other professionals are discovering the pleasures of living in a neighborhood that still retains much of its heritage. In the capital city's Yanaka District, public and private efforts have succeeded in preserving eighty temples, old shops, traditional wooden houses, and gardens. People have continued to live in the community despite strong pressures by developers to raze the old structures and put up modern buildings. The city authorities continue to be concerned about dangers from fire, earthquakes, and other calamities, but the insistent residents have clung to their traditional community and so far resisted changes. As public authorities have recognized the value of keeping traditional culture alive in a very urban setting, things are looking very good for the residents of the Yanaka District.

Another good example of inner-city redevelopment was the restoration of the Yuyuan temple and bazaar in Shanghai as a tourist and shopping center. Located within the 2-hectare site were (1) the Temple of the City God, (2) a classical Chinese garden, (3) a bazaar, and (4) traditional residential quarters. In redeveloping the site, the Shanghai Institute of Urban Planning and Design was guided by the following approach:

> The preservation of the traditional and historical features of the architecture is not only embodied in the form, scale and color of the buildings but also in the whole architectural environment—the development and reapplication of the traditional spatial forms and sequence. It should be focused on the design of the whole environmental space. (Xiong 1994, 48)

Following this approach, the Yuyuan complex preserved the exterior of old structures while modernizing plumbing, electricity, sanitation, and other facilities. The human scale of the whole landscape was maintained, for no new high-rise structures were built in the area. The narrow lanes and streets were designed for temple worshipers and shoppers and were kept free of motorized transport. By design, "the spatial composition of the Yuyuan Shopping Center is of a series of spatial nodes (places for gathering such as squares) consisting of spatial nodes and pedestrian paths. Its best composition is of a network type . . . the traditional Chinese shopping streets embody this network feature; but modern streets have destroyed this feature because of accession of car flows" (Xiong 1994, 49). The redevelopment approach also renovated the residential quarters so that most of the people selling things and operating businesses in the Yuyuan complex could continue living in the area, thereby maintaining the spirit of community life in the neighborhood.

The Yuyuan complex has shown that paying special attention to cultural factors in redeveloping an inner-city area could result in an aesthetically pleasing and at the same time economically viable solution. It is hoped that, despite the development pressures created by rapid tourism development, similar efforts at heritage conservation will be pursued in other Asian mega-urban regions in the future. Hopefully, such efforts will avoid the "one size fits all" urban renewal approaches focused on the razing of old structures and the construction of "modern" buildings that have proven so disastrous in North America. In this regard, the design and character of the inner cities of many old European urban regions may serve as better models for Asian planners and urban designers in the future.

An entirely different type of inner-city redevelopment is posed by deteriorating urban cores in city-regions like Bangkok, Dhaka, Jakarta, Karachi, Manila, and Mumbai, whose inner cities are inhabited by desperately poor individuals living in congested old houses or in makeshift shanties built on vacant lots, abandoned industrial sites, or along the banks of rivers and canals. In the inner-city *kampungs* of Jakarta and other Indonesian cities, community-upgrading efforts have improved the lives of poverty-stricken residents. This has been achieved by interventions, such as cleaning up and dredging canals, the construction of footpaths, launching community-based efforts for the collection and disposal of solid waste, and the provision of artesian wells and standpipes to make clean water available to people. In the slums of Metro Manila, the zonal improvement program also organizes poor urban communities to help them improve their livelihood, gain access to water and sanitation services, and develop their physical surroundings. The community mortgage program has also enabled poor urban families to buy the land they have been squatting on and to build their own housing.

A controversial issue in inner-city redevelopment is the forced resettlement of poor families to peripheral sites. In all infrastructure projects funded by the World Bank and the Asian Development Bank, eviction and relocation are not allowed unless the people to be relocated are provided with land and housing arrangements acceptable to them. In Indonesian and Philippine cities, the "land sharing" or "land readjustment" approach has been found very useful in accommodating people onsite rather than resettling them elsewhere. In this approach, a smaller section of the inner-city land located as close as possible to the original site is set aside for building houses that will accommodate the original residents. High-density housing is designed, built, and made available to the people affected by the scheme. The cleared land is then used for high-end development, and some of the "profits" from the scheme are used to cross-subsidize housing for poor residents. In this way, the lives of poor people are not adversely affected too much but the inner-city land is developed.

These innovative approaches to inner-city redevelopment show that the "hole in the doughnut" development pattern that is such a serious concern in North American cities can be prevented in Asian mega-urban regions. The ancient histories of some Asian cities provide them with culturally important heritage buildings and relics that can be developed as national symbols for nation building and for tourism. The cultural traditions of high-density living in inner cities serve to maintain the vitality of harmoniously cooperative communities. A number of governmental approaches have been successful in providing shelter and basic urban services to even the poor people who live in inner cities. As Asian mega-urban regions continue to grow and expand in the future, therefore, they will most likely pursue integrated areawide plans and schemes that will balance the redevelopment of inner cities with peripheral area development.

Voices from Below: People's Involvement in Regional Governance

Traditionally, urban governance is concerned with balancing efficiency in service delivery with openness and responsiveness to citizen interests through democratic participation, social inclusion, and transparent decision-making processes. Advocates of decentralizing authority and responsibility to local government units believe that citizens' views are best heard by institutions that make "grassroots democracy" workable. They look to the increasingly important roles of civil society groups in articulating and aggregating interests to make local governments more responsive to people's demands.

Unfortunately, as mega-urban regions grow and expand territorially, the problems that face them tend to become larger, more complex, and more costly. Diseases and environmental pollution do not respect political or administrative boundaries. Traffic regulation requires the active involvement and collaboration of transport managers and police forces belonging to different local government units. The spread of crime, juvenile delinquency, drugs, prostitution, HIV/AIDS, and other problems calls for integrated co-operative action and coordination. The need to provide adequate and reliable supplies of potable water and to dispose of sewage and gray water are best met at an areawide and regional level. Relying on the voluntary cooperation and goodwill of disparate local government units to solve the many areawide problems confronting mega-urban regions might be idealistic and democratic, but it will most likely cause delays, duplication of efforts, inefficiency, and waste.

Some countries, such as the Philippines, have adopted governance mechanisms based on the voluntary federation of local government units to form metropolitan governments. The 1987 Philippine Constitution stipulated that a group of cities and municipalities may set up a government that takes the form of a metropolitan federation, provided that such a structure is approved by the citizens in a plebiscite. The Metro Manila Development Authority (MMDA) was created under this constitutional mandate. It is made up of fourteen cities operating under their own individual charters and three municipalities belonging to three provinces. The MMDA covers a territory of 636 square kilometers with a population of 10.8 million. Policymaking in the MMDA is vested in the Metro Manila Council, which is composed of all the mayors of the constituent cities and municipalities. The chair of the MMDA is appointed by the president of the Philippines and is a member of the Cabinet. He exercises executive powers, assisted by a general manager and three assistant general managers in charge of planning, finance and administration, and operations (Bautista-Cruz 2001).

The statute creating the MMDA, Republic Act 7924, provided that the MMDA "shall perform planning, monitoring and coordinating functions, and in the process exercise regulatory and supervisory authority over the delivery of metro-wide services within Metro Manila without diminution of the autonomy of the local government units concerning purely local matters." The metro-wide services placed under the MMDA's jurisdiction were development planning, traffic and transport management, flood control and sewerage management, solid waste disposal and management, urban renewal, zoning and land use planning, health and sanitation, urban protection and pollution control, and public safety. Despite this seemingly large number of functions vested in the MMDA, however, it has remained a very weak institution, mainly because of the way the local government units have interpreted the phrase "without diminution of the autonomy of the local government units concerning purely local matters." The internal contradiction in the law itself that vested areawide functions to MMDA and yet stipulated that there should be no diminution of authority of local units has created many tensions and problems. Many of the local government units in Greater Manila have justified most of their functions as "purely local matters" and have taken them out of the MMDA's jurisdiction.

After more than a decade of metropolitan governance in Metro Manila, it is apparent that the system is not working very well. Local mayors and councils participating in decision making within the MMDA have tended to protect their own local interests rather than agree to policies and programs that would benefit the whole national capital region. For example, when the MMDA tried an experiment to limit the number of vehicles on the road, a number-coding scheme was used. Vehicles with plates ending in an odd number could be operated only on odd-numbered days, and those ending in even numbers on even-numbered days. However, the city governments of Makati and Mandaluyong refused to enforce the regulations within their boundaries, and the experiment proved to be less than successful. Similarly, repeated MMDA efforts to find a suburban site for a sanitary landfill for the disposal of the metropolitan area's garbage have been frustrated by local units that refuse to have the facility within their territories. In fact, local citizens, with the support of their elected officials, have forcibly closed some of the existing dumps. They have also barred the entry of garbage trucks into their jurisdictional areas.

The experience with participatory regional governance in Metro Manila indicates that while its democratic ideals and aspirations might be applauded, in practice, the approach does not make for efficient and effective governance. With local government units, municipal and city officials, private business groups, and even civil society leaders pushing only for their particularistic interests, achieving even a workable consensus becomes extremely difficult. Public decision making takes up a lot of time, and bureaucratically induced delays are common. Even after long bargaining sessions and attempts at mutual accommodation of specific interests, policy outcomes have been unsatisfactory and often not acceptable to all stakeholders. Most important of all, governance becomes interest-driven and may become marked by rent seeking. The public interest then gets lost in the transactional processes of bargaining, accommodation, and horse trading.

Rule from the Top: Unified Governance

People who favor institutionalized efficiency in delivering urban services believe that although the decentralization of authority is very useful, such delegation needs to be vested in governance bodies that have sufficient power and financial and managerial capabilities to actually carry out governance functions. If left to their own devices, local government units tend to pursue particularistic and selfish interests, such as those reflected in not-in-my-back-yard-ism and local bossism. Individually, most local government units do not have adequate financial, organizational, and managerial resources to deal with urban problems. Unless authority and power as well as adequate financial and managerial resources are vested in an areawide or regional body, mega-urban regions would not be able to adequately cope with the problems confronting them.

Because of the need to effectively solve areawide problems and the apparent failure of local government federations to cooperatively deal with those problems, central, state, or provincial governments in Asia may consider establishing unified city-region governance institutions in the future. These efforts to introduce areawide interventions may start with the formulation of regional development plans.

This trend is already apparent in the case of the Tokyo Megalopolis, where the Tokyo Metropolitan Government (TMG) has joined forces with adjoining local government units in the formulation of an integrated plan and the adoption of a strategy that seeks coordinated action to solve areawide problems. The Japanese authorities have set up a coordination mechanism, whereby representatives from TMG, three prefectures (Saitama, Chiba, and Kanagawa), and three cities (Yokohama, Kasawaki, and Chiba) participate in a permanent consultative organ. The mechanism will not only deal with common problems but will also "bolster the revenue source for the improvement of social overhead capital" in the whole mega-urban region. This coordination structure does not yet constitute an instrument for unified governance, but there are hopes that a unified structure might be operational by 2025.

In Greater Jakarta, the Indonesian government has invested almost $1 billion to develop the Jabotabek region through a regional development plan that is an operational elaboration of the Fourth National Five-Year Plan (Repelita IV). The plan proposes a single agency to coordinate planned activities carried out by three levels of government (central, provincial, and local). The agency would (1) provide a forum for all local agencies involved; (2) undertake independent and objective evaluations of alternative development options; and (3) maintain and translate an overall development strategy into basic guiding policies, principles, and criteria for sector development. This agency would be charged with the coordination of all infrastructure development planning in Jabotabek as a whole and empowered to make choices between alternative sectors (Jabotabek 2003).

The Government of Bangladesh has also started to establish a coordination mechanism to help provide much needed services in its capital city of Dhaka. In 1996, the government established a "Coordination Committee," headed by the minister of local government as convenor and the mayor of Dhaka City as co-convenor, to coordinate all the line departments and agencies of the central and local governments operating in the city-region. The main functions placed under the coordinating jurisdiction of the committee were traffic congestion, water supply, drainage, and health. To assist the committee in its tasks, the Asian Development Bank has approved a technical assistance project to promote better urban governance. The government and the Asian Development Bank regard the committee's establishment as the "first step to establish the proposed Metropolitan Government in the city of Dhaka" (Haque Bhuiyan 1999, 3–4).

These examples clearly indicate that more and more urban agglomerations in Asia are starting to appreciate the need for areawide coordinated action in mega-urban regions and that some may even be contemplating the establishment of unified mega-urban governance structures in the future to achieve areawide development through rational comprehensive planning and the coordinated management of large-scale urban services. They also seek to take advantage of the economic benefits arising from economies of scale and the stronger tax base and higher credit rating associated with metropolitan amalgamation. In pursuing this policy option, urban authorities will most likely face opposition from advocates of local autonomy and decentralization, who argue that setting up large upper-tier governance structures above municipalities and cities tend to diminish opportunities for public participation. However, as the problems arising from local government fragmentation and uncoordinated action become more apparent, the trend toward regional planning and development may accelerate.

To achieve unified regional governance, experience in Asia has shown that efficient and coordinated action requires the intervention of higher levels of government (central or provincial/state) to bring about coordinated action among local units. This authority can be incorporated in legislation. It can take the form of infusions of financial resources through grants-in-aid or other fiscal policy mechanisms. It can be shown in the provision of infrastructure and basic services that shape the city-region area. It can be implemented by the adoption and enforcement of enforcement mechanisms, such as land use plans, zoning regulations, building codes, and performance standards. The support of local government units will of course be crucial in the final stages of development, but at least initially, some higher governmental authority might be needed to "knock heads together" and clearly show the advantages and merits of coordinated regionwide action.

The process of establishing unified regional governance structures in Asian city-regions will probably go by stages. The first stage will most likely take the form of a comprehensive regional planning exercise that analyzes development trends, identifies mega-urban region problems, and then proposes pragmatic solutions. The second stage might involve the identification of urban service functions that are, of their very nature, regionwide in character. Such functions may include strategic planning, land use controls, and the locational aspects of investment decisions. A third stage may take the form of setting up functionally specific agencies to manage individual functions, such as water, sewerage and sanitation, transportation, open space and parks, energy provision, and environmental pollution control. Fourth and finally, an overarching metropolitan or regional organization may be set up to effectively manage and coordinate the activities of the various functional units. This whole process may take years to evolve, or it can suddenly come about by the imposition of authority by higher levels of government. Whatever form the process takes, it is clear from the city-region case studies covered in this book that unified regional governance is greatly needed to effectively and efficiently coordinate development in Asia's mega-urban regions.

The Promise of Civil Society

One of the most notable developments in some Asian urban agglomerations has been the emergence of civil society groups made up of NGOs, CBOs, and people's organizations. To pursue the democratic goals advocated by many international agencies and financial institutions, foreign aid and technical assistance have been focused on supporting these civil society groups, which have been very active in policy areas such as poverty alleviation, environment, gender and development, and basic human rights.

Governmental reorganization reforms have been adopted in many Asian urban governments to include these civil society groups in public decision making. In the Philippines, the Local Government Code of 1991 provided that sectoral representatives of the poor people, labor, youth, women, and others had to be elected to municipal and city councils. Separate elections were also held for youth (people age 15–24 years) to select their representatives in councils at the *barangay* (community), municipal, city, and metropolitan government levels.

An innovative approach to civil society activism is seen in Mumbai and other cities in India, where a group called the Alliance has been in operation since 1987. The Alliance is made up of three partners: (1) SPARC, an NGO formed by social work professionals; (2) the National Slum Dwellers Federation, a CBO active since 1974; and (c) Mahila Milan, an organization of poor women set up in 1986. The Alliance is committed to pursuing programs designed to achieve secure tenure in land, access to services, and affordable housing (UNCHS 2001, 171).

A great deal of the success of the Alliance lies in enabling its members to improve their living conditions rests on an explicit policy not to directly engage in electoral politics. Unlike civil society groups in other Asian cities that trade their votes for benefits and eventually become adjuncts of political parties, the Alliance enters into working arrangements with local and central government bureaucracies that are charged with urban development. For example, the Alliance has developed links with autonomous organizations like India Railways, Mumbai Electric Supply and Transport, and the Port Authority. Because the bureaucratic organizations are the ones in charge of programs such as housing loans, slum rehabilitation, and real estate regulations, the Alliance is able to work with them directly on issues of mutual concern. Interestingly, the politics of the Alliance has been described as one of "accommodation, negotiation and long term pressure rather than of confrontation or threats of political reprisal" (UNCHS 2001, 172).

The most important promise of civil society groups in urban governance lies in their willingness to engage in scaling up activities above the purely local level. Past efforts in public participation—as noted above in relation to decentralization measures targeted at the lowest level of governmental activity—is the inability of NGOs and CBOs to rise above their small-scale concerns. Because they are dependent on voluntary efforts and meager local resources, traditional NGOs and CBOs usually do not have the human and financial resources to keep up their sustained efforts. In this regard, it is worth noting that international bodies like the International Monetary Fund and the World Bank have engaged in poverty alleviation programs that are directly supportive of civil society groups. Bilateral agencies such as the Canadian International Development Agency and the U.S. Agency for International Development have also been supporting civil society groups in developing-country cities. With such international assistance, some civil society groups might be able to help poor urban groups in their efforts to scale up their activities.

A National System of Cities

Although mega-urban regions are dominating economic and social development in nation-states, small and medium-sized cities in Asia are often expanding at even higher rates. In some ways, the rapid growth of these small and medium-sized cities is most welcome because it deflects population from mega-urban regions. In many cases, the growth of alternative urban nodes is the result of successful "national urban strategies." These strategies have been implemented through (1) the provision of infrastructure and urban services (including housing) by central and provincial or state governments; (2) incentives to the private sector to invest more in alternative urban nodes; (3) the mobilization of local support in designated centers; and (4) legislative edicts covering land use controls, zoning codes, subdivision regulations, and performance standards.

A country that has consistently pursued a policy of decentralizing growth from the capital city is South Korea. Rising up from the Korean War, the country saw rapid economic development, which was initially centered in Pusan, Seoul, and Taegu. Partly because of a concern that Seoul, located close to the border with North Korea, was vulnerable to military attack, the Korean government pursued an official policy to develop growth centers in southern regions, focused on Chungbuk, Jeonbuk, Kwangju, Kyungnam, and Taejeon. The policy was implemented through formal directives embodied in the Provincial Industry Development Act of 1970, the National Land Utilization and Management Act of 1972, the Population Dispersal Plan for Seoul (1975), the Population Redistribution Plan for the Capital Region (1977), the First National Land Development Plan (1972–81), the Third and Fourth Five-Year Economic Development Plans (1972–76; 1976–81), the Restriction on Construction of Public and Large Buildings in the Capital Region (1982), and the Capital Region Readjustment Plan (1984). In addition, South Korea has also passed two additional National Land Development Plans providing for the decentralization of Seoul and the capital region and aspiring for national regional balance (Sung 1996, 170).

Despite the persistence of macroeconomic forces enhancing the further development of the Seoul metropolitan area, South Korea's conscious policy to decentralize growth to other urban centers throughout the whole national landscape seems to have been effective. The growth rate of the population within the formal boundaries of Seoul has declined to –0.4 percent. In the meantime, other centers, such as Kyungnam, Pusan, Taegu, and Taejeon, have increased their populations. Of course, urban areas on Seoul's periphery, such as those in Incheon–Kyunggi, have continued to grow, signifying the potential need for a possible redefinition of Seoul's metropolitan boundaries. However, as a whole, Korea's population dispersal policy seems to have been successful, helping somewhat in making the urban problems of Seoul more solvable.

Another country that has consciously tried to encourage development in regions far from the national capital is Thailand. In pursuing a National Urban Development Policy, the Thai government has focused attention on seven development regions that were designed to counter urban growth in the Bangkok Metropolitan Region. Thai planners are projecting that, despite concerted efforts, the Bangkok Metropolitan Region will continue to absorb about 33 percent of the national population increase during the period 1990–2010. However, the national strategy also expects that the northeast region would absorb 24.6 percent and the southern region would absorb 19.3 of the national population increase.

Solving the problems of Asian mega-urban regions, therefore, does not have to be confined to the immediate vicinity of such regions. A national urban strategy can effectively reduce the growth rate of city-region populations. It can make other urban nodes more attractive to investors by providing infrastructure, energy, housing, and other inputs. Such a strategy might also help encourage the development of multinodal mega-urban regions by concentrating investments in nodes not too far from dominant mega-cities. Though market forces exert a tremendous influence on the eventual shape of urban settlements, explicitly stated and consciously directed investment policies, land use control measures, and the building of urban infrastructure and services at planned sites can effectively influence mega-urban development patterns.

Who Pays for City-Region Development?

Dealing with the many problems of Asian mega-urban regions requires vast financial resources. Using methods that parallel those used by the World Bank in estimating infrastructure costs, the Asian Development Bank estimated that between 1995 and 2020, Asian countries would need $6.9 trillion to meet the costs of urban infrastructure. This huge amount would meet the costs of water supply, wastewater management and sanitation, solid waste management, urban drainage and flood control, and urban roads and traffic management. It does not include the costs of affordable housing and mass transit systems (Brockman and Williams 1996, 49).

Because of the heavy concentration of economic activities in mega-cities and mega-urban regions, the bulk of governmental revenue is usually generated in such regions. In Jakarta, for example, where only 4.6 percent of Indonesia's population lives, more than one-third of total domestic and international investments and 20 percent of total national employment is concentrated in the national capital. If other areas in the Jabotabek region are added, the region's share of investments and employment will more than double (Jabotabek 2003).

Despite the potentials for raising public revenue in mega-urban regions, local governments in such areas, as a rule, are heavily dependent on central governments for financial resources. In the Philippines, for example, more than 50 percent of local government revenues comes from transfers and grants from the central government. Even in relatively well off Japan, the central government collects 60 percent of all governmental revenue and transfers 30 percent of that to local units. Local taxes account for only one-third of local revenues, although a wealthy unit like the Tokyo Metropolitan Government gets about 70 percent of its resources from local taxes (Vogel 2001, 119). One Japanese authority has argued that this system whereby the central government collects and distributes tax revenues to local government units is tending to make local government units in Japan less competitive in the world economy. He has proposed that urban areas would be better off if they were allowed to develop by relying more on their own resources and capabilities (Ohmae 1995).

The financial situation in Asian mega-urban regions is made extremely difficult by the concentration of revenue-raising powers in the central government. Though many Asian governments have decentralized responsibility for urban services to local government units, the transfer of responsibility has not been accompanied by equivalent grants of fiscal authority. As pointed out by the UN Center for Human Settlements, devolving the management of infrastructure to local governments without granting them an adequate tax base to support the associated costs has led to serious service deficiencies or the total collapse of the systems and loss of physical assets as a result of overload and lack of maintenance (UNCHS 2001, 152).

The future development of financial capabilities in mega-urban regions will depend very heavily on the realization that adequate authority for raising revenue and building up local capacity to manage urban finances is needed in most Asian mega-urban regions. In some countries, such as China, the responsibility for delivering urban services is now vested in local governance structures. The mayor of an extended municipality like Shanghai, for example, has the authority to approve projects that do not exceed $50 million. Metropolitan governments in the Philippines, like Metro Manila or Metro Cebu, are allowed to float bonds and borrow domestically or internationally to finance big infrastructure projects. The grant of fiscal authority to governmental bodies in these large urban agglomerations is justified because they have sufficient economic resources to enable them to adequately exercise such authority. The financial strength of large city-region authorities is also enhanced by the improvement of their credit ratings arising from the pooling of the assets of constituent local government units and their much richer tax bases.

It is common in urban management to make a distinction between financing systems for operating or recurrent expenditures and investments in long-term capital works, such as water supply, mass transit, ports and harbors, and solid waste disposal. Because local government units are often dependent on shared resources from the central government, their capacity to influence the pattern of operating expenditures is often quite limited. However, many do have the capacity to make more flexible decisions for capital investments. In China, for example, many local government units have control over urban land and have used land availability as an incentive for foreign investors to locate within their jurisdictions. By using land surveys, land titling, land registration, and simple procedures for land value appraisals, Chinese local government units have been able to increase collections from real estate taxes. In Indonesia, relatively simple systems for adjusting land valuations have made it possible for local government units to "recover" some of the benefits accruing to landowners from the installation of public infrastructure and services (roads, ports, harbors) by taxing the increases in land values arising from these improvements.

In the Philippines, supporters of the Local Government Code of 1991 have criticized the overdependence of local officials on internal revenue allotments, encouraging these local officials to instead mobilize local assets, especially land, in setting up public–private partnerships. Local governments have also been encouraged to use their borrowing authority for capital investments rather than relying on "pork barrel" allocations from national politicians. In some urban areas, big-ticket capital projects have been funded under build–operate–transfer and build–operate–own–manage schemes. Special concessions and contracts for land development or the operation and management of public–private enterprises have also been found effective in augmenting local finance capabilities.

In recent years, a great deal of attention has been focused in Asian mega-urban regions on the use of user charges for financing urban services. Such charges include fees for services rendered, such as water supply, electricity, and garbage collection and disposal. They involve charges for governmental permission to engage in certain occupations or activities (license fees, building permits). Income is also obtained from the use of local government property (rental fees for market stalls). A review of experience in Asia reveals that local governments do not usually maximize income from various user charges. In some instances, they also find it time consuming and difficult to collect these charges. One approach that has been found useful in some countries is the "bundling" of collections from a number of services. For example, in communities around the Subic Bay Special Economic Zone in the Philippines, the municipal government includes charges for garbage collection and disposal in monthly bills for water and sewerage. Aside from the efficiency achieved by this simplified system, the local government is also able to work out a system of "cross-subsidy," whereby a service that people are more inclined to pay for (water) benefits another system where collections are more difficult (garbage collection and disposal).

Future mega-urban region governments in Asia will most likely see a greater role played by the private sector in financing and managing urban services. The initial experience with privatization of water and sewerage systems in Manila and Jakarta has not been too encouraging. However, privately managed and financed toll roads, electricity, telephone, gas, and rapid transit systems have been quite successful. Private enterprise has made available to urban projects technical expertise, vast financial resources, and professional management capabilities. Public–private partnerships may also be useful as an approach to financing mega-urban capital projects in the future.

City-Regions in an Era of Globalization

Globalization as manifested in its various forms is intimately linked to the growth and functioning of big cities and mega-urban regions. It is in city-regions where people congregate at high densities that social and economic changes are rapidly happening. At the same time, the rapid growth of mega-urban regions is also affecting globalization. As noted by the UN Center for Human Settlements:

> It is in cities where global operations are centralized and where one can see most clearly the phenomena associated with their activities: changes in the structure of employment, the formation of powerful partnerships, the development of monumental real estate, the emergence of new forms of local governance, the effects of organized crime, the expansion of corruption, the fragmentation of informal networks, and the spatial isolation and social exclusion of certain population groups. The characteristics of cities and their surrounding regions, in turn, help shape globalization; for example, by providing a suitable labor force, making available the required physical and technological infrastructure, creating a stable and accommodating regulatory environment, offering the bundle of necessary support services, contributing financial incentives and possessing the institutional capacity without which globalization cannot occur. (UNCHS 2001, xxxi)

Globalization forces are centered in cities, and they have profound effects on the physical form as well as the socioeconomic makeup of mega-urban regions. In theory, globalization is expected to be directly correlated with (1) more rapid rates of economic development and growth of very large "global cities," (2) reduced inequalities among social classes and various regions, and (3) improved changes for the development of a liberal democratic way of life (Sen 2002). This study of Asian mega-urban regions suggests, however, that the positive effects of globalization are not always realized and apply to different places in different ways. Though tangible benefits from globalization have been achieved (e.g., the reduction in mortality rates due to global diffusion of medical knowledge, increased food production based on shared agricultural technologies, improved environmental protection and conservation), the benefits from these achievements have not been equally and equitably shared among all classes and groups within a city-region or a country. In fact, empirical data are tending to show that inequality in mega-urban regions is growing wider and spatial polarization is occurring, with rich people living in gated communities and poor residents in marginal settlements (UNCHS 2001, xxxi).

It has been suggested that the emergence of global cities linked together by economic, informational, political, and financial ties has served to weaken the nation-state. The dominant influence of global actors (multinational corporations, international financing institutions, networks of agglutinated business elites) is supposed to have resulted in the "hollowing out of the state" and its capture by particularistic local interests closely allied with international power holders. In the case of the Asian mega-urban regions covered in this study, however, it has been shown that though most of them aspire to global city status, some of their leaders are strongly committed to their national institution-building roles. The city-regions lead their countries in the drive toward economic development. They are the centers of innovation and the generators of social change. They play, and will most likely continue to play, a highly significant role in the development of nation-states in which they are embedded.

Most important of all, city-regions may play a very important role in the spread of norms of democratic governance, the value of environmental protection, and the ideals of social justice and basic human rights. As Aristotle said centuries ago, "City air makes man free." It is that commitment to *civitas,* the right to citizenship in a free community and assuming responsibility for actions that uphold the common good, that makes citizens' involvement the keystone for city-region development. Mega-urban regions and megalopolitan areas already are, and will continue to be, the dominant forms of settlements in the new millennium. Their planning and governance provide the main instruments for achieving their fullest development potentials.

References

Abrams, Charles. 1964. *Man's Struggle for Shelter in an Urbanizing World.* Cambridge, Mass.: MIT Press.

Abueva, Jose V. 1959. *Focus on the Barrio: The Story behind the Birth of the Philippine Community Development Program under President Ramon Magsaysay.* Manila: Institute of Public Administration, University of the Philippines.

Anderson, T. L., and P. Snyder. 1997. *Water Markets: Priming the Invisible Pump.* Washington, D.C.: Cato Institute.

Angel, Shlomo. 1977. The Low-Income Housing Delivery System in Asia. In *Low-Income Housing: Technology and Policy,* ed. R. P. Pama, S. Angel, and J. H. de Goede. Bangkok: Asian Institute of Technology.

———. 2000. *Housing Policy Matters: A Global Analysis.* Oxford: Oxford University Press.

Argo, Teti. 1999. Thirsty Downstream: The Provision of Clean Water in Jakarta, Indonesia. Ph.D. dissertation, School of Community and Regional Planning, University of British Columbia, Vancouver.

Argo, Teti, and Aprodicio Laquian. 2004. Privatization of Water Utilities and Its Effects on the Urban Poor in Jakarta Raya and Metro Manila. Paper presented at Forum on Urban Infrastructure and Public Service Delivery for the Urban Poor, Regional Focus: Asia, India Habitat Centre, New Delhi, June 24–25.

Arlosoroff, Saul. 1998. Water Demand Management. In *Promoting Sustainable Consumption in Asian Cities,* ed. United Nations Center for Human Settlement (Habitat). Fukuoka: Habitat Fukuoka Office.

Ashraf, Ali, and Leslie Green. 1972. Calcutta. In *Great Cities of the World: Their Government, Politics and Planning,* ed. William A. Robson and D. E. Regan. London: George Allen and Unwin.

Asian Development Bank. 1993. *Water Utilities Data Book.* Manila: ADB Case Studies for the Mega-City Regional Consultation.

Asiaweek. 2000. Asia's Best Cities, 2000. Available at http://www/asiaweek.com/features/asiacities2000.

Badami, Madhav, Geetam Tiwari, and Dinesh Mohan. 2004. Access and Mobility for the Urban Poor in India: Bridging the Gap Between Policy and Needs. Paper presented

423

at Forum on Urban Infrastructure and Public Service Delivery for the Urban Poor, Regional Focus: Asia, India Habitat Centre, New Delhi, June 24–25.

Banerjee, Tridib, and Sigrid Schenk. 1984. Lower Order Cities and National Urbanization Policies: China and India. In *Equity with Growth? Planning Perspectives for Small Towns in Developing Countries,* ed. H. Detlef Kammeier and Peter J. Swan. Bangkok: Asian Institute of Technology.

Bao Guilan. 1992. Socio- and Psychological Analysis of the Inhabitants of Shanghai. In *The Research on Human Settlements in Shanghai,* ed. Zheng Shiling. Shanghai: College of Architecture and Urban Planning, Tongji University.

Batley, Richard. 2001. Public–Private Partnership for Urban Services. In *The Challenge of Urban Government, Policies and Practices,* ed. Mila Freire and Richard Stren. Washington, D.C.: World Bank Institute.

Bautista-Cruz, Corazon. 2001. *Development Planning in Metropolitan Manila.* Makati City: Metropolitan Manila Development Authority.

Beijing Municipal Government. 1987. *The Beijing Master Plan.* Beijing. Beijing Municipal Planning Bureau.

Booth, William. 2003. Thirsty Cities Look Seaward for More Water. *Washington Post,* March 30.

Brandon, C., and R. Ramankutty. 1993. *Toward an Environmental Strategy for Asia.* Washington, D.C.: World Bank.

Bray, David John. 1996. Urban Transport. In *Urban Infrastructure Finance,* ed. Royston Brockman and Allen Williams. Manila: Water Supply, Urban Development, and Housing Division, Asian Development Bank.

Breese, Gerald. 1966. *Urbanization in Developing Countries.* Englewood Cliffs, N.J.: Prentice Hall.

Brockman, Royston, and Allen Williams, eds. 1996. *Urban Infrastructure Finance,* Manila: Asian Development Bank.

Brown, Fred. 2001. Pedestrians: The Need for a New Approach. In *Modern Transport in Hong Kong for the 21st Century,* ed. Anthony Gar-On Yeh, Peter R. Hills, and Simon Ka-Wing Ng. Hong Kong: Centre of Urban Planning and Environmental Management, University of Hong Kong.

Bukit, N. T. 1995. Water Quality Conservation for the Citarum River in West Java. *Water, Science and Technology* 31, no. 9: 1–10.

Button, K., and W. Rotherngatter. 1993. Global Environmental Degradation: The Role of Transport. In *Transport, the Environment and Sustainable Development,* ed. D. Banister and K. Button. London: E & FN Spon.

Cai Jianming. 2000. Peri-Urban Agriculture Development in China: A New Approach in Xiaotongshan, Beijing. Institute of Geographical Sciences and Natural Resource Research, Beijing.

Cairncross, Sandy, and Richard G. Feachem. 1983. *Environmental Health Engineering in the Tropics: An Introductory Text.* Chichester: John Wiley & Sons.

Campanella, Thomas J., Ming Zhang, Tunney Lee, and Nien Dak Sze. 2002. The Pearl River Delta: A Evolving Region. In *Building a Competitive Pearl River Delta Region: Cooperation, Coordination, and Planning,* ed. Anthony Gar-On Yeh, Yok-Shiu F. Lee, Tunney Lee, and Nien Dak Sze. Hong Kong: Centre of Urban Planning and Environmental Management, University of Hong Kong.

Campbell, Tim. 2002. Banking on Decentralization in Continents of Cities: Taking Stock of Lessons, Looking Forward to Reform. In *Democratic Governance and Urban Sus-*

tainability, ed. Joseph S. Tulchin, Diana H. Varat and Blair A. Ruble. Washington, D.C.: Woodrow Wilson International Center for Scholars.

Carino, Ledivina. 1986. *Bureaucratic Corruption in Asia: Causes, Consequences and Control.* Manila: College of Public Administration, University of the Philippines.

CDGK (City District Government of Karachi). 2004. *Devolution Plan for Karachi.* Karachi: City District Government of Karachi. Available at http://www.karachicity.gov.pk.

Cheung, Peter T. Y. 2002. Managing the Hong Kong–Guangdong Relationship: Issues and Challenges. In *Building a Competitive Pearl River Delta Region: Cooperation, Coordination, and Planning,* ed. Anthony Gar-On Yeh, Yok-Shiu F. Lee, Tunney Lee, and Nien Dak Sze. Hong Kong: Centre of Urban Planning and Environmental Management, University of Hong Kong.

Choong Tet Sieu. 1998. How to Make Cities Work. *Asiaweek,* December 11, 40–45.

Clark, Robin. 1993. *Water: The International Crisis,* Cambridge, Mass.: MIT Press.

Constantino-David, Karina. 1998. From the Present Looking Back: A History of Philippine NGOs. In *Civil Society and the Philippine State,* ed. G. Sidney Silliman and Leila Garner Noble. Quezon City: Ateneo de Manila University Press.

Coronel, Sheila. 1998. *Pork and Other Perks: Corruption and Governance in the Philippines.* Quezon City: Philippine Center for Investigative Journalism.

———. 2000. *Betrayal of the Public Trust, Investigative Reports on Corruption.* Quezon City: Philippine Center for Investigative Journalism.

Cui Gonghao. 1995. Development of Shanghai and the Yangtze Delta. In *Chinese Cities and China's Development: A Preview of the Future Role of Hong Kong,* ed. Anthony Gar-On Yeh and Chai-Kwong Mak. Hong Kong: Centre of Urban Planning and Environmental Management, University of Hong Kong.

Daly, Herman, and Kenneth N. Townsend, eds. 1993. *Valuing the Earth: Economics, Ecology, Ethics.* Cambridge, Mass.: MIT Press.

Datta, Abhijit, and J. N. Khosla. 1972. Delhi. In *Great Cities of the World: Their Government, Politics and Planning,* ed. William A. Robson and D. E. Regan. London: George Allen and Unwin.

Davis, Kingsley, and Hilda H. Golden. 1955. Urbanization and the Development of Pre-Industrial Areas. *Economic Development and Cultural Change* 3: 24–32.

Delhi Traffic Police. 2004. *Traffic Statistics.* Available at http://www.terrin.org/urban/delhi.

Dharmapatni, Ida Ayu, and Tommy Firman. 1995. Problems and Challenges of Mega-Urban Regions in Indonesia: The Case of Jabotabek and the Bandung Metropolitan Area. In *The Mega-Urban Regions of Southeast Asia,* ed. T. G. McGee and Ira M. Robinson. Vancouver: University of British Columbia Press.

DKI Jakarta (Daerah Khusus Ibukota Jakarta). 1984. Perda 5. *Development Plan, Jakarta.* Jakarta: DKI.

Dollar, David. 2004. How to Reduce Poverty: Lessons from China. *Yale Global,* January 6.

Dong Liming. 1985. Beijing: The Development of a Socialist Capital. In *Chinese Cities: the Growth of the Metropolis since 1949,* ed. Victor F. S. Sit. Hong Kong: Oxford University Press.

Dowding, K., P. Dunleavy, D. King, and H. Margetts. 1995. Rational Choice and Community Power Structures. *Political Studies* 43, no. 2: 267–77.

Downs, Anthony. 2004. Traffic: Why It's Getting Worse, What Government Can Do. In

Cities and Suburbs. Washington, D.C.: Brookings Institution. Available at http://www.brookings.edu/comm/policybriefs.

Duggal, V. K., and G. K. Pandey. 2002. Air Quality Management in Delhi. Paper presented at Seminar on Better Air Quality in Asian and Pacific Rim Cities (BAQ 2002), Hong Kong, December 16–18.

Duran, Leoncio. 2001. Planning in a Changing Environment: The Case of Marilao in the Philippines. *Urban Agriculture Magazine,* no. 4 (July): 40–41.

Dwyer, Dennis J. 1974. *The City in the Third World.* London: Macmillan.

———. 1975. *People and Housing in Third World Cities: Perspectives on the Problems of Spontaneous Settlements.* London: Longman.

Easter, K. W., and G. Feder. 1997. Water Institutions, Incentives and Markets. In *Decentralization and Coordination of Water Resources Management,* ed. D. D. Parker and Y. Tsur. Boston: Kluwer Academic Publishers.

Ebanks, Edward, and Chaoze Cheng. 1990. China: A Unique Urbanization Model. *Asia Pacific Population Journal* 5, no. 3 (September): 29–50.

Ebel, Robert D., and François Vaillancourt. 2001. Fiscal Decentralization and Financing Urban Governments: Framing the Problems. In *The Challenge of Urban Government, Policies and Practices,* ed. Mila Freire and Richard Stren. Washington, D.C.: World Bank Institute.

Enright, Michael J., Kam-mun Chang, Edith E. Scott, and Wen-hui Zhu. 2003. *Hong Kong and the Pearl River Delta: The Economic Interaction.* Hong Kong: 2022 Foundation.

Ensink, Joroen, Tariq Mahmood, Wim van der Hoek, Liqa Raschid-Sally, and Felix Amerasinghe. 2002. Use of Untreated Wastewater in Peri-Urban Agriculture in Pakistan: Risks and Opportunities. Technical Report, International Water Management Institute, Colombo.

Environment and Urbanization. 1999. Sustainable Development Revisited II. *Environment and Urbanization* 11, no. 2 (October): 3–9.

Esguerra, George. 1994. Balanced Urban Transport Development Opportunities for Metro Manila. *Toyota Quarterly Review,* no. 8 (July) (The Wheel Extended).

Fei Xiaotong. 1984. *Exploitation of Small Cities and Towns,* Nanjing: Jiangsu People's Publishing House.

Fong, Alex. 2002. Port Planning for the Pearl River Delta Region: A Hong Kong Perspective. In *Building a Competitive Pearl River Delta Region: Cooperation, Coordination, and Planning,* ed. Anthony Gar-On Yeh, Yok-Shiu Lee, Tunney Lee, and Nien Dak Sze. Hong Kong: Centre of Urban Planning and Environmental Management, University of Hong Kong.

Foo Suan Tiek. 1998. Managing Transport Demand in Asian Cities. In *Promoting Sustainable Consumption in Asian Cities,* ed. United Nations Center for Human Settlement (Habitat). Fukuoka: Habitat Fukuoka Office.

Forester, J. 1989. *Planning in the Face of Power.* Berkeley: University of California Press.

Forstall, Richard, and Victor Jones. 1970. Selected Demographic, Economic and Governmental Aspects of the Contemporary Metropolis. In *Metropolitan Problems: International Perspectives,* ed. Simon Miles. Toronto: Methuen.

Fouracre, P. R., G. D. Jacobs, and D. A. C. Maunders. Characteristics of Conventional Public Transport Services in Third World Cities. *Traffic Engineering Control* 27, no. 12 (1996): 6–11.

French, R. A.. and F. E. Hamilton. 1979. *The Socialist City: Spatial Structure and Urban Policy.* New York: John Wiley & Sons.

Frick, Francis. 2000. *A Seaside Arcology of Southern China.* Vancouver: Office of Urban Agriculture, City Farmer Canada.

Friedmann, John. 1987. *Planning in the Public Domain: From Knowledge to Action.* Princeton, N.J.: Princeton University Press.

———. 1992. *Empowerment: The Politics of Alternative Development.* Cambridge, Mass.: Blackwell.

———. 1998. The Common Good: Assessing the Performance of Cities. In *City, Space and Globalization: An International Perspective,* ed. Hemalata Dandekar. Ann Arbor: University of Michigan Press.

Frischtak, Leila L. 1994. *Governing Capacity and Economic Reform in Developing Countries.* Technical Paper 254. Washington, D.C.: World Bank.

Fukami, Takatsune. 2000. The Urban Renewal Projects in Japan: Non-Residential Projects. In *Planning for a Better Living Urban Environment in Asia,* ed. Anthony Gar-On Yeh and Mee Kam Ng. Burlington, Vt.: Ashgate Publishing.

Fung, Victor. 2002. Hong Kong and the Pearl River Delta: Competing Together. In *Building a Competitive Pearl River Delta Region: Cooperation, Coordination, and Planning,* ed. Anthony Gar-On Yeh, Yok-Shiu F. Lee, Tunney Lee, and Nien Dak Sze. Hong Kong: Centre of Urban Planning and Environmental Management, University of Hong Kong.

Garreau, Joel. 1991. *Edge City: Life on the New Frontier.* New York: Doubleday.

Gaylican, Christine, and Agnes Donato. 2002. We Can No Longer Save Maynilad. *Philippine Daily Inquirer,* December 11.

Ginsburg, Norton. 1972. Planning the Future of the Asian City. In *The City as a Centre for Change in Asia,* ed. D. J. Dwyer. Hong Kong: Hong Kong University Press.

Ginsburg, Norton, B. Koppel, and T. G. McGee, eds. 1991. *The Extended Metropolis: Settlement Transition in Asia.* Honolulu: University of Hawaii Press.

Glasmeier, Amy. 1988. Factors Governing the Development of High-Tech Industry Agglomerations: A Tale of Two Cities. *Regional Studies* 22, no. 4: 287–301.

Goldstein, Sidney. 1994. Demographic Issues and Data Needs for Mega-City Research. In *Mega-City Growth and the Future,* ed. Roland Fuchs, Ellen Brennan, Joseph Chamie, Fu-chen Lo, and Joha I. Uitto. Tokyo: United Nations University Press.

Goodman, John B., and G. W. Loveman. 1991. Does Privatization Serve the Public Interest? *Harvard Business Review* 69, no. 5: 26–38.

Gottman, Jean. 1961. *Megalopolis: The Urbanized Northeastern Seaboard of the United States.* New York: Twentieth Century Fund and Kraus International Publications.

Goude, Andrew. 1990. *The Human Impact on the Natural Environment.* Cambridge, Mass.: MIT Press.

Grekel, Koreann. 1995. *Implementation of Community-Managed Water Supply and Sanitation Programs for Low-Income Communities: A Case Study of Indonesia.* Student Paper 29. Toronto: University Consortium on the Environment.

Gulyani, Sumila. 2001. The Demand Side Approach to Planning Water Supply. In *The Challenge of Urban Government: Policies and Practices,* ed. Mila Freire and Richard Stren. Washington, D.C.: World Bank Institute.

Hall, Peter. 1988. *Cities of Tomorrow.* New York: Blackwell.

———. 1992. *Urban and Regional Planning.* New York: Routledge.

Halliday, Deborah. 1995. The Human Side of Development: A Study of Migration, Housing and Community Satisfaction in Pudong New Area, People's Republic of

China. Master's thesis, School of Community and Regional Planning, University of British Columbia, Vancouver.

Hamer, Andrew. 1994. Economic Impacts of Third World Mega-Cities: Is Size the Issue? In *Mega-City Growth and the Future,* ed. Roland Fuchs, Ellen Brennan, Joseph Chamie, Fu-chen Lo, and Joha I. Uitto. Tokyo: United Nations University Press.

———. 1995. Urban China: Looking Forward, Looking Back. In *Chinese Cities and China's Development: A Preview of the Future Role of Hong Kong,* ed. Anthony Gar-On Yeh and Chai-Kwong Mak. Hong Kong: Centre of Urban Planning and Environmental Management, University of Hong Kong.

Hamm, Bernd, and Pandurang K. Muttagi, eds. 1999. *Sustainable Development and the Future of Cities.* New Delhi: Oxford and IBP Publishing Company.

Haque Bhuiyan, Mohamed Shamshul. 1999. Dhaka City, Bangladesh. Paper presented at Asian Development Strategy Conference, Tokyo.

Hardoy, Ana, and Ricardo Schusterman. 2000. New Models for the Privatization of Water and Sanitation for the Urban Poor. *Environment and Urbanization* 12, no. 2 (October): 63–75.

Harsono, Andreas. 2003. Water and Politics in the Fall of Suharto. Center for Public Integrity; http://www.icij.org/water.

Hasan, Arif. 2002. A Model for Government-Community Partnership in Building Sewage Systems for Urban Areas: The Experience of the Orangi Pilot Project Research and Training Institute (OPP-RTI), Karachi. *Water Science and Technology* 45, no. 8: 199–216.

Hau, Timothy. 2001. Demand-Side Measures and Road Pricing. In *Modern Transport in Hong Kong for the 21st Century,* ed. Anthony Gar-On Yeh, Peter Hills, and Simon Ka-Wing Ng. Hong Kong: Centre of Urban Planning and Environmental Management, Hong Kong University.

Hauser, Philip. 1957. *Urbanization in Asia and the Far East.* UNESCO Tensions and Technology Series. Calcutta: UNESCO.

Houn, Franklin W. 1973. *A Short History of Chinese Communism.* Englewood Cliffs, N.J.: Prentice Hall.

Howard, Ebenezer. 1965. *Garden Cities of Tomorrow.* Cambridge, Mass.: MIT Press.

Howard, Michael. 1993. *Asia's Environmental Crisis.* Boulder, Colo.: Westview Press.

Hsing You-tien. 1998. *Making Capitalism in China: The Taiwan Connection.* New York: Oxford University Press.

HUDCC (Housing and Urban Development Coordinating Council). 1995. *Metropolitan Manila Management Study.* Manila: Local Government Development Foundation.

Ibon Foundation. 2004. Water Crisis in Metro Manila: What's New? *Cyberdyaryo.* Available at http://www.codewan.com.ph.

Ikaputra, Kunihiro Narumi, and Takahiro Hisa. 2000. Preserving Traditional Architecture: Noble Residential Development Area Development in Java. In *Planning for a Better Living Urban Environment in Asia,* ed. Anthony Gar-On Yeh and Mee Kam Ng. Burlington, Vt.: Ashgate Publishing.

Institute for Research on Environment and the Economy. 1993. *Ecological Economics: Emergence of a New Development Paradigm.* Ottawa: University of Ottawa and the Canadian International Development Agency.

International Labor Organization. 1995. New Challenges and Opportunities for the Informal Sector. Background paper for a seminar on the informal sector, held in Metro Manila, November 28–29.

IREE (Institute for Research on Environment and the Economy). 1993. *Ecological Economics: Emergence of a New Development Paradigm*. Ottawa: University of Ottawa and the Canadian International Development Agency.

Islam, Nazrul, and Salma Shafi. 2004. Solid Waste Management and the Urban Poor in Dhaka. Paper presented at Forum on Urban Infrastructure and Public Service Delivery for the Urban Poor, Regional Focus: Asia, India Habitat Centre, New Delhi, June 24–25.

Iyer, Narayan. 2002. Efforts to Reduce Pollution from 2-Wheelers in India and Across Asia. Paper presented at Seminar on Better Air Quality in Asian and Pacific Rim Cities (BAQ 2002), Hong Kong, December 16–18.

Jabotabek. 2003. *Growth Centres and Population of Jabotabek in 2005*. Rencana Umum Tata Ruang (General Spatial Plan). Jakarta: Development Cooperation Board, Jabotabek. Available at http://www.unu.edu/unupress/unupbooks/uul.

Jain, A. K. 1996a. Calcutta: The Mega-Crucible. In *The Indian Mega-City and Economic Reforms*. New Delhi: Management Publishing Company.

———. 1996b. *The Indian Mega-City and Economic Reforms*. New Delhi: Management Publishing Company.

Jauregui-Roxas, Miguel. 2002. Mexico's Actions Towards the Implementation of the Monterrey Consensus. In *Global Agenda, 2002–2003: Meeting the Challenges*, ed. World Bank. Background Paper for the Annual Meetings of the World Bank and International Monetary Fund. Washington, D.C.: World Bank

Johnson, E. A. J. 1970. *The Organization of Space in Developing Countries*. Cambridge, Mass.: Harvard University Press.

Kammaier, Detlef, and Peter J. Swan, eds. 1984. *Equity with Growth? Planning Perspectives for Small Towns in Developing Countries*. Bangkok: Asian Institute of Technology.

Kaothien, Utis. 1995. The Bangkok Metropolitan Region: Policies and Issues in the Seventh Plan. In *The Mega-Urban Regions of Southeast Asia*, ed. T. G. McGee and Ira M. Robinson. Vancouver: University of British Columbia Press.

Karyoedi, Mochtarram. 1995. The Neighborhood Housing Redevelopment of Industri Dalam Area: Toward Comprehensive Urban Renewal of Bandung Inner City. Paper presented at International Workshop on Neighborhood Redevelopment, Zhongshan University, Guangzhou, September 16–20.

Khan, Shahed Anwer. 1992. Eviction, the Right to Shelter and the Urban Poor: A Study of Factors Influencing Eviction of Informal Settlements in Bangkok, Karachi and Seoul. Ph.D. dissertation, Human Settlements Development Division, Asian Institute of Technology, Bangkok.

Khan, Shahier. 2003. Reckless Urban Growth Chokes Bangladesh Capital. *One World;* http://www.oneworld.net.

Kim, Won Bae. 1999. National Competitiveness and Governance of Seoul, Korea. In *Urban and Regional Governance in Pacific Asia*, ed. John Friedmann. Vancouver: Institute of Asian Research, University of British Columbia.

Klitgaard, Robert, Ronald Maclean-Abaroa, and H. Lindsey Parris. 2000. *Corrupt Cities: A Practical Guide to Cure and Prevention*. Washington, D.C.: World Bank Institute.

KMDA (Kolkata Metropolitan Development Authority). 2004. Evolution of Kolkata Metropolitan Area. Available at http://www.cmdaonline.com/evolution.html.

Koc, Mustafa, Rod MacRae, Luc J. A. Mougeot, and Jennifer Welsh. 1999. *For Hunger-Proof Cities: Sustainable Food Systems*. Ottawa: International Development Research Centre.

Kokpol, Orathai. 1996. Thailand. In *The Changing Nature of Local Government in Developing Countries,* ed. Patricia McCarney. Toronto: Centre for Urban and Community Studies, University of Toronto.

Korff, Rudiger. 1989. *Bangkok and Modernity.* Bangkok: Social Research Institute, Chulalongkorn University.

Koswara, Mustaram. 1997. Urban Housing and Infrastructure Provision Financing in Indonesia. In *Urbanization in Large Developing Countries: China, Indonesia, Brazil and India,* ed. Gavin Joness and Pravin Visaria. Oxford: Clarendon Press.

Kundu, Nitai. 1994. *Planning the Metropolis: A Public Policy Perspective.* Calcutta: Minerva Associates.

Kwon, Tai-joon. 1972. Future Development Stages for Seoul. In *The City as a Centre of Change in Asia,* ed. D. J. Dwyer. Hong Kong: Hong University Press.

Lam Kin-che and Shu Tao. 1996. Environmental Quality and Pollution Control. In *Shanghai: Transformation and Modernization under China's Open Policy,* ed. Yueman Yeung and Sung Yun-wing. Hong Kong: Chinese University Press.

Landingin, Roel. 2003. *Loaves, Fishes and Dirty Dishes: Manila's Privatized Water Can't Handle the Pressure.* Washington, D.C.: Center for Public Integrity. Available at http://www.icij.org.

Laquian, Aprodicio. 1966. *The City in Nation-Building: Politics and Administration in Metropolitan Manila.* Manila: Institute of Public Administration, University of the Philippines.

———. 1969. *Slums Are for People: the Barrio Magsaysay Pilot Project in Philippine Urban Community Development.* Honolulu: East–West Center Press.

———. 1971. *Rural–Urban Migrants and Metropolitan Development.* Toronto: International Association for Metropolitan Research and Development (Intermet).

———. 1976. Whither Sites and Services? *Science* 192, no. 4243: 950–55.

———. 1983a. *Basic Housing: Policies for Sites, Services and Shelter in Developing Countries.* Ottawa: International Development Research Centre.

———. 1983b. Sites, Services and Shelter: An Evaluation. *Habitat International* 7, nos. 5–6: 216–25.

———. 1994. Social and Welfare Impacts of Mega-City Development. In *Mega-city Growth and the Future,* ed. Roland Fuchs, Ellen Brennan, Joseph Chamie, Fu-chen Lo, and Joha I. Uitto. Tokyo: United Nations University Press.

———. 1995. The Governance of Mega-Urban Regions. In *The Mega-Urban Regions of Southeast Asia,* ed. T. G. McGee and Ira M. Robinson. Vancouver: University of British Columbia Press.

———. 1996. The Multi-Ethnic and Multicultural City: An Asian Perspective. *International Social Science Journal* 47, no. 1 (March): 43–54.

———. 2002a. Metro Manila: People's Participation and Social Inclusion in a City of Villages. In *Urban Governance around the World,* ed. Blair Ruble, Richard Stren, Joseph Tulchin and Diana Varat. Washington, D.C.: Woodrow Wilson International Center for Scholars.

———. 2002b. Urban Governance: Some Lessons Learned. In *Democratic Governance and Urban Sustainability,* ed. Joseph S. Tulchin, Diana H. Varat and Blair A. Ruble. Washington, D.C.: Woodrow Wilson International Center for Scholars.

———. 2004. Who Are the Poor and How Are They Being Served in Asian Cities? Paper presented at Forum on Urban Infrastructure and Public Service Delivery for the Urban Poor, Regional Focus: Asia, India Habitat Centre, New Delhi, June 24–25.

Laquian, Aprodicio, and Eleanor R. Laquian. 2002. *The Erap Tragedy: Tales from the Snake Pit.* Manila: Anvil Publications.

Leaf, Michael. 1995. Inner City Redevelopment in China. *Cities* 12, no. 1: 12–20.

Lee, Rance. 1986. Bureaucratic Corruption in Asia: The Problem of Incongruence between Legal Norms and Folk Norms. In *Bureaucratic Corruption in Asia, Causes, Consequences and Control,* ed. Ledivina Carino. Manila: College of Public Administration, University of the Philippines.

Leftwich, Adrian. 1994. Governance, the State and the Politics of Development. *Development and Change* 19, no. 5: 299–316.

Liang Ssu-ch'eng. 1984. *A Pictorial History of Chinese Architecture,* ed. Wilma Fairbank. Cambridge, Mass.: Massachusetts Institute of Technology.

Lin, George. 1997. *Red Capitalism in South China: Growth and Development of the Pearl River Delta.* Vancouver: University of British Columbia Press.

———. 2002. The Growth and Structural Change of Chinese Cities: A Contextual and Geographic Analysis. *Cities* 19, no. 5: 299–316.

Lipton, Michael. 1977. *Why Poor People Stay Poor: Urban Bias in National Development.* Cambridge, Mass.: Harvard University Press.

Liu Yang. 1995. Environmental Aspects of Beijing's Old and Dilapidated Housing Renewal. *China City Planning Review* 11, no. 1 (March): 45–55.

Li Ying. 1997. The Housing Delivery Systems in Beijing: An International Perspective. Ph.D. dissertation, School of Community and Regional Planning, Faculty of Graduate Studies, University of British Columbia, Vancouver.

Maclaren, Virginia. 2004. Solid Waste Management in Asian Cities: Implications for the Urban Poor. Paper presented at Forum on Urban Infrastructure and Public Service Delivery for the Urban Poor, Regional Focus: Asia, India Habitat Centre, New Delhi, June 24–25.

Mangin, William. 1970. *Peasants in Cities: Readings in the Anthropology of Urbanization,* Boston: Houghton Mifflin.

Mao Qizhi. 1996. Small Town Development and Planning in the Beijing Metropolitan Region. Paper presented at International Workshop on Small Town Development, Tongji University, Shanghai, April 17–20.

Marshall, Alfred. 1920. *Principles of Economics,* 8th ed. London: Macmillan.

Marton, Andrew. 1996. Restless Landscapes: Spatial Economic Restructuring in China's Lower Yangzi Delta. Ph.D. dissertation, Department of Geography, Faculty of Arts, University of British Columbia, Vancouver.

Mathur, Om Prakash. 1996. Governing Cities in India, Nepal and Sri Lanka: The Challenge of Poverty and Globalization. In *Cities and Governance: New Directions in Latin America, Asia and Africa,* ed. Patricia L. McCarney. Toronto: Centre for Urban and Community Studies, University of Toronto.

MMC (Millennium Challenge Corporation). 2004. *The Millennium Challenge Account.* Available at http://www/mca.gov.

McCarney, Patricia, ed. 1996a. *The Changing Nature of Local Government in Developing Countries.* Toronto: Centre for Urban and Community Studies, University of Toronto.

———. 1996b. Reviving Local Government: The Neglected Tier in Development. In *The Changing Nature of Local Government in Developing Countries,* ed. Patricia McCarney. Toronto: Centre for Urban and Community Studies, University of Toronto.

McCarney, Patricia, Mohamed Alfani, and Alfredo Rodriguez. 1995. Towards an Understanding of Governance: The Emergence of an Idea and Its Implications for Urban

Research in Developing Countries. In *Urban Research in the Developing World: Perspectives on the City,* vol. 4, ed. Richard Stren and Judith K. Bell. Toronto: Centre for Urban and Community Studies, University of Toronto.

McDowell, Mark. 1993. Energy Strategies and Environmental Constraints in China's Modernization. In *Asia's Environmental Crisis,* ed. Michael C. Howard. Boulder, Colo.: Westview Press.

McGee, T. G. 1967. *The Southeast Asian City: A Social Geography of the Primate Cities of Southeast Asia.* London: G. Bell and Sons.

―――. 1995. Metrofitting the Emerging Mega-urban Regions of ASEAN: An Overview. In *The Mega-Urban Regions of Southeast Asia,* ed. T. G. McGee and Ira M. Robinson. Vancouver: University of British Columbia Press.

McGee, T. G., and C. Greenberg. 1992. The Emergence of Extended Metropolitan Regions in ASEAN, 1960–1980: An Exploratory Outline. In *Regional Development and Change in Southeast Asia in the 1990s,* ed. Amara Pongsapich, Michael C. Howard, and Jacques Amyot. Bangkok: Social Research Institute, Chulalongkorn University.

McGee, T. G., and Ira M. Robinson, eds. 1995. *The Mega-Urban Regions of Southeast Asia.* Vancouver: University of British Columbia Press.

Meng Xiaochen. 1995. Prosperity, Development and Sustainability: A Case Study of Shenzhen, China. Paper presented at Senior International Seminar on China's Small Town Development, Beijing, November 13–17.

Midgley, P. 1994. *Urban Transport in Asia: An Operational Agenda for the 1990s.* Washington, D.C.: World Bank.

Ministry of Construction, China. 2004. *Human Settlements Country Profile, China.* Beijing: Department of Urban and Regional Planning.

MMRDA (Mumbai Metropolitan Regional Development Authority). 2002. *Mumbai Urban Transport Project.* Report PID 8175. Washington, D.C.: World Bank.

Mok, Victor. 1996. Industrial Development. In *Shanghai: Transformation and Modernization under China's Open Policy,* ed. Yue-man Yeung and Sung Yun-wing. Hong Kong: Chinese University Press.

Monroe, James S., and Reed Wicander. 1997. *The Changing Earth: Exploring Geology and Evolution.* Belmont, Calif.: Wadsworth Publishing Company and West Publishing Company.

Morato, Edwardo, Jr. 1991. Alternative Delivery Systems for Poverty Alleviation. In *Reaching Out Effectively: Improving the Design, Management and Implementation of Poverty Alleviation Programmes,* ed. Ismael P. Getubig Jr. and M. Khalid Shamss. Kuala Lumpur: Asian and Pacific Development Centre.

Moulaert, F., and E. A. Swyngedouw. 1989. A Regulation Approach to the Geography of Flexible Production Systems. *Environment and Planning: Society and Space* 7: 327–45.

Mumford, Lewis. 1961. *The City in History.* New York: Harcourt, Brace and World.

NESDB (National Economic and Social Development Board). 1982. *The Fifth National Economic and Social Development Plan (1982–1986).* Bangkok: NESDB.

―――. 1990. *National Urban Development Policy Framework, Vol. 1, Final Report, Bangkok: Joint NESDB, UNDP and Thailand Development Research Institute (TDRI) Project.* Bangkok: NESDB.

―――. 1991. *National Urban Development Policy Framework.* Final Report, Joint UN Development Program–NESDB–Thailand Development Research Institute Project. Bangkok: NESDB.

Newman, P. W. G., and J. R. Kenworthy. 1989. *Cities and Automobile Dependence: A Sourcebook.* Aldershot, U.K.: Gower.

Ng, Ava. 2002. "Cross-Border Planning: The Interface between Hong Kong and the Mainland. In *Building a Competitive Pearl River Delta Region: Cooperation, Coordination, and Planning,* ed. Anthony Gar-On Yeh, Yok-Shiu F. Lee, Tunney Lee, and Nien Dak Sze. Hong Kong: Centre of Urban Planning and Environmental Management, University of Hong Kong.

Ng Mee Kam. 2000. An Extended Metropolis? A Growth Triangle? Towards Better Planning for the Hong Kong and Pearl River Delta Region. In *Planning for a Better Living Urban Environment in Asia,* ed. Anthony Gar-On Yeh and Mee Kam Ng. Burlington, Vt.: Ashgate Publishing.

Nguyen Quang Vinh. 1996. Social Implications of Ho Chi Minh Inner City Redevelopment Process. Paper presented at International Workshop on the Future of the Asian City, Institute of Social Sciences and Humanities, Ho Chi Minh City, December 2–7.

Nickum, J. E., and K. W. Easter, eds. 1994. *Metropolitan Water Use and Conflicts in Asia and the Pacific.* Boulder, Colo.: Westview Press.

Nourse, Mary A. 1943. *A Short History of the Chinese.* New York: New York Home Library. Originally published in 1935 as *The Four Hundred Million,* by Bobs-Merrill Company.

Ohmae, Kenichi. 1995. *The End of the Nation State: The Rise of Regional Economies,* New York: Free Press.

Olds, Kris. 1995. Pacific Rim Mega-Projects and the Global Cultural Economy: Tales from Vancouver and Shanghai. Ph.D. dissertation, Department of Geography, University of Bristol. Bristol, U.K.

Orangi Pilot Project. 1998. *Proposal for a Sewage Disposal System for Karachi.* Research and Training Institute, Orangi Pilot Project. Karachi: City Press.

Osaka Prefectural Government. 2000. *Rebuilding Osaka: Doubling Its Vitality, Comprehensive Plan for 21st Century Osaka.* Osaka: Office of the Governor of Osaka Prefecture.

———. 2002. *Traffic in Osaka.* Osaka: Traffic Policy Office.

Overby, R. 1985. The Urban Economic Environmental Challenge: Improvement of Human Welfare by Building and Managing Urban Ecosystems. Paper presented at the POLMET 85 Urban Environment Conference, sponsored by World Bank, Washington.

Pachauri, R. K., and A. Sen. 1998. Problems, Challenges and Prospects for Sustainable Management of Energy Demand in Asian Cities. In *Promoting Sustainable Consumption in Asian Cities,* ed. United Nations Center for Human Settlement (Habitat). Fukuoka: Habitat Fukuoka Office.

Pearl River Delta Economic Zone Planning Committee. 1996. *Plan for the Pearl River Delta Economic Zone of Guangdong Province.* (Original in Chinese.) Guangzhou: Guangdong Economy Press,

Peattie, Lisa. 1968. *The View from the Barrio.* Ann Arbor: University of Michigan Press.

———. 1982. Some Second Thoughts on Sites and Services. *Habitat International* 13, no. 3: 23–49.

Polese, Mario. 2000. Learning from Each Other: Policy Choices and the Social Sustainability of Cities. In *The Social Sustainability of Cities: Diversity and the Management of Change,* ed. Mario Polese and Richard Stren. Toronto: University of Toronto Press.

Pudong New Area Administration. 1991. *Shanghai Pudong New Area: Investment Environment and Development Prospect.* Shanghai: Shanghai Municipal Planning Bureau.

Pym, Christopher. 1968. *The Ancient Civilization of Angkor.* New York: New American Library.

Qian Guan. 1996. Lilong Housing: A Traditional Settlement Form. Master's thesis, School of Architecture, McGill University, Montreal.

Ray, Kalyan. 1998. Promoting Sustainable Consumption in Asian Cities. In *Promoting Sustainable Consumption in Asian Cities,* ed. United Nations Center for Human Settlement (Habitat). Fukuoka: Habitat Fukuoka Office.

Reader, John, and Harvey Croze. 1977. *Pyramids of Life: An Investigation of Nature's Fearful Symmetry.* London: William Collins Sons.

Rees, William. 1992. Ecological Footprints and Appropriated Carrying Capacity: What Urban Economics Leaves Out. *Environment and Urbanization* 4, no. 2 (October): 121–30.

———. 1994. Achieving Sustainability: Reforms or Transformation? *Journal of Planning Literature* 9, no. 3: 113–19.

———. 1998. Understanding Sustainable Development. In *Sustainable Development and the Future of Cities,* ed. Bernd Hamm and Pandurang K. Muttagi. New Delhi: Oxford and UBH Publishing Company.

Rees, William, and Mark Roseland. 1998. Sustainable Communities: Planning for the 21st Century. In *Sustainable Development and the Future of Cities,* ed. Bernd Hamm and Pandurang K. Muttagi. New Delhi: Oxford and UBH Publishing Company.

Rees, William, and Mathis Wackernagel. 1996. *Our Ecological Footprint: Reducing Human Impact on the Earth.* Gabriola Island, B.C.: New Society Publishers.

Reforma, Mila. 1977. An Evaluation of the Tondo Dagat-Dagatan Development Project: A Research Design. National Housing Authority, Manila.

Remenyi, Joe. 2000. *Poverty Reduction and Urban Renewal through Urban Agriculture and Microfinance: A Case Study of Dhaka, Bangladesh.* World Bank Technical Study. Washington, D.C.: World Bank.

Robben, P. M. 1987. Measurement of Population Dynamics Following Squatter Settlement Improvement in Ashok Nagar, Madras. In *Shelter Upgrading for the Urban Poor: Evaluation of Third World Experience,* ed. R. J. Skinner, J. L. Taylor, and E. A. Wegelin. Manila: Island Publishing House.

Rocamora, Joel. 2002. A Clash of Ideologies: International Capitalism and the State in the Wake of the Asian Crisis. In *Democratic Governance and Social Inequality,* ed. Joseph S. Tulchin and Amelia Brown. Boulder, Colo.: Lynne Reinner Publishers.

Rodrik, Dani. 1994. King Kong Meets Godzilla: The World Bank and the East Asian Miracle. In *Miracle or Design? Lessons from the East Asian Experience,* ed. A. Fishlow, G. Gwin, S. Haggard, and R. Wade. Policy Essay 11.Washington, D.C.: Overseas Development Council.

Rondinelli, Dennis. 1984. Small Towns in Developing Countries: Potential Centers of Growth, Transformation and Integration. In *Equity with Growth? Planning Perspectives for Small Towns in Developing Countries,* ed. H. Detlef Kammaier and Peter J. Swan. Bangkok: Asian Institute of Technology.

Rosegrant, M. W., and R. S. Meinzen-Dick. 1997. Water Resources in the Asia-Pacific Region: Managing Scarcity. *Asia Pacific Literature* 10, no. 2: 32–53.

Roth, G. *The Private Provision of Public Services in Developing Countries.* Washington, D.C.: World Bank, 1987.

Roth, L. 2000. An Economic Approach to Urban Development and Transportation in Metro Manila. Manila: Linköping University. Available at http://www.ep.liu.se.

Roy, Ananya. 2002. Marketized? Feminized? Medieval? Urban Governance in an Era of Liberalization. In *Democratic Governance and Urban Sustainability,* ed. Joseph S. Tulchin, Diana H. Varat, and Blair A. Ruble. Washington, D.C.: Woodrow Wilson International Center for Scholars.

Royama, Masamichi. 1972. Tokyo and Osaka. In *Great Cities of the World: Their Government, Politics and Planning,* ed. William A. Robson and D. E. Regan. London: George Allen and Unwin.

Ruble, Blair A., Richard E. Stren, Joseph S. Tulchin, and Diana Varat, eds. 2001. *Urban Governance around the World.* Washington, D.C.: Woodrow Wilson International Center for Scholars.

Ruble, Blair, Joseph Tulchin, and Allison M. Garland. 1996. Introduction: Globalism and Local Realities—Five Paths to the Urban Future. In *Preparing for the Urban Future: Global Pressures and Local Forces,* ed. Michael A. Cohen, Blair A. Ruble, Joseph Tulchin, and Allison M. Garland. Washington, D.C.: Woodrow Wilson Center Press.

Sancton, Andrew. 1994. *Governing Canada's City Regions: Adapting Form to Function.* Montreal: Institute for Research on Public Policy.

Sassen, Saskia. 1991. *The Global City: New York, London, Tokyo.* Princeton, N.J.: Princeton University Press.

———. 1994. *Cities in a World Economy.* London: Pine Forge Press.

Saxenian, Anna Lee. 1989. The Cheshire Cat's Grin: Innovation, Regional Development and the Cambridge Case. *Economy and Society* 18, no. 4 (November): 448–77.

Sazanami, Hidehiko. 2000. Challenges and Future Prospects of Planning for a Better Living Environment in the Large Cities of Asia. In *Planning for a Better Living Urban Environment in Asia,* ed. Anthony Gar-On Yeh and Mee Kam Ng. Burlington, Vt.: Ashgate Publishing.

Scott, Mel. 1971. *American City Planning since 1890.* Berkeley: University of California Press.

Sen, Amartya. 2002. How to Judge Globalism. *The American Prospect,* winter, A2–A5

Seoul City Government. 2000. Seoul's Urban Transportation Policy and Rail Transit Plan, Present and Future. *Japan Railway and Transport Review,* October.

Serageldin, Ismail. 1994. *Water Supply, Sanitation and Environmental Sustainability: The Financing Challenge.* Washington, D.C.: World Bank.

———. 1995. *Nurturing Development: Aid and Cooperation in Today's Changing World.* Washington, D.C.: World Bank.

Shah, Asad. 1996. Urban Trends and the Emergence of the Mega-City. In *The Future of Asian Cities,* ed. Jeffrey R. Stubbs. Manila: Asian Development Bank.

Shanghai Institute of Comprehensive Urban Transport Planning. 1994. Outline of the Comprehensive Urban Transport Planning for Shanghai. *China City Planning Review* 10, no. 2 (June): 52–55.

Shi Peijun, Lin Hui, and Liang Jinshe. 1996. Shanghai as a Regional Hub. In *Shanghai: Transformation and Modernization under China's Open Policy,* ed. Yue-man Yeung and Sung Yun-wing. Hong Kong: Chinese University Press.

Shiu Sin-por and Yang Chun. 2002. A Study on Developing the Hong Kong–Shenzhen Border Zone. In *Building a Competitive Pearl River Delta Region: Cooperation, Coordination, and Planning,* ed. Anthony Gar-On Yeh, Yok-shiu Lee, Tunney Lee, and Nien Dak Sze. Hong Kong: Centre of Urban Planning and Environmental Management, University of Hong Kong.

Silas, J. 1984. The Kampung Improvement Programme in Indonesia: A Comparative

Case Study of Jakarta and Surabaya. In *Low-Income Housing in the Developing World: The Role of Sites and Services and Settlement Upgrading,* ed. G. K. Payne. Chichester: John Wiley & Sons.

———. 1989. Community Participation in Urban Development: A Case Study from Indonesia. In *Community Participation in Urban Management: The Asian Experience,* ed. M. Bamberger and K. Shams. Kuala Lumpur: APDC and RDI–World Bank.

———. 1994. Impact Assessment of Kampung Improvement Program in Urban III. Paper presented at IBRD Evaluation Seminar, Surabaya, November 20–21.

Sit, Victor. 1985. *Chinese Cities: The Growth of the Metropolis since 1949.* Hong Kong: Oxford University Press.

Sivaramakrishnan, K. C. 1996. Urban Governance: Changing Realities. In *Preparing for the Urban Future: Global Pressures and Local Forces,* ed. Michael A. Cohen, Blair A. Ruble, Joseph Tulchin, and Allison M. Garland. Washington, D.C.: Woodrow Wilson Center Press.

———. 2001. Confronting Urban Issues with a Metropolitan View in Mumbai, India. In *Urban Governance around the World,* ed. Blair Ruble, Richard Stren, Joseph Tulchin and Diana Varat. Washington, D.C.: Woodrow Wilson International Center for Scholars.

Sivaramakrishnan, K. C., and Leslie Green. 1986. *Metropolitan Management: The Asian Experience.* Oxford: Oxford University Press.

Sjoberg, Gideon. 1960. *The Preindustrial City: Past and Present,* New York: Free Press.

Smart Growth Network. 2003. *Getting to Smart Growth: 100 Policies for Implementation.* Washington, D.C.: International City/County Management Association, U.S. Environmental Protection Agency, and Smart Growth Network.

Soegijoko, Budhy Tjahjati S. 1981. *Public Transportation in Bandung.* Bandung: Department of Planning, Institute of Technology.

———. 1996. Jabotabek and Globalization. In *Emerging World Cities in Pacific Asia,* ed. Fu-chen Lo and Yue-man Yeung. Tokyo: United Nations University Press.

Sohail, M. 2000. Urban Public Transport and Sustainable Development for the Poor: A Case Study of Karachi, Pakistan. Water Engineering and Development Centre, Loughborough, U.K.

Spiller, Pablo T., and Willliam D. Savedoff. 1999. Government Opportunism and the Provision of Water. In *Spilled Water: Institutional Commitment in the Provision of Water Services,* ed. William Savedoff and Pablo Spiller. Washington, D.C.: Inter-American Development Bank.

Sternstein, Larry. 1972. Planning the Future of Bangkok. In *The City as a Centre of Change in Asia,* ed. D. J. Dwyer. Hong Kong: Hong University Press.

Stokke, K. 1997. Authoritarianism in the Age of Market Liberalism in Sri Lanka. *Antipode* 24, no. 4: 437–55.

Stren, Richard. 2001. Introduction. In *Urban Governance around the World,* ed. Blair Ruble, Richard Stren, Joseph Tulchin and Diana Varat. Washington, D.C.: Woodrow Wilson International Center for Scholars.

Sung Woong Hong. 1996. Seoul: A Global City in a Nation of Rapid Growth. In *Emerging World Cities in Pacific Asia,* ed. Fu-chen Lo and Yue-man Yeung. Tokyo: United Nations University Press.

Sun Wen-bin and Wong Siu-lun. 2002. The Development of Private Enterprise in Contemporary China: Institutional Foundations and Limitations. *China Review* 2, no. 2 (fall): 65–91.

Swyngedouw, E. 1996. The Contradiction of Urban Water Provision. *Third World Planning Review* 17, no. 4: 65–80.

Takahashi, Junjiro, and Noriyuki Sugiura. 1996. The Japanese Urban System and the Growing Centrality of Tokyo in the Global Economy. In *Emerging World Cities in Pacific Asia,* ed. Fu-chen Lo and Yue-man Yeung. Tokyo: United Nations University Press.

Tan Ying. 1994. Social Aspects of Beijing's Old and Dilapidated Housing Renewal. *China City Planning Review* 10, no. 4 (December): 45–55.

Tapales, Proserpina. 1993. *Devolution and Empowerment: The Local Government Code of 1991 and Local Autonomy in the Philippines.* Quezon City: Philippine Center for Integrative and Development Studies, University of the Philippines.

———. 1996. The Philippines. In *The Changing Nature of Local Government in Developing Countries,* ed. Patricia McCarney. Toronto: Centre for Urban and Community Studies, University of Toronto.

Taubman, Wolfgang. 2002. Urban Administration, Urban Development and Migrant Enclaves: The Case of Guangzhou. In *Resource Management, Urbanization and Governance in Hong Kong and the Zhujiang Delta,* ed. Wong Kwan-jiu and Shen Jianfa. Hong Kong: Chinese University Press.

Taylor, J. L. 1987. Evaluation of the Jakarta Kampung Improvement Program. In *Shelter Upgrading and the Urban Poor: Evaluation of the World Experience,* ed. R. J. Skinner, J. L. Taylor, and E. A. Wegelin. Manila: Island Publishing House.

Thomas, Vinod, Mansoor Dailami, Ashok Dhareshwar, Daniel Kaufmann, Nalin Kishor, Ramon Lopez, and Yan Wang. 2000. *The Quality of Growth.* New York: Oxford University Press.

Tinker, Irene. 1997. *Street Foods: Urban Food and Employment in Developing Countries.* Oxford: Oxford University Press.

Tiwari, Geetam. 2002. Bus Priority Lanes for Delhi. In *Urban Transport for Growing Cities: High Capacity Bus Systems,* ed. Geetam Tiwari. New Delhi: Macmillan India.

Tokyo Bureau of City Planning. 2003. *The Tokyo Plan 2000.* Tokyo: Tokyo Bureau of City Planning. Available at http: //www.toshikei.metro.tokyo.

Tokyo Metropolitan Government. 2003. *Transportation,* Tokyo: Bureau of City Planning.

Tongji University. 1995. *A Survey of Nanshi District, Shanghai.* Shanghai: Faculty of Architecture and Urban Planning.

———. 1996a. The Human Settlement of Small Towns in Metropolitan Shanghai. Report submitted to Asian Urban Research Network, Faculty of Architecture and Urban Planning, Shanghai.

———. 1996b. The Renovation of Shanghai Old Residential Areas and Buildings. Report submitted to Asian Urban Research Network by the Faculty of Architecture and Urban Planning, Tongji University, Shanghai.

Turner, John F. C. 1965. Lima's Barriadas and Corralones: Suburbs vs. Slums. *Ekistics* 19, no. 12: 152–55.

———. 1968. The Squatter Settlement: An Architecture that Works. *Architectural Design* 38, no. 8: 357–60.

———. 1976. *Housing by People: Towards Autonomy in Building Environments.* New York: Pantheon Books.

Turner, John F. C., and R. Fichter, eds. 1972. *Freedom to Build.* New York: Macmillan.

UNCHS (United Nations Center for Human Settlements; Habitat). 1996. *An Urbanizing World: Global Report on Human Settlements, 1996.* Oxford: Oxford University Press.

————. 2001. *Cities in a Globalizing World: Global Report on Human Settlements, 2001.* London: Earthscan Publications.

UNDP (United Nations Development Program). 2002. *Promoting Good Governance in the Arab States,* New York: United Nations Office for Project Services.

UNICEF (United Nations Children's Fund). 1993. *Planning for Health and Socio-Economic Benefits from Water and Environment Sanitation Programs.* Workshop Summary. New York: UNICEF.

United Nations. 1986. *Population Growth and Policies in Mega-Cities: Bombay.* Population Policy Paper 6. New York: Department of International Economic and Social Affairs, United Nations.

————. 1987a. *Population Growth and Policies in Mega-Cities: Bangkok.* Population Policy Paper 10. New York: Department of International Economic and Social Affairs, United Nations.

————. 1987b. *Population Growth and Policies in Mega-Cities: Dhaka.* Population Policy Paper 8. New York: Department of International Economic and Social Affairs, United Nations.

————. 1988. *Population Growth and Policies in Mega-Cities: Karachi.* Population Policy Paper 13. New York: Department of International Economic and Social Affairs, United Nations.

————. 1989. *Population Growth and Policies in Mega-Cities: Jakarta.* Population Policy Paper 18. New York: Department of International Economic and Social Affairs, United Nations.

————. 1998a. *World Population Prospects: The 1996 Revision.* New York: Population Division, Department of Economic and Social Affairs, United Nations.

————. 1998b. *World Urbanization Prospects: The 1996 Revision.* New York: Population Division, Department of Economic and Social Affairs, United Nations.

————. 2001. *World Urbanization Prospects, the 2001 Revision,* New York: Population Division, Department of Economic and Social Affairs, United Nations.

Van Horen, Basil. 1996. Informal Settlement Upgrading in Durban, South Africa: Building Institutional Capacity to Sustain the Improvement Process. Ph.D. dissertation, School of Community and Regional Planning, University of British Columbia, Vancouver.

————. 2004. Community Upgrading and Institutional Capacity Building to Benefit the Urban Poor in Asia. Paper presented at Forum on Urban Infrastructure and Public Service Delivery for the Urban Poor, Regional Focus: Asia, India Habitat Centre, New Delhi, June 24–25.

Villanueva, Hector. 2002. Maynilad's Water Woes. *Manila Bulletin,* December 3.

Vogel, Ronald K. 2001. Decentralization and Urban Governance: Reforming Tokyo Metropolitan Government. In *Urban Governance around the World,* ed. Blair Ruble, Richard Stren, Joseph Tulchin, and Diana Varat. Washington, D.C.: Woodrow Wilson International Center for Scholars.

Walsh, Annmarie Hauck. 1969. *The Urban Challenge to Government.* New York: Frederick A. Praeger.

Wang, James, and Cherry Ho. 2002. Competition, Cooperation and Governance of Airports in the Greater Pearl River Delta Region. In *Building a Competitive Pearl River Delta Region: Cooperation, Coordination, and Planning,* ed. Anthony Gar-On Yeh, Yok-Shiu F. Lee, Tunney Lee, and Nien Dak Sze. Hong Kong: Centre of Urban Planning and Environmental Management, University of Hong Kong.

Wang, Jixian James, and Crystal Chan. 2004. Public Transport and Planned High-Density Living in Hong Kong: Do They Help the Poor? Paper presented at Forum on Urban Infrastructure and Public Service Delivery for the Urban Poor, Regional Focus: Asia, India Habitat Centre, New Delhi, June 24–25.

Wang Cun. 1990. The Development of Information Activities in the Special Economic Zones of China. *Journal of Information Science* 16: 393–98.

Wang Jian. 1995. Some Issues of China's Long Term Economic Development. In *Chinese Cities and China's Development: A Preview of the Future Role of Hong Kong*, ed. Anthony Gar-On Yeh and Chai-Kwong Mak. Hong Kong: Centre of Urban Planning and Environmental Management, University of Hong Kong.

Wardrop Engineering. 1995. Second Subic Bay Freeport Project, Final Report." Report Submitted to World Bank and Subic Bay Metropolitan Authority, Washington and Winnipeg.

WCED (World Commission on Environment and Development). 1987. *Our Common Future* (Brundtland Commission Report). Oxford: Oxford University Press.

Wickramanayake, Ebel, and Hu Biliang. 1993. *Emergence of Rural Industrial Township Enterprises in China.* Working Paper 42. Bangkok: Human Settlements Development Division, Asian Institute of Technology.

Widianto, Bambang. 1993. Solid Waste Management in Jakarta: Problems and Alternatives at the Community Level. Major paper, master's in environmental sciences, Faculty of Environmental Studies, York University, Toronto.

Wirth, Louis. 1938. Urbanism as a Way of Life. *American Journal of Sociology* 44, no. 1 (July): 1–24.

Witty, David. 1998. Identifying a More Appropriate Role for the Canadian Planning Profession. Ph.D. dissertation, School of Community and Regional Planning, Faculty of Graduate Studies, University of British Columbia, Vancouver.

Wong, Francis, and Eddie Hui. 2000. *Housing Reform in Southern China: Shenzhen and Guangzhou.* Hong Kong: Department of Building and Real Estate, Hong Kong Polytechnic University.

Wong Kam Sing. 1996. Dwelling Densification and "Greenness": Hong Kong's High Density Housing and Resources Conservation. M.S. thesis, School of Architecture, University of British Columbia, Vancouver.

World Bank. 1993a. *The East Asian Economic Miracle: Economic Growth and Public Policy.* New York: Oxford University Press.

———. 1993b. *Indonesia: Urban Public Infrastructure Services.* Washington, D.C.: World Bank.

———. 1994. *Indonesia: Sustaining Development—A Country Study Report.* Washington, D.C.: World Bank.

———. 1995. *Better Urban Services: Finding the Right Incentives.* New York: Oxford University Press.

———. 2000. *Transport Strategy Review.* Washington, D.C.: World Bank.

———. 2002a. *Financing for Sustainable Development.* Washington, D.C.: International Monetary Fund, UN Environment Program, and Environment Department of the World Bank.

———. 2002b. *Global Agenda 2002–2003: Meeting the Challenges.* Document for the Annual Meetings of the World Bank and International Monetary Fund. Washington, D.C.: World Bank.

World Bank–Netherlands Water Partnership Program. 2002. *Stimulating Innovative Performance and Supporting World Bank Operations in Water Management,* Washington, D.C.: World Bank and Netherlands Ministry of Foreign Affairs.

World Health Organization. 1988. *Health Education in Food Safety.* Geneva: World Health Organization.

————. 1992. *Our Planet, Our Health: Report of the WHO Commission on Health and the Environment,* Geneva.

Wright, Arthur. 1977. The Cosmology of the Chinese City. In *The City in Late Imperial China,* ed. William G. Skinner. Stanford, Calif.: Stanford University Press.

Wu Chung-tong. 2000. Whither Asian Planning Education? In *Planning for a Better Living Urban Environment in Asia,* ed. Anthony Gar-On Yeh and Mee Kam Ng. Burlington, Vt.: Ashgate Publishing.

Wu Liangyong. 1986. *A Brief History of Ancient Chinese City Planning.* Kassel, West Germany: Urbs et Region Publication.

————. 1999. *Rehabilitating the Old City of Beijing: A Project in the Ju'er Hutong Neighbourhood.* Vancouver: University of British Columbia Press.

Wu Liangyong and Mao Qizhi. 1993. On the Integrated Development of Beijing and Some Potential Growth Areas in the Beijing Metropolitan Region. Paper presented at International Workshop on Metropolitan Development, Tsinghua University, Beijing, October 12–14.

Xiong Luxia. 1994. The Planning of Shanghai Yuyuan Tourist and Shopping Center. *China City Planning Review* 10, no. 2 (June): 47–51.

Xue Desheng. 1996. *Industry of Renhe Town : Development and Linkage.* Working Paper 9. Guangzhou: Centre for Urban and Regional Studies, Zhongshan University.

Xu Xueqiang and Xu Yongjian. 2002. A Study on an Integrated Cross-Border Transport Network for the Pearl River Delta. In *Building a Competitive Pearl River Delta Region: Cooperation, Coordination, and Planning,* ed. Anthony Gar-On Yeh, Yok-Shiu F. Lee, Tunney Lee, and Nien Dak Sze. Hong Kong: Centre of Urban Planning and Environmental Management, University of Hong Kong.

Yan Xiaopei. 1995a. *The Satellite Towns of Metropolitan Guangzhou: Evolution, Inherent Links with the Central City Tendencies—A Case Study of Renhe Town.* Working Paper 3, Asian Urban Research Network Project. Guangzhou: Centre for Urban and Regional Studies, Zhongshan University.

————. 1995b. *A Study of the Migrant Labor Force of China in Recent Years: A Case Study of Nanhai City of Guangdong Province.* Working Paper 13, Asian Urban Research Network Project. Guangzhou: Centre for Urban and Regional Studies, Zhongshan University.

Yan Zhongmin. 1985. Shanghai: The Growth and Shifting Emphasis of China's Largest City. In *Chinese Cities: the Growth of the Metropolis since 1949,* ed. Victor F. S. Sit. Hong Kong: Oxford University Press.

Yee, Francis. 1992. Economic and Urban Changes in the Shenzhen Special Economic Zone, 1979–1986. Ph.D. dissertation, Department of Geography, University of British Columbia, Vancouver.

Yeh, Anthony Gar-On. 1995. *Planning Hong Kong for the 21st Century: A Preview of the Future Role of Hong Kong.* Hong Kong: Centre for Urban Planning and Environmental Management, University of Hong Kong.

Yeh, Anthony Gar-On, Peter Hills, and Simon Ka-Wing Ng, eds. 2001. *Modern Trans-*

port in Hong Kong for the 21st Century. Hong Kong: Centre of Urban Planning and Environmental Management, University of Hong Kong.

Yeh, Anthony Gar-On, Yok Shiu Lee, Tunney Lee, and Nien Dak Sze, eds. 2002. *Building a Competitive Pearl River Delta Region: Cooperation, Coordination, and Planning.* Hong Kong: Centre of Urban Planning and Environmental Management, University of Hong Kong.

Yeh, Anthony Gar-On, and Xia Li. 1996. An Integrated Remote Sensing and GIS Approach in the Monitoring and Evaluation of Rapid Urban Growth for Sustainable Development in the Pearl River Delta, China. *International Planning Studies* 2, no. 2: 195–222.

Yeh, Anthony Gar-On, and Fulong Wu. 1996. The New Land Development Process and Urban Development in Chinese Cities. *International Journal of Urban and Regional Research* 20, no. 2: 330–53.

Yeh, Stephen H. K. 1975. *Public Housing in Singapore: A Multi-disciplinary Study.* Singapore: Singapore University Press.

Yeh, Stephen H. K., and Aprodicio Laquian, eds. 1979. *Housing Asia's Millions: Problems, Policies and Prospects for Low Cost Housing in Southeast Asia,* Ottawa: International Development Research Centre.

Ye Shun-zan. 1986. City and Town Development in the Beijing-Tianjin-Tangshan Region. *Economic Geography* 3, no. 1 (spring): 37–41.

Yeung Yue-man. 1990. *Changing Cities of Pacific Asia: A Scholarly Interpretation.* Hong Kong: Chinese University Press.

Yin Yonguan and Mark Wang. 2000. China's Urban Environmental Sustainability in a Global Context. In *Consuming Cities: The Urban Environment in the Global Economy after the Rio Declaration,* ed. Nicholas Low, B. Gleason, I. Elander, and R. Lidskog. New York: Routledge.

Yu, Verna. 2003. In Modern Beijing, Officials Seek to Save Space for the Past. *South China Morning Post,* October 30, A-8.

Yu Minfei and Shai Feng. 1995. A Study of the Reconstruction of Shanghai's Old Residential Areas. Report to the Asian Urban Research Network from the College of Architecture and Urban Planning, Tongji University, Shanghai.

Zhang Jie. 1993. Neighborhood Redevelopment in the Inner City Areas of Beijing. Paper presented at International Workshop on Mega-Urban Region Development, Tsinghua University, Beijing, November 24–27.

Zhang Jinggan. 1993. Two Strategic Diversions in the Urban Development of Beijing. *China City Planning Review* 9, no. 4 (December): 10–14.

Zhao Bingshi, Chen Baorong, and Zhang Jie. 1992. An Introduction to Beijing and Its Metropolitan Region. Paper presented at Regional Workshop on Metropolitan and Regional Planning, Chulalongkorn University, Bangkok, June 29–July 3.

Bibliography

Books and Monographs

Abrams, Charles. *Man's Struggle for Shelter in an Urbanizing World.* Cambridge, Mass.: MIT Press, 1964.

Abueva, Jose V. *Focus on the Barrio: The Story behind the Birth of the Philippine Community Development Program under President Ramon Magsaysay.* Manila: Institute of Public Administration, University of the Philippines, 1959.

Anderson, T. L., and P. Snyder. *Water Markets: Priming the Invisible Pump.* Washington, D.C.: Cato Institute, 1997.

Angel, Shlomo. *Housing Policy Matters: A Global Analysis.* Oxford: Oxford University Press, 2000.

Armstrong-Wright, A. *Public Transport in Third World Cities.* London: Her Majesty's Stationery Office, 1993.

Bannister, D., and K. Button, eds. *Transport, the Environment, and Sustainable Development.* London: E. & F.N. Spon, 1993.

Barross, Paul, and Jan van der Linden, eds. *The Transformation of Land Supply in Third World Cities.* Brookfield, Vt.: Gower Publishing Company, 1993.

Brandon, C., and R. Ramankutty. *Toward an Environmental Strategy for Asia,* Washington, D.C.: World Bank, 1993.

Breese. Gerald. *Urbanization in Developing Countries.* Englewood Cliffs, N.J.: Prentice Hall, 1966.

Breheny, M. J., ed. *Sustainable Development and Urban Form.* London: European Research in Regional Science, 1992.

Brockman, Royston, and Allen Williams, eds. *Urban Infrastructure Finance.* Manila: Water Supply, Urban Development, and Housing Division, Asian Development Bank, 1996.

Caoili, Manuel A. *The Origins of Metropolitan Manila: A Political and Social Analysis.* Quezon City: New Day Publishers, 1988.

Carino, Ledivina V. *Bureaucratic Corruption in Asia: Causes, Consequences and Control.* Manila: College of Public Administration, University of the Philippines, 1986.

Castells, Manuel. *The Informational City: Information, Technology, Economic Restructuring and the Urban-Regional Process.* Oxford: Blackwell, 1989.

————. *The Power of Identify.* Oxford: Blackwell, 1997.

————. *The Rise of the Network Society.* Oxford: Blackwell, 1996.

Chandoke, S. K. *Habitation and Environment, Inter-Actions, Inter-Relations and Adjustments.* New Delhi: Har-anand Publications, 1994.

Childe, Gordon V. *The Dawn of European Civilization.* London: Routledge and Kegan Paul, 1957.

Clark, Robin. *Water: The International Crisis.* Cambridge, Mass.: MIT Press, 1993.

Cohen, Michael, Blair A. Ruble, Joseph H. Tulchin, and Allison M. Garland, eds. *Preparing for the Urban Future: Global Pressures and Local Forces.* Washington, D.C.: Woodrow Wilson Center Press, 1996.

Coronel, Sheila. *Betrayal of the Public Trust: Investigative Reports on Corruption.* Manila: Philippine Center for Investigative Journalism, 2000.

————. *Pork and Other Perks: Corruption and Governance in the Philippines.* Quezon City: Philippine Center for Investigative Journalism, 1998.

Corson, Walter. *The Global Economy Handbook.* Boston: Beacon Press, 1990.

Daly, Herman, and Kenneth N. Townsend, eds. *Valuing the Earth: Economics, Ecology, Ethics.* Cambridge, Mass.: MIT Press, 1993.

Dandekar, Hemalata, ed. *City, Space and Globalization: An International Perspective.* Ann Arbor: College of Architecture and Planning, University of Michigan, 1998.

Dimitriou, Harry T., ed. *Moving Away from the Motor Vehicle: The German and Hong Kong Experience.* Hong Kong: Centre of Urban Planning and Environmental Management, University of Hong Kong, 1994.

Dwyer, Dennis J. *The City in the Third World.* London: Macmillan, 1974.

————. *People and Housing in Third World Cities: Perspectives on the Problems of Spontaneous Settlements.* London: Longman, 1975.

Enright, Michael J., Ka-mun Chang, Edith E. Scott, and Wen-hui Zhu. *Hong Kong and the Pearl River Delta: The Economic Interaction.* Hong Kong: 2022 Foundation, 2003.

Fei Xiaotong. *Exploitation of Small Cities and Towns.* Nanjing: Jiangsu People's Publishing House, 1984.

Forester, J. *Planning in the Face of Power.* Berkeley: University of California Press, 1989.

Freire, Mila, and Richard Stren, eds. *The Challenge of Urban Government: Policies and Practices.* Washington, D.C.: World Bank Institute, 2001.

French, R. A.. and F. E. Hamilton. *The Socialist City: Spatial Structure and Urban Policy.* New York: John Wiley & Sons, 1979.

Friedmann, John. *Empowerment: The Politics of Alternative Development.* Cambridge, Mass.: Blackwell, 1992.

————. *Planning in the Public Domain: From Knowledge to Action.* Princeton, N.J.: Princeton University Press, 1987.

————, ed. *Urban and Regional Governance in Pacific Asia.* Vancouver: Institute of Asian Research, University of British Columbia, 1999.

Frischtak, Leila L. *Governance Capacity and Economic Reform in Developing Countries.* Technical Paper 254. Washington, D.C.: World Bank, 1994.

Fuchs, Roland, Ellen Brennan, Joseph Chamie, Fu-chen Lo, and Joha I. Uitto, eds. *Mega-City Growth and the Future.* Tokyo: United Nations University Press, 1994.

Garreau, Joel. *Edge City: Life on the New Frontier.* New York: Doubleday, 1991.

Getubig, Ismael P., and M. Khalid Shams, eds. *Reaching Out Effectively: Improving the*

Design, Management and Implementation of Poverty Alleviation Programmes. Kuala Lumpur: Asian and Pacific Development Centre, 1991.

Ginsburg, Norton, B. Koppel, and T. G. McGee, eds. *The Extended Metropolis: Settlement Transition in Asia.* Honolulu: University of Hawaii Press, 1991.

Glickman, N. J. *The Growth and Management of the Japanese Urban System.* New York: Academic Press, 1979.

Gottman, Jean. *Megalopolis: The Urbanized Northeastern Seaboard of the United States.* New York: Twentieth Century Fund and Kraus International Publications, 1961.

Goude, Andrew. *The Human Impact on the Natural Environment.* Cambridge, Mass.: MIT Press, 1990.

Hainsworth, Geoffrey, ed. *Localized Poverty Reduction in Viet Nam.* Vancouver: Centre for Southeast Asia Research, University of British Columbia, 1999.

Hall, Peter. *Cities of Tomorrow.* New York: Blackwell, 1988.

———. *Urban and Regional Planning.* New York: Routledge, 1992.

Hamm, Bernd, and Pandurang K. Muttagi, eds. *Sustainable Development and the Future of Cities.* New Delhi: Oxford and IBH Publishing Company, 1999.

Hauser, Philip M., ed. *Urbanization in Asia and the Far East.* Tensions and Technology Series. Calcutta: UNESCO, 1957.

Hershkowitz, Allen, and Eugene Salerni. *Garbage Management in Japan: Leading the Way.* New York: Inform, Inc., 1987.

Houn, Franklin W. *A Short History of Chinese Communism.* Englewood Cliffs, N.J.: Prentice Hall, 1973.

Howard, Ebenezer. *Garden Cities of Tomorrow.* Cambridge, Mass.: MIT Press, 1965.

Howard, Michael. *Asia's Environmental Crisis,* Boulder, Colo.: Westview Press, 1993.

Hsing, You-tien. *Making Capitalism in China: The Taiwan Connection.* Oxford: Oxford University Press, 1998.

Institute for Research on Environment and the Economy. *Ecological Economics: Emergence of a New Development Paradigm.* Ottawa: University of Ottawa and the Canadian International Development Agency, 1993.

Institute for Research in Public Policy. *Governing Canada's City-Regions: Adapting Form to Function.* Monograph Series on City-Regions 2. Montreal: Institute for Research in Public Policy, 1994.

Jain, A. K. *The Indian Mega-City and Economic Reforms,* New Delhi: Management Publishing Company, 1996.

Johnson, E. A. J. *The Organization of Space in Developing Countries.* Cambridge, Mass.: Harvard University Press, 1970.

Jones, Gavin, and Pravin Visaria, eds. *Urbanization in Large Developing Countries: China, Indonesia, Brazil, and India.* Oxford: Clarendon Press, 1997.

Kammeier, H. Detlef, and Peter J. Swan, eds. *Equity with Growth? Planning Perspectives for Small Towns in Developing Countries.* Bangkok: Asian Institute of Technology, 1984.

Kasarda, John D., and Allan M. Parnell, eds. *Third World Cities: Problems, Policies and Prospects.* Newbury Park, Calif.: Sage Publications, 1993.

Klitgaard, Robert, Ronald Maclean-Abaroa, and H. Lindsey Parris. *Corrupt Cities: A Practical Guide to Cure and Prevention.* Washington, D.C.: World Bank Institute, 2000.

Koc, Mustafa, Rod MacRae, Luc J. A. Mougeot, and Jennifer Welsh. *For Hunger-Proof Cities: Sustainable Food Systems.* Ottawa: International Development Research Centre, 1999.

Korff, Rudiger. *Bangkok and Modernity.* Bangkok: Social Research Institute, Chulalongkorn University, 1989.

Kundu, Nitai. *Planning the Metropolis: A Public Policy Perspective.* Calcutta: Minerva Associates, 1994.

Laquian, Aprodicio. *Administrative Aspects of Urbanization.* Document ST/TAO/M/51. New York: Public Administration Division, Department of Economic and Social Affairs, United Nations, 1970.

———. *Basic Housing: Policies for Urban Sites, Services and Shelter in Developing Countries.* Ottawa: International Development Research Centre, 1983.

———. *The City in Nation-Building: Politics and Administration in Metropolitan Manila.* Manila: School of Public Administration, University of the Philippines, 1966.

———. *Rural–Urban Migrants and Metropolitan Development.* Toronto: International Association for Metropolitan Research and Development (Intermet), 1971.

———. *Slums Are for People: The Barrio Magsaysay Pilot Project in Philippine Urban Community Development.* Honolulu: East–West Center Press, 1969.

Laquian, Aprodicio, and Eleanor R. Laquian. *The Erap Tragedy: Tales from the Snake Pit.* Manila: Anvil Publications, 2002.

Laquian, Aprodicio, and Stephen H. K. Yeh, eds. *Housing Asia's Millions: Problems, Policies and Prospects for Low-Cost Housing in Southeast Asia.* Ottawa: International Development Research Centre, 1979.

Liang Ssu-ch'eng. *A Pictorial History of Chinese Architecture.* Edited by Wilma Fairbank.Cambridge, Mass.: MIT Press, 1984.

Lin, George. *Red Capitalism in South China.* Vancouver: University of British Columbia Press, 1997.

Lincoln, Y., and E. Guba. *Naturalistic Inquiry.* Beverley Hills, Calif.: Sage Publications, 1985.

Lipton, Michael. *Why Poor People Stay Poor: Urban Bias in National Development.* Cambridge, Mass.: Harvard University Press, 1977.

Lo Fu-chen and Kemal Salih. *Growth Pole Strategy and Regional Development Policy: Asian Experiences and Alternative Approaches,* Oxford: Pergamon Press, 1978.

Lo Fu-chen and Yue-man Yeung, eds. *Emerging World Cities in Pacific Asia.* Tokyo: United Nations University Press, 1996.

Mangin, William. *Peasants in Cities: Readings in the Anthropology of Urbanization.* Boston: Houghton Mifflin, 1970.

Mara, Duncan, and Sandy Cairncross. *Guidelines for the Safe Use of Wastewater and Excreta in Agriculture and Aquaculture.* Geneva: World Health Organization, 1989.

Marshall, Alfred. *Principles of Economics.* 8th ed. London: Macmillan, 1920.

McCarney, Patricia, ed. *The Changing Nature of Local Government in Developing Countries.* Toronto: Centre for Urban and Community Studies, University of Toronto, 1996.

———, ed. *Cities and Governance: New Directions in Latin America, Asia and Africa.* Toronto: Centre for Urban and Community Studies, University of Toronto, 1990.

McGee, T. G. *The Southeast Asian City: A Social Geography of the Primate Cities of Southeast Asia.* London: G. Bell and Sons, 1967.

McGee, T. G., and Ira M. Robinson, eds. *The Mega-Urban Regions of Southeast Asia.* Vancouver: University of British Columbia Press, 1995.

Micklin, Michael, ed. *Natural Resources, Environment and Development in Ecological Perspective: A Sourcebook for Teaching and Research.* Hong Kong: Centre of Urban Planning and Environmental Management, University of Hong Kong, 1996.

Midgley, P. *Urban Transport in Asia: An Operational Agenda for the 1990s.* Washington, D.C.: World Bank, 1994.

Miles, Simon, *Metropolitan Problems: International Perspectives.* London: Methuen, 1970.

Monroe, James S., and Reed Wicander. *The Changing Earth: Exploring Geology and Evolution.* Belmont, Calif.: Wadsworth Publishing Company and West Publishing Company, 1997.

Mumford, Lewis. *The City in History.* New York: Harcourt, Brace & World, 1961.

Myers, David J., and Henry A. Dietz. *Capital City Politics in Latin America: Democratization and Empowerment.* Boulder, Colo.: Lynne Reinner Publishers, 2002.

Newman, P. W. G., and J. R. Kenworthy. *Cities and Automobile Dependence: A Sourcebook.* Aldershot, U.K.: Gower, 1989.

Nickum, J. E., and K. W. Easter, eds. *Metropolitan Water Use Conflicts in Asia and the Pacific.* Boulder, Colo.: Westview Press, 1994.

Nourse, Mary A. *A Short History of the Chinese.* New York: New York Home Library, 1943. Originally published in 1935 as *The Four Hundred Million,* by Bobs-Merrill Company.

Orangi Pilot Project. *Proposal for a Sewage Disposal System for Karachi.* Research and Training Institute, Orangi Pilot Project. Karachi: City Press, 1998.

Pama, R. P., S. Angel, and J.H. de Goede. *Low Income Housing: Technology and Policy.* Bangkok: Asian Institute of Technology, 1977.

Payne, G. K., ed. *Low-Income Housing in the Developing World: The Role of Sites and Services and Settlement Upgrading.* Chichester: John Wiley & Sons, 1984.

Pearce, David W., and R. Kerry Turner. *Economics of Natural Resources and the Environment.* Baltimore: Johns Hopkins University Press, 1990.

Peattie, Lisa. *The View from the Barrio.* Ann Arbor: University of Michigan Press, 1968.

Pleskovic, Boris, and Nicholas Stern, eds. *Annual World Bank Conference on Development Economics 2001/2002.* New York: World Bank, 2002.

Pongsapich, Amara, Michael C. Howard, and Jacques Amyot, eds. *Regional Development and Change in Southeast Asia in the 1990s.* Bangkok: Social Research Institute, Chulalongkorn University, 1992.

Pym, Christopher. *The Ancient Civilization of Angkor.* New York: New American Library, 1968.

Reader, John, and Harvey Croze. *Pyramids of Life: An Investigation of Nature's Fearful Symmetry.* London: William Collins Sons, 1977.

Rees, William, and Mathis Wackernagel. *Our Ecological Footprint, Reducing Human Impact on the Earth.* Gabriola Island, B.C.: New Society Publishers, 1996.

Ruble, Blair, Richard E. Stren, Joseph S. Tulchin, and Diana Varat, eds. *Urban Governance around the World.* Washington, D.C.: Woodrow Wilson International Center for Scholars, 2001.

Rybczynski, Witold, Chongrak Polsapert, and Michael McGarry, eds. *Low Cost Technology Options for Sanitation: A State-of-the-Art Review and Annotated Bibliography.* Ottawa: International Development Research Centre, 1978.

Sassen, Saskia. *Cities in a World Economy.* London: Pine Forge Press, 1994.

————. *The Global City: New York, London, Tokyo,* Princeton, N.J.: Princeton University Press, 1991.

Scott, Mel. *American City Planning since 1890.* Berkeley: University of California Press, 1971.

Serageldin, Ismail. *Nurturing Development: Aid and Cooperation in Today's Changing World.* Washington, D.C.: World Bank, 1995.

————. *Water Supply, Sanitation and Environmental Sustainability: The Financing Challenge.* Washington, D.C.: World Bank, 1994.

Silliman, G. Sidney, and Leila Garner Noble, eds. *Civil Society and the Philippine State.* Quezon City: Ateneo de Manila University Press, 1998.

Sit, Victor. *Chinese Cities: The Growth of the Metropolis since 1949.* Hong Kong: Oxford University Press, 1985.

Sivaramakrishnan, K. C., and Leslie Green. *Metropolitan Management: The Asian Experience.* Oxford: Oxford University Press, 1986.

Sjoberg, Gideon. *The Preindustrial City: Past and Present.* New York: Free Press, 1960.

Skinner, R. J., J. L. Taylor, and E. A. Wegelin, eds. *Shelter Upgrading for the Urban Poor: Evaluation of Third World Experience.* Manila: Island Publishing House, 1987.

Skinner, William G. *The City in Late Imperial China.* Stanford, Calif.: Stanford University Press, 1977.

Smart Growth Network. *Getting to Smart Growth: 100 Policies for Implementation.* Washington, D.C.: International City/County Management Association, U.S. Environmental Protection Agency, and Smart Growth Network, 2003.

Smith, Patrick, H. Peter Oberlander, and Tom Hutton, eds. *Urban Solutions to Global Problems.* Vancouver: Centre for Human Settlements, University of British Columbia, 1996.

Soegijoko, Budhy Tjahjati. *Public Transportation in Bandung.* Bandung: Institute of Technology, Department of Planning, 1981.

Soto, Hernando de. *The Mystery of Capital: Why Capitalism Triumphs in the West and Fails Everywhere Else.* New York: Basic Books, 2000.

————. *The Other Path.* Paris: I. B. Tauris, 1989.

Stren, Richard, and Judith K. Bell, eds. *Urban Research in the Developing World: Perspectives on the City,* vol. 4. Toronto: Centre for Urban and Community Studies, University of Toronto, 1995.

Swedish Environmental Protection Agency. *Biological-Chemical Characterization of Industrial Wastewater.* Solna, Sweden: Information Department, Naturvardsverket, 1990.

Tapales, Proserpina D. *Devolution and Empowerment: The Local Government Code of 1991 and Local Autonomy in the Philippines.* Quezon City: Philippine Center for Integrative and Development Studies, University of the Philippines, 1993.

Thomas, Vinod, Mansoor Dailami, Ashok Dhareshwar, Daniel Kaufmann, Nalin Kishor, Ramon Lopez, and Yan Wang. *The Quality of Growth.* New York: Oxford University Press, 2000.

Turner, John F. C. *Housing by People: Towards Autonomous Building Environments.* New York: Pantheon Books, 1976.

Turner, John F. C., and R. Fichter, eds. *Freedom to Build.* New York: Macmillan, 1972.

Turner, Ralph. *The Great Cultural Traditions: The Ancient Cities.* New York: McGraw Hill, 1941.

United Nations. *Population Growth and Policies in Mega-Cities: Bangkok.* Population Policy Paper 10. New York: Department of International Economic and Social Affairs, United Nations, 1987.
———. *Population Growth and Policies in Mega-Cities: Bombay.* Population Policy Paper 6. New York: Department of International Economic and Social Affairs, United Nations, 1986.
———. *Population Growth and Policies in Mega-Cities: Calcutta.* Population Policy Paper 1. New York: Department of International Economic and Social Affairs, United Nations, 1986.
———. *Population Growth and Policies in Mega-Cities: Dhaka.* Population Policy Paper 8. New York: Department of International Economic and Social Affairs, United Nations, 1987.
———. *Population Growth and Policies in Mega-Cities: Jakarta.* Population Policy Paper 18. New York: Department of International Economic and Social Affairs, United Nations, 1989.
———. *Population Growth and Policies in Mega-Cities: Karachi.* Population Policy 13. New York: Department of International Economic and Social Affairs, United Nations, 1988.
———. *2000 Revision of World Population Prospects.* New York: Department of Economic and Social Affairs, United Nations, 2002.
———. *World Population Prospects: The 1996 Revision.* Population Division Document ST/ESA/SER.A/167. New York: Department of Economic and Social Affairs, United Nations, 1998.
———. *World Urbanization Prospects: The 1996 Revision.* Population Division Document ST/ESA/SER.A/170. New York: Department of Economic and Social Affairs, United Nations, 1998.
———. *World Urbanization Prospects: The 2001 Revision,* New York: Department of Economic and Social Affairs, United Nations, 2001.
United Nations Center for Human Settlements (Habitat). *Cities in a Globalizing World: Global Report on Human Settlements, 2001.* London: Earthscan Publications, 2001.
———. *An Urbanizing World: Global Report on Human Settlements, 1996.* Oxford: Oxford University Press, 1996.
United Nations Children's Fund. *Planning for Health and Socio-Economic Benefits from Water and Environment Sanitation Programs.* New York: United Nations Children's Fund, 1993.
United Nations Development Program. *Promoting Good Governance in the Arab States.* New York: United Nations Office for Project Services, 2002.
Walsh, Annmarie Hauck. *The Urban Challenge to Government.* New York: Frederick A. Praeger, 1969.
Wong Kwan-yiu and Shen Jianfa, eds. *Resource Management, Urbanization and Governance in Hong Kong and the Zhujiang Delta.* Hong Kong: Chinese University Press, 2002.
World Bank. *Better Urban Services: Finding the Right Incentives.* New York: Oxford University Press, 1995.
———. *Financing for Sustainable Development.* Washington, D.C.: International Monetary Fund, UN Environment Program, and Environment Department of the World Bank, 2002.

————. *Indonesia: Sustaining Development—A Country Study Report.* Washington, D.C.: World Bank, 1994.

————. *Indonesia: Urban Public Infrastructure Services.* Washington, D.C.: World Bank, 1993.

World Commission on Environment and Development. *Our Common Future* (The Brundtland Commission Report). Oxford: Oxford University Press, 1987.

World Health Organization. *Health Education in Food Safety.* Geneva: World Health Organization, 1988.

————. *The International Drinking Water Supply and Sanitation Decade: Review of Mid-Decade Progress.* Geneva: World Health Organization, 1987.

————. *Our Planet, Our Health: Report of the WHO Commission on Health and Environment.* Geneva: World Health Organization, 1992.

Wu Liangyong. *A Brief History of Ancient Chinese City Planning.* Kassel, West Germany: Urbs et Region Publication, 1986.

————. *Rehabilitating the Old City of Beijing: A Project in the Ju'er Hutong Neighbourhood.* Vancouver: University of British Columbia Press, 1999.

Yeh, Anthony Gar-On, ed. *Planning Hong Kong for the 21st Century: A Preview of the Future Role of Hong Kong.* Hong Kong: Centre of Urban Planning and Environmental Management, University of Hong Kong, 1995.

Yeh, Anthony Gar-On, and Chai-Kwong Mak, eds. *Chinese Cities and China's Development: A Preview of the Future Role of Hong Kong.* Hong Kong: Centre of Urban Planning and Environmental Management, University of Hong Kong, 1995.

Yeh, Anthony Gar-On, Peter Hills, and Simon Ka-Wing Ng. *Modern Transport in Hong Kong for the 21st Century.* Hong Kong: Centre of Urban Planning and Environmental Management, University of Hong Kong, 2001.

Yeh, Anthony Gar-On, and Mee Kam Ng, eds. *Planning for a Better Living Urban Environment in Asia.* Burlington, Vt: Ashgate Publishing, 2000.

Yeh, Anthony Gar-On, Yok Shiu Lee, Tunney Lee, and Nien Dak Sze, eds. *Building a Competitive Pearl River Delta Region: Cooperation, Coordination, and Planning.* Hong Kong: Centre of Urban Planning and Environmental Management, University of Hong Kong, 2002.

Yeh, Stephen H. K. *Public Housing in Singapore: A Multi-Disciplinary Study.* Singapore: University of Singapore Press, 1975.

Yeh, Stephen H. K., and Aprodicio Laquian, eds. *Housing Asia's Millions: Problems, Policies and Prospects for Low Cost Housing in Southeast Asia.* Ottawa: International Development Research Centre, 1979.

Yeung Yue-man. *Changing Cities of Pacific Asia: A Scholarly Interpretation.* Hong Kong: Chinese University Press, 1990.

Yeung Yue-man and David K. Y. Chau, eds. *Guangdong: Survey of a Province Undergoing Rapid Change.* Hong Kong: Chinese University Press, 1994.

Yeung Yue-man and C. P. Lo, eds. *Changing South-East Asian Cities: Readings on Urbanization.* Singapore: Oxford University Press, 1976.

Yeung, Yue-man and Sung Yun-ming, eds. *Shanghai: Transformation and Modernization under China's Open Policy.* Hong Kong: Chinese University Press, 1996.

Yeung, Yue-man and Timothy Wong. *Fifty Years of Public Housing in Hong Kong: A Golden Jubilee Review and Appraisal.* Hong Kong: Hong Kong Housing Authority and Chinese University Press, 2003.

Book Chapters

Amin, A. T. M. Nurul. "The Compulsions of Accommodating the Informal Sector in the Asian Metropolises and Changes Necessary in the Urban Planning Paradigm." In *Planning for a Better Urban Living Environment in Asia,* ed. Anthony Gar-On Yeh and Mee Kam Ng. Burlington, Vt.: Ashgate Publishing, 2000.

Angel, Shlomo. "The Low Income Housing Delivery System in Asia." In *Low Income Housing: Technology and Policy,* ed. R. P. Pama, S. Angel, and J. H. de Goede. Bangkok: Asian Institute of Technology, 1977.

Arlosoroff, Saul. "Water Demand Management." In *Promoting Sustainable Consumption in Asian Cities,* ed. United Nations Center for Human Settlements (Habitat). Nairobi: United Nations Center for Human Settlements and Habitat Fukuoka Office, 1998.

Asian Engineering Consultants. "Public Transport Network Systems Study," Bangkok, 1994. Quoted in "Urban Transport," by David John Bray, in *Urban Infrastructure Finance,* ed. Royston Brockman and Allen Williams. Manila: Water Supply, Urban Development, and Housing Division, Asian Development Bank, 1996.

Ashraf, Ali, and Leslie Green. "Calcutta." In *Great Cities of the World: Their Government, Politics and Planning,* ed. William A. Robson and D. E. Regan. London: George Allen and Unwin, 1972.

Banerjee, Tridib, and Sigrid Schenk. "Lower Order Cities and National Urbanization Policies: China and India." In *Equity with Growth? Planning Perspectives for Small Towns in Developing Countries,* ed. H. Detlef Kammeier and Peter J. Swan. Bangkok: Asian Institute of Technology, 1984.

Bao Guilan. "Socio- and Psychological Analysis of the Inhabitants of Shanghai." In *The Research on Human Settlements in Shanghai,* ed. Zheng Shiling. Shanghai: College of Architecture and Urban Planning, Tongji University, 1992.

Batley, Richard. "Public-Private Partnerships for Urban Services." In *The Challenge of Urban Government, Policies and Practices,* ed. Mila Freire and Richard Stren. Washington, D.C.: World Bank Institute, 2001.

Bray, David John. "Urban Transport." In *Urban Infrastructure Finance,* ed. Royston Brockman and Allen Williams. Manila: Water Supply, Urban Development, and Housing Division, Asian Development Bank, 1996.

Brennan, Ellen. "Mega-City Management and Innovation Strategies: Regional Views." In *Mega-City Growth and the Future,* ed. Roland Fuchs, Ellen Brennan, Joseph Chamie, Fu-chen Lo, and Joha I. Uitto. Tokyo: United Nations University Press, 1994.

Brennan-Galvin, Ellen. "In Search of Sustainable Cities." In *Democratic Governance and Urban Sustainability,* ed. Joseph S. Tulchin, Diana H. Varat and Blair A. Ruble. Washington, D.C.: Woodrow Wilson International Center for Scholars, 2002.

Burgell, Galia, and Guy Burgell. "Global Trends and City Policies: Friends or Foes of Urban Development?" In *Preparing for the Urban Future: Global Pressures and Local Forces,* ed. Michael A. Cohen, Blair A. Ruble, Joseph Tulchin, and Allison M. Garland. Washington, D.C.: Woodrow Wilson Center Press, 1996.

Button, K., and W. Rotherngatter. "Global Environmental Degradation: The Role of Transport." In *Transport, the Environment and Sustainable Development,* ed. D. Bannister and K. Button. London: E & F. N. Spon, 1993.

Campanella, Thomas J., Ming Zhang, Tunney Lee, and Nien Dak Sze. "The Pearl River Delta: An Evolving Region." In *Building a Competitive Pearl River Delta Region: Cooperation, Coordination, and Planning,* ed. Anthony Gar-On Yeh, Yok-Shiu F. Lee, Tunney Lee, and Nien Dak Sze. Hong Kong: Centre of Urban Planning and Environmental Management, University of Hong Kong, 2002.

Campbell, Tim. "Banking on Decentralization in Continents of Cities: Taking Stock of Lessons, Looking Forward to Reform." In *Democratic Governance and Urban Sustainability,* ed. Joseph S. Tulchin, Diana H. Varat, and Blair A. Ruble. Washington, D.C.: Woodrow Wilson International Center for Scholars, 2002.

Cheung, Peter T. Y. "Managing the Hong Kong–Guangdong Relationship: Issues and Challenges." In *Building a Competitive Pearl River Delta Region: Cooperation, Coordination, and Planning,* ed. Anthony Gar-On Yeh, Yok-shiu F. Lee, Tunney Lee, and Nien Dak Sze. Hong Kong: Centre of Urban Planning and Environmental Management, University of Hong Kong, 2002.

Clinard, Marshall, and B. Chatterjee. "Urban Community Development in India: The Delhi Pilot Project." In *India's Urban Future,* ed. Roy Turner. Berkeley and Los Angeles: University of California Press, 1961.

Constantino-David, Karina. "From the Present Looking Back: A History of Philippine NGOs." In *Civil Society and the Philippine State,* ed. G. Sidney Silliman and Leila Garner Noble. Quezon City: Ateneo de Manila University Press, 1998.

Cui Gonghao. "Development of Shanghai and the Yangtze Delta." In *Chinese Cities and China's Development: A Preview of the Future Role of Hong Kong,* ed. Anthony Gar-On Yeh and Chai-Kwong Mak. Hong Kong: Centre of Urban Planning and Environmental Management, University of Hong Kong, 1995.

Daly, Herman. "Introduction to Essays Toward a Steady-State Economy." In *Valuing the Earth: Economics, Ecology, Ethics,* ed. Herman Daly and Kenneth N. Townsend. Cambridge, Mass.: MIT Press, 1993.

Datta, Abhijit, and J. N. Khosla. "Delhi." In *Great Cities of the World: Their Government, Politics and Planning,* ed. William A. Robson and D. E. Regan. London: George Allen and Unwin, 1972.

Dharmapatni, Ida Ayu, and Tommy Firman. "Problems and Challenges of Mega-Urban Regions in Indonesia: The Case of Jabotabek and the Bandung Metropolitan Area." In *The Mega-Urban Regions of Southeast Asia,* ed. T. G. McGee and Ira M. Robinson. Vancouver: University of British Columbia Press, 1995.

Dong Liming. "Beijing: The Development of a Socialist Capital." In *Chinese Cities: The Growth of the Metropolis since 1949,* ed. Victor F.S. Sit. Hong Kong: Oxford University Press, 1985.

Easter, K. W., and G. Feder. "Water Institutions, Incentives and Markets." In *Decentralization and Coordination of Water Resources Management,* ed. D. D. Parker and Y. Tsur. Boston: Kluwer Academic Publishers, 1997.

Ebel, Robert D., and François Vaillancourt. "Fiscal Decentralization and Financing Urban Governments: Framing the Problems." In *The Challenge of Urban Government: Policies and Practices,* ed. Mila Freire and Richard Stren. Washington, D.C.: World Bank Institute, 2001.

Fan, Cindy. "Permanent Migrants, Temporary Migrants, and the Labour Market in Chinese Cities." In *Resource Management, Urbanization and Governance in Hong Kong and the Zhujiang Delta,* ed. Kwan-yiu Wong and Jianfa Shen. Hong Kong: Chinese University Press, 2002.

Findley, Sally E. "The Third World City: Development Policy and Issues." In *Third World Cities: Problems, Policies and Prospects,* ed. John D. Kasarda and Allan M. Parnell. Newbury Park, Calif.: Sage Publications, 1993.

Fong, Alex. "Port Planning for the Pearl River Delta Region: A Hong Kong Perspective." In *Building a Competitive Pearl River Delta Region: Cooperation, Coordination, and Planning,* ed. Anthony Gar-On Yeh, Yok-Shiu Lee, Tunney Lee, and Nien Dak Sze. Hong Kong: Centre of Urban Planning and Environmental Management, University of Hong Kong, 2002.

Foo Tuan Seik. "Managing Transport Demand in Asian Cities." In *Promoting Sustainable Consumption in Asian Cities,* ed. United Nations Center for Human Settlements (Habitat). Fukuoka: Habitat Fukuoka Office, 1998.

Forstall, Richard, and Victor Jones. "Selected Demographic, Economic and Governmental Aspects of the Contemporary Metropolis." In *Metropolitan Problems: International Perspectives,* ed. Simon Miles. Toronto: Methuen Publications, 1970.

Friedmann, John. "The Common Good: Assessing the Performance of Cities." In *City, Space, and Globalization: An International Perspective,* ed. Hemalata Dandekar. Ann Arbor: University of Michigan Press, 1998.

Fukami, Takatsune. "The Urban Renewal Projects in Japan: Non-residential Projects." In *Planning for a Better Living Urban Environment in Asia,* ed. Anthony Gar-On Yeh and Mee Kam Ng. Burlington, Vt.: Ashgate Publishing, 2000.

Fung, Victor. "Hong Kong and the Pearl River Delta: Competing Together." In *Building a Competitive Pearl River Delta Region: Cooperation, Coordination, and Planning,* ed. Anthony Gar-On Yeh, Yok-Shiu Lee, Tunney Lee, and Nien Dak Sze. Hong Kong: Centre of Urban Planning and Environmental Management, University of Hong Kong, 2002.

Ginsburg, Norton. "Planning the Future of the Asian City." In *The City as a Centre for Change in Asia,* ed. D. J. Dwyer. Hong Kong: Hong Kong University Press, 1972.

Goldstein, Sidney. "Demographic Issues and Data Needs for Mega-City Research." In *Mega-City Growth and the Future,* ed. Roland Fuchs, Ellen Brennan, Joseph Chamie, Fu-chen Lo, and Joha I. Uitto. Tokyo: United Nations University Press, 1994.

Gulyani, Sumila. "The Demand Side Approach to Planning Water Supply." In *The Challenge of Urban Government: Policies and Practices,* ed. Mila Freire and Richard Stren. Washington, D.C.: World Bank Institute, 2001.

Hamer, Andrew. "Economic Impacts of Third World Mega-Cities: Is Size the Issue?" In *Mega-City Growth and the Future,* ed. Roland Fuchs, Ellen Brennan, Joseph Chamie, Fu-chen Lo, and Joha I. Uitto. Tokyo: United Nations University Press, 1994.

———. "Urban China: Looking Forward, Looking Back." In *Chinese Cities and China's Development: A Preview of the Future Role of Hong Kong,* ed. Anthony Gar-On Yeh and Chai-Kwong Mak. Hong Kong: Centre of Urban Planning and Environmental Management, University of Hong Kong, 1995.

Hau, Timothy. "Demand-Side Measures and Road Pricing." In *Modern Transport in Hong Kong for the 21st Century,* ed. Anthony Gar-On Yeh, Peter Hills, and Simon Ka-Wing Ng. Hong Kong: Centre of Urban Planning and Environmental Management, Hong Kong University, 2001.

Ikaputra, Kunihiro Narumi, and Takahiro Hisa. "Preserving Traditional Architecture: Noble Residential Area Development in Java." In *Planning for a Better Urban Living Environment in Asia,* ed. Anthony Gar-On Yeh, and Mee Kam Ng. Burlington, Vt.: Ashgate Publishing, 2000.

Jain, A. K. "Calcutta: The Mega-Crucible." In *The Indian Mega-City and Economic Reforms.* New Delhi: Management Publishing Company, 1996.

Jauregui-Roxas, Miguel. "Mexico's Actions Towards the Implementation of the Monterrey Consensus." In *Global Agenda, 2002–2003: Meeting the Challenges,* ed. World Bank. Background Paper for the Annual Meetings of the World Bank and International Monetary Fund. Washington, D.C.: World Bank, 2002.

Kamo, Toshio. "Urban-Regional Governance in the Age of Globalization: The Case of Metropolitan Dhaka." In *Urban and Regional Governance in Pacific Asia,* ed. John Friedmann. Vancouver: Institute of Asian Research, University of British Columbia, 1999.

Kaothien, Utis. "The Bangkok Metropolitan Region: Policies and Issues in the Seventh Plan." In *The Mega-Urban Regions of Southeast Asia,* ed. T. G. McGee and Ira M. Robinson. Vancouver: University of British Columbia Press, 1995.

Kim Won Bae. "National Competitiveness and Governance of Seoul, Korea." In *Urban and Regional Governance in Pacific Asia,* ed. John Friedmann. Vancouver: Institute of Asian Research, University of British Columbia, 1999.

Kokpol, Orathai. "Thailand." In *The Changing Nature of Local Government in Developing Countries,* ed. Patricia McCarney. Toronto: Centre for Urban and Community Studies, University of Toronto, 1996.

Krongkaew, Medhi. "The Changing Urban System in a Fast-Growing City and Economy: The Case of Bangkok and Thailand." In *Emerging World Cities in Pacific Asia,* ed. Fu-chen Lo and Yue-man Yeung. Tokyo: United Nations University Press, 1996.

Kwon Tai-joon. 1972. "Future Development Stages for Seoul." In *The City as a Centre for Change in Asia,* ed. D. J. Dwyer. Hong Kong: Hong Kong University Press, 1972.

Lam Kin-che and Shu Tao. "Environmental Quality and Pollution Control." In *Shanghai: Transformation and Modernization Under China's Open Policy,* ed. Yue-man Yeung and Sung Yun-wing. Hong Kong: Chinese University Press, 1996.

Laquian, Aprodicio. "The Asian City and the Political Process." In *The City as a Centre for Change in Asia,* ed. D. J. Dwyer. Hong Kong: Hong Kong University Press, 1972.

———. "The Effects of National Urban Strategy and Regional Development Policy on Urban Growth in China." In *Urbanization in Large Developing Countries, China, Indonesia, Brazil and India,* ed. Gavin W. Jones and Pravin Visaria. Oxford: Clarendon Press, 1997.

———. "The Governance of Mega-Urban Regions." In *The Mega-Urban Regions of Southeast Asia,* ed. T. G. McGee and Ira M. Robinson. Vancouver: University of British Columbia Press, 1995.

———. "Manila." In *Great Cities of the World: Their Government, Politics and Planning,* ed. William A. Robson and D. E. Regan. London: George Allen and Unwin, 1972.

———. "Metro Manila: People's Participation and Social Inclusion in a City of Villages." In *Urban Governance around the World,* ed. Blair Ruble, Richard Stren, Joseph Tulchin, and Diana Varat. Washington, D.C.: Woodrow Wilson International Center for Scholars, 2002.

———. "The Pearl River Delta in the World Perspective." In *Planning Hong Kong for the 21st Century: A Preview of the Future Role of Hong Kong,* ed. Anthony Gar-On Yeh. Hong Kong: University of Hong Press, 1996.

———. "Review and Evaluation of Urban Accommodationist Policies in Population

Distribution." In *Population Distribution Policies in Developing Countries,* ed. United Nations New York: UN Populations Fund, 1981.

———. "Sites, Services and Shelter: An Evaluation." In *Action Planning and Responsive Design,* ed. Wendy Aldhous, Steven Groak, Babar Mumtaz, and Michael Safier. London: Pergamon Press, 1983.

———. "Social and Welfare Impacts of Mega-City Development." In *Mega-City Growth and the Future,* ed. Roland Fuchs, Ellen Brennan, Joseph Chamie, Fu-chen Lo, and Joha I. Uitto. Tokyo: United Nations University Press, 1994.

———. "Urbanisation in China." In *Population and Development Planning in China,* ed. Wang Jiye and Terence H. Hull. North Sydney, Australia: Allen and Unwin, 1991.

———. "Urban Governance: Some Lessons Learned." In *Democratic Governance and Urban Sustainability,* ed. Joseph S. Tulchin, Diana H. Varat, and Blair A. Ruble. Washington, D.C.: Woodrow Wilson International Center for Scholars, 2002.

———. "Urban Tensions in Southeast Asia in the 70s." In *Population, Politics and Development in Southeast Asia,* ed. H. Howard Wriggins and James Guyot. Lexington, Ky.: Lexington Books, 1973.

Lee Boon Thong. "Challenges of Super-Induced Development: The Mega-Urban Region of Kuala Lumpur-Klang Valley." In *The Mega-urban Regions of Southeast Asia,* ed. T. G. McGee and Ira M. Robinson. Vancouver: University of British Columbia Press, 1995.

Lee, Rance. "Bureaucratic Corruption in Asia: The Problem of Incongruence between Legal Norms and Folk Norms." In *Bureaucratic Corruption in Asia, Causes, Consequences and Control,* ed. Ledivina Carino. Manila: College of Public Administration, University of the Philippines, 1986.

Li Si-ming and Siu Yat-ming. "Fertility of Migrants and Non-Migrants in Dongguan and Meizhou: A Study of the Impact of Regional Development and Inter-Regional Migration on Fertility and Behavior in China." In *Resource Management, Urbanization and Governance in Hong Kong and the Zhujiang Delta,* ed. Wong Kwan-jiu and Shen Jianfa. Hong Kong: Chinese University Press, 2002.

Liu Junde. "Study on the Innovation in the Administrative Organization and Management of the Metropolitan Areas in Mainland China, with Special Reference to the Pearl River Delta." In *Resource Management, Urbanization and Governance in Hong Kong and the Zhujiang Delta,* ed. Wong Kwau-jiu and Shen Jianfa. Hong Kong: Chinese University Press, 2002.

Mathur, Om Prakash. "Governing Cities in India, Nepal and Sri Lanka: The Challenge of Poverty and Globalization," In *Cities and Governance: New Directions in Latin America, Asia and Africa,* ed. Patricia L. McCarney. Toronto: Centre for Urban and Community Studies, University of Toronto, 1996.

McCarney, Patricia L. "Reviving Local Government: The Neglected Tier in Development." In *The Changing Nature of Local Government in Developing Countries,* ed. Patricia L. McCarney. Toronto: Centre for Urban and Community Studies, University of Toronto, 1996.

McCarney, Patricia, Mohamed Alfani, and Alfredo Rodriguez. "Towards an Understanding of Governance: The Emergence of an Idea and Its Implications for Urban Research in Developing Countries." In *Urban Research in the Developing World: Perspectives on the City,* vol. 4, ed. Richard Stren and Judith K. Bell. Toronto: Centre for Urban and Community Studies, University of Toronto, 1995.

McDowell, Mark. "Energy Strategies and Environmental Constraints in China's Modernization." In *Asia's Environmental Crisis,* ed. Michael C. Howard. Boulder, Colo.: Westview Press, 1993.

McGee, T. G. "The Emergence of Desakota Regions in Asia: Expanding a Hypothesis." In *The Extended Metropolis: Settlement Transition in Asia,* ed. N. Ginsburg, B. Koppel, and T. G. McGee. Honolulu: University of Hawaii Press, 1991.

———. "Metrofitting the Emerging Mega-Urban Regions of ASEAN: An Overview." In *The Mega-Urban Regions of Southeast Asia,* ed. T. G. McGee and Ira M. Robinson. Vancouver: University of British Columbia Press, 1995.

McGee, T. G., and C. Greenberg. "The Emergence of Extended Metropolitan Regions in ASEAN, 1960-1980: An Exploratory Outline." In *Regional Development and Change in Southeast Asia in the 1990s,* ed. Amara Pongsapich, Michael C. Howard and Jacques Amyot. Bangkok: Social Research Institute, Chulalongkorn University, 1992.

Meier, Richard. "Relations of Technology to the Design of Very Large Cities," In *India's Urba`n Future,* ed. Roy Turner. Berkeley: University of California Press, 1961.

Mitra, Banashree Chatterji. "Land Supply for Low Income Housing in Delhi." In *The Transformation of Land Supply in Third World Cities,* ed. Paul Barross and Jan van der Linden. Brookfield, Vt.: Gower Publishing, 1990.

Mok, Victor. "Industrial Development." In *Shanghai: Transformation and Modernization under China's Open Policy,* ed. Yue-man Yeung and Sung Yun-wing. Hong Kong: Chinese University Press, 1996.

Morato, Edwardo, Jr. "Alternative Delivery Systems for Poverty Alleviation." In *Reaching Out Effectively: Improving the Design, Management and Implementation of Poverty Alleviation Programmes,* ed. Ismael P. Getubig Jr. and M. Khalid Shams. Kuala Lumpur: Asian and Pacific Development Centre, 1991.

Ng, Ava. "Cross-Border Planning: The Interface Between Hong Kong and the Mainland." In *Building a Competitive Pearl River Delta Region: Cooperation, Coordination, and Planning,* ed. Anthony Gar-On Yeh, Yok-Shiu Lee, Tunney Lee, and Nien Dak Sze. Hong Kong: Centre of Urban Planning and Environmental Management, University of Hong Kong, 2002.

Ng Mee Kam. "An Extended Metropolis? A Growth Triangle? Towards Better Planning for the Hong Kong and Pearl River Delta Region." In *Planning for a Better Living Urban Environment in Asia,* ed. Anthony Gar-On Yeh and Mee Kam Ng. Burlington, Vt.: Ashgate Publishing, 2000.

Ocampo, Romeo. "The Metro Manila Mega-Region." In *The Mega-Urban Regions of Southeast Asia,* ed. T. G. McGee and Ira M. Robinson. Vancouver: University of British Columbia Press, 1995.

O'Rourke, Kevin H. "Globalization and Inequality: Historical Trends." In *Annual World Bank Conference on Development Economics,2001–2002,* ed. Boris Pleskovic and Nicholas Stern. New York: Oxford University Press, 2002.

Owens, S. E. "Energy, Environmental Sustainability and Land Use Planning." In *Sustainable Development and Urban Form,* ed. M. J. Breheny. London: European Research in Regional Science, 1992.

Pachauri, R. K., and A. Sen. "Problems, Challenges and Prospects for Sustainable Management of Energy Demand in Asian Cities." In *Promoting Sustainable Consumption in Asian Cities,* ed. United Nations Center for Human Settlements (Habitat). Fukuoka: Habitat Fukuoka Office, 1998.

Pendakur, Setty. "Gridlock in the Slopopolis: Congestion Management and Sustainable Development." In *The Mega-Urban Regions of Southeast Asia,* ed. T. G. McGee and Ira M. Robinson. Vancouver: University of British Columbia Press, 1995.

Polese, Mario. "Learning from Each Other: Policy Choices and the Social Sustainability of Cities." In *The Social Sustainability of Cities: Diversity and the Management of Change,* ed. Mario Polese and Richard Stren. Toronto: University of Toronto Press, 2000.

Ray, Kalyan. "Promoting Sustainable Consumption in Asian Cities." In *Promoting Sustainable Consumption in Asian Cities,* ed. United Nations Center for Human Settlements (Habitat). Fukuoka: Habitat Fukuoka Office, 1998.

Rees, William E. "Understanding Sustainable Development." In *Sustainable Development and the Future of Cities,* ed. Bernd Hamm and Pandurang K. Muttagi. New Delhi: Oxford and UBH Publishing Company, 1999.

Rees, William E., and Mark Roseland. "Sustainable Communities: Planning for the 21st Century." In *Sustainable Development and the Future of Cities,* ed. Bernd Hamm and Pandurang K. Muttagi. New Delhi: Oxford and UBH Publishing Company, 1999.

Richardson, Harry W. "Efficiency and Welfare in LDC Mega-Cities." In *Third World Cities: Problems, Policies and Prospects,* ed. John D. Kasarda and Allan M. Parnell. Newbury Park, Calif.: Sage Publications, 1993.

Robben, P. M. "Measurement of Population Dynamics Following Squatter Settlement Improvement in Ashok Nagar, Madras." In *Shelter Upgrading for the Urban Poor: Evaluation of Third World Experience,* ed. R. J. Skinner, J. L. Taylor, and E. A. Wegelin. Manila: Island Publishing House, 1987.

Robinson, Ira M. "Emerging Spatial Patterns in ASEAN Mega-Urban Regions: Alternative Strategies." In *The Mega-Urban Regions of Southeast Asia,* ed. T. G. McGee and Ira M. Robinson. Vancouver: University of British Columbia Press, 1995.

Rocamora, Joel. "A Clash of Ideologies: International Capitalism and the State in the Wake of the Asian Crisis." In *Democratic Governance and Social Inequality,* ed. Joseph S. Tulchin and Amelia Brown. Boulder, Colo.: Lynne Rienner Publishers, 2002.

Rondinelli, Dennis. "Small Towns in Developing Countries: Potential Centers of Growth, Transformation and Integration." In *Equity with Growth? Planning Perspectives for Small Towns in Developing Countries,* ed. H. Detlef Kammaier and Peter J. Swan. Bangkok: Asian Institute of Technology, 1984.

Rosser, Colin. "Housing and Planned Urban Change: The Calcutta Experience." In *The City as a Centre for Change in Asia,* ed. D. J. Dwyer. Hong Kong: Hong Kong University Press, 1972.

Roy, Ananya. "Marketized? Feminized? Medieval? Urban Governance in an Era of Liberalization." In *Democratic Governance and Urban Sustainability,* ed. Joseph S. Tulchin, Diana H. Varat, and Blair A. Ruble. Washington, D.C.: Woodrow Wilson International Center for Scholars, 2002.

Royama Masamichi. "Tokyo and Osaka." In *Great Cities of the World: Their Government, Politics and Planning,* ed. William A. Robson and D. E. Regan. London: George Allen and Unwin, 1972.

Ruble, Blair, Joseph S. Tulchin, and Allison M. Garland. "Introduction: Globalism and Local Realities—Five Paths to the Urban Future." In *Preparing for the Urban Future: Global Pressures and Local Forces,* ed. Michael A. Cohen, Blair A. Ruble, Joseph H.

Tulchin, and Allison M. Garland. Washington, D.C.: Woodrow Wilson Center Press, 1996.

Sazanami, Hidehiko. "Challenges and Future Prospects of Planning for a Better Living Environment in the Large Cities of Asia." In *Planning for a Better Urban Living Environment in Asia,* ed. Anthony Gar-On Yeh, and Mee Kam Ng. Burlington, Vt.: Ashgate Publishing, 2000.

Shah, Asad. "Urban Trends and the Emergence of the Megacity." In *The Future of Asian Cities,* ed. Jeffrey R. Stubbs. Manila: Asian Development Bank, 1996.

Shi Peijun, Lin Hui, and Liang Jinshe. "Shanghai as a Regional Hub." In *Shanghai: Transformation and Modernization under China's Open Policy,* ed. Yue-man Yeung and Sung Yun-wing. Hong Kong: Chinese University Press, 1996.

Shiu Sin-por and Yang Cun. "A Study on Developing the Hong Kong -Shenzhen Border Zone." In *Building a Competitive Pearl River Delta Region: Cooperation, Coordination, and Planning,* ed. Anthony Gar-On Yeh, Yok-Shiu Lee, Tunney Lee, and Nien Dak Sze. Hong Kong: Centre of Urban Planning and Environmental Management, University of Hong Kong, 2002.

Silas, J. "The Kampung Improvement Programme in Indonesia: A Comparative Case Study of Jakarta and Surabaya." In *Low Income Housing in the Developing World: The Role of Sites and Services and Settlement Upgrading,* ed. G. K. Payne. Chichester: John Wiley & Sons, 1984.

Sivaramakrishnan, K. C. "Confronting Urban Issues with a Metropolitan View in Mumbai, India." In *Urban Governance around the World,* ed. Blair Ruble, Richard Stren, Joseph Tulchin, and Diana Varat. Washington, D.C.: Woodrow Wilson International Center for Scholars, 2002.

―――. "Urban Governance: Changing Realities." In *Preparing for the Urban Future: Global Pressures and Local Forces,* ed. Michael A. Cohen, Blair A. Ruble, Joseph H. Tulchin, and Allison M. Garland. Washington, D.C.: Woodrow Wilson Center Press, 1996.

Soegijoko Budhy Tjahjati S. "Jabotabek and Globalization." In *Emerging World Cities in Pacific Asia,* ed. Fu-chen Lo and Yue-man Yeung. Tokyo: United Nations University Press, 1996.

Spiller, Pablo T., and William D. Savedoff. "Government Opportunism and the Provision of Water." In *Spilled Water: Institutional Commitment in the Provision of Water Services,* ed. William Savedoff and Pablo Spiller. Washington, D.C.: Inter-American Development Bank, 1999.

Sternstein, Larry. " Planning the Future of Bangkok." In *The City as a Centre for Change in Asia,* ed. D. J. Dwyer. Hong Kong: Hong Kong University Press, 1972.

Stren, Richard. "Introduction." In *Urban Governance around the World,* ed. Blair Ruble, Richard Stren, Joseph Tulchin, and Diana Varat. Washington, D.C.: Woodrow Wilson International Center for Scholars, 2002.

―――. "Local Governance and the Development of Associational Life: An Exploration." In *Democratic Governance and Urban Sustainability,* ed. Joseph S. Tulchin, Diana H. Varat, and Blair A. Ruble. Washington, D.C.: Woodrow Wilson International Center for Scholars, 2002.

Sung Woong Hong. " Seoul: a Global City in a Nation of Rapid Growth." In *Emerging World Cities in Pacific Asia,* ed. Fu-chen Lo and Yue-man Yeung. Tokyo: United Nations University Press, 1996.

Sung Yun-wing. "Economic Integration of Hong Kong and the Zhujiang Delta." In *Re-*

source Management, Urbanization and Governance in Hong Kong and the Zhujiang Delta, ed. Wong Kwau-jiu and Shen Jianfa. Hong Kong: Chinese University Press, 2002.

Takahashi Junjiro and Noriyuki Sugiura. "The Japanese Urban System and the Growing Centrality of Tokyo in the Global Economy." In *Emerging World Cities in Pacific Asia,* ed. Fu-chen Lo and Yue-man Yeung. Tokyo: United Nations University Press, 1996.

Tapales, Proserpina. "The Philippines." In *The Changing Nature of Local Government in Developing Countries,* ed. Patricia L. McCarney. Toronto: Centre for Urban and Community Studies, University of Toronto, 1996.

Taubmann, Wolfgang. "Urban Administration, Urban Development and Migrant Enclaves: The Case of Guangzhou." In *Resource Management, Urbanization and Governance in Hong Kong and the Zhujiang Delta,* ed. Wong Kwau-jiu and Shen Jianfa. Hong Kong: Chinese University Press, 2002.

Taylor, J. L. "Evaluation of the Jakarta Kampung Improvement Program." In *Shelter Upgrading and the Urban Poor: Evaluation of Third World Experience,* ed. R. J. Skinner, J. L. Taylor, and E. A. Wegelin. Manila: Island Publishing House, 1987.

Tiwari, Geetam. "Bus Priority Lanes for Delhi." In *Urban Transport for Growing Cities: High Capacity Bus Systems,* ed. Geetam Tiwari. New Delhi: Macmillan India, 2002.

Vogel, Ronald K. "Decentralization and Urban Governance: Reforming Tokyo Metropolitan Government." In *Urban Governance around the World,* ed. Blair Ruble, Richard Stren, Joseph Tulchin, and Diana Varat. Washington, D.C.: Woodrow Wilson International Center for Scholars, 2002.

Wang, James, and Cherry Ho. "Competition, Cooperation and Governance of Airports in the Greater Pearl River Delta Region." In *Building a Competitive Pearl River Delta Region: Cooperation, Coordination, and Planning,* ed. Anthony Gar-On Yeh, Yok-Shiu Lee, Tunney Lee, and Nien Dak Sze. Hong Kong: Centre of Urban Planning and Environmental Management, University of Hong Kong, 2002.

Wang Jian. "Some Issues of China's Long Term Economic Development." In *Chinese Cities and China's Development: A Preview of the Future Role of Hong Kong,* ed. Anthony Gar-On Yeh and Chai-Kwong Mak. Hong Kong: Centre of Urban Planning and Environmental Management, University of Hong Kong, 1995.

Wright, Arthur. "The Cosmology of the Chinese City." In *The City in Late Imperial China,* ed. William G. Skinner. Stanford, Calif.: Stanford University Press, 1977.

Wu Chung-tong. "Whither Asian Planning Education?" In *Planning for a Better Urban Living Environment in Asia,* ed. Anthony Gar-On Yeh, and Mee Kam Ng. Burlington, Vt.: Ashgate Publishing, 2000.

Xu Xueqiang and Xu Yongjian. "A Study on an Integrated Cross-Border Transport Network for the Pearl River Delta." In *Building a Competitive Pearl River Delta Region: Cooperation, Coordination, and Planning,* ed. Anthony Gar-On Yeh, Yok-Shiu Lee, Tunney Lee, and Nien Dak Sze. Hong Kong: Centre of Urban Planning and Environmental Management, University of Hong Kong, 2002.

Yan Zhongmin. "Shanghai: The Growth and Shifting Emphasis of China's Largest City." In *Chinese Cities: The Growth of the Metropolis Since 1949,* ed. Victor F.Sit. Hong Kong: Oxford University Press, 1985.

Ye Shun-zan. "Development Prospect of North China's Coastal Region and Beijing-Tianjin Conurbation." In *Chinese Cities and China's Development: A Preview of the Future Role of Hong Kong,* ed. Anthony Gar-On Yeh and Chai-Kwong Mak. Hong

Kong: Centre of Urban Planning and Environmental Management, University of Hong Kong, 1995.

Yin Yonguan and Mark Wang. "China's Urban Environmental Sustainability in a Global Context." In *Consuming Cities: The Urban Environment in the Global Economy after the Rio Declaration,* ed. Nicholas Low, B. Gleason, I. Elander, and R. Lidskog. New York: Routledge, 2000.

Journal, Magazine, and Newspaper Articles

Asiaweek, February 28, 1992.

Bukit, N. T. "Water Quality Conservation for the Citarum River in West Java" *Water, Science and Technology* 31, no. 9 (1995): 1–10.

Brockerhoff, M. "Urban Growth in Developing Countries: A Review of Projections and Revisions." *Population and Development Review* 25, no. 4 (1999): 757–78.

Calumpita, Ronnie. "69% of Water Supply Lost to Leaks, Illegal Connections." *Manila Times,* January 31, 2004.

China Daily. "New Rules to Standardize Housing Services," October 17, 2001; http://www.china.org.cn.

China Labor Bulletin (Hong Kong). "Residence Registration to Stay; Migration Eased." February 26, 2002. http://www.china-labour.org.

Choi Songsu. "Evaluation of Urban and Regional Policies of China." *Villes en Developpement,* no. 60–61, June–September 2003, 6–8.

Choong Tet Sieu. "How to Make Cities Work," *Asiaweek,* December 11, 1998, 40–45.

Dawn Internet Edition (Karachi). "Karachi: Transport Project of City in Doldrums." October 28, 2003.

Dollar, David. "How to Reduce Poverty: Lessons from China." *Yale Global,* January 6, 2004.

Dowding, K., P. Dunleavy, D. King, and H. Margetts. "Rational Choice and Community Power Structures." *Political Studies* 43, no. 2 (1995): 267–77.

Downs, Anthony. "Traffic: Why It's Getting Worse, What Government Can Do." In *Cities and Suburbs.* Washington, D.C.: Brookings Institution, 2004. Available at http://www.brookings.edu/comm/policybriefs.

Duran, Leoncio. "Planning in a Changing Environment: The Case of Marilao in the Philippines." *Urban Agriculture Magazine,* no. 4 (July 2001): 40–41.

Ebanks, Edward, and Chaoze Cheng. "China: A Unique Urbanization Model." *Asia Pacific Population Journal* 5, no. 3 (September 1990): 29–50.

Environment and Urbanization. "Sustainable Development Revisited II." Vol. 11, no. 2 (October 1999): 3–9.

Esguerra, George. "Balanced Urban Transport Development Opportunities for Metro Manila: The Wheel Extended." *Toyota Quarterly Review,* no. 88, July 1994.

Firman, Tommy, and Ida Ayu Dharmapatni. "The Emergence of Extended Metropolitan Regions in Indonesia: Jabotabek and Bandung Metropolitan Area." *Review of Urban and Regional Development Studies* 7 (1995): 167–88.

Gaylican, Christine, and Agnes Donato. "We Can No Longer Save Maynilad." *Philippine Daily Inquirer,* December 11, 2002.

Gilbert, Alan. "On the Mystery of Capital and the Myths of Hernando de Soto: What Difference Does Legal Title Make?" *IDPR* 24, no. 1 (2002): 1–17.

Glasmeier, Amy. "Factors Governing the Development of High-Tech Industry Agglomerations: A Tale of Two Cities." *Regional Studies* 22, no. 4 (1988): 287–301.

Goodman, John B., and G. W. Loveman. "Does Privatization Serve the Public Interest?" *Harvard Business Review* 69, no. 5 (1991): 26–38.

Hardoy, Ana, and Ricardo Schusterman. "New Models for the Privatization of Water and Sanitation for the Urban Poor." *Environment and Urbanization* 12, no. 2 (October 2000): 63–75.

Harsono, Andreas. "Water and Politics in the Fall of Suharto." Center for Public Integrity, 2003; http://www.icij.org/water.

Hasan, Arif. "A Model for Government–Community Partnership in Building Sewage Systems for Urban Areas: The Experience of the Orangi Pilot Project-Research and Training Institute (OPP-RTI), Karachi." *Water Science and Technology* 45, no. 8 (2002): 199–216.

Horn, Robert. "Leap Bangkok's Traffic with a Single Bound." *Time Asia,* July 3, 2000.

Ibon Foundation. "Water Crisis in Metro Manila: What's New?" *Cyberdyaryo,* January 21, 2004; http://www.codewan.com.ph.

Kaothien, Utis. "Regional and Urbanisation Policy in Thailand: The Tertiary Sector as a Leading Sector in Regional Development." *Urban Studies* 29, no. 6 (1991): 1027–43.

Landingin, Roel. "Loaves, Fishes and Dirty Dishes: Manila's Privatized Water Can't Handle the Pressure." Center for Public Integrity, 2003; http://www.icij.org/water.

Laquian, Aprodicio. "China and Vietnam: Urban Strategies in Societies in Transition." *Third World Planning Review* 18, no. 1 (1996): iii–xii.

———. "The Multi-Ethnic and Multicultural City: An Asian Perspective." *International Social Science Journal* 47, no. 1 (March 1996): 43–54.

———. "Sites, Services and Shelter: An Evaluation." *Habitat International* 7, nos. 5–6 (1983): 216–25.

———. "Whither Sites and Services?" *Science* 92, no. 4243 (1976): 950–55.

Lawson, Alistair. "Dhaka Bans Polluting Baby Taxis." BBC News On Line, 2003; http://www.bbcnewsonline.com.

Leaf, Michael. "Inner City Redevelopment in China." *Cities* 12, no. 1 (1995).

Leftwich, Adrian. "Governance, the State and the Politics of Development." *Development and Change* 25 (1994): 363–86.

Lin, George. "The Growth and Structural Change of Chinese Cities: A Contextual and Geographic Analysis." *Cities* 19, no. 5 (2002): 299–316.

Liu Yang. "Environmental Aspects of Beijing's Old and Dilapidated Housing Renewal." *China City Planning Review* 11, no. 1 (March 1995): 45–55.

Malaya (Manila). "Color Coding Abolition Tried Out for Three Weeks." January 31, 2003, 5.

———. "Government Seeks Funding for Clear Air." February 4, 2003, 6.

Manila Bulletin. "MWSS Sets Public Consultation." December 3, 2002.

———."100 PUBs Using CNG to Ply EDSA by October." *Manila Bulletin,* August 13, 2003, 5.

Manila Times. "Minding the Store at Maynilad," July 2, 2004; http://www.manilatimes.net.

Millennium Challenge Corporation. *The Millennium Challenge Account.* Available at http://www.mca.gov.

Moulaert, F., and E.,A. Swyngedouw. "A Regulation Approach to the Geography of Flexible Production Systems." *Environment and Planning* 7 (1989): 327–45.

Peattie, Lisa. "Some Second Thoughts on Sites and Services." *Habitat International* 13, no. 3 (1982): 23–49.

People's Daily Online. "China Reports Booming Housing Sales in First Half of 2003." July 24, 2003; http://english.peopledaily.com.cn.

Philippine Daily Inquirer. "WB Study Says RP Spends $1.5 Billion Because of Air Pollution." January 20, 2003, 5.

Rees, William E. "Achieving Sustainability: Reform or Transformation?" *Journal of Planning Literature* 9, no. 3 (1994).

————. "Ecological Footprints and Appropriated Carrying Capacity: What Urban Economics Leaves Out." *Environment and Urbanization* 4, no. 2 (October 1992): 121–30.

Rosegrant, M. W., and R. S. Meinzein-Dick. "Water Resources in the Asia-Pacific Region: Managing Scarcity." *Asia Pacific Literature* 10, no. 2 (1997): 32–53.

Saxenian, Anna Lee. "The Cheshire Cat's Grin: Innovation, Regional Development and the Cambridge Case." *Economy and Society* 18, no. 4 (November 1989): 448–77.

Sen, Amartya. "How to Judge Globalism." *The American Prospect,* winter 2002, A2–A5.

Shanghai Institute of Comprehensive Urban Transport Planning. "Outline of the Comprehensive Urban Transport Planning for Shanghai." *China City Planning Review* 10, no. 2 (June 1994): 53–55.

Stokke, K. "Authoritarianism in the Age of Market Liberalism in Sri Lanka." *Antipode* 24, no. 4 (1997): 437–55.

Sun Wen-bin and Wong Siu-lun. "The Development of Private Enterprise in Contemporary China: Institutional Foundations and Limitations." *China Review* 2, no. 2 (fall 2002): 65–91.

Swyngedouw, E. "The Contradiction of Urban Water Provision." *Third World Planning Review* 17, no. 4 (1996): 65–80.

Tan Ying. "Social Aspects of Beijing's Old and Dilapidated Housing Renewal." *China City Planning Review* 10, no. 4 (December 1994): 45–55.

Turner, John F. C. "Lima's Barriadas and Corralones: Suburbs vs. Slums." *Ekistics* 19, no. 12 (1965): 152–55.

————. 1968. "The Squatter Settlement: An Architecture That Works." *Architectural Design* 38, no. 8 (1965): 357–60.

Villanueva, Hector. "Maynilad's Water Woes." *Manila Bulletin,* December 3, 2002.

Wang Cun. "The Development of Information Activities in the Special Economic Zones of China." *Journal of Information Science* 16 (1990): 393–98.

Wirth, Louis. "Urbanism as a Way of Life." *American Journal of Sociology* 44, no. 1 (July 1938): 1–24.

Ye, Shun-zan. "City and Town Development in the Beijing-Tianjin-Tangshan Region." *Economic Geography* 3, no. 1 (spring 1986).

Yeh, Anthony Gar-On, and Fulong Wu. "The New Land Development Process and Urban Development in Chinese Cities." *International Journal of Urban and Regional Research* 20, no. 2 (1996): 330–53.

Yeh, Anthony Gar-On, and Xia Li. "An Integrated Remote Sensing and GIS Approach in the Monitoring and Evaluation of Rapid Urban Growth for Sustainable Development in the Pearl River Delta, China." *International Planning Studies* 2, no. 2 (1996): 195–222.

Yu, Verna. "In Modern Beijing, Officials Seek to Save Space for the Past." *South China Morning Post,* October 30, 2003, A-8.

Xie Yichun and Frank J. Costa. "Urban Planning in Socialist China: Theory and Practice." *Cities,* May 1993, 102–14.

Zhang Dan. "The World Paper." *Hong Kong Standard,* November 23, 1996.

Public Documents and Technical Reports

Ali, Mubarik, and Fe Porciuncula. "Urban and Peri-Urban Agriculture in Metro Manila: Resources and Opportunities for Food Production." Technical Bulletin 26, Asian Vegetable Research and Development Center. School of Australian and International Studies, Deakin University, Geelong, Victoria, 2001.

Asia/Pacific Research Center. "The Urban Dynamics of East Asia." Institute for International Studies, Stanford University, Stanford, Calif., 2003.

Asian Development Bank. *Review of the Scope for Bank Assistance to Urban Transport.* Manila: Asian Development Bank, 1989.

———. *Water Utilities Data Book.* ADB Case Study for the Mega-City Regional Consultation. Manila: Asian Development Bank, 1993.

Cai Jianming. "Peri-Urban Agriculture Development in China: A New Approach in Xiaotangshan, Beijing." Institute of Geographical Sciences and Natural Resource Research, Beijing, 2000.

Chinese Science Society. *The Sustainable Development Strategy of Bohai Rim Region.* (Original in Chinese.) Beijing: Chinese Science Society, 1995.

DKI (Daerah Khusus Ibukota Jakarta). Perda 5. *Development Plan, Jakarta.* Jakarta: DKI, 1984.

Ensink, Joroen, Tariq Mahmood, Wim van der Hoek, Liqa Raschid-Sally, and Felix Amerasinghe. "Use of Untreated Wastewater in Peri-Urban Agriculture I Pakistan: Risks and Opportunities." Technical Report, International Water Management Institute, Colombo, 2002.

Fouracre, P. R., G. D. Jacobs, and D. A. C. Maunders. "Characteristics of Conventional Public Transport Services in Third World Cities." *Traffic Engineering Control* 27, no. 12 (1996): 6–11.

Frick, Francis. *A Seaside Arcology for Southern China.* Vancouver: Office of Urban Agriculture, City Farmer Canada, 2000.

Gertler, L. "A Re-Examination of the Scope and Limitations of Planing Theory and Practice." In *Proceedings of the First Oxford-Waterloo Research Seminar, Planning and Design in British Columbia and Canada,* vol. 2, ed. George Rich. Ottawa: Canadian Institute of Planners, 1987.

Government of the Philippines. *Statistical Yearbook.* Manila: National Statistical Coordination Board, 2001.

HUDCC (Housing and Urban Development Coordinating Council). *Metropolitan Manila Management Study.* Report submitted to World Bank under Technical Grant 05-28782PH. Manila: Local Government Development Foundation, 1995.

Inocencio, Arlene. "Public–Private Partnerships in Metro Manila, Philippines." Asian Development Bank, Manila, 2003; http://www.adb.org/Documents.

Jiang Zhenshen and Liu Fengchen. "Small Towns in China and the Problem of Municipal Solid Waste Disposal." China Agricultural University, Beijing, 2003. Also published in *Waste Management World Magazine,* September–October 2003.

Kahaner, D. K. "Economic-Industrial Overview of Northeast China." Asian Technology Information Program, Tokyo, 1995.

MMRDA (Mumbai Metropolitan Regional Development Authority). *Mumbai Urban Transport Project.* Report PID 8175. Washington, D.C.: World Bank, 2002.

National Agricultural Census Office of China. *Rural Town Districts and Their Socio-Economic Conditions.* Agricultural Census Communiqué 4. Beijing: National Agricultural Census Office of China, 2002.

National Building Museum. *On Track: Transit and the American City.* Exhibition brochure. Washington, D.C.: National Building Museum, 2002.

National Economic and Social Development Board (Thailand). *The Fifth National Economic and Social Development Plan (1982–1986).* Bangkok: National Economic and Social Development Board, 1982.

———. *National Urban Development Policy Framework, Vol. 1, Final Report, Bangkok: Joint NESDB, UNDP and Thailand Development Research Institute (TDRI) Project.* Bangkok: National Economic and Social Development Board, 1990.

Orangi Pilot Project. *Proposal for a Sewage Disposal System for Karachi.* Karachi: City Press for the Research and Training Institute, 1998.

Osaka Prefectural Government. *Rebuilding Osaka, Doubling Its Vitality: Comprehensive Plan for 21st Century Osaka.* Osaka: Office of the Governor of Osaka Prefecture, 2000.

Pearl River Delta Economic Zone Planning Committee. *Plan for the Pearl River Delta Economic Zone of Guangdong Province.* (Original in Chinese.) Guangzhou: Guangdong Economy Press, 1996.

Pudong New Area Administration. *Shanghai Pudong New Area: Investment Environment and Development Prospect.* Shanghai: Pudong New Area Administration, 1991.

Ragragio, Junio. "Understanding Slums: Case Studies for the Global Report 2003." Nairobi: United Nations Center for Human Settlements, 2002.

Remenyi, Joe. *Poverty Reduction and Urban Renewal through Urban Agriculture and Microfinance: A Case Study of Dhaka, Bangladesh.* Technical Study. Washington, DC: World Bank, 2000.

Roth, G. *The Private Provision of Public Services in Developing Countries.* Washington, D.C.: World Bank, 1987.

Sohail, M. "Urban Public Transport and Sustainable Development for the Poor: A Case Study of Karachi, Pakistan." Water Engineering and Development Centre, Loughborough, U.K., 2000.

Tokyo Bureau of City Planning. *Outline of the Tokyo Megalopolitan Concept.* Tokyo: Tokyo Bureau of City Planning, 2003. Available at http://www.toshikei.metro.tokyo.

———. *The Tokyo Plan 2000.* Tokyo: Tokyo Bureau of City Planning, 2003. Available at http://www.toshikei.metro.tokyo.

Tokyo Metropolitan Government. *Transportation,* Tokyo: Tokyo Bureau of City Planning, 2003.

World Bank. *East Asia and the Pacific Sector Notes: Thailand Urban Development,* Washington, D.C.: World Bank, 2002.

————. *Global Agenda 2002–2003: Meeting the Challenges.* Document for the Annual Meetings of the World Bank and International Monetary Fund. Washington, D.C.: World Bank, 2002.

————. *India: Mumbai Urban Transport Project.* Report PIC 8175. Washington, D.C.: World Bank, 2002.

World Bank–Netherlands Water Partnership Program. *Stimulating Innovative Performance and Supporting World Bank Operations in Water Management.* Washington, D.C.: World Bank and Netherlands Ministry of Foreign Affairs, 2002.

Unpublished Materials

Ajero, M.Y. "Future Emissions of Metro Manila." Paper given at the Mega-City Project Conference of the Institute for Global Environmental Strategies, Kitakyushu, Japan, 2002.

Akbar, H., M. Delwar, and Basil van Horen. "Institutional Reform for Water Supply to the Poor in Dhaka, Bangladesh." Paper issued by Department of Geography, University of Queensland, Brisbane, 2003.

Argo, Teti. "Scarcity of Water Supply in Metropolitan Jakarta: Assessing Competition Between Sources." Report Submitted to the Asian Urban Research Network Project, Centre for Human Settlements, University of British Columbia, Vancouver, 1998.

————. "Thirsty Downstream: The Provision of Clean Water in Jakarta, Indonesia." Ph.D. dissertation, School of Community and Regional Planning, University of British Columbia, Vancouver, 1999.

Argo, Teti, and Aprodicio Laquian. "Privatization of Water Utilities and Its Effects on the Urban Poor in Jakarta Raya and Metro Manila." Paper presented at Forum on Urban Infrastructure and Public Service Delivery for the Urban Poor, Regional Focus: Asia, India Habitat Centre, New Delhi, June 24–25, 2004.

Badami, Madhav, Geetam Tiwari, and Dinesh Mohan. "Access and Mobility for the Urban Poor in India: Bridging the Gap between Policy and Needs." Paper presented at Forum on Urban Infrastructure and Public Service Delivery for the Urban Poor, Regional Focus: Asia, India Habitat Centre, New Delhi, June 24–25, 2004.

Bartone, Carl. "Urban Waste Water and Sanitation: Responding to Household and Community Demand." Paper presented at Second Annual World Bank Conference on Environmentally Sustainable Development, Washington, September 19–21, 1994.

Cal, Primitivo. "Impact of Metro Manila Transport on the Poor." Paper issued by School of Urban and Regional Planning, University of the Philippines and Eastern Asia Society for Transportation Studies, Quezon City, 1998.

Changrien, Phaibul, and Robert J. Stimson. "Bangkok: Jewel in Thailand's Crown." National Institute of Development Administration and Queensland University of Technology, Bangkok, no date.

Chinese Science Society. *The Sustainable Development Strategy of the Bohai Rim Region* (in Chinese), quoted in "Hydrological Metabolism and Water Resources Management of the Beijing Metropolitan Region in the Hai River Basin," unpublished research paper by Lee Sung Ho submitted for MSc. degree, Department of Geography and Institute for Environmental Studies, University of Toronto, 1998, 36.

Duggal, V. K., and G. K. Pandey. "Air Quality Management in Delhi." Paper presented at Seminar on Better Air Quality in Asian and Pacific Rim Cities (BAQ 2002), Hong Kong, December 16–18, 2002.

Grekel, Koreann. *Implementation of Community-Managed Water Supply and Sanitation Programs for Low-Income Communities: A Case Study in Indonesia.* Student Paper 29. Toronto: University Consortium on the Environment, 1995.

Hall, Peter. "Can Cities Be Sustainable?" Paper presented at Second Annual World Bank Conference on Environmentally Sustainable Development, Washington, September 19–21, 1994.

Halliday, Deborah. "The Human Side of Development: A Study of Migration, Housing and Community Satisfaction in Pudong New Area, People's Republic of China." Master's thesis, School of Community and Regional Planning, University of British Columbia, Vancouver, 1995.

Han Xiaohui. "*Siheyuan* or Courtyard Housing in China," Master's thesis, School of Architecture, Faculty of Graduate Studies, University of British Columbia, Vancouver, 1997.

Islam, Nazrul, and Salma Shafi. "Solid Waste Management and the Urban Poor in Dhaka." Paper presented at Forum on Urban Infrastructure and Public Service Delivery for the Urban Poor, Regional Focus: Asia, India Habitat Centre, New Delhi, June 24–25, 2004.

Iyer, Narayan. "Efforts to Reduce Pollution from 2-Wheelers in India and Across Asia." Paper presented at Seminar on Better Air Quality in Asian and Pacific Rim Cities (BAQ 2002), Hong Kong, December 16–18, 2002.

Karyoedi, Mochtarram. "The Neighborhood Housing Redevelopment of Industri Dalam Area: Toward Comprehensive Urban Renewal of Bandung Inner City." Paper Presented at International Workshop on Neighborhood Redevelopment, Zhongshan University, Guangzhou, September 16–20, 1995.

Khan, Shahed Anwer. "Evictions, the Right to Shelter and the Urban Poor: A Study of Factors Influencing Eviction of Informal Settlements in Bangkok, Karachi and Seoul." Ph.D. thesis, Human Settlements Development Division, Asian Institute of Technology, Bangkok, 1992.

Khan, Shahier. "Reckless Urban Growth Chokes Bangladesh Capital." *One World,* 2003; http://www.oneworld.net).

Laquian, Aprodicio. "Who Are the Poor and How Are They Being Served in Asian Cities?" Paper presented at Forum on Urban Infrastructure and Public Service Delivery for the Urban Poor, Regional Focus: Asia, India Habitat Centre, New Delhi, June 24–25, 2004.

Leaf, Michael L. "Land Regulation and Housing Development in Jakarta, Indonesia: From the Big Village to the Modern City." Ph.D. dissertation, Department of City and Regional Planning, University of California at Berkeley, 1991.

Lee Sung Ho. "Hydrological Metabolism and Water Resources Management of the Beijing Metropolitan Region in the Hai River Basin." Research paper submitted for the MSc. degree, Graduate Department of Geography and Institute of Environmental Studies, University of Toronto, Toronto, 1998.

Li Ying. "The Housing Delivery Systems in Beijing: An International Perspective." Ph.D. dissertation, School of Community and Regional Planning, Faculty of Graduate Studies, University of British Columbia, Vancouver, 1997.

Maclaren, Virginia. "Solid Waste Management in Asian Cities: Implications for the Urban Poor." Paper presented at Forum on Urban Infrastructure and Public Service Delivery for the Urban Poor, Regional Focus: Asia, India Habitat Centre, New Delhi, June 24–25, 2004.

Mao Qizhi. "Small Town Development and Planning in the Beijing Metropolitan Region," Paper presented at International Workshop on Small Town Development, Tongji University, Shanghai, April 17–20, 1996.

Marton, Andrew. "Restless Landscapes: Spatial Economic Restructuring in China's Lower Yangzi Delta." Ph.D. dissertation, Department of Geography, Faculty of Arts, University of British Columbia, Vancouver, 1996.

Meng Xiaochen. "Prosperity, Development and Sustainability: A Case Study of Shenzhen, China." Paper presented at Senior International Seminar on China's Small Town Development, Beijing, November 13–17, 1995.

Nishida, Yuko. "Tokyo's Experience toward Cleaner Air." Paper presented at Seminar on Better Air Quality in Asian and Pacific Rim Cities (BAQ 2002), Hong Kong, December 16–18, 2002.

Nguyen Quang Vinh. "Social Implications of Ho Chi Minh Inner City Redevelopment Process," Paper presented at International Workshop on the Future of the Asian Inner City, sponsored by the Vietnam Academy for Social Sciences and Humanities and the Asian Urban Research Network Project, Ho Chi Minh City, December 2–7, 1996.

Olds, Kris. "Pacific Rim Mega-Projects and the Global Cultural Economy: Tales from Vancouver and Shanghai." Ph.D. thesis, Department of Geography, University of Bristol, 1995.

Overby, R. "The Urban Economic Environmental Challenge: Improvement of Human Welfare by Building and Managing Urban Ecosystems." Paper presented at POLMET 85 Urban Environment Conference, sponsored by World Bank, Washington, 1985.

Pendakur, Setty. "Congestion Management, Non-Motorized Transport, and Sustainable Cities." Paper presented at Non-Motorized Transport Seminar, Washington, May 12, 1992.

Peng, Zhong-Ren. "Urban Transportation Strategies in Chinese Cities and Their Impacts on the Urban Poor." Paper presented at Forum on Urban Infrastructure and Public Service Delivery for the Urban Poor, Regional Focus: Asia, India Habitat Centre, New Delhi, June 24–25, 2004.

Qian, Guan. "Lilong Housing: A Traditional Settlement Form," Master's thesis, School of Architecture, McGill University, Montreal, 1996.

Railway Technology. "Manila Light Right Extension, Philippines." Available at http://www.railway-technology.com/projects/manila.

Reforma, Mila. "An Evaluation of the Tondo Dagat-Dagatan Development Project: A Research Design." National Housing Authority, Manila, 1977.

Sayeg, Philip. *Successful Conversion to Unleaded Gasoline in Thailand.* Technical Working Paper 410. Washington, D.C.: World Bank, 1992.

Tongji University. "On the Development of Metropolitan Shanghai." Report submitted to Asian Urban Research Network, Faculty of Architecture and Urban Planning, Shanghai, 1997.

———. "The Human Settlement of Small Towns in Metropolitan Shanghai." Special Report submitted to Asian Urban Research Network, Faculty of Architecture and Urban Planning, Shanghai, 1996.

————. "The Renovation of Shanghai Old Residential Areas and Buildings." Report submitted to Asian Urban Research Network, Faculty of Architecture and Urban Planning, Shanghai, 1996.

Turner, John F. C. "Uncontrolled Urban Settlement: Problems and Policies." Paper presented at Inter-Regional Seminar on Development Policies and Planning in Relation to Urbanization, Pittsburgh, 1968.

Uranza, Rogelio. "The Role of Traffic Engineering and Management in Metro Manila." Paper given at International Conference on Transport Planning, Demand Management and Air Quality, Asian Development Bank, Manila, February 26–27, 2001.

Van Horen, Basil. "Community Upgrading and Institutional Capacity Building to Benefit the Urban Poor in Asia." Paper presented at Forum on Urban Infrastructure and Public Service Delivery for the Urban Poor, Regional Focus: Asia, India Habitat Centre, New Delhi, June 24–25, 2004.

————. "Informal Settlement Upgrading in Durban, South Africa: Building Institutional Capacity to Sustain the Improvement Process." Ph.D. thesis, School of Community and Regional Planning, Faculty of Graduate Studies, University of British Columbia, Vancouver, 1996.

Wang, Jixian James, and Crystal Chan. "Public Transport and Planned High-Density Living in Hong Kong: Do They Help the Poor?" Paper presented at Forum on Urban Infrastructure and Public Service Delivery for the Urban Poor, Regional Focus: Asia, India Habitat Centre, New Delhi, June 24–25, 2004.

Wardrop Engineering. "Second Subic Bay Freeport Project, Final Report." Report Submitted to World Bank and Subic Bay Metropolitan Authority, Washington and Winnipeg, 1995.

Wickramanayake, Ebel, and Hu Biliang. *Emergence of Rural Industrial Township Enterprises in China.* Working Paper 42. Bangkok: Human Settlements Development Division, Asian Institute of Technology, 1993.

Widianto, Bambang. "Solid Waste Management in Jakarta: Problems and Alternatives at the Community Level." Major paper, master's in environmental studies, Faculty of Environmental Studies, York University, Toronto, 1993.

Witty, David. "Identifying a More Appropriate Role for the Canadian Planning Profession." Ph.D. dissertation, School of Community and Regional Planning, Faculty of Graduate Studies, University of British Columbia, Vancouver, 1998.

Wong, Francis, and Eddie Hui. "Housing Reform in Southern China: Shenzhen and Guangzhou." Department of Building and Real Estate, Hong Kong Polytechnic University, Hong Kong, 2000.

Wong Kam Sing. "Dwelling Densification and Greenness: Hong Kong's High Density Housing and Resource Conservation." M.S. thesis, School of Architecture, University of British Columbia, Vancouver, 1996.

Wu Liangyong and Mao Qizhi. "On the Integrated Development of Beijing and Some Potential Growth Areas in the Beijing Metropolitan Region." Paper presented at International Workshop on Metropolitan Development, Tsinghua University, Beijing, October 12–14, 1993.

Xue Desheng. "Industry of Renhe Town: Development and Linkage." Working Paper 9, Centre for Urban and Regional Studies, Zhongshan University, Guangzhou, 1996.

Yan Xiaopei. "The Satellite Towns of Metropolitan Guangzhou: Evolution, Inherent Links with the Central City, and Tendencies—A Case Study of Renhe Town." Working Paper 3, Asian Urban Research Network Project, Centre for Urban and Regional Studies, Zhongshan University, Guangzhou, 1995.

———. "A Study of the Migrant Labor Force of China in Recent Years: A Case Study of Nanhai City of Guangdong Province." Working Paper 13, Asian Urban Research Network Project, Centre for Urban and Regional Studies, Zhongshan University, Guangzhou, 1995.

Yee, Francis L. "Economic and Urban Changes in the Shenzhen Special Economic Zone, 1979–1986." Ph.D. dissertation, Department of Geography, University of British Columbia, Vancouver, 1992.

Yu Minfei. "A Survey of Living Environment of the Relocated Residents Before and After Their Resettlement Arising from Urban Renewal in the Older Districts of Shanghai." Paper Presented at the International Workshop on Neighborhood Redevelopment in the Context of the Central City, sponsored by Zhongshan University, Guangzhou, September 1995.

Yu Minfei and Shai Feng. "A Study of the Reconstruction of Shanghai's Old Residential Areas." Report submitted to Asian Urban Research Network Project, Faculty of Architecture and Urban Planning, Tongji University, Shanghai, June 1995.

Zhang Jie. "Neighborhood Redevelopment in the Inner City Areas of Beijing." Paper presented at International Workshop on Mega-Urban Region Development, sponsored by Asian Urban Research Network and Tsinghua University, Beijing, November 24–27, 1993.

Zhao Bingshi, Chen Baorong, and Zhang Jie. "An Introduction to Beijing and Its Metropolitan Region." Paper presented at Regional Workshop on Metropolitan and Regional Planning, sponsored by Asian Urban Research Network and Chulalongkorn University, Bangkok, June 29–July 3, 1992.

Index

accountability and governance, 142, 155–58

acid rain, 177

agencies' responsibilities, 119–24

Agenda 21, 182

agriculture, 170–76; land lost to urban use, 172–73, 328–29, 384; use of "night soil," 173–74, 318; wastewater reuse in, 226; and water resource issues, 223. *See also* urban agriculture

airport construction, 81, 103, 389

Alliance (India), 414

alternative energy sources and fuels, 178–79, 268–69, 397–98

Angel, Shlomo, 368–69

Angkor Wat and Angkor Thom (Cambodia), 38, 56–67

Annan, Kofi A., 143

Asian Coalition on Housing Rights, 196

Asian Development Bank, 228, 232, 238, 312, 354, 376, 403, 407, 412, 416

Asian mega-cities, 1–8

Asian Urban Research Network: establishment of, xxiii; research focus of, xxv–xxvi, 49–50; study of relocated urban residents, 306–7; study of small town development, 323, 324

Asiaweek survey on Asian cities (1998), 42–43

automobiles: effect of use of, 94, 180, 259, 383–84; limiting use of, 180–81, 183–84, 241, 245, 267, 395; maintenance problems, 251–52; manufacturing of, 182, 245, 246, 345. *See also* mobility

autonomous local governance, 44, 113, 119, 131, 158–60

Bagong Barangay Housing Project (Manila), 356

Baguio: flood-risk housing in, 83; "garden city" planning in, 59; planning of, 39, 55, 60

"balance sheet," 143–44

Bandung, 33, 99, 102, 296. *See also* Jakarta

Bangalore, planning of, 39, 55, 59

Bangkok: agricultural use of urban waste in, 174; in competition with HK-PRD region, 73; and environmental planning, 103; governance in, 118, 124; and greenbelts, 170, 171; growth of, 33–34; high-density nodes in, 197; housing in, 349, 351–52, 354, 356; inner-city redevelopment in, 93, 198, 314; and jurisdictional fragmentation, 145; market forces on development of, 85; natural disasters and emergencies in, 252; and peripheral

471